A Bibliography of Novels

Related to American Frontier

and Colonial History

A Bibliography of Novels
Related to American Frontier
and Colonial History

~~~

by
Jack Warner VanDerhoof

The Whitston Publishing Company
Incorporated
Troy, New York
1971

Dedicated

to

Harry J. Carman

who
always had time
even
when none was available

PREFACE

American colonial history embraces the chronological period from the beginnings to 1789, the end of the Confederation period. To 1763 the area of concern was the New World, thus activity of both European colonials and original inhabitants in the Western hemisphere falls into the area treated by this bibliography. After 1763, the area is the present limits of the continental United States. Also included are those novels written by Americans during the period, ?-1789.

American frontier history embraces the chronological period, ?-to date. I have rejected the obvious limit of 1890 suggested by Turner's Thesis and the Census Bureau. "Frontier" is understood to be both place and process. The place is essentially the continental limits of the United States, though some attention has been given to Alaska and Hawaii. As process, titles were included if I considered them important for or bearing on the transition from savagery to civilization. Thus contemporary farm problems are legitimate aspects of the frontier process. Included also are titles not qualified under the broad rules established. If a writer, for example, has done a title or a series of titles fitting into colonial or frontier and then leaves for the sophisticated modern areas, such later titles were included.

Short stories are not included, valuable as they are, and some are more valuable than many of novels included. It was difficult to exclude the work of Dorothy Johnson (e.g. Indian Country and Hanging Tree). Her sensitivity to and reflection of Indian-white relations and other problems of the West have made important contributions to a valid understanding of America's past. Mary Murfree, writing under the pseudonym of Charles Egbert Craddock, brought agony to the decision process. In The Tennessee Mountains is not a novel but a work which set the tradition for treatment of mountain folk in American writing. To exclude her forced rejection of Alfred Quin's Wolfville stories and Mary Austin's marvelous The Land of Little Rain. Then what of the marginal works at once history and fiction such as John Ise's moving account of The Sod and The Stubble? The forty-ninth parallel also served as a bibliographical scalpel, cutting out Harold Bindloss and his Canadian tales. If Zane Grey is included why not his counterpart for the Canadian West, William Bryon Mowery (e.g. Resurrection River)? I reply with a sentence written by C. L. Sonnichsen: "But of course we could debate these matters all night if we had a night to debate in." The Civil War (American style) was excluded because R. A. Lively's fine work, Ficton Fights the Civil War is available. If a work fell into that time period, 1860-1865, and appeared to be given essentially to the West rather than the war, it was included.

In respect to juvenilia the general rule was to exclude it the closer it came to the present. Sometimes only one or two representative titles of an author were used, a device intended to illuminate the path rather than light the entire journey.

The touchstone for all decisions was usefulness rather than absolute consistency and an opening of avenues rather a closing of passageways. In many instances inclusion or exclusion of a title depended on the moment of decision. A title might be excluded on first notice then inserted or included than removed. This does not obviate personal error and ignorance.

Bibliographies are academic icebergs. What constitutes colonial, what frontier, and what juvenilia are the portion riding above the water. The submerged two-thirds consists of such questions as what is history, what is a historical novel, and what is historical fiction. When Edwin Fussell quotes Caroline Kirkland's response to a question about how much the term "west" really includes as "I have never been able to discover its limits", she speaks, for me, to the larger question, "What is a historical novel?" for I have not been able to discover its limits.

Any novel is a historical novel either because it deals with some aspect of past reality, imagined reality, or past imagination or is itself of the past. Such an eclectic posture offers advantages to a bibliographer. He can include many additional titles and need not make as many difficult inclusion-exclusion decisions. It enables one to move with minimum difficulty from the position of György Lukács reflected in THE HISTORICAL NOVEL, (translated from the German by Hannah and Stanley Mitchell):

> What matters therefore in the historical novel is not the retelling of great historical events, but the poetic awakening of the people who figured in those events. What matters is that we should re-experience the social and human motives which led men to think, feel and act just as they did in historical reality.
> . . . .
> The historical novel therefore has to <u>demonstrate</u> by <u>artistic</u> means that historical circumstances and characters existed in precisely such and such a way. What Scott has called very superficially "Authenticity of local color" is in actual fact this demonstration of historical reality

to that expressed by Brander Matthews in the HISTORICAL NOVEL AND OTHER ESSAY'S:"...the really trustworthy historical novels are those which were a-writing while the history was a-making." If neither the extreme position of Lukács, shaped by Hegelian alienation and Marxian dialectic nor the simple and homey statement by Matthews suits there is the position held by Ernest Leisy in THE AMERICAN HISTORICAL NOVEL:

> A historical novel is a novel the action of which is laid in an earlier time--how much earlier, remains an

open question, but it must be in the readily iden-
tifiable past time. Sir Walter Scott, who in theory
and practice laid the foundations of the modern historical novel, set the interval at half a century.
But in America-so rapid are changes here--a generation
appears sufficient to render a preceding period historical.

MECHANICS

Each entry is numbered except cross references.

Books are entered by the author's surname when known,
otherwise by unidentified pseudonyms. If both are
lacking, i.e. surname or pseudonym, then the entry is
by title exclusive of articles.

If an author uses his legal name and a pseudonym or
pseudonyms the following rule applies: titles are
arranged chronologically under the legal name then under
pseudonyms taken alphabetically.

The title citation is the full citation as given in the
National Union Catalog or other reliable source. On
several occasions ellipses are used in sub-titles.

The place of publication is the first one cited for the
first edition. If the first one cited is foreign and
there is an American publisher given for the same year
the latter is given preference.

If more than one publisher is given for the first
edition the same rule used for place of publication
was used in this case.

The date of publication is the date of publication for
the first edition if it is known.

Annotations were used to present succintly place, time,
content, and/or theme of the work.

Attention is called to several bibliographic problems.
Peter Field is a "house name" and two authors were known
to have written under this pseudonym. How many others
wrote under this pseudonym I do not know. It was not
possible to determine which titles belonged to E. B.
Mann and which to Fred East. A letter sent to the
publisher asking for more information about this problem
was dismissed with the curt reply that this was a "house
name" and carried with it some secret classification.
Therefore the titles of doubtful authorship are listed
under the pseudonym.

In the case of Leslie Scott and Oscar Schisgall writing
under the pseudonym of Jackson Cole the three titles
were listed under each of the men. Thus items numbered

5286, 5287, and 5293 are repeated as items 5357, 5358, and 5359.

Feike Frederick Feikema legally changed his name to Frederick F. Manfred but all his works appear under the entry, Feikema, Feike Fredrick.

On occasion use is made of references such as "Gaston--first southwestern novel:" Gaston refers to author's or compiler's last name in the Bibliographical Aids list. (see entry #2181).

ACKNOWLEDGMENTS

Many helped in many ways. One of Russell Sage College's grants enabled me to give several months of uninterrupted attention to the task during the summer of 1970. Margaret S. Tompkins, Reference Librarian, and Joseph Menditto, Head of Technical Services, both gave unstintingly of their professional expertise and evidenced genuine interest so that many times drudgery gave way to enjoyment and stagnation was erased by progress. Stephen Goode, Director of Libraries, encouraged the person and the work in many ways with a multiplicity of motivation.

My wife, Evelyn, and our daughter, Susan, lived with me as I searched and arranged cards. They also searched and arranged cards and encouraged rather than discouraged my efforts. My daughter, Lynne, and son, Douglas, were always interested.

A. Stanley Trickett, not only an adviser and influential teacher during my undergraduate days but also a friend and professional companion for three decades, influenced me through his library, personality, and interest.

I thank all those mentioned and appreciate the contribution of the unmentioned. The errors of commission and omission are mine. Western titles are as plentiful as the Sioux and twice as elusive. Colonial tales were oft as lost as the pilgrims who strayed from the narrow path. I have many more titles than I missed; and, I have missed many more titles than I wished.

Haynersville, New York   Jack VanDerhoof
December, 1970

BIBLIOGRAPHICAL AIDS

Baker, Ernest A.. History in fiction. a guide to the best historical romances, sagas, novels and tales. New York: Dutton, n.d..

Bay, Jens Christian. Handful of western books. Cedar Rapids, Iowa: Privately printed for friends of the Torch Press. 1935.

---A second handful of western books. Cedar Rapids, Iowa: Privately printed. 1936.

---A third handful of western books. Cedar Rapids, Iowa: Privately printed. 1937.

Blacke, Irwin R.. The old west in fiction. New York: Obolensky, 1961.

Blaine, Harold A.. "The frontiersman in american prose fiction 1800-1860". Unpublished Ph D dissertation from Western Reserve. 1935.

Blake, Nelson Manfred. Novelists' america; fiction as history 1910-1940. Syracuse, New York: Syracuse University. 1969.

Bone, Robert. Negro novel in america. New Haven, Connecticut: Yale Press, 1958.

Brown, Herbert Ross. The sentimental novel in america 1789-1860. Durham, North Carolina: Duke University, 1940.

Bryan, William Alfred. George washington in american literature 1775-1865. New York: Columbia, 1952.

Campbell, Harry Modean and Elton, Foster R.. Elizabeth maddox roberts, american novelist. Norman, Oklahoma: University of Oklahoma Press, 1956.

Coan, Otis W. and Lillard, Richard G.. America in fiction; an annotated list of novels that interpret aspects of life in the united states, canada, and mexico. 5th Edition. Palo Alto, California: Pacific Books, 1967.

Cooper, Frederic Taber. Some american story tellers. New. York: Holt, 1911.

---Some english story tellers. New York: Holt, 1912.

Davidson, Levette J. and Bostwick, Prudence. The literature of the rocky mountain west 1803-1903. Caldwell, Idaho: Caxton, 1939.

Dickinson, A. T. Jr.. American historical fiction, 2nd edition. New York: Scarecrow Press, 1963.

Easton, Robert. Max brand, the big "westerner". Norman, Oklahoma, 1970.

Eisinger, Chester E.. Fiction of the forties. Chicago: University Chicago Press, 1963.

Fidell, Estelle A. and Flory, Esther V. Fiction catalogue: a list of 4,097 works of fiction in the english language with annotations, 7th edition. New York: H. W. Wilson, 1961.

Flanagan, John T.. "A bibliography of middle western farm novels". Minnesota History XXIII (1942).

Folsom, James K.. The american western novel. New Haven: College and University Press, 1966.

Forester, E. M.. Aspects of the modern novel. New York: Harcourt, 1927.

Fussell, Edwin. Frontier: american literature and the american west. Princeton: Princeton University Press, 1965.

Gaston, Edwin W. Jr.. The early novel of the southwest. Albuquerque, New Mexico: University of New Mexico, 1961.

Gerstenberger, Donna and Hendrick, George. The american novel 1789-1959: a checklist of twentieth-century criticism. Denver, Colorado: Swallow, 1961.

Gohdes, Clarence. Bibliographical guide to the study of the literature of the u.s.a., 3rd edition. Durham, North Carolina: Duke University, 1970.

Griswold, William M.. A descriptive list of novels and tales dealing with american country life. Cambridge, Massachusetts: Griswold, 1890.

---A descriptive list of novels and tales dealing with the history of north america. Cambridge, Massachusetts: Griswold, 1895.

Guthrie, A. B.. The blue hen's chick; a life in context. New York: McGraw, 1964.

Hazard, Lucy Lockwood. The frontier in american literature. New York: Crowell, 1927.

Hubbell, Jay Broadus. Virginia life in fiction. Dallas,
Texas: n.p., 1922.

---The south in american literature. Chapel Hill, North
Carolina: Duke University, 1954.

Hughes, H. Stuart. History as art and as science. twin
vistas on the past. [Aushen, Ruth Nanda, ed. World
Perspective Series, Vol. 32] New York: Harper, 1964.

Hutchinson, W. H.. A bar cross liar. bibliography of
eugene manlove rhodes who loved the west-that-was when he
was young. Stillwater, Oklahoma: Redlands Press, 1959.

Johnson, James Gibson. Southern fiction prior to 1860; an
attempt at a first-hand bibliography. Charlottesville,
Virginia: Michil Co., 1909.

Karolides, Nicholas T.. The pioneer in the american novel
1900-1950. Norman, Oklahoma: University of Oklahoma,
1967.

Keiser, Albert. The indian in american literature. New
York: Oxford, 1933.

Kerr, Elizabeth Margaret. Bibliography of the sequence novel.
Minneapolis, Minnesota: University of Minnesota Press, 1950.

Leisy, Ernest E.. The american historical novel. Norman,
Oklahoma: University of Oklahoma, 1950.

Lenrow, Elbert. Reader's guide to prose fiction; an intro-
ductory essay with bibliographies of 1500 novels. New
York: Appleton, 1940.

Levin, David. In defense of historical literature. essays
on american history, autobiography, drama and fiction.
New York: Hill and Wang, 1967.

Lively, Robert W.. Fiction fights the civil war. Chapel
Hill, North Carolina: University North Carolina Press, 1957.

Loshe, Lillie Deming. The early american novel. New York:
Columbia University, 1907.

Lukács, György. The historical novel. Boston: Beacon, 1963.

McGarry, Daniel and White, Sarah. Historical fiction guide.
Denver, Colorado, Scarcrow, 1963.

Marble, Annie (Russell). A study of the modern novel, british
and american since 1900. Appleton, 1928.

Matthews, Brander. The historical novel and other essays.
New York: Scribner's, 1901.

Meyer, Roy W.. The middlewest farm novel in 20th century. Lincoln: University of Nebraska, 1964.

Nield, Jonathan. A guide to the best historical novels and tales, 5th edition. London: Macmillan, 1929.

Overton, Grant. The women who make our novels. New York: Dodd, 1928.

Pearson, Edmund Lester. Dime novels; or, following an old trail in popular literature. Boston: Little, 1929.

Rusk, Ralph Leslie. The literature of the middle western frontier. New York: Columbia, 1925.

Steckmesser, Kent Ladd. The western hero in history and legend. Norman, Oklahoma: University of Oklahoma, 1965.

Stuckey, William Joseph. The pulitizer prize novels; a critical backward look. Norman, Oklahoma: University of Oklahoma, 1966.

VanEvery, Dale. Our country then; tales of our first frontier. New York: Holt, 1958.

VanPatten, N.. Index to bibliographies of american and british authors 1923-1932. Stanford, California: Stanford University Press, 1934.

Wagenknecht, Edward. Cavalcade of the american novel; from the birth of the nation to the middle of the twentieth century. New York: Holt, 1952.

Warfel, Harry. Charles brockden brown, american gothic novelist. Gainesville, Florida: University of Florida, 1949.

Weber, Olga S.. Literary and library prizes, 5th edition. New York: Bowker, 1963.

Wegelin, Oscar. Early american fiction, 1774-1830. a compilation of the titles of works of fiction, by writers born or residing in north america, north of the mexican border and printed previous to 1831. 3rd edition. New York: Smith, 1929.

Wright, Lyle H.. American fiction 1851-1875. a contribution toward a bibliography. San Marino, California: Huntington Library, 1957.

---American fiction 1774-1850. a contribution toward a bibliography, 2nd edition revised. San Marina, California: Huntington Library, 1969.

---American fiction 1876-1900. a contribution toward a bibliography. San Marina, California: Huntington Library, 1966.

1   Abby, Edward (1927-   ). The brave cowboy; an old tale
      in a new time. New York: Dodd, 1956. 277p.

2   ---Fire on the mountain. New York: Dial, 1962. 211p.
            Western Heritage Award--Wrangler Trophy--Outstand-
      ing Western Novel--1963.

3   Abbot, Charles Conrad (1843-1919). A colonial wooing.
      Philadelphia: Lippincott, 1895. 241p.
            Quakers--Burlington County, New Jersey--Critical.

4   ---The hermit of nottingham; a novel. Philadelphia:
      Lippincott, 1897. 275p.

5   Abbot, Mrs. Jane Ludlow (1881-   ). Folly farm.
      Philadelphia: Lippincott, 1935. 314p.
            Thirteen year old girl--1809-1812--From Phil-
      adelphia area to new home in wilderness near Buffalo,
      New York--Romance--Juvenile.

6   ---River's rim; a novel. Philadelphia: Lippincott, 1950.
      254p.
            Romance set during War 1812 pivoting about Niagara
      frontier--An American loyal to patriot's cause is sus-
      pected of disloyalty because of relatives--McCarthyism
      of an earlier moment--Not too good.

7   Abbott, Johnston. LaRoux. New York: Macmillan, 1924.
      340p.
            Adventure of French girl in New France--Search for
      man who robbed her father--Iriquois.

8   ---The seigneurs of la saulaye; gentlemen adventurers of
      new france two centuries ago. New York: Macmillan,
      1928. 379p.
            Romantic novel--New France--Story told in grand
      manner.

9   Adams, Andy (1859-1935). Log of a cowboy; a narrative
      of the old trail days. Boston: Houghton, 1903. 387p.
            Log of a cattle drive--Most complete factual
      account in literature of this western activity--Texas
      to Wyoming.

10 ---The outlet. New York: Houghton, 1905. 371p.
    Cattle, Indians, Cowboys, Railroads, 1880's--
    Sharp methods of railway companies, contractors and
    congressional lobbyists concerned with cattle drives.

11 ---Reed anthony, cowman; an autobiography. Boston:
    Houghton, 1907. 384p.
    Confederate veteran rancher in Texas after the
    Civil War.

12 ---Wells brothers; the young cattle kings. Boston:
    Houghton, 1911. 356p.
    Two orphan boys--Nebraska--1800's--Stirring
    adventure--Juvenile.

13 ---The ranch on the beaver; a sequal to wells brothers;
    the young cattle kings. Boston: Houghton, 1927. 307p.
    Teen age boys--Ranch life--Prairie fire--Wild
    horses--Rodeo--Cattle--Juvenile.

14 Adams, Clifton. The desperado. New York: Fawcett, 1950.
    163p.
        Western

15 ---A noose for the desperado. New York: Fawcett, 1951.
    166p.
        Western

16 ---Six gun boss. New York: Random, 1952. 244p.
        Western

17 ---Two gun law. New York: Fawcett, 1954. 174p.
        Western

18 ---Death's sweet song. New York: Fawcett, 1955. 144p.
        Western

19 ---The dangerous days of kiowa jones. New York: Doubleday,
    1963. 192p.
        Western

20 ---Doomsday creek. New York: Doubleday, 1964. 181p.
        Western

21 ---The hottest forth of july in the history of hangtree
    county. New York: Doubleday, 1964. 182p.
        Western

22 ---The grabhorn bounty. New York: Doubleday, 1965. 185p.
        Western

23 ---Shorty. New York: Doubleday, 1966. 185p.
        Western

24 ---The most dangerous profession. New York: Doubleday,
    1967. 189p.

25   ---A partnership with death.   Ace, 1967.   192p.
          Western

26   ---pseud. Randall Clay.   When oil ran red.   New York:
          Pennant, 1954.   168p.
          Western

27   Adams, Frank Davis.   Life and times of buckshot south;
          and of his friends and colleague, phineas j. courtney,
          and their mutal companion, laura morse, to say nothing
          of their intrepid adversary mr. aaron cosgrove of the
          starling detective agency.   New York: Dutton, 1959.
          251p.
              Western--Satire--Spoofs last days of outlaws--
          Colorado--1903--Good.

28   Adams, Frank Ramsey (1883-   ).   Five fridays.   Boston:
          Small, 1915.   339p.
          Western

29   ---King's crew.   New York: R. Long and R. R. Smith, 1932.
          332p.
          Western

30   ---Gunsight ranch.   New York: Doubleday, 1939.   275p.
          Western

31   ---Arizona feud.   New York: Doubleday, 1941.   278p.
          Mystery with western setting.

32   Adams, Henry Austin.   Westchester; a tale of the revolution.
          St. Louis, Missouri: Herder, 1899.   264p.

33   Adams, James Douglas.   Cap'n ezara, privateer.   New York:
          Harcourt, 1940.   248p.
              Two farm boys--Eve War of 1812--Newburyport
          shipyard--Juvenile.

34   Adams, John Turville (1805-1882).   The lost hunter; a
          tale of early times.   New York: Derby, 1856.   462p.
              Indians, N. A.--Island off Connecticut--1635.

35   ---The white chief among the red men; or, the knight of
          the golden melice.   a historical romance.   New York:
          Derby, 1859.   473p.
              Sir Christopher Gardiner, (1630-32)--Pequot
          War 1637--Also published under title, the knight of
          the golden malice; a historical romance.   New York:
          Derby, 1857.   473p.

36   Adams, Marshall.   They fought for liberty.   New York:
          Dodge, 1937.   250p.
              Romance--American Revolution--Juvenile.

37   Adams, Samuel Hopkins (1871-1958).   Gorgeous hussy.

Boston: Houghton, 1934. 549p.
Mrs. Margaret L. (O'Neal) Timberlare Eaton.

38   ---The harvey girls. New York: Random, 1942. 327p.
Based on Fred Harvey restaurant and girls--1891--
Sandrock Mountain territory.

39   ---Canal town; a novel. New York: Random, 1944. 466p.
Palmyra, New York 1820's--Doctor comes to canal
town and tries to reform practices to fight malaria
and dysentery--Author used Walter Edmonds' notes on
Erie Canal--Good portrait of canal town.

40   ---Banner by the wayside. New York: Random, 1947. 442p.
Endurance Andrews, foundling and Jans Quintard,
ex-Harvard student in touring theatre group 1840's
along Erie Canal.

41   ---The pony express. New York: Random, 1950. 185p.
Juvenile

42   ---The santa fé trail. New York: Random, 1951. 181p.
First wagon expedition--Wm. Becknell (ca.1790-
1832)--Not as good as Holling's Tree in the Trail--
Juvenile.

43   ---Wagons to the wilderness; a story of westward expansion.
Philadelphia: Winston, 1954. 182p.
Thirteen year old boy 1822 Captain Mabbitts
trading expedition--Juvenile.

44   ---Chingo smith of the erie canal. New York: Random,
1958. 275p.
1816--Juvenile.

45   Ainsworth, Edward Maddin (1902-   ). Eagles fly west.
New York: Macmillan, 1946. 447p.
Lt. Shane Malone reporter for James Gordon
Bennett of New York Herald in 1846--To California
for gold rush--Picture of Spanish-American world.

46   Ainsworth, William Harrison (1805-1882). John law,
the protector. London: Chapman Hall, 1864. 3 vols.
Mississippi Bubble--1705-1729--John Law (1671-
1729).

47   Albert, Edna. Little pilgrim to penn's woods. New
York: Longmans, 1930. 300p.
Young German girl, Selinda, from Wertheim,
Germany, to Pennsylvania--Juvenile.

48   Alden, Joseph. The old revolutionary soldier. New York:
Gates, 1848. 152p.

49   Alderman, Clifford Lindsey. To fame unknown. New York:
Appleton, 1954. 360p.

4

Romance of French-Indian War--Last phase--Mili-
tary, social, economic problem and love--Good research.

50 ---Joseph brant; chief of the six nations. New York:
Messner, 1958. 192p.
Indians with British--American Revolution--Joseph
Brant (1742-1807).

51 ---The silver keys. New York: Putnam, 1960. 319p.
Sir William Phips--1675-1700--Good Jacobean
London background--Romance--Pirates--Treasure.

52 ---The vengeance of abel wright. New York: Doubleday,
1964. 192p.
King Philip's War--1675-76--Juvenile.

53 Aldis, Mrs. Dorothy (Keeley) (1896-   ). Ride the wild
waves; a true story of adventure. New York: Putnam,
1957. 182p.
Colonial Massachusetts--Juvenile.

54 Aldrich, Bess Streeter (1881-1954) [1911-1918) pseud.
Steven, Margaret Dean]. The rim of the prairie.
New York: Appleton, 1925. 352p.
Pioneers and romance in Nebraska--Realistic.

55 ---A lantern in her hand. New York: Appleton, 1928.
306p.
Pioneer in Nebraska 1865-1900--Log cabin in Iowa--
Good account of early stages of community growth--
Sentimental.

56 ---A white bird flying. New York: Appleton, 1931.
335p.
Sequel to Lantern In Her Hand--Recreate spirit
of descendants of early Scotch and German settlers--
Nebraska.

57 ---Spring came on forever. New York: D. Appleton-Century,
1935. 332p.
German-Americans to Nebraska--Sweep of four generations.

58 ---Song of years. New York: D. Appleton, 1939. 490p.
Pioneer life in Iowa, 1854-1865--Nine children
in the family.

59 ---Lieutenant's lady. New York: D. Appleton-Century,
1942. 275p.
Based on diary of wife of army officer who lives
on frontier at fort on Missouri River during 1830's.
and 1840's.

60 Aldrich, Mrs. Clara Chapline (Thomas) pseud. Aldrich,
Darragh. Peter good for nothing; a story of the
minnesota logging camps. New York: Macmillan, 1929.
351p.

5

Minnesota logging--Romance.

Aldrich, Darragh pseud. see Aldrich, Mrs. Clara Chapline
Thomas

61 Alexander, Charles Wesley pseud. Bradshaw, Wellesley.
Saved by buffalo bill during the ghost dances of the
wild indians of dakota. Philadelphia: Old Franklin
Publishing House, 1891. 78p.

Alexander, William, jt. author, see Cormack, Maribelle

62 Alfriend, Mary Bethel (Mrs). Sanluis of apalache; a tale
of early american life. Boston: Chapman and Grimes,
1939. 241p.
Florida--1765-1763.

63 ---Juan ortiz; gentleman of seville, a novel. Boston:
Chapman and Grimes, 1941. 289p.
Fictional biography--Served as guide and in-
terpreter with DeSota--Lived for ten years in Florida.

64 Allee, Mrs. Marjorie (Hill). Judith lankester. Boston:
Houghton, 1930. 241p.
First of Lankester Series--Juvenile.

65 ---The road to carolina. Boston: Houghton, 1932. 240p.
Sequel to Tristam Coffin--Lad and northern
Quaker Uncle trapped in Carolina during Civil War--
Juvenile.

66 ---A house of her own. Boston: Houghton, 1934. 220p.
Second of Lankester Series--1850's-1860's--
Backwoods of Indiana--School teacher--Juvenile.

67 ---Off to philadelphia! Boston: Houghton, 1936. 214p.
Third of Lankester girls Series--Steam packet--
Indiana to Philadelphia--Juvenile.

68 ---Runaway linda. Boston: Houghton, 1939. 220p.
Teen age boy and girl--1875--Escape "Uncle"
who has Indiana farm--Juvenile.

Allen, Don B. jt. author, see Allen, Terry D.

69 Allen, Dexter. Jaguar and the golden stag. New York:
Coward, 1954. 340p.
First novel--Mexico--Nezahuapilli (1476)--Prince
Nezahual, emperor of Anahuac--#1 of Trilogy.

70 ---Coil of serpent; a novel. New York: Coward, 1955. 314p.
Follows Jaguar and Golden Stag--Not as good as
first novel--#2 of Trilogy.

71 ---Valley of eagles; a novel. New York: Coward-McCann,
       1957. 256p.
       #3 of Trilogy--Based on Prescott's Conquest of
       Mexico--Ends three years after Cortes.

72 Allen, Henry (1912-   ) pseud. Fisher, Clay. Red bliz-
       zard; a novel of the north plains sioux. New York:
       Simon and Schuster, 1951. 250p.

73 ---War bonnet; a novel of mountain man war and arapaho
       intrigue along the old medicine road. Boston:
       Houghton, 1953. 180p.

74 ---Yellow hair; a novel of indian warfare in the arkansas
       valley of 1868, and the fate-foreshadowing, willful
       way of george a. custer eight years before an angry
       history caught up with him on the banks of montana's
       little big horn. Boston: Houghton, 1953. 194p.

75 ---The tall men. Boston: Houghton, 1954. 182p.
       Western

76 ---The big pasture; a novel of new lands and old emotions,
       the forgotten story of montana's first range war.
       Boston: Houghton, 1955. 215p.

77 ---The brass command; an account of a career officer's
       last chance, and of the base-metal rewards of military
       ambition in an indian territory garrison of the late
       1870's. Boston: Houghton, 1955. 218p.

78 ---The blue mustang; a novel inspired by one of the most
       remarkable rides in the history of the southwest.
       Boston: Houghton, 1956. 246p.

79 ---Yellowstone kelly. Boston: Houghton, 1957. 246p.
       Luther Sage Kelly (1849-1928).

80 ---The crossing. Boston: Houghton, 1958. 314p.
       Civil War.

81 ---Niño, the legend of "apache kid." New York: Morrow,
       1961. 190p.
       Apache Kid.

82 ---The pitchfork patrol. New York: Macmillan, 1962. 181p.
       Western

83 ---Valley of the bear; a novel of the north plains sioux.
       Boston: Houghton, 1964. 184p.

84 Allen, Henry (1912-   ) pseud. Henry, Will. No sur-
       vivors, a novel. New York: Random House, 1950. 344p.
       Custer--Sioux--Pro-Indian--Custer critical pic-
       ture--Details good--Romance--Climax Battle of Little
       Big Horn (1876).

85 ---Wolf eye, the bad one. New York: Messner, 1951.
173p.
Western

86 ---To follow a flag. New York: Random, 1953. 241p.

87 ---Death of legend. New York: Random, 1954. 244p.
Jesse W. James (1847-1882).

88 ---The fourth horseman; a novel of old arizona. New York:
Random House, 1954. 242p.
Western

89 ---Who rides with wyatt; the strange and lonely story of
the last of the great lawmen. New York: Random,
1955. 241p.
Wyatt Berry Stapp Earp (1848-1929).

90 ---The north star. New York: Random, 1956. 213p.

91 ---The texas rangers. New York: Random, 1957. 181p.
Western

92 ---Orphan of the north. New York: Random, 1958. 176p.

93 ---Reckoning at yankee hat. New York: Random, 1958.
232p.
Henry Plummer (d. 1864).

94 ---The seven men at mimbres springs. New York: Random,
1958. 217p.
Western

95 ---From where the sun now stands. New York: Random,
1960. 279p.
Joseph, Nez Percé, chief (1850-1904)--Golden
Spur Award 1961 for Best Western Historical Novel.

96 ---The feleen brand. New York: Bantam, 1962. 184p.
Western

97 ---San juan hill. New York: Random, 1962. 276p.
Spanish-American War--1898.

98 ---The gates of the mountains. New York: Random, 1963.
306p.
Golden Spur Award--Best Western historical
novel--1964.

99 ---Mackenna's gold. New York: Random, 1963. 276p.

100 ---In the land of the mandans. Philadelphia: Chilton,
1965. 150p.

101 ---The last warpath. New York: Random, 1966. 242p.
Cheyenne 1680-1696.

8

102   ---Sons of the western frontier. Philadelphia: Chilton,
         1966. 303p.
               Western

103   ---One more river to cross; the life and the legend
         of isom dart. New York: Random, 1967. 256p.
               Series of Outlaw Adventures--Arkansas slave to
         west--Western about Negro.

104   ---Alias butch cassidy. New York: Random, 1968.
         209p.
               George LeRoy Parker (1867-   ).

105   ---The day fort larking fell. Philadelphia: Chilton,
         1968. 215p.

106   ---Maheo's children; the legend of little dried river.
         Philadelphia: Chilton, 1968. 148p.
               Battle of Sand Creek (1864).

107   Alderman, Clifford Lindsey. The arch of stars. New
         York: Appleton, 1950. 410p.
               First novel--American Revolution--Hampshire
         Grants, Vermont--Ethan Allen and Seth Warner.

108   Allen, Hervey (1889-1949), [full name William Hervey
         Allen]. Anthony adverse. New York: Farrar, 1933.
         1224p.
               1775-1830 Scot to America and world-wide ad-
         ventures--Good historical romance.

109   ---The forest and the fort. New York: Rinehart, 1943.
         344p.
               First in series--Salathiel Albine returns to
         white world in 1763--Ft. Pitt.

110   ---Bedford village. New York: Farrar, 1944. 305p.
               Second of series--November 1763-Autumn 1764--
         Albine's life with whites and his wife Melissa--
         Bedford Village--Mountains east of Pittsburg--
         Not up to Forest and Fort.

111   ---Toward morning. New York: Rinehart, 1948. 458p.
               Third of series--Sequel Bedford Village--
         Pennsylvania pioneer life before Revolution--S.
         Albine and common-in-law-wife Melissa--Costume
         piece--1765.

112   ---The city in the dawn. New York: Rinehart, 1950.
         696p.
               Abridgement of Trilogy of Forest and Fort,
         Bedford Village and Toward the Morning.

113   Allen, James Lane (1849-1925). John gray; a kentucky
         tale of the olden time. Philadelphia: Lippincott,
         1893. 218p.

9

Some included in <u>Choir Invisible</u>.

114 ---<u>Choir invisible</u>. New York: Macmillan, 1897. 361p.
Story of Kentucky during last part of 18th
century and first part of 19th century--A hopeless
romance--Love and renunciation--Rural Kentucky.

115 Allen, John Houghton. <u>Southwest</u>. Philadelphia:
Lippincott, 1952. 220p.
Frontier life--Texas.

116 Allen, Merritt Parmelee (1892-   ). <u>Black rain</u>.
New York: Longmans, 1939. 213p.
1763--Siege of Detroit--Pontiac, Ottawa Chief
(d. 1769)--Juvenile.

117 ---<u>Western star; a story of jim bridger</u>. New York:
Longmans, 1941. 186p.
Fictionalized biography--James Bridger (1804-
1881)--Juvenile.

118 ---<u>The green cockade</u>. New York: Longmans, 1942. 199p.
New Hampshire Grants--Ethan Allen--Dan Morgan--
Green Mountain Boys--Yorkers--Juvenile.

119 ---<u>Suntrail</u>. New York: Longmans, 1943. 198p.
Fictional account of Jebediah Smith--Juvenile.

120 ---<u>Red heritage</u>. New York: Longmans, 1946. 314p.
Youth with General Herkimer at Oriskany--
American Revolution--Juvenile.

121 ---<u>The spirit of the eagle</u>. New York: Longmans, 1947.
234p.
Youth with Mountain Men--Far West--Benjamin
Louis Eulalie de Bonneville--Juvenile.

122 ---<u>Battle lanterns</u>. New York: Longmans, 1949. 279p.
Youth with Francis Marion--Slave on West In-
dian plantation--Revolutionary era--Juvenile.

123 --<u>The wilderness way</u>. New York: Longmans, 1954. 246p.
With LaSalle down Mississippi River--Juvenile.

124 ---<u>East of astoria</u>. New York: Longmans, 1956. 250p.
Astor Fur Company--Astoria--1810--Overland
return trip to St. Louis, Missouri--Robert Stuart--
Juvenile.

125 ---<u>Silver wolf</u>. New York: Longmans, 1951. 216p.
Santa Fé Trail--Christopher "Kit" Carson--
Juvenile.

Allen, T. D. <u>pseud</u>. see Allen, Terry D. and Don B.

10

126   Allen, Terry D. and Allen, Don B. pseud. Allen, T. D..
      Doctor in buckskin. New York: Harper, 1951. 277p.
            Based on Marcus Whitman and discredited story
      of Reverand Henry Spaulding an associate--Cf. The Way
      West.

127   ---Troubled border. New York: Harper, 1954. 275p.
            John McLoughlin of Hudson Bay Fur Company--
      Ft. Vancouver on Columbia River.

      Allen, William Hervey, see Allen, Hervey

128   Allerton, James Martin. Hawk's nest; or, the last of
      the cahoonshees. a tale of the delaware valley and
      historical romance of 1690. Port Jervis, New York:
      Gazette Book and Job Print, 1892. 246p.

129   Allis, Marguerite. Not without peril. New York: Putnam,
      1941. 405p.
            One of better novels--Jemima Sartwell Howe (1713?-
      1805) main character as early settler of Vermont--
      True story--Indian captivity.

130   ---The splendour stays; an historical novel based on
      the lives of the seven hart sisters of saybrook,
      connecticut. New York: Putnam, 1942. 497p.
            First of extended Connecticut family series.

131   ---All in good time. New York: Putnam, 1944. 309p.
            Connecticut clockmaker and wife--Job Hubbard
      and Elvira Stone--Post-Revolutionary era--Litchfield--
      Sound Americana.

132   ---Water over the dam. New York: Putnam, 1947. 376p.
            Connecticut 1820's building of Farmington Canal--
      Mt. Nebo's and New Haven 1825-1848--Titus Dodd--Orphan
      boy working in general store.

133   ---The bridge. New York: Putnam, 1949. 307p.
            Connecticut--1840-1876--Lord family operates
      steamship to New York City--Ships out--Railroad in.

134   ---Now we are free. New York: Putnam, 1952. 307p.
            #1 of Trilogy--From Connecticut to Ohio
      County lands by Revolutionary soldiers after the war--
      Western Reserve--1789-1810.

135   ---To keep us free. New York: Putnam, 1953. 344p.
            #2 of Trilogy--Sequel to Now We are Free--
      Early life on Ohio frontier 1797-1860--Substantial
      work.

136   ---Brave pursuit. New York: Putnam, 1954. 312p.
            #3 of Trilogy--1802-1820--Early Ohio River
      trade--Early days of statehood--Education on frontier.

11

137 ---The rising storm, a novel. New York: Putnam, 1955.
312p.
Field family series continued--1830-1863--
Abolition in Ohio--Twin brothers holding opposite
views of slavery find conflict over underground
railroad--Cincinnati.

138 ---Free soil. New York: Putnam, 1958. 288p.
Lafayette Field to Kansas frontier--John Brown--
Kansas 1850's.

139 Altrocchi, Mrs. Julia (Cooley) (1893-   ). Wolves
against the moon. New York: Macmillan, 1940. 572p.
First novel based in part on brief family
chronicle by Frances R. Howe--1794-1834 French homestead in old Northwest--Mackinac to New Orleans,
to Detroit--Fur trade money later in real estate and
lake transportation--Good Ottawa tribal customs.

140 Altsheler, Joseph Alexander (1862-1919). The hidden
mine. New York: J. S. Tait, 1896. 273p.
Western Life Series No. 2--Wrote many Juveniles.

141 ---A soldier of manhattan, and his adventures at ticonderoga and quebec. New York: Appleton, 1897. 316p.
French-Indian War--Battle of Quebec--Romance
English officer and French maiden--Capture of Ticonderoga.

142 ---The sun of saratoga; a romance of burgoyne's surrender. New York: Appleton, 1897.
1777--Capitulation of General Burgoyne.

143 ---A herald of the west; an american story of 1811-1815.
New York: Appleton, 1898. 359p.
War 1812--British attacks on Washington, D. C.
and New Orleans--Anti-England.

144 ---The rainbow of gold. New York: Continental, 1898.
228p.

145 ---In hostile red; a romance of the monmouth campaign.
New York: Doubleday, 1900. 340p.
Battle Monmouth 1778.

146 ---The wilderness road; a romance of st. clair's defeat
and wayne's victory. New York: Appleton, 1901. 379p.
Arthur St. Clair (1734-1818)--Anthony Wayne
(1743-1796).

147 ---My captive; a novel. New York: Appleton, 1902. 281p.
American Revolution in the South.

148 ---The free rangers; a story of early days along the
mississippi. New York: Appleton, 1909. 364p.
Sequel to Forest Runner--Spanish control and
intrigue--Mississippi River.

12

149 ---The young trailers; a story of early kentucky.
New York: Appleton, 1907. 331p.

150 ---The forest runners; a story of the great war trail
in early kentucky. New York: Appleton, 1908. 362p.
Juvenile series adventure, sequel to Young
Trailers.

151 ---The recovery; a story of kentucky. New York:
Lovell, 1908. 353p.

152 ---The last of the chiefs; a story of the great sioux
war. New York: Appleton, 1909. 336p.
Two boys--Caravan to West--Custer's Last Stand--
Montana--Dakota Indian Wars 1876.

153 ---The horsemen of the plains; a story of the great
cheyenne war. New York: Macmillan, 1910. 390p.

154 ---The rifleman of the ohio; a story of early days along
the beautiful river. New York: Appleton, 1910.
354p.
Continues characters of Young Trailers, Forest
Rangers and Free Runners.

155 ---The quest of the four; a story of the comanches and
buena vista. New York: Appleton, 1911. 385p.

156 ---The scouts of valley; a story of wyoming and the
chemung. New York: Appleton, 1911. 362p.
Wyoming Valley of Pennsylvania--Six nations--
Juvenile.

157 ---The border water; a story of the great chiefs last
stand. New York: Appleton, 1912. 370p.
Last of "Young Trailers Series"--Juvenile.

158 ---The texan star; a story of a great fight for liberty.
New York: Appleton, 1912. 372p.
Texas Revolution--Juvenile.

159 ---Apache gold; a story of the strange southwest.
New York: Appleton, 1913. 382p.
Boys search for treasure--Juvenile.

160 ---The texan scouts; a story of the alamo and goliad.
New York: Appleton, 1913. 355p.
Sequel to Texan Star--Escape Alamo during
"fall"--to New Orleans--Juvenile.

161 ---The texan triumph; a romance of the san jacinto
campaign. New York: Appleton, 1913. 356p.
Last of Trilogy--Ned Fulton's Texas adventures--
Juvenile.

162 ---The hunters of the hills; a story of the great

french and indian war. New York: Appleton, 1916.
359p.
    French-Indian War--1755-1763--Juvenile Series--#1.

163 ---The keeper of the trail; a story of the great woods.
New York: Appleton, 1916. 323p.
Young Trailers Series.

164 ---The eyes of the woods; a story of the ancient wilderness. New York: Appleton, 1917. 318p.
Young Trailer Series.

165 ---The rulers of the lakes; a story of george and champlain. New York: Appleton, 1917. 332p.
    From Braddock's defeat at Duquesne to Colonial success on Lake George--#2 of French-Indian Series--Juvenile.

166 ---The shadow of the north; a story of old new york and a lost campaign. New York: Appleton, 1917. 357p.
French-Indian War Series #3.

167 ---The great sioux trail; a story of mountain and plain.
New York: Appleton, 1918. 340p.
    Sioux country--Treasure hunting--Romance--First of post-Civil War group.

168 ---The lost hunters; a story of wild man and a great beast. New York: Appleton, 1918. 341p.
Sequel to Sioux Trail.

169 ---The masters of the peaks; a story of the great north woods. New York: Appleton, 1918. 310p.
    Sequel to Rulers of the Lakes--From victory at Lake George to fall of Fort William Henry.
#4 of French-Indian Series.

170 ---The lords of the wild; a story of the old new york border. New York: Appleton, 1919. 297p.
    #5 of French-Indian Series--Ends with fall of Ticonderoga--Adirondack Region.

171 ---The sun of quebec; a story of a great crisis.
New York: Appleton, 1919. 333p.
    #6 of French-Indian Series--To capture of Quebec--Assumes reader knows some history.

172 Alves, Juliet. Huldah. New York: Scribner's, 1942.
365p.
    Backwoods North Carolina girl marries Virginia aristocrat--To Kentucky frontier--Post-Revolution--Good color--Honest.

173 Ambrose and eleanor; or, the disinherited pair. a tale of the revolution. [Anonymous]. New York:

Clausman, 1834. 2 vols.
Battle of Brandywine--Melodramatic--Romance.

174 Amelia; or, the faithless briton. an original novel
to which is added Amelia; or, malevolence defeated
and Miss seward's monody on major andré. [Annoymous].
Boston: Spotswood and Wayne, 1798. 61p.
Oldest American tale of Revolution.

175 Ames, Joseph Bushnell (1878-1928). The treasure of the
canyon; a story of adventure in arizona. New York:
Holt, 1907. 330p.
Juvenile

176 ---Pete, cow-puncher; a story of the texas plains.
New York: Holt, 1908. 324p.
Young New Yorker to Texas Plains rather than to
Yale and Wall Street. Clean, honest boy story--
Juvenile.

177 ---Curley of the circle bar. New York: Century, 1919.
263p.
Western--Juvenile.

178 ---Curley and the aztec gold. New York: Century, 1920.
268p.
Western--Juvenile.

179 ---Shoe bar stratton. New York: Century, 1922. 354p.
Western--Juvenile.

180 ---The man from painted post. New York: Century, 1923.
336p.
Western

181 ---Curly graham, cow puncher. New York: Century, 1924.
321p.
Western

182 ---Clearport boys. New York: Century, 1925. 304p.

183 ---Loudon from laramie. New York: Century, 1925. 374p.
Western

184 ---The lone hand. New York: Century, 1926. 368p.
Western

185 ---The mounted troop. New York: Century, 1926. 212p.

186 ---The stranger from cheyenne. New York: Century, 1927.
354p.
Western--Good story.

187 ---Chaps and chukkers. New York: Century, 1928. 383p.
Western

188   ---The flying v mystery. New York: Century, 1928. 207p.
       Western--Mystery.

189   ---The bladed barrier. New York: Century, 1929. 393p.
       Mystery--Western Adventure.

190   Ames, Merlin McMain (1879-   ). The fork in the trail.
       Philadelphia: McKay, 1948. 348p.
       Wisconsin frontier--1890-1900--Juvenile.

191   The amorous intrigues and adventures of aaron burr.
       [Annoymous]. New York: Published for the proprietors,
       ca. 1861. 100p.
       Wright--"a scurrilous story."

192   Anderson, Mrs. Ada (Woodruff). Heart of the red firs;
       a story of the pacific northwest. Boston: Little,
       1907. 313p.
       Completion of Northern Pacific Road to Coast.

193   ---The strain of white. Boston: Little, 1909. 300p.
       Frontier life Pacific Northwest 1850's--Heroine
       a Yakima chief's sister and an army officer.

194   Anderson, Nephi. Added upon; a story. Salt Lake City,
       Utah: Deseret News Pub., 1898. 140p.
       Mormon principles.

       Andrews, Charles Robert Douglas Hardy, see Andrews,
       Robert Douglas

195   Andrews, Marietta (Minnigerove) (1869-1931), Mrs. Eliaphet
       Fraser Andrews. The seventh wave. New York:
       Boni, 1930. 261p.
       Four generations of pioneer family--Sketchy.

196   Andrews, Ned. Jerky; the story of two boys in the old
       west. New York: Morrow, 1936. 295p.
       Author a cattleman--Juvenile for older boys--
       Arizona.

197   ---The lost "chicken henry". New York: Morrow, 1937.
       276p.
       Juvenile

198   ---Little stranger; the story of a western pony.
       New York: Morrow, 1941. 248p.
       Juvenile

199   ---Cowdog. New York: Morrow, 1946. 222p.
       Western--Lone Ranger fans--Juvenile.

200   Andrews, Robert Douglas (1903-   ). Great day in the
       morning. New York: Coward, 1950. 341p.
       1850 Colorado gold--Attempt to pull Colorado

into Civil War on side of the South--Hero Owen
Pentecost--Southern to Denver 1858--Started <u>Georgia</u>
<u>Conspiracy</u>.

201 ---<u>Burning gold</u>. New York: Doubleday, 1945. 403p.
Good Pirate story--Daniel DeFoe, Captain William Dampier--Dr. Thomas Dover--to West Indies--
cross Isthmus--to London.

202 <u>Annals of the empire city; from its colonial days</u>
<u>to the present. tale 1: the quadroon; or, new-york</u>
<u>under the english</u>. By a New Yorker [Annoymous].
New York: Trow, 1852. 238p.
Black Plot--1741.

203 Anness, Milford E. <u>Song of metamoris; a story that</u>
<u>remains of a people who passed this way</u>. Caldwell,
Idaho: Caxton, 1964. 509p.
Delaware Indians in Indiana 1810.

204 ---<u>Forever the song</u>. Caldwell, Idaho: Caxton, 1967.
304p.
Indians in North America.

205 Anthony, Wilder. <u>Star of the hills</u>. New York: Macauly,
1927. 317p.
Spanish-American conflicts in California--
Espionage--Romance--Adventure.

206 Aplington, Kate Adele. <u>Pilgrims of the plains; a</u>
<u>romance of the santa fé trail</u>. Chicago: Browne,
1913. 400p.
Story is diary of young girl's trip from
Illinois to New Mexico--19th Century.

207 Appel, David. <u>Comanche; the story of america's most</u>
<u>heroic horse</u>. Cleveland: World, 1951. 224p.
First person narrative of horse Commanche only
survivor of Battle of Little Big Horn.

208 Arbuckle, Dorothy Fry. <u>The after-harvest festival; a</u>
<u>story of a girl of the old kankakee</u>. New York:
Dodd, 1955. 248p.
1863--Indians--Frontier--Twelve year old
daughter of French trapper--Juvenile.

209 Archer, George W. pseud. Bendbow, Hesper. <u>More than</u>
<u>she could bear; a story of the gachupin war in texas</u>
<u>a.d. 1812-1813</u>. Philadelphia: Claxton, 1872.
43p.
Texas--1810-1821.

210 Armer, Mrs. Laura (Adams) (1874-   ). <u>Waterless</u>
<u>mountain</u>. New York: Longsmans, 1931. 212p.
Author lived and worked among Navaho for years--
1930's era--Story of younger brother, sensitive,

beauty loving Navaho boy--Training under uncle for
office of Medicine Priest--Won Longman's Juvenile
Fiction Contest 1931.

211   ---Dark circle of branches.   New York: Longmans, 1933.
212p.
1862--Removal of Navajos to exile--Na Nai
small Navaho learns culture from medicine man uncle--
Very good.

212   ---Southwest.   New York: Longmans, 1935.   224p.
Navaho

213   ---The traders' children.   New York: Longmans, 1937.
241p.
Life of Black Mountain trading post--150 miles
from railroad--Story of trader's children--Spanish-
American--Navaho--Sheep raising.

214   ---Farthest west.   New York: Longmans, 1939.   190p.
California school children--Save redwoods from
destruction--Juvenile.

215   Armstrong, William.   An american nobleman; a story of
the canaan wilderness.   Chicago: Shulte, 1892.   277p.
Kentucky mountaineer.

216   Arnold, Adelaide Wilson.   A son of the first people.
New York: Macmillan, 1940.   248p.
Eight year old boy sent to government school--
Juvenile.

217   Arnold, Elliott (1912-   ).   Blood brother.   New York:
Duell, 1947.   558p.
Sympathetic to Indian cause--Chiricahua, Arizona
after Gadsden Purchase--Cochise and Tom Jeffers--
Description of Camp Grant Massacre--Apache Wars--
1856-1870.

218   ---The time of the gringo.   New York: Knopf, 1953.   612p.
Old Santa Fé--Exciting narrative of New Mexico--
Mexican War--1845-1848--Stunning--Excellent--Rise of
Manuel Armijo, Mexican Governor of New Mexico.

219   ---White falcon.   New York: Knopf, 1955.   246p.
Juvenile for older boys--John Tanner (1780?-
1847)--Late 1700's taken by Ottawa--Lived with
Chippewas--Red River.

220   ---Broken arrow.   New York: Duell, 1954.   246p.
Apache Wars--Has much of Blood Brother material
in it.

221   Arntson, Herbert E. (1911-   ).   Adam gray: stowaway;
a story of the china trade.   New York: Watts, 1961.
195p.

18

"Around the Horn"--Juvenile.

222   Arrington, Alfred W. pseud. Summerfield, Charles (1810-
      1867). The desperadoes of the southwest; contain-
      ing an account of the cane hill murders, together
      with the lives of several of the most notorious
      regulators and moderates of that region. New York:
      Graham, 1847. 48p.
         Southwest in transition--Lynch law.

223   ---The rangers and regulators of tanaha; or, life among
      the lawless. New York: DeWitt, 1856. 397p.
         Pioneer Texas--Published later 1884 under title
      of A Faithful Lover--Judge Alfred W. Arrington
      (1810-1867) came to Arkansas from North Carolina
      in 1819, Methodist Preacher 1828-1834, Arkansas
      Leg--Moved to Texas--Circuit Judge 1850-56--
      Published 1892 as Rangers and Regulators.

224   ---A faithful lover. New York: Carleton, 1884. 396p.
         Published in 1856 as The Rangers and the Reg-
      ulators of Tanaha; or, life among the Lawless.

      Arthur, Burt pseud. see Arthur, Herbert

225   Arthur, Herbert [originally Shappiro, Herbert Arthur].
      The black rider; a mustang marshall western. New York:
      Arcadia, 1941. 248p.
         Western

226   ---The valley of death; a mustang marshall western.
      New York: Arcadia, 1941. 256p.
         Western

227   ---Chenango pass; a mustang marshall western. New York:
      Arcadia, 1942. 256p.
         Western

228   ---Mustang marshall. New York: Phoenix, 1943. 253p.
         Western

229   ---Trouble at moon pass. New York: Phoenix, 1943. 256p.
         Western

230   ---Silver city rangers. New York: Phoenix, 1944. 254p.
         Western

231   ---Gunsmoke over utah. New York: Phoenix, 1945. 256p.
         Western

232   ---High pockets. New York: McBride, 1946. 160p.
         Western

233   ---The texan. New York: McBride, 1946. 217p.
         Western

234   ---The buckaroo. New York: Arcadia, 1947. 223p.
       Western

235   ---Boss of the far west. New York: Phoenix, 1948. 250p.
       Western

236   ---The long west trail. New York: Phoenix, 1948. 256p.
       Western

237   ---Sheriff of lonesome. New York: Phoenix, 1948. 255p.
       Western

238   ---The killer. New York: Doubleday, 1952. 185p.
       Western

239   ---pseud. Arthur, Burt. Nevada. New York: Doubleday,
       1949. 221p.
       Western

240   ---Stirrups in the dust. New York: Doubleday, 1950.
       223p.
       Western

241   ---Trouble town. New York: Doubleday, 1950. 190p.
       Western

242   ---Thunder valley. New York: Doubleday, 1951. 188p.
       Western

243   ---pseud. Herbert, Arthur. Bugles in the night; an
       historical novel of the west. New York: Rinehart,
       1950. 250p.
       Western

244   ---Freedom run. New York: Rinehart, 1951. 249p.
            Far West 1870--Same hero as Bugles in the Night--
       Repel Russian invasion of California after Alaskan
       purchase--Horse opera--Russian variations.

245   ---The gun slinger. New York: Rinehart, 1951. 217p.
       Western

246   Ashland, Aria. Muscoma; or, faith campbell. a romance
       of the revolution. Boston: Hotchkiss, 1848. 100p.

247   ---The rebel scout; a romance of the revolution.
       New York: Stringer, 1852-55ca. 109p.

248   Ashton, John. The adventures and discourses of captain
       john smith sometime president of virginia and admiral
       of new england. New York: Cassell, 1883. 309p.
       Fictional Biography.

249   Aspden, Don. Barney's barges. New York: Holiday House,
       1944. 192p.
            War 1812--Barges defend Tidewater--John Rutledge
       horse boy on Tidewater ferry--Juvenile.

20

250   Aswell, Mary (White) (1902-   ). Abigail. New York:
       Crowell, 1959. 306p.
                    Quaker daughter in rebellion against the quiet
       life--Early settlement of Vermont.

251   Atherton, Gertrude Franklin (Horn) (1857-1948). The
       doomswoman. New York: Tait, Sons & Co., 1893. 263p.
                    First novel--Romance Old California--1840.

252   ---The californians. London: Lane, 1898. 351p.
                    Writes of her native land--Magdalene Yorba,
       daughter of Spanish mother and New England father.

253   ---The valiant runaways. New York: Dodd, 1898. 276p.
                    Romance--California--before entered Union--
       Spaniards.

254   ---The conqueror; being the true and romantic story
       of alexander hamilton. New York, Macmillan, 1902.
       546p.
                    Pro-Hamilton--Good history based on Hamilton's
       papers--Biography dramatized.

255   ---pseud. Lin, Frank. Rezánov. New York: The Authors
       and Newspaper Association, 1906. 320p.
                    California--1764-1807--Romance--Russian diplomat
       and daughter of Commandante of Presidio.

256   Atkins, Harry. A later son, a different daughter.
       New York: McGraw, 1968. 146p.
                    Set on Texas desert

       Atkinson, Eleanor Blake pseud. see Pratt, Mrs. Eleanor
       Blake (Atkinson)(1899-   ).

257   Atkinson, Mrs. Eleanor (1863-   ). Johnny appleseed;
       the romance of the power. New York: Harper, 1915.
       340p.
                    Jonathan Chapman--1774-1845--Juvenile.

258   ---Hearts undaunted; a romance of four frontiers.
       New York: Harper, 1917. 348p.
                    Midwest frontier--founding of Chicago--Iriquois.

259   Atkinson, Oriana (Torrey). The twin cousins; a novel.
       Indianapolis: Bobbs, 1951. 320p.
                    Catskill area--frontier--construction of Sus-
       quehanna Turnpike--Juvenile.

260   ---The golden season. Indianapolis: Bobbs, 1953. 309p.
                    Rush to Ohio 1790's--Juvenile.

261   Attwood, Adeline. Treasure of the sun. Boston: Houghton,
       1953. 218p.
                    Peruvian Indians know of location of Inca trea-
       sure--detail of customs of Inca.

21

Atwood, Dascomb pseud. see White, Mrs. Georgia (Atwood)

262 Auslander, Joseph (1897-   ). My uncle jan; a novel.
New York: Longmans, 1948. 236p.
Czech immigrants to Wisconsin in 1800's.

263 Austin, Anne (1895-   ). Jackson street. New York:
Greenberg, 1927. 298p.
Poor girl--Railroad yards--Texas City.

Austin, Frank pseud. see Faust, Fredrick Schiller

264 Austin, Mrs. Jane (Goodwin) (1831-1894). A nameless
nobleman. Boston: Osgood, 1881. 369p.
Plymouth--1676-1677 woven from family tradition--
Juvenile.

265 ---The desmond hundred. Boston: Osgood, 1882. 330p.
Juvenile

266 ---Standish of standish; a story of the pilgrims.
Boston: Houghton, 1889. 422p.
Pilgrims, 1620-27--Juvenile.

267 ---Dr. lebaron and his daughters; a story of the old
colony. Boston: Houghton, 1890. 460p.
Plymouth 1670's to American Revolution--Juvenile.

268 ---Betty alden; the first-born daughter of the pilgrims.
Boston: Houghton, 1891. 384p.
Juvenile

269 Austin, John Osborne. The journal of william jefferay,
gentleman. born at chiddingly, old england...1591;
died newport, new england...1675...a diary that
might have been. edited by john osborne austin.
Providence, Rhode Island: Freeman, 1899. 189p.

270 Austin, Mrs. Mary Hunter (1868-1934). Isidro. New
York: Grosset and Dunlap, 1904. 424p.
Romance in California during time of Franciscan
missionaries under Mexican rule--Indian and Spanish
settlers--Well wrought story by Indian authority
with good local color--Austin lived on slopes of
Sierras and edge of Mohave Desert.

271 ---Starry adventure. Boston: Houghton, 1931. 420p.
Son of college professor to Southwest for
health--Indians--Spaniards-Immigrants--Sangre de
Cristo Mountains.

272 Averill, Charles E.. The mexican ranchero; or, the maid
of the chapparal. a romance of the mexican war.
Boston: Gleason, 1847. 100p.

273 ---The secret service ship; or, the fall of san juan

d'Vlloa. a thrilling tale of the mexican war.
Boston: Gleason, 1848. 100p.

274 ---Kit carson, prince of gold hunters; or, the adventures
of the sacramento. a tale of the new el dorado
founded on actual facts. Boston: Williams, 1849.
124p.
Steckmesser suggests served as sterotype for
Kit Carson pictures in literature.

275 ---Life in california; or, the treasure seekers expedition. a sequel to kit carson. Boston: Williams,
1849. 108p.

276 Aydelotte, Dora (1878-   ). Long furrows. New York:
Appleton, 1935. 262p.
Farm family, Shelby County, Iowa--1890's seen
through eldest daughter teenager--Fair picture--
rural Methodist Church.

277 ---Trumpets calling. New York: Appleton, 1938. 391p.
1889-1900 Land rush in Cherokee Strip in Okla-
homa--Pioneer story--Good natured novel rè frontier.

278 ---Full harvest. New York: Appleton, 1939. 333p.
Sequel to Long Furrows--Move to town then
return to farm--Feminine point of view.

279 ---Run of the stars. New York: Appleton, 1940. 340p.
Oklahoma 1889--Rancher v. Nester--Romance--
Good background.

280 ---Across the prairie. New York: Appleton, 1941. 267p.
Small town in Kansas--Widow Travis main char-
acter--Strong on characters, weak on plot--1880.

281 Babcock, Mrs. Bernie (Smade) (1868-   ). The soul
     of anne rutledge; abraham lincoln's romance.
     Philadelphia: Lippincott, 1919. 322p.
          Abraham Lincoln romance--1831-1835--Illinois.

282 ---The heart of george washington. Philadelphia, 1932.

283 Babcock, William Henry (1849-1922). The tower of wye;
     a romance. Philadelphia: Coates, 1901. 330p.
          Early colonists on Atlantic Coast.

284 Babson, Mrs. Naomi Lane. The yankee bodleys. New York:
     Reynal, 1936. 339p.
          Chronicle--1845-1925--Massachusetts Coast.

285 ---I am lidian. New York: Harcourt, 1951. 311p.
          Lady of ninety reflects on first thirty years
     of her life--1840's from Massachusetts across plains
     to Montana--pioneer mores.

     Bacheller, Addison Irving, see Bacheller, Irving

286 Bacheller, Irving (1859-1950). The master of silence.
     New York: Webster, 1892. 176p.
          Romance

287 ---Eben holden; a tale of the north country. Boston:
     Lathrop, 1900. 432p.
          Adirondacks--farm land--St. Lawrence--beginnings
     of Civil War--Lincoln and Horace Greeley.

288 ---D'ri and i; a tale of daring deeds in the second
     war with the british. Boston: Lothrop, 1901. 362p.
          War of 1812--Memoirs of Colonel Ramm Bell--
     St. Lawrence.

289 ---Silas strong, emperor of the woods. New York:
     Grossett, 1906. 339p.
          Plea for the forests.

290 ---The light in the clearing; a tale of the north country
     in the time of silas wright. Indianapolis: Bobbs,
     1917. 414p.
          Silas Wright--Northern New York State--first
     half of nineteenth century--simple homespun life.

291 ---A man for the ages; the story of the builders of
     democracy. Indianapolis: Bobbs, 1919. 416p.
          A. Lincoln's formative years--1831-1847.

24

292 ---In the days of poor richard. Indianapolis: Bobbs,
1922. 414p.
Pro-Franklin--American Revolution--well doc-
umented--Patriotic novel--England and America.

293 ---A candle in the wilderness; a tale of the beginning
of new england. Indianapolis: Bobbs, 1930. 318p.
Massachusetts and New York c.1635--Indians v.
Colonists--Romance and adventure--Sound historical
novel.

294 ---The master of chaos. Indianapolis: Bobbs, 1932.
326p.
American Revolution--Washington's male secretary
loves daughter of Loyalist.

295 ---The harvesting. New York: Stokes, 1934. 303p.
New community in north country--1874.

296 ---The winds of god; a tale of the north country.
New York: Rinehart, 1941. 318p.

297 The bachelor's surrender [Annoymous]. Boston: Loring,
1880. 137p.
California Ranch.

298 Bacon, delia salter the bride of fort edward; founded
on an incident of the revolution. [Annoymous].
New York: Colman, 1839. 174p.
Series of dialogues.

299 Baer, Warren. Carmine; or, the trader at the fort.
Galveston: Advocate Publishing Co., 1872. 140p.
Texas setting.

300 ---The sentinel at the pass; a novel. Galveston:
Printed at the "News" steam job office, 1873.
98p.

301 Bailey, Alice Cooper. Sun gold; a story of the hawaiian
islands. Boston: Houghton, 1930. 267p.

302 Bailey, Mrs. Alice Ward pseud. Ward, A. B. (1857-   ).
The sage brush parson. Boston: Little, 1906. 390p.
Touching story--Nevada mining town.

303 Bailey, Henry Christopher (1878-   ). Gentleman
adventurer. New York: Doran, 1915. 345p.
Pirates--English--French--West Indies--
Close of seventeenth century.

304 Bailey, Paul Dayton (1906-   ). For time and all
eternity. New York: Doubleday, 1964. 400p.
Mormons--1870-1880.

305 ---The claws of the hawk; the incredible life of

25

wahker the ute. Los Angeles: Westernlore, 1966. 358p.
Walkara--Ute chief--(1808ca.-1855).

306 Baker, Charles Henry (1895-   ). Blood of the lamb.
New York: Rinehart, 1946. 275p.
First novel--Florida "cracker" country--Merrimac,
Florida--attempts to do for Florida what Jesse Stuart
did for Kentucky.

307 Baker, Charlotte (Mrs. Roger Montgomery). Venture of
the thunderbird; story of a voyage from norfolk,
virginia to the northwest coast of america in the
ship thunderbird, commanded by john audley, begun
in 1800 and terminated one year later. New York:
McKay, 1954. 243p.
For 12-16 year old--China trade.

308 Baker, Elizabeth Whitemore. Stocky, boy of west texas.
Philadelphia: Winston, 1945. 188p.
Buffalo hunter through Comanche territory to
find orphan boy--1878--Juvenile.

309 Baker, Howard. Orange valley. New York: Coward-McCann,
1931. 344p.
First novel--San Joaquin Valley--pioneer family
tries to start fruit ranch--Sober and careful.

310 Baker, Mrs. Karle Wilson (1878-   ) pseud. Wilson,
Charlotte. Family style. New York: Coward-McCann,
1937. 307p.
From farming to oil in eastern Texas.

311 ---Star of the wilderness; a novel. New York: Coward-
McCann, 1942. 508p.
Early days in Texas--Nacagdoches--Paul and Jessie
McAlpine--through eyes of woman.

312 Baker, Olaf. Buffalo barty. New York: Dodd, 1932.
267p.
Barty taken by Blackfeet--Juvenile.

313 Baker, William Mumford. The virginians in texas; a
story for young folks and old folks. New York:
Harper, 1878. 169p.

314 ---Blessed saint certainty; a story. Boston: Roberts,
1881. 445p.
Western trading post.

315 Balch, Frederick Homer. The bridge of the gods; a
romance of indian oregon. Chicago: McClurg, 1890.
280p.
Willamette Valley.

316 Balch, Glenn (1902-   ). Riders of the rio grande;
a cattle-rustling mystery story.

New York: Crowell, 1937. 289p.
Juvenile

317 ---Tiger roan. New York: Crowell, 1938. 236p.
Roan horse story--Juvenile.

318 ---Indian paint; the story of an indian pony. New
York: Crowell, 1942. 244p.
Indians--Juvenile.

319 Baldwin, Leland DeWitt (1897-   ). The delectable
country. New York: Furman, 1939. 715p.
Whiskey insurrection Pittsburgh--Riverman's
adventure in Ohio Valley--Based on three historical
monographs--1790.

320 Baldwin, Lydia Wood. A yankee-school teacher in virginia;
a tale of the old dominion in the transition state.
New York: Funk-Wagnalls, 1884. 238p.

321 Balestier, Charles Wolcott (1861-1891). A victorious
defeat; a romance. New York: Harper, 1886. 349p.
Moravians in Pennsylvania--Post-Revolution.

322 ---Benefits forgot. New York: Lovell, 1891. 438p.
Rocky Mountain mining camps.

Balestier, Wolcott (1861-1891), see Balestier, Charles
Wolcott

Ball, Zachary pseud., see Masters, Kelly Ray

Ballard, Todhunter, see Ballard, Willis Todhunter

323 Ballard, Willis Todhunter (1903-   ). Incident at
sun mountain. Boston: Houghton, 1952. 248p.
Western

324 ---West of quarantine. Boston: Houghton, 1952. 250p.
Western

325 ---High iron. Boston: Houghton, 1953. 252p.
Western

326 ---Rawhide gunman; a western novel. New York:
Popular Library, 1954. 158p.
Western

327 ---Trigger trail; a western novel. New York:
Popular Library, 1955. 144p.
Western

328 ---The long trail back. New York: Doubleday, 1960.
188p.
Western

329 ---The night riders. New York: Doubleday, 1961. 190p.
     Western

330 ---Gopher gold. New York: Doubleday, 1962. 192p.
     Western

331 ---Westward the monitors roar. New York: Doubleday,
     1963. 185p.
     Western

332 ---Gold in california. New York: Doubleday, 1965.
     364p.
     Golden Spur Award as one of two best Western
     Historical Novels-1966.

333 ---pseud. Hunter, John. West of justice. Boston:
     Houghton, 1954. 185p.
     Western

334 ---Ride the south wind. New York: Permabooks, 1957.
     151p.
     Western

335 ---Desperation valley; a novel of the cherokee strip.
     Western

     Ballew, Charles pseud. see Snow, Charles Horace

336 Ballou, John. The lady of the west; or, the gold seekers.
     Cincinnati: Moore, 1855. 544p.

337 Ballou, Maturin Murray pseud. Lieutenant Murray.
     Fanny campbell, the female pirate captain. a tale
     of the revolution. Boston: Gleason, 1845. 100p.
     Mollie Pitcher of Manmouth.

338 Bandelier, Adolph Francis Alphonse (1840-1914). The
     delight makers. New York: Dodd, 1890. 490p.
     Author was archaelogist and hispanic scholar--
     Sound ethnological base--Belight Makers-Koshare
     semi-secret society has power of gift of rain--
     Remarkable book about Pueblo and Navajo Indians--
     Life in ancient Pueblos.

339 ---The gilded man (el dorado) and other pictures of
     the spanish occupancy of america. New York:
     Appleton, 1893. 302p.
     El Dorado Legend.

340 Bangs, Nickerson. The ormsteads; a novel of three
     generations. New York: Kinsey, 1939. 298p.
     Chronicle--Western New York.

341 Banks, Nancy Huston. Oldfield; a kentucky tale of the
     last century. New York: Macmillan, 1902. 43p.
     Life and manners.

28

342   ---Round anvil rock; a romance. New York: Macmillan,
      1903. 356p.
            Kentucky--ca. 1810--Peter Cartwright--Battle
      of Tippecanoe--Philip Alston.

343   Banks, Polan. Black ivory. New York: Harper, 1926.
      305p.
            Jean LaFitte--War of 1812.

344   ---The gentleman from america. New York: Cape and
      Smith, 1930. 439p.
            Romance based on B. Franklin in France pre-
      Revolution.

345   Banvard, Joseph (1810-1887). Priscilla; or, trials
      for the truth. an historic tale of the puritans and
      the baptists. Boston: Heath and Graves, 1854. 405p.
            Puritans v. Baptists--Baptist view point--
      Indians.

346   Barber, Elsie (Oakes) (1914-   ). Hunt for heaven.
      New York: Macmillan, 1950. 230p.
            1890's--Communal living--Pennsylvania farm.

347   Barbeau, Charles Marius (1883-   ). Mountain cloud.
      Caldwell, Idaho: Caxton, 1944. 300p.
            French Canadian trader--Hudson's Bay Company--
      Wolf tribe.

      Bardwell, Denver pseud. see Sayers, James Denson

348   Barker, Benjamin. Ellen grafton, the lily of lexington;
      or, the bride of liberty. a romance of the revolution.
      Boston: Gleason's, 1846. 100p.
            Dime novel--little on Revolution.

349   ---The dwarf of the channel; or, the commodore's daugh-
      ter. a nautical romance of the revolution. Boston:
      Gleason's, 1846. 100p.

350   ---The female spy; or, the child of the brigade. a
      romance of the revolution. Boston: Gleason's, 1846.
      100p.

351   ---The indian bucanier; or the trapper's daughter. a
      romance of oregon. Boston: Gleason's, 1847. 50p.
            Columbia River settlement.

352   Barker, Roland (1905-   ) and Doerflinger, William.
      The middle passage. New York: Macmillan, 1939.
      410p.
            Slave trade--Napoleonic Era--light historical
      tale.

353   Barker, Shirley [Frances]. Peace, my daughters. New
      York: Crown, 1949. 248p.

                              29

1691 Witchcraft. Devil disguised as shoe maker.

354 ---Rivers parting; a novel. New York: Crown, 1950.
311p.
Romance--New Hampshire 1630-1640--John Scarlock
leaves farm in Nottingham to go to New Hampshire--
Royalist--anti-Massachusetts Puritan.

355 ---Fire and hammer; a tale of love and violence. New
York: Crown, 1953. 339p.
Revolutionary War--Quakers in Bucks County
Pennsylvania, and New Jersey--Outlaws harassing
patriots--Tory view point--History good.

356 ---Tomorrow the new moon. Indianapolis: Bobbs, 1955.
354p.
Puritans 1630-1700--Three cousins from Isle of
Man go to Martha's Vineyard.

357 ---Liza bowie. New York: Random, 1956. 245p.
Armada--1588-1590.

358 ---Swear by apollo. New York: Random, 1958. 306p.
Doctor from America to Edinburg--Medical train-
ing--Revolutionary Era--Ends with Lexington and
Concord.

359 ---The last gentleman. New York: Random, 1960. 341p.
Governor James Wentworth (1737-1820) of New
Hampshire--Loyalist--sends aid to General Gage in
Boston--1775--Romance.

360 ---The road to bunker hill. New York: Duell, 1962. 181p.
Revolution--1775-1789--Juvenile.

361 ---Strange wives. New York: Crown, 1963. 377p.
Jews to Rhode Island.

362 Barnes, Percy Raymond (1880-   ). Crum elbow folks.
Philadelphia: Lippincott, 1938. 283p.
Country life--Quaker custom--Hudson River--1838.

Barnacle, Captain pseud. see Newell, Charles Martin

363 Barney, Mrs. Helen Corse. Fruit in his season. New York:
Crown, 1951. 246p.
First novel--Quakers from Virginia to Ohio--
Oppose slavery--American Revolution.

364 ---Green rose of furley. New York: Crown, 1953. 247p.
Civil War Romance--Quaker girl's farm a station
on the underground railroad.

365 Baron, Alexander (1918-   ) originally Alec Bernstein.
The golden princess. New York: Washburn, 1954. 378p.
Marina, mistress of and interpreter for Cortez.

30

pivot for very good work.

366   Barr, Amelia Edith (Huddleston) (1831-1919). <u>Bow of</u>
      <u>orange ribbon</u>. New York: Dodd, 1886. 445p.
              1756--Romance Dutch girl and British officer--
      Followed by <u>Maid of Maiden Lane</u>.

367   ---<u>Remember the alamo</u>. New York: Dodd, 1888. 431p.
              Texas 1835-1836--Attack on Alamo--Davy Crockett--
      Sam Houston--Santa Anna.

368   ---<u>The maid of maiden lane; a sequel to the bow of</u>
      <u>orange ribbon</u> . New York: Dodd, 1900. 338p.
              Romance--1791-1792.

369   ---<u>The strawberry handkerchief; a romance of the stamp</u>
      <u>act</u>. New York: Dodd, 1908. 368p.
              Historical Romance--New York City--Stamp Act--
      1765.

370   ---<u>The house on cherry street</u>. New York: Dodd, 1909.
      375p.
              Political contest--New York Colony.

371   ---<u>A maid of old new york; a romance of peter stuyves-</u>
      <u>ant's time</u>. New York: Dodd, 1911. 377p.
              Latter part of seventeenth century--Amsterdam--
      Peter Stuyvesant central figure.

372   Barrett, Wilson (1848-1904) and Barron Elwyn.   <u>In old</u>
      <u>new york; a romance</u>. Boston: Page, 1900. 410p.
              New York City 1750's.

373   Barrett, Monte. <u>Sun in their eyes; a novel of texas</u>
      <u>in 1812</u>. Indianapolis: Bobbs, 1944. 319p.
              Stirring tale.

374   ---<u>Tempered blade</u>. Indianapolis: Bobbs, 1946. 317p.
              James Bowie (1799-1836)--Covers period 1815-
      1836--Alamo--Sandbar Duel.

375   ---<u>Smoke up the valley; an historical novel of texas</u>
      <u>in the 70's</u>. Indianapolis: Bobbs, 1949. 344p.
              Romance and Adventure.

      Barrington, F. Clinton <u>pseud</u>. see Lewis, Julius Warren

      Barron, Elwyn (1855-   ) jt. author, see Barrett, Wilson

376   Barrow, Elizabeth N. <u>The fortunes of war; being por-</u>
      <u>tions of many letters and journals written...during...</u>
      <u>the time of the struggle for the independence of the</u>
      <u>colonies</u>. New York: Holt, 1900. 268p.

377   Barry, Jane. <u>The long march</u>. New York: Appleton, 1955.
      316p.

31

Historical romance--Revolution in North Carolina and Virginia--1779-1782--Daniel Morgan (1736?-1802)--Battle of Cowpens.

378 ---The carolinians. New York: Doubleday, 1959. 318p.
Historical romance--Loyalists in South Carolina--1776-1789--One of better frontier novels.

379 ---A time in the sun. New York: Doubleday, 1962. 384p.
1870 Tuscon, Arizona--Arizona--Apache, Mexican Americans--Romance white girl and part Indian fellow--Indian Wars.

380 ---A shadow of eagles. New York: Doubleday, 1964. 424p.
1877 Mexico-Texas Border.

381 Barrymore, Lionel (1878-   ). Mr. cantonwine; a moral tale. Boston: Little, 1953. 218p.
Itinerant Evangelist wandering thru mid-west first half 19th century.

382 Barth, John. The sot weed factor. New York: Doubleday, 1960. 806p.
Picaresque novel of young man, twin sister, and tutor--England and Maryland--17th century--Barth "Moral allegory cloaked in material of American colonial history."

383 Bartlett, Arthur C.. Yankee doodle; a story of a pioneer boy and his dog. Boston: Wilde, 1936. 318p.
Boy and dog in Maine--Early days of Republic--Juvenile.

384 Bartlett, Lanier and Bartlett, Virginia Stivers.
Adios! New York: Morrow, 1929. 309p.
California desperados--1846.

Bartlett, Virginia Stivers, Jt. author, see Bartlett, Lanier

385 Basket, James Newton. As the light led. New York: Macmillan, 1900. 392p.
Northern Missouri late 1860's.

Bass, Frank pseud. see Peeples, Samuel Anthony

386 Bass, Milton R. Jory. New York: Putnam, 1969. 255p.
Adolescent gun slinger--West of 1870's--cf. Portis, True Grit.

387 Basso, [Joseph] Hamilton (1904-   ). Cinnamon seed. New York: Scribner's, 1934. 379p.
Southern plantation, Louisiana--Reflections on past.

388 Bates, Josephine White. A blind lead; the story of

32

a mine. Philadelphia: Lippincott, 1888. 250p.
Mining in Rockies.

389 ---A nameless wrestler. Philadelphia: Lippincott,
1889. 215p.
Mining--Washington Territory.

390 Baume, Frederic Ehrenfried (1900-   ). Yankee woman.
New York: Dodd, 1945. 259p.
First novel--three generations--Barbary Coast
gold rush years up to 1906--Yankee woman, wife of
Maine sea captain.

Baxter, George Owen pseud. see Faust, Fredrick Schiller

391 Bayliss, Marguerite Farlee (1895-   ). The bolinvars.
New York: Holt, 1944. 384p.
Romance and mystery--New Jersey and Virginia--
1810's.

392 Baylor, Frances Courtney (1848-1920). Behind the blue
ridge; a homely narrative. Philadelphia: Lippincott,
1887. 313p.

393 Beach, Mrs. Rebecca (Gibbons) (1823-1893). The puritan
and the quaker; a story of colonial times. New York:
Putnam, 1879. 393p.
Pro-Quaker

394 Beach, Rex Ellingwood (1877-1949). The spoilers.
New York: Harper, 1906. 313p.
Alaska mining--Shades of Jack London.

395 ---The silver horde; a novel. New York: Harper, 1909.
389p.
Alaska--Salmon canning.

396 ---Iron trail;an alaskan romance. New York: Harper,
1913. 390p.
Stirring story--Romance and adventure--
Alaska railroading.

397 ---Flowing gold. New York: Harper, 1922. 377p.
Texas oil.

398 ---Wild pastures. New York: Farrar, 1935. 313p.
Western with Florida setting.

399 ---Valley of thunder. New York: Farrar, 1939. 326p.
Love and adventure in Alaska of twentieth
century.

400 ---The world in his arms. New York: Putnam, 1946.
214p.
Alaska--1850's--Russians--Fur poachers--
Romance--Adventure--All equal Hollywood.

401 Bean, Mrs. Amelia. The fancher train. New York:
Doubleday, 1958. 356p.
Author native of Utah--Indictment of Mormons--
"function of history and fiction to humanize the
facts"--Jed Smith--1857--Mountain Meadow Massacre--
Golden Spur Award 1959 for best Western Historical
Novel.

402 ---The feud. New York: Doubleday, 1960. 287p.
Arizona Territory--1885--Graham-Tewksbury
feud--Sheepmen v. cattlemen.

403 ---Time for outrage. New York: Doubleday, 1967. 456p.
Lincoln County, New Mexico Territory--Late
1870's--Violence and lawlessness--Strong novel.

404 Beardsley, Charles E. The victims of tyranny. Buffalo:
[?], 1847. 2 vols.
1812--Niagara frontier.

405 Beater, Jack and Roberts, MacLennan. Sea avenger.
New York: Dell, 1957. 256p.
José Gasparilla (Pirate)--Florida.

406 Beater, Jack [assumed name] [real name Orlando Beater].
The gasparilla story; a life of josé gaspar, the
pirate of florida, with frequent reference to history.
Fort Meyers, Florida: 1952. 68p.
José Gaspar--1756-1821.

Beater, Orlando, see Beater, Jack

407 Beatty, John (1922-   ) and Patricia. Campion towers.
New York: Macmillan, 1965. 293p.
Fifteen year old girl from Massachusetts Bay
to England--Cromwellian age--Civil War--"research
good not novel".

Beatty, Patricia jt. author, see Beatty, John

408 Beaumont, de La Bonniniére, Gustave Auguste de. (1802-
1866). Marie: or, slavery in the united states:
a novel of jacksonian america. Paris: Hauman, 1835.
2 vols.
Joint author with A. de Tocqueville in Democracy
In America.

409 Bechdolt, Frederick Ritchie (1874-   ). The hard
rock man. New York: Moffat, 1910. 224p.
Western

410 ---When the west was young. New York: Century, 1922.
309p.
Western

411 ---Riders of the san pedro. New York: Doubleday, 1931.
320p.

34

Western--Gold Rush--San Pedro Valley.

412 ---Horse thief trail. New York: Doubleday, 1932. 304p.
Western

413 ---The tree of death. New York: Doubleday, 1937. 277p.
Western

414 ---Bold raiders of the west. New York: Doubleday, 1940.
269p.
New Mexico--Civil War.

415 ---Danger on the border. New York: Doubleday, 1940.
280p.
Western

416 ---Hot gold. New York: Doubleday, 1941. 273p.
Western

417 ---Riot at red water. New York: Doubleday, 1941. 269p.
Western

418 ---The hills of fear. New York: Doubleday, 1943. 280p.
Western

419 ---Dry gulch canyon. New York: Phoenix, 1946. 255p.
Western

Bedford, Donald F. pseud. see Friede, Donald

420 Bedford-Jones, Henry James O'Brien (1887-   ). The
conquest. Elgin, New York: Donald Cook, 1914. 95p.
Pierre Espirit Radisson (1620?-1710).

421 ---Mesa trail. New York: Doubleday, 1920. 244p.
Western--Mining.

422 ---The star woman. New York: Dodd, 1924. 293p.
England v. France--Hudson Bay area--Good writing--
"outstanding novel of the year".

423 Beebe, Elswyth Thane (Ricker) (Mrs. Wm. Beebe) (1900-   )
[pseud. Thane, Elswyth]. Dawn's early light. New
York: Duell, 1943. 317p.
First of Williamsburg Pentalogy written 1943-
1948--Revolution in Virginia--1774-1779.

424 ---Yankee stranger. New York: Duell, 1944. 306p.
Second of Pentalogy--Civil War--Virginia--
Romance.

425 ---Ever after. New York: Duell, 1945. 334p.
Third of Pentalogy--Sequel to Yankee Stranger.

426 ---The light heart. New York: Duell, 1947. 341p.
Fourth of Pentalogy--Sequel to Ever After--

Ends during World War I.

427 ---Kissing kin. New York: Duell, 1948. 374p.
    Fifth of Pentalogy of Williamsburg family
    (Spragues)--1914-1934.

428 Beebe, Ralph. Who fought and bled. New York: Coward,
    1941. 329p.
    War of 1812--General Hull--Ohio--Detroit.

429 Beers, Lorna Doone (Mrs. C. R. Chambers). Prairie
    fires. New York: Dutton, 1925. 367p.
    Fictionalized account of Nonpartisan League in
    North Dakota--1912-1916--Romance--cf. Montross;
    East of Eden.

430 ---A humble lear. New York: Dutton, 1929. 381p.
    Reworks Shakespeare's theme in Blue Hern Town-
    ship, Hennepin County, Minnesota--1890.

431 ---The crystal cornerstone. New York: Harper, 1953.
    218p.
    Sixteen year old joins George Washingtons
    Revolutionary army--Juvenile.

432 Belden, Mrs. Jessie Perry (VanZile) (1857-1910).
    Antonia. Boston: Page, 1901. 258p.
    Dutch colonials--Hudson River Valley--1640-
    1650.

433 Belisle, David W.. The american family robinson; or,
    the adventures of a family lost in the great desert
    of the west. Philadelphia: Hazard, 1854. 360p.

434 Belisle, Orvilla S.. The prophets; or, mormonism
    unveiled. Philadelphia: Smith, 1855. 412p.
    Anti-Mormon.

435 Belknap, Jeremy. The foresters, an american tale:
    being a sequel to the history of john bull the
    clothier, in a series of letters to a friend.
    Boston: Thomas and Andrews, 1792. 216p.
    Allegory of American history.

436 Bell, Alfreda Eva. Boadicea, the mormon wife; life
    scenes in utah. Baltimore: Orton, 1855. 97p.

437 Bell, Ed (1910-   ). Fish on steeple. New York:
    Farrar, 1935. 312p.
    Picture of small Tennessee mountain town--
    cf. February Hill and Not for Heaven.

438 Bell, Jessica LaFarge (1884?-   ). Ward's land; a
    story of the wards in kansas in the days of the
    civil war. San Antonio: Naylor Co., 1967. 272p.
    Kansas Civil War--Juvenile.

439 Bell, Kensil. <u>Secret mission for valley forge</u>. New
     York: Dodd, 1955. 246p.
          Fifteen year old New Jersey boy serves as
     guide for Anthony Wayne--Foraging expedition for
     George Washington--Juvenile.

440 Bell, Margaret Elizabeth (1898-   ). <u>Enemies in icy
     strait</u>. New York: Morrow, 1945. 206p.
          Adventure in Alaska--Juvenile.

441 ---<u>Watch for a tall white sail; a novel</u>. New York:
     Morrow, 1948. 222p.
          Pioneer experiences in Alaska--Juvenile for
     girls.

442 Bell, Sallie. <u>Marcel armand, a romance of old louisiana;
     being the story of a lieutenant of jean lafitte's
     pirate band and of elbee rochelle, a lady of new
     orleans, with whom he fell in love and thereby
     acquired a mortal enemy</u>. Boston: Page, 1935. 343p.
          Romance--Good history--New Orleans.

443 Bell, Sydney. <u>Wives of the prophet</u>. New York: Macaulay,
     1935. 394p.
          Life story of Emma first wife of Joseph Smith
     (1805-1844)--Dramatic.

444 Bellamy, Edward (1850-1898). <u>Duke of stockbridge;
     a romance of shay's rebellion</u>. New York: Silver
     Burdett, 1900. 371p.
          Proletarian Romance--Shay's Rebellion 1786-1787.

445 Bellaman, Henry (1882-   ). <u>King's row</u>. New York:
     Simon and Schuster, 1940. 674p.
          Small midwestern town life at turn of century
     (1900).

446 ---<u>Floods of spring</u>. New York: Simon and Schuster,
     1942. 374p.
          Pennsylvania Dutch--Missouri--Based on a family
     history--Character study.

     Bend Palmer <u>pseud.</u> see Putnam, George Palmer (1887-   )

     Bendbow, Hesper <u>pseud.</u> see Archer, George W.

447 Benefield, Barry (1877-   ). <u>Bugles in the night</u>.
     New York: Century, 1927. 309p.
          Juvenile

448 ---<u>Little clown lost</u>. New York: Century, 1928. 317p.
          Juvenile

449 ---<u>Valiant is the word for carrie</u>. New York: Reynal,
     1935. 292p.
          Juvenile

450 ---Eddie and the archangel mike. New York: Reynal,
   1943. 310p.
   Juvenile

451 Benét, Laura. The hidden valley. New York: Dodd, 1938.
   207p.
   White boy--Red boy--Yosemite Valley--Frémont
   in California--Juvenile.

452 Benét, Stephen Vincent. Spanish bayonet. New York:
   Doran, 1926. 268p.
   Romance--Pre-Revolution--English attempts to
   colonize Florida with Minorcan Greeks and Italians--
   Indentured servants.

453 Bengsston, Frans Gunnar (1894-   ) trans. Meyer, Michael.
   Long ships; a saga of the viking age. New York:
   Knopf, 1954. 503p.
   Excellent tale of Vikings--980-1010--England--
   Spain--Byzantium--Russia.

454 Benjamin, Mrs. Nora. Fathom five; a story of bermuda.
   New York: Random, 1939. 241p.
   Episodes in lives of Carroll family 1609
   to date--Juvenile.

455 Bennet, Robert Ames (1870-   ). A volunteer with pike;
   the true narrative of one dr. john robinson and of
   his love for the fair señorita vollois. Chicago:
   McClurg, 1909. 453p.
   Zebulon Montgomery Pike (1779-1813).

456 ---The quarterbreed. Chicago: Browne, 1914. 347p.
   Western

457 ---The bloom of cactus. New York: Doubleday, 1920. 248p.
   Western--Romance.

458 ---Waters of strife. New York: Watt, 1921. 295p.
   Western

459 ---Tyrrell of the cow country. Chicago: McClurg, 1923.
   355p.
   Western

460 ---Branded. Chicago: McClurg, 1924. 307p.
   Western--Romance.

461 ---The two-gun man. Chicago: McClurg, 1924. 348p.
   Western

462 ---The cattle baron. Chicago: McClurg, 1925. 295p.
   Western--Northwest Colorado.

463 ---The rough rider. Chicago: McClurg, 1925. 302p.
   Western

464 ---The boss of the diamond a. Chicago: McClurg, 1926.
    319p.
        Western

465 ---Go-getter gary. Chicago: McClurg, 1926. 303p.
        Western

466 ---Ken, the courageous. Chicago: McClurg, 1927. 290p.
        Western

467 ---On the rustler trail. Chicago: McClurg, 1927. 278p.
        Western

468 ---The tenderfoot. Chicago: McClurg, 1928. 361p.
        Western

469 ---The border wolf. New York: Watt, 1931. 296p.
        Western

470 ---The roped wolf. New York: Watt, 1931. 283p.
        Western

471 ---Caught in the wild. New York: Washburn, 1932. 305p.
        Western

472 ---The gold wolf. New York: Watt, 1932. 309p.
        Western

473 ---Feud of the cattle kings. New York: Washburn, 1933.
    297p.
        Western

474 ---The hunted wolf. New York: Washburn, 1933. 303p.
        Western

475 ---Guns on the rio grande. New York: Washburn, 1934.
    300p.
        Western

476 ---Texas Man. New York: Washburn, 1934. 304p.
        Western

477 ---Death rides the range. New York: Washburn, 1935.
    294p.
        Western

478 ---Horsethief hole. New York: Washburn, 1936. 311p.
        Western

479 ---Man against mustang. New York: Washburn, 1936. 309p.
        Western

480 ---Crossed trails. New York: Washburn, 1937. 311p.
        Western

481 ---Hot lead. New York: Washburn, 1937. 297p.
        Western

482 ---The gun fighter. New York: Washburn, 1938. 297p.
Western

483 ---The brand blotters. New York: Washburn, 1939. 302p.
Western

484 ---Sheepman's gold. New York: Washburn, 1939. 316p.
Western

Bennett, Dwight pseud. see Newton, Dwight Bennett
(1916-   )

485 Bennett, Emerson (1822-1905). Mike fink: a legend
of the ohio. Cincinnati: Robinson, 1848. 102p.
Ohio River.

486 ---Kate clarendon; or, neocromancy in the wilderness.
a tale of little miami. Cincinnati: Stratton,
1848. 135p.

487 ---The renegade. Cincinnati: Robinson, 1848. 138p.
Kentucky border life--Simon Girty (1741-1818)--
Published in 1854 under title Ella Barnwell: a
Historical Romance of Border Life.

488 ---The trapper's bride; or spirit of adventure.
Cincinnati: Stratton, 1848. 154p.

489 ---The prairie flower; or, adventures in the far west.
Cincinnati: Stratton, 1849. 128p.
Two Harvard chums set out for Oregon--Paperback
novel.

490 ---Leni-leoti;or, adventures in the far west. Cincinnati:
Stratton, 1849. 117p.
Sequel to The Prairie Flower .

491 ---The bandits of the osage: a western romance. Cincinnati: Stratton, 1850. 130p.
Western

492 ---The forest rose; a tale of the frontier. Cincinnati:
James, 1850. 111p.

493 ---The traitor; or, the fate of ambition. Cincinnati:
1850. 2pts.
American Revolution.

494 ---The female spy; or, treason in the camp. Cincinnati:
Stratton, 1851. 112p.
Benedict Arnold (1741-1801) and John André
(1751-1780)--Romance in Cooper tradition.

495 ---The league of the miami. Louisville: Hagan, n.d..
116p. Preface December 1850.

496 ---The pioneer's daughter; a tale of indian captivity.
     Philadelphia: Peterson, 1851. 96p.

497 ---Rosalie dupont; or, treason in the camp. Cincinnati:
     Stratton, 1851. 109p.
          American Revolution--Sequel to The Female Spy.

498 ---The fair rebel; a tale of colonial times. Cincinnati:
     Rulison, 1853. 98p.
          Bacon's Rebellion--1676.

499 ---Ella barnwell: a historical romance of border life.
     Cincinnati: James, 1854. 112p.
          Published in 1848 as The Renegade.

500 ---Viola; or, adventures in the far south-west.
     Philadelphia: Peterson, 1854. 226p.
          Texas during provincial period--Dime novel.

501 ---Clara moreland; or, adventures in the far south-west.
     Philadelphia: Peterson, 1853. 334p.

502 ---The bride of the wilderness. Philadelphia: Peterson,
     1854. 325p.

503 ---Forest and prairie; or, life on the frontier.
     Philadelphia: Potter, 1860. 111p.

504 ---The traitor; or, the fate of ambition. Cincinnati:
     James, 1860. 2 vol.
          Aaron Burr (1756-1836).

505 ---The phantom of the forest: a tale of the dark and
     bloody ground. Author's Revised Edition.
     Philadelphia: Potter, 1868. 503p.

506 ---The outlaw's daughter; or, adventures in the south.
     Philadelphia: Claxton, 1874. 343p.

507 Bennett, William P. The sky-sifter, the great chief-
     tainess and "medicine woman" of the mohawks: remark-
     able adventures and experiences of her white foster
     son...scenes in canada, in the states, on the great
     lakes, on the plains, and in california. Oakland,
     California: Pacific Press, 1892. 302p.
          Wright--"Author is not William Porter Bennett".

     Benson, Percival Ramsey see Benson, Ramsey (1866-   ).

508 Benson, Ramsey (1866-   ). Hill country; the story
     of j. j. hill and the awakening of the west. New
     York: Stokes, 1928. 356p.
          Biographical novel--Swedish settlement western
     Minnesota--Farmers' Alliance.

509 Berger, Thomas (1924-   ). Little big man. New York:
     Dial, 1964. 440p.

41

Very important novel--"Pecos Picaresque"--a
feeling of life of white and red people in American
west--Excellent work--Western Heritage--Wrangler
Award Outstanding Western Novel--1965.

510 Bernard, Paul (1911-   ). Genesee castle. Philadelphia:
     Dorrance, 1970. 152p.
     Revolutionary Era--General Sullivan marches
     against Iriquois--Summer 1779.

     Bernstein, Alec see Baron, Alexander

511 Berry, Abel B.. The last penacook; a tale of provincial
     times. Boston: Lothrop, 1887. 180p.
     Pre-American Revolution.

512 Berry, Don. Trask, a novel. New York: Viking, 1960.
     373p.
     Oregon Territory--1840's--Based on experience of
     Elbridge Trask, fur trapper turned farmer--Good book.

513 ---Moontrap, a novel. New York: Viking, 1962. 339p.
     Oregon Country--1850's--"Spur Award" from
     Western Fiction Writers of America--1963--Not as
     good as Trask.

514 ---To build a ship; a novel. New York: Viking, 1963.
     209p.
     Oregon Coast--1850's--Pioneers build ship
     because provisioning ship will not return.

515 ---Mountain men; the trappers of the great fur trading
     era 1822-1843. New York: Macmillan, 1966. Unpaged.
     Trappers--Juvenile.

     Berry, Erick pseud. see Best, Mrs. Allena (Champlin)

516 Berry, Raymond. Dusty rivers. Philadelphia: Macrae,
     1934. 294p.
     Western

517 ---The holding of recapture valley. Philadelphia:
     Macrae, 1934. 286p.
     Western

518 ---Smoky waters. Philadelphia: Macrae, 1935. 287p.
     Western

519 ---Crimson roundup. New York: Greenberg, 1938. 256p.
     Western

520 Berry, Wendell. Nathan coulter. Boston: Houghton, 1960.
     204p.
     First novel--Coulter family--Kentucky tobacco
     country.

521 Besant, Sir Walter (1836-1901). For faith and freedom.
     New York: Harper, 1889. 383p.
         Puritans--James II--Monmouth's Rebellion--
     Exiles to Barbados--1662-1688.

522 Bessie, Alvah Cecil (1901-   ). Dwell in the wilderness.
     New York: Covivi, 1935. 468p.
         Chronicle of family life three generations--
     1876-1925--Michigan town--cf. with Josephine Herbst
     "The Executioner Waits".

523 Best, Mrs. Allena (Champlain)(1892-   ). Seven beaver
     skins; a story of the dutch in new amsterdam. Phil-
     adelphia: Winston, 1948. 275p.
         First of "Land of Free Series"--Fur trade--
     Falconry.

524 ---pseud. Berry, Erick. Homespun. Boston: Lothrop,
     1937. 309p.
         New York State--1820's and 1830's--Pioneering
     activities--New Orleans--Santa Fé--Canada--Juvenile.

525 ---Go and find wind. New York: Oxford, 1939. 251p.
         #1 of Trilogy on transportation--Mystic, Conn-
     ecticut--1849--Clipper ships.

526 ---Lock her through. New York: Oxford, 1940. 246p.
         #2 of Trilogy on transportation Erie Canal--
     Mohawk Turnpike--Juvenile (12-16).

527 ---Harvest of the hudson. New York: Macmillan, 1945.   239p.
             New York life prior to American Revolution--
     Juvenile.

528 Best, Herbert (1894-   ). Young'un. New York:
     Macmillan, 1944. 271p.
         Late 18th century--New York pioneer girl--
     Lake Champlain--Fur trading.

529 ---Border iron. New York: Viking, 1945. 219p.
         1740--New York--Massachusetts border--Juvenile.

530 ---Whistle, daughter, whistle. New York: Macmillan,
     1947. 300p.
         Lake Champlain area--lady from Albany visits
     her grandmother.

531 ---The long portage; a story of ticonderoga and lord
     howe. New York: Viking, 1948. 250p.
         Young lad with Roger's Rangers--French-Indian
     War--1755-1763--William Howe (1729-1814) fifth
     viscount.

532 Beverley-Giddings, Arthur Raymond (1899-   ). Rival
     shores. New York: Morrow, 1956. 320p.

Frontier is eastern shore Maryland and Delaware--
love and conflict eve of American Revolution--Loyalist
underground escape route.

533 Bickham, Jack M. *The padre must die*. New York:
Doubleday, 1967. 185p.
Western

534 ---*The war on charity ross*. New York: Doubleday, 1967.
191p.
Western

535 ---*Target: charity ross*. New York: Doubleday, 1968. 192p.
Western

Bigly, Cantell A. pseud. see Peck, George Washington

536 Bindloss, Harold. *Sweetwater ranch*. New York: Stokes,
1935. 311p.
Romance--adventure--Saskatchewan prairie--
northern timber lands.

537 Bingham, Edfrid A. *The heart of thunder mountain*.
Boston: Little, 1916. 360p.
Western

538 Bingham, Kate (Boyles) (1876-   ) and Boyles, Virgil
Dillin (1872-   ). *Langford of the three bars*.
Chicago: McClurg, 1907. 277p.
Western

539 ---*The homesteaders*. Chicago: McClurg, 1909. 345p.
Western

540 ---*The spirit trail*. Chicago: McClurg, 1910. 416p.
1870's--Romance--Missionary to Sioux--
Adventures.

541 ---*A daughter of the badlands*. Boston: Stratford, 1922.
259p.
Romance

542 Binns, Archie (1899-   ). *The laurels are cut down*.
New York: Reynal, 1937. 332p.
Pioneering Pacific northwest--Close 19th century.

543 ---*The land is bright*. New York: Scribner's, 1939. 345p.
1850--Oregon Trail--Chronicle of Illinois farm
family.

544 ---*Mighty mountain*. New York: Scribner's, 1940. 440p.
1850's--Washington Territory--Good regional
novel--Indian's struggle to keep land.

545 ---*The timber beast*. New York: Scribner, 1944. 345p.
Contempory--Lumber industry around Puget Sound.

44

546 ---You rolling river. New York: Scribner, 1947. 342p.
        Life at mouth of Columbia River--Astoria--1865ca.

547 ---The headwaters. New York: Duell, 1957. 280p.
        Pioneer life--San Juan island chain east of
Vancouver.

548 Bird, Robert Montgomery (1806-1854). Calavar; or, the
knight of the conquest: a romance of mexico.
Philadelphia: Carey, 1834. 2 vols.
        Conquest of Mexico--1519-1540--Conquistadors.

549 ---Hawks of hawk-hollow. Philadelphia: Carey, 1835.
2 vols.
        Romance Delaware Water Gap 1780--Tradition of
Pennsylvania.

550 ---The infidel; or, the fall of mexico. Philadelphia:
Carey, 1835. 2 vols.
        Mexican Conquest--1519-1540--Sequel to Calavar...

551 ---Nick of the woods; or, the jibbenainosay; a tale of
kentucky. Philadelphia: Carey, 1837. 2 vols.
        Indian uprising--Cruel debased--Nick=Quaker
hero--Indians are real--Spirited picture.

552 Birney, Hoffman (1891-   ). King of the mesa.
Philadelphia: Penn, 1927. 300p.
        Western

553 ---The masked rider. Philadelphia: Penn, 1928. 297p.
        Western

554 ---The cañon of lost waters. Philadelphia: Penn, 1930.
305p.
        Western

555 ---Tu'Kwi of the peaceful people. Philadelphia: Penn,
1931. 279p.
        Navaho

556 ---Barrier ranch. Philadelphia: Penn, 1933. 302p.
        Western--Mystery.

557 ---Forgotten cañyon. Philadelphia: Penn, 1934. 306p.
        Western--Colorado.

558 ---Grim journey; a story of the adventures of the emi-
grating company known as the donner party, which in
the year 1846, crossed the plains from independence,
missouri to california, with an account of their
sufferings upon the desert of the great salt lake and
their final tragic fate when many suffered death on
the head waters of the truckee river in the sierra
nevada mountains. the narrative from the lips of a
survivor, mr. eddy, late of illinois, who lost wife

45

and children by horrible fate, and who participated in the rescue of his late companions of the migration. New York: Minton, 1934. 275p.

559 ---Ay-chee, son of the desert. Philadelphia: Penn, 1935. 112p.
     Navaho--Juvenile.

560 ---Eagle in the sun. New York: Putnam, 1935. 312p.
     Mexican War 1845-1848--Captures flavor of Santa Fé.

561 ---A stranger in black butte. Philadelphia: Penn, 1936. 309p.
     Western

562 ---Dead man's trail. Philadelphia: Penn, 1937. 307p.
     Western

563 ---Ann carmeny. New York: Putnam, 1941. 423p.
     Romance--Southwest--1860's--Better than most westerns.

564 Birney, Hoffman (1891-   ). pseud. Kent, David. The dice of god. New York: Holt, 1956. 350p.
     Battle of Little Big Horn--1876--Based on Custer--Politics.

565 Bishop, Curtis Kent (1912-   ) pseud. Carroll, Curt. Golden herd. New York: Morrow, 1950. 249p.
     Romance of Carl Miller, son of German who went to Texas 1840 and niece of wealthy rancher--Real not all fictional--Western.

566 Blackbeard, a page from the colonial history of philadelphia. [Anonymous]. New York: Harper, 1835. 2 vols.
     Captain E. Teach--1732.

567 Blackburn, Thomas Wakefield. A good day to die. New York: McKay, 1967. 269p.
     1890-1891--Last stand of Sioux over Standing Rock, and Pine Ridge reservations and Walker Lake Nevada--Somber tale of despair and divided loyalty--Ghost Dance--Sitting Bulls death--Wounded Knee--Buffalo Bill--Fredrick Remington.

568 Blacker, Irwin R. Westering. Cleveland: World Pub., 1958. 282p.
     Wagon train to Oregon--1845.

569 ---Taos. Cleveland, Ohio: World Pub., 1959. 478p.
     1680--New Mexico--Fictional reconstruction of rebellion of Pueblo--Based on legend and records.

570 ---The bold conquistadores. Indianapolis: Bobbs, 1961. 191p.

Spanish exploration--Juvenile.

Blake, Eleanor see Pratt, Mrs. Eleanor Blake (Atkinson) (1899-   )

571 Blake, Forrester [Avery] (1912-   ). Johnny christmas; a novel. New York: Morrow, 1948. 278p.
    1836-1846--Frontiersmen--Mexicans--Indians-- Spanish Trail to California.

572 ---Wilderness passage. New York: Random, 1953. 310p.
    Utah territory--Mormons v. United States-- Whites v. Reds.

573 ---The franciscan. New York: Doubleday, 1963. 302p.
    Missionary in Southwest--1675.

574 Blasco, Ibáñez Vicente [trans. Livingston, Arthur].
    Unknown lands; the story of columbus. New York: Dutton, 1929. 270p.
    Two young lovers pose as brothers--Sail on first voyage by Columbus to America.

575 ---The knight of the virgin. New York: Dutton, 1930. 305p.
    Sequel to Unknown Lands--Don Alonso de Ojeda with Columbus on second voyage--Good historical foundation.

576 Blassingame, Wyatt. Live from the devil. New York: Doubleday, 1959. 408p.
    Florida frontier--1900-1940--Rise of cattle baron--Mythical county of Tonekka--Western different setting and time.

577 ---The golden geyser. New York: Doubleday, 1961. 335p.
    1920's--Florida real estate boom--Money.

578 Bleecker, Ann Eliza (Schuyler). The history of maria kittle...in a letter to miss ten eyck. Hartford: E. Babcock (printer), 1797. 70p.

579 Bloom, Margaret (1893-   ). Down the ohio. Chicago: Whitman, 1938. 201p.
    Thirteen year old boy from Shenandoah to Kentucky of "dark and bloody ground"--Pioneering in Ohio.

Bloom, Rolfe, jt. author, see Ullman, Allan

580 Bloundelle-Burton, John Edward (1850-1917). A gentleman adventurer; a story of panama. London: Melrose, 1895. 287p.
    1698--Founded on plan to seize Panama from Spaniards--Buccaneering--Adventure.

581 ---The hispaniola plate (1683-1893). New York: Cassell, 1895. 352p.

47

Buccaneers--Loss of ship off San Domingo--
1683--Search for and recovery in 19th century of
manuscript.

582 ---Across the salt seas; a romance of the war of
succession. Chicago: Stone, 1897. 446p.
War of Spanish Succession 1701-1714--
(Queen Ann's War).

583 ---The land of bondage. London: White, 1904. 318p.
Indentured servants to colonial Virginia.

584 Boesch, Mark J. Beyond the muskingum. Philadelphia:
Winston, 1952. 214p.
Teen age boy to frontier forests--Ohio.

585 Bojer, Johan (1872-   ). [Trans. from Norwegian by
Muir, Jesse.] The last of the vikings. New York:
Century, 1923. 302p.
Epic of sea.

586 ---[Trans. from Norwegian by Jayne, A. G.]. The emigrants
New York: Century, 1925. 351p.
Norwegians to Red River, North Dakota--Convin-
cing--Accurate.

587 Bolster, Evelyn (Mrs. Forrest Barnes) (1909-   ).
Come gentle spring. New York: Vanguard, 1942. 378p.
Second novel--Idaho--Pastoral.

588 Bolton, Ivy May (1879-   ). Rebels in bondage.
New York: Longmans, 1938. 234p.
Two English school girls--Exiled to Albany,
New York area--Bonded maids--Dutch.

589 ---Tennessee outpost. New York: Longmans, 1939. 244p.
Tennessee when held by Spain.

590 ---Wayfaring lad. New York: Messner, 1948. 192p.
Boy from Watauga, Tennessee to Virginia--
Indians--Juvenile.

Bonnamy, Francis pseud. see Walz, Jay

591 Bonner, Geraldine (1870-1930). Hard pan; a story of
bonanza fortunes. New York: Century, 1900. 279p.
San Francisco

592 ---The pioneer; a tale of two states. Indianapolis:
Bobbs, 1905. 392p.
Early days of Americans in California and Nevada.

593 ---The emigrant trail. New York: Duffield, 1910. 496p.
1848--Trip from Missouri to California.

Bonner, Michael pseud. see Glasscock, Anne Bonner

48

594   Bonney, Edward. The banditti of the prairies; or, the murder's doom! a tale of the mississippi valley. Chicago: Bonney, 1850. 196p.

595   Bontemps, Arna Wendell (1902-   ). Black thunder. New York: Macmillan, 1936. 298p.
          Good slave revolt--Gabriel, Virginia--1800-1810--Powerful--1100 slaves plan to seize Richmond.

596   The book of algoonah: being a concise account of the early people of the continent of america known as mound builders. St. Louis, Missouri: Little, 1884. 353p. [Anonymous]

597   Borden, Lucille (Papin) (1873-   ). Kings highway. New York: Macmillan, 1941. 485p.
          Refugees from Elizabethan England to New World.

598   Borland, Barbara Dodge. The greater hunger. New York: Appleton, 1962. 406p.
          Massachusetts Bay Company--1629--Minor epic brave men and women.

599   Borland, Hal Glen (1900-   ). High, wide, and lonesome. Philadelphia: Lippincott, 1956. 251p.
          1910--Boy nine describes life on Colorado plains homestead--Charming Narrative.

600   ---The amulet. Philadelphia: Lippincott, 1957. 224p.
          Plains--Civil War--Missouri.

601   ---The seventh winter. Philadelphia: Lippincott, 1959. 256p.
          Adult western--Colorado cattlemen--1870's.

602   ---When the legends die. Philadelphia: Lippincott, 1963. 288p.
          Coming of age of Indian boy--Southwest Colorado--Small time rodeo--Good.

      Borland, Harold Glen see Borland, Hal Glen

603   Bosworth, Allan R. Sancho of the long, long horns. New York: Doubleday, 1947. 206p.
          Texas ranch and long drive.

604   Bosworth, Allan Bernard pseud. Bosworth, Jim. The long way north. New York: Doubleday, 1959. 188p.
          Western--Cattle drive--Texas to Montana.

      Bosworth, Jim pseud. see Bosworth, Allan Bernard

605   Bothwell, Jean. Tree house at seven oaks; a story of the flat water country in 1853. New York: Abelard, 1957. 239p.
          1853--Young lad of sixteen to Nebraska--

Indian unrest--Kansas-Nebraska Act--intrigue.

606   Botsford, Eva Bell. <u>Lucky; a tale of the western prairie.</u> Buffalo: Peter Paul Book Co., 1895. 167p.

Bowen, Marjorie <u>pseud.</u> see Long, Gabrille

Bower, B. M. <u>pseud.</u> see Sinclair, Mrs. Bertha (Muzzy) (1874-   )

607   Bowie, Sam. <u>Gunlock.</u> New York: Universal, 1968. 155p.
    Western

608   Bowles, John (1833-1900). <u>The stormy petrel; an historical romance.</u> New York: Lovell, 1892. 349p.
    Former Kentucky slave owner with John Brown in Kansas.

609   Bowyer, Mrs. Edith M. (Nicholl). <u>The human touch. a tale of the great southwest.</u> Boston: Lothrop, 1905. 409p.

610   Bowyer, James T.. <u>The witch of jamestown; a story of colonial virginia.</u> Richmond, Virginia: Randolph, 1890. 151p.
    English writer.

611   Boyce, Burke (1901-   ). <u>Perilous night.</u> New York: Viking, 1942. 560p.
    First novel--One of best on American Revolution-- Set in narrow valley across Hudson River from Westchester.

612   ---<u>Man from mt. vernon.</u> New York: Harper, 1961. 338p.
    George Washington--Before Lexington and Concord through Yorktown--Uneven.

613   ---<u>Morning of a hero; a novel.</u> New York: Harper, 1963. 340p.
    George Washington--1750's--French-Indian Conflict Virginia and Ohio Valley.

614   Boyd, Aubrey. <u>Smoky pass.</u> New York: Dutton, 1932. 313p.
    Melodramatic--Yukon--1897-1898.

615   Boyd, James (1888-   ). <u>Drums.</u> New York: Scribner's, 1925. 490p.
    Excellent--Solid reconstruction--North Carolina 1771-1781--Scots--John Paul Jones--Morgan's men.

616   ---<u>Marching on.</u> New York: Scribner's, 1927. 426p.
    Southern soldier--Civil War--Descendant of one of characters in <u>Drums.</u>

617   ---<u>Long hunt.</u> New York: Scribner's, 1930. 376p.

Post Revolution--Tennessee and North Carolina--
Mississippi and beyond--Early 1800's--Excellent.

618 ---Roll river. New York: Scribner's, 1935. 603p.
        Chronicle of four generations--Pennsylvania
    family.

619 ---Bitter creek. New York: Scribner's, 1939. 422p.
        Thirteen year old boy in revolt against father--
    1880-1890.

620 Boyd, Marion Margaret (Mrs. Walter Havighurst).   Strange
    island. Cleveland: World Pub., 1957. 219p.
        Aaron Burr's Conspiracy--Blennerhasset Island--
    Story of Faith Arnold--Governess to Burr's children--
    Juvenile.

    Boyd, Marion Margaret (Mrs. W. Havighurst) jt. author,
    see Havighurst, Walter

621 Boyd, Thomas Alexander (1898-1935).   Samuel drummond.
    New York: Scribner's, 1925. 308p.
        True-to-life story of Ohio farmer--About time
    Civil War.

622 ---Simon girty, the white savage. New York: Minton,
    1928. 252p.
        Fictional reconstruction life of white renegade
    of Revolution--1741-1818--Indian Wars (1750-1815).

623 ---Shadow of the long knives; a novel. New York:
    Scribner's, 1928. 354p.
        Carefully done--Angus McDermott scout and
    interpreter for British--Ohio Indians--American
    Revolution--Romance.

624 Boyles, C. S. (1905-   ) pseud. Brown, Will C..
    The nameless breed. New York: Macmillan, 1960.
    154p.
        Western--Golden Spur Award 1961--Best Western.

    Boyles, Kate see Bingham, Mrs. Kate (Boyles)

    Boyles, Virgil D. jt. author, see Bingham, Mrs. Kate Boyles

625 Brace, John Pierce (1793-1872).   The dawn of the pale
    faces; or, two centuries ago. New York: Appleton,
    1853. 288p.
        People of Hartford, Connecticut and Indians--
    1650.

    Brace, Timothy pseud. see Pratt, Theodore

626 Brackenridge, Hugh Henry (1748-1816).   Modern chivalry:
    containing the adventures of captain john farrago,
    and teague o'brien, his servant. Philadelphia:

M'Culoch, 1792, 1793, 1797.
First extended use of backwood's life in American fiction--Washington appears as President--1787--Gaston p. 24--Satirized American Frontier--Only early American novel still entertaining and valuable document of colonial time.

627 Brackett, Leigh. Follow the free wind. New York: Doubleday, 1963. 215p.
Golden Spur Award Best Western Novel-1964.

628 Bradbury, Osgood. Lucelle; or, the young iroquois! a tale of the indian wars. Boston: Williams, 1845. 75p.

629 ---Isabelle; or, the emigrant's daughter. a tale of boston and the west. Boston: Gleason, 1848. 100p.

630 ---Manita of the pictured rocks; or, the copper speculation. a tale of lake superior. Boston: Gleason, 1848. 100p.

631 ---Pontiac; or, the last battle of the ottawa chief. a tale of the west. Boston: Gleason, 1848. 100p.

632 ---Therese; or, the iroquois maiden. a tale of new york city and of forest life. Boston: Williams, 1852. 100p.

633 ---The beautiful half-breed; or, the border rovers. a tale of 1812. New York: DeWitt, 1867. 100p.

634 Bradford, Roark (1896-   ). This side of jordan. New York: Harper, 1929. 255p.
First novel--Good--Cf. Black April and Scarlet Sister Mary--Slaves lower Mississippi cotton growing.

635 ---John henry. New York: Harper, 1931. 225p.
John Bunyan of negroes of lower Mississippi River--Tall tales.

636 ---Kingdom coming. New York: Harper, 1933. 319p.
Louisiana Plantation--Negro--Civil War--Very good.

Bradshaw, Wellesley pseud. see Alexander, Charles Wesley

637 Brady, Cyrus Townsend (1861-1920). For love of country. a story of land and sea in the days of the revolution. New York: Scribner, 1898. 354p.
American Revolution--Romance and adventure--Wrote many juveniles.

638 ---For the freedom of the sea; a romance of the war of 1812. New York: Collier, 1899. 354p.

639   ---The grip of honor; a story of paul jones and the american revolution. New York: Scribner, 1900.   246p.

640   ---The quiberon touch; a romance of the days when "the great lord hawke" was king of the sea. New York: Appleton, 1901.   410p.
          Taking Quebec--ca. 1759-1763--Edward Hawke, 1st Baron (1705-1781).

641   ---When blades are out and love's afield; a comedy of cross purposes in the carolinas. Philadelphia: Lippincott, 1901.   305p.
          American Revolution.

642   ---In the wasp's nest, the story of a sea waif in the war of 1812. New York: Scribner's, 1902.   327p.

643   ---The bishop; being some account of his strange adventures on the plains. New York: Harper, 1903.   301p.
          Western romance--Adventure.

644   ---In the war with mexico, a mid-shipman's adventures on ship and shore. New York: Scribner's, 1903.   313p.

645   ---Sir henry morgan, buccaneer; a romance of the spanish main. New York: Dillingham, 1903.   446p.

646   ---The chalice of courage; a romance of colorado. New York: Dodd, 1912.   382p.

647   ---West wind; a story of red men and white in old wyoming. Chicago: McClurg, 1912.   389p.
          Ranchers and cavalry rescue white girl--Sioux camp.

648   ---Arizona; a romance of the great southwest. New York: Dodd, 1914.   326p.
          Melodrama

649   ---Britton of the seventh; a romance of custer and the great northwest. Chicago: McClurg, 1914.   391p.
          One of last novels in heroic tradition-- Major Reno hero not Custer.

650   ---The little angel of canyon creek. New York: Revell, 1914.   292p.

651   ---A baby of the frontier. New York: Revell, 1915.   286p.
          United States Troops v. Cheyenne.

652   ---"By the world forgot"; a double romance of the east and the west. Chicago: McClurg, 1917.   344p.

653 Brainard, John Garidner Calkins (1796-1828). Fort
     braddock letters; or, a tale of the french and indian
     wars in america at the beginning of the eighteenth
     century. Worcester, Massachusetts: Dorr, 1827. 98p.

654 Braley, Berton (1882-1966). Shoestring. New York:
     Sears, 1931. 310p.
          West--Copper mine--Poker playing.

655 Branch, Edward Payson. Plain people; a story of the
     western reserve. New York: Publishers' Printing,
     1892. 293p.

656 Branch, Houston and Waters, Frank (1902-   ). River
     lady. New York: Farrar, 1942. 374p.
          Saga of frontier life--Lumbering days on Miss-
     issippi River.

657 ---Diamond head. New York: Farrar, 1948. 371p.
          Romance--Whaling in Pacific by New Englanders.

     Brand, Max pseud. see Faust, Fredrick Schiller

658 Brandon, Curris. David woodburn, the mountain missionary.
     Boston: Hoyt, 1865. 310p.
          Wisconsin Frontier.

     Brearley, William H. jt. author, see Kelley, Adelaide
     (Skeel)

659 Breck, John. When hell came through. New York:
     Harpers, 1929. 321p.
          Western--Union Pacific--Indians.

     Breck, Vivian pseud. see Breckenfeld, Vivian Gurney

660 Breckenfeld, Vivian Gurney pseud. Breck, Vivian.
     High trail. New York: Doubleday, 1948. 214p.
          Western

661 ---Hoof beats on the trail. New York: Doubleday, 1950.
     238p.
          Western

     Breneman, Mary Worthy pseud. Thurston, Mary Worthy and
     Breneman, Muriel see Thurston, Mary Worthy

     Breneman, Muriel jt.author, see Thurston, Mary Worthy

     Brentano, Lowell jt.author, see Lancaster, Bruce

662 Breslin, Howard. Tamarack tree. New York: McGraw,
     1947. 438p.
          Political rally--Stratton, Vermont--1840--
     Daniel Webster.

663   ---Bright battalions. New York: McGraw, 1953. 325p.
        French-Indian War (1754-1763)--Lakes Champlain
    and George--Romantic adventure.

664   ---Silver oar. New York: Crowell, 1954. 310p.
        Colonial America to Boston--1689--Sir Edmund
    Andros--Glorious Revolution in colony.

665   ---Shad run. New York: Crowell, 1955. 276p.
        Ratification of Constitution of the United
    States--Poughkeepsie, New York--1787-1789.

666   ---pseud. Niall, Michael. Bad day at black rock.
    New York: Fawcett, 1954. 143p.
        Western

667 Bretherton, Vivien. Rock and the wind. New York:
    Dutton, 1942. 618p.
        Kansas girl to Oregon 1860's--Romantic adventure.

668 Brewer, Charles. Retribution at last; a mormon tragedy
    of the rockies. Cincinnati: Editor Pub. Co., 1899.
    101p.

669 Brick, John. Troubled spring. New York: Farrar, 1950.
    279p.
        Civil War veteran from Andersonville to Newburgh,
    New York--Good picture of Hudson River Valley life.

670   ---The raid. New York: Farrar, 1951. 308p.
        Authentic tale Hudson Valley frontier life--
    American Revolution--Butler's Rangers take woman
    captive--Rescue--Romance--Joseph Brant (1779).

671   ---Homer crist; a novel of highland county. New York:
    Farrar, 1952. 255p.
        New York--1833-1872--Chronicle.

672   ---The rifleman; a novel. New York: Doubleday, 1953.
    349p.
        Pennsylvania--Schoharie--American Revolution--
    Timothy Murphy 1751-1818.

673   ---King's rangers. New York: Doubleday, 1954. 290p.
        Butler's Rangers--Upper New York--Tory view of
    American Revolution.

674   ---The strong men. New York: Doubleday, 1959. 360p.
        American Revolution--Deerkill, New York--Gen-
    erals Wayne and Steuben--Battle of Monmouth.

675   ---Tomahawk trail. New York: Duell, 1962. 149p.
        Sullivan Indian Campaign 1779--Juvenile.

676 The brigantine; or, admiral lowe. a tale of the seven-
     teenth century by an american. [Anonymous]. New York:
     Crowen, 1839. 201p.

677 Briggs, William Harlowe (1876-1952). Dakota in the
     morning. New York: Farrar, 1942. 277p.
          Boy tells of growth of South Dakota frontier
     town.

678 Brigham, Johnson (1846-   ). The sinclairs of old
     fort des moines; a historical romance. Cedar Rapids,
     Iowa: Torch, 1927. 245p.
          Fort Des Moines, Iowa--1840's.

679 Bright, Robert. The life and death of little jo.
     New York: Doubleday, 1944. 216p.
          Mexicans in isolated village in New Mexico.

680 Brill, Ethel Claire (1877-   ). Red river trail.
     Philadelphia: Macrae, 1927. 310p.

681 ---Rupahu's warning; a story of the great sioux outbreak.
     Philadelphia: Macrae, 1931. 286p.
          Dakota Indians--1862-1865--Juvenile.

682 ---White brother; a story of the pontiac uprising: told
     by alan davidson, called nekah by the ojibways. New
     York: Holt, 1932. 250p.
          1763-1765--Juvenile.

683 ---Madeleine takes command. New York: McGraw, 1946.
     204p.
          Marie Magdelaine Jarret de Verchères (1678-
     1747)--Juvenile.

684 ---Copper country adventure. New York: McGraw, 1949.
     213p.
          Upper peninsula--Michigan--1850--Juvenile.

685 Brinig, Myron (1900-   ). The sun sets in the west.
     New York: Farrar, 1935. 360p.
          Montana mining country.

686 ---The gambler takes a wife. New York: Farrar, 1943.
     309p.
          Montana frontier town 1880's.

687 Brink, Mrs. Carol (Ryrie) (1895-   ). Caddie woodlawn.
     New York: Macmillan, 1935. 270p.
          One year in life of author's grandmother on
     Wisconsin frontier--1864--Age eleven.

688 ---Buffalo coat; a novel. New York: Macmillan, 1944.
     421p.
          Opportunity, Idaho--1890.

689 ---Strangers in the forest. New York: Macmillan, 1959.
314p.
Bundy Jones--Conservationist with Governor
Pinchot--Early twentieth century.

690 Brinkerhoff, Henry R. Nah-nee-ta; a tale of the navajos.
Washington: Soulé, 1886. 236p.

691 Brisbane, Abbott Hall. Ralphton; or, the young carolinian of 1776. a romance on the philosophy of
politics. Charlestown: Burges, 1848. 242p.

692 Bristow, Gwen (Mrs. Bruce Manning) (1903-   ). Deep
summer. New York: Crowell, 1937. 329p.
#1 of Trilogy--Louisiana--1775-1800--Emergence
of plantations.

693 ---Handsome road. New York: Crowell, 1938. 384p.
#2 of Louisiana Trilogy--Sequel to Deep Summer.

694 ---The side of glory. New York: Crowell, 1940. 400p.
#3 of Louisiana Trilogy--Fine love story--
1885--Aristocrats unite with plebians by marriage.

695 ---Jubilee trail. New York: Crowell, 1950. 564p.
Santa Fé Trail--1844-1849--Trek of gentle
girl and trader husband.

696 ---Celia garth. New York: Crowell, 1959. 406p.
Charleston, South Carolina last years of
American Revolution--Spy for Marion--Romance.

697 Broderick, Therese pseud. Schreimer, Tin. The brand;
a tale of the flathead reservation. Seattle,
Washington: Harriman, 1909. 271p.
Informed, sympathetic tale of New York girl
working on Flathead Reservation.

698 Brodhead, Eva Wilder (McGlasson). Diana's livery.
New York: Harper, 1891. 286p.
Shakers in Kentucky.

699 Bromfield, Louis (1896-1956). The farm. New York:
Harper, 1933. 346p.
Ohio family chronicle of four generations--
Reminiscences and geneological information--Valuable
recreation of past--1815-1915.

700 ---Wild is the river. New York: Harper, 1941. 326p.
New Orleans--Civil War.

701 ---Mrs. parkington. New York: Harper, 1942. 330p.
Portrait of New York grand dame--Age 84 in
1942--Rise from Leaping Rock, Nevada--Married Robber
Baron.

57

702 ---Colorado. New York: Harper, 1947. 263p.
      Silver City--1880's.

703 ---The wild country; a novel. New York: Harper, 1948.
      274p.
           18th century tale of seduction and revenge
      set in 20th century Missouri farm.

704 Bronson, Edgar Beecher. The vanguard. New York:
      Doran, 1914. 316p.
           Based on notes of Corporal Stocking, mine and
      coach guard--1840-1865--Michigan--Santa Fé Trail.

705 Brook farm; the amusing and memorable of american
      country life. [Anonymous]. New York: Carter, 1860.
      208p.
           Utopian Community.

706 Brooks, Elbridge S. The master of the stronghearts;
      a story of custer's last rally. New York: Dutton,
      1898. 314p.
           One of earliest attempts at full length fic-
      tional interpretation of Custer--Heroic portrait--
      Juvenile.

707 ---A son of the revolution; being the story of young
      tom edwards, adventurer...in the days of burr's
      conspiracy. Boston: Wilde, 1898. 301p.
           Relationship of Burr's conspiracy to national
      expansion.

    Brown, Caroline pseud. see Krout, Caroline Virginia

708 Brown, Charles Brockden (1771-1810). Wieland; or, the
      transformation of an american tale. New York:
      Caritat, 1798. 298p.
           European seeking conversion of Indian emigrates
      to New World--Savagery meets civilization--Picture of
      Alleghany Region.

709 ---Edgar huntley; or, memoirs of a sleep walker.
      Philadelphia: Maxwell, 1799. 3 vols.
           Picture of Delaware Indians.

710 ---Ormond; or, the secret witness. New York: Caritat,
      1799. 338p.
           Early statement of West as condition of soul
      rather than physiographical.

711 Brown, Dee. Wave high the banner; a novel based on
      life of davy crockett. Philadelphia: Macrae, 1942.
      367p.
           Davy Crockett (1786-1836)--Straightford story.

712 Brown, Harry Peter M'Nab (1917-   ). The stars in

                              58

their course. New York: Knopf, 1960. 362p.
1879--Southwest--Better than average.

713 Brown, Helen Dawes. A civilian attaché; a story of a
     frontier army post. New York: Scribner's, 1899.
     161p.

714 Brown, J. P. S.. Jim kane. New York: Dial, 1970. 384p.
     First novel--Day-to-day life of modern cowboy.

715 Brown, Joe David. The freeholder. New York: Morrow,
     1949. 340p.
         Bonded servant to America to Civil War--Carolina
     plantation overseer to Alabama 1861--Sons hate
     slavery.

716 Brown, Katherine Holland (-1931). Diane; a romance
     of the icarian settlement on the mississippi river.
     New York: Doubleday, 1904. 440p.
         1856--End of Cabet's popularity--Good descript-
     ion of commune--John Brown--Abolitionists.

717 ---The father. New York: Day, 1928. 368p.
         Abolitionists from New England to Illinois--
     1850's--$25,000 prize novel.

718 Brown, Mrs. Marion Marsh. Frontier beacon. Philadel-
     phia: Westminister Press, 1952. 187p.
         Nebraska Territory--Slavery questions--Juvenile.

719 Brown, Stirling Wilson. In the limestone valley;
     pen pictures of early days in western wisconsin.
     West Salem [?] Wisconsin: 1900. 214p.

     Brown, Will C. pseud. see Boyles, C. S.

720 Brown, William Hill. The power of sympathy; or, the
     triumph of nature, founded on truth. Boston:
     Thomas, 1789. 2 vols.
         First American novel--Earlier references
     attributed to Sarah Morton--Epistolary form.

721 Brown, William Wells (1815-   ). Clotel; or, the
     president's daughter, a narrative of slave life in
     the united states. Boston: Red Path, 1864. 104p.
         Author former slave--First known novel by
     American Negro--Based on legend Jefferson sold own
     slave children.

722 Browne, John Ross. Adventures in apache country. a
     tour through arizona and sonora, with notes on the
     silver regions of nevada. New York: Harper, 1869.
     535p.

723 Browning, Meshach. Forty-four years of the life of a

59

hunter; being reminiscences of meshach browning, a maryland hunter. Philadelphia: Lippincott, 1859. 400p.

724 Bruff, Nancy (Mrs. E. T. Clarke). The manatee. New York: Dutton, 1945. 251p.
First novel--Nantucket whaling--Sadistic.

725 Bryan, Mary Edwards. Manch. New York: Appleton, 1880. 309p.
Comanches.

726 Bryson, John Gordon (1900-   ). Valiant libertine. New York: Appleton, 1942. 427p.
Boston and Quebec--Profligate--Boston Siege 1775-1776.

727 Buchan, John. Salute to adventurers. New York: Doran, 1917. 348p.
Scotsman to Virginia--1690--Adventure story.

728 Buck, James Smith, by the prophet James. The chronicles of the land of columbia, commonly called america. from the landing of the pilgrim fathers to the second reign of ulysses the I, a period of two hundred and fifty-two years. Milwaukee: Stearns, 1876. 112p.

729 Buck, Pearl pseud. Sedges, John. The townsman. New York: Day, 1945. 384p.
Kansas--Building of a town--Good pioneer story--Based on true development of town--Post-Civil War.

730 Buckingham, Henry A. Harry burnham, the young continental; or, memoirs of an american officer during the campaigns of the revolution, and sometime member of washington's staff. New York: Burgess, 1851. 256p.
George Washington frequently appears.

Buckmaster, Henrietta pseud. see Henkle, Henrietta (Mrs. P. J. Stephens)

731 Budd, Mrs. Lillian. Land of strangers. Philadelphia: Lippincott, 1953. 369p.
Man from Sweden to America--19th century romance.

732 Buel, James William. Life and marvelous adventures of wild bill, the scout. Chicago: Belford, 1880. 92p.

733 ---The border outlaws; an authentic and thrilling history of the most noted bandits of ancient or modern times, the younger brothers jesse and frank james, and their comrades in crime. St. Louis, Missouri: Historical Pub. Co., 1881. 288p.

734 ---Heroes of the plains; or, lives and wonderful adven-

tures of wild bill, buffalo bill, kit carson...and
other celebrated indian fighters...including a...
history of gen. custer's famous "last fight".
St. Louis, Missouri: Historical Pub. Co., 1881. 548p.

735 Bull, Katherine Thomas (Jarboe) pseud. Thomas, Kate.
Aila. San Francisco: Doxey, 1896. 278p.
Early California.

736 Bulla, Clyde Robert. The secret valley. New York:
Crowell, 1949. 100p.
1849--Family of four from Missouri to California--
Juvenile.

Bullis, Franklin Howar, jt. author, see Pearson, Molly
(Winston)

Bull-us, Hector pseud. see Paulding, James Kirke (1778-
1860)

737 Bunce, William Harvey (1903-   ). Dragon prows westward.
New York: Harcourt, 1946. 199p.
Viking lad to Vineland--Captured by Iriquois--
Adventure--Juvenile.

Buntline, Ned pseud. see Judson, Edward Zane Carroll

738 Burdett, Charles. Margaret moncrieffe; the first love
of aaron burr: a romance of the revolution. New
York: Derby, 1860. 437p.

739 Burgess, Jackson. Pillar of cloud. New York: Putnam,
1957. 254p.
Kansas crossing to Cherry Creek, Colorado--
1858--Written as uncompleted memoirs of Judge Garvin
Cooper.

740 Burgwyn, Collinson Pierrepont Edwards. The hugenot
lovers; a tale of the old dominion. Richmond,
Virginia: Pub. by Author, 1889. 219p.

741 Burks, Arthur J. pseud. MacArthur, Burke. Rivers into
wilderness. New York: Mohawk, 1932. 295p.
Depicts life on barren homestead state of
Washington--Good.

742 Burlingham, Roger (1889-1967). Three bags full. New
York: Harcourt, 1936. 637p.
Hendrik Van Huyten, friend and brother-in-law
Pieter de Groot to New York wilderness to establish
Glenvil--Late 1700's to 1920--cf. Drums Along The
Mohawk.

743 Burman, Ben Lucien (1894-   ). Steam boat round the
bend. New York: Farrar, 1933. 308p.
Romance Bayou couple--Shanty boat life.

61

744   ---Blow for a landing. Boston: Houghton, 1938. 320p.
      Mississippi River Life--Shantyman.

745   ---Every where i roam. New York: Doubleday, 1949. 304p.
      Allegorical tale--Capt. Asa from Cumberlands in
      Kentucky.

746   Burmeister, Mrs. Kate. The indian maiden's dream ;
      a novel. Kansas City, Missouri: Pub. by Author,
      1895. 182p.

747   Burnett, Mrs. Frances Hodgson (1849-1924). In connection
      with the dewilloughby claim. New York: Scribner's,
      1899. 445p.
      Country life--Tennessee--1861--Juvenile.

748   Burnett, William Riley (1899-   ). Iron man. New
      York: Dial, 1930. 312p.
      Western

749   ---Saint Johnson. New York: Dial, 1930. 305p.
      Western

750   ---The dark command; a kansas iliad. New York: Knopf,
      1938. 396p.
      Free Soilers v. Quantrill (1837-1865) Kansas
      and Missouri--"Sack of Lawrence".

751   ---Adobe walls; a novel of the last apache rising.
      New York: Knopf, 1953. 279p.
      Western--Last of Apache Revolts--1883-1886--
      Generals Crook and Miles.

752   ---Captain lightfoot. New York: Knopf, 1954. 297p.
      Michael Martin 1795-1821.

753   ---Pale moon. New York: Knopf, 1956. 276p.
      Western

754   ---Bitterground. New York: Knopf, 1957. 245p.
      Western

755   ---Underdog. New York: Knopf, 1957. 242p.
      Western

756   ---Mi Amigo; a novel of the southwest. New York:
      Knopf, 1959. 241p.
      Western--Southwest--Lincoln County-1878--
      Billy The Kid (Wm. Bonney)--Excellent.

757   ---The goldseekers. New York: Doubleday, 1962. 282p.
      Western

      Burns, Tex pseud. see L'Amour, Louis

758 Burns, Walter Noble. Saga of billy the kid. New York:
     Doubleday, 1926. 322p.
          Folklore and myth--Base for 1930 movie--Fic-
     tional biography.

759 Burr, Mrs. Anna Robeson (Brown) (1873-   ). The golden
     quicksand; a novel of santa fé. New York: Appleton,
     1936. 267p.
          Pentitentes--Indians--Spain--1840's--Mexican
     War.

760 Burress, John. Bugle in the wilderness. New York:
     Vanguard, 1958. 222p.
          Four Mile, Missouri--Twelve year old boy and
     father--Realistic--Compassionate account of back-
     woods life.

761 Burroughs, Edgar Rice (1875-1950). Apache devil.
     Tarzana, California: Burroughs, 1933. 310p.
          Geronimo pivot of story--Real devil is white
     man with Apache--1896.

762 Burt, Katherine (Newlin) (1882-   ). Close pursuit.
     New York: Scribner's, 1946. 320p.
          Romance--Williamsburg, Virginia--Wm. Fyfe--
     T. Jefferson--Patrick Henry.

763 Burton, Carl D.. Satan's rock. New York: Appleton,
     1954. 262p.
          First novel--Kentucky mountain country--
     Southern regional literature.

764 Burton, Frederick Russell (1861-1909). Strongheart;
     a novel. New York: Dillingham, 1908. 393p.
          Ojibways--White missionaries--Based on play by
     Wm. C. DeMille.

765 ---Red cloud of the lakes; a novel. New York: Dillingham,
     1909. 374p.
          Three generations--Ojibway--Real Indian in
     fiction.

766 Burton, Mrs. Katherine (Kurz). Paradise planters;
     the story of brook farm. New York: Longmans, 1939.
     336p.
          Utopian Community.

767 Burton, Maria Amparo (Ruiz) pseud. Loyal C.. The
     squatter and the don; a novel descriptive of contem-
     porary occurrences in california. San Francisco:
     Carson, 1885. 421p.

768 Burts, Robert (-1839). The scourge of the ocean;
     a story of the atlantic by an officer of the u. s.

63

navy. Philadelphia: Carey, 1837. 2 vols.
Sea tale American Revolution--Cooper style.

769 ---The sea king; a nautical romance. Philadelphia:
Hart, 1851. 203p.

770 Busch, Niven Don (1903-   ). Duel in the sun. New
York: Morrow, 1944. 246p.
Southwest frontier 1880's--Pearl Chavez.

771 ---The furies. New York: Dial, 1948. 352p.
Western

772 Busey, Garreta Helen (1893-   ). The windbreak.
New York: Funk, 1938. 350p.
Illinois prairie life--1860-1914--Regional
literature.

773 Bushnell, Oswald Andrew. Return of lono; a novel of
captain cook's last voyage. Boston: Little, 1956.
290p.
James Cook (1728-1779)--Search for Northwest
Passage--Hawaiian Island.

774 ---Molokai. Cleveland: World Pub. Co., 1963. 539p.
Father Damien--Leper colony--Molokay, Hawaiian
Islands.

775 Bushnell, William H.. Prairie fire! a tale of early
illinois. Chicago: Sloan, 1855. 96p.

776 ---Ah-Meek, the beaver; or, the copper-hunters of
lake superior. New York: American News, 1867. 104p.

777 Buster, Green B.. Brighter sun; an historical account
of the struggles of a man to free himself and his
family from human bondage. New York: Pagent, 1954.
282p.
Based on life of Garret Buster (1809-1903)--
Underground Railroad--Slavery--Kentucky plantation.

778 Butler, Beverly. Song of the voyageur. New York:
Dodd, 1955. 247p.
First novel--Wisconsin 1830's--Massachusetts
girl--Juvenile.

779 ---The silver key. New York: Dodd, 1961. 239p.
Eastern girl to Welsh community in Wisconsin--
Underground Railroad--Juvenile.

780 ---Feather in the wind. New York: Dodd, 1965. 243p.
Wisconsin Territory-1832--Blackhawk--Sauk--
Romance--Juvenile.

781 Butters, Mrs. Dorothy Gilman. Witch's silver.

Philadelphia: Macrae, 1959. 190p.
Puritan Arbella Hewitt--Witches--Juvenile.

782 The buttonwoods; or, the refugees of the revolution.
a historical sketch. [Anonymous]. Philadelphia:
Harmstead, 1849. 95p.

783 Buxbaum, Katherine. Iowa outpost. Philadelphia:
Dorrance, 1948. 253p.
German--Mennonites--Iowa--1900--Family life.

"By a Texan" see Ganilh, Anthony

"By a Yankee" pseud. see Ingraham, Joseph Holt

784 Bynner, Edwin Lassetter (1842-1893). Agnes surriage.
Boston: Houghton, 1886. 418p.
Port of Boston--Romance--1755 ca.

785 ---Penelope's suitors. Boston: Ticknor, 1887. 68p.
Diary Penelope Pelham, wife of Governor Buckley
of Massachusetts.

786 ---The begum's daughter. Boston: Little, 1890. 473p.
Leisler's Revolt--1689-1690--New Amsterdam--
Good story.

787 ---Zachary phips. Boston: Houghton, 1892. 512p.
Boston boy with Aaron Burr--1804--War of 1812.

788 Byrd, Sigman and Sutherland, John. The valiant. New
York: Jason Press, 1955. 315p.
Nez Perce v. whites--Oregon Territory--1850's--
Tribute to Nez Perce.

789 Cabell, James Branch (1879-1958). First gentleman of america; a comedy of conquest. New York: Farrar, 1942. 309p.
     Nemattanon, Prince of Ajacan (Virginia) with Spanish to Florida and Spain--Legend based.

790 Cable, George Washington (1844-1925). The grandissimes; a story of creole life. New York: Scribner's, 1880. 448p.
     Louisiana--D'Iberville's expedition and exploration party 1699-1700?

791 ---Dr. sevier. Boston: Osgood, 1885. 473p.
     Pre-Civil War--New Orleans.

792 ---Gideon's band; a tale of the mississippi. New York: Scribner's, 1914. 500p.
     Pre-Civil War--Local scenes and color--Most on riverboat.

793 Cahill, Holger. The shadow of my hand. New York: Harcourt, 1956. 409p.
     Veteran of two wars to wheat country of North Dakota--Melodramatic and strong.

     Caillou, Alan pseud. see Lyle-Smith, Alan

794 Cain, James Mallahan (1892-   ). Past all dishonor. New York: Knopf, 1946. 232p.
     Virginia City--1860's--Melodramatic.

     Caldwell, Janet Taylor see Caldwell, Taylor (1900-   )

795 Caldwell, Taylor (1900-   ). Dynasty of death. New York: Scribner's, 1938. 797p.
     #1 of Trilogy--Pennsylvania firearms family through the Civil War--1837-1914--#2 of Trilogy--The Eagles Gather (1940)--#3 of Trilogy--The Final Hour (1944).

796 ---This side of innocence. New York: Scribner's, 1946. 499p.
     Up-State New York--1868-1880--Social novel.

797 ---Let love come last. New York: Scribner's, 1949. 408p.
     Self-made lumber magnate 1879-1907.

798 ---Never victorious, never defeated. New York: McGraw,
     1954. 549p.
          Railroad empire building--Victorian--1865-1940.

799 ---pseud. Reiner, Max. The wide house. New York:
     Scribner's, 1945. 533p.
          Up-State New York--1850's--Intolerance--
     Religious and racial.

800 Call, Hughie (Florence). The shorn lamb. Boston:
     Houghton, 1969. 199p.
          Montana ranch country widow tries to run large
     sheep ranch--Happy ending.

801 Cameron, Caddo pseud.. Rangers is powerful hard to kill.
     New York: Doubleday, 1936. 304p.
          Western

802 ---It's hell to be a ranger. New York: Doubleday, 1937.
     305p.
          Western

803 ---At the end of a texas rope. New York: Doubleday,
     1938. 306p.
          Western

804 ---Due for a hanging. New York: Doubleday, 1939. 277p.
          Western

805 ---Ghosts on the range tonight. New York: Carlton House,
     1941. 303p.
          Western

806 Cameron, Leslie Georgiana (1886-1958) pseud. Leslie, Ann
     George. Dancing saints. New York: Doubleday, 1943.
     307p.
          First novel--Mother leaves boy of eight with
     Shakers.

807 Cameron, Margaret (1867-   ). Johndover. New York:
     Harper, 1924. 483p.
          Gold Rush--California.

808 Campbell, Eugene. The long whip. New York: Scribner's,
     1934. 361p.
          English blacksmith to America 1830--Dies wealthy.

809 Campbell, Evelyn Murray. The knight of lonely land.
     Boston: Little, 1921. 302p.
          Western

810 ---The vanishing rider. New York: Dial, 1932. 302p.
          Western

811 ---Tall grass. New York: Dial, 1933. 304p.
          Western

67

812   Campbell, Mrs. Grace MacLennan (Grant). The higher hill.
      New York: Duell, 1945. 320p.
      Pioneer life--Scots in Ontario--War 1812--In
      tradition of Annie Swann, Amelia Barr and Wilson Evans.

813   Campbell, Marie. Cloud walking. New York: Farrar, 1942.
      272p.
      Understanding story of the heirs of Daniel
      Boone--Kentucky mountains.

814   Campbell, Mrs. Patricia (1901-   ). Eliza. Seattle,
      Washington: Superior, 1947. 349p.
      Society girl from Philadelphia to frontier
      Pacific Northwest--1870's and 1880's.

815   ---By sun and candlelight. New York: Macmillan, 1955.
      280p.
      Lumbering--Puget Sound--Late 19th century.

816   ---Royal anne tree. New York: Macmillan, 1956. 252p.
      Washington Territory pre Civil War--Young girl
      marries middle aged farmer--Pioneer story of Olympia.

817   Campbell, Thomas Bowyer (1887-   ). Old miss. Boston:
      Houghton, 1929. 302p.
      Chronicle of Virginia life--Woman's experiences.

818   Campbell, Walter S. pseud. Vestal, Stanley. 'Dobe walls;
      a story of kit carson's southwest. Boston: Houghton,
      1929. 314p.
      Brent's Fort and Santa Fé Trail--1840's.

819   ---Revolt on the border. Boston: Houghton, 1938. 246p.
      Kearny and New Mexico--Santa Fé--1846--Romantic
      tale.

820   ---Jim bridger, mountain man; a biography. New York:
      Morrow, 1946. 333p.
      Fictionalized--Jim Bridger (1804-1881).

821   Canfield, Chauncey deLeon (1843-1909). The diary of
      forty-niner. New York: Shepard, 1906. 231p.
      "The diary purported to be the experiences of
      Alfred T. Jackson, a pioneer miner who...worked on
      Rock Creek, Nevada County, California".

822   ---The city of six. Chicago: McClurg, 1910. 365p.
      California placer miners 1849--Good story.

823   Canfield, William Walker (1855-1937). The white seneca.
      New York: Dutton, 1911. 281p.
      White boy's life with Iriquois--Cayugas v. Seneca.

824   Cann, Marion Stuart. On skidd's branch; a tale of
      kentucky mountains. Scranton, Pennsylvania: Republican
      1884. 56p.

825   Cannon, Blanche. Nothing ever happens sunday morning.
       New York: Putnam, 1948. 281p.
          1900--Flashbacks--Utah Mormon family.

826   Cannon, Mrs. Cornelia (James) (1876-   ). The pueblo
       boy; a story of coronado's search for the seven
       cities of cibola. Boston: Houghton, 1926. 197p.
          1540--Twelve year old Indian boy with Coronado
       (1510-1549).

827   ---Red rust. Boston: Little, 1928. 320p.
          First novel--Swedes in Minnesota--Rust resistant
       wheat--Regional piece--Sentimental.

828   ---The pueblo girl; the story of coronado on the rio
       grande. Boston: Houghton, 1929. 174p.

829   ---Lazaro in the pueblos; the story of antonio de
       espejos expedition into new mexico. Boston:
       Houghton, 1931. 196p.

830   ---The fight for the pueblo; the story of oñate's
       expedition and the founding of santa fé. Boston:
       Houghton, 1934. 208p.
          Juan de Oñate (1595-1622).

831   Cannon, LeGrande, jr. (1899-   ). A mighty fortress.
       New York: Farrar, 1937. 336p.
          Abolitionists--New Hampshire and Boston.

832   ---Look to the mountain. New York: Holt, 1942. 565p.
          Excellent--New England--1769-1777--New Hampshire
       land grants in area of Mount Chocorua--Bruce Lan-
       caster "...one of finest historical novels [he] read."

833   ---Come home at even. New York: Holt, 1951. 283p.
          Four people--Settle Salem--1630's--Roger Williams
       appears--Beautiful book.

       Cantrell, Wade B. pseud. see Hogan, Robert J.

834   Cantwell, Robert. The land of plenty. New York: Farrar,
       1934. 369p.
          Strike of workers in western lumber mill--
       Proletarian approach.

835   Canzeau, Mrs. William Leslie pseud. Montgomery, Cora.
       Eagle pass; or, life on the border. New York:
       Putnam, 1852. 188p.
          Texas

836   Capps, Benjamin (1922-   ). Trail to ogallala. New
       York: Duell, 1964. 279p.
          First novel--Daily detail of one of last big
       cattle drives pre-fencing--Good local color--Golden
       Spur Award Best Western 1965.

                                 69

837   ---Sam chance; a novel. New York: Duell, 1965. 261p.
       Archtypal cattleman--West Texas--Post Civil War--
       Good portrait of West--Golden Spur Award Best Western
       1966.

838   ---A woman of the people; a novel. New York: Duell,
       1966. 242p.
       White girl captive of Commanche.

839   ---The brothers of uterica; a novel. New York: Meredith,
       1967. 310p.
       Americans and Europeans fail in Utopian community
       of Uterica in northern Texas in 1850's--Mature and
       valuable examination of the failure.

840   ---The white man's road. New York: Harper, 1969. 256p.
       Young Comanche as conquered race on Oklahoma
       Reservation--Life 1890's.

841   Carb, David (1885-   ). Sunrise in the west. New York:
       Brewer, 1931. 384p.

842   Carder, Leigh. Border guns. New York: Covici, 1935.
       306p.
       Western

843   ---Outlaw justice. New York: Covici, 1935. 317p.
       Western

       Carder, Michael pseud. see Fluharty, Vernon L. (1907-   )

       Cargoe, Richard pseud. see Payne, Pierre Stephen Robert

844   Carhart, Arthur Hawthorne (1892-   ). Drum up the dawn.
       New York: Dodd, 1937. 294p.
       Zebulon Pike negotiates with Spanish governor--
       Santa Fé.

845   ---pseud. Thorne, Hart. Bronc twister. New York: Dodd,
       1937. 270p.
       Western

846   ---Saddle men of the c. bit brand. New York: Dodd, 1937.
       262p.
       Western

       Carleton, S. pseud. see Jones, Susan Carleton

847   Carlisle, Helen Grace. We begin. New York: Smith,
       1932. 390p.
       Separatist's family from Holland to America--
       1606-1641--Research good--Romance.

       Carlton, Robert, Esq. pseud. see Hall, Baynard Rush

70

848   Carmer, Carl Lamson (1893-   ). Genesee fever. New
       York: Farrar, 1941. 360p.
           Genesee Region--1790--School teacher sides
       with rebels in Whiskey Rebellion.

849   Carpenter, Edmund Janes. A woman of shawmut; a romance
       of colonial times. Boston: Little, 1891. 234p.
           Puritan romance.

850   Carpenter, William Henry (1813-1899). Clairborne the
       rebel; a romance of maryland, under the proprietary.
       New York: Ferrett, 1845. 104p.
           1632-1661.

851   ---Ruth emsley, the betrothed maiden; a tale of the
       virginia massacre. Philadelphia: Hart, 1850. 130p.
           White captives--Rescue--1622.

852   ---The regicide's daughter; a tale of two worlds.
       Philadelphia: Lippincott, 1851. 213p.
           1670's

853   Carr, Harriett H. Against the wind. New York: Macmillan,
       1955. 214p.
           Boys--Homesteading--North Dakota--Early 1900's.

854   ---Where the turnpike starts. New York: Macmillan,
       1955. 216p.
           Michigan--1835--Juvenile.

855   ---Wheels for conquest. New York: Macmillan, 1957.
       185p.
           Pittsburgh--Conestoga wagon trade--Pennsylvania
       Dutch--Good atmosphere.

856   Carr, John Dickson. The devil in velvet. New York:
       Harper, 1951. 335p.
           Restoration Era.

857   Carr, Mrs. Lorraine. Mother of the smiths. New York:
       Macmillan, 1940. 296p.
           First novel--Taos, New Mexico--Pioneer from
       Texas.

858   Carr, Mary [Anonymous, by A Lady of Philadelphia].
       The last resource; or, female fortitude. a novel
       founded on recent facts in the western parts of
       pennsylvania. Philadelphia: 1809. [?].

859   Carr, Mary Jane. Young mac of fort vancouver. New York:
       Crowell, 1940. 238p.
           1830's--Hudson Bay Company--Boy's life--Juvenile.

860   Carra, Emma pseud.. The hermit of the hudson; or, the
       farmer's daughter. a tale of the seventeenth century.
       Boston: Gleason, 1848. 100p.

861 ---Viroqua; or, the flower of the ottawas. a tale of the west. Boston: Gleason, 1848. 100p.

Carroll, Curt see Bishop, Curtis Kent (1912-   )

862 Carroll, Mrs. Gladys Hasty (1904-   ). A few foolish ones. New York: Macmillan, 1935. 384p.
     Small farming community in Southern Maine--1870-1930--Life on farm and town.

863 ---As the earth turns. New York: Macmillan, 1936. 339p.
     Farm novel--New England locale.

864 ---Dunnybrook. New York: Macmillan, 1943. 389p.
     Maine farm family--American Revolution to 1940--Based on author's family.

865 Carruth, Fred Hayden (1862-1932). The voyage of the rattle trap. New York: Harper, 1897. 207p.
     Nebraska--Wyoming--Black Hills.

866 ---Track's end; being the narratives of judson pitcher's strange winter spent there as told by himself and edited by hayden carruth. New York: Harper, 1911. 229p.
     Adventure for boys--Railroad--Dakota Territory--Juvenile.

867 Carse, Robert (1903-   ). Great venture. New York: Scribner's, 1952. 239p.
     Scottish attempt to set colony at Darien 17th century--Juvenile.

868 ---The beckoning waters. New York: Scribner's, 1953. 438p.
     Panorama life Great Lakes 1876-1932.

869 ---Great circle. New York: Scribner's, 1956. 243p.
     Whaling ship from Salem in 1840 to South Seas--Author licensed mate.

870 Carson, Katharine. Mrs. Pennington. New York: Putnam, 1939. 312p.
     Small town family in Kentucky--1880's--Chautauquas

871 Carter, Jefferson. Madam constantia; the romance of a prisoner of war in the revolution (south carolina). New York: Longmans, 1919. 285p.
     British view--Goddaughter of Madison risks life of patriotic lover.

872 Carter, John Henton. The man at the wheel. St. Louis: Carter, 1898. 187p.
     Steamboats on Mississippi River.

873   Carteret, John Dunloe. <u>A fortune hunter; or, the old</u>
      <u>stone corral. a tale of the old santa fe trail.</u>
      Cincinnati: Printed for the Author, 1888. 290p.

874   Caruthers, William Alexander (1802-1846). <u>The cavaliers</u>
      <u>of virginia; or, the recluse of jamestown. an</u>
      <u>historical romance of the old dominion.</u> New York:
      Harper, 1834-35.
             Romance based on Bacon's Rebellion--1675-1676--
      Bacon wins--Based on Burk's, <u>History of Virginia.</u>

875   ---<u>The kentuckian in new york; or, the adventures of</u>
      <u>three southerners.</u> New York: Harper, 1834. 2 vols.
             Epistolary--Two South Carolina gentleman journey
      to New York.

876   ---<u>The knight of the horse shoe; a traditionary tale</u>
      <u>of the cocked hat gentry in the old dominion.</u>
      Weptumka, Alabama: Yancey, 1845. 284p.
             Best novel--Governor Alexander Spotswood (1676-
      1740) of Virginia explores back country--Order of
      Cocked Hat Gentry--Scout Red Jarvis--Good character.

877   Case, Robert Ormond. <u>Riders of the grande ronde.</u>
      New York: Doubleday, 1928. 373p.
             Western

878   ---<u>The yukon drive.</u> New York: Doubleday, 1930. 359p.
             Gold Rush--1898.

879   ---<u>Whispering valley.</u> New York: Doubleday, 1932. 311p.
             Western

880   ---<u>Big timber; a novel.</u> Philadelphia: Macrae, 1937.
      271p.

881   ---<u>Wings north.</u> New York: Doubleday, 1938. 280p.
             Mystery--Adventure--Canada.

882   ---<u>Golden portage.</u> New York: Doubleday, 1940. 276p.
             Western

883   ---<u>West of barter river.</u> New York: Doubleday, 1941.
      272p.
             Western

884   ---<u>White victory.</u> New York: Doubleday, 1943. 210p.
             Western

885   Case, Victoria. <u>The quiet life of mrs. general lane.</u>
      New York: Doubleday, 1952. 319p.
             Fictionalized biography--Joseph Lane (1801-
      1881)--Polly Lane (1820ca.-1876)--Mexican War--
      Oregon statehood fight.

886   <u>Cassimer sarol; a tale.</u> Charleston: Wiley, 1835. 264p.

War of 1812--Wright "Attributed to Bernard H. Reynolds...".

887 Castle, Mrs. Marian (Johnson). Deborah. New York: Morrow, 1946. 372p.
Three generations of women Dakota farm family-- 1890-1930.

888 ---The golden fury. New York: Morrow, 1949. 329p.
Gospel spreader--Colorado boomtown--1890's.

889 ---Roxana. New York: Morrow, 1955. 344p.
Colorado mining country--1879-1880.

890 Castle, William and Joseph, Robert. Hero's oak; a novel. New York: Reader's Press, 1945. 334p.
Family of Polish immigrants to Vermont--1910-1936.

Castleton, D. R. pseud. see Derby, Caroline Rosina

891 Castor, Henry. The spanglers. New York: Doubleday, 1948. 308p.
Romance and adventure Pennsylvania Dutch family--1860's.

892 ---The year of the spaniard; a novel of 1898. New York: Doubleday, 1950. 274p.
War--Pokes fun at Rough Riders--Two college friends.

893 Cather, Willa Sibert (1875-1947). O pioneers! New York: Houghton, 1913. 308p.
Important work--Distinguished farm novel-- Prairie immigrant life toward end of 19th century-- Daughter runs Nebraska farm after father's death.

894 ---My ántonia. Boston: Houghton, 1918. 418p.
One of great farm novels--Nebraska 1880's- 1890's--Bohemian girl conquers life and prairies-- An important American novel.

895 ---The professor's house. New York: Knopf, 1925. 283p.
In part deals with ancient cliff city in New Mexico.

896 ---Death comes for the archbishop. New York: Knopf, 1927. 303p.
Does for New Mexico what My Ántonia did for Nebraska--Archbishop Lamy subject of novel--Great book.

897 ---Shadows on the rock. New York: Knopf, 1931. 280p.
Details of administration--Delicate tones-- Frontenac--1670-1698--Quebec.

74

898   ---Sapphira and the slave girl. New York: Knopf, 1940.
       295p.
          Virginia lady is wife of miller on the frontier--
       Not one of her better efforts--Loudon County--1856.

899   Catherwood, Mrs. Mary (Hartwell) (1847-1902). Romance
       of dollard. New York: Century, 1889. 206p.
          Man saves New France from Iriquois in 1660's--
       Francis Parkman gave full approval to historical
       accuracy--First real success.

900   ---The story of tonty. Chicago: McClurg, 1890. 227p.
          Henri de Tonti (d. 1704)--One armed lieutenant
       of LaSalle (1643-1687?)--Canada and Texas.

901   ---The lady of fort st. john. Boston: Houghton, 1891.
       284p.
          Acadia--Based on records--Feud of two families--
       Fort St. John.

902   ---Old kaskaskia;[a novel.] Boston: Houghton, 1893.   200p.
          Illinois

903   ---The white islander. New York: Century, 1893.   164p.
          Mackinac--Romance--Indian Wars.

904   ---Spanish peggy; a story of young illinois.   Chicago:
       Stone, 1899. 85p.
          A. Lincoln (1809-1865).

905   ---Lazarre. Indianapolis: Bowen, 1901. 436p.
          Legend that son of Louis XVI found among Indians
       in Illinois--1795--Tecumseh--Johnny Appleseed.

906   Catlin, Henry Guy. Yellow pine basin; the story of a
       prospector. New York: Richmond, 1897. 214p.

907   Cato, Max. Oil king. New York: Simon, 1970. 288p.
          Texas dynasty chronicle.

908   Caudill, Harry M. (1922-   ). Dark hill to westward;
       the saga of jennie wiley. Boston: Little, 1969.
       197p.
          1789--Woman carried away by maurading Indians
       escapes after a year of captivity--Jennie (Sellards)
       Wiley (d.1831).

909   Caudill, Rebecca (Mrs. James Sterling Ayars) (1899-   ).
       Tree of freedom. New York: Viking, 1949. 279p.
          Pioneers from Carolina to homestead in Kentucky--
       1780--Juvenile.

910   Cauffman, Stanley Hart. At the sign of the silver ship.
       Philadelphia: Penn, 1925. 333p.
          Inn near Philadelphia--Romance--Intrigue--Adven-
       ture--Colonial era--Juvenile.

911   ---The adventures of polydore. Philadelphia: Penn,
      1930. 339p.
            Romance--Colonial--Good idiom of period.

912   Cave, Claire. Wild peach. New York: Gramercy, 1937.
      254p.
            Western

913   Chalmers, Harvey. West to the setting sun. New York:
      Macmillan, 1944. 362p.
            Joseph (Thayendanegea) Brant--(1742-1807)--
      Fictionalized biography--People of the Long house--
      Six nations.

914   ---Drums against frontenac. New York: Smith, 1949. 440p.
            General Bradstreet to Frontenac--1758--Facts good.

915   Chamberlain, George Agnew (1879-   ). Scudda-hoo!
      scudda-hay!. Indianapolis: Bobbs, 1946. 208p.
            New Jersey farm boy--Mules.

916   Chambers, Robert William (1865-1933). Cardigan; a novel.
      New York: Harper, 1901. 512p.
            American Revolution--New York State--Romance--
      1744-1773.

917   ---The maid-at-arms; a novel. New York: Harper, 1902.
      342p.
            Popular novel of American Revolution--Tryon
      County--Ft. Stanwick--Loyalists get aid from Indians.

918   ---The reckoning. New York: Appleton, 1905. 386p.
            Wealthy land owners in New York State after
      the Revolution--Oneidas.

919   ---The hidden children. New York: Appleton, 1914.
      650p.
            Gypsy girl follows hero member of Morgan's
      Rifles--Adventure--Border warfare--Western New York.

920   ---The little red foot. New York: Doran, 1921. 351p.
            Love story based on John Drogue--Former overseer
      for Sir William Johnson--New York--1774-1782.

921   ---America; or, the sacrifice. a romance of the american
      revolution. New York: Grosset, 1924. 399p.

922   ---The man they hanged. New York: Appleton, 1926.
      416p.
            Late 17th century--New York City--Kind portrait
      of Captain Kidd--Romance.

923   ---The drums of aulone. New York: Appleton, 1927. 347p.
            Heroine Michelle de Maniscamp, daughter of Count
      d'Aulone--Huguenots chased from France to England and
      Canada.

924 ---<u>The rogue's moon</u>. New York: Appleton, 1928. 274p.
Girl disguised as boy--Pirates--Adventure.

925 ---<u>The sun hawk</u>. New York: Appleton, 1928. 342p.
Richard Stanhope, son of Prince Rupert, tells
of his adventures--1630's--Sabatini style--Romance.

926 ---<u>The happy parrot</u>. New York: Appleton, 1929. 334p.
Slave trade--War 1812--Juvenile.

927 ---<u>The painted minx</u>. New York: Appleton, 1930. 306p.
American Revolution--1777-1788--Life in New York.

928 ---<u>The rake and the hussy</u>. New York: Appleton, 1930.
440p.
Romance Joshua Brooke, aide to A. Jackson and
Naia, patriot--New Orleans--War 1812.

929 ---<u>Gitana</u>. New York: Appleton, 1931. 363p.
Mexican War--1845-1848--Ends with Battle of
Beuna Vista--Good history.

930 ---<u>War paint and rouge</u>. New York: Appleton, 1931. 376p.
Romance--French-Indian War (1755-1763).

931 ---<u>Love and the lieutenant</u>. New York: Appleton, 1935.
402p.
One of his better romances--American Revolution--
British soldier with Burgoyne falls in love with
American girl.

932 Champney, Elizabeth (Williams) (1880-1922). <u>Rosemary and</u>
<u>rue</u>. Boston: Osgood, 1881. 292p.
American Revolution.

933 ---<u>Great-grandmother's girls in new mexico, 1670-1680</u>.
Boston: Estes, 1888. 330p.
Juvenile

934 Chanslor, Roy (1899-1964). <u>The ballad of cat ballou</u>.
Boston: Little, 1956. 334p.
Western based on <u>The Ballad of Cat Ballou</u>.

935 Chapman, Arthur (1873-1935). <u>Mystery ranch</u>. Boston:
Houghton, 1921. 305p.
Western--Mystery.

936 ---<u>John crews</u>. Boston: Houghton, 1926. 303p.
Frontier life--Ft. Laramie, Wyoming--Danites--
Indians.

937 Chapman, C. I. A.. <u>Franklin's oath; a tale of wyoming</u>
<u>one hundred years ago</u>. Pittston, Pennsylvania:
Hart, 1880. 110p.

77

938 Chapman, Elisabeth (Cobb). She was a lady. Indianapolis:
     Bobbs, 1934. 316p.
          Cinderella story--Montana ranch--Author daughter
     of Irwin S. Cobb.

939 Chapman, Harry James (1856-   ). Lords of acadia.
     Boston: Small, 1925. 356p.
          King William's War (1689-1697)--French Acadia--
     English Sagadahock.

     Chapman, Maristan pseud. see Chapman, Mary Stanton
     (Isley) (1895-   ) pseud. of Chapman, John Stanton
     Higham and Chapman, Mary (Isley)

940 Chapman, Mary Stanton (Isley) (1895-   ) pseud. Chapman,
     Maristan. Rogue's march. Philadelphia: Lippincott,
     1949. 384p.
          American Revolution--Romance--Tory has Whig
     daughter--Battle of King's Mountain 1780--Western
     Carolina--Tennessee.

941 ---Tennessee hazard. Philadelphia: Lippincott, 1953.
     367p.
          Spanish conspiracy--Ratification of Constitution--
     Tennessee frontier about 1787-1788--Wilkinson's
     conspiracy.

942 Charbonneau, Louis. Down from the mountain. New York:
     Doubleday, 1969. 360p.
          Wagon train--Ft. Laramie to Rockies--1860's.

943 Charnley, Mitchell Vaughn. Jean lafitte, gentleman
     smuggler. New York: Viking, 1934. 240p.
          Jean LaFitte (1780?-1826?)--Juvenile.

944 Charters, Mrs. Zelda Stewart. Barbary brew; a romantic
     novel. New York: Stackpole, 1937. 361p.
          Henty style--Romance and adventure--Barbary
     States--1800's.

945 Chase, Jessie (Anderson) (1865-   ). A daughter of
     the revolution. Boston: Badger, 1910. 128p.
          Royalist child to colonies before American
     Revolution.

946 Chase, Mary Ellen (1887-   ). Virginia of elk creek
     valley. Boston: Page. 1917. 297p.
          Western

947 ---Silas crockett. New York: Macmillan, 1935. 404p.
          Four generations of New England family--
     Clipper ship era--Maine culture.

948 Chateaubriand, François Auguste René, Viscounte de
     (1768-1848). Atala; or, the amours of two indians,

in the wilds of america. London: Lee, 1802. 129p.
Published in France 1801--Natchez-Mississippi
region.

949 Cheavens, Martha Louise (Mrs. Hugh Joel S. Chuck)
(1898-   ). Crosswinds. Boston: Houghton, 1948.
278p.
Texas-Mexican border--Contemporary--Minister
and family.

950 Cheavins, Frank (1905-   ). Arron lie still; a novel.
Dallas: Story Book Press, 1950. 302p.
Texas history.

951 Cheney, Brainard. Lightwood. Boston: Houghton, 1939.
369p.
Post Civil War--Georgia--Farmers v. Yankee-
owned corporation--Piney Woods.

952 ---River rogue. Boston: Houghton, 1942. 443p.
Logging in back country of eastern Georgia
1880's--Vibrant.

953 Cheney, Mrs. Harriet Vaughn (Foster). A peep at the
pilgrims in sixteen hundred thirty-six. a tale of
olden times. Boston: Wells, 1824. 2 vols.
Plymouth, England to Boston, Massachusetts.

954 ---The rivals of acadia; an old story of the new world.
Boston: Wells, 1827. 271p.
D'Aulney v. LaTour--1643.

955 Chesebro', Caroline. Victoria: or, the world overcome.
New York: Derby, 1856. 465p.
Witchcraft--New England--1650-1680.

956 Cheshire, Gifford Paul (1905-   ). Starlight basin.
New York: Random, 1954. 236p.
Western

957 ---River of gold; oregon and the challenge of the
gold rush. New York: Aladdin, 1955. 192p.
Juvenile

958 ---Gunmaster. New York: Graphic, 1956. 159p.
Western

959 ---Year of the gun; an original western. New York:
Dell, 1957. 192p.
Western

960 ---Edge of the desert. New York: Doubleday, 1958. 188p.
Western

961 ---The sudden guns. New York: Doubleday, 1959. 190p.
Western

79

962 ---Thunder on the mountain. New York: Doubleday, 1960.
192p.
Western

963 ---Black list. New York: Doubleday, 1962. 188p.
Western

964 ---Stronghold. New York: Doubleday, 1963. 192p.
Western

965 ---Wenatchee bend. New York: Doubleday, 1966. 191p.
Western

966 ---Ambush at bedrock. New York: Doubleday, 1969. 189p.
Western

967 ---pseud. Pendleton, Ford. Outlaw justice. Hasbrouck
Heights, New Jersey: Graphic, 1954. 190p.
Western

968 ---Vengeance trail. New York: Avalon, 1958. 224p.
Western

969 ---pseud. Merriman Chad. Fury on the plains. New York:
Fawcett, 1954. 144p.
Western

970 ---The avengers. New York: Ballantine, 1959. 141p.
Western

971 ---Bunch quitter. New York: Ballantine, 1959. 143p.
Western

972 ---Gunpoint ransom. London: Ward, 1961. 157p.
Western

973 ---Rogue river. New York: Ballantine, 1962. 127p.
Western

974 ---the harsh range. New York: Ballantine, 1963. 191p.
Western

975 Cheshire, Gifford Paul and Overholser, Wyane D. pseuds.
Merriman, Chad and Leighton, Lee. Colorado gold.
New York: Ballantine, 1958. 159p.
Western

976 Chevalier, Elizabeth (Pickett). Redskin. New York:
Grosset, 1929. 275p.

977 ---Drivin' woman. New York: Macmillan, 1942. 652p.
1865-1915--Kentucky tobacco planter--New York
financier--cf. Gone With The Wind and Show Me A Land.

978 Chevigny, Hector. Lost empire; the life and the adventures of nikolai petrovich rezánov. New York:

80

Macmillan, 1937. 356p.
Nikolai Petrovich Rezánov (1764-1807)--Alaska
from Russia to United States.

979 Chidester, Ann (1919-   ). <u>Moon gap</u>. New York:
Doubleday, 1950. 254p.
Ghost town in Nevada--Good description.

980 Chidsey, Donald Barr (1902-   ). <u>Pistols in the morning</u>.
New York: Day, 1930. 282p.
Romance and adventure--Riverboat gambler and
Creole beauty.

981 ---<u>Stronghold</u>. New York: Doubleday, 1948. 343p.
Connecticut opposition to Jefferson's embargo--
Impressment--Martinique.

982 ---<u>Captain adam</u>. New York: Crown, 1953. 318p.
Romance days of Queen Anne--Pirates--Smugglers.

983 ---<u>Lord of the isles</u>. New York: Crown, 1954. 287p.
Hawaii--1820--Queen Kaahumanu--Religion--
Romance.

984 ---<u>Edge of piracy; a novel</u>. New York: Crown, 1964. 284p.
American Revolution.

985 ---<u>The legion of the lost</u>. New York: Crown, 1967. 284p.
Captain Kidd--1690's.

986 Child, Frank Samuel (1854-1922). <u>Colonial witch; being</u>
<u>a study of the black art in colony of connecticut</u>.
New York: Baker, 1897. 307p.
Puritans in Connecticut--Fanaticism--Rich
social setting.

987 ---<u>A puritan wooing; a tale of the great awakening</u>
<u>in new england</u>. New York: Baker, 1898. 305p.

988 ---<u>An unknown patriot; a story of the secret service</u>.
Boston: Houghton, 1899. 396p.
American Revolution.

989 ---<u>Friend or foe; a tale of connecticut during the war</u>
<u>of 1812</u>. Boston: Houghton, 1900. 328p.

990 Child, Mrs. Lydia Maria (Francis) (1802-1880). <u>Hobomok,</u>
<u>a tale of early times</u>. Boston: Cummings, 1824.
188p.
Massachusetts during Endicott's governorship--
1628-1630--Apes Cooper.

991 ---<u>The rebels; or, boston before the revolution</u>. Boston:
Cummings, 1825. 304p.
Stamp Act agitation.

81

992   Chisholm, Arthur Murray (1872-   ). The boss of
      wind river. New York: Doubleday, 1911. 340p.
      Romance--Lumbering.

993   Choate, Florence and Curtis, Elizabeth. Lysbet; a
      story of old new york. Philadelphia: Lippincott,
      1947. 220p.
      Girl taken by Indians to Mohawk Valley--
      Dutch in New York.

994   The christian indian; or, times of the first settlers.
      [Anonymous]. New York: Collins, 1825. 251p.
      Defense of Massachusetts--Indians.

995   Christian, William Asbury. Marah; a story of old
      virginia. Richmond, Virginia: Jenkins, 1903. 386p.

996   Christie, Robert Cleland Hamilton. The trembling
      land. New York: Doubleday, 1959. 288p.
      Western

997   Churchill, Winston (1871-1947). Richard carvel. New
      York: Macmillan, 1899. 538p.
      Sea action during the Revolution--Georgian
      London--Maryland--Contemporary language--Good.

998   ---The crisis. New York: Macmillan, 1901. 522p.
      Missouri during the Civil War.

999   ---The crossing. New York: Macmillan, 1904. 598p.
      George Rogers Clark in the Old Northwest--
      1780-1804.

1000 ---Coniston. New York: Macmillan, 1906. 534p.
      Corruption--New Hampshire politics during
      Jacksonian period.

1001 Cicchetti, Mrs. Janet (O'Daniel). O genesee. Phil-
      adelphia: Lippincott, 1957. 350p.
      Fairchild family left Albany, New York for
      Genesee--1799--Pioneering--War of 1812--Romance--
      Adventure.

1002 Cicchetti, Janet and Ressler, Lillian pseud. Janet,
      Lillian. Touchstone. New York: Rinehart, 1947.
      346p.
      1849--San Francisco and Sacramento--Two women.

1003 ---The city beyond devil's gate. New York: Random,
      1951. 263p.
      Virginia City, Nevada--1860's--Comstock Lode--
      Melodrama for women.

1004 Clagett, John. Cradle of the sun. New York: Crown,
      1952. 304p.
      First novel.

Romance set in New World with Mayas, conquis-
todors--Some of inquisition in Spain--Very good--
Spanish officer becomes Yucatan leader.

1005 ---Buckskin cavalier. New York: Crown, 1954. 216p.
Girl taken by Indians near Fort Pitt--Wild-
erness Road.

1006 Clark, Charlotte (Moon). Baby rue; her adventures and
misadventures, her friends and her enemies. Boston:
Roberts, 1881. 318p.
Western frontier life.

1007 Clark, Dorothy (Park) and McMeekin Isabella (McClennan)
pseud. McMeekin, Clark. Show me a land. New York:
Appleton, 1940. 441p.
Virginia--Kentucky-- 1816- 1875--Horse raising--
Politics.

1008 ---Reckon with the river. New York: Appleton, 1941.
392p.
Aaron Burr--Blennerhassett--Ohio Valley frontier life.

1009 ---Red raskall. New York: Appleton, 1943. 311p.
Tale of adventure--England and Virginia-- 1816.

1010 ---Gaudy's ladies. New York: Appleton, 1948. 297p.
Louisville, Kentucky--Early 19th century.

1011 ---The october fox. New York: Putnam, 1956. 310p.
Kentucky family 1890's.

1012 ---The fair brothers; a novel. New York: Putnam,
1961. 288p.
Kentucky family life-- 1875 first run of Derby.

1013 Clark, Ellery Harding (1874- 1949). The strength of
the hills; a story of andrew jackson, and of the
pioneers of tennessee. New York: Crowell, 1929.
350p.
Andrew Jackson basis of story--Opens 1776--
Ends 1829.

1014 Clark, Frederick Thickstun. On cloud mountain; a
novel. New York: Harper, 1894. 230p.
Colorado

1015 ---The mistress of the ranch; a novel. New York:
Harper, 1897. 357p.
Rio Grande

1016 ---pseud. Thickstun, Frederick. A mexican girl.
Boston: Ticknor, 1888. 287p.
California mining.

83

1017   Clark, Howard. The mill on mad river. Boston: Little,
        1948. 278p.
        Clockmaking--Waterbury, Connecticut--1810.

1018   Clark, Imogen. The domine's garden; story of old new
        york. London: Murray, 1901. 380p.
        Social life in Dutch Colonial New York--1757--
        Tragic note.

1019   ---God's puppets; an eighteenth century romance of
        new york city. (A Story of Old New York). New
        York: Scribner's, 1901. 381p.
        Dutch Dominie Ryerssen, parson of Garden
        Street Church--1757--Clark one of first to use this
        era and material.

1020   Clark, Susie Champney. Lorita, an alaska maiden.
        Boston: Lee, 1892. 171p.

1021   Clark, Valma (1894-   ). Horn of plenty. New York:
        Duell, 1945. 247p.
        Family life--Farming area of upstate New York.

1022   Clark, Walter VanTilburg (1909-   ). The ox-bow
        incident. New York: Random, 1940. 309p.
        First novel--People real--Lynching--Two cow-
        boys ride into town and join posse--Important con-
        tribution to further understanding of male psychology
        on frontier--Excellent--Wyoming or Nevada--1880's.

1023   ---The city of trembling leaves. New York: Random,
        1945. 690p.
        Reno, Nevada.

1024   ---The track of the cat; a novel. New York: Random,
        1949. 404p.
        Nevada Ranch--Symbolism good and evil.

1025   Clarke, Gipsy (Mrs. P. M. Clarke). Out yonder.
        New York: Crowell, 1935. 317p.
        First novel--Western.

1026   Clarke, Mary Stetson. The iron peacock. New York:
        Viking, 1966. 251p.
        Iron works--Saugus River--Massachusetts Bay--
        Juvenile.

        Clavers, Mary pseud. see Kirkland, Mrs. Caroline
        Matilda (Stansbury) (1801-1864)

1027   Clay, Grover. Hester of the hills; a romance of the
        ozark mountain. Boston: Page, 1907. 410p.
        Northerner marries a "cracker"--Romance--
        Missouri.

84

Clay, John Wood   jt. author, see Mulford. Clarence Edward

1028   Cleary, Kate (McPhelim).   Like a gallant lady.   Chicago:
       Way, 1897. 292p.
          Nebraska farm.

Cleeve, Lucas pseud. see Kingscote, Mrs. Georgiana
   (Wolff)

Cleland, Mrs. Mabel (Goodwin), jt. author, see Ogley,
   Mrs. Dorothy (Cleland)

1029   Clemens, Jeremiah (1814-1865).   Bernard lile; an
       historical romance, embracing the periods of the
       texas revolution, and the mexican war.   Philadelphia:
       Lippincott, 1856. 287p.

1030   ---Mustang gray; a romance.   Philadelphia: Lippincott,
       1859. 296p.
          Anglo-American-Mexican conflict--One of few
       based on real person.

1031   ---The rivals; a tale of the times of aaron burr and
       alexander hamilton.   New York: Lippincott, 1860.
       286p.
          A. Burr (1756-1836) v. A. Hamilton (1757-1804)--
       American Revolution--Hamilton, evil--Burr, good--
       Published in 1900 under title An American Colonel.

1032   Clemens, Samuel pseud. Twain, Mark.   Life on the
       mississippi.   Boston: Osgood, 1883. 624p.
          Classic on age of steamboat.

1033   Clevenger, G. A..   Spring may be late.   New York:
       Phoenix, 1936. 254p.
          Denver setting for romance--Western.

1034   Clinton, Park.   Glanmore; a romance of the revolution.
       New York: Stearns, 1853. 102p.
          Bandit of Saratoga Lake.

1035   Clippinger, John Albert.   Pedagogue of widow's gulch;
       or, the adventurers of a pioneer school teacher in
       a secluded vale in california where married men
       could not live and where widows did not die.
       Sacramento: Young, 1876. 207p.

1036   Cluff, Tom.   Minutemen of the sea.   Chicago: Follett,
       1955. 223p.
          Five days before Battle of Bunker Hill--Jeremiah
       O'Brien (1744-1818)--Take British cutter--Juvenile.

1037   Clugston, Katharine.   Wilderness road, virginia.
       New York: Blue Ribbon, 1937. 309p.
          Daniel Boone (1734-1830)--From CBS radio show--
       Juvenile.

85

1038 Coates, Grace Stone (1881-   ). Black cherries.
New York: Knopf, 1931. 213p.
Kansas farm life--Through eyes of a child.

1039 Coates, Robert M.. The outlaw years; the history of
land pirates of natchez trace. New York: Macauly,
1930. 308p.
Land pirates of Natchez Trace.

1040 Coatsworth, Elizabeth Jane (Mrs. Henry Beston Sheahan)
(1893-   ). Sword of the wilderness. New York:
Macmillan, 1936. 160p.
White taken by Abenakis--War in New England--
Maine and Canada--1689--Juvenile.

1041 ---Here i stay. New York: Coward, 1938. 246p.
Maine to Ohio--1817--Daughter of Tory stays on
land in Maine--Juvenile.

1042 ---A toast to the king. New York: Coward, 1940. 159p.
Three orphaned Tories and Christmas--American
Revolution--Juvenile.

1043 ---The last fort; a story of the french voyageurs.
Philadelphia: Winston, 1952. 250p.
Land of Free Series--Juvenile.

1044 ---Mountain bride; an incredible tale. New York:
Pantheon, 1954. 153p.
Maine legend--Katahdin Mountain--Juvenile.

Cobb, Mrs. Elisabeth see Chapman, Elisabeth (Cobb)

1045 Cobb, Irvin Shrewsbury (1876-1944). Chivalry peak.
New York: Cosmopolitan, 1927. 314p.
Southern migrants to poor holdings in Western
hills--Chase--Robbery.

1046 ---Red likker. New York: Cosmopolitan, 1929. 339p.
Distillery in Kentucky--1790 through 1930's.

1047 Cobb, Joseph Beckham (1819-1858). The creole; or,
siege of new orleans. an historical romance.
Philadelphia: Hart, 1850. 131p.

1048 Cobb, Margaret Smith. Blaxine, half breed girl.
New York: Neale, 1910. 253p.
California coastal ranges setting--Romance.

1049 Cobb, Sylvanus. The golden eagle; or, the privateer
of '76. a tale of the revolution. Boston: Gleason,
1850. 100p.
Contains also two other tales.

1050 ---Olivia trevett; or, the patriot cruiser. a story of

the american revolution. New York: French, 185-?.
100p.

1051 ---Orlando chester; or, the adventures of a young
hunter. a story of old virginia's early days.
Boston: Gleason, 1852. 100p.
1755-1775.

1052 Coblentz, Catherine (Cate) (Mrs. W. W. Coblentz) (1897-).
The bells of leyden sing. New York: Longmans, 1944.
259p.
English exiles leave Holland 1609 for America--
Juvenile.

1053 Cochran, Hamilton. Windward passage. Indianapolis:
Bobbs, 1942. 313p.
Henry Morgan's raid on Panama--1671.

1054 ---Captain ebony. Indianapolis: Bobbs, 1943. 430p.
Virginia gentleman turned "black birder"--
1840's--Danish West Indies.

1055 ---Silver shoals. Indianapolis: Bobbs, 1945. 320p.
Treasure hunting--New England and Bahamas--
Sir William Phips.

1056 ---Rogue's holiday; a novel. Indianapolis: Bobbs,
1947. 297p.
Romance early 18th century--Lt. British navy
and American girl--Edward Teach (Blackbeard).

1057 Cochran, Louis (1899-). Son of haman. Caldwell,
Idaho: Caxton, 1937. 330p.
People of Yazoo River delta--Post Civil War--
#1 of proposed Trilogy.

1058 ---Fool of god; a novel based upon the life of alexander
campbell. New York: Duell, 1958. 413p.
Biographical novel of Alexander Campbell
(1764-1824)--Founder of Disciples of Christ.

1059 Cocke, Sarah Cobb (Johnson) (Mrs. Lucian Howard Cocke).
The master of the hills; a tale of the georgia
mountains. New York: Dutton, 1917. 327p.
Two generations of Georgia 1860-1900--
"Grey Eagle" mountaineer.

Cody, Al pseud. see Joscelyn, Archie

1060 Cody, Hiran Alfred. The frontiersman; a tale of the
yukon. New York: Hodder, 1910. 342p.
Medical missionary--Alaska--1910.

1061 ---The chief of the ranges; a tale of the yukon. New
York: Doran, 1913. 303p.

White fur traders--Chilcat and Ayana Tribes--
Yukon before whites came.

Cody, John pseud. see Repp, Edward Earl

Cody, Stone pseud. see Mount, Thomas Ernest

1062 Coffin, Charles Carleton (1823-1896). Daughters of
the revolution and their times, 1769-1776; a
historical romance. Boston: Houghton, 1895. 387p.
All major New England events of start of
American Revolution--Juvenile.

1063 Coffin, Robert Peter Tristram (1892-1955). Lost
paradise; a boyhood on the maine coast farm. New
York: Macmillan, 1934. 284p.
Salt water farm.

1064 ---John dawn. New York: Macmillan, 1936. 307p.
Maine ship building--Post Revolutionary Era.

1065 Cogswell, Frederick Hull. The regicides; a tale of
early colonial times. New York: Colonial Pub.,
1896. 363p.

1066 Cohen, Octavius Roy (1891-   ). Borrasca. New York:
Macmillan, 1953. 310p.
Comstock Lode--1868 through 1870's--Virginia
City, Nevada.

1067 Colby, Merle Estes (1902-   ). All ye people. New
York: Viking, 1931. 429p.
Panoramic--Pioneers--East--West--South-1810--
Social and economic life ca.1810--Eastern farming
and Western pioneering--Valuable as history.

1068 ---The new road. New York: Viking, 1933. 310p.
Frontier town in Ohio in early days--1820-1838--
Maumee River--Romance.

1069 Cole, Cornelius. California three hundred and fifty
years ago; manuelo's narrative, translated from
the portuguese, by a pioneer. San Francisco:
Carson, 1888. 333p.

Cole, Jackson pseud. see Scott, Leslie

Cole, Jackson pseud. see Schisgall, Oscar (1901-   )

1070 Coleman, Gilbert Payson. Captain at fifteen. New York:
Appleton, 1911. 309p.
Young man on merchant vessel--1774.

1071 Collins, Norman Richard. Black ivory; being the story
of ralph rudd, his early adventures, perils and mis-
fortunes on land and sea.

New York: Duell, 1948. 305p.
Last days of slave trade--Juvenile.

1072 Collins, Paul Valorous. A country romance. Milwaukee,
Wisconsin: Yewdale, 1896. 138p.
To promote J. I. Case threshing machine.

1073 Colony, Horatio. Free forester; a novel of pioneer
kentucky. Boston: Little, 1935. 302p.
Swashbuckling men during and after American
Revolution.

Colt, Clem pseud. see Nye, Nelson Coral (1907-   )

1074 Colter, Eli. Adventures of hawke travis; episodes
in the life of a gunman. New York: Macmillan, 1931.
220p.
Fictionalized biography of western "badman"--
Good western.

1075 ---Bad man's trail. New York: King, 1931. 271p.
Western

1076 ---Outlaw blood. New York: King, 1932. 284p.
Western

1077 ---Three killers. New York: King, 1932. 286p.
Western

1078 ---The outcasts of lazy s. New York: King, 1933. 286p.
Western

1079 ---Blood on the range. New York: Dodge, 1939. 256p.
Western

1080 ---Canyon rattlers. New York: Dodge, 1939. 256p.
Western

1081 Colver, Alice Mary (Ross) (1892-   ). The measure of
the years. New York: Dodd, 1954. 332p.
First family in Stockbridge, Massachusetts.

1082 ---There is a season. New York: Dodd, 1957. 306p.
Sequel to The Measure of the Years--1756-1770--
Stockbridge, Massachusetts and Charles-Town, South
Carolina.

1083 Colver, Anne (1908-   ). Listen for the voices; a
novel of concord. New York: Farrar, 1939. 387p.
Concord, Massachusetts--1840's--Emerson.

1084 ---Theodosia, daughter of aaron burr. New York: Farrar,
1941. 291p.

1085 Comfort, Mildred Houghton (1886-   ). Winter on the

89

johnny smoker. New York: Morrow, 1943. 218p.
1874--Winter spent on "side-wheeler"--Juvenile.

1086 ---Treasure on the johnny smoker. New York: Morrow,
1947. 219p.
Sequel to Winter on the Johnny Smoker--
(1943)--Fur trading--Freight carrying--Upper Mississippi 1870's--Juvenile.

1087 Comfort, Will Levington (1878-1932). Routledge rides
alone. Philadelphia: Lippincott, 1910. 310p.
Western

1088 ---Somewhere south in sonora; a novel. Boston: Houghton,
1925. 236p.
Western

1089 ---Apache. New York: Dutton, 1931. 274p.
Fictionalized biography of Mangas Coloradas
Apache Chief (d. 1836?)--Ranks with La Farges
Laughing Boy.

1090 Comstock, Sarah. The soddy. New York: Doubleday,
1912. 370p.
Family--Romance--Sod house symbol for spirit
that makes and builds new country.

1091 ---Speak to the earth. New York: Doubleday, 1927.
330p.
Salesgirl to sheep ranch in Dakota Bad Lands--
Picture of New West.

1092 Conner, Mrs. Aletha (Caldwell). Pisces' child.
Dallas, Texas: Southwest Press, 1934. 187p.
Oklahoma--Local color.

1093 Connolly, (Capt.) James (1842-   ). Magic of the
sea; or, commodore john barry in the making.
St. Louis: Herder, 1911. 554p.
American Revolution.

Connor, Ralph pseud. see Gordon, Charles William

1094 The conspiracy of aaron burr; a historical romance.
[Anonymous]. New York: Simmons, 1854. 311p.

1095 Constant, Alberta Wilson. Oklahoma run. New York:
Crowell, 1955. 374p.
1891--Land rush.

1096 Constantin-Weyer, Maurice (1881-   ). The half breed.
New York: Macauly, 1930. 310p.
Louis David Riel (1844-1885)--Red River Reb-
ellion (1869-1870).

90

1097 ---The french adventurer; the life and exploits of
      la salle. New York: Macauly, 1931. 255p.
          1643-1687.

1098 Conway, William B.. The cottage on the cliff; a tale
      of the revolution. Ebensburg, Pennsylvania:
      Morgan, 1838. 144p.
          Delaware

1099 Cook, Fannie. Boot-heel doctor. New York: Dodd, 1941.
      268p.
          Southeastern Missouri--Sharecroppers--Fine
      regional novel.

1100 Cook, Roberta St. Clair. The thing about clarissa.
      Indianapolis: Bobbs, 1958. 247p.
          Contrast life in ladys' seminary in Philadelphia
      with Ohio frontier--1837.

      Cook, Will see Cook, William Everett

1101 Cook, William Everett. Prairie guns. New York: Popular,
      1954. 168p.
          Western

1102 ---Apache ambush. New York: Dodd, 1955. 216p.
          Western

1103 ---Fury at painted rock; a western novel. New York:
      Popular, 1955. 159p.
          Western

1104 ---The fighting texan; a western novel. New York:
      Popular, 1956. 158p.
          Western

1105 ---Sabrina kane; a novel of frontier illinois. New
      York: Dodd, 1956. 279p.

1106 ---Elizabeth by name. New York: Dodd, 1958. 308p.
          Frontier trading--Post-Texas--Civil War Era.

1107 ---Comanche captives. New York: Bantam, 1960. 121p.
          Western

1108 ---The tough texan. New York: Bantam, 1963. 152p.
          Western

1109 ---pseud. Everett, Wade. First command. New York:
      Ballantine, 1959. 142p.
          Western

1110 ---Fort starke. New York: Ballantine, 1959. 159p.
          Western

1111 ---pseud. Keene, James. The texas pistol. New York:
Random, 1955. 238p.

1112 ---The brass and the blue. New York: Random, 1956.
247p.
Western

1113 ---Justice, my brother! a novel of oklahoma in the early
nineteen hundreds. New York: Random, 1957. 245p.
Western

1114 ---Seven for vengeance. New York: Random, 1958.
239p.
Western

1115 ---Iron man, iron horse. New York: Doubleday, 1960.
191p.
Western

1116 ---pseud. Peace, Frank. Easy money. New York: Permabooks, 1955. 170p.
Western

1117 ---The brass brigade; a western novel of renegade
apaches. New York: Permabooks, 1956. 186p.
Western

1118 Cooke, David Coxe (1917-   ). The post of honor.
New York: Putnam, 1958. 254p.
Authentic picture white-Indian relations--
1868--Uprising Apache.

Cooke, Grace MacGowan jt. author, see MacGowan, Alice

1119 Cooke, John Esten (1830-1886). Leather stocking and
silk; or, hunter john myers and his times. New
York: Harper, 1854. 408p.
Shenandoah--Martinsburg, West Virginia--
Cooke connecting link earlier and later Virginia
novelists.

1120 ---Virginia comedians; or, old days in the old dominion.
ed. from the mss. of c. effingham, esq. New York:
Appleton, 1854. 2 vols.
One of early works fixing romanticism of plantation novels--Effingham pseud.--Society before
American Revolution--His best and best by Virginian
before Civil War.

1121 ---The youth of jefferson; or, a chronicle of college
scrapes at williamsburg, in virginia, a.d. 1764.
New York: Redfield, 1854. 249p.

1122 ---The last of the foresters; or, humors on the border.
a story of the old virginia frontier. New York:

Derby, 1856. 419p.
1755-1775.

1123 ---Henry st. john, gentleman of "flower of hundreds"
in the county of prince george, virginia. a tale
1774-'75. New York: Harper, 1859. 503p.
        Published under title Bonnybel Vane (1883)--
Shenandoah 1774-1775--Sequel to The Virginia Comedians.

1124 ---Fairfax; or, the master of greenway court. a
chronicle of the valley of the shenandoah. New
York: Carleton, 1868. 405p.
        Romantic account of George Washington's youth--
1748-1751--Also published under title, Lord Fairfax; or, The Master of Greenway Court--1892.

1125 ---Doctor vandyke; a novel. New York: Appleton, 1872.
142p.
        Williamsburg ca. 1772.

1126 ---Justin harley; a romance of old virginia. Philadelphia: Today, 1874. 301p.
        Hubbell suggests this anticipates Mary Johns-
ton's, To Have and To Hold.

1127 ---Canolles; the fortune of a partisan of '81. Detroit:
Smith, 1877. 313p.
        Romance set in Virginia during Revolution--
1781.

1128 ---The virginia bohemians; a novel. New York: Harper,
1880. 233p.

1129 ---My lady pokahontas; a true relation of virginia.
written by anas todkill, puritan and pilgrim.
Boston: Houghton, 1885. 190p.
        Anas Todkill pseud.--Pocohontas (d. 1617).

1130 Cooke, Mrs. Rose (Terry) (1827-1892). Steadfast;
the story of a saint and sinner. Boston: Ticknor,
1889. 426p.
        New England minister to Connecticut Valley--
1700's.

1131 Cooley, Ellen Hodges. The boom of a western city.
Boston: Lee, 1897. 89p.
        Fargo, North Dakota.

1132 Collidge, Asenath Carver. Prophet of peace. Water-
town, New York: Hungerford, 1907. 236p.
        Quaker-Puritan romance.

1133 Coolidge, Dane (1873-1940). Hidden water. Chicago:
McClurg, 1910. 483p.

Western--Sheepmen v. Cattlemen--Arizona.

1134 ---The texican. Chicago: McClurg, 1911. 368p.
Western

1135 ---Bat wing bowles. New York: Stokes. 1914. 296p.
Western

1136 ---The desert trail. New York: Watt, 1915. 279p.
Western

1137 ---Rimrock jones. New York: Watt, 1917. 311p.
Western

1138 ---The fighting fool; a tale of the western frontier.
New York: Dutton, 1918. 291p.
Western

1139 ---Shadow mountain. New York: Watt, 1919. 311p.
Western

1140 ---Silver and gold; a story of luck and love in a
western mining camp. New York: Dutton, 1919. 260p.
Western

1141 ---Wun post. New York: Dutton, 1920. 273p.
Western

1142 ---The man-killers. New York: Dutton, 1921. 243p.
Western

1143 ---Lost wagons. New York: Dutton, 1923. 256p.
Western--Mining.

1144 ---The scalp-lock. New York: Dutton, 1924. 253p.
Western--Well written.

1145 ---Lorenzo the magnificent; the riders from texas.
New York: Dutton, 1925. 320p.
Western

1146 ---Not afraid. New York: Dutton, 1926. 299p.
Western

1147 ---Under the sun. New York: Dutton, 1926. 294p.
Western

1148 ---Gun-smoke. New York: Dutton, 1928. 231p.
Western

1149 ---War paint. New York: Dutton, 1929. 274p.
Western

1150 ---Horse-ketchum. New York: Dutton, 1930. 236p.
Western

1151 ---Maverick makers. New York: Dutton, 1931. 278p.
         Western

1152 ---Sheriff killer. New York: Dutton, 1932. 286p.
         Western

1153 ---Jess roundtree, texas ranger. New York: Dutton, 1933.
         252p.
         Western

1154 ---The fighting danites. New York: Dutton, 1934. 284p.
         Western--Mormons on Arizona Line.

1155 ---Silverhat. New York: Dutton, 1934. 255p.
         Western

1156 ---Long rope. New York: Dutton, 1935. 254p.
         Western--One of his best.

1157 ---Wolf's candle. New York: Dutton, 1935. 256p.
         Western

1158 ---Rawhide johnny. New York: Dutton, 1936. 282p.
         Western

1159 ---Snake bite jones. New York: Dutton, 1936. 280p.
         Western

1160 ---Ranger two-rifles. New York: Dutton, 1937. 248p.
         Western

1161 ---The trail of gold. New York: Dutton, 1937. 252p.
         Western

1162 ---Comanche chaser. New York: Dutton, 1938. 255p.
         Western

1163 ---Hell's hip pocket. New York: Dutton, 1938. 251p
         Western

1164 ---Gringo gold; a story of joaquin murieta, the bandit.
         New York: Dutton, 1939. 249p.
              Joaquin Murrieta (1828or9-1853)--California
         Gold Rush.

1165 ---Wally laughs-easy. New York: Dutton, 1939. 249p.
         Western

1166 ---Bloody head. New York: Dutton, 1940. 254p.
         Western

1167 ---Yaqui drums. New York: Dutton, 1940. 250p.
         May be his best effort.

1168 ---Bear paw. New York: Dutton, 1941. 252p.
         Western

1169   Coolidge, Herbert (1874-   ). Pancho mcclish.
        Chicago: McClurg, 1912. 341p.
        Itinerant horse dealer through Southwest.

1170   Cooper, Courtney Ryley (1886-   ). The cross-cut.
        Boston: Little, 1921. 321p.
        Mining--Western Colorado.

1171   ---The white desert. Boston: Little, 1922. 301p.
        Adventure--Colorado Timberland.

1172   ---The last frontier. Boston: Little, 1923. 304p.
        Pivots about Wild Bill Hickok--Opening of
        West--Beth Holliday.

1173   ---Oklahoma; a novel. Boston: Little, 1926. 303p.
        Homesteading rush with "Pawnee Bill" (Major
        Gordon Lillie)--Romance.

1174   ---The golden bubble. Boston: Little, 1928. 302p.
        Romance--Denver gold fields--1859.

1175   ---Poor man's gold. Boston: Little, 1936. 282p.
        Alaska border.

1176   ---The pioneers. Boston: Little, 1938. 309p.
        Kit Carson races British to Oregon--1842--
        Thriller.

        Cooper, Frank pseud. see Simms, William Gilmore

1177   Cooper, James Fenimore (1789-1851). The spy; a tale
        of the neutral ground. New York: Grattan, 1821.
        2 vols.
        Colonial frontier--Westchester County, New
        York State--Bryan"...first noteworthy historical
        romance using American scene..."--Cooper's second
        novel--Westchester County, New York--1780.

1178   ---The pilot; a tale of the sea. New York: Wiley,
        1823. 2 vols.
        First use of naval affairs in historical
        fiction in United States--Nautical romance--Paul
        Jones (1747-1792).

1179   ---The pioneers; or, the sources of the susquehanna;
        a descriptive tale by the author of "precaution."
        New York: Wiley, 1823. 2 vols.
        Tale #4 in Leatherstocking Tales--Natty Bumpo
        age 70 at Otsego where he passed his boyhood.

1180   ---Lionel lincoln; or, the leaguer of boston by the
        author of "precaution". New York: Wiley, 1825-1824.
        2 vols.
        1775

1181   ---Last of the mohicans; a narrative of 1757. Phil-
       adelphia: [?], 1826. 2 vols.
             Tale #2 Leatherstocking Series--Second to be
       written--French-Indian War (1756-1757).

1182   ---The prairie; a tale. Philadelphia: Carey, 1827.
       2 vols.
             Tale #5 Leatherstocking Series--Bumpo trapper
       upper Missouri River.

1183   ---The red rover. New York: Putnam, 1827. 469p.
             Adventure--Pirate fights for country during
       Revolution.

1184   ---The wept of wish-ton-wish; a tale. Philadelphia:
       Carey, 1829. 2 vols.
             King Philips War 1675-76--Published under
       The Wept of Wish-ton-Wish The Heathcotes.

1185   ---The water witch; or, the skimmer of the seas.
       Philadelphia: Carey, 1831. 2 vols.
             Pirates--1710-1720.

1186   ---Mercedes of castile; or, the voyage to cathay.
       Philadelphia: Lea, 1840. 2 vols.
             Columbus Voyage--Late 15th century.

1187   ---The pathfinder; or, the inland sea. Philadelphia:
       Lea, 1840. 2 vols.
             Tale #3 Leatherstocking Series--Lake Ontario--
       Romance.

1188   ---The deerslayer; or, the first war-path. Philadelphia:
       Lea, 1841. 2 vols.
             Tale #1 Leatherstocking Series--Last written
       in series--Youth of Natty Bumpo.

1189   ---Wyandotté; or, the hutted knoll. Philadelphia:
       Lea, 1843. 2 vols.
             New York--1770's.

1190   ---The chainbearer; or, the little page manuscripts.
       New York: Burgess, 1845. 2 vols.
             #2 of Anti-Rent War Trilogy--Romance--Surveying--
       1750-1829.

1191   ---Satanstoe; or, the little page manuscripts. a tale
       of the colony. New York: Burgess, 1845. 2 vols.
             Part #1 of Trilogy--Anti-Rent War in New York
       State--1750-1829.

1192   ---Redskins; or, indian and inj[G]in, being the con-
       clusion of the little page manuscripts. New York:
       Burgess, 1846. 2 vols.
             #3 of Anti-Rent War Trilogy--1829-1845.

97

1193 ---The oak openings; or, the bee hunter. New York:
Burgess, 1848. 2 vols.
Last of frontier stories--Michigan--War of 1812.

1194 Cooper, Miss Jamie Lee. The horn and the forest.
Indianapolis: Bobbs, 1963. 256p.

1195 ---Rapaho. Indianapolis: Bobbs, 1967. 203p.
Story of brave old buffalo hunter and his
reliving of old days of lore and legend not reality--
reality he is Hutch, broken sod-buster.

1196 Cooper, Kent (1880-1965). Anna zenger, mother of
freedom. New York: Farrar, 1946. 345p.
Anna Zenger (1704?-1751)--Peter Zenger (1680?-
1746).

1197 Cooper, Madison Alexander. Sironia texas. Boston:
Houghton, 1952. 2 vols.

1198 ---The haunted hacienda. Boston: Houghton, 1955.
303p.
First novel--West Texas--1880's.

1199 Cooper, S. M.. Life in the forest; or, the trials
and sufferings of a pioneer. Philadelphia: Perry,
1854. 155p.
Colonial Era.

1200 The cooper's son; or, the prize of virtue. a tale
of the revolution. [Anonymous]. Boston: French,
1846. 139p.

1201 Corbett, Elizabeth Frances (1887-   ). Light of
other days; a novel of mount royal. New York:
Appleton, 1938. 361p.
Three generations Irish family in America--
1846--Mt. Royal.

1202 ---She was carrie eaton; a novel about the young mrs.
meigs. New York: Appleton, 1938. 320p.
Ohio small city life--1870's.

1203 ---Early summer. New York: Appleton, 1942. 321p.
Rural Illinois.

1204 ---Golden grain. New York: Appleton, 1943. 334p.
Sequel to "Faye's Folly"--Illinois town 1880's.

1205 ---Eve and christopher. New York: Doubleday, 1949.
253p.
Daughter of Wisconsin lumber baron 1890's.

1206 Corcoran, Charles. Blackrobe. Milwaukee: Bruce,
1938. 377p.

Jacques Marquette (1637-1675)--Two journeys
down Mississippi River.

1207 Corcoran, William (1901-   ). Blow desert winds!
New York: Appleton, 1935. 311p.
Western

1208 ---Golden horizons. Philadelphia: Macrae, 1937.
282p.
Western--Kansas and introduction of winter
wheat.

Cord, Barry pseud. see Germano, Peter

1209 Corey, Paul (1903-   ). Three miles square. Indianapolis: Bobbs, 1939. 448p.
#1 of Mantz Trilogy--Widow and children.

1210 ---The road returns. Indianapolis: Bobbs, 1940. 457p.
#2 of Mantz Trilogy--Sequel to Three Miles
Square--Continues story of widow Mantz and children--
World War I and 1920's.

1211 ---County seat. Indianapolis: Bobbs, 1941. 418p.
#3 of Mantz Trilogy--Ends 1930's--Important
contribution to farm novel.

1212 ---The red tractor. New York: Morrow, 1944. 248p.
Small farm v. absentee owner--1940.

1213 ---Acres of antaeus. New York: Holt, 1946. 388p.
Farm mortgage war--Advent of large corporate
agricultural organization--Small farmer out.

1214 Corle, Edwin (1906-1956). Fig tree john. New York:
Liveright, 1935. 318p.
Agocho (White River Apache)--Settles Salton
Sea--Good on Indian--1906.

1215 ---People on earth. New York: Random, 1937. 401p.
Navajo--Southwest--Indian lad has white edu-
cation--Return to people.

1216 ---Coarse gold. New York: Dutton, 1942. 250p.
Nevada mining town--Two phases--Gold Rush
(1892-1900)--1942 rebuild town with World War II
and tungsten.

1217 ---Billy the kid. New York: Duell, 1953. 293p.
Fictionalized biography of William Bonney
(1859-1881).

1218 Cormack, Maribelle and Alexander, William Prindle.
Land for my sons; a frontier tale of the american
revolution. New York: Appleton, 1939. 311p.

Roadway to West--Surveyor with George Washington.

1219   Cornelius, Mrs. Mary Ann (Mann).   Littlewolf; a tale
       of the western frontier.   Cincinnati: Journal, 1872.
       458p.
              Minnesota

1220   Coryell, Hubert Vansant (1889-   ).   Tan-ta-ka;[kills-
       with-a-knife.] Boston: Little, 1934. 305p.
              Twelve year old boy taken by Sioux--Thriller.

1221   ---Indian brother.   New York: Harcourt, 1935. 348p.
              Twins taken by Indians--1713--Jesuits against
       the crown--Sébastien Rasles (1657-1724)--Juvenile.

1222   ---The scalp hunters.   New York: Harcourt, 1936. 277p.
              Maine--1700's--John Lovewell (1691-1725)--
       Pigwacket fight (1725).

1223   ---Klondike gold.   New York: Macmillan, 1938. 319p.
              Fifteen year old joins Klondike rush--1898--
       Juvenile.

1224   Costain, Thomas Bertram (1885-   ).   For my great
       folly; a novel.   New York: Putnam, 1942. 504p.
              Seventeenth century English free booter--
       John Ward (1603-1615).

1225   ---High towers.   New York: Doubleday, 1949. 371p.
              New France--1697--Montreal to New Orleans--
       Nine LeMoyne Brothers--Good historical base.

1226   Coulter, James W.   The larger faith; a novel.   Chicago:
       Kerr, 1898. 285p.
              Ranch--New Mexico--Religion.

1227   Countryman, Asa.   A tale of the wyoming and missouri
       valley.   Great Bend, Kansas: Democrat, 1897. 149p.

1228   Courlander, Harold (1908-   ).   The african; a novel.
       New York: Crown, 1967. 311p.
              Life of slave in South--Attention to pre-
       slave African experience--This is most important
       contribution.

1229   Covert, Mrs. Alice Lent (1913-   ).   Return to dust.
       New York: Kinsey, 1939. 204p.
              First novel--Oklahoma dust bowl.

1230   ---End of reckoning.   New York: Kinsey, 1942. 314p.
              Oklahoma town from settlement through 1930's--
       Saloon keeper rises to Senate.

1231   Cox, William Robert (1901-   ).   Comanche moon; a novel
       of the west.   New York: McGraw, 1959. 244p.
              Western

100

1232   Crabb, Alfred Leland (1884-   ). Dinner at belmont;
       a novel of captured nashville. Indianapolis: Bobbs,
       1942. 385p.
            #3 of Nashville Saga--1858-1865.

1233   ---Supper at the maxwell house; a novel of recaptured
       nashville. Indianapolis: Bobbs, 1943. 372p.
            #4 of Nashville Saga.

1234   ---Breakfast at the hermitage; a novel of nashville
       rebuilding. Indianapolis: Bobbs, 1945. 312p.
            #5 of Nashville Saga--Reconstruction Era.

1235   ---Lodging at the st. cloud; a tale of occupied
       nashville. Indianapolis: Bobbs, 1946. 255p.
            #2 of Nashville Saga--Civil War.

1236   ---Home to the hermitage; a novel of andrew and rachel
       jackson. Indianapolis: Bobbs, 1948. 318p.
            War of 1812 to 1829 presidency.

1237   ---Home to kentucky; a novel of henry clay. Indiana-
       polis: Bobbs, 1953. 339p.
            Fictionalized biography--1777-1852.

1238   ---Journey to nashville. Indianapolis: Bobbs, 1957.
       291p.
            #1 of Nashville Saga--Founding of Nashville.

1239   Crabb, Richard. Empire on the platte. Cleveland:
       World, 1967. 373p.
            Mormons--1880--Oregon Trail--Platte Valley.

       Craddock, Charles Egbert pseud. see Murfree, Mary
       Noailles

1240   Craig, Benjamin Franklin. The border ruffian; or,
       kansas and missouri. an historical western story
       of the present time, with interesting conversations
       between jeff and abe on the subject of slavery.
       Cincinnati: Pub. for the Author, 1863. 234p.

1241   ---The rough diamond. Kansas City, Missouri: Ramey,
       1880. 214p.
            One hundred year chronicle of Kentucky pioneer
       family.

1242   Craine, Edith Janice (1881-   ). The victors. New
       York: Duffield, 1933. 254p.
            Spanish conquest of South America--Follow
       Memoir's of Garcilasso de Vega (ca.1540-ca.1616),
       son of Spanish Captain and Inca Princess--Peru-
       1522-1548.

1243   ---pseud. Daru, Juliska. Conquistador. New York:

101

Duffield, 1931. 288p.
Pedro Ciezade Leon--Follows adventures as
recorded in Travels--To New World at age of thirteen.

Crane, Robert pseud. see Robertson, Frank Chester (1890-

1244   Cranston, Paul. To heaven on horseback; the romantic
story of narcissa whitman. New York: Messner,
1952. 255p.
First novel--Fictionalized biography of Narcissa (Prentiss) Whitman (1808-1847)--To Oregon
country as missionary.

1245   Craven, Braxton pseud. Vernon, Charles. Mary barker.
(2nd Edition) Raleigh, North Carolina: Branson,
1865. 72p.

1246   Crawford, Phyllis (1899-   ). Walking on gold. New
York: Messner, 1940. 284p.
California Gold Rush--1849--Juvenile.

1247   Crichton, Kyle Samuel pseud. Forsythe, Robert (1896-   ).
The proud people; a novel. New York: Scribner's,
1944. 368p.
Family of Spaniards living in New Mexico--
1941--Ancestor there in 1598.

1248   Criss, Mildred (Mrs. G. L. Catlin) (1890-   ).
Jefferson's daughter. New York: Dodd, 1948. 278p.
Fictionalized biography of Martha Jefferson
(1772-1836), oldest daughter of Thomas Jefferson.

1249   Cronyan, George William (1888-   ). '49; a novel of
gold. Philadelphia: Dorrance, 1925. 278p.
Local color--Fire--Flood--Gold Rush.

1250   Cross, Ruth. Soldier of good fortune; an historical
novel. Dallas, Texas: Upshaw, 1936. 347p.
Louis St. Denis (1676-1744, to American Southwest pre-1763--Romance.

Cross, Stewart pseud. see Drago, Harry Sinclair (1888-   )

1251   Crowley, Mary Catherine. A daughter of new france;
with some account of the gallant sieur cadillac
and his colony on the detroit. Boston: Little,
1901. 409p.
Antoine de la Mothe Cadillac (1656ca.-1730?).

1252   ---The heroine of the strait; a romance of detroit
in the time of pontiac. Boston: Little, 1902.
373p.
Ca.1763-1765--Red Coat v. Red Skin.

1253   ---Love thrives in war; a romance of the frontier in 1812.

Boston: Little, 1903. 340p.

1254 Crowley, Michael. Horseshoe range. New York: McBride, 1936. 295p.
Western

1255 Crownfield, Gertrude (1867-1945). Alison blair. New York: Dutton, 1927. 301p.
Young girls to New York with Sir William Johnson--Captured by Indians during French-Indian War.

1256 ---Where glory waits; the romance of mary vining and anthony wayne. Philadelphia: Lippincott, 1934. 319p.
Mary Vining (1756-1821)--Anthony Wayne (1745-1796)--Revolution.

1257 ---Conquering kitty; a romance of the sassafras river. Philadelphia: Lippincott, 1935. 307p.
Eastern shore of Maryland--Romance.

1258 ---Traitor's torch. Philadelphia: Lippincott, 1935. 301p.
Fourteen year old girl flees to Connecticut from Long Island--Tories--Revolution--Juvenile.

1259 ---King's pardon. Philadelphia: Lippincott, 1937. 317p.
New Castle and Delaware Coast--1637--Juvenile.

1260 -- Diantha's signet ring; being the story of a maid of early williamsburg in his majesty's colony of virginia. New York: Crowell, 1939. 172p.
1718

1261 ---Lone star rising. New York: Crowell, 1940. 338p.
Texas v. Mexico--1835--Fifteen year old girl--Juvenile.

1262 ---Proud lady. Philadelphia: Lippincott, 1942. 256p.
Settlement of New Castle, Delaware--1669-1670.

1263 Croy, Homer (1883-   ). R.F.D. no 3. New York: Harper, 1924. 349p.
Missouri rural life 1920's--cf. Zury work.

1264 ---River girl; a realistic romance of the high days of mississippi steamboating. New York: Harper, 1931. 320p.
Romance--Racing--Rivalry.

1265 ---The lady from colorado; a novel based on the true story of the washerwoman who became the first titled lady of colorado. New York: Duell, 1957. 277p.
Based on fact--Life of Kattie Lawder--1880's--

103

Cinderella theme western setting--Lady Catherine
Gralton (Lawder) Moon (d. 1926).

1266 Crozier, Robert Haskins. Golden rule; a tale of texas.
      Richmond, Virginia: Whittet, 1900. 179p.

1267 Crum, Mrs. Gertrude (Bosworth). The strumpet wind.
      New York: Covici, 1938. 290p.
           First novel--Waitress from Texas town to
      California.

1268 Crumpton, M. Nataline. The silver buckle; a story
      of the revolutionary days. Philadelphia: Altemus,
      1889. 89p.

1269 Cullum, Ridgwell (1867-   ). The story of the foss
      river ranch; a tale of the northwest. Boston:
      Page, 1903. 326p.

1270 ---The watchers of the plains; a tale of the western
      prairies. Philadelphia: Jacobs, 1909. 374p.
           Western

1271 ---The one-way trail; a story of the cattle country.
      Philadelphia: Jacobs, 1911. 415p.
           Western

1272 ---The golden woman; the story of a western mining camp.
      Philadelphia: Jacobs, 1913. 447p.
           Montana Hills.

1273 ---The night-riders; a romance of early montana.
      Philadelphia: Jacobs, 1913. 426p.
           Western

1274 ---The way of the strong. Philadelphia: Jacobs, 1914.
      447p.
           Alaska--Southern California--Alberta.

1275 ---The triumph of john kars; a story of the yukon.
      Philadelphia: Jacobs, 1917. 437p.
           Adventure--Mystery--Romance.

1276 ---The law of the gun. Philadelphia: Jacobs, 1919.
      420p.
           Mystery--Gold and copper fields of Canada.

1277 ---The luck of the kid. New York: Putnam, 1923. 365p.
           Mystery and adventure--Yukon--Gold Trail.

1278 ---Child of the north. New York: Doran, 1926. 348p.
           Gold--North country.

1279 ---The wolf pack. Philadelphia: Lippincott, 1927. 320p.
           Backwoods melodrama--Murder et. al.

104

1280 ---The mystery of the barren lands. Philadelphia:
Lippincott, 1928. 318p.
Hudson Bay.

1281 ---The tiger of cloud river. Philadelphia: Lippincott,
1929. 313p.
Western

1282 Culp, John H.. Born of the sun. New York: Sloane,
1959. 444p.
Western--First cattle drives from Texas in
1870's.

1283 ---The men of gonzales. New York: Sloane, 1960. 244p.
Siege of Alamo-1836--Based on historical fact--
Thirty-two men from Gonzales to relief of Alamo.

1284 ---The restless land. New York: Sloane, 1962. 438p.
Western

1285 ---The bright feathers. New York: Holt, 1965. 283p.
Western

1286 ---A whistle in the wind; a novel. New York: Holt,
1968. 281p.
Western--Texas 1850-1870.

1287 Cunningham, Eugene (1896-   ). The trail to apacaz.
London: Utwin, 1924. 256p.
Western

1288 ---Diamond river man. Boston: Houghton, 1934. 270p.
Western

1289 ---Texas sheriff; a novel of the territory. Boston:
Houghton, 1934. 298p.
Western

1290 ---Quick triggers. Boston: Houghton, 1935. 264p.
Western

1291 ---Whistling lead. Boston: Houghton, 1936. 271p.
Western

1292 ---Texas triggers. Boston: Houghton, 1938. 260p.
Western

1293 ---Gun bulldogger. Boston: Houghton, 1939. 248p.
Western

1294 ---Red range. Boston: Houghton, 1939. 302p.
Western

1295 Cunningham, John M.. Warhorse; a novel of the old west.
New York: Macmillan, 1956. 384p.
Western--Superior.

1296 Cunningham, William (1901-   ). The green corn rebel-
     lion. New York: Vanguard, 1935. 302p.
     1917--Oklahoma.

1297 Curry, Peggy (Simson). So far from spring; a novel.
     New York: Viking, 1956. 344p.

1298 ---The oil patch. New York: McGraw, 1959. 325p.
     Wyoming oil drilling--1930's.

1299 Curtis, Alice (Turner) (Mrs. Irving Curtis). The
     frontier girl of pennsylvania. Philadelphia:
     Penn, 1937. 277p.
     Girl from Philadelphia to wilderness--Upper
     reaches of Delaware River--1690.

     Curtis, Elizabeth jt. author, see Choate, Florence

1300 Curtis, Jack. The kloochman; a novel. New York:
     Simon, 1966. 286p.
     First novel--Alaska--"Klooch" means street-
     walker--Artic Circle.

1301 Curtis, Newton Mallory. The black plumed riflemen;
     a tale of the revolution. New York: Burgess, 1846.
     125p.

1302 ---The patrol of the mountain; a tale of the revolution.
     New York: Williams, 1847. 112p.

1303 ---The ranger of ravenstream; a tale of the revolution.
     New York: Williams, 1847. 118p.

1304 ---The scout of silver pond; a tale of the revolution.
     New York: Williams, 1847. 110p.

1305 ---The marksmen of monmouth; a tale of the revolution.
     Troy: Willard, 1848. 127p.
     Prolific writer--Washington does not meet Lee.

1306 Curwood, James Oliver (1878-1927). The courage of
     captain plum. Indianapolis: Bobbs, 1908. 319p.
     Mormon colony--Beaver Island, Lake Michigan--
     Melodramatic--Romantic adventure.

1307 ---Gold hunters; a story of life and adventure in
     the hudson bay wilds. Indianapolis: Bobbs, 1909.
     328p.
     Continuation of "Wolf Hunters"--Juvenile.

1308 ---The honor of the big snows. Indianapolis: Bobbs,
     1911. 317p.
     Frozen north--Juvenile.

1309 ---God's country-and the woman. New York: Doubleday,

106

1915. 347p.
Romance of North woods.

1310 ---Grizzly king; a romance of the wild. New York:
Doubleday, 1916. 234p.
Companion piece to "Kazan".

1311 ---The courage of marge o'doone. New York: Doubleday,
1918. 309p.
Action in northern forests.

1312 ---Plains of abraham. New York: Doubleday, 1928. 316p.
Last of his many novels--New France--Roman-
ticized treatment of French-Indian War.

1313 Cushing, Mrs. Eliza Lanesford (Foster) (1794-   ).
Saratoga; a tale of the revolution.
Boston: Cummings, 1824. 2 vols.
British officer with Burgoyne--Romance.

1314 ---Yorktown; an historical romance. Boston: Wells,
1826. 2 vols.
Follows J. F. Cooper--Siege-1781--Gothic
Romance.

1315 Cushman, Dan. Montana here i be! New York: Macmillan,
1950. 173p.
Cowboy "Robin Hood" tall tale--Fun--Author
former western cow puncher.

1316 ---Badlands justice. New York: Macmillan, 1951. 190p.
Western

1317 ---The ripper from rawhide. New York: Macmillan,
1952. 196p.
Western

1318 ---Stay away, joe; a novel. New York: Viking, 1952.
249p.
French Canadian--Indian--Comic.

1319 ---The fastest gun. New York: Dell, 1955. 190p.
Western

1320 ---The silver mountain. New York: Appleton, 1957.
442p.
Montana 1880's-1890's--Poor man's determination
to rise to wealth and power--Golden Spur Award for
Best Western Historical Novel 1958.

1321 ---Tall wyoming. New York: Dell, 1957. 192p.
Western

1322 ---Brothers in kickapoo. New York: McGraw, 1962. 252p.
Western

107

D

1323   Dabney, Owen P.. <u>True story of the lost shackle; or,</u>
       <u>seven years with the indians</u>. Salem, Oregon:
       Capital, 1897. 98p.

1324   Daggett, Mary (Stewart) (Mrs. Charles Stewart Daggett).
       <u>Mariposilla; a novel</u>. Chicago: Rand McNally, 1895.
       268p.
             California--San Gabriel Valley.

1325   Daggett, Rollin Mallory. <u>Braxton's bar; a tale of</u>
       <u>pioneer years in california</u>. New York: Carleton,
       1882. 453p.

1326   Dahl, Borghild Margarethe. <u>Homecoming</u>. New York:
       Dutton, 1953. 251p.
             From Norway to Minneapolis--Young girl and
       parents.

1327   Dale, Virginia. <u>Honeyfogling time</u>.. New York:
       Harper, 1946. 262p.
             Mid-western town--"Good ole days"--Juvenile.

1328   Dalgliesh, Alice (1893-   ). <u>Adam and the golden</u>
       <u>cock</u>. New York: Scribner's, 1959. 64p.
             Connecticut--1781--Juvenile.

1329   Daly, Robert Welter (1916-   ). <u>Guns of yorktown</u>.
       New York: Dodd, 1953. 181p.
             Young American with French fleet--1781--Juvenile.

1330   Dana, Francis. <u>Leonora of the yawmish; a novel</u>. New
       York: Harper, 1897. 310p.
             Pacific northwest.

       Dana, Mary S. B. <u>pseud</u>. see Shendler, Mary Stanley
       (Palmer) Dana

1331   Daniel, Hawthorne (1890-   ). <u>In the favour of the</u>
       <u>king</u>. New York: Doubleday, 1922. 269p.
             Search for Seven Cities of Cibola--New Galacia,
       province of Mexico--New Spain--Romance and adventure--
       1500.

1332   Daniels, Harriet McDoval (1874-1959). <u>Muller hill</u>.
       New York: Knopf, 1943. 402p.
             French aristocrat married New York society
       girl--To wilderness in Oneida--Disappears--Lewis
       Anathe Miller.

108

Daniels, John S. pseud. see Overholser, Wayne D.

1333   Darby, Ada Claire (1883-1953). Yonder the golden
       gate; a story of old san francisco. New York:
       Stokes, 1939. 341p.
              Missouri boy to California gold fields--Juvenile.

1334   Daring donald mckay; or, the last war-trail of the
       modocs. the romance of the life of donald mckay,
       government scout and chief of the warm spring indians.
       [Anonymous]. (2nd Edition) Chicago: Rounds, 1881.
       108p.

       Daru, Juliska pseud. see Craine, Edith Janice

       d'Aubertevil, Hilliard see Hilliard d'Aubertevil

1335   David, Evan John (1881-   ). As runs the glass.
       New York: Harper, 1943. 312p.
              Romance--Fortunes of Maine sea-faring family--
       Post-Revolutionary period.

1336   Davidson, L.. The disturber. New York: Macmillan,
       1964. 341p.
              Merry Mount, Massachusetts Bay Colony--Thomas
       Morton (1575-1646).

1337   Davidson, Louis B. and Doherty, Edward J.. Captain
       marooner. New York: Crowell, 1952. 368p.
              Based on actual mutiny on whaler "Globe" out
       of Nantucket 1822.

1338   Daviess, Maria Thompson (1872-1924). The matrix.
       New York: Century, 1920. 260p.
              Romance Kentucky Bluegrass--Thomas Lincoln
       and Nancy Hanks (1784-1818)--"Pious memorial".

1339   Davis, Burke. The ragged ones. New York: Rinehart,
       1951. 336p.
              American Revolution--Southern Campaign--1781--
       Generals Morgan and Greene.

1340   ---Yorktown. New York: Rinehart, 1952. 306p.
              American Revolution--Central figure Peter
       Spargo makes lieutenant--Escape from prison ship
       off Long Island--Good romance.

1341   Davis, Clyde Brion. Nebraska coast. New York: Farrar,
       1939. 423p.
              York state farmer west to Nebraska during
       Civil War--Travel by Erie Canal.

       Davis, Don pseud. see Dresser, Davis (1904-   )

1342   Davis, Mrs. Dorothy Salisbury. Men of no property.

New York: Scribner's, 1956. 438p.
Irish immigrants to New York State--1848
through Civil War--Excellent.

1343   Davis, Harold Lenoir (1896-   ). Honey in the horn.
New York: Harper, 1935. 380p.
Oregon homestead ca.1900--Received Pulitzer
Prize in 1936--Harper Prize Novel.

1344   ---Beulah land. New York: Morrow, 1949. 314p.
Cherokees west from North Carolina--Trip cross
country--Beulah Land=Indian Country--1850.

1345   ---Winds of morning. New York: Morrow, 1952. 344p.
Mature work about young man who learns of
life from an old herder--Columbia River country--
1920's--Excellent narrative.

1346   ---The distant music. New York: Morrow, 1957. 311p.
Poetic story of development of Columbia River
country.

1347   Davis, James Francis. The road to san jacinto.
Indianapolis: Bobbs, 1936. 334p.
Texas Revolution--1835-1836--Georgian searches
for father's murderer--Romance with Quaker girl--
Good.

1348   Davis, John (1774-1854). The farmer of new jersey;
or, a picture of domestic life. by the translator
of buonaparte's campaign, author of ferdinand and
elizabeth. New York: Furman, 1800. 70p.

1349   ---The wanderings of william; or, the inconstancy of
youth. Philadelphia: Rawle, 1801. 299p.
Sequel to The Farmer of New Jersey.

1350   ---The first settlers of virginia; an historical novel,
exhibiting a view of the rise and progress of the
colony at jamestown. a picture of indian manners,
the countenance of the country, and its natural
1351   productions. New York: Riley, 1805. 284p.
Pre-Waverley.

1352   Davis, Julia (Mrs. Paul West). No other white man.
New York: Dutton, 1937. 242p.
Lewis and Clark Expedition--Sacagawea--Juvenile.

1353   ---Cloud on the land. New York: Rinehart, 1951. 404p.
#1 of Trilogy about MacLeods of Virginia--
Plantation owner marries anti-slavery girl--Post War--
1812--Long western trip--Romance.

1354   ---Bridle the wind. New York: Rinehart, 1953. 247p.
#2 of MacLeod Trilogy--Sequel to Cloud on the

Land--Fugitive slave.

1354　---Eagle on the sun. New York: Rinehart, 1956. 314p.
　　　　#3 of MacLeod Trilogy--Sequel to Bridle The Wind--
　　　　Mexican War--Romance.

1355　Davis, Kenneth Sydney (1912-　). Morning in kansas.
　　　　New York: Doubleday, 1952. 382p.
　　　　Three part novel--Kansas town--Family flash
　　　　back to 1858--Contemporary--Good feeling for the
　　　　land.

1356　Davis, Mary Elizabeth (Moragne). The british partizan;
　　　　a tale of the times of old. Augusta, Georgia:
　　　　Thompson, 1839. 150p.
　　　　American Revolution--Georgia.

1357　Davis, Mrs. Mary Evelyn (Moore) (1852-1909). Under
　　　　the man-fig. Boston: Houghton, 1895. 323p.

1358　---The wire cutters. Boston: Houghton, 1899. 373p.
　　　　Texas--Cattle.

1359　Davis, Paxton (1925-　). The seasons of heroes;
　　　　a novel. New York: Morrow, 1967. 276p.
　　　　Chronicle of three generations of Virginia
　　　　family--19th and 20th centuries.

1360　Davis, Robert (1881-　). Gid granger. New York:
　　　　Holiday, 1945. 179p.
　　　　Vermont farm--World War II.

1361　Davis, William Stearns (1877-　). Gilman of redford;
　　　　a story of boston and harvard college on the eve of
　　　　the revolutionary war, 1770-1775. New York: Mac-
　　　　millan, 1927. 533p.
　　　　Romance--Excellent.

1362　Dawes, Rufus (1803-1859). Nix's mate; an historical
　　　　romance of america. New York: Coleman, 1839. 2 vols.
　　　　Massachusetts Bay Colony--Revolt against royal
　　　　oppression--Howard--Andros--1688-1689.

1363　Dawson, Cleo (Mrs. George Edwin Smith). She came to
　　　　the valley. New York: Morrow, 1943. 388p.
　　　　Rio Grande--1905-1914.

1364　Dawson, Coningsby William (1883-1959). Inspiration
　　　　valley. New York: Knopf, 1935. 286p.
　　　　Canada Rockies--Dukhobors--Romance.

Dawson, Peter pseud. see Glidden, Jonathan H. (1907-　)

1365　Day, Holman Francis (1865-1935). King spruce; a novel.
　　　　New York: Harper, 1908. 371p.

Maine timber--College man v. lumber baron--
Melodramatic--Romance and adventure.

1366 ---The red lane; a romance of the border. New York:
       Harper, 1912. 398p.
       Canadian area--Romance.

Dazey, Charles jt. author, see Marshall, Edward

1367 Dean, Frederic Alva. The heroines of petoséga; a novel.
       New York: Hawthorne, 1889. 283p.
       Upper Michigan--Three thousand years ago.

1368 Dean, Leon W. (1889-   ). I became a ranger. New
       York: Farrar, 1945. 240p.
       French-Indian War--Roger's Rangers--Juvenile.

1369 ---Guns over champlain. New York: Rinehart, 1946. 245p.
       War of 1812--Vermont--Juvenile.

1370 ---Royalton raid. New York: Rinehart, 1949. 241p.
       Vermont lad taken by British and Indians 1780--
       Escapes from Canada--Juvenile.

1371 ---White ox; being a story of one ezra button and the
       adventures that befell him in the neighborhood of
       lake champlain in new england. New York: Ariel,
       1953. 177p.
       Revolutionary era--New Hampshire Grants--
       Juvenile.

1372 DeAngeli, Mrs. Marguerite. Thee, hannah! New York:
       Doubleday, 1940. 88p.
       Philadelphia--Quaker--Juvenile.

1373 Deasy, Mary. The hour of spring. Boston: Little,
       1948. 368p.
       Family chronicle--Irish-American--Midwest--
       1870-1928.

1374 Debo, Angie (1890-   ). Prairie city; the story of
       an american community. New York: Knopf, 1944. 245p.
       Oklahoma--Founding by "run"--1889-1940's.

1375 The debtor's prison; a tale of a revolutionary soldier.
       [Anonymous]. New York: Greene, 1834. 164p.
       Wright--"Appleton and Roorbach attribute to Asa
       Greene".

1376 De Capite, Raymond. The coming of fabrizze. New York:
       McKay, 1960. 208p.
       First novel--Italian immigrants to Cleveland,
       Ohio--1920's.

1377 Decker, Malcolm Grove. The rebel and the turncoat.
       New York: Whittlesey, 1949. 250p.

American Revolution--New York City and Phila-
delphia--1775--Juvenile.

1378 Decker, William. To be a man; a novel. Boston: Little,
      1967. 239p.
            Story of Roscoe Banks from childhood to death--
      Roaming cowboy--Action from Texas to Montana--1890's-
      1950's--On par with Ross Santee and Frank Dobie.

1379 Defoe, Daniel (1661-1731). The history and remarkable
      life of the truly honorable colonel jacques, commonly
      called colonel jack, who was born a gentleman, put
      prentice to a pick-pocket, was six and twenty years
      a thief, and then kidnapped to virginia. came back
      a merchant, was five times married to four whores;
      went into the wars, behav'd bravely, got preferment,
      was made colonel of a regiment, came over and fled
      with the chevalier, is still abroad completing a
      life of wonders, and resolves to dye a general.
      London: Brotherton, 1722. 399p.

1380 DeForest, John William (1826-1906). Miss ravenel's
      conversion from secession to loyalty. New York:
      Harper, 1865.
            Gaston "first realistic novel in modern sense"--
      Civil War era.

1381 ---Overland; a novel. New York: Sheldon, 1872. 209p.
            New Mexico and California frontier.

1382 ---A lover's revolt. New York: Longmans, 1898. 417p.
            American Revolution--Massachusetts--Romance.

1383 Degenhard, William. The regulators; being an account
      of the late insurrections in massachusetts known
      as shay's rebellion as witnessed by warren hascott,
      esq. also conveying some idea of the interior cir-
      cumstances of massachusetts and other sections of
      the newly founded united states of america. New
      York: Dial, 1943. 598p.
            1786-1787--One of best dealing with Daniel
      Shay.

1384 DeJong, David Cornell (1905-1967). Light sons and
      dark. New York: Harper, 1940. 329p.
            American family on almost worthless midwest
      farm--Realistic--cf. Winesburg, Ohio.

1385 De La Rhue, Treviño (1894-   ). Spanish trails to
      california. Caldwell, Idaho: Caxton, 1937. 285p.
            Spanish immigration to American southwest--
      1760.

1386 De Lesdernier, Mrs. Emily Pierpont. Fannie st. john;
      a romantic incident of the american revolution.

New York: Hurd, 1874. 63p.

DeLeuze, Bernard pseud. see Sabran, Jean

1387 Delmar, Vina (1905-   ). The big family. New York:
Harcourt, 1961. 382p.
Chronicle of Slidell family from Revolution
through 1870--Judah Benjamin (1811-1884).

Deming, Kirk pseud. see Drago, Harry Sinclair (1888-   )

1388 Denison, Mrs. Mary (Andrews). The days and ways of
the cocked hats; or, the dawn of the revolution.
New York: Rollo, 1860. 383p.
Boston life--1770's.

1389 ---The lover's trials; or, the days before the revolution. Philadelphia: Peterson, 1865. 383p.
Sir Edmund Andros--Rebellion 1688-1689.

1390 Denison, Thomas Stewart (1848-1911). The man behind;
a novel. Chicago: Denison, 1888. 311p.
Southwest.

1391 ---My invisible partner. Chicago: Rand, 1898. 231p.
New Mexico mining.

Denver, Drake C. pseud. see Nye, Nelson Coral (1907-   )

1392 Derby, Caroline Rosina pseud. Castleton, D. R..
Salem; a tale of the seventeenth century. New York:
Harper, 1874. 336p.
Witchcraft and trials.

1393 Derleth, August William (1909-   ). Still is the
summer night. New York: Scribner's, 1937. 356p.
Sac Prairie, Wisconsin Series #1 written
#8 in order--1880's.

1394 ---Wind over wisconsin. New York: Scribner's, 1938.
391p.
Sac Prairie, Wisconsin Series--#2 written
#3 in order--1830's--Black Hawk War.

1395 ---Restless is the river. New York: Scribner's, 1939.
514p.
Sac Prairie, Wisconsin Series--#3 written #4
in order--1839-1850--Early settlement.

1396 ---Bright journey. New York: Scribner's, 1940. 424p.
Sac Prairie, Wisconsin Series--#4 written #1
in order--1800-1812--Fur trading--Old northwest.

1397 ---Evening in spring. New York: Scribner's, 1941. 308p.
Sac Prairie, Wisconsin Series--#5 written #10
in order--1926.

114

1398 ---Sweet genevieve. New York: Scribner's, 1942. 301p.
Sac Prairie, Wisconsin Series--#6 written #9
in order--1910-1918--Romance.

1399 ---Shadow of night. New York: Scribner's, 1943. 354p.
Sac Prairie, Wisconsin Series--#7 written #6
in order--1850--French emigrés and German refugees.

1400 ---The shield of the valiant. New York: Scribner's,
1945. 511p.
Sac Prairie, Wisconsin Series--#8 written #11
in order--1940's.

1401 ---The house on the mound. New York: Duell, 1958. 335p.
Sac Prairie, Wisconsin Series--#9 written #2
in order--1812-1830.

1402 ---The hills stand watch. New York: Duell, 1960. 337p.
Sac Prairie, Wisconsin Series--#10 written #5
in order--1840's--Lead mining.

1403 ---The wind leans west. New York: Candlelight, 1969.
323p.
Sac Prairie, Wisconsin Series #11 written
#7 in order--1836-1853--Politics--Banking.

1404 Devereux, Mary (-1914). Betty peach; a tale of
colonial days. Marblehead, Massachusetts: Graves,
1896. 144p.
Juvenile

1405 ---From kingdom to colony. Boston: Little, 1899. 382p.
New England life early days of the American
Revolution.

1406 ---Lafitte of louisiana. Boston: Little, 1902. 427p.
1815--French--New Orleans--Jean LaFitte (1780?-
1826?).

Devighne, Harry jt. author, see White, Stewart Edward

1407 Devon, John. O western wind. New York: Putnam, 1957.
320p.
Cornwall, England and Plymouth in New World--
Founding of Merry Mount.

1408 DeVoto, Bernard Augustine (1897-1955). The house of
sun-goes-down. New York: Macmillan, 1928. 408p.
Southerners to West after Civil War--Land-
mining--Sans gunmen and rustlers.

1409 Dewlen, Al. The night of the tiger. New York: McGraw,
1956. 264p.
First novel--Western.

1410   Dickson, Harris (1868-   ). The black wolf's breed;
        a story of france in the old world and the new,
        happening in the reign of louis XIV. Indianapolis:
        Bobbs, 1899. 288p.
            ca. 1680--Europeans among Indians.

1411   ---The siege of lady resolute; a novel. New York:
        Harper, 1902. 378p.
            Legend of merchant who wishes to become prince
        of Louisana--Era of Louis XIV (1643-1715).

1412   ---Gabrille transgressor. Philadelphia: Lippincott,
        1906. 374p.
            Turkish prince and French girl to colonial
        New Orleans.

1413   ---Children of the river; a romance of old new orleans.
        New York: Sears, 1928. 326p.

        Dickson, Helen see Reynolds, Helen Mary Greenwood
        (Campbell) (1884-   )

1414   Dieter, William. The white land. New York: Knopf,
        1970. 269p.
            First novel--Montana--1880's--Western morality
        play.

1415   Dillon Mrs. Mary C. (Johnson). The rose of old st.
        louis. New York: Century, 1904. 406p.
            Louisiana Purchase--1803.

1416   ---The patience of john morland. New York: Burt, 1909.
        406p.
            Men of middle period all appear.

1417   ---Miss livingston's companion; a love story of old
        new york. New York: Century, 1911. 434p.
            Romance--A. Hamilton--J. F. Cooper--Washington
        Irving--A. Burr.

1418   Disosway, Ella Taylor. South meadows; a tale of long
        ago. Philadelphia: Porter, 1874. 280p.
            Cotton Mather--Massachusetts--17th century.

1419   Dix, Beulah Marie (1876-   ). Soldier rigdale; how
        he sailed in the "mayflower" and how he served
        miles standish. New York: Macmillan, 1899. 323p.
            1620--Juvenile.

1420   ---The making of christopher ferringham. New York:
        Macmillan, 1901. 453p.
            Puritans and Quakers--Massachusetts--1652.

1421   Dixon, Thomas Jr. (1864-1953). The one woman; a story
        of modern utopia. New York: Doubleday, 1903. 350p.

116

1422   ---Comrades; a story of social adventure in california.
       New York: Doubleday, 1909. 319p.
             Socialistic colony on a deserted island.

1423   ---The man in gray; a romance of the north and south.
       New York: Appleton, 1921. 427p.
             Events leading to Civil War.

1424   ---The torch; a story of the paranoiac who caused a
       great war. New York: The Author, 1927. 125p.
             John Brown (1800-1859)--Written for the screen.

1425   ---The sun virgin. New York: Liveright, 1929. 306p.
             Peru--1522-1548--Francisco Pizzaro (1470?-1541).

1426   Dobson, Ruth Lininger. Straw in the wind. New York:
       Dodd, 1937. 226p.
             First novel--Indiana--Small farming community--
       Amish Mennonites.

1427   Dodge, Mrs. Constance (Woodbury) (1896-   ). The
       dark stranger. Philadelphia: Penn, 1940. 439p.
             From Scotland 1745 to Carolina plantation--
       Indians and Bon Homme Richards--Sword play--Gun
       fire--Romance.

1428   ---Weathercock. New York: Dodd, 1942. 370p.
             North Carolina--Matriarchy of plantation--
       Revolution--Battle of Alamance.

1429   ---In adam's fall; a novel. Philadelphia: Macrae,
       1946. 494p.
             Salem witchcraft hunt 1690's--Based on records.

1430   Dodge, Louis (1870-   ). The american. New York:
       Messner, 1934. 634p.
             Pioneer life--1850's--From Illinois to Calif-
       ornia gold fields.

       Doerflinger, William jt. author, see Barker, Roland

       Doherty, Edward J. jt. author, see Davidison, Louis B.

1431   Doherty, Ethel and Long, Leslie. Seeds of time. New
       York: Dutton, 1938. 376p.
             1880's-1930's--From Nebraska farm to east and
       the return.

1432   Dohrman, Richard. The last of the maidens; a novel.
       New York: Holt, 1969. 304p.

1433   Dole, Edmund Pearson. Hiwa; a tale of ancient
       hawaii. New York: Harper, 1900. 107p.

1434   Donaldson, James Lowry. Sergeant atkins; a tale of adventure founded on fact. [By an Officer of the United States Army]. Philadelphia: Lippincott, 1871. 317p.
         Seminole War--1835-1842.

Donaldson, Lois, jt. author, see Sperry, Portia Howe

1435   Doneghy, Dagmar (Mrs. Joseph Warren Beach). The border; a missouri saga. New York: Morrow, 1931. 343p.
         First novel--Mother and six small sons on Kansas-Missouri border during Civil War.

1436   Doner, Mary Frances (Mrs. C. L. Parzant). Ravenswood; a story of the impact of a family and an industry on a great lakes town. New York: Doubleday, 1948. 254p.
         Chronicle Michigan family--Salt making.

1437   Donovan, Josephine. Black soil. Boston: Stratford, 1930. 320p.
         First novel--Irish to Iowa prairie land--German--Dutch--Austrian--Catholic community.

1438   Doone, Radko (1896-   ). Nuvat the brave; an eskimo robinson crusoe. Philadelphia: Macrae, 1934. 194p.
         Juvenile

1439   Dorrance, Mrs. Ethel Arnold (Smith) (1880-   ) and Dorrance, James French. Glory rides the range. New York: Macaulay, 1920. 308p.
         Western--Mystery.

1440   Dorrance, James French (1879-1961). The golden alaskan. New York: Macaulay, 1931. 311p.
         Nome setting for mystery.

Dorrance, James French see Dorrance, Mrs. Ethel Arnold (Smith) jt. author.

1441   Dorrance, Ward Allison (1904-   ). The sundowners. New York: Scribner's, 1942. 343p.
         Life nineteen year old boy--Life Jefferson City, Missouri.

1442   Dorsey, Mrs. Anna Hanson (McKenney). Coaina, the rose of the algonquins. New York: O'Shea, 1867. 145p.

1443   Dougall, Lily (1858-1923). The mormon prophet. New York: Appleton, 1899. 427p.
         Pro-Joseph Smith (1805-1844).

1444   Douglas, Mrs. Marjory (Stoneman). Freedom river, florida. New York: Scribner's, 1953. 264p.

Florida history--Negro--Seminole--Quaker--
Juvenile.

1445 Dowdey, Clifford (1904-   ). Bugles blow no more.
Boston: Little, 1937. 493p.
Richmond, Virginia Trilogy--#1 written #2 in
order--Social history.

1446 ---Gamble's hundred. Boston: Little, 1939. 367p.
Richmond, Virginia Trilogy--#2 written #1 in
order--Tidewater 1700-1730--Costume piece.

1447 ---Sing for a penny. Boston: Little, 1941. 366p.
Richmond, Virginia Trilogy--#3 written #3 in
order--1880's and 1890's--Sociology of post war
south.

1448 ---Tidewater. Boston: Little, 1943. 332p.
Western Tennessee after 1837.

1449 Downes, Mrs. Anne Miller. The eagle's song. Phil-
adelphia: Lippincott, 1949. 320p.
Colonial era to World War I--Mohawk Valley town--
Two families.

1450 ---The pilgrim soul. Philadelphia: Lippincott, 1952.
251p.
Mt. Manchester, New Hampshire--1820-1870--
Pioneers.

1451 ---The quality of mercy. Philadelphia: Lippincott,
1959. 317p.
Philadelphia and Kentucky--1813--Jackson v.
Creeks.

1452 Downey, Fairfax Davis (1893-   ). Army mule. New
York: Dodd, 1945. 192p.
Arizona--1870's--Apache Wars (1872-1873).

1453 ---Cavalry mount. New York: Dodd, 1947. 227p.
Texas--Indian Wars--1866-1895--Juvenile.

1454 Downing, John Hyatt (1888-   ). A prayer for tomorrow.
New York: Putnam, 1938. 342p.
South Dakota wheat farmers--Homespun American
life--Cattle and lumber.

1455 ---Hope of living. New York: Putnam, 1939. 311p.
Homesteading--South Dakota.

1456 ---Sioux city; a novel. New York: Putnam, 1940. 314p.
Meat packing--1880's.

1457 ---The harvest is late. New York: Hampton, 1944. 308p.
South Dakota--Small town--1920-1921--Farm
Bank--Depression.

1458   Doyle, Sir Arthur Conan (1859-1930). The refugees;
       a tale of two continents. New York: Harper, 1893.
       365p.
                Huguenot romance--1675.

1459   Drago, Harry Sinclair (1888-   ). Suzanna; a romance
       of early california. New York: Macaulay, 1922. 286p.
                1835--Haciendas--Descendents of conquistadores.

1460   ---Smoke of the .45. New York: Macaulay, 1923. 311p.
       Western

1461   ---Following the grass. New York: Macaulay, 1924. 320p.
       Western

1462   ---The desert hawk. New York: Macaulay, 1927. 315p.
       Western

1463   ---Where the loon calls. New York: Macaulay, 1928.
       317p.
                Early French settlements--Lake Erie--Toledo--
       Detroit.

1464   ---Guardians of the sage. New York: Macaulay, 1932.
       255p.
       Western

1465   -- Desert water. New York: Macaualy, 1933.
       251p.
       Western

1466   ---Montana road. New York: Morrow, 1935. 306p.
       Western

1467   ---Trigger gospel. New York: Macaulay, 1935.
       250p.
       Western

1468   ---Buckskin empire. New York: Doubleday, 1942. 268p.
       Western

1469   ---River of gold. New York: Dodd, 1945. 235p.
       Western

1470   ---The drifting kid. New York: Doubleday, 1947. 185p.
       Western

1471   ---Pay-off at black hawk. New York: Permabooks, 1956.
       154p.
       Western

1472   ---Decision at broken butte. New York: Permabooks,
       1957. 136p.
       Western

1473 ---<u>Wild grass</u>. New York: Permabooks, 1957. 169p.
Western

1474 ---<u>Buckskin affair</u>. New York: Doubelday, 1958. 190p.
Western

1475 ---<u>Fenced off</u>. New York: Doubleday, 1959. 192p.
Western

1476 ---<u>Many beavers; the story of a cree indian boy</u>. New
York: Dodd, 1967. 126p.
Western

1477 --- jt. author, Noel, Joseph. <u>Whispering sage</u>. New York:
Century, 1922. 304p.
Western

1478 ---<u>pseud</u>. Cross, Stewart. <u>This way to hell</u>. New York:
Macaulay, 1933. 288p.
Western

1479 ---<u>pseud</u>. Deming, Kirk. <u>Colt lightin'</u>. New York:
Macaulay, 1938. 253p.

1480 ---<u>Grass means fight</u>. New York: Macaulay, 1938. 253p.
Western

1481 ---<u>pseud</u>. Ermine, Will. <u>Laramie rides alone</u>. New
York: Morrow, 1934. 276p.
Western

1482 ---<u>Lobo law</u>. New York: Macaulay, 1935. 279p.
Western

1483 ---<u>Plundered range</u>. New York: Morrow, 1936. 278p.
Western

1484 ---<u>Prairie smoke</u>. New York: Green Circle, 1936. 253p.
Western

1485 ---<u>Wind river outlaw</u>. New York: Green Circle, 1936.
256p.
Western

1486 ---<u>Barbed-wire empire</u>. New York: Green Circle, 1937.
256p.
Western

1487 ---<u>Lawless legion</u>. New York: Macaulay, 1938. 288p.
Western

1488 ---<u>Trail trouble</u>. New York: Green Circle, 1938. 256p.
Western

1489 ---<u>Cowboy say your prayers!</u> New York: Morrow, 1939. 274p.
Western

1490 ---Rustler's moon. New York: Morrow, 1939. 271p.
        Western

1491 ---Singing lariat. New York: Morrow, 1939. 281p.
        Western

1492 ---Boss of the plain. New York: Morrow, 1940. 282p.
        Western

1493 ---Rider of the midnight range. New York: Morrow, 1940.
        283p.
        Western

1494 ---Watchdog of thunder river. New York: Morrow, 1941.
        252p.
        Western

1495 ---My gun is law. New York: Morrow, 1942. 251p.
        Western

1496 ---Brave in saddle. New York: Morrow, 1943. 220p.
        Western

1497 ---Stagecoach kingdom. New York: Doubleday, 1943.
        240p.
        Western

1498 ---The iron bronc. New York: Jefferson House, 1944.
        187p.
        Western

1499 ---Rusted range. New York: Morrow, 1944. 220p.
        Western

1500 ---Buckskin marshal. New York: Jefferson House, 1945.
        187p.
        Western

1501 ---Outlaw on horse back. New York: Doubleday, 1946.
        184p.
        Western

1502 ---Apache crossing. New York: Doubleday, 1950. 219p.
        Western

1503 ---Busted range. New York: Jefferson House, 1951.
        220p.
        Western

1504 ---Boss of the plains. New York: Jefferson House, 1952.
        282p.
        Western

1505 ---Longhorn empire. New York: Doubleday, 1953. 186p.
        Western

1506 ---War on the saddle rock. New York: Jefferson House,
      1953. 188p.
      Western

1507 ---Frenchman's river. New York: Permabooks, 1955. 169p.
      Western

1508 ---pseud. Lomax, Bliss. Closed range. New York: Mac-
      aulay, 1936. 254p.
      Western

1509 ---Canyon of golden skulls. New York: Macaulay, 1937.
      255p.
      Western

1510 ---The law bringers. New York: Macaulay, 1937. 317p.
      Western

1511 ---Mavericks of the plains. New York: Greenberg, 1938.
      250p.
      Western

1512 ---Colt comrades. New York: Doubleday, 1939. 279p.
      Western

1513 ---Gringo gunfire. New York: Doubleday, 1940. 282p.
      Western

1514 ---The leather burners. New York: Doubleday, 1940.
      273p.
      Western

1515 ---Pardners of the bad lands. New York: Doubleday,
      1942. 281p.
      Western

1516 ---Horse thief creek. New York: Doubleday, 1944. 179p.
      Western

1517 ---Rusty guns. New York: Dodd, 1944. 222p.
      Western

1518 ---Saddle hawks. New York: Doubleday, 1944. 181p.
      Western

1519 ---Outlaw river. New York: Dodd, 1945. 215p.
      Western

1520 ---The phantom corral. New York: Dodd, 1946. 212p.
      Western

1521 ---Trail dust. New York: Dodd, 1947. 218p.
      Western

1522 ---Shadow mountain. New York: Dodd, 1948. 214p.
Western

1523 ---The fight for the sweetwater. New York: Dodd, 1950.
212p.
Western

1524 ---Guns along the yellowstone. New York: Dodd, 1952.
254p.
Western

1525 ---Riders of the buffalo grass. New York: Dodd, 1952.
244p.
Western

1526 ---The loner; an original western. New York: Dell,
1956. 160p.
Western

1527 ---Stranger with a gun. New York: Dodd, 1957. 214p.
Western

1528 ---Last call for a gun fighter. New York: Dodd, 1958.
213p.
Western

1529 ---Appointment on the yellowstone. New York: Dodd, 1959.
209p.
Western

Drago, Sinclair see Drago, Harry Sinclair (1888-   )

1530 Drake, Henry Burgess. The schooner california. New
York: Harper, 1927. 318p.
Youth to California gold fields--Adventure--
Juvenile.

1531 Drake, Samuel Adams (1833-1905). Captain nelson; a
romance of colonial days. New York: Harper, 1876. 172p
Boston--1688.

1532 ---The young vigilantes; a story of california life in
the fifties. Boston: Lee, 1904. 284p.

1533 Dresser, Davis (1904-   ). Death rides the pecos.
New York: Morrow, 1940. 249p.
Western

1534 ---The hangmen of sleepy valley. New York: Morrow, 1940.
250p.
Western

1535 ---Two-gun rio kid. New York: Morrow, 1941. 248p.
Western

1536 ---pseud. Davis, Don. Return of the rio kid. New York:
      Morrow, 1940. 281p.
            Western

1537 Driscoll, Charles Benedict (1885-1951). Kansas irish.
      New York: Macmillan, 1943. 359p.
            Wichita--Childhood in Kansas.

1538 DuBois, Constance Goddard. Martha corey; a tale of
      salem witchcraft. Chicago: McClurg, 1890. 314p.
            Moves from England to Massachusetts.

1539 ---Columbus and beatriz; a novel. Chicago: McClurg,
      1892. 297p.

1540 DuBois, Theodora (McCormick) (1890-   ). Freedom's
      way. New York: Funk, 1953. 450p.
            Young gentleman from England to America--
      Indentured servant--Romance--Early 1770's.

1541 Dudley, Albertus True (1866-1955). A spy of '76.
      Boston: Lothrop, 1933. 323p.
            Juvenile

1542 Duffus, Robert Luther (1888-   ). Jornada. New
      York: Covici, 1935. 313p.
            Mexican War (1845-1848).

1543 Duffy, Owen. Walter warren; or, the adventurer of
      the northern wilds. New York: Stringer, 1854. 105p.

1544 Duganne, Augustine Joseph Hickey. The bravo's daughter;
      or, the tory of carolina. a romance of the american
      revolution. New York: Winchester, 1850. 92p.
            Siege of Charleston--1780.

1545 Duke, Seymour R.. Osceola; or, facts and fiction. a
      tale of the seminole war. New York: Harper, 1838.
      150p.
            1836-1837.

1546 Dulles, Foster Rhea (1900-   ). Harpoon; the story
      of a whaling voyage. Boston: Houghton, 1935. 230p.
            Juvenile

1547 Duncan, David (1913-   ). Yes, my darling daughters.
      New York: Doubleday, 1959. 238p.
            Utopian colony--Free love.

1548 Duncan, Norman. The measure of a man; a tale of the
      big woods. New York: Revell, 1911. 356p.
            Religion--Lumber camps.

1549 Duncan, Thomas William (1905-   ). Big river, big man.
      Philadelphia: Lippincott, 1959. 1022p.

19th century--Upper Mississippi River.

1550 Dunham, Bertha Mabel. Trail of the conestoga. New
      York: Macmillan, 1924. 342p.
      Mennonites from Pennsylvania to Ontario,
      Canada--Early 19th century.

1551 ---Toward sodom. New York: Macmillan, 1928. 336p.
      Mennonite community--Pioneering in Canada.

1552 Duniway, Mrs. Abigail (Scott). Captain gray's company;
      or, crossing the plains and living in oregon.
      Portland, Oregon: McCormick, 1859. 342p.

1553 Dunn, Joseph Allan Elphinstone (1872-   ). Jim morse,
      gold hunter. Boston: Small, 1920. 266p.

1554 ---Turquoise cañon. New York: Doubleday, 1920. 241p.
      Western

1555 ---Man trap. New York: Doubleday, 1921. 294p.
      Mining--Indians--Pueblo--Juvenile.

1556 ---Rimrock trail. Indianapolis: Bobbs, 1922. 397p.
      Western

1557 ---Buffalo boy. New York: Grosset, 1929. 224p.
      Western--Juvenile.

1558 ---Young eagle of the trail. New York: Grosset, 1931.
      216p.
      Western--Juvenile.

1559 Dunn, Robert. The youngest world; a novel of the
      frontier. New York: Dodd, 1914. 492p.
      Alaska--Juvenile.

1560 Dunsing, Dorothy May (Mrs. William Byron Mowery).
      War chant. New York: Longmans, 1954. 176p.
      Second Seminole War--1836--Ft. Tampa--Juvenile.

1561 Dupuy, Eliza Ann (1814?-1881). The conspirator. New
      York: Appleton, 1850. 299p.
      Aaron Burr (1756-1836).

1562 ---Ashleigh; a tale of the olden time. Cincinnati:
      Pearson. 1854. 112p.
      New Hampshire v. New York--1775.

1563 ---The huguenot exiles; or, the times of louis XIV.
      a historical novel. New York: Harper, 1856. 453p.

1564 ---All for love; or, the outlaw's bride. Philadelphia:
      Peterson, 1873. 415p.
      Western

126

1565   Dwight, Allan. <u>Drums in the forest</u>.   New York: Mac-
         millan, 1936.   255p.
              French boy--St. Lawrence and west--Pre-1763⁰.

1566   Dye, Mrs. Eva (Emery) (1855-   ).   <u>McLoughlin and
         old oregon; a chronicle</u>.   Chicago: McClurg, 1900.
         381p.

1567   ---<u>The conquest; the true story of lewis and clark</u>.
         Chicago, McClurg, 1902.   443p.
              Meriwether Lewis (1774-1809)--William Clark
         (1770-1838).

1568   Dykeman, Wilma.   <u>The tall woman</u>.   New York: Holt,
         1962.   315p.
              Pioneer North Carolina--1864-1896--Good reg-
         ional background.

E. A. B. S. see Shackleford, Miss E. A. B.

1569   East, Fred pseud. Field, Peter. Dry-gulch adams.
      New York: Morrow, 1934. 282p.
      Western

1570   ---Gringo guns. New York: Morrow, 1935. 307p.
      Western

1571   ---The boss of the lazy 9. New York: Morrow, 1936.
      246p.
      Western

1572   ---The outlaw of eagle's nest. New York: Morrow, 1938.
      276p.
      Western

1573   ---Doctor two-guns. New York: Morrow, 1939. 284p.
      Western

1574   ---The tender foot kid. New York: Morrow, 1939. 280p.
      Western

1575   ---Law badge. New York: Morrow, 1940. 279p.
      Western

1576   ---Fight for powder valley! New York: Morrow, 1942.
      248p.
      Western

1577   ---Law man of powder valley. New York: Morrow, 1942.
      247p.
      Western

1578   ---Powder valley payoff. New York: Morrow, 1942. 242p.
      Western

1579   ---Trail south from powder valley. New York: Morrow,
      1942. 251p.
      Western

1580   ---Powder valley vengeance. New York: Morrow, 1943.
      248p.
      Western

1581   ---Smoking iron. New York: Morrow, 1943. 215p.
      Western

1582 ---End of the trail. New York: Morrow, 1945. 186p.
Western

1583 ---Powder valley showdown. New York: Morrow, 1945.
186p.
Western

1584 ---Trail from needle rock; a powder valley western.
New York: Morrow, 1947. 220p.
Western

1585 ---pseud. Manning, Roy. Trigger trail; a western
novel. Philadelphia: Smith, 1945. 224p.
Western

1586 ---Vengeance valley. Philadelphia: Smith, 1946. 248p.
Western

1587 ---Tangled trail. Philadelphia: Smith, 1947. 224p.
Western--Issued in 1954 as The Shoot Out at
Sentinel Park.

1588 ---Renegade ranch. Philadelphia: Macrae, 1948. 224p.
Western

1589 ---Six gun sheriff. Philadelphia: Smith, 1948. 231p.
Western

1590 ---Red range. Philadelphia: Macrae, 1950. 256p.
Western

1591 ---pseud. West, Tom. Powdersmoke pay-off. New York:
Dutton, 1948. 218p.
Western

1592 ---Spectre spread. New York: Dutton, 1948. 224p.
Western

1593 ---Botched brand. New York: Dutton, 1949. 222p.
Western

1594 ---Ghost gold. New York: Dutton, 1950. 221p.
Western

1595 ---Flaming feud. New York: Dutton, 1951. 217p.
Western

1596 ---Vulture valley. New York: Dutton, 1951. 219p.
Western

1597 ---Ghost gun. New York: Dutton, 1952. 206p.
Western

1598 ---Gunsmoke gold. New York: Dutton, 1952. 224p.
Western

1599   ---Lobo legacy. New York: Ace, 1954. 154p.
        Western--May have appeared in 1946 as The
        one shot kid.

1600   Eastman, Elaine (Goodale) (1863-   ). Yellow star;
        a story of east and west. Boston: Little, 1911.
        272p.
            Indian girl--For girls.

1601   Easton, Robert Olney. The happy man. New York: Viking,
        1943. 221p.
            First novel--California cattle ranch.

1602   Eaton, Evelyn Sybil Mary (1902-   ). Restless are the
        sails. New York: Harper, 1941. 348p.
            Siege of Louisburg--1745--Romance.

1603   ---The sea is so wide. New York: Harper, 1943. 281p.
            Acadians from Nova Scotia (1755)--Williamsburg
        life--Romance.

1604   ---Give me your golden hand. New York: Farrar, 1951.
        309p.
            Bonded servant to America during American
        Revolution.

1605   Eaton, Geoffrey Dell (1894-   ). Back furrow. New
        York: Putnam, 1925. 332p.
            Michigan farm life--1900-1925--Meyer, "signif-
        icant as strongest attack on farm life in whole
        body of farm fiction".

1606   Eckenrode, Hamilton James (1881-   ). Bottom rail
        on top; a novel of the old south. New York: Green-
        berg, 1935. 274p.
            Author Virginan historian.

1607   Eckert, Allan W. The frontiersman; a narrative. Boston:
        Little, 1967. 626p.
            First in projected series, "The Winning of
        America Narratove History"--1750-1815--Indian Wars--
        Tecumseh--Simon Kenton (1755-1836).

1608   ---Wilderness empire. Boston: Little, 1969. 640p.
            Second in series--American frontier--1730-
        1774--Sir William Johnson--Main figure--Chief Pont-
        iac (Obwondiyag)--Chief Brant.

1609   Edgerton, Mrs. Lucile Selk. Pillars of gold. New
        York: Knopf, 1941. 408p.

1610   Edith; or, the quaker's daughter. a tale of puritan
        times. by one of her descendents. [Anonymous]. New
        York: Mason, 1856. 407p.
            Boston

130

1611   Edmonds, Walter Dumaux (1903-   ). Rome haul.
       Boston: Little, 1929. 347p.
           First novel--Erie Canal--1850's--Realistic
       atmosphere--Broad canvas.

1612   ---Big barn. Boston: Little, 1930. 333p.
           Black River Valley--Erie Canal--Farm life--
       1860's--Pioneer country people--Good regional work.

1613   ---Erie water. Boston: Little, 1933. 506p.
           New York life 1817-1825--Romance--Good period
       study.

1614   ---Drums along the mohawk. Boston: Little, 1936. 592p.
           American Revolution--1776-1784--Mohawk Valley--
       Battle of Oriskany (1777)--Excellent.

1615   ---Chad hanna. Boston: Little, 1940. 548p.
           Mohawk Valley, New York--1830's--Orphan joins
       travelling circus.

1616   ---Tom whipple. New York: Dodd, 1942. 70p.
           Taken from story in Lydia Maria Child's
       Letters from New York.

1617   ---Two logs crossing; john haskell's story. New York:
       Dodd, 1943. 82p.
           Boy must care for family--Aided by Indian
       trapper--Juvenile.

1618   ---Wilderness clearing. New York: Dodd, 1944. 156p.
           American Revolution--Mohawk Valley, New York--
       1777--Excellent--Juvenile.

1619   ---In the hands of the senecas. Boston: Little, 1947.
       213p.
           Finger Lakes, New York--1770's.

1620   ---The wedding journey. Boston: Little, 1947. 118p.
           Wedding trip--Packet boat--Erie Canal--1835.

1621   ---The boyds of black river. New York: Dodd, 1953.
       248p.
           Horse breeders--Upper New York--1900's--Coming
       of "horseless carriage".

1622   ---The musket and the cross; the struggle of france
       and england for north america. Boston: Little,
       1968. 514p.
           Narrative--1609-1689.

1623   Edwardes, Tickner (1865-   ). Tansy. New York:
       Dutton, 1914?. 336p.
           Sheep ranch.

1624 Edwards, Elisha Jay. Shad and shed; or, the remarkable adventures of the puritan brothers. Washington: U.S. Service Pub, 1889. 261p.
Late 17th century.

1625 Eggleston, Edward (1837-1902). Hoosier schoolmaster; a novel. New York: Judd, 1871. 276p.
Indiana pioneer life--1850.

1626 ---The end of the world; a love story. New York: Judd, 1872. 299p.
Millerites in Indiana--1843.

1627 ---The circuit rider; a tale of the heroic age. New York: Scribner's, 1874. 332p.
Author was Methodist circuit rider--1800-1825.

1628 ---Roxy. New York: Scribner's, 1878. 432p.
Tippecanoe Campaign--Southern Indiana--1811.

1629 ---The hoosier school-boy. New York: Scribner's, 1883. 181p.
Indiana and Ohio life--ca. 1840--Problem of getting an education on frontier.

1630 ---The graysons; a story of illinois. New York: Century, 1888. 362p.
Daily life--Rural Illinois--1850.

1631 Eggleston, George Cary (1839-1911). A carolina cavalier. Boston: Lothrop, 1901. 448p.
American Revolution--1779-1780.

1632 ---Irene of the mountains; a romance of old virginia. Boston: Lothrop, 1909. 437p.

E. G. L. see Lindsey, E. G.

1633 Ehle, John (1925-   ). Lion on the hearth. New York: Harper, 1961. 406p.

1634 ---The land breakers. New York: Harper, 1964. 407p.
Pioneer life in mountain country of Carolina-Tennessee border 1779-1784--Good recreation of pioneer past.

1635 Ehrlich, Leonard. God's angry man. New York: Simon, 1932. 401p.
First novel--Remarkable--John Brown (1800-1859).

1636 Eifert, Mrs. Virginia Louise (Snider) (1911-   ). Three rivers south; the story of young abe lincoln. New York: Dodd, 1953. 176p.
#3 of Trilogy--Flat boat down the Mississippi River--1831--Juvenile.

1637 ---The buffalo trace. New York: Dodd, 1955. 193p.
#1 of Trilogy--Lincoln's grandfather basis--
1780's from Virginia to Kentucky--Juvenile.

1638 ---Out of the wilderness; young abe lincoln. New
York: Dodd, 1956. 214p.
#2 of Trilogy--Third to be written.

1639 Eisele, Wilbert Edwin pseud. Lyndon, Ross. The real
wild bill, famous scout and knight chivalric of
the plains. a true story of pioneer life in the
far west. Denver, Colorado: Andre, 1931. 364p.
Old school western--James Butler Hickok--
(1837-1876).

1640 Ellen woodville; or, life in the west. [Anonymous].
New York: Langley, 1844. 160p.

1641 Ellerbe, Rose (1862-   ). Ropes of sand. Hollywood,
California: Fischer, 1925. 395p.
California--Pioneer--Catholics--Indians.

1642 Elliott, Mrs. Sarah Barnwell. A simple heart. New
York: Ireland, 1887. 69p.
Pioneer town in Texas.

1643 Elliott, Thomas Rose. Hugh layal; a romance of the up
country. New York: Macmillan, 1927. 263p.
Canadian northwest--Red River--Romance--Mystery.

1644 Ellis, Edward Sylvester (1840-1916). The haunted
wood; a legend of mohawk in 1778. New York:
Chapman, 1866. 120p.

1645 ---Ned in the block-house; a tale of early days in
the west. Philadelphia: Porter, 1883. 327p.

1646 ---Life on the mountain and prairie. New York: Munro,
1884. 31p.

1647 ---The lost trail. Philadelphia: Porter, 1884. 378p.

1648 ---Ned in the woods; a tale of the early days in the
west. Philadelphia: Porter, 1884. 290p.

1649 ---Ned on the river. Philadelphia: Porter, 1884. 300p.

1650 ---Camp-fire and wigwam. Philadelphia: Porter, 1885.
388p.

1651 ---Foot-prints in the forest. Philadelphia: Porter,
1886. 387p.

1652 ---The camp in the mountains. Philadelphia: Porter,
1887. 366p.

1653 ---The hunters of the ozark. Philadelphia: Porter, 1887. 410p.

1654 ---The last war trail. Philadelphia: Porter, 1887. 376p.

1655 ---Wyoming. Philadelphia: Porter, 1888. 321p.

1656 ---Storm mountain. Philadelphia: Porter, 1889. 357p.

1657 ---The cabin in the clearing; a tale of the frontier. Philadelphia: Porter, 1890. 438p.

1658 ---Arthur helmuth. New York: U.S. Book, 1891. 306p.

1659 ---Check 2134. New York: U.S. Book, 1891. 275p.

1660 ---Across texas. Philadelphia: Porter, 1893. 349p.

1661 ---Lena-wingo, the mohawk; a sequel to The wilderness fugitives. St. Paul: Price, 1893. 248p.

1662 ---The river fugitives. St. Paul: Price, 1893. 256p.

1663 ---The wilderness fugitives; a sequel to the River fugitives. St. Paul: Price, 1893. 253p.

1664 ---Among the esquimaux; or, adventures under the artic circle. Philadelphia: Penn, 1894. 317p.

1665 ---The path in the ravine. Philadelphia: Porter, 1895. 319p.

1666 ---The young ranchers; or, fighting the sioux. Philadelphia: Coates, 1895. 284p.

1667 ---The phantom of the river; a sequel to Shod with silence . Philadelphia: Coates, 1896. 352p.

1668 ---Shod with silence; a tale of the frontier. Philadelphia: Coates, 1896. 363p.

1669 ---Uncrowning a king; a tale of king philip's war. New York: Amsterdam, 1896. 312p.

1670 ---In the days of the pioneers; sequel to the Phantom of the river . Philadelphia: Coates, 1897. 368p.

1671 ---Cowmen and rustlers; a story of the wyoming cattle ranges. Philadelphia: Coates, 1898. 322p.

1672 ---Klondike nuggets and how two boys secured them. New York: Doubleday, 1898. 255p.

1673 ---Two boys in wyoming; a tale of adventure.

Philadelphia: Coates, 1898. 399p.

1674 ---Iron heart, war chief of the iriquois. Philadelphia:
      Coates, 1899. 386p.

1675 ---Blazing arrow; a tale of the frontier. Philadelphia:
      Coates, 1900. 289p.

1676 ---The boy patriot; a story of jack, the young friend
      of washington. New York: Burt, 1900. 302p.

1677 ---Red plume. New York: Mershon, 1900. 385p.

1678 ---Red eagle; a tale of the frontier. Philadelphia:
      Coates, 1901. 296p.

1679 ---An american king; a story of king philip's war.
      Philadelphia: Coates, 1903. 482p.

1680 ---The cromwell of virginia; a story of bacon's rebel-
      lion. Philadelphia: Coates, 1904. 380p.

1681 ---The last emperor of the old dominion. Philadelphia:
      Coates, 1904. 365p.

1682 ---Patriot and tory. Boston: Estes, 1904. 311p.

1683 ---Deerfoot in the forest. Philadelphia: Winston,
      1905. 366p.

1684 ---Deerfoot in the mountains. Philadelphia: Winston,
      1905. 363p.

1685 ---Deerfoot on the prairies. Philadelphia: Winston,
      1905. 366p.

1686 ---The forest messengers. Philadelphia: Winston,
      1907. 340p.

1687 ---Seth jones of new hampshire. New York: Dillingham,
      1907. 282p.

1688 ---Tam; or, holding the fort. Chicago: Winston, 1907.
      351p.

1689 ---Off the reservation; or, caught in an apache raid.
      Philadelphia: Winston, 1908. 331p.

1690 ---The story of red feather; a tale of the american
      frontier. New York: McLoughlin, 1908. 132p.

1691 ---Trailing geronimo; or, campaigning with crook.
      Philadelphia: Winston, 1908. 353p.

1692 ---Alden among the indians; or, the search for the

missing pony express rider. Philadelphia: Winston, 1909. 323p.

1693 ---The forest spy; a tale of the war of 1812. New York: Hurst, 1910. 249p.

1694 ---The frontier angel; a romance of kentucky rangers' life. New York: Hurst, 1910. 251p.

1695 ---Nathan todd; or, the fate of the sioux captive. New York: Hurst, 1910. 247p.

1696 ---The hunter's cabin; an episode in the early settle-ments of southern ohio. New York: Hurst, 1911. 256p.

1697 ---Irona; or, life on the southwest border. New York: Hurst, 1911. 245p.

1698 ---Oonomoo, the huron. New York: Hurst, 1911. 256p.

1699 ---The ranger; or, the fugitivies of the border. New York: Hurst, 1911. 224p.

1700 ---Rifleman of the miami. New York: Hurst, 1912. 272p.

1701 ---The boy patrol around the council fire. Philadelphia: Winston, 1913. 314p.

1702 ---"Remember the alamo". Philadelphia: Winston, 1914. 342p.

1703 ---The three arrows. Philadelphia: Winston, 1914. 332p.

1704 ---pseud. Gordon, Colonel H.R..Pontiac, chief of the ottawas; a tale of the siege of detroit. New York: Dutton, 1897. 300p.

1705 ---Tecumseh, chief of the shawnoes[sic]; a tale of the war of 1812. New York: Dutton, 1898. 312p.

1706 ---Osceola, chief of the seminoles. New York: Dutton, 1899. 322p.

1707 ---Red jacket, the last of the senecas. New York: Dutton, 1900. 347p.

1708 ---Logan the mingo; a story of the frontier. New York: Dutton, 1902. 337p.

1709 ---Black partridge; or, the fall of fort dearborn. New York: Dutton, 1906. 302p.

1710 ---pseud. Hawthorne, Captain R. M.. Hurricane gulch; a tale of the aosta and bufferville trail. New York: Collier, 1892. 144p.

1711   ---pseud. Jayne, Lieutenant R. H.. On the trail of
       geronimo; or, in the apache country. New York:
       Lovell, 1889. 323p.

1712   ---The white mustang. New York: Lovell, 1889. 342p.

1713   ---Lost in the wilderness. St. Paul: Price, 1892. 265p.

1714   ---Through apache land. St. Paul: Price, 1893. 334p.

1715   ---The cave in the mountain; a sequel to In the pecos
       country. New York: Merriam, 1894. 295p.

1716   ---In the pecos country. New York: Merriam, 1894. 303p.

1717   ---pseud. Lisle, Seward D.. Teddy and towser; a story
       of early days in california. Philadelphia: Coates,
       1904. 352p.

1718   Ellis, John Brackenridge (1870-   ). Arkinsaw cousins;
       a story of the ozarks. New York: Holt, 1908. 328p.

1719   Ellis, William Donahue. Bounty lands. Cleveland:
       World, 1952. 492p.
            First novel--Revolutionary soldiers to old
       Northwest--Take up new land--Sound work.

1720   ---Jonathan blair, bounty lands lawyer. Cleveland:
       World, 1954. 464p.
            Sequel to Bounty Lands--Eastern lawyer defends
       settlers' interest--Mesopotamia territory--Better
       than first novel.

1721   ---The brooks legend. New York: Crowell, 1958. 467p.
            #3 in series--Some characters from Bounty Lands
       and Jonathan Blair--Life in Ohio territory.

1722   Ellison, Nina E.. Nadine; a romance of two lives.
       Nashville, Tennessee: Gospel Advocate Pub. Co.,
       1897. 343p.
            Kentucky--San Francisco--Alaska.

1723   Ellsberg, Edward (1891-   ). Captain paul. New York:
       Dodd, 1941. 607p.
            John Paul Jones (1747-1792)--Privateer to
       "Serapis".

       Ellsworth, Elmer pseud. see Thayer, Tiffany

1724   Elston, Allan Vaughn (1887-   ). Come out and fight!
       New York: Doubleday, 1941. 275p.
            First western novel.

1725   ---Guns on the cimarron. Philadelphia: Macrae, 1943.
       255p.

Western--Author former cowboy.

1726 ---Hit the saddle; a western novel. Philadelphia:
Macrae, 1947. 254p.
Western

1727 ---The sheriff of san miguel. Philadelphia: Lippincott,
1949. 222p.
Western

1728 ---Deadline at durango. Philadelphia: Lippincott, 1950.
224p.
Western

1729 ---Grass and gold. Philadelphia: Lippincott, 1951.
222p.
Western

1730 ---Roundup on the picketwire. Philadelphia: Lippincott,
1952. 224p.
Western

1731 ---Saddle up for sunlight. Philadelphia: Lippincott,
1952. 221p.
Western

1732 ---Stage road to denver. Philadelphia: Lippincott,
1953. 223p.
Western

1733 ---Long lope to lander. Philadelphia: Lippincott,
1954. 229p.
Western

1734 ---Wagon wheel gap. Philadelphia: Lippincott, 1954.
224p.
Western

1735 ---Forbidden valley. Philadelphia: Lippincott, 1955.
221p.
Western

1736 ---The wyoming bubble. Philadelphia: Lippincott, 1955.
222p.
Western

1737 ---Last stage to aspen. Philadelphia: Lippincott, 1956.
220p.
Western

1738 ---The marked men. Philadelphia: Lippincott, 1956.
221p.
Western

1739 ---Grand mesa. Philadelphia: Lippincott, 1957. 220p.
Western

1740 ---Rio grande deadline. Philadelphia: Lippincott,
        1957. 222p.
        Western

1741 ---Wyoming manhunt. Philadelphia: Lippincott, 1958.
        222p.
        Western

1742 ---Gun law at laramie. Philadelphia: Lippincott, 1959.
        223p.
        Western

1743 ---Montana masquerade. Philadelphia: Lippincott, 1959.
        222p.
        Western

1744 ---Beyond the bitterroots. Philadelphia: Lippincott,
        1960. 218p.
        Western

1745 ---Sagebrush serenade. Philadelphia: Lippincott, 1960.
        219p.
        Western

1746 ---Roundup on the yellowstone. Philadelphia: Lippincott,
        1962. 215p.
        Western

1747 ---Treasure coach from deadwood. Philadelphia: Lippin-
        cott, 1962. 224p.
        Western

1748 ---The land seekers. Philadelphia: Lippincott, 1964.
        223p.
        Western

1749 Elwood, Muriel (1902-   ). Heritage of the river; an
        historical novel of early montreal. New York:
        Scribner's, 1945. 310p.
        "Court Life" at Quebec--Late 17th century--
        Romance and adventure.

1750 ---Deeper the heritage. New York: Scribner's, 1946.
        344p.
        New France--1700's--Romance and adventure.

1751 ---Against the tide. Indianapolis: Bobbs, 1950. 331p.
            American to Los Angeles area--Rancher--Loves
        Spanish girl.

1752 ---Web of destiny. Indianapolis: Bobbs, 1951. 311p.
            French-Indian War (1755-1763).

1753 Embree, Charles Fleming (1874-1905). A dream of a
        throne; the story of a mexican revolt. Boston:

Little, 1900. 464p.
Mexican Wars--1821-1861.

1754 Emerson, Caroline Dwight (1891-   ). The magic tunnel;
a story of old new york. New York: Stokes, 1940.
120p.
New Amsterdam--1664--Juvenile.

1755 Emerson, Mrs. Elizabeth (Holaday). The good crop.
New York: Longmans, 1946. 297p.
Chronicle--Quaker family--Eastern Illinois--
1840-1860.

1756 ---The garnered sheaves. New York: Longmans, 1948.
264p.
Sequel to Good Crop--ca. 1900.

1757 Emerson, Lucien Waldo (1902-   ). Cimarron bend.
New York: Macaulay, 1936. 256p.
Western

1758 ---Rawhide. New York: Morrow, 1936. 263p.
Western--First novel.

1759 Emma bartlett; or, prejudice and fanaticism. By an
American Lady. [Anonymous]. Cincinnati: Moore,
1856. 502p.
Anti-Abolitionist--Anti-know nothing.

1760 Emmett, Elizabeth. The land he loved; a story of old
narragansett. New York: Macmillan, 1940. 291p.
New England lady came from London--1726--
Juvenile.

1761 Emmons, Mrs. Della Florence (Gould). Sacajawea of
the shoshones. Portland, Oregon: Binfords, 1943.
316p.
Girl Scout book--Lewis and Clark Expedition--
Sacajawea (1786-1884)--Juvenile.

1762 ---Nothing in life is free; through naches pass to
puget sound. a historical novel of pioneer west.
Minneapolis: Northwestern, 1953. 315p.
Selected as official book commemorating
Washington Territorial Centennial.

1763 ---Leschi of the nisquallies. Minneapolis: Denison,
1965. 416p.
Indian Chief (d. 1858)--Juvenile.

1764 Engle, Paul (1908-   ). Always the land. New York:
Random, 1941. 326p.
First novel of poet--Iowa farming--Horse breed-
ing--Horse trading.

1765   Engstrand, Stuart David (1905-   ). The invaders.
        New York: Knopf, 1937. 265p.
            First novel--Truck farming--Middle west.

1766   ---They sought for paradise. New York: Harper, 1939.
        272p.
            Janssonists--Illinois--1846--Mature love story.

1767   Erdman, Loula Grace. The years of the locust. New York:
        Dodd, 1947. 234p.
            Missouri farm life--Third of thirteen novels
        written between 1944-1960.

1768   ---The edge of time. New York: Dodd, 1950. 275p.
            Wagon trip to Texas Panhandle--1885--Young
        couple.

1769   ---The wind blows free. New York: Dodd, 1952. 242p.
            Life Texas Plains--1890's.

1770   ---The far journey. New York: Dodd, 1955. 282p.
            Covered wagon journey to Texas from Missouri--
        1885.

1771   ---The wide horizon; a story of the texas panhandle.
        New York: Dodd, 1956. 245p.
            Sequel to The Wind Blows Free--1890's.

1772   ---The short summer. New York: Dodd, 1958. 304p.
            Missouri town life--1914.

1773   ---The good land. New York: Dodd, 1959. 182p.
            Third book ré Pierce family pioneers in Texas
        Panhandle--Sequel to Wide Horizon--1910 era.

1774   Erickson, Howard. Son of earth. New York: Dial, 1933.
        310p.
            First novel--Danish immigrant--Iowa farm--
        1900-1925.

        Ermine, Will pseud. see Drago, Harry Sinclair (1888-   )

1775   Ernewein, Leslie Charles (1900-   ). Gunsmoke galoot.
        New York: Phoenix, 1941. 255p.
            First western.

1776   ---Boss of panamint. New York: Phoenix, 1942. 254p.
            Western

1777   ---Kincaid of red butte. New York: Phoenix, 1942.
        251p.
            Western

1778   ---The faro kid. New York: Phoenix, 1944. 255p.
            Western

141

1779 ---Bullet breed. New York: McBride, 1946. 148p.
       Western

1780 ---Rio renegade. New York: McBride, 1946. 221p.
       Western

1781 ---High gun. Greenwich, Connecticut: Fawcett, 1956.
       144p.
            Golden Spur Award 1957 for Best Western.

1782 ---Warrior basin. New York: Doubleday, 1959. 188p.
       Western

1783 Erskine, Mrs. Dorothy Ward. Big ride. New York:
       Crowell, 1958. 207p.
            First Spanish colonizing expedition to Calif-
       ornia--1775--Juvenile.

1784 Erskine, John (1879-   ). Give me liberty; the story
       of an innocent bystander. New York: Stokes, 1940.
       313p.
            Pre-Revolutionary politics--1759-1775--Main
       character an admirer of Patrick Henry.

1785 Erskine, Laurie York (1894-   ). The laughing rider.
       New York: Appleton, 1924. 306p.
       Western--Romance.

1786 ---Valor of the range. New York: Appleton, 1925. 282p.
       Western--Young adults.

1787 Ertz, Susan. Proselyte. New York: Appleton, 1933.
       359p.
            Hand cart brigade--Pro-Mormon--Serious fiction.

1788 Esperanza; my journey thither and what i found there.
       [Anonymous]. Cincinnati: Valentine, 1860. 332p.
       Utopian--Free love.

1789 Ethridge, Willie (Snow) (Mrs. M. F. Ethridge). Summer
       thunder. New York: Coward, 1959. 319p.
            James Edward Oglethorpe (1696-1785)--Georgia
       settlement--1730's--Romance--Good research.

1790 Eunson, Dale. Homestead. New York: Farrar, 1935.
       311p.
            Montana--Early 1900's--Cattlemen v. homesteaders.

1791 Eustis, Helen. The fool killer. New York: Doubleday,
       1954. 219p.
            Good picture--Twelve year old boy American
       midwest--Post-Civil War--cf. Catcher In The Rye.

     Evan, Paul pseud. see Lehman, Paul Evan

                              142

Evans, Augusta Jane (1835-1909) see Wilson, Augusta
   Jane (Evans)

Evans, Evan pseud. see Faust, Frederick S. (1892-1944)

1792 Evans, Florence (Wilkinson). The lady of the flag
      flowers. Chicago: Stone, 1899. 364p.
         Romance--Huron maiden.

1793 Evans, Muriel Naomi (1908-   ) pseud. Newsom, Ed.
      Ride the high places. Boston: Little, 1954. 294p.
      Western

1794 ---Wagons to tucson. Boston: Little, 1954. 276p.
      Western

1795 ---Cherokee. Boston: Little, 1955. 238p.
      Western

1796 Evarts, Hal George (1887-   ). Tumbleweeds. Boston:
      Little, 1923. 297p.
         Opening of Cherokee Strip--Romance.

1797 ---Spanish acres. Boston: Little, 1925. 303p.
      Western

1798 ---Painted stallion. Boston: Little, 1926. 267p.
      Western

1799 ---The moccasin telegraph. Boston: Little, 1927.
      275p.
         Artic Circle.

1800 ---Fur brigade; a story of the trappers of the early
      west. Boston: Little, 1928. 279p.
         Romantic thriller--1815-1835.

1801 ---Tomahawk rights. Boston: Little, 1929. 319p.
         Days of Daniel Boone--Good Indian point of view.

1802 ---The shaggy legion. Boston: Little, 1930. 307p.
         Narrative of vanishing of buffalo herds--
      Romance--Author Kansas born and bred--Has historic
      value.

1803 ---Shortgrass. Boston: Little, 1932. 309p.
      Western

1804 ---Wolf dog. New York: Doubleday, 1935. 304p.

Everett, Wade pseud. see Cook, William Everett

Everitt, Pell John Leggett jt. author, see Perry,
   Clair Willard

143

1805 Everson, Florence McClurg and Power, Effie Louise.
Early days in ohio; a story of a pioneer family of
the western reserve. New York: Dutton, 1928. 265p.
Cleveland and vicinity.

1806 Ewell, Alice Maude. A white guard to satan; being an
account of mine own adventures and observation in
that time of the trouble in virginia now called
bacon's rebellion, which same did take place in...
1676 by mistress elizabeth godstowe. recovered by
a. m. ewell. Boston: Houghton, 1900. 187p.

Expension Agent see Morford, Henry

1807 Eyssen, Mrs. Marguerite. Go-devil. New York: Doubleday,
1947. 314p.
Opening oil country in Pennsylvania.

1808 Eyster, Mrs. Nellie (Blessing) (-1922). A colonial
boy; or, the treasures of an old link closet.
Boston: Lothrop, 1889. 294p.
Two boys--1880's and colonial era--Diary--
Juvenile.

1809 ---A chinese quaker; an unfictious novel. New York:
Revell, 1902. 377p.
Chinese in California.

144

1810   Fairbank, Janet Ayer.   The bright land.   Boston:
       Houghton, 1932.   525p.
              New Hampshire girls and woman to pioneer life
       Galena, Illinois--1830's.

1811   Falkner, William C.   The white rose of memphis; a novel.
       New York: Carleton, 1881.   531p.
              Steamboat on Mississippi River.

1812   ---The little brick church; a novel.   Philadelphia:
       Lippincott, 1882.   429p.
              Before and during American Revolution.

1813   Faralla, Dana.   A circle of trees.   Philadelphia:
       Lippincott, 1955.   221p.
              Danish to Minnesota prairie--1800's.

1814   Fargo, Lucile Foster (1880-   ).   Prairie girl.   New
       York: Dodd, 1937.   276p.
              Dakota town--1800's and 1890's--World's Fair--
       Women's Rights--Blizzard--Juvenile.

1815   ---Come, colors come.   New York: Dodd, 1940.   283p.
              Coeur d'Alene mining country of northern Idaho--
       1880's--Juvenile.

1816   ---Prairie chautauqua.   New York: Dodd, 1943.   254p.
              Chautauqua--Duck Lake, South Dakota--Juvenile.

1817   Farmer, James Eugene (1867-1915).   Brinton eliot; from
       yale to yorktown.   New York: Macmillan, 1902.   395p.
              Anti-British--1767-1776.

1818   Farnol, Jeffery (1878-   ).   A pageant of victory.
       Boston: Little, 1936.   371p.
              Chronicle--Three generations of Falconbridge
       family.

1819   Farrar, Rowena Rutherford.   Bend your heads all; a novel.
       New York: Holt, 1965.   288p.
              Revolutionary era--Pioneering in Nashville,
       Tennessee.

1820   Farrell, Cliff.   Follow the new grass.   New York:
       Random, 1955.   264p.
              Western

1821   ---West with the missouri.   New York: Random, 1955.   264p.
              Western

145

1822 ---Santa fé wagon boss. New York: Doubleday, 1958.
189p.
Western

1823 ---Ride the wild trail. New York: Doubleday, 1959.
191p.
Western

1824 ---Fort deception. New York: Doubleday, 1960. 189p.
Western

1825 ---The lean rider. New York: Doubleday, 1960. 192p.
Western

1826 ---Trail of the tattered star; a historical novel of
the west. New York: Doubleday, 1961. 190p.
Western

1827 ---The walking hills. New York: Doubleday, 1962. 183p.
Western

1828 ---Ride the wild country. New York: Doubleday, 1963.
192p.
Western

1829 ---Return of the long riders. New York: Doubleday,
1964. 192p.
Western

1830 ---Bucko. New York: Doubleday, 1965. 192p.
Western

1831 ---Cross-fire. New York: Doubleday, 1965. 192p.
Western

1832 ---Comanch'. New York: Doubleday, 1966. 188p.
Western

1833 ---The guns of judgment day. New York: Doubleday,
1967. 190p.
Western

1834 Farris, Jack (1921-   ). Ramey. Philadelphia:
Lippincott, 1953. 250p.

1835 ---A man to ride with. Philadelphia: Lippincott, 1957.
222p.
"Half-breed"--Pioneer life Vermont.

1836 Fast, Howard Melvin (1914-   ). Two valleys. New
York: Dial, 1933. 293p.
American Revolution--Fort Pitt area.

1837 ---Strange yesterday. New York: Dodd, 1934. 273p.
Chronicle of five generations--Colonial era to
date.

1838 ---Conceived in liberty; a novel of valley forge.
      New York: Simon, 1939. 389p.
           American Revolution--Grim--Realistic--Valley
      Forge, Pennsylvania--Experienced through private frc
      Mohawk Valley.

1839 ---Haym solomon, son of liberty. New York: Messner,
      1941. 243p.
           1740-1785.

1840 ---The last frontier. New York: Duell, 1941. 307p.
           Cheyenne--Flight from Oklahoma to Montana--
      1878--Reservation life.

1841 ---The tall hunter. New York: Harper, 1942. 103p.
           Daniel Boone--Kentucky--John Chapman (1774-
      1845)--Juvenile.

1842 ---Unvanquished. New York: Duell, 1942. 316p.
           American Revolution--From Battle of Brooklyn
      to Trenton--Good picture of George Washington.

1843 ---Citizen tom paine. New York: Duell, 1943. 341p.
           1737-1809--Vivid picture.

1844 ---Freedom road. New York: Duell, 1944. 263p.
           Reconstruction--South--Whites and blacks
      work together for a few years.

1845 ---The proud and the free. Boston: Little, 1950.
      311p.
           Revolt of 11th Regiment of Pennsylvania Line
      on New Year's Day 1781--General Wayne--Well drawn--
      Persuasive novel.

1846 ---April morning; a novel. New York: Crown, 1961.
      184p.
           American Revolution--Lexington-Concord--Very
      good--Fifteen year old tells of experiences in
      realistic fashion.

1847 Faulkner, Fritz. Windless sky. New York: Covici,
      1937. 225p.
           First novel-- 1870 backwoods American settlement.

1848 Faulkner, Nancy. Undecided heart. New York: Double-
      day, 1957. 207p.
           Virginia--American Revolution--Romance--Girl's
      father Tory--Brother and boyfriend patriots--Juvenile.

1849 ---Tomahawk shadow. New York: Doubleday, 1959. 215p.
           King Philip's War--Rhode Island--Roger Williams--
      Juvenile.

1850 Faulkner, William (1897-1962). "Absalom, absalom!"

New York: Random, 1936. 384p.
Mississippi plantation--1830's.

1851   Faust, Fredrick Schiller (1892-1944). Dan barry's
       daughter. New York: Putnam, 1924. 353p.
       Western

1852   ---pseud. Austin, Frank. The return of the rancher.
       New York: Dodd, 1933. 268p.
       Western

1853   ---The sheriff rides. New York: Dodd, 1934. 299p.
       Western

1854   ---King of the range. New York: Dodd, 1935. 300p.
       Western

1855   ---pseud. Baxter, George Owen. Free range lanning; a
       western story. New York: Chelsea, 1921. 303p.
       Western

1856   ---Donnegan; a western story. New York: Chelsea, 1923.
       320p.
              Western

1857   ---The long, long trail; a western story. New York:
       Chelsea, 1923. 320p.
       Western

1858   ---The range-land avenger; a western story. New York:
       Chelsea, 1924. 319p.
       Western

1859   ---The shadow of silver tip. New York: Chelsea, 1925.
       311p.
              Western

1860   ---Train's trust; a western story. New York: Burt,
       1925. 320p.
       Western

1861   ---Wooden guns; a western story. New York: Chelsea,
       1925. 318p.
       Western

1862   ---The whispering outlaw; a western story. New York:
       Chelsea, 1926. 320p.
       Western

1863   ---The trail to san triste; a western story. New York:
       Chelsea, 1927. 318p.
       Western

1864   ---Tiger men. New York: Macaulay, 1929. 309p.
       Western

1865 ---The killers. New York: Macaulay, 1931. 310p.
     Western

1866 ---Call of the blood. New York: Macaulay, 1934. 316p.
     Western

1867 ---Red devil of the range. New York: Macaulay, 1934.
     320p.
     Western

1868 ---Brother of the cheyennes. New York: Macaulay, 1935.
     320p.
     Western

1869 ---pseud. Brand, Max. The untamed. New York: Putnam,
     1919. 374p.
     Western

1870 ---The night horseman. New York: Putnam, 1920. 379p.
     Western

1871 ---Trailin'! New York: Putnam, 1920. 375p.
     Western

1872 ---The seventh man. New York: Putnam, 1921. 332p.
     Western

1873 ---Alcatraz. New York: Putnam, 1923. 325p.
     Western

1874 ---Fire-brain. New York: Putnam, 1926. 391p.
     Western

1875 ---The blue jay. New York: Dodd, 1927. 267p.
     Western

1876 ---Pillar mountain; a western story. New York: Dodd,
     1928. 314p.
     Western

1877 ---Pleasant jim. New York: Dodd, 1928. 276p.
     Western

1878 ---The gun tamer. New York: Dodd, 1929. 283p.
     Western

1879 ---Mistral. New York: Dodd, 1929. 315p.
     Western

1880 ---Destry rides again. New York: Dodd, 1930. 296p.
     Western

1881 ---Mystery ranch. New York: Dodd, 1930. 270p.
     Western

1882 ---The happy valley. New York: Dodd, 1931. 289p.
Western

1883 ---Smiling charlie. New York: Dodd, 1931. 312p.
Western

1884 ---The jackson trail. New York: Dodd, 1932. 285p.
Western

1885 ---Twenty notches. New York: Dodd, 1932. 271p.
Western

1886 ---Valley vultures. New York: Dodd, 1932. 310p.
Western

1887 ---The longhorn feud. New York: Dodd, 1933. 280p.
Western

1888 ---The outlaw. New York: Dodd, 1933. 298p.
Western

1889 ---Slow joe. New York: Dodd, 1933. 299p.
Western

1890 ---The thunderer. New York: Dearydale, 1933. 202p.
Western

1891 ---Brothers on the trail. New York: Dodd, 1934. 234p.
Western

1892 ---The rancher's revenge. New York: Dodd, 1934. 309p.
Western

1893 ---Timbal gulch trail. New York: Dodd, 1934. 257p.
Western

1894 ---Hunted riders. New York: Dodd, 1935. 300p.
Western

1895 ---Rustlers of beacon creek. New York: Dodd, 1935.
300p.
Western

1896 ---The seven of diamonds. New York: Dodd, 1935. 301p.
Western

1897 ---Happy jack. New York: Dodd, 1936. 309p.
Western

1898 ---The king bird rides. New York: Dodd, 1936. 302p.
Western

1899 ---South of rio grande. New York: Dodd, 1936. 302p.
Western

1900 ---Six golden angels. New York: Dodd, 1937. 269p.
Western

1901 ---The streak. New York: Dodd, 1937. 264p.
Western

1902 ---Trouble trail. New York: Dodd, 1937. 304p.
Western

1903 ---Dead or alive. New York: Dodd, 1938. 300p.
Western

1904 ---The iron trail. New York: Dodd, 1938. 295p.
Western

1905 ---Singing guns. New York: Dodd, 1938. 280p.
Western

1906 ---Fightin' fool. New York: Dodd, 1939. 246p.
Western

1907 ---Gunman's gold. New York: Dodd, 1939. 277p.
Western

1908 ---Marble face. New York: Dodd, 1939. 280p.
Western

1909 ---Danger trail. New York: Dodd, 1940. 311p.
Western

1910 ---The dude. New York: Dodd, 1940. 298p.
Western

1911 ---Riders of the plains. New York: Dodd, 1940. 279p.
Western

1912 ---The border kid. New York: Dodd, 1941. 303p.
Western

1913 ---The long chance. New York: Dodd, 1941. 299p.
Western

1914 ---Vengeance trail. New York: Dodd, 1941. 305p.
Western

1915 ---The man from mustang; a silvertip story. New York:
Dodd, 1942. 252p.
Western

1916 ---Silvertip. New York: Dodd, 1942. 226p.
Western

1917 ---Silvertip's strike. New York: Dodd, 1942. 226p.
Western

1918 ---Silvertip's trap. New York: Dodd, 1943. 216p.
Western

1919 ---Valley of vanishing men. New York: Dodd, 1947.
199p.
Western

1920 ---Larramee's ranch. New York: Watts, 1967. 207p.
Western--c. 1924.

1921 ---Rippon rides double. New York: Dodd, 1968. 216p.
Western--Since death of Faust his material
which appeared in magazines now being published--
c. 1930.

1922 ---The stingaree. New York: Dodd, 1968. 256p.
Western--c. 1930.

1923 ---Thunder moon. New York: Dodd, 1969. 180p.
Western--c. 1927.

1924 ---pseud. Evan Evans. The border bandit. New York:
Harper, 1926. 245p.
Western

1925 ---Montana rides! New York: Harper, 1933. 300p.
Western

1926 ---Montana rides again. New York: Harper, 1934. 253p.
Western

1927 ---Song of the whip. New York: Harper, 1936. 261p.
Western

1928 ---The rescue of broken arrow. New York: Harper,
1948. 249p.
Western

1929 Fay, Theodore Sedgwick (1807-1898). Herbert wendall;
a tale of the revolution. New York: Harper, 1835.
2 vols.
Wright "An advertisement attributes this title
to T. S. Fay".

1930 ---Hoboken; a romance of new york. New York: Harper,
1843. 2 vols.
Moralistic romance.

Fearing, Kenneth jt. author, see Friede, Donald

1931 Feikema, Feike Fredrick (1912-   ). The golden
bowl. St. Paul, Minnesota: Webb, 1944. 226p.
Oklahoma farmer.

1932 ---This is the year. New York: Doubleday, 1947. 623p.

Detailed chronicle of Frisan farmer in northwest Iowa--1916-1936--Meyer,"One of the most sig-
nificant farm novels in recent years".

1933 ---Lord grizzly. New York: McGraw, 1954. 281p.
Hugh Glass, mountain man--1820's--Clawed by
grizzly.

1934 ---Conquering horse; a novel. New York: McDowell, 1959.
355p.
Yankton Sioux--Horse culture--Boy's search for
vision regarding manhood.

1935 ---Scarlet plume. New York: Trident, 1964. 365p.
Massacre of missionaries.

1936 Feld, Rose Caroline (1895-   ). Heritage. New York:
Knopf, 1928. 300p.
First novel--Three generations--New Hampshire
farm.

1937 Felton, Ronald Oliver pseud. Welch, Ronald. Mohawk
valley. New York: Criterion, 1958. 226p.
French-Indian War (1754-1763)--Juvenile.

1938 Ferber, Edna (1887-1968). Cimarron. New York: Doubleday, 1930. 388p.
Oklahoma--1889-1930--Opening of Cherokee Strip.

1939 ---American beauty. New York: Doubleday, 1931. 313p.
Chronicle of slow decadence of family and farm--
Two hundred years--1700 Captain Oakes in Connecticut.

1940 ---Come and get it. New York: Doubleday, 1935. 518p.
Chronicle--American family--1850-1929--Wis-
consin lumbering.

1941 ---Great son. New York: Doubleday, 1945. 281p.
Chronicle four generations--Seattle family--
1851-1941.

1942 ---Ice palace. New York: Doubleday, 1958. 411p.
Chronicle--Alaska--Pioneer to statehood.

1943 Ferguson, Blanche Smith. Boxwood. Philadelphia:
Penn, 1935. 314p.
Maryland aristocrat v. lumber-oil millionaire--
Western.

1944 Ferguson, Thompson B.. The jayhawkers; a tale of the
border war. kansas in the early days. Guthrie,
Oklahoma: State Capital Printing Co., 1892. 415p.

1945 Fergusson, Harvey (1890-   ). Blood of the conquerors.
New York: Knopf, 1921. 265p.

153

#1 of Trilogy--First novel--Decay of Spanish
family--One of southwest's first authentic realists.

1946 ---Wolf song. New York: Knopf, 1927. 206p.
#2 of Trilogy southwest--Kit Carson--Sam Lash--
Mountain men--Good color.

1947 ---In those days; an impression of change. New York:
Knopf, 1929. 267p.
#3 of Trilogy southwest--Rio Grande--Days of
wagon trains to 1920's.

1948 ---Footloose mcgarnigle. New York: Knopf, 1930. 274p.
Life in artist colonies of Sante Fé and Taos.

1949 ---Followers of the sun; a trilogy of the santa fé
trail. wolf song, in those days, the blood of
conquerors. New York: Knopf, 1936. 75p.

1950 ---The life of riley. New York: Knopf, 1937. 328p.
Son of saloon keeper--Southwest frontier town.

1951 ---Grant of kingdom; a novel. New York: Morrow,
1950. 311p.
Centers about Lucien Maxwell Land Grant
1,750,000 acres--Wide sweep of western history--
Excellent.

1952 ---The conquest of don pedro. New York: Morrow, 1954.
250p.
Frontier town New Mexico--1865-1870's--Four-
teenth of published works--Social history.

1953 Fernald, Mrs. Helen(Clark). Smoke blows west. New
York: Longmans, 1937. 288p.
Neosho Bend, Kansas--1866--Railroad right-
of-way--From father's manuscript--Juvenile.

1954 ---and Slocombe, Edwin M.. The scarlet fringe.
New York: Longmans, 1931. 236p.
Peruvian Conquest (1522-1548)--How Paullu--
Descendent first rulers of Incas--Fine story.

1955 Ferrell, Elizabeth and Ferrell, Margaret. Full of
thy riches. New York: Mill, 1944. 315p.
Quaker girl and elderly husband--From Philadelphia to West Virginia--1860's--Romance.

Ferrell, Margaret jt. author, see Ferrell, Elizabeth

1956 Fessenden, Laura Dayton (-1924). A colonial dame;
a pen-picture of colonial days and ways. Chicago:
Rand McNally, 1897. 116p.

1957 Feuchtwanger, Lion (1884-1958). Proud destiny; a novel.

154

New York: Viking, 1947.   625p.
       B. Franklin--Beaumarchais--Parisian society.

1958   Field, Ben (1901-   ).   The outside leaf.   New York:
      Reynal, 1943.   237p.
          First novel--Tobacco grower--Connecticut Valley--
      Son of Jewish immigrant.

1959   ---The last freshet.   New York: Doubleday, 1948.   280p.
          Logging--Upper Delaware River--Regional.

1960   Field, Mrs. Elsie (Kimmell).   Prairie winter.   New
      York: Lothrop, 1959.   160p.
          Early 1900 family from Iowa to Dakota land
      claim--Homesteading days.

Field, Frank Chester pseud. see Robertson, Frank Chester

1961   Field, Peter pseud. East, Fred (1895-   ).   Repp,
      edward; mustang mesa.   [np], 1937.
          National Union Catalog List 1953-1957 states
      that Field, Peter is pseudonym for Mann, E. B. and
      East, Fred--Titles carried under Field, Peter for
      these years.

1962   ---Canyon of death.   New York: Jefferson, 1953.   215p.
      Western

1963   ---Dig the spurs deep; a powder valley western.   New
      York: Jefferson, 1953.   215p.
      Western

1964   ---Guns roaring west; a powder valley western.   New
      York: Jefferson, 1953.   224p.
      Western

1965   ---Montana maverick; a powder valley western.   New
      York: Jefferson, 1953.   217p.
      Western

1966   ---Maverick's return.   New York: Jefferson, 1954.   217p.
      Western

1967   ---Powder valley deadlock.   New York: Jefferson, 1954.
      246p.
      Western

1968   ---Powder valley stampede.   New York: Jefferson, 1954.
      213p.
      Western

1969   ---Ride for trinidad; a powder valley western.   New
      York: Jefferson, 1954.   246p.
      Western

1970 ---Breakneck pass; a powder valley western. New
York: Jefferson, 1955. 224p.
Western

1971 ---Outlaw of castle canyon; a powder valley western.
New York: Jefferson, 1955. 224p.
Western

1972 ---Rawhide rider; a powder valley western. New York:
Jefferson, 1955. 252p.
Western

1973 ---Saddles to santa fe! a powder valley western. New
York: Jefferson, 1955. 224p.
Western

1974 ---Powder valley renegade. New York: Jefferson, 1956.
248p.
Western

1975 ---Strike for tomahawk; a powder valley western. New
York: Jefferson, 1956. 252p.
Western

1976 ---Wild horse lightning; a powder valley western.
New York: Jefferson, 1956. 256p.
Western

1977 ---Guns for grizzly flat; a powder valley western.
New York: Jefferson, 1957. 253p.
Western

1978 ---Man from robber's roost; a powder valley western.
New York: Jefferson, 1957. 224p.
Western

1979 ---Powder valley manhunt. New York: Jefferson, 1957.
249p.
Western

1980 ---Raiders at medicine bow. New York: Jefferson, 1957.
224p.
Western

1981 ---Sheriff wanted! New York: Pocket, 1957 [c.1949].
150p.
Western

1982 ---Hangman's trail; a powder valley western. New
York: Jefferson, 1958. 223p.
Western

1983 ---Rimrock riders. New York: Jefferson, 1958. 250p.
Western

1984 ---<u>Rustler's rock</u>. New York: Jefferson, 1958. 250p.
       Western

1985 ---<u>Sagebrush swindle</u>. New York: Jefferson, 1958.
       224p.
           Western

1986 ---<u>Drive for devil's river; a powder valley western</u>.
       New York: Jefferson, 1959. 253p.
           Western

1987 ---<u>Outlaw express; a powder valley western</u>. New York:
       Jefferson, 1959. 252p.
           Western

1988 ---<u>Trail to troublesome; a powder valley western</u>.
       New York: Jefferson, 1959. 254p.
           Western

1989 ---<u>Doublecross canyon</u>. New York: Jefferson, 1960.
       252p.
           Western

1990 ---<u>Powder valley plunder</u>. New York: Jefferson, 1960.
       255p.
           Western

1991 ---<u>Rattlesnake range</u>. New York: Jefferson, 1961.
       253p.
           Western

1992 ---<u>Wolf pack trail</u>. New York: Jefferson, 1961. 253p.
           Western

1993 ---<u>Cougar canyon; a powder valley western</u>. New York:
       Jefferson, 1962. 223p.
           Western

1994 ---<u>The outlaw herd</u>. New York: Jefferson, 1962. 252p.
           Western

1995 ---<u>Powder valley ransom</u>. New York: Jefferson, 1962.
       223p.
           Western

1996 ---<u>Outlaw deputy</u>. New York: Jefferson, 1963. 223p.
           Western

1997 ---<u>Powder valley getaway</u>. New York: Jefferson, 1963.
       223p.
           Western

1998 ---<u>Trail through tascosa</u>. New York: Jefferson, 1963.
       224p.
           Western

157

1999 ---Rustlers' empire. New York: Jefferson, 1964. 190p.
      Western

2000 ---Feud at silvermine. New York: Jefferson, 1965. 221p.
      Western

2001 Field, Rachael Lyman. Hitty; her first hundred years.
      New York: Macmillan, 1929. 207p.
          Memoirs of wooden doll--Starts in Maine.

2002 Fields, Mrs. Ada M.. Altha; or, shells from the strand.
      Boston: French, 1856. 300p.

2003 Fields, Johathan. Memoirs of dunstan barr. New York:
      Coward, 1959. 382p.
          Chronicle family and land--Four generations--
      Rural Illinois--1890-1929.

2004 Fierro Blanco, Antonio de (trans. de Steiguer, Walter).
      Journey of the flame, being an account of one year
      in the life of señor don juan obrigón, known during
      the past years in the three californias as juan
      colorado, and to the indiada of the same as the
      flame, born at san josé arroyo, lower california,
      mexico, in 1798, and having seen three centuries of
      change customs and manners, died alone in 1902 at
      the great cardon, near rosario, mexico, with his
      face toward the south. Boston: Houghton, 1933. 294p.
          Understanding of Mexican temper--Vaquero--1810--
      Excellent.

2005 Findley, Mrs. Francine. Treeless eden. New York:
      King, 1934. 416p.
          Sacramento Valley, California--Ranching 1860's.

2006 ---From what dark roots. New York: Harper, 1940. 292p.
          Family chronicle--Southerner to Malone, New
      York--1839-1860.

2007 Finger, Charles Joseph (1871-1941). Courageous
      companions. New York: Longmans, 1929. 304p.
          English boy sails with Magellan--Colorful--
      Excellent--Juvenile.

2008 ---Cape horn snorter; a story of the war of 1812 and of
      gallant days with captain porter of the u. s. frigate,
      essex. Boston: Houghton, 1939. 263p.
          New England shippers--David Porter (1780-1843).

2009 Finney, Mrs. Gertrude Elva (Bridgeman). Muskets along
      the chickhominy. New York: Longmans, 1953. 242p.
          Virginia--Bacon's Rebellion--Exiles return to
      get land--Juvenile.

2010 ---The plums hang high. New York: Longmans, 1955. 312p.

English to middle-west--Two generations--1868-
1890.

2011 ---Is this my love? New York: Longmans, 1956. 228p.
Girl to Jamestown, Virginia as bride--Juvenile.

2012 ---Stormy winter. New York: Longmans, 1959. 246p.
San Juan Island, Puget Sound--1840's-1850's--
Boundary dispute--Juvenile.

2013 Fish, Rachel Ann. The running iron. New York: Coward,
1957. 380p.
Chronicle--Family to Wisconsin territory--
1860's--Indians--Cattle wars.

2014 Fisher, Mrs. Ann (Benson) (1898-   ). Cathedral
in the sun. New York: Carlyle, 1940. 408p.
Chronicle--Three generations--San Carlos
Borromeo Mission--1818-1882.

Fisher, Clay pseud. see Allen, Henry (1912-   )

Fisher, Evelyn Anne (Benson) (1898-   ) see Fisher,
Anne (Benson)

2015 Fisher, John. To dream again. New York: Holt, 1933.
282p.
Hawaiian Islands--Last days of monarchy.

2016 Fisher, Vardis Alvero (1895-   ). Toilers of the hills.
Boston: Houghton, 1928. 361p.
First book of prose--Repressive effect of
frontier life in Idaho hills--Very good.

2017 ---Dark bridwell. Boston: Houghton, 1931. 376p.
Idaho homestead--Powerful story--Twenty-one
years.

2018 ---In tragic life. Caldwell, Idaho: Caxton, 1932. 464p.
#1 of Vridar Hunter Tetralogy--Western farm
life.

2019 ---Passions spin the plot. Caldwell, Idaho: Caxton,
1934. 428p.
#2 of Hunter Tetralogy--Salt Lake.

2020 ---We are betrayed. New York: Doubleday, 1935. 369p.
#3 of Hunter Tetralogy.

2021 ---No villian need be. New York: Doubleday, 1936.
387p.
#4 of Hunter Tetralogy.

2022 ---Children of god; an american epic. New York: Harper,
1939. 769p.

Mormonism--Beginnings through migration--
Joseph Smith--Author from Mormon country.

2023 ---City of illusion; a novel. New York: Harper, 1941.
382p.
Virginia City, Nevada--Comstock Lode--Mrs.
Eilley (Orrum) Bowers (d.1903).

2024 ---The mothers; a saga of american courage. New York:
Vanguard, 1943. 334p.
Donner Party--1846--Follows record closely--
cf. Stewart, Ordeal By Hunger.

2025 ---Pemican; a novel of the hudson's bay company.
New York: Doubleday, 1956. 319p.
David McDonald hunter for company--Exciting
story.

2026 ---Tale of valor; a novel of the lewis and clark
expedition. New York: Doubleday, 1958. 456p.
Follows diary closely--Eight thousand mile
round trip--1804-1805.

2027 ---Orphans in gethsemane; a novel of the past in
the present. Denver: Swallow, 1960. 987p.
Twelfth in Testament of Man Series--Auto-
biographical.

2028 ---Mountain men; a novel of male and female in the
early american west. New York: Morrow, 1965.
372p.
Mountain Men--Rockies--1830's--Routine--
Indians--Sam Minard--Golden Spur Award one of
two best western historical novels--1966--West-
ern Heritage Wrangler Award outstanding western
novel--1966.

Flack, Marjorie jt. author, see Lomen, Helen

2029 Flannagan, Roy Catesby (1897-   ). Forest cavalier;
a romance of america's first frontier and of bacon's
rebellion. Indianapolis: Bobbs, 1952. 377p.
Virginia--1676.

2030 Fleishmann, Glen. While rivers flow. New York:
Macmillan, 1963. 489p.
Northern Georgia and Cherokee land.

2031 Fleming, A. M.. A soldier of the confederacy. Boston:
Meador, 1934. 345p.
Sam Houston--Texas--1836-1865--Plantation life.

2032 Fleming, Berry (1899-   ). The conqueror's stone.
New York: Day, 1927. 299p.
Plantation--Gentleman pirate--Carolina--1766--
Mystery.

2033   ---The lightwood tree. Philadelphia: Lippincott,
        1947. 378p.
            A Georgia community--1742, 1783, 1863, 1943.

2034   Fletcher, Mrs. Inglis (Clark) (1888-   ). Raleigh's
        eden; a novel. Indianapolis: Bobbs, 1940. 662p.
            First of long Carolina series--North Carolina--
        1765-1785--Coast plantation.

2035   ---Men of albemarle. Indianapolis: Bobbs, 1942. 566p.
            Carolina series--North Carolina 1710-1712--
        Morals and manners.

2036   ---Lusty wind for carolina. Indianapolis: Bobbs, 1944.
        509p.
            Carolina settlers--Huguenot settlers--Cape
        Fear--Adventure.

2037   ---Toil of the brave. Indianapolis: Bobbs, 1946.
        547p.
            Carolina series--Albemarle, North Carolina--
        American Revolution--1779-1780--Ends with King's
        Mountain--Romance--Adventure.

2038   ---Roanoke hundred; a novel. New York: Garden City
        Books, 1948. 492p.
            Based on Grenville Expedition to Roanoke--
        1585-1586--Sir Richard Grenville (1542-1591)--
        Life Elizabethian court--Very good.

2039   ---Bennett's welcome. New York: Garden City Books,
        1950. 451p.
            Carolina series--Sixth in series--North Carol-
        ina 1651-1652--Captain in army of Charles II to
        Virginia as indentured servant--Careful research.

2040   ---Queen's gift. Indianapolis: Bobbs, 1952. 448p.
            Carolina series--Seventh--North Carolina--
        Constitution of United States pivot--Details of
        ratification--1788-1789.

2041   ---The scotswoman. Indianapolis: Bobbs, 1954. 480p.
            Carolina series--North Carolina--1770's--
        Flora MacDonald (1722-1790).

2042   ---Wind in the forest. Indianapolis: Bobbs, 1957.
        448p.
            Carolina series--Regulator insurrection (1766-
        1771)--Ninth of series--Frontier v. tidewater.

2043   ---Cormorant's brood. Philadelphia: Lippincott,
        1959. 345p.
            Carolina series--Career of unscrupulus Gov-
        ernor George Burrington--Albemarle region.

2044 ---Wicked lady. Indianapolis: Bobbs, 1962. 256p.
American Revolution.

2045 ---Rogue's harbour. Indianapolis: Bobbs, 1964. 242p.

2046 Fletcher, John Gould (1886-   ). John smith--also
pocahontas. New York: Bretano's, 1928. 303p.
John Smith (1580-1631)--Pocohontas (d.1617).

2047 Flint, Margaret (1891-   ). The old ashburn place.
New York: Dodd, 1936. 301p.
New England farm novel.

2048 Flint, Timothy (1780-1840). Frances berrian; or, the
mexican patriot. Boston: Cummings, 1826. 2 vols.
Mexico, old and new--1815-1825--Second southwestern novel--Heroic deeds--Louisiana, Texas and
New Mexico.

2049 ---The life and adventures of arthur clenning...
Philadelphia: Towar, 1828. 2vols. in one.
Steal from DeFoe's, Robinson Crusoe--Man and
bride return from adventure to Birkbeck settlement
in Illinois.

2050 ---George mason, the young backwoodsman; or, 'don't
give up the ship'. a story of the mississippi.
Boston: Hilliard, 1829. 167p.
Mississippi and southwest.

2051 ---The lost child. Boston: Putnam, [1830?].
Not listed in Wright.

2052 ---The shoshonee valley; a romance. Cincinnati:
Flint, 1830. 2 vols.
First novel about mountain men--Antedates
W. Irving's Astoria by six years.

2053 Flisch, Julia A.. Old hurricane; a novel. New York:
Crowell, 1925. 356p.
Epic of soil--Land grant system of Georgia--
Pre-Civil War.

2054 Flood, Charles. Monmouth; a novel. Boston: Houghton,
1961. 349p.
American Revolution--1777-1778--Valley Forge--
Carefully researched.

2055 Fluharty, Vernon L. (1907-   ) pseud. Carder, Michael.
Cimarron crossing. Philadelphia: Macrae, 1951.
253p.
Western

2056 ---Action at war bow valley. Philadelphia: Macrae, 1952.
221p.
Western

162

2057 ---Return of the outlaw. Philadelphia: Macrae, 1954.
      221p.
            Western

2058 ---Decision at sundown. Philadelphia: Macrae, 1955.
      221p.
            Western

2059 ---pseud. O'Mara, Jim. Trial by gunsmoke. New York:
      Dutton, 1949. 254p.
            Western

2060 ---Wall of guns. New York: Dutton, 1950. 256p.
            Western

2061 ---Free grass. New York: Dutton, 1951. 252p.
            Western

2062 ---Death at war dance. New York: Dutton, 1952. 218p.
            Western

2063 ---Rustler of the owlhorns. New York: Dutton, 1952.
      224p.
            Western

2064 Flynn, Robert. North to yesterday. New York: Knopf,
      1967. 338p.
            First novel--Trail drive--Texas to Kansas--
      Bitter western.

2065 Foley, Pearl. The octagon crystal. New York: Carrier,
      1929. 273p.
            Chief Red Hawk--Last of Narragansetts.

2066 Foote, Mrs. Mary (Hallock) (1847-   ). The led-horse
      claim; a romance of the mining camp. Boston:
      Osgood, 1883. 279p.
            Western

2067 ---The royal americans. Boston: Houghton, 1910. 386p.
            Girl motherless after 1756 raid on Fort Ontario--
      Life in Dutch and English villages.

2068 ---A picked company; a novel. Boston: Houghton, 1912.
      416p.

2069 ---The valley road. Boston: Houghton, 1915. 359p.
            Mining--California--English man and family.

2070 Foote, Shelby. Tournament. New York: Dial, 1949.
      238p.
            Delta planter and family--Revive plantation
      after Civil War.

2071 Footner, Hulbert (1879-1944). The fur bringers; a

                              163

story of the canadian northwest. New York: McCann, 1920. 313p.
Trading posts--Indians--"Half breeds".

2072 ---A backwoods princess. New York: Doran, 1927. 320p.
Girl runs trading post--Romance--Adventure.

2073 ---Sailor of fortune; the life and adventures of commodore barney, u.s.n. New York: Harper, 1940. 323p.
Fictionalized biography--1759-1818.

2074 Forbes, Esther. A mirror for witches, in which is reflected the life, machinations, and death of famous doll bilby, who with a more than feminine perversity, preferred a demon to a mortal lover. here is also told how and why a righteous and most awful judgment befell her, destroying both corporeal body and immortal soul. Boston: Houghton, 1928. 213p.
Excellent--Salem witchcraft--1690's.

2075 ---Paradise. New York: Harcourt, 1937. 556p.
Panorama Puritan life--Established Canaan-- 1639--From Boston--Earthy picture--King Philip's War.

2076 ---General's lady. New York: Harcourt, 1938. 394p.
American Revolution--Wife of American general loves a British officer--1780-1781.

2077 ---Johnny tremain; a novel for old and young. Boston: Houghton, 1943. 256p.
American Revolution--Boston--Hero--Young boy apprenticed to silversmith.

2078 ---Running of the tide. Boston: Houghton, 1948. 632p.
Salem ship captain's--Salem life 1795-1812-- Golden age--Romance.

2079 ---Rainbow on the road. Boston: Houghton, 1953. 343p.
Itinerant portrait painter--New England 1830's-- Identity confusion with highwayman.

2080 Forbes-Lindsay, Charles Harcourt Ainslie (1860-   ). John smith, gentleman adventurer. Philadelphia: Lippincott, 1907. 304p.
1580-1631.

2081 Ford, Charles. Death sails with magellan. New York: Random, 1937. 363p.
Sailor with Magellan marooned on Guam--Rescued-- Magellan (d. 1521) pictured as meglomanic.

2082 Ford, Mrs. Elisabeth. No hour of history; a novel. New York: Washburn, 1940. 330p.

164

Chronicle--1630--World War I--Iowa.

2083 Ford, Paul Leicester (1865-1902). The honorable peter
sterling and what people thought of him. New York:
Holt, 1894. 417p.

2084 ---Janice meredith; a story of the american revolution.
New York: Dodd, 1899. 536p.
Romance--New Jersey and New York--1774 through
1781--All major figures appear.

2085 Foreman, Leonard London (1901-   ). Don desperado.
New York: Dutton, 1941. 285p.
Western

2086 ---The renegade. New York: Dutton, 1942. 285p.
Western

2087 ---The road to san jacinto. New York: Dutton, 1943.
285p.
Texas to 1846--Romance.

2088 ---Gunning for trouble. New York: Dutton, 1953. 191p.
Western

2089 ---Arrow in the dust. New York: Dell, 1954. 190p.
Western

2090 ---Woman of the avalon. New York: Dell, 1955. 191p.
Western

2091 ---Lone hand. New York: Dell, 1956. 192p.
Western

2092 ---Return of the texan. New York: Ballantine, 1958.
155p.
Western

2093 ---Desparation trail. New York: Doubleday, 1959. 190p.
Western

2094 ---Long rider. New York: Doubleday, 1961. 192p.
Western

2095 ---Spanish grant. New York: Doubleday, 1962. 191p.
Western

2096 ---Farewell to texas. New York: Doubleday, 1964. 180p.
Western

2097 ---The mustang trail. New York: Doubleday, 1965. 189p.
Western

2098 ---The silver flame. New York: Doubleday, 1966. 190p.
Western

2099   ---<u>Rogue's legacy</u>. New York: Doubleday, 1968.   167p.
        Western

2100   Forester, Cecil Scott (1899-   ). <u>To the indies</u>.
        Boston: Little, 1940.   298p.
        Cristoforo Colombo--Third voyage--Returns
        broken and in chains.

2101   ---<u>Captain from connecticut</u>. Boston: Little, 1941.
        344p.
        Blockade running--Jefferson's administration.

        Forester, Frank <u>pseud</u>. see Herbert, Henry William

2102   Forrest, Williams. <u>Trail of tears</u>. New York: Crown,
        1959.   247p.
        Cherokee Indians--Gold discovered on their
        land--John Ross--Removal to Oklahoma territory--
        1830's.

        Forsythe, Robert <u>pseud</u>. see Crichton, Kyle Samuel

2103   Fort, John Porter (1888-   ). <u>Stone daugherty</u>. New
        York: Dodd, 1929.   307p.
        Pioneer's v. Indians--Grim picture--Forest
        frontier.

2104   ---<u>God in the straw pen</u>. New York: Dodd, 1931.   234p.
        Methodist revival--Georgia--1830--Good on camp
        meeting--Powerful book.

2105   Fosdick, William Whiteman. <u>Malmiztic; the toltec and
        the cavaliers of the cross</u>. Cincinnati: Moore,
        1851.   356p.
        Montezuma--Cortes--16th century.

2106   Foster, Bennett. <u>Seven slash range</u>. New York: Morrow,
        1936.   274p.
        First western.

2107   ---<u>The cow thief trail</u>. New York: Morrow, 1937.   279p.
        Western

2108   ---<u>Pay-off at ladron</u>. New York: Morrow, 1937.   283p.
        Western

2109   ---<u>Badlands</u>. New York: Morrow, 1938.   282p.
        Western

2110   ---<u>Turn loose your wolf; a novel of the west</u>. New York:
        Morrow, 1938.   304p.
        Western

2111   ---<u>Blackleg range</u>. New York: Morrow, 1939.   279p.
        Western

2112 ---The mustangers. New York: Morrow, 1939. 284p.
      Western

2113 ---Rider of the rifle rock. New York: Morrow, 1939.
      279p.
      Western

2114 ---The owl hoot trail. New York: Morrow, 1940. 282p.
      Western

2115 ---Powdersmoke fence. New York: Doubleday, 1940. 277p.
      Western

2116 ---Dust of the trail. New York: Doubleday, 1941. 275p.
      Western

2117 ---The maverick. New York: Doubleday, 1942. 268p.
      Western

2118 ---Winter quarters. New York: Doubleday, 1942. 278p.
      Western

2119 ---Man tracks. New York: Doubleday, 1943. 249p.
      Western

2120 ---Turn loose your wolf. New York: Jefferson, 1948.
      304p.
      Western

2121 Foulke, William Dudley (1848-1935). Maya; a story
      of yucatan. New York: Putnam, 1900. 219p.
      Romance--16th century.

2122 Foust, Juana. Prairie chronicle. New York: Putnam,
      1932. 248p.
      Four generations--Collins clan--Southern planter
      and Cherokee wife--To Oklahoma and New Mexico--
      Panoramic.

2123 Fowler, Gene (1891-   ). Salute to yesterday. New
      York: Random, 1937. 365p.
      Picaresque tale--Denver--Modern--Old western
      rivals.

2124 Fox, Frances Barton pseud. Renard, Frances. Ridgeways.
      New York: Stokes, 1933. 463p.
      Chronicle Kentucky family--Five generations.

2125 Fox, John Jr. (1862-1919). The kentuckians; a novel.
      New York: Harper, 1898. 227p.
      Feud

2126 ---The little shepard of kingdom come. New York:
      Scribner's, 1903. 404p.
      Kentucky mountain people.

2127 ---Erskine dale, pioneer. New York: Scribner's, 1920.
          White boy raised by Indians--Two worlds--
      Juvenile.

2128 Fox, Marion. The bountiful hour. New York: Lane,
      1912. 320p.
          Romance--18th century--Girl's life from age
      six to marriage.

2129 Fraetas, Josiah A. pseud. Melville, J.. Ethan allen;
      or, the king's men. an historical novel. New York:
      Graham, 1846. 108p.

2130 ---The buckskin; or, the camp of the besiegers. a
      tale of the revolution. New York: Graham, 1847.
      98p.
          G. Washington and secret agents--Romance--
      Role of Washington similar to Mr. Harper in Cooper's
      The Spy.

2131 France, Lewis Browne. Over the old trail; a novel.
      Boston: Arena, 1895. 339p.
          Colorado mining.

2132 Frances pseud.. With the churchman early day. Lamoni,
      Iowa: 1891. 391p.
          Mormons to 1844.

2133 Franklin, Frieda Kenyon (1921-   ). The cleft in the
      rock. New York: Crowell, 1955. 250p.
          Alaska--Bridge building.

2134 Fraser, Georgia. Crow-step. New York: Witter, 1910.
      401p.
          Romance--New York--American Revolution.

2135 ---Princess royal. New York: Vinal, 1926. 103p.
          Pocahontas (d.1617).

2136 ---The white captain. Boston: Little, 1930. 319p.
          John Smith (1580-1631).

2137 Fraser, Mary Crawford (Mrs. Hugh Fraser). In the
      shadow of the lord; a romance of the washingtons.
      New York: Holt, 1906. 428p.

2138 Fraser, William Alexander (1859-   ). Red meekins.
      New York: Doran, 1921. 297p.
          Western

2139 Frazee, Theo D.. The farmer's niece; a romance of the
      mexican war. Newark, New Jersey: Heinz, 1892. 232p.

2140 Frazier, Mrs. Neta (Lohnes) (1890-   ). Young bill

168

fargo. New York: Longmans, 1956. 202p.
Lad sixteen--Journey with parents to Pacific
northwest-- 1869--Juvenile.

2141 Frazee, Steve. Shining mountains. New York: Rinehart,
1951. 248p.
Gold rush to Colorado--Post-Civil War--Adventure.

2142 ---Cry coyote. New York: Macmillan, 1955. 202p.
Western

2143 ---Spur to the smoke. New York: Perma Books, 1955.
208p.
Western

2144 ---Tumbling range woman. New York: Perma Books, 1956.
182p.
Western

2145 ---Desert guns. New York: Dell, 1957. 192p.
Western

2146 ---The alamo. New York: Hearst, 1960. 160p.
Western

2147 ---Hellsgrin. New York: Rinehart, 1960. 251p.
Western

2148 ---pseud. Jennings, Dean. Range trouble. New York:
Phoenix, 1951. 222p.
Western

2149 Frederic, Harold (1856-1898). Seth's brother's wife;
a study of life in greater new york. New York:
Scribner's, 1887. 405p.

2150 ---In the valley. New York: Scribner's, 1890. 427p.
Mohawk Valley, New York-- 1757- 1780--Dutchman
opposed to British tells story--Battle of Oriskany.

2151 ---The copperhead. New York: Scribner's, 1893. 197p.
New York farmer opposed to abolitionists.

2152 Frederick, John Towner (1893-   ). Druida. New York:
Knopf, 1923. 286p.
First novel--Farming--Red River Valley--Daughter
of farmer--Coarse.

2153 ---Green bush. New York: Knopf, 1925. 304p.
Defense of farming--Theme is "reconciliation
to the soil".

Freedgood, Morton jt. author, see Freedgood, Stanley

2154 Freedgood, Stanley and Freedgood, Morton pseud. Morton,

169

Stanley. Yankee trader; a novel. New York:
Sheridan House, 1947. 343p.
Connecticut trader--Pre-Revolution.

2155 Freeman, Mrs. Mary Eleanor (Wilkins) (1852-1930).
In colonial times; the adventures of ann, the bound
girl of samuel wales of braintree, in the province
of massachusetts bay. Boston: Lothrop, 1899. 115p.

2156 ---The heart's highway; a romance of virginia in the
seventeenth century. New York: Doubleday, 1900.
308p.
Tobacco riots after Bacon's Rebellion--1682.

2157 French, Alice pseud. Thanet, Octave. By inheritance.
Indianapolis: Bobbs, 1910. 394p.

2158 ---Expiation. New York: Scribner's, 1890. 215p.

2159 French, Allen (1870-1946). The colonials; being a
narrative of events chiefly connected with the
siege and evacuation of the town of boston in
new england. New York: Doubleday, 1902. 504p.
Anti-British--1772-1776--Historical details--
Events leading to Revolution.

2160 French, James Strange (1807-1886) .
Elkswatawa; or, the prophet of the west. a tale
of the frontier. New York: Harper, 1836. 2 vols.
Supposed author Timothy Flint--Kentucky hunter--
Tecumseh--1812-1814.

2161 French, Mrs. Maida (Parlow). Boughs bend over. New
York: Doubleday, 1944. 246p.
Saga of settlement of American loyalists who
fled from Albany at close of Revolution--To grants
in Canadian forests.

2162 Frey, Ruby Frazier (Parsons). Red morning. New York:
Putnam, 1946. 380p.
First novel--1750-1763--Ohio territory--French-
Indian War--John Frazier--Real character.

2163 Friede, Donald, Jones, H. Bedford, and Fearing, Kenneth
pseud. Bedford, Donald F.. John barry. New York:
Creative Age, 1947. 418p.
California--1846-1850--Rescue of the Donner
Party.

2164 Friedenthal, Richard [trans.] Lumley, Charles Hope.
White gods. New York: Harper, 1931. 424p.
(1485-1547)--Cortés and his mistress--Fiction-
alized account.

2165 Friel, Arthur Olney (1885-1959). Hard wood.

Philadelphia: Penn, 1925. 333p.
Shawangunk Mountains--Upper New York--Hudson
Valley frontier--Canal era.

2166 Friend, Oscar J.. Round-up; a story of ranchmen,
cowboys, rustlers, and bad-men happening in the
days when the great southwest was being won for
civilization. Chicago: McClurg, 1924. 373p.
Western

2167 Friermood, Mrs. Elizabeth Hamilton. Hoosier heritage.
New York: Doubleday, 1954. 221p.
From Indiana to Missouri and Kansas--Girl--
1879--Juvenile.

2168 Friesen, Gordon (1909-   ). Flamethrowers. Caldwell,
Idaho: Caxton, 1936. 490p.
Young man from Mennonite village in Kansas
off to Oklahoma college--Russian-German community.

2169 Fritz, Jean. Early thunder. New York: Coward, 1967.
255p.
Salem, Massachusetts--Tory boy converted to
patriot cause--American Revolution--Juvenile.

2170 Frost, Elizabeth (Hollister) Mrs. W. D. Blair. This
side of land; an island epic. New York: Coward,
1942. 464p.
Epic of Nantucket--Early 1800's--Diary of
Kezia Fanning (1775-1820)--Original idiom of island.

2171 Frost, John. Border wars of the west; comprising the
frontier wars of pennsylvania, virginia, kentucky,
ohio, indiana, illinois, tennessee and wisconsin.
Auburn: Derby, 1853. 608p.

2172 Frye, Pearl. Captain gallant; a biographical novel
based on the life of john paul jones. Boston:
Little, 1956. 324p.
J. P. Jones (1747-1792)--Good picture of era.

2173 Fuller, Edmund (1914-   ). A star pointed north.
New York: Harper, 1946. 361p.
Fictionalized biography--Frederick Douglass
(1817?-1895)--Abolitionist.

2174 Fuller, Hulbert. Vivian of virginia; being the memoirs
of our first rebellion by john vivian, esq. of
middle plantation, virginia. Boston: Lamson, 1897.
377p.
Bacon's Rebellion-1676.

2175 Fuller, Iola. The loon feather. New York: Harcourt,
1940. 419p.
Mackinac--Indian life on Lake Huron--

171

Early 1800's--Told by Oneta, daughter of Tecumseh--
Fictionalized biography--Fiction winner in Avery
and Jule Hopwood award contest 1939 at University
of Michigan.

2176 ---The shining trail. New York: Duell, 1943. 442p.
Black Hawk War--1832--Lead discovered on
Sauk Lands.

2177 ---The gilded torch. New York: Putnam, 1957. 343p.
Twin brothers with LaSalle (1643-1687)--Ex-
ploration--1680's and 1690's.

2178 Furman, Garrit. Redfield; a long island
tale of the seventeenth century. New York:
Wilder, 1825. 214p.

2179 Furnas, Joseph Chamberlain (1905-   ). The devil's
rainbow. New York: Harper, 1962. 341p.
Joseph Smith (1805-1844)--Smith as paranoic--
Good.

2180 Furnas, Marth Edith (Mrs. S. E. Stauffer) (1904-   ).
The far country. New York: Harper, 1947. 304p.
Diary form--Overland to California in 1840's--
Great migration.

2181   "G_____m," "F___nm". <u>L'Heroine du texas</u>. Paris:
Plancher, 1819. [trans.] by Joseph, Donald.
Book Club of Texas, 1937.
      Gaston--First southwestern novel--Author thought
to be member of Texas colony--Trinty River--1816-
1818.

2182   Gabriel, Gilbert Wolf (1890-   ). <u>I, james lewis</u>.
New York: Doubleday, 1932. 334p.
      Clerk on ship, "Tonquin"--Fur trading exped-
ition to Astor's Oregon 1811--Indian massacre.

2183   ---<u>I thee wed</u>. New York: Macmillan, 1948. 340p.
      Asylum in Pennsylvania for Marie Antoinette--
Her double part of escape plot--Susquehanna.

2184   Gaither, Mrs. Frances Ormond (Jones) (1889-1955).
<u>The painted arrow</u>. New York: Macmillan, 1931.
244p.
      Louisiana--Colonial period.

2185   ---<u>The scarlet coat</u>. New York: Macmillan, 1934.
205p.
      Boy from Canada with LaSalle (1643-1687).

2186   ---<u>Follow the drinking gourd</u>. New York: Macmillan,
1940. 270p.
      Drinking gourd =The great dipper, guide for
runaway slaves--Georgia and Alabama--Pre-Civil War--
Underground railroad.

2187   ---<u>The red cock crows</u>. New York: Macmillan, 1944.
313p.
      Northern schoolteacher describes Mississippi--
1835--Related to <u>John Brown's Body</u> and <u>Strange
Fruit</u>.

2188   ---<u>Double muscadine</u>. New York: Macmillan, 1949.
335p.
      Trial of yellow slave--Mississippi--1850's--
Good descriptions--Compassion.

2189   Gale, Elizabeth. <u>Katrina vanost and the silver rose</u>.
New York: Putnam, 1934. 294p.
      Twelve year old Dutch girl to New Amsterdam--
Juvenile.

2190   ---<u>The winged boat</u>. New York: Putnam, 1942. 190p.

Hudson's--"Half Moon"--Tribal life of Hudson
River Indians--Juvenile.

2191 The gambler; or, memoirs of a british officer, distinguished in the war of the american revolution. [Anon-
ymous]. 2nd Edition. Washington: Duane, 1802. 94p.

2192 Ganilh, Anthony. "By a Texan", pseud. Myrthe, A. T. or
Ganilh, Anthony. Mexico versus texas; a descriptive
novel, most of the characters of which consist of
living persons. Philadelphia: Siegfried, 1838. 348p.
Texas Revolution (1835-1836)--Published later
under title Ambrosio de Letinez; or, The first
Texian novel. 1842.

2193 ---Ambrosio de letinez; or, the first texian novel...
with incident's of the war of independence. New
York: Frances, 1842. 2 vols.
See Mexico verses Texas.

2194 Gann, Walter. The trail boss. Boston: Houghton, 1937.
244p.
Western

2195 Garangula, the ongua-honwa chief; a tale of indian life
among the mohawks and onondagas, two hundred years
ago. By a citizen of Milwaukee [Anonymous].
Milwaukee: Strickland, 1857. 160p.

2196 Gardiner, Dorothy. The golden lady. New York: Doubleday, 1936. 498p.
Daughter of gambler--From gold mining camps
in Colorado to English beauty--Returns Colorado
after World War I--cf. Karsner, Silver Dollar and
Fowler, Timberline.

2197 ---Snow-water. New York: Doubleday, 1939. 360p.
Chronicle of founder of Bartorville, Colorado--
Daniel Bartor (1868-1934).

2198 ---Great betrayal. New York: Doubleday, 1949. 301p.
Sand Creek Massacre 1864.

2199 Gardner, Mrs. H. C.. Mehetabel; a story of revolution.
New York: Nelson, 1875. 372p.

Garland, George pseud. see Roark, Garland

2200 Garland, Hamlin (1860-1940). A little norsk; or,
ol' pap's flaxen. New York: Appleton, 1892. 157p.

2201 ---A spoil of office; a story of the modern west.
Boston: Arena, 1892. 385p.
Populist movement 1890's--Good.

174

2202   ---Rose of dutcher's coolly. Chicago: Stone, 1895.
       403p.
              Success story--Leave farm--Succeed in city.

2203   ---Jason edwards; an average man. New York: Appleton,
       1897. 213p.
              New Hampshire--Farm not an escape for surplus
       urban population.

2204   ---Boy life on the prairies. New York: Macmillan, 1899.
       423p.

2205   ---The eagle's heart. New York: Appleton, 1900. 369p.
              Plains life.

2206   ---The captain of gray-horse troop; a novel. New York:
       Harper, 1902. 414p.
              Cattlemen v. Cheyenne--Montana--1890's.

2207   ---The long trail; a story of the northwest wilderness.
       New York: Harpers, 1907. 262p.
              Klondike Gold Rush--1898--Boy.

2208   ---The moccasin ranch; a story of dakota. New York:
       Harper, 1909. 136p.
              From Illinois to unbroken west--Romantic nov-
       elette--Impact of frontier on woman.

2209   ---Cavanagh, forest ranger; a romance of the mountain
       west. New York: Harper, 1910. 300p.
              Passing of old west ranger--Conservation.

2210   ---The forester's daughter; a romance of the bear-
       tooth range. New York: Harper, 1914. 286p.
              Forestry--Girl in Colorado mountains.

2211   ---Trail-makers of the middle border. New York:
       Macmillan, 1926. 426p.
              Maine and pioneering days in Wisconsin--
       Story of Garland's father.

2212   ---Back-trailers from the middle border. New York:
       Macmillan, 1928. 379p.
              Last of series--Son of Middle Border, Daughter
       of Middle Border, Trailmakers of the Middle Border--
       Return to east--Retreat from frontier.

2213   Gardner, Claud (1891-   ). Wetback; a novel. New
       York: Coward, 1947. 215p.
              Mexican farm laborers.

2214   ---Cornbread aristocrat. New York: Creative Age, 1950.
       328p.
              Early period--Arkansas territory.

175

2215   Garnett, David (1892-   ). Pocahontas; the nonparell
       of virginia. New York: Harcourt, 1933. 344p.
       Essentially Cooke interpretation.

2216   Garrett, Garet (1878-   ). Satan's bushel. New York:
       Dutton, 1924. 207p.
       Commodity speculation.

2217   Garst, Mrs. Doris (Shannon). Joe meek, man of the west.
       New York: Messner, 1954. 179p.
       Fictionalized biography--Joe Meek (1810-1875)--
       Trapper--Indian fighter--First U. S. Marshal in
       Oregon--Juvenile.

2218   Garth, David. Fire on the wind. New York: Putnam,
       1951. 378p.
       Michigan timber--Post Civil War--Romance--
       Railroad--Logging.

2219   Gash, Abram Dale. The false star; a tale of the
       occident. Chicago: Conkey, 1899. 578p.
       Anti-Mormon--Set in Utah.

2220   Gates, Doris (1901-   ). North fork. New York:
       Viking, 1945. 211p.
       Sierra Nevadas--Heir to lumber mills--Friend-
       ship of young lad with Indian boy.

2221   ---River ranch. New York: Viking, 1949. 160p.
       Modern cattle ranch--Rustlers--Trucks.

2222   Gates, Eleanor (Mrs. F. F. Moore) (1875-1951).
       The plow-woman. New York: McClure, 1906. 364p.
       Two Texas girls to Dakota claim--Romantic
       triangle.

2223   ---Pa hardy. New York: Green Circle Books, 1936.
       313p.
       Miner hit it rich in California--Local color.

2224   Gates, Henry Leyford (1880-   ). Paintrock canyon.
       New York: McBride, 1934. 287p.
       Western

2225   ---Riders to the dust. New York: McBride, 1936. 248p.
       Western

2226   Gay, Margaret Cooper. Hatchet in the sky; a novel.
       New York: Simon, 1954. 500p.
       Ojibway Indians under Chief Pontiac--Detroit--
       1763-64--French-Indian War--Pontiac's conspiracy.

2227   Gayarré, Charles Étienne Arthur. Aubert dubayet; or,
       the two sister republics. Boston: Osgood, 1882. 479p.
       Romance--American and French Revolutions.

2228   Gazer, Giles pseud.. Fredrick de algeroy; the hero
        of camden plains. a revolutionary tale. New York:
        Collins, 1825. 235p.
        Gothic tale--Battle of Camden--Kidnapping.

2229   Gébler, Ernest. The plymouth adventure; a chronicle
        of voyage of the mayflower. New York: Doubleday,
        1950. 377p.
        Reconstructed farm letters, journals, and
        histories--True picture--Documentary chronicle--
        Author Czech-Irish never in America.

2230   Gendron, Val. Powder and hides. New York: Longmans,
        1954. 230p.
        Plains Indians--Juvenile.

2231   Germano, Peter. Trail boss from texas. New York:
        Phoenix, 1948. 254p.
        First western.

2232   ---pseud. Cord, Barry. The gunsmoke trail. New York:
        Phoenix, 1951. 222p.
        Western

2233   ---Shadow valley. New York: Phoenix, 1951. 224p.
        Western

2234   ---Mesquite johnny. New York: Arcadia, 1952. 223p.
        Western

2235   ---Trail to sundown. New York: Arcadia, 1953. 220p.
        Western

2236   ---Cain basin. New York: Arcadia, 1954. 224p.
        Western

2237   ---The sagebrush kid. New York: Arcadia, 1954. 224p.
        Western

2238   ---Boss of barbed wire. New York: Arcadia, 1955.
        223p.
        Western

2239   ---Dry range. New York: Arcadia, 1955. 224p.
        Western

2240   ---The guns of hammer. New York: Arcadia, 1956. 224p.
        Western

2241   ---The gunshy kid. New York: Arcadia, 1957. 224p.
        Western

2242   ---Sheriff of big hat. New York: Arcadia, 1957. 224p.
        Western

2243 ---Concho valley. New York: Arcadia, 1958. 221p.
       Western

2244 ---A ranger called solitary. New York: Arcadia, 1966.
       189p.
       Western

2245 ---Canyon showdown. New York: Arcadia, 1967. 192p.
       Western

2246 ---Trouble in peaceful valley. New York: Arcadia,
       1968. 191p.
       Western

2247 ---pseud. Kane, Jim. Spanish gold. New York: Arcadia,
       1963. 221p.
       Western

2248 ---Lost canyon. New York: Arcadia, 1964. 191p.
       Western

2249 ---Red river sheriff. New York: Arcadia, 1965. 190p.
       Western

2250 ---Rendezvous at bitter wells. New York: Arcadia,
       1966. 191p.
       Western

2251 Gerson, Noel Bertram (1914-   ). Savage gentleman.
       New York: Doubleday, 1950. 306p.
            Queen Anne's War 1702-1713--People near Schen-
       ectady, New York--Benjamin Church (1639-1718).

2252 ---The mohawk ladder. New York: Doubleday, 1951.
       276p.
            Spanish Succession War 1701-1714 or Queen
       Anne's War.

2253 ---The cumberland rifles. New York: Doubleday, 1952.
       314p.
            Romance--Tennessee--1796--Free state of Franklin.

2254 ---The golden eagle. New York: Doubleday, 1953.
       313p.
            Mexican War (1845-1848)--Secret agent.

2255 ---The forest lord; a romantic adventure of 18th
       century charleston. New York: Doubleday, 1955.
       318p.
            English playboy shanghied to Charleston,
       South Carolina--Aratomahon--Chief of Westoes.

2256 ---The highwayman. New York: Doubleday, 1955. 288p.
            King George's War 1744-48--Capture of Louis-
       berg.

178

2257 ---Daughter of eve. New York: Doubleday, 1958. 320p.
　　　　　Pocahontas (d. 1617) based on Smith--Pocahontas
　　　is paragon.

2258 ---The land is bright. New York: Doubleday, 1961.
　　　356p.
　　　　　First years of Plymouth, Massachusetts--Wm.
　　　Bradford (1588-1657).

2259 ---Give me liberty; a novel of patrick henry. New
　　　York: Doubleday, 1966. 347p.
　　　　　1736-1799.

2260 ---I'll storm hell; a biographical novel of "mad
　　　anthony" wayne. New York: Doubleday, 1967. 302p.
　　　　　Anthony Wayne 1745-1796--Biographical novel.

2261 ---San houston; a biographical novel. New York:
　　　Doubleday, 1968. 297p.
　　　　　Sam Houston and events leading to Civil War.

2262 ---pseud. Vaughn, Carter. The invincibles. New York:
　　　Doubleday, 1958. 319p.
　　　　　King George's War 1744-1748--Financial scheming--
　　　Louisburg expedition.

2263 ---The wilderness. New York: Doubleday, 1959. 288p.
　　　　　King George's War 1744-1748.

2264 ---Scoundrel's brigade. New York: Doubleday, 1962.
　　　259p.
　　　　　Unit organized by George Washington to ferret
　　　out enemy counterfeiters--Melodrama--American
　　　Revolution.

2265 ---Dragon cove. New York: Doubleday, 1964. 248p.
　　　　　Rhode Island resistance--American Revolution.

2266 ---Roanoke warrior. New York: Doubleday, 1965. 251p.
　　　　　Tuscarora Indians Wars 1711-1713--North
　　　Carolina.

2267 ---Fortress fury; a romantic adventure of the 18th
　　　century. New York: Doubleday, 1966. 254p.
　　　　　Alleghany Mountains.

2268 ---The silver saber. New York: Doubleday, 1967. 248p.
　　　　　Indentured servant--Delaware 1680-1713.

2269 ---The river devils. New York: Doubleday, 1968. 239p.
　　　　　Mississippi barge men--Spain holds Louisiana.

2270 ---The seneca hostage. New York: Doubleday, 1969.
　　　234p.
　　　　　Romantic adventure--1753--Englishman taken by
　　　Indians.

2271 Gessner, Robert Joseph (1907-   ). Broken arrow.
New York: Farrar, 1933. 280p.
Levi Horse-Afraid--Oglala Sioux--Question of
agency Indian.

2272 ---Treason. New York: Scribner's, 1944. 383p.
Benedict Arnold (1741-1801)--Reasons why he
betrayed country--Parallel present.

2273 Gibbons, Robert Faucett. Bright is the morning. New
York: Knopf, 1943. 339p.
Well-to-do Alabama farm.

2274 Gibbons, Stella (1902-   ). Cold comfort farm. New
York: Longmans, 1932. 307p.
Satire of Seth's Brother's Wife.

2275 Gibbs, George Fort (1870-   ). In search of
mademoiselle. Philadelphia: Coates, 1901. 373p.
French and Spanish rivalry in early Florida--
Published in 1926 under title The Love of Mademoiselle.

2276 ---The flame of courage. New York: Appleton, 1926.
326p.
Romance--Actress of Rouen banished to Canada
by Madame de Pompodour--Pre-French-Indian War.

2277 ---The shores of romance. New York: Appleton, 1928.
292p.
New Orleans--War of 1812--Romance--Naval
officer and Jean LaFitte love same girl.

2278 ---Old philadelphia. New York: Appleton, 1931. 4 vol.
Four short romances--The Loyal Rebel-1770's--
Super Cargo-1790's--Autumn-1830's--North Star-1850's.

2279 Gibson, Eva Katherine (Clapp). A lucky mishap; a novel.
Chicago: Belford, 1883. 276p.
Kansas and Colorado.

2280 ---A woman's triumph; a true story of western life.
Chicago: Andrews, 1885. 80p.

2281 Gibson, Mrs. Jewel (1904-   ). Black gold. New
York: Random, 1950. 329p.
Texas oil boom--1900.

2282 Gibson, Katherine (1893-   ). Arrow fly home. New
York: Longmans, 1945. 146p.
Two white children with Shawnee--Days of Corn-
stalk and Logan--Juvenile.

2283 Giles, Henry Earl. Harbin's ridge. Boston: Houghton,
1951. 233p.
First novel--Kentucky hill people--cf. Jesse

Stuart--James Still--Elizabeth Roberts.

2284   Giles, Mrs. Janice Holt. Enduring hills. Philadelphia:
       Westminister, 1950. 256p.
              Kentucky Mountain region.

2285   ---Miss willie. Philadelphia: Westminister, 1951. 268p.
              Sequel to Enduring Hills, 1950--Schoolmarm from
       Texas to Piney Ridge, Kentucky.

2286   ---The Kentuckians. Boston: Houghton, 1953. 272p.
              #1 series of Kentucky--Kentucky part of Virginia
       --1769-1777--Opening by North Carolina speculators--
       Cherokee.

2287   ---The plum thicket. Boston: Houghton, 1954. 284p.
              Farm and village life in Arkansas ca.1900.

2288   ---Hannah fowler. Boston: Houghton, 1956. 312p.
              #2 of Kentucky series--To Boonesborough in
       1778--Women in Kentucky--Johnny Osage son of Fowler--
       Oklahoma 1820's.

2289   ---The believers. Boston: Houghton, 1957. 302p.
              #3 of Kentucky series--Rebecca Fowler daughter
       of Hannah Fowler--Follows husband to Kentucky--
       Shaker colony--1800's.

2290   ---The land beyond the mountains. Boston: Houghton,
       1958. 308p.
              #4 of Kentucky series--1783-1792--Wilkinson's
       treason--Cass Cartwright settlement near Frankfort--
       Romance.

2291   ---Johnny osage. Boston: Houghton, 1960. 313p.
              #5 of series--Son of Hannah Fowler--Osage--
       Pawnee--Cherokee--Trading post.

2292   ---Savanna. Boston: Houghton, 1961. 304p.
              #6 of series--Fort Gibson, Arkansas territory
       (Oklahoma)--Savanna-granddaughter of Hannah Fowler.

2293   ---Voyage to santa fé. Boston: Houghton, 1962. 327p.
              Wife of trader to Santa Fé.

2294   ---Six-horse hitch. Boston: Houghton, 1969. 448p.
              Overland mail--Stage coach drivers--1860's.

Giles, John Clifford jt. author, see Palmer, Bruce

2295   Gill, George Creswell. Beyond the blue grass; a
       kentucky novel. New York: Neale, 1908. 223p.
              Hills of Génseng country--Rural.

2296   Gill, Tom. Death rides the mesa. New York: Farrar,

181

1934. 309p.
Western

2297 ---<u>Starlight pass</u>. New York: Farrar, 1935. 316p.
Western

2298 ---<u>Red earth</u>. New York: Farrar, 1937. 314p.
Western

2299 ---<u>Firebrand</u>. New York: Farrar, 1939. 309p.
Western

2300 Gillmor, Frances (1903-   ). <u>Windsinger</u>. New York:
Minton, 1930. 218p.
Navajo prophet--Leader of tribal chants.

2301 ---<u>Fruit out of rock</u>. New York: Duell, 1940. 269p.
Arizona fruit growing region.

2302 Gillum, Charles W.. <u>Man goeth forth</u>. Boston: Humphries,
1932. 362p.
John Broadwood--From 1867 to death--Life of
pioneer.

2303 Gilman, Peter. <u>Diamond head; a novel</u>. New York:
Coward, 1960. 416p.
First novel--Hawaii--Not as good as Michener.

2304 Gilman, Samuel C.. <u>The story of a western claim;
a tale of how two boys solved the indian question</u>.
Philadelphia: Lippincott, 1893. 201p.
Juvenile

2305 Gipson, Frederick Benjamin (1908-   ). <u>Old yeller</u>.
New York: Harper, 1956. 158p.
Boy and dog--Life Texas prairie farm--1860.

2306 ---<u>Savage sam</u>. New York: Harper, 1962. 214p.
Fifteen year old boy and six year old girl--
Taken by Indians--Dog leads people to rescue.

2307 Glasgow, Ellen Anderson Gholson (1874-1945). <u>Barren
ground</u>. New York: Doubleday, 1925. 511p.
Realistic novel of south--Virginia--Great novel.

2308 ---<u>Vein of iron</u>. New York: Harcourt, 1935. 462p.
Great Valley of Virginia--1900-1932--Scot-
Presbyterians--Depression.

2309 Glaspell, Susan (Mrs. Norman Matson) (1882-1948).
<u>Brooks evans</u>. New York: Stokes, 1928. 312p.
Chronicle three generations--Prairie farm girl.

2310 Glasscock, Anne Bonner. <u>The disturbing death of
jenkin delaney</u>. New York: Doubleday, 1966. 181p.
Western

182

2311   ---pseud. Bonner, Michail. Kennedy's gold. New York:
       Doubleday, 1960. 191p.
       Western

2312   ---The iron noose. New York: Doubleday, 1961. 186p.
       Western

2313   ---Shadow of a hawk. New York: Doubleday, 1963. 206p.
       Western

2314   Gleason, Riner. The boy from nowhere. Philadelphia:
       Westminister, 1954. 192p.
       Western--Juvenile.

2315   Glidden, Frederick Dilley (1908-   ). Silver rock.
       Boston: Houghton, 1953. 179p.
       Western

2316   ---pseud. Short, Luke. The feud at single shot. New
       York: Farrar, 1936. 311p.
       Western

2317   ---Raiders of the rimrock. New York: Doubleday, 1939.
       275p.
       Western

2318   ---Dead freight for piute. New York: Doubleday, 1940.
       275p.
       Western

2319   ---Hard money. New York: Doubleday, 1940. 267p.
       Western

2320   ---War on the cimarron. New York: Doubleday, 1940.
       269p.
       Western

2321   ---Gunman's chance. New York: Doubleday, 1941. 302p.
       Western

2322   ---Hardcase. New York: Doubleday, 1942. 275p.
       Western

2323   ---Ride the man down. New York: Doubleday, 1942. 279p.
       Western

2324   ---Sunset graze. New York: Doubleday, 1942. 280p.
       Western

2325   ---Ramrod. New York: Macmillan, 1943. 232p.
       Western

2326   ---And the wind blows free. New York: Macmillan, 1945.
       172p.
       Western

2327 ---<u>Coroner creek</u>. New York: Macmillan, 1946. 222p.
       Western

2328 ---<u>Station west</u>. Boston: Houghton, 1947. 220p.
       Western

2329 ---<u>High vermilion</u>. Boston: Houghton, 1948. 218p.
       Western

2330 ---<u>Ambush</u>. Boston: Houghton, 1949. 249p.
       Western

2331 ---<u>Fiddlefoot</u>. Boston: Houghton, 1949. 264p.
       Western

2332 ---<u>Vengeance valley</u>. Boston: Houghton, 1950. 219p.
       Western

2333 ---<u>Barren land murders</u>. New York: Fawcett, 1951. 189p.
       Western

2334 ---<u>Play a lone hand</u>. Boston: Houghton, 1951. 218p.
       Western

2335 ---<u>Saddle by starlight</u>. Boston: Houghton, 1952. 169p.
       Western

2336 ---<u>Marauder's moon</u>. New York: Dell, 1954. 223p.
       Western

2337 ---<u>Bought with a gun</u>. New York: Dell, 1955. 190p.
       Western

2338 ---<u>Rimrock</u>. New York: Random, 1955. 238p.
       Western

2339 ---<u>The branded man</u>. New York: Dell, 1956. 192p.
       Western

2340 ---<u>The whip</u>. New York: Bantam, 1957. 118p.
       Western

2341 ---<u>Summer of the smoke</u>. New York: Bantam, 1958. 122p.
       Western

2342 ---<u>The some day country</u>. New York: Bantam, 1964. 123p.
       Western

2343 Glidden, Jonathan H. (1907-   ) pseud. Dawson, Peter.
       <u>Gunsmoke graze</u>. New York: Dodd, 1942. 275p.
       Western

2344 ---<u>Long ride</u>. New York: Dodd, 1942. 233p.
       Western

2345 ---Trail boss. New York: Dodd, 1943. 298p.
       Western

2346 ---High country. New York: Dodd, 1947. 214p.
       Western

2347 ---Royal gorge. New York: Dodd, 1948. 212p.
       Western

2348 ---Renegade canyon. New York: Dodd, 1949. 220p.
       Western

2349 ---Stirrup boss. New York: Dodd, 1949. 224p.
       Western

2350 ---Ruler of the range. New York: Dodd, 1951. 214p.
       Western

2351 ---Dead man pass. New York: Dodd, 1954. 213p.
       Western

2352 ---Big outfit. New York: Dodd, 1955. 210p.
       Western

2353 ---Man on the buckskin. New York: Dodd, 1957. 212p.
       Western

2354 ---Treachery at rock point; an original western. New
       York: Dell, 1957. 190p.
       Western

2355 ---Bloody gold. New York: Bantam, 1963. 121p.
       Western

2356 Goddard, Gloria (Mrs. Clement Wood) (1897-   ).
       These lord's descendants. New York: Stokes, 1930.
       394p.
              Chronicle--Several generations--Colonial--
       California--World War I--Romance.

2357 Goff, George Paul. Johnny quickstep's whaling voyage.
       San Francisco: 1894. 240p.
       Juvenile.

2358 Gooden, Arthur Henry (1879-   ). Wayne of the flying w.
       New York: Kinsey, 1934. 275p.
       Western

2359 ---Valley of the kings. New York: Kinsey, 1935. 292p.
       Western

2360 ---Smoke tree range. New York: Kinsey, 1936. 280p.
       Western

2361 ---Donovan rides. New York: Macaulay, 1937. 256p.
       Western

185

2362 ---<u>Boss of circle b</u>. London: Harrap, 1938. 247p.
Western

2363 ---<u>Cross knife ranch</u>. New York: Phoenix, 1939. 255p.
Western

2364 ---<u>Tenderfoot boss</u>. London: Harrap, 1939. 283p.
Western

2365 ---<u>The trail of vengeance</u>. New York: Phoenix, 1939.
252p.
Western

2366 ---<u>The range hawk</u>. New York: Carlton, 1940. 310p.
Western

2367 ---<u>Painted buttes</u>. New York: Carlton, 1941. 298p.
Western

2368 ---<u>Roaring river range</u>. Boston: Houghton, 1942. 254p.
Western

2369 ---<u>Guns on the high mesa</u>. Boston: Houghton, 1943.
243p.
Western

2370 ---<u>The valley of dry bones</u>. Boston: Houghton, 1945.
237p.
Western

2371 ---<u>The shadowed trail</u>. Boston: Houghton, 1946. 241p.
Western

2372 ---<u>Trouble in the saddle</u>. Boston: Houghton, 1948.
258p.
Western

2373 ---<u>Call of the range</u>. Philadelphia: Macrae, 1951.
256p.
Western

2374 ---<u>Ride for hell pass</u>. London: Hodder, 1956. 189p.
Western

2375 ---<u>pseud</u>. Rider, Brett. <u>Boss of the ok</u>. New York:
Phoenix, 1940. 254p.
Western

2376 ---<u>Circle c moves in; a western novel</u>. Philadelphia:
Macrae, 1944. 252p.
Western

2377 ---<u>Death stalks the range; a western novel</u>. Philadelphia: Macrae, 1945. 249p.
Western

2378 ---Circle c carries on; a western novel. Philadelphia:
Macrae, 1948. 256p.
Western

2379 ---No benefit of law; a western novel. Philadelphia:
Macrae, 1949. 254p.
Western

2380 ---Law of the gun. Philadelphia: Macrae, 1950. 252p.
Western

2381 ---The long trail. Philadelphia: Macrae, 1952. 223p.
Western

2382 Goodhue, James M.. Struck a lead; an historical tale
of the upper lead region. Chicago: Jameson, 1883.
115p.
Wisconsin-Illinois border.

2383 Goodridge, Roberts, Theodore (1877-   ). Brothers
of peril; a story of old new foundland. Boston:
Page, 1905. 327p.

2384 ---A captain of raleigh's; a romance. Boston: Page,
1911. 351p.

2385 ---The wasp. New York: Dillingham, 1914. 352p.
Piracy--Seventeenth century--Adventure.

2386 Goodwin, Charles Carroll. The comstock club. Salt
Lake City, Utah: Tribune, 1891. 288p.
Mining--Nevada and California.

2387 ---The wedge of gold. Salt Lake City, Utah: Tribune,
1893. 283p.
Comstock Lode.

2388 Goodwin, Harold Leland (1914-   ). The feathered cape.
Philadelphia: Westminister, 1947. 188p.
Massachusetts boy prisoner by British--To
Hawaii--Escapes--Stays--1792--Juvenile.

2389 Goodwin, Mrs. Maud (Wilder) (1856-1935). The head
of a hundred in the colony of virginia; being an
account of certain passages in the life of humphrey
huntoon, esq., sometyme an officer in the colony
of virginia. Boston: Little, 1895. 225p.
Autobiographical form--Courtly style of Eliz-
abethan romance--Maids to Virginia.

2390 ---White aprons'; a romance of bacon's rebellion,
virginia, 1676. Boston: Little, 1896. 339p..

2391 ---Sir christopher; a romance of a maryland manor in
1644. Boston: Little, 1901. 411p.

Somersetshire Knight.

2392 Goodwyn, Frank (1911-   ). The magic of limping john;
a story of the mexican border country. New York:
Farrar, 1944. 275p.
   Mexican characters--Folkways--Ranch ways.

2393 ---Black bull. New York: Doubleday, 1958. 264p.
   Mexican Vaqueros--Texas cowboys--Fiction but
also documentary.

2394 Gordon, Caroline (1895-   ). Penhally. New York:
Scribner's, 1931. 282p.
   First novel--Chronicle--Kentucky manor--1826
to date--Try to keep up estate.

2395 ---Green centuries. New York: Scribner's, 1941. 469p.
   Pre-Revolution--Tennessee-Kentucky frontier--
Holston River area.

2396 Gordon, Charles William (1860-1937) pseud. Connor,
Ralph. The sky pilot; a tale of the foothills.
New York: Revell, 1899. 300p.
   Minister to frontier village--Foothills of
Rockies.

2397 ---The runner; a romance of the niagras. New York:
Doubleday, 1929. 481p.
   War of 1812.

2398 ---The rock and the river; a romance of quebec. New
York: Dodd, 1931. 377p.
   War of 1812 from Canadian point of view--Events--
leading to conflict.

2399 ---Torches through the bush. New York: Dodd, 1934.
300p.
   Scottish highlanders to eastern Ottawa.

2400 ---The rebel loyalist. New York: Dodd, 1935. 328p.
   American Revolution--Tory hero--Romance.

Gordon, Colonel H. R. pseud. see Ellis, Edward Sylvester
1840-1916

2401 Gordon, Homer King. Code of men; a western story. New
York: Crowell, 1926. 341p.
   Western

2402 Gordon, Virginia. A man should rejoice. Philadelphia:
Westminister, 1943. 360p.
   Mississippi Valley days of Black Hawk--Every-
day record.

2403 Gordon, William John. Englishman's haven. New York:

Appleton, 1892. 288p.
1745-1758 Louisbourg.

2404 Gorman, Herbert Sherman (1893-1954). The wine of
san lorenzo. New York: Farrar, 1945. 472p.
Mexican War (1845-1848)--Mexican view.

Grady, Tex pseud. see Webb, Jack

2405 Gragg, Frances and Putnam, George Palmer. Golden
valley; a novel of california. New York: Duell,
1950. 206p.

2406 Graham, Effie. "Passin' on" party. Chicago: McClurg,
1912. 183p.
Former slaves and bondsmen freeholders in
the west.

2407 Graham, Lewis and Olmstead, Edwin. The unsinkable
mrs. jay; a novel. New York: Covici, 1934. 308p.
Molly Brown of Leadville and Denver leaves
and conquers the world.

Grant, Allan pseud. see Smith, Arthur Douglas Howden

2408 Grant, Blanch Chloe (1874-   ). Dona Iona; a story
of old taos and santa fé. New York: Funk, 1941.
323p.
1830's and 1840's.

2409 Grant, Bruce (1893-   ). Longhorn; a story of the
chisholm trail. Cleveland: World, 1956. 215p.
Western--Juvenile.

2410 Grant, Dorothy (Fremont) (1900-   ). Margaret brent,
adventurer; a novel. New York: Longmans, 1944.
293p.
Catholic woman in Maryland--1600-1661.

2411 ---Night of decision; a novel of colonial new york.
New York: Longmans, 1946. 279p.
New York under Catholic Governor--Thomas
Dongan (1683-1690)--Leisler's Revolt--Melodrama--
Leisler is villain.

2412 Graves, Robert (1895-   ). Sergeant lamb's america.
New York: Random, 1940. 380p.
British soldier under Burgoyne--Roger Lamb
(1756-1830)--Irish author debunks army life--Told
in first person.

2413 ---Proceed sergeant lamb. New York: Random, 1941.
322p.
Sequel to Sergeant Lamb's America--Serves under
Cornwallis after Saratoga.

2414   ---The islands of unwisdom. New York: Doubleday,
        1949. 328p.
            Spanish expedition to establish colony Solomon
        Islands--1595--Alvaro Mendaña de Neira (d.1595).

        Gray, Carl pseud. see Park, Charles Caldwell 1860

        Gray, Elizabeth Janet see Vining, Elizabeth (Grey)
        1902

        Gray, Robertson pseud. see Raymond, Rossiter Worthington

2415   Gray, Stanley. Half that glory. New York: Macmillan,
        1941. 468p.
            Young Virginian with Beaumarchais--Seeks aid
        for colonies--American Revolution.

2416   Gray, Westmoreland. Rolling stone. Indianapolis:
        Bobbs, 1932. 310p.
            Western--Mystery.

2417   ---Danger range. Indianapolis: Bobbs, 1933. 318p.
            Western--Mystery.

2418   ---Manhunt trail. Philadelphia: Lippincott, 1934.
        288p.
            Western

2419   ---Hell's stamping ground. Philadelphia: Lippincott,
        1935. 296p.
            Western

        Grayson, Eldred, Esq. pseud. see Hare, Robert

2420   Grebanier, Mrs. Frances (Vinciquerra) (1900-   )
        pseud. Winwar, Frances. Gallow's hill. New York:
        Holt, 1937. 292p.
            Salem witchcraft--1690's--Based on records--
        Romance.

2421   Grebenc, Lucile. The time of change. New York: Double-
        day, 1938. 268p.
            Widow and baby farm life--Connecticut--1815-
        1825.

2422   Greeley, Robert F.. The child of the islands; or,
        the shipwrecked gold seekers. New York: Strenger,
        1850. 87p.

2423   ---The partisan's oath; or, the trooper's revenge.
        a tale of the revolution. New York: Bunce, 185?.
        96p.

2424   Green, Gerald. The sword and the sun; the story of
        spanish civil wars in peru. New York: Scribner's,

1953. 363p.
Conquistadores--Peru--Diego de Almagro (1520-1542).

2425 Green, Miss M. P. pseud. Parker, Gay. The fight for dominion; a romance of our first war with spain. New York: Herrick, 1899. 316p.

2426 Greene, Josiah E. (1911-   ). Not in our stars. New York: Macmillan, 1945. 588p. Large dairy farm in east--1940.

2427 Greene, Mrs. Marjorie Sherman. Cowboy of the ramapos. New York: Abelard, 1956. 189p. American Revolution--Orange County, New York-- Food for Washington taken by tory "cowboys"-- Juvenile.

2428 Greene, Sarah Pratt (McLean). Last chance junction, far, far west; a novel. Boston: Cupples and Hurd. Algonquin Press, 1889. 258p. Western

2429 Greenhood, David. The hill. New York: Duell, 1943. 266p. San Francisco--Wabash Hill--Talk to old residents.

2430 Gregg, F. M.. The founding of a nation; the story of the pilgrim fathers, their voyage on the mayflower, their early struggles, hardships, dangers, and the beginnings of american democracy. New York: Doran, 1915. 481p. Mayflower Pilgrims v. Puritans.

2431 Gregor, Elmer Russell (1878-1954). Camping in the maine woods; adventures of two boys in the maine wood. New York: Harper, 1912. 379p.

2432 ---Camping on western trails; adventures of two boys in the rocky mountains. New York: Harper, 1913. 332p. Juvenile

2433 ---The red arrow; an indian tale. New York: Harper, 1915. 282p. Western prairie--White Otter--Grandson Sioux Chief--Juvenile.

2434 ---White otter. New York: Appleton, 1917. 312p. Sequel to "The Red Arrow"--Indian life before whites appear.

2435 ---Running fox. New York: Appleton, 1918. 317p.

2436 ---The war trail. New York: Appleton, 1921. 257p.
Juvenile

2437 ---The white wolf. New York: Appleton, 1921. 267p.
Juvenile

2438 ---Spotted deer. New York: Appleton, 1922. 239p.
Juvenile

2439 ---Three sioux scouts. New York: Appleton, 1922.
252p.
Juvenile

2440 ---Jim mason, backwoods man. New York: Appleton, 1923.
282p.
Juvenile

2441 ---Jim mason, scout. New York: Appleton, 1923. 273p.
Juvenile

2442 ---Captain jim mason. New York: Appleton, 1924. 252p.
Juvenile

2443 ---The medicine buffalo. New York: Appleton, 1925.
263p.
Juvenile

2444 ---Mason and his rangers. New York: Appleton, 1926.
244p.
Juvenile--Lake George.

2445 ---The war eagle. New York: Appleton, 1926. 223p.
Juvenile

2446 ---The mystery trail. New York: Appleton, 1927. 224p.
Juvenile

2447 ---The war chief. New York: Appleton, 1927. 236p.
Juvenile

2448 ---Three wilderness scouts. New York: Appleton, 1928.
238p.
Juvenile

2449 ---The spotted pony. New York: Appleton, 1930. 237p.
Juvenile

2450 Gregory, Jackson (1882- 1943). Under handicap; a novel.
New York: Harper, 1914. 321p.
Western

2451 ---The outlaw. New York: Dodd, 1916. 328p.
Western

2452 ---The short cut. New York: Dodd, 1916. 383p.
Western

2453   ---Wolfbreed. New York: Dodd, 1917. 296p.
       Western

2454   ---The joyous trouble maker. New York: Dodd, 1918.
       330p.
       Western

2455   ---Six feet four. New York: Dodd, 1918. 295p.
       Western

2456   ---Bells of san juan. New York: Scribner's, 1919.
       337p.
       Western scenario.

2457   ---Judith of blue lake ranch. New York: Scribner's,
       1919. 393p.
       Western

2458   ---Man to man. New York: Scribner's, 1920. 367p.
       Western

2459   ---Desert valley. New York: Scribner's, 1921. 318p.
       Western

2460   ---The everlasting whisper; a tale of the california
       wilderness. New York: Scribner's, 1922. 375p.
       Western

2461   ---Timber-wolf. New York: Scribner's, 1923. 333p.
       Western

2462   ---The maid of the mountain; a romance of the california
       wilderness. New York: Scribner's, 1925. 331p.
       Western

2463   ---The desert thoroughbred; a romance of the california
       desert country. New York: Scribner's, 1926. 331p.
       Western--Mystery.

2464   ---Captain cavalier. New York: Scribner's, 1927. 300p.
       Western

2465   ---Emerald trails. New York: Scribner's, 1928. 309p.
       Western

2466   ---Redwood and gold. New York: Dodd, 1928. 306p.
       Western

2467   ---Mystery at spanish hacienda. New York: Dodd, 1929.
       293p.
       Western

2468   ---Sentinel of the desert. New York: Dodd, 1929. 310p.
       Western

2469 ---The trail to paradise. New York: Dodd, 1920. 282p.
Western

2470 ---The silver star. New York: Dodd, 1931. 306p.
Western

2471 ---Riders across the border. New York: Dodd, 1932.
286p.
Western

2472 ---Ru, the conqueror. New York: Scribner's, 1933.
289p.

2473 ---Shadow on the mesa. New York: Dodd, 1933. 287p.
Western

2474 ---High courage. New York: Dodd, 1934. 280p.
Western

2475 ---Lords of the coast. New York: Dodd, 1935. 340p.
Romance early days of California.

2476 ---Valley of adventure. New York: Dodd, 1935. 297p.
Western

2477 --- Into the sunset. New York: Dodd, 1936. 262p.
Western

2478 ---Mountain men. New York: Dodd, 1936. 282p.
Western

2479 ---Dark valley. New York: Dodd, 1937. 274p.
Western

2480 ---Sudden bill dorn. New York: Dodd, 1937. 270p.
Western

2481 ---Marshal of sundown. New York: Dodd, 1938. 266p.
Western

2482 ---Mysterious rancho. New York: Dodd, 1938. 248p.
Western

2483 ---Powder smoke on wandering river. New York: Dodd,
1938. 279p.
Western

2484 ---Mad o'hara of wild river. New York: Dodd, 1939.
272p.
Western

2485 ---Rocky bend. New York: Dodd, 1939. 249p.
Western

2486 ---Secret valley. New York: Dodd, 1939. 256p.
Western sans cowboys.

194

2487 ---The far call. New York: Dodd, 1940. 263p.
      Western

2488 ---The girl at the crossroads. New York: Dodd, 1940.
      225p.
      Western

2489 --- I must ride alone. New York: Dodd, 1940. 245p.
      Western

2490 ---Ace in the hole. New York: Dodd, 1941. 245p.
      Western

2491 ---Guardians of the trail. New York: Dodd, 1941.
      265p.
      Western

2492 ---The red law. New York: Dodd, 1941. 244p.
      Western

2493 ---Border line. New York: Dodd, 1942. 248p.
      Western

2494 ---The man from texas. New York: Dodd, 1942. 259p.
      Western

2495 ---Two in the wilderness. New York: Dodd, 1942. 258p.
      Western

2496 ---Lonely trail. New York: Dodd, 1943. 243p.
      Western

2497 ---The man from painted rock. New York: Dodd, 1943.
      214p.
      Western

2498 ---Aces wild at golden eagle. Philadelphia: Blakiston,
      1944. 236p.
      Western

2499 ---The hermit of thunder king. New York: Dodd, 1945.
      200p.
      Western

2500 Grew, David. The sorrel stallion. New York: Scribner's,
      1932. 321p.
      Western

2501 Grey, Katherine. Rolling wheels. Boston: Little,
      1932. 339p.
      Indiana to California via covered wagon--
      Good--Juvenile.

2502 ---Hills of gold. Boston: Little, 1933. 338p.
      Sequence to Rolling Wheels--Gold--Santa Clara,
      California--Juvenile.

2503   Grey, Zane (1872-1939). Betty Zane. New York: Francis,
        1903. 291p.
                Elizabeth Zane (1759?-1847?)--Migration from
        Virginia to Ohio--Simon Girty.

2504   ---The spirit of the border; a romance of the early
        settlers in the ohio valley. New York: Burt, 1906.
        266p.

2505   ---The last of the plainsmen. New York: Outing, 1908.
        314p.
                Western--Record of trip Zane Grey took with
        Buffalo Jones (1844-1919).

2506   ---The last trail; a story of early days in the ohio
        valley. New York: Burt, 1909. 300p.

2507   ---The heritage of the desert; a novel. New York:
        Harper, 1910. 297p.
                Western

2508   ---The young lion hunter. New York: Harper, 1911.
        277p.
                Forest preserves--Utah.

2509   ---Riders of the purple sage; a novel. New York:
        Harper, 1912. 334p.
                Western

2510   ---Desert gold; a romance of the border. New York:
        Harper, 1913. 325p.
                Western

2511   ---The light of western stars; a romance. New York:
        Grosset, 1914. 388p.
                Western

2512   ---The lone star ranger; a romance of the border.
        New York: Harper, 1915. 372p.
                Western

2513   ---The rainbow trail; a romance. New York: Harper,
        1915. 372p.
                Western--Mormon.

2514   ---The border legion. New York: Harper, 1916. 365p.
                Western

2515   ---Wildfire. New York: Harper, 1917. 320p.
                Western

2516   ---The u. p. trail; a novel. New York: Harper, 1918.
        408p.
                Published 1938 under title The Roaring U. P.
        Trail.

2517   ---The man of the forest; a novel. New York: Harper,
         1920. 382p.
         Western

2518   ---The mysterious rider; a novel. New York: Harper,
         1921. 335p.
         Western

2519   ---To the last man. New York: Harper, 1922. 310p.
         Western

2520   ---Wanderer of the wasteland. New York: Harper, 1923.
         419p.
         Western

2521   ---The call of the canyon. New York: Harper, 1924.
         291p.
         Western

2522   ---The thundering herd. New York: Harper, 1925. 400p.
         Western

2523   ---The vanishing american. New York: Harper, 1925.
         308p.
         Western

2524   ---Under the tonto rim. New York: Harper, 1926. 281p.
         Western

2525   ---Forlorn river; a romance. New York: Harper, 1927.
         338p.
         Western

2526   ---Valley of wild horses. New York: Harper, 1927.
         244p.
         Western

2527   ---"Nevada"; a romance of the west. New York: Harper,
         1928. 365p.
         Western

2528   ---Wild horse mesa. New York: Harper, 1928. 365p.
         Western

2529   ---Fighting caravans. New York: Harper, 1929. 361p.
         Western

2530   ---The shepherd of guadaloupe. New York: Harper, 1930.
         335p.
         New Mexico--Ranch--Post World War I.

2531   ---The wolf-tracker. New York: Harper, 1930. 98p.
         Western

2532   ---The dude ranger. New York: Grosset, 1931. 240p.
         Western

2533 ---Sunset pass. New York: Harper, 1931. 349p.
      Western

2534 ---Arizona ames. New York: Harper, 1932. 310p.
      Western

2535 ---The drift fence. New York: Harper, 1932. 314p.
      Western

2536 ---Robber's roost. New York: Harper, 1932. 295p.
      Western

2537 ---Wyoming. New York: Harper, 1932. 249p.
      Western

2538 ---The hash knife outfit. New York: Harper, 1933.
      323p.
      Western

2539 ---Code of the west. New York: Harper, 1934. 309p.
      Western

2540 ---Thunder mountain. New York: Harper, 1935. 309p.
      Western

2541 ---The lost wagon train. New York: Harper, 1936.
      401p.
      Western

2542 ---The trail driver. New York: Harper, 1936. 302p.
      Western

2543 ---West of the pecos. New York: Harper, 1937. 314p.
      Western

2544 ---The heritage of the desert. New York: Grosset,
      1938. 298p.
      Western

2545 ---Majesty's rancho. New York: Harper, 1938. 297p.
      Western

2546 ---Raiders of spanish peaks. New York: Harper, 1938.
      332p.
      Western

2547 ---Knights of the range. New York: Harper, 1939.
      308p.
      Western

2548 ---Western union. New York: Harper, 1939. 297p.
      Western

2549 ---30,000 on the hoof. New York: Harper, 1940. 304p.
      Western

2550 ---Twin sombreros. New York: Harper, 1940. 301p.
       Western

2551 ---Stairs of sand. New York: Harper, 1943. 321p.
       Western

2552 ---Shadow on the trail. New York: Harper, 1946. 278p.
       Western

2553 ---The maverick queen. New York: Grosset, 1950. 246p.
       Western

2554 ---Lost pueblo. New York: Harper, 1954. 249p.
       Western

2555 ---Black mesa. New York: Harper, 1955. 244p.
       Western

2556 ---Stranger from the tonto. New York: Harper, 1956.
       216p.
       Western

2557 ---The fugitive trail. New York: Harper, 1957. 215p.
       Western

2558 ---The arizona clan. New York: Harper, 1958. 211p.
       Western

2559 ---Horse hill heaven. New York: Harper, 1959. 216p.
       Western

2560 Griffin, Henry Farrand. The white cockade. New York:
       Greystone, 1941. 359p.
              Yankee sea captain and French royalist--
       Pre-1763.

2561 ---Paradise street. New York: Appleton, 1943. 364p.
              New Bedford--1830's--Romance.

2562 Griffis, William Elliot. The pathfinders of the rev-
       olution; a story of the great march into the wilder-
       ness and lake region of new york in 1779. Boston:
       Wilde, 1900. 316p.

2563 Griggs, Sutton Elbert. Imperium in imperia. Cincinn-
       ati: Editor Publishing, 1899. 265p.
              Texas as a Negro Republic.

2564 Grinstead, Durward (1894-   ). Elva. New York:
       Covici, 1929. 353p.
              Spread of Salem witchcraft hysteria.

2565 Grinstead, Frances. The high road. New York: Double-
       day, 1945. 214p.
              First novel--Regional--Missouri backwoods ca.1910.

199

2566 Grinstead, Jesse Edward (1866-   ). King of hualpi
      valley. New York: Dodge, 1940. 255p.
      Western

2567 ---The killers of green's cove. New York: Dodge,
      1941. 254p.
      Western

2568 Grissom, Irene Welsh. The superintendent. New York:
      Harriman, 1910. 228p.
      Western Washington--Feminine tale of sawmill--
      Temperance for young people--Juvenile.

2569 Griswold, Francis (1902-   ). The tides of malvern.
      New York: Morrow, 1930. 333p.
      Chronicle--Romance--Southern family eighteenth
      century to 1930.

2570 ---A sea island lady. New York: Morrow, 1939. 964p.
      Chronicle--Southern family Civil War-1920--
      Beaufort, South Carolina.

      Groom, Lillian (Ressler) see Cicchetti, Janet, jt. author

2571 Groseclose, Elgin Earl (1899-   ). The firedrake;
      a novel. Philadelphia: Lippincott, 1942. 354p.
      Clipper ship--1850.

2572 Grove, Fred. Flame of the osage. New York: Pyramid,
      1958. 192p.
      Western

2573 ---Sun dance. New York: Ballantine, 1958. 189p.
      Western

2574 ---Comanche captives. New York: Ballantine, 1962. [?].
      Western--Golden Spur Award for best Western--
      1963.

2575 ---Buffalo spring. New York: Doubleday, 1967. 191p.
      Western

2576 Gruber, Frank. Buffalo box; a simon lash mystery.
      New York: Farrar, 1942. 279p.
      Western

2577 ---The gift horse; a johnny fletcher mystery. New York:
      Farrar, 1942. 283p.
      Western

2578 ---Gunsight. New York: Dodd, 1942. 223p.
      Western

2579 ---Fighting man. New York: Rinehart, 1948. 188p.
      Western

2580 ---Broken lance. New York: Rinehart, 1949. 217p.
        Western

2581 ---The leather duke. New York: Rinehart, 1949. 247p.
        Western

2582 ---Fort starvation. New York: Rinehart, 1953. 217p.
        Western

2583 ---Bitter sage. New York: Rinehart, 1954. 217p.
        Western

2584 ---Bugles west. New York: Rinehart, 1954. 249p.
        Western

2585 ---Johnny vengeance. New York: Rinehart, 1954. 248p.
        Western

2586 ---The highwayman. New York: Rinehart, 1955. 252p.
        Western

2587 ---Buffalo grass; a novel of kansas. New York: Rine-
        hart, 1956. 249p.
        Western

2588 ---Lonesome river. New York: Rinehart, 1957. 242p.
        Western

2589 ---The town tamer. New York: Rinehart, 1957. 221p.
        Western

2590 ---The marshal. New York: Rinehart, 1958. 251p.
        Western

2591 ---The bushwhackers. New York: Rinehart, 1959. 220p.
        Western

       Gulick, Bill see Gulick, Grover C.

2592 Gulick, Grover C.. Bend of the snake. Boston: Hough-
        ton, 1950. 274p.
        Western

2593 ---A drum calls west. Boston: Houghton, 1951. 246p.
        Western

2594 ---White men, red men, and mountain men. Boston:
        Houghton, 1955. 216p.
        Western

2595 ---The land beyond. Boston: Houghton, 1958. 234p.
        Western

2596 ---The moon-eyed appalossa. New York: Doubleday, 1962.
        191p.
        Western

2597   ---The hallelujah train. New York: Doubleday, 1963.
       192p.
              Western appeared in 1956 as The Hallelujah Trail.

       Gunn, Tom pseud. see McDowell, Syl

2598   Guthrie, Alfred Bertram (1901-   ). The big sky.
       New York: Sloane, 1947. 386p.
              #1 of Trilogy--Opening American West--1830-
       1843--Major work--Excellent.

2599   ---The way west. New York: Sloane, 1949. 340p.
              #2 of Trilogy--Wagon train from Independence,
       Missouri to Oregon--1840's.

2600   ---These thousand hills. Boston: Houghton, 1956.
       346p.
              #3 of Trilogy--Cattle trail Boise City to
       Montana--Sequel to Way West.

2601   Guy, Earl. Heaven is a sunswept hill. New York:
       Macmillan, 1943. 220p.
              First novel--River bottom farmers--Flood
       rescue work.

202

H. H. pseud. see Jackson, Helen Hunt

2602 Habberton, John. The jericho road; a story of western life. Chicago: Jansen, 1877. 222p.

2603 Hagedorn, Hermann (1882-1964). Rough riders; a romance. New York: Harper, 1927. 508p.
Spanish-American War.

2604 Haggard, Sir Henry Rider (1856-1925). Montezuma's daughter. New York: Longmans, 1893. 328p.
Spanish Inquisition--Cortez--1519-1520.

2605 ---The virgin of the sun. New York: Doubleday, 1898. 294p.
Conquest of Peru--Pizzaro.

2606 Haig-Brown, Roderick Langmere Haig (1908-   ). Timber; a novel of pacific coast loggers. New York: Morrow, 1942. 410p.

2607 Haines, Edwin I.. The exquisite siren; the romance of peggy shippen and major andré. Philadelphia: Lippincott, 1938. 444p.
Tory wife of Benedict Arnold (1760-1804)-- Love for André.

2608 Haines, Thorton Jenkins. Rich and judkin's wooing; a tale of virginia in the revolution. New York: Neely, 1898. 266p.

2609 Haines, William Wister (1908-   ). The winter war; a historical novel. Boston: Little, 1961. 274p.
Criticism of George Custer--Nelson Miles-- (1839-1925)--Indian conflicts (1866-1895)--Golden Spur Award, Best Western Historical Novel-1962.

2610 Haislip, Harvey. Sailor named jones; a novel of america's greatest captain. New York: Doubleday, 1957. 311p.
First novel and first of Trilogy--Special attention to 1777-1779--Author retired navy captain.

2611 ---Prize master. New York: Doubleday, 1959. 283p.
#2 of Trilogy--Sequel to Sailor Named Jones-- American Revolution--Romance and adventure.

2612 ---Sea road to yorktown. New York: Doubleday, 1960. 288p.

#3 of Trilogy--Sequel to Prize Master--
Privateering--American Revolution.

Haldeman-Julius, Mrs. Anna Marcet(1888-   ) jt.
author, see Haldeman-Julius, Emanuel (1889-   )

2613   Haldeman-Julius, Emanuel and Anna Marcet.   Dust.
New York: Brentano's, 1921.   251p.
Tragedy of Kansas woman on farm--Husband
coarse and soulless--Good.

2614   Hale, Edward Everett (1822-1909).   Philip nolan's
friends; a story of the change of western empire.
New York: Scribner's, 1877.   395p.
Louisiana Purchase--1803.

2615   ---East and west; a story of new-born ohio.   New York:
Cassell, 1892.   267p.
End of eighteenth century.

2616   Hale, Randolph.   Prodigal bandit.   New York: Dodge,
1940.   256p.
First novel--Western

2617   ---Gun king of melted rocks.   New York: Dodge, 1941.
255p.
Western

2618   Hall, Baynard Rush pseud. Carlton, Robert, Esq..
The new purchase; or, seven and a half years in the
far west.   New York: Appleton, 1843.   2 vols.

2619   Hall, Charles Winslow.   Twice taken; an historical
romance of the maritime british provinces.   Boston:
Lee, 1867.   242p.
Siege of Louisburg--1745-1758.

2620   ---Cartagena; or, the lost brigade. a story of heroism
in the british war with spain, 1740-1742.   Boston:
Wolff, 1898.   574p.

2621   Hall, James (1793-1868).   The harpe's head; a legend
of kentucky.   Philadelphia: Key, 1833.   256p.
Harpe brothers--Outlaws in Mississippi Valley--
1834 appeared under title Kentucky.

2622   ---The wilderness and the warpath.   New York: Wiley,
1849.   174p.

2623   Hall, Marshall R..   The valley of strife.   Boston:
Small, 1925.   292p.
Western

2624   ---Storm of the old frontier.   Philadelphia: Altemus,
1927.   302p.

2625   Hall, Oakley Maxwell pseud. Manor, Jason. Warlock.
       New York: Viking, 1958. 471p.
              Southwest-1880's--Tombstone--Wyatt Earp legend--
       Serious work with western theme--cf. stature with
       Ox-bow Incident--Excellent.

2626   Hall, Rubylea. The great tide. New York: Duell,
       1947. 535p.
              First novel--Florida plantation--1830's and
       1840's--Many details--Fever--Hurricane.

2627   Hall, Ruth (1858-   ). The black gown. Boston:
       Houghton, 1900. 318p.
              French-Indian War (1754-1763)--Albany, New York.

2628   ---The golden arrow; a story of roger william's day.
       Boston: Houghton, 1901. 316p.
              Roger Williams (1604-1683)--Anne Hutchinson--
       Indians.

2629   Halleran, Eugene Edward (1905-   ). No range is free.
       Philadelphia: Macrae, 1944. 255p.
       Western

2630   ---Prairie guns. Philadelphia: Macrae, 1944. 256p.
       Western

2631   ---Outposts of vengeance. Philadelphia: Macrae, 1945.
       237p.
       Western

2632   ---Double cross trail; a western novel. Philadelphia:
       Macrae, 1946. 219p.
       Western

2633   ---Shadow of the badlands. Philadelphia: Macrae,
       1946. 236p.
       Western

2634   ---Outlaw guns; a western novel. Philadelphia: Macrae,
       1947. 239p.
       Western

2635   ---Outlaw trail. Philadelphia: Macrae, 1949. 252p.
       Western

2636   ---Rustler's canyon; a western novel. Philadelphia:
       Macrae, 1949. 253p.
       Western

2637   ---High prairie. Philadelphia: Macrae, 1950. 251p.
       Western

2638   ---Smoky range. Philadelphia: Lippincott, 1951. 210p.
       Western

2639 ---Straw boss. Philadelphia: Lippincott, 1952. 211p.
Western

2640 ---Winter ambush. Philadelphia: Macrae, 1954. 217p.
Western

2641 ---Blazing border. Philadelphia: Macrae, 1955. 224p.
Western

2642 ---Devil's canyon. New York: Ballantine, 1956. 155p.
Western

2643 ---Wagon captain. New York: Ballantine, 1956. 150p.
Western

2644 --- The hostile hills. New York: Ballantine, 1957. 155p.
Western

2645 --- Spanish ridge. New York: Ballantine, 1957. 159p.
Western

2646 ---Shadow of the big horn. New York: Ballantine, 1960.
160p.
Western

2647 ---Blood brand; a new western. London: Hammond, 1961.
186p.
Western--Reissued 1968 under Gringo Gun.

2648 ---Indian fighter. New York: Ballantine, 1964. 156p.
Golden Spur Award Best Western Historical
Novel-1965.

2649 Hallet, Richard Matthews (1887-1967). The canyon
of the fools. New York: Harper, 1922. 409p.
Western

2650 ---Michael beam. Boston: Houghton, 1939. 451p.
Black Hawk War--Point of view of Illinois
recruit.

2651 Halyard, Harry pseud. The heroine of tampico; or,
wildfire the wanderer. a tale of mexican war.
Boston: Gleason, 1847. 100p.
1845-1848.

2652 ---The chieftan of churubusco; or, the spectre of the
cathedral. a romance of the mexican war. Boston:
Gleason, 1848. 100p.
1845-1848.

2653 ---Geraldine; or, the gipsey of germantown. a national
and military romance. Boston: Gleason, 1848. 100p.

2654 ---The haunted bride; or, the witch of gallows hill.

a romance of olden time. Boston: Gleason, 1848.
100p.
　　　Salem--1691.

2655　---The mexican spy; or, the bride of buena vista.
a tale of the mexican war. Boston: Gleason, 1848.
100p.
　　　1845-1848.

2656　---The ocean monarch; or, the ranger of the gulf. a
mexican romance. Boston: Gleason, 1848. 100p.
1845-1848.

2657　---The rover of the reef; or, the nymph of the night-
ingale. a romance of massachusetts bay. Boston:
Gleason, 1848. 100p.
　　　Colonial era.

2658　---The warrior queen; or, the buccaneer of the brazos!
a romance of mexico. Boston: Gleason, 1848. 100p.
1845-1848.

2659　Ham, Tom (1912-　　　). Give us this valley. New York:
Macmillan, 1952. 304p.
　　　1837--Pennsylvania couple to Georgia by schooner
wagon--Pioneer story.

2660　Hamele, Ottamar. When destiny called; a story of the
doniphan expedition in the mexican war. San Antonio,
Texas: Naylor, 1948. 236p.
　　　Missouri mounted volunteers--Santa Fé to northern Mexico--1846-1847.

2661　Hamill, Mrs. Katherine Bernie (King) (1877-　　　).
Flower of monterey; a romance of the california.
Boston: Page, 1921. 341p.
　　　Spanish missionary--American girl--Romance
with "Boston" (New England trader).

2662　---Swamp shadow. New York: Knopf, 1936. 237p.
　　　Mississippi gulf people.

2663　Hamilton, George W.. Kit caffrey's grit; a story of
texas. Cincinnati: Standard, 1895. 233p.

2664　Hamilton, Harry. Banjo on my knee; a novel. Indianapolis: Bobbs, 1936. 320p.
　　　Shanty-river life.

2665　---Thunder in the wilderness. Indianapolis: Bobbs,
1949. 304p.
　　　Mississippi Valley--1760's--French and Indian
War--Colorful.

2666　Hammand, Esther Barstow. Road to endor. New York:

Farrar, 1940. 434p.
London, Barbados, Salem--1680's and 1690's--
Samuel Pariss--Witchcraft--Plague--Fire.

2667 Hammond, William Alexander. Lal; a novel. New York:
Appleton, 1884. 466p.
Western

2668 Hancock, Albert Elmer (1870-   ). Bronson of the
rabble; a novel. Philadelphia: Lippincott, 1909.
321p.
Philadelphia 1812--Blacksmith's son--Romance.

2669 Hand, Mrs. Matilda Butler. Romance of old cape may.
Philadelphia: Dorrance, 1928. 280p.
American Revolution--Philadelphia and southern
New Jersey.

2670 Hanes, Frank Borden. The fleet rabble; a novel of the
nez perce war. New York: Page, 1961. 368p.
Chief Joseph v. Army--1877.

2671 Hankins, Arthur Preston. The heritage of the hills.
New York: Dodd, 1922. 307p.
Western

2672 ---Falcon of squawtooth; a western story. New York:
Chelsea, 1923. 318p.
Western

2673 ---Canyon gold. New York: Macaulay, 1925. 312p.
Western

2674 ---The lucky bug lode. New York: Macaulay, 1926. 317p.
Western

2675 Hankins, Colonel. Dakota land; or, the beauty of st.
paul. an original illustrated, historic, and romantic
work...to which is added;"a round of pleasure," with
interesting notes of travel...forming a comprehensive
guide to the great north-west. New York: Hankins,
1868. 460p.

2676 Hankins, Robert Maxwell (1905-   ). Lonesome river
justice. Philadelphia: Macrae, 1943. 250p.
Western

2677 Hanna, Evelyn. Blackberry winter. New York: Dutton,
1938. 428p.
Chronicle--Rise and fall southern family--1799-
1865--Marlow County, Georgia.

2678 Hannigan, Dennis. The swamp steed; or, the days of
marion and his merry men. a romance of the american
revolution. New York: Dewitt, 1852. 198p.

Flora MacDonald--Moultrie-- 1778-1781.

2679 Hannum, Mrs. Alberta (Pierson) (1906-   ). Roseanna
      mccoy. New York: Holt, 1947. 256p.
          Hatfield-McCoy feud-- 1880--Romance.

2680 The hapless orphan; or, innocent victim of revenge.
          a novel founded on incidents in real life, in a
          series of letters from caroline francis to maria
          b____. By an American Lady. [Anonymous]. Boston:
          np., 1793. [?]
             Philadelphia

2681 Harbaugh, Thomas Cholmers (1849-1924). For freedom's
          cause; or, on to saratoga. Philadelphia: McKay,
          1910. 244p.
             American Revolution.

2682 ---Following mad anthony wayne; or, the drums of
          germantown. Philadelphia: McKay, 1912. 262p.
             American Revolution.

2683 ---The young captains; or, prisoners of the king. a
          stirring tale of philadelphia. Philadelphia:
          McKay, 1913. 223p.
             American Revolution.

      Hardin, Clement pseud. see Newton, Dwight Bennett

      Hardin, Dave pseud. see Holmes, Llewellyn Perry

      Hardy, Stuart pseud. see Schisgall, Oscar (1901-   )

2684 Hare, Robert pseud. Grayson, Eldred, Esq.. Standish
          the puritan; a tale of the american revolution.
          New York: Harper, 1850. 320p.
             Collegians to war--With English--With patriots.

2685 --- Overing; or, the heir of wycherly. a historical
          romance. New York: Cornish, 1852. 416p.
             Rhode Island.

2686 Hargreaves, Sheba. The cabin at trail's end; a story
          of oregon. New York: Harper, 1928. 341p.
             Life 1843--Willamette Valley--Very good.

2687 ---Heroine of the prairies; a romance of the oregon
          trail. New York: Harper, 1930. 288p.
             Authentic portrait-- 1848.

      Harland, Marion pseud. see Terhune, Mrs. Mary Virginia
          (Hawes)

2688 Harlin, Amos R.. For here is my fortune. New York:
          McGraw, 1946. 290p.

209

Ozark's--Early twentieth century--Series of
autobiographical anecdotes.

2689 Harper, Martha Rebecca (Barnhart). <u>Red silk pantalettes</u>.
New York: Longmans, 1946. 228p.
Punxsutawney, Pennsylvania 1850's--Juvenile.

2690 Harper, Robert S.. <u>Trumpet in the wilderness</u>. New
York: Mill, 1940. 346p.
War of 1812--Battle of Lake Erie high point--
Frontier warfare--Ohio.

2691 Harrington, Mrs. Isis L.. <u>Komoki of the cliffs</u>. New
York: Scribner's, 1934. 95p.
Hopi Indians--Juvenile.

2692 Harris, Mrs. Bernice (Kelly) (1894-   ). <u>Sweet</u>
<u>beulah land</u>. New York: Doubleday, 1943. 389p.
North Carolina--Between sea and Virginia line--
White share croppers.

2693 ---<u>Hearthstones; a novel of the roanoke river country</u>
<u>in north carolina</u>. New York: Doubleday, 1948.
273p.
Two deserters in two wars--Civil and World
War II--Haw Island.

2694 Harris, Cyril Beverly (1891-   ). <u>Trumpets at dawn</u>.
New York: Scribner's, 1938. 429p.
American Revolution--Class rivalry--Generation
gap--Psychological implications of war--1776-1783.

2695 ---<u>Richard pryne</u>. New York: Scribner's, 1941. 414p.
American Revolution--American spy in and
around New York--Based on S. Culper Jr. notes.

2696 ---<u>One braver thing</u>. New York: Scribner's, 1942.
416p.
Loyalists exiled after American Revolution--
New Jersey doctor and four children to Nova Scotia--
Heroic story--Author native of Nova Scotia.

2697 ---<u>Street of knives</u>. Boston: Little, 1950. 370p.
Burr's Conspiracy (1805-1807)--Aaron Burr
(1756-1836)--Theodosia (Burr) Alston (1783-1813)--
Blennerhassett.

2698 Harris, John (1911-   ) and Harris, Margaret (Plumlee)
(1912-   ). <u>The medicine whip</u>. New York: Morrow,
1952. 250p.
West--Wyoming after Civil War.

2699 ---<u>Arrow in the moon</u>. New York: Morrow, 1954. 312p.
West--Dull Knife and tribe--Nebraska cattlemen.

210

2700   ---Chant of the hawk. New York: Random, 1959. 308p.
           Wyoming State Historical Society Fiction Award--
       Forts Platte and Laramie.

2701   Harris, Mrs. Laura B.. Bride of the river. New York:
           Crowell, 1956. 310p.
           1837-1860--Plantation girl marries riverboat
       man--Underground railroad.

       Harris, Margaret (Plumlee) (1912-   ) jt. author,
           see Harris, John (1911-   )

2702   Harris, Walter Butler. Pioneer life in california.
           Stockton, California: Berdine, 1884. 98p.
           Social life in and around mines.

2703   Harrison, C. William. Boothill trail. New York:
           Phoenix, 1940. 256p.
           Western

2704   ---Puncher pards. New York: Phoenix, 1942. 253p.
           Western

2705   Harrison, Constance. Flower de hundred; the story of
           a virginia plantation. New York: Cassell, 1890.
           301p.
           Colonial piece.

2706   ---A son of the old dominion. Boston: Wolffe, 1897.
           355p.
           Colonial

2707   Harrison, Samuel Bertram. Yonder lies jericho. New
           York: Appleton, 1933. 313p.
           Jewish immigrant from St. Louis to Texas--
       Close of Civil War.

2708   ---White king. New York: Doubleday, 1950. 335p.
           Gerrit Judd (1803-1873) to Hawaii 1827--
       Medical missionary.

2709   Harriss, Robert Preston (1903-   ). The foxes.
           Boston: Houghton, 1936. 239p.
           Fox hunting--Decayed South Carolina plantation--
       Low country color.

2710   Harsha, William Justin. Ploughed under; the story
           of an indian chief, told by himself. New York:
           Fords, 1881. 268p.

2711   Harry, Robert Reese. Island boy; a story of ancient
           hawaii. New York: Lothrop, 1956. 209p.
           Juvenile

2712   Hart, Alan. In the lives of men. New York: Norton,
           1937. 451p.

211

Panorama of Puget Sound life 1890-1907--
Panic '93--Spanish American War--Alaska gold rush.

2713　Hart, Edwin Kirkman. The sleeping sentinel of valley
forge; a romance of the revolution. Philadelphia:
n.p. 1897. 37p.

2714　Hart, Jerome Alfred (1854-　　). A vigilante girl.
Chicago: McClurg, 1910. 397p.
California--Transitional period to law and
order--Romance--Adventure.

2715　---The galconda bonanza. San Francisco: Pioneer,
1923. 315p.
Mining

2716　Hart, Mildred Burcham. Dead woman's shoes. New York:
Crowell, 1932. 305p.
First novel--Second marriage of young Nebraska
farmer.

2717　---Strange harvest. Caldwell, Idaho: Caxton, 1936.
344p.
German-Americans--Nebraska--1900ca.

2718　Hart, William Surrey (1874-1946). Hoofbeats. New York:
Dial, 1933. 231p.
Western

2719　Harte, Bret (1839-1902). Gabriel conroy; a novel.
Hartford, Connecticut: American, 1876. 466p.
California--Lawless west of 1850's.

2720　---Thankful blossom; a romance of the jerseys, 1779.
Boston: Osgood, 1877. 158p.
American Revolution.

2721　---The story of a mine. Boston: Osgood, 1878. 172p.

2722　---The argonauts of north liberty. Boston: Houghton,
1888. 206p.

2723　---A waif of the plains. Boston: Houghton, 1890. 231p.

2724　---Susy; a story of the plains. Boston: Houghton,
1893. 264p.

Harte, Francis Bret (1836-1902) see Harte, Bret

2725　Hatch, Richard Warren. Leave the salt earth. New
York: Covici, 1933. 345p.
#2 of series--Bradford family farm--Massa-
chusetts coast. #1 was Into The Wind (1929).

2726　Hatcher, Harlan Henthorne (1898-　　). Patterns of

wolfpen. Indianapolis: Bobbs, 1934. 332p.
Chronicle of family--1785-1885--Kentucky
Valley.

2727 Hauck, Mrs. Louise (Platt) pseud. Landon, Louise.
Wild grape; a novel of the ozarks. Philadelphia:
Penn, 1931. 293p.
Romantic tale--Italian-Americans to Missouri.

2728 Havard, Aline (1889-   ). The regicide's children.
New York: Scribner's, 1927. 271p.
Vanes at Hartford--1689--Juvenile.

2729 Havighurst, Walter Edwin (1901-   ). The quiet shore.
New York: Macmillan, 1937. 284p.
Lake Erie--Ohio from swamp land to farm land.

2730 ---The winds of spring. New York: Macmillan, 1940.
323p.
Wisconsin--Pioneer days--1840-1870--Agassiz
in log cabin.

2731 ---and Boyd, Marion Margaret (Mrs. W. Havighurst).
High prairie. New York: Farrar, 1944. 239p.
Dakota and Wisconsin--1867--Norwegians.

2732 Havill, Edward (1907-   ). Big ember; a novel.
New York: Harper, 1947. 238p.
Sioux attack on Minnesota Norwegian settlement--
1862.

2733 Hawkes, Clarence (1869-1954). King of the thundering
herd; the biography of an american bison. Philadelphia: Jacobs, 1911. 299p.
Biography of beast of the plains--1870's--
Northwest Missouri and northeast Kansas.

2734 ---Patches; a wyoming cow pony. Springfield, Massa-
chusetts: Bradley, 1928. 268p.
Sixteen year old boy west to uncle's ranch--
Juvenile.

2735 Hawkins, Anne. To the swift; a novel. New York:
Harper, 1949. 296p.
Pony Express--Piutes.

2736 Hawley, Zoa Grace. A boy rides with custer. Boston:
Little, 1938. 295p.
1875-1876--Indian--White reconciliation--
Juvenile.

2737 Hawthorne, Hildegarde (Mrs. J. M. Oskison). Lone
rider. New York: Longmans, 1933. 264p.
Western--Juvenile.

2738   ---On the golden trail. New York: Longmans, 1936.
          302p.
             Western--Juvenile.

2739   ---Rising thunder; the story of jack jouett of virginia.
          New York: Longmans, 1937. 272p.
             John Jouett (1754-1822)--Ride through Virginia
          to save Revolutionary leaders from Tarleton Raiders--
          Juvenile.

2740   ---No road too long. New York: Longmans, 1940. 261p.
             John Frémont--Third expedition--1845--Great
          Salt Lake--California--Oregon--Juvenile.

2741   Hawthorne, Nathaniel (1804-1864). The scarlet letter.
          Boston: Ticknor, 1850. 322p.
             Classic of Puritan mores--Romance.

2742   ---The house of seven gables. Boston: Ticknor, 1851.
          344p.
             Salem early nineteenth century.

2743   ---Blithedale romance. Boston: Ticknor, 1852. 288p.
             Largely autobiographical--Margaret Fuller--
          Brook Farm communal experiment--George Ripley--1841.

       Hawthorne, Captain R. M. pseud. see Ellis, Edward
          Sylvester (1840-1916)

2744   Haycox, Ernest (1899-1950). Free grass. New York:
          Doubleday, 1929. 274p.
             Western

2745   ---Chaffee of roaring horse. New York: Doubleday,
          1930. 291p.
             Western

2746   ---Whispering range. New York: Doubleday, 1930. 320p.
             Western

2747   ---Starlight rider. New York: Doubleday, 1933. 309p.
             Western

2748   ---Riders west. New York: Doubleday, 1934. 296p.
             Western

2749   ---Rough air. New York: Doubleday, 1934. 310p.
             Western

2750   ---Silver desert. New York: Doubleday, 1935. 310p.
             Western

2751   ---Trail smoke. New York: Doubleday, 1936. 293p.
             Western

2752 ---Deep west. Boston: Little, 1937. 301p.
      Western

2753 ---Trouble shooter. New York: Doubleday, 1937. 291p.
      Western

2754 ---Man in the saddle. Boston: Little, 1938. 307p.
      Western

2755 ---Sundown jim. Boston: Little, 1938. 292p.
      Western

2756 ---The border trumpet. Boston: Little, 1939. 306p.
      Western

2758 ---Saddle and ride. Boston: Little, 1940. 291p.
      Western

2759 ---Rim of the desert. Boston: Little, 1941. 305p.
      Western

2760 ---Trail town. Boston: Little, 1941. 298p.
      Western

2761 ---Alder gulch. Boston: Little, 1942. 302p.
      Western

2762 ---Action by night. Boston: Little, 1943. 286p.
      Western

2763 ---The wild bunch. Boston: Little, 1943. 245p.
      Western

2764 ---Bugles in the afternoon. Boston: Little, 1944.
      306p.
            Western--Sioux Campaign--1876--7th Cavalry--
      Anti-Custer--Smeckmesser "...one of best historical
      westerns ever written.....".

2765 ---Canyon passage. Boston: Little, 1945. 264p.
      Western

2766 ---Long storm. Boston: Little, 1946. 296p.
            Portland, Oregon during Civil War--Knights
      of the Golden Circle.

2767 ---Earthbreakers. Boston: Little, 1952. 405p.
            Western--Last written before death--Serious
      novelist--Panoramic--Best western of the year.

2768 ---Murder on the frontier. Boston: Little, 1952. 173p.
      Western

2769 ---The adventurers. Boston: Little, 1954. 332p.
      Western

2770 ---A rider of the high mesa. New York: Popular Library, 1956. 128p.
Western

2771 ---Outlaw guns. New York: Pyramid, 1964c.. 173p.
Western

2772 Hayes, Charles Edward (1912-   ). The four winds. New York: Macmillan, 1942. 379p.
Rural "Studs Lonigan"--Poverty--Irish-Catholic community in Kansas.

2773 Hays, Hoffman Reynolds. The takers of the city. New York: Reynal, 1946. 376p.
Mexico--1500's--Bartolomé de las Casas main figure--Dominicans.

Hazel, Harry pseud. see Jones, John Beauchamp

2774 Heald, Mrs. Sarah E.. by S.E.H.. The eagle's plume; a story of the early days of vermont. Philadelphia: Sunshine, 1890. 112p.

Heath, Elizabeth Alden pseud. see Holton, Edith Austin

2775 Heath, James Ewell. Edge-hill; or, the family of the fitzroyals; a novel. Richmond: White, 1828. 2 vols.
Virginia--1781--Cornwallis--Lafayette--Lee.

2776 Hedden, Worth Tuttle. Wives of high pasture. New York: Doubleday, 1944. 285p.
Account of life in branch of Oneida community--1857.

2777 Heifetz, Harold. Jeremiah thunder. New York: Doubleday, 1968. 187p.
New Mexico--Past and present--Pueblo Indians.

2778 Hémon, Louis (1880-1913). Maria chapdelaine; a tale of the lake st. john country. New York: Macmillan, 1921. 288p. [trans. W. H. Blake].
French Catholics on Candian forest frontier.

2779 Henderson, George C.. The killers. New York: Greenberg, 1935. 250p.

2780 ---Singing lead. New York: Greenberg, 1936. 256p.
Western

2781 ---Whizz fargo, gunfighter. New York: Phoenix, 1937. 256p.
Western

2782 ---Trigger trail. New York: Phoenix, 1938. 258p.
Western

2783 ---The cowpokes of bitter creek. New York: Phoenix, 1939. 257p.
    Western

2784 Henderson, George Wylie. Ollie Miss; a novel. New York: Stokes, 1935. 276p.
    Negroes--Cotton growing--Deep south.

2785 Henderson, Nola. This much is mine! New York: Smith, 1934. 328p.
    Romance--Rural Oklahoma.

2786 Hendryx, James Beardsley (1880-). The promise; a tale of the great northwest. New York: Burt, 1915. 419p.
    Romance

2787 ---Connie morgan in alaska. New York: Putnam, 1916. 341p.

2788 ---The gun-brand. New York: Putnam, 1917. 417p.
    Western

2789 ---The texan; a story of the cattle country. New York: Burt, 1918. 392p.
    Western

2790 ---The gold girl. New York: Putnam, 1920. 349p.
    Western

2791 ---Prairie flowers. New York: Putnam, 1920. 315p.
    Western

2792 ---Snowdrift; a story of the strong cold. New York: Putnam, 1922. 381p.

2793 ---Connie morgan in the cattle country. New York: Putnam, 1923. 307p.

2794 ---North. New York: Putnam, 1923. 334p.
    Alaska--Gold--Romance--Adventure.

2795 ---At the foot of the rainbow. New York: Putnam, 1924. 331p.

2796 ---Without gloves. New York: Putnam, 1924. 389p.

2797 ---Oak and iron of these be the breed of the north. New York: Putnam, 1925. 369p.

2798 ---Frozen inlet post. New York: Doubleday, 1927. 282p.
    Hudson Bay Company.

2799 ---Gold-and the mounted. New York: Doubleday, 1928. 278p.

2800 ---Man of the north. New York: Doubleday, 1929. 297p.

2801 ---Blood on the yukon trail; a novel of corporal downey of the mounted. New York: Doubleday, 1930. 305p.

2802 ---Corporal downey takes the trail. New York: Doubleday, 1931. 320p.

2803 ---Raw gold. New York: Doubleday, 1933. 307p.
       Yukon-1850's.

2804 ---The yukon kid. New York: Doubleday, 1934. 294p.
       1892

2805 ---Outlaws of halfaday creek. New York: Doubleday, 1935. 299p.
       Western

2806 ---Connie morgan in the artic. New York: Putnam, 1936. 239p.

2807 ---Grubstake gold. New York: Doubleday, 1936. 300p.

2808 ---Blood of the north. New York: Doubleday, 1938. 278p.

2809 ---Black john of halfaday creek. New York: Doubleday, 1939. 305p.
       Western

2810 ---Edge of beyond. New York: Doubleday, 1939. 276p.
       Yukon

2811 ---The czar of halfday creek. New York: Doubleday, 1940. 271p.
       Western

2812 ---Hard rock man. New York: Carlton, 1940. 286p.
       Klondike Gold Rush.

2813 ---Gambler's chance. New York: Carlton, 1941. 269p.

2814 ---Law and order on halfaday creek. New York: Carlton, 1941. 308p.
       Western

2815 ---Gold and guns on halfaday creek. New York: Carlton, 1942. 280p.
       Western

2816 ---Skulldugery on halfaday creek. New York: Doubleday, 1946. 271p.
       Western

2817 ---Justice on halfaday creek. New York: Doubleday, 1949. 220p.

218

2818 ---Murder in the outlands. New York: Doubleday, 1949.
      218p.

2819 ---Badmen on halfaday creek. New York: Doubleday, 1950.
      216p.
         Western

2820 ---Murder on halfaday creek. New York: Doubleday, 1951.
      191p.
         Western

2821 ---On the rim of the artic. New York: Doubleday, 1951.
      191p.

2822 ---Sourdough gold. New York: Doubleday, 1952. 190p.

2823 ---Gold is where you find it. New York: Doubleday,
      1953. 191p.
         Western

2824 ---Intrigue on halfaday creek. New York: Doubleday,
      1953. 186p.
         Western

2825 ---Good men and bad. New York: Doubleday, 1954.
      192p.
         Western

2826 Henkle, Henrietta (Mrs. P. J. Stephens) (1909-   )
      pseud. Buckmaster, Henrietta. Deep river. New
      York: Harcourt, 1944. 481p.
         Georgia 1858-1860--Mountaineer educated leads
      fight against slavery--Pro-union.

2827 ---Fire in the heart. New York: Harcourt, 1948.
      351p.
         English woman weds Georgia plantation owner--
      Frances Anne Kemble (1809-1893)--Pre-Civil War.

2828 Hennagin, Allie D.. Third daughter. New York: Nelson,
      1954. 189p.
         Oregon--1860's--Juvenile.

2829 Henri, Mrs. Florette. Kings mountain. New York:
      Doubleday, 1950. 340p.
         First novel--American Revolution--Battle King's
      Mountain (1780).

      Henry, Will pseud. see Allen, Henry (1912-   )

2830 Henshaw, Nevil Gratiot. Aline of the grand woods; a
      story of louisiana. New York: Outing, 1909. 491p.
         Cajuns--Louisiana.

2831 Henty, George Alfred (1832-1902). With wolfe in canada;

or, the winning of a continent. New York: Burt,
189?. 401p.
Lad of 17 aide of Washington--Juvenile.

2832　Hentz, Nicholas Marcellus. Tadeuskund, the last king
of the lenape. an historical tale. [Anonymous].
Boston: Cummings, 1825. 276p.
Pennsylvania--French-Indian War (1754-1763).

2833　Hepburn, Andrew. Letter of marque. Boston: Little,
1959. 342p.
American privateer--War of 1812.

Herbert, Arthur pseud. see Arthur, Herbert

2834　Herbert, Henry William (1807-1858). The innocent
witch; a continuation of Ruth whaley; or, the
fair puritan. a romance of the bay province.
Boston: Williams, 1845. 50p.
Colonial Era.

2835　---The revolt of boston; a continuation of Ruth whaley;
or, the fair puritan. a romance of the bay province.
Boston: Williams, 1845. 48p.

2836　---Ruth whaley; or, the fair puritan. a romance of
the bay province. Boston: Williams, 1845. 72p.

2837　---pseud. Forester, Frank. The deerstalkers; or,
circumstantial evidence. a tale of the southwestern counties. Philadelphia: Cary, 1849. 198p.

2838　Hergesheimer, Joseph (1880-1954). Mountain blood;
a novel. New York: Kennerley, 1915. 312p.
Third generation Scots in highlands of Virginia--
Romance.

2839　---Java head. New York: Knopf, 1919. 255p.
1840's--Salem sailor returns home with Chinese
wife.

2840　---Balisand. New York: Knopf, 1924. 371p.
Virginia--1782--Romance--Hero Federalist.

2841　---The limestone tree. New York: Knopf, 1931. 386p.
Chronicle Kentucky family--Eighteenth and
nineteenth century--Gabriel Sash.

Hersch, Helen Virginia (Davis) see Hersch, Virginia
(1896-　　)

2842　Hersch, Virginia Davis (1896-　　). Storm beach.
Boston: Houghton, 1933. 275p.
Chronicle--Jewish family--Charleston, South
Carolina--Early nineteenth century.

2843 ---The seven cities of gold. New York: Duell, 1946.
243p.
Francisco Coronado(1510-1549)--Second exped-
ition--Mexico to Kansas--Colorful.

2844 Hess, Fjeril (1893-   ). Leather pants. New York:
Macmillan, 1941. 278p.
Dry farming--Cowboys--Current.

2845 Heuman, William. Captain mcrae; a novel of the northwest frontier. New York: Morrow, 1954. 192p.
Sioux on warpath.

2846 ---Missouri river boy. New York: Dodd, 1959. 153p.
1868--Life on river boat--Cub pilot.

2847 Hewes, Mrs. Agnes Danforth. Glory of the seas. New
York: Knopf, 1933. 315p.
Boston--Pre-Civil War--Romance--Adventure--
Juvenile.

2848 Hewlett, John Henry (1905-   ). Cross on the moon.
New York: McGraw, 1946. 316p.
Rural Georgia community--Narrow religious
views.

2849 Heyer, Georgette (1902-   ). Beauvallet. New York:
Longmans, 1930. 348p.
Sir Nicholas Beauvallet--Super pirate--Scourge
of Spanish Main--Romance--Adventure.

2850 Hicks, Clifton. The little lion. New York: Island
Workship, 1946. 256p.
Frontier--1850's-1870's--Upper New York State
and Iowa.

2851 Hicks, John (1918-   ). The long whip. New York:
McKay, 1969. 344p.
Black slave with union black militia--1850
through reconstruction.

2852 Hildreth, Harry Dean. Wauneta; an indian story of
happiness as a mental condition. Chicago: Donohue,
1894. 182p.

2853 Hill, Beveridge. The story of a cañon. Boston: Arena,
1895. 452p.
Colorado--Silver.

2854 Hill, Francis. Once on a summer range. New York:
Macmillan, 1918. 328p.
1888--Montana--Sheepherder--Romance--Melodrama.

2855 Hilliard d'Auberteuil. Mis macrae, roman historique.
Philadelphia: 1784. 146p.

221

Losche "first novel both written and published
in America"--American Revolution--Sabin..."probably
published at Brussels"--Based on story of Jane McCrae.

Hilliard, John Northern jt. author, see Mason, Grace
Sartwell

2856 Hilton, Francis W.. The long rope. New York: Kinsey,
1935. 282p.
Western

2857 ---The mañana kid. New York: Kinsey, 1939. 274p.
Western

2858 Hinckley, Helen (Mrs. Ivan Jones) (1903-   ). The
mountains are mine. New York: Vanguard, 1946.
394p.
Mormon girl age eleven to Salt Lake City in
wagon train--Ends when she is age twenty--Good on
Mormons.

2859 Hinkle, Thomas Clark (1876-   ). Tawny; a dog of the
old west. New York: Morrow, 1927. 238p.
Kansas plains--Dog story.

2860 ---Bing; the story of a tramp dog. New York: Morrow,
1932. 224p.
Kansas-- 1880's.

2861 ---Hurricane pinto; the story of an outlaw horse.
New York: Morrow, 1935. 257p.
Boy--Horse--cf. Will James.

2862 ---Barry; the story of a wolf dog. New York: Morrow,
1938. 242p.
Juvenile

2863 ---Dusty; the story of a wild dog. New York: Morrow,
1940. 252p.
Western plains.

2864 ---Old nick and bob; two dogs of the west. New York:
Morrow, 1941. 239p.
Western plains.

2865 ---Mustang; a horse of the old west. New York: Morrow,
1942. 247p.

2866 ---Shep; a collie of the old west. New York: Morrow,
1943. 224p.
Kansas setting.

2867 Hinsdale, Harriet (1900-   ). Be my love. New York:
Creative Age, 1950. 376p.
American Revolution from viewpoint of British

222

colonial officers--Cinderella romance--Sir Charles
Franklin (1716-1768)--Lady Franklin (1726-1783).

2868 Hitchcock, Enos (1745-1803). Memoirs of the bloomsgrove
family in a series of letters to a respectable citizen of philadelphia; containing sentiments on a mode
of domestic education, suited to the present state
of society, government, and manners in the united
states of america; and on the dignity of the female
character, interspersed with a variety of interesting
anecdotes. Boston: Thomas, 1790. 2 vols.

2869 Hittell, Theodore Henry (1830-1917). Adventures of
james capen adams, mountaineer and grizzly bear
hunter of california. San Francisco: Towne, 1860.
378p.
         Juvenile

2870 Hobart, Mrs. Alice Tisdale (Nourse) (1882-1967).
The cup and the sword. Indianapolis: Bobbs, 1942.
400p.
         Family chronicle--Grapes and wine--California--
1920-1940.

Hobart, Bayne see Hobart, Donald Bayne

2871 Hobart, Donald Bayne. Arizona outlaw. New York:
Arcadia, 1961. 223p.
         Western

2872 ---Sinister ranch. New York: Arcadia, 1968. 192p.
         Western

2873 Hodge, Jane (Aiken). Here comes a candle. New York:
Doubleday, 1967. 264p.
         Gothic--Romance--War of 1812--New England
plan of secession.

2874 Hodges, M. C.. The mestico; or, the warpath and its
incidents. a story of the creek indian disturbances
of 1836. New York: Graham, 1850. 204p.

2875 Hoffine, Lyla. White buffalo; a story of the northwest fur trade. New York: Longmans, 1939. 284p.
         Manuel Lisa (1772-1820)--Juvenile.

2876 Hoffman, Charles Fenno (1806-1884). Wild scenes in
the forest and prairie. London: Bentley, 1839.
2 vols.

2877 ---Greyslaer; a romance of the mohawk. New York:
Harper, 1840. 2 vols.
         Revolution Era--New York State--Mohawk Valley.

2878 Hoffman, Paul. Seven yesterdays. New York: Harper,
1933. 226p.

Boyhood--Rome or Utica, New York--Autobiograph-
ical novel.

2879 Hogan, Pendleton (1907-   ). The dark comes early.
      New York: Washburn, 1934. 357p.
      Texas Revolution--Mexican War--Romance.

2880 Hogan, Ray (1908-   ). The life and death of clay
      allison. New York: New American Library, 1961.
      160p.
           Clay Allison (d. 1887).

2881 Hogan, Robert J.. Two-gun law. New York: Dodd, 1950.
      210p.
      Western

2882 ---Apache landing. New York: Dodd, 1951. 256p.
      Western

2883 ---The challenge of smoke wade. New York: Dodd, 1951.
      255p.
      Western

2884 ---Renegade gun. New York: Dodd, 1952. 216p.
      Western

2885 ---Stampede canyon. New York: Dodd, 1952. 248p.
      Western

2886 ---Howl at the moon. Boston: Houghton, 1953. 202p.
           Pioneer life--Prairies--Juvenile.

2887 ---Savage rebel. New York: Dodd, 1953. 245p.
      Western

2888 ---Night rider's moon. New York: Dodd, 1954. 215p.
      Western

2889 ---Texas guns. New York: Dodd, 1954. 218p.
      Western

2890 ---pseud. Cantrell, Wade B.. Brand of cain. New
      York: Pyramid, 1955. 159p.
      Western

2891 ---pseud. Jasper, Bob. Feud at sundown. Boston:
      Houghton, 1951. 246p.
      Western

2892 Hogeboom, Amy (1891-   ) and Ware, John Fleming
      (1891-   ). One life to lose. New York: Lothrop,
      1942. 284p.
           Nathan Hale (1755-1776)--Juvenile.

2893 Holbrook, Elizabeth. Old 'kaskia days; a novel...

kaskasia;jesuit mission founded 1680-86, under
british rule, 1763, a county of virginia, 1778,
northwestern territory, 1787, territory of indiana,
1802, territory of illinois, 1809, state of illinois,
1818. Chicago: Schulte, 1893. 295p.

2894 Holford, Castell N.. Aristopia; a romance history of
      the new world. Boston: Arena, 1895. 234p.

2895 Holland, Josiah Gilbert (1819-1881). The bay-path;
      a tale of new england colonial life. New York:
      Putnam, 1857. 418p.
          Connecticut Valley--1638--Puritan intolerance--
      Quiet portrait.

2896 Holland, Rupert Sargent (1878-1952). The blue heron's
      feather; a story of a dutch boy in the american
      colony of new netherland. Philadelphia: Lippincott,
      1917. 301p.
          Son taken by Indians--Hudson Valley--Mohawks.

2897 ---The rider in the green mask. Philadelphia: Lippincott,
      1926. 288p.
          Privateering--Adventure and mystery.

2898 ---The pirate of the gulf. Philadelphia: Lippincott,
      1929. 270p.
          Jean LaFitte (1780?-1826?).

2899 Holling, Holling Clancy. Tree in the trail. Boston:
      Houghton, 1942. 63p.
          Cottonwood tree--1610-1834--Juvenile.

2900 ---Seabird. Boston: Houghton, 1948. 58p.
          Three generations of carved seabird--Whaling
      to flying--Juvenile.

2901 Hollister, Gideon Hiram (1817-1881). Mount hope; or,
      philip king of the wampanoags. an historical romance.
      New York: Harper, 1851. 280p.
          Metacomet (d.1676)--Fugitive regicides--Goffe
      and Whalley.

2902 Holmes, Llewellyn Perry (1895-   ). Roaring range.
      New York: Greenberg, 1935. 250p.
          Western

2903 ---Destiny range. New York: Greenberg, 1936. 256p.
          Western

2904 ---The law of kyger gorge. New York: Greenberg, 1936.
      252p.
          Western

2905 ---Bloody saddles. New York: Greenberg, 1937. 250p.
          Western

2906   ---Outlaws of boardman's flat. New York: Phoenix,
       1941. 256p.
          Western

2907   ---Flame of sunset. New York: Curl, 1947. 224p.
          Western

2908   ---Desert rails. New York: Simon, 1949. 241p.
          Western

2909   ---Water, grass and gunsmoke. New York: Doubleday,
       1949. 218p.
          Western

2910   ---Black sage. New York: Doubleday, 1950. 220p.
          Western

2911   ---Dead man's saddle. New York: Doubleday, 1951.
       221p.
          Western

2912   ---Summer range. New York: Doubleday, 1951. 190p.
          Western

2913   ---Apache desert. New York: Doubleday, 1952. 192p.
          Western

2914   ---High starlight. New York: Doubleday, 1952. 189p.
          Western

2915   ---Delta deputy. New York: Doubleday, 1953. 187p.
          Western

2916   ---Somewhere they die. Boston: Little, 1955. 211p.
          Western--Golden Spur Award 1956 for Best Western.

2917   ---Modoc; the last sundown. New York: Dodd, 1957.
       213p.
          Western

2918   ---Catch and saddle. New York: Dodd, 1959. 214p.
          Western

2919   ---Hill smoke. New York: Dodd, 1959. 214p.
          Western

2920   ---Night marshal. New York: Dodd, 1961. 212p.
          Western

2921   ---pseud. Hardin, Dave. Brandon's empire. New York:
       Ballantine, 1953. 180p.
          Western

2922   ---pseud. Stuart, Matt. Dusty wagons. Philadelphia:
       Lippincott, 1949. 206p.
          Western

2923 ---Bonanza gulch. Philadelphia: Lippincott, 1950. 217p.
        Western

2924 ---Gunsmoke showdown. Philadelphia: Lippincott,
        1951. 210p.
        Western

2925 ---Gun law at vermillion. Philadelphia: Lippincott,
        1951. 219p.
        Western

2926 ---The smoky trail. Philadelphia: Lippincott, 1951.
        221p.
        Western

2927 ---Sunset rider. Philadelphia: Lippincott, 1952. 214p.
        Western

2928 ---Wire in the wind. Philadelphia: Lippincott, 1952.
        216p.
        Western

2929 ---Deep hills. Philadelphia: Lippincott, 1953. 187p.
        Western

2930 ---The lonely law. New York: Dodd, 1957. 216p.
        Western

2931 ---The plunderers. New York: Dodd, 1957. 210p.
        Western

2932 ---Wild summit. New York: Dodd, 1958. 212p.
        Western

2933 ---Tough saddle. New York: Dodd, 1959. 218p.
        Western

2934 ---Warrior creek. New York: Dodd, 1960. 214p.
        Western

2935 Holmes, Mrs. Mary Jane (Hawes). Ethelyn's mistake;
        or, the home in the west. a novel. New York:
        Carleton, 1869. 380p.
        Iowa

2936 Holmes, Richard Sill (1842-1912). The victor; a novel.
        New York: Revell, 1908. 320p.
        Pennsylvania mountains--Discovery of oil--
        Romance--Murder.

2937 Holmes, Thomas K.. The man from tall timber. New York:
        Sully, 1919. 434p.
        Western

2938 ---The heart of canyon pass. New York: Sully, 1921. 312p.
        Western--Mining.

2939 Holt, Felix. The gabriel horn. New York: Dutton,
      1951. 221p.
      First novel--Westward trek of settlers--Early
      nineteenth century--Tennessee River--Kentucky.

2940 ---Dan'l boone kissed me. New York: Dutton, 1954. 248p.
      Romance--Adventure.

2941 Holton, Edith Austin (1891-   ). pseud. Heath, Elizabeth
      Alden. Time and the hour. New York: Putnam, 1946. 310
      Chronicle--Five generations--Penmingtons--
      Early 1800's--Cape Cod.

2942 Hood, Margaret Page. Tequila. New York: Coward, 1950. 3
      New Mexico--1900ca.

2943 Hoogstraat, Moore E. von. Where the sage and catus grow.
      Chicago: Scroll, 1900. 243p.
      Mining--Mohave Desert.

2944 Hooker, Mrs. Forrestine Cooper (1867-1932). The long
      dim trail. New York: Knopf, 1920. 364p.
      Western

2945 ---Star, the story of an indian pony. New York: Doubleday
      1922. 191p.
      Comanche--Quanah Parker (1854-1911).

2946 ---When geronimo rode. New York: Doubleday, 1924. 325p.
      Western

2947 Hooker, William Francis (1856-1938). Branded men and
      women; story of a western town. Boston: Badger,
      1921. 305p.
      Western

2948 Hooper, Johnson Jones (1815?-1863). Some adventures
      of captain simon suggs, late of the tallapoosa vol-
      unteers; together with "taking the census", and
      other alabama sketches. Philadelphia: Carey, 1845. 20
      Old southwest--Flush times--Ostensibly a
      campaign biography.

2949 Hopkins, Joseph G. E.. Patriot's progress. New York:
      Scribner's, 1961. 245p.
      American Revolution--Young physican's family
      marked by divided loyalties--Massachusetts 1774-1776.

2950 ---Retreat recall. New York: Scribner's, 1966. 223p.
      American Revolution--Sequel to Patriot's Progress

2951 Hopkins, Pauline Bradford (Mackie). Mademoiselle de
      berny; a story of valley forge. Boston: Lamson,
      1897. 272p.
      American Revolution.

228

2952 ---Ye lyttle salem maide; a story of witchcraft.
Boston: Wolffe, 1898. 321p.
1690's.

2953 ---A georgian actress. Boston: Page, 1900. 296p.
George III Era.

2954 Hopkins, Samuel. The youth of the old dominion.
Boston: Jewett, 1856. 473p.
Jamestown, Virginia--Bacon's Rebellion.

2955 Hopkins, Squire D. pseud. Vic St. L. (Jeune Hopkins).
The mysterious hunter; or, the last of the aztecs.
Chicago: Jeune Hopkins Co., 1892. 293p.

Hoppus, Mary A. M. see Marks, Mary A. M. (Hoppus)

2956 Hopson, William L.. Gun-thrower. New York: Phoenix,
1940. 256p.
Western

2957 ---Cowpoke justice. New York: Phoenix, 1941. 254p.
Western

2958 ---The laughing vaquero. New York: Phoenix, 1943. 254p.
Western

2959 ---Sunset ranch. New York: Phoenix, 1943. 256p.
Western

2960 ---Silver gulch. New York: Phoenix, 1944. 256p.
Western

2961 ---Hell's horseman. New York: Phoenix, 1946. 256p.
Western

2962 ---Rambling top hand. New York: Phoenix, 1946. 256p.
Western

2963 ---The gringo bandit. New York: Phoenix, 1947. 255p.
Western

2964 ---Straight from boot hill. New York: Phoenix, 1947.
254p.
Western

2965 ---Arizona roundup. New York: Phoenix, 1948. 255p.
Western

2966 ---NP puncher. New York: Phoenix, 1948. 254p.
Western

2967 ---The tombstone stage. New York: Phoenix, 1948. 256p.
Western

2968 ---The border raider. New York: Phoenix, 1949. 261p.
Western

2969 ---Horse thief masquerade. New York: Phoenix, 1949.
256p.
Western

2970 ---Yucca city outlaw. New York: Phoenix, 1949. 251p.
Western

2971 ---The last apaches. New York: Bourgey, 1951. 255p.
Western

2972 ---Gunfighters pay. New York: Bourgey, 1952. 253p.
Western

2973 ---High saddle. New York: Arcadia, 1952. 221p.
Western

2974 ---Cow thief empire. New York: Arcadia, 1953. 224p.
Western

2975 ---Cry viva! New York: Bourgey, 1953. 255p.
Western

2976 ---Apache kill. New York: Avalon, 1954. 256p.
Western

2977 ---A gunman rode north. New York: Avalon, 1954. 253p.
Western

2978 ---Trouble rides tall. New York: Fawcett, 1955. 159p.
Western

2979 ---pseud. Sims, John. The new cowhand. New York:
Phoenix, 1949. 250p.
Western

2980 ---Outlaw of hidden valley. New York: Phoenix, 1949.
252p.
Western

2981 ---Desert campfire. New York: Phoenix, 1951. 223p.
Western

2982 ---Hangtree range. New York: Arcadia, 1952. 221p.
Western

2983 Horan, James David. King's rebel. New York: Crown,
1953. 376p.
American Revolution--Hero is British officer--
Weds rebel girl--New York Indians--Cherry Valley
Massacre.

2984 ---The shadow catcher. New York: Crown, 1961. 405p.

Fur trade--West--Western Heritage-Wrangler
Award Outstanding Western Novel-1962.

2985 Horgan, Paul (1903-   ). Main line west. New York:
Harper, 1936. 306p.
Western America--Mobility.

2986 ---A lamp on the plains. New York: Harper, 1937. 373p.
New Mexico--Sequel to Main Line West.

2987 ---A distant trumpet. New York: Farrar, 1960. 629p.
Life on Arizona army post--1880's--Apache.

Horne, Howard pseud. see Payne, Robert

2988 Hosmer, James Kendall.(1834-1927). How thankful was
bewitched. New York: Putnam, 1894. 299p.
Invasion of Massachusetts--Queene Anne's War.

2989 Hotchkiss, Chauncey Crafts (1852-1920). In defiance
of the king; a romance of the american revolution.
New York: Appleton, 1895. 312p.

2990 ---A colonial free lance. New York: Appleton, 1897.
312p.

2991 ---The strength of the weak; a romance. New York:
Appleton, 1902. 371p.
French-Indian War (1754-1763)--General Braddock--
Sir William Johnson.

2992 Hough, Emerson (1857-1923). The girl at halfway house;
a story of the plains. New York: Appleton, 1900. 371p.
Romance--Hero Union captain.

2993 ---The mississippi bubble; how the star of good fortune
rose and set and rose again by a woman's grace, for
one john law of lauriston; a novel. Indianapolis:
Bowen, 1902. 452p.
John Law (1671-1729)--Romance--Iriquois--New
France--1704-1729.

2994 ---Heart's desire; the story of a contented town,
certain peculiar citizens, and two fortunate lovers;
a novel. New York: Macmillan, 1905. 367p.
Rough western life--Utopia--Eden.

2995 ---54-40 or fight. Indianapolis: Bobbs, 1909. 402p.
Oregon Treaty--Texas boundary dispute--Romance.

2996 ---The magnificent adventure; this being the story of
the world's greatest exploration, and the romance of
a very gallant gentleman; a novel. New York: Appleton, 1916. 355p.
Louisiana Purchase--Lewis and Clark--Burr's

231

Conspiracy--Hero-Meriwether Lewis (1774-1809)--
Theodosia Burr is heroine.

2997 ---The sagebrusher; a story of the west. New York:
Appleton, 1919. 318p.
Western

2998 ---Covered wagon. New York: Appleton, 1922. 378p.
Missouri to Oregon--1848--Romance.

2999 ---North of 36. New York: Appleton, 1923. 429p.
Cattle drive and life in cowtown--Idealized--
Reconstruction era--Will Bill-symbolic peace officer.

3000 ---Mother of gold. New York: Appleton, 1924. 326p.
Western

3001 Hough, Frank. Renown. New York: Carrick, 1938. 497p.
Benedict Arnold (1741-1801)--Generally sympathetic.

3002 ---If not victory. New York: Carrick, 1939. 335p.
American Revolution--Westchester County, New
York--War from view of "common man"--Divided loyalty.

3003 ---The neutral ground. Philadelphia: Lippincott, 1941.
526p.
American Revolution--Westchester County, New
York--Sequel to If Not Victory.

3004 Hough, Henry Beetle (1896-   ). Long anchorage;
a new bedford story. New York: Appleton, 1947. 309p.
From whaling to textiles--1847-1922.

3005 ---The new england story; a novel. New York: Random,
1958. 277p.
Chronicle--Three generations--New England
whaling family--1800's.

3006 Houston, Margaret Bell (Mrs. M. L. Kauffman). Magic
valley. New York: Appleton, 1934. 310p.
Western

3007 Houston, Margaret Bell (Mrs. William H. Probert).
Cottonwoods grow tall. New York: Crown, 1958. 247p.
Texas ranching--1890's--day-to-day--Well told
story.

3008 Houston, Noel. The great promise; a novel. New York:
Reynal, 1946. 502p.
Oklahoma Territory--1897--Land lottery.

3009 How, Louis (1873-1947). The penitentes of san rafael;
a tale of the san luis valley. Indianapolis: Bowen,
1900. 381p.
New Mexico.

3010 Howard, Elizabeth. Adventure for alison. New York:
        Lothrop, 1942. 216p.
            Scottish brother and sister to Jacobite brother
        in America--Juvenile.

3011 ---Summer under sail. New York: Morrow, 1947. 213p.
            Sailing ships on Great Lakes--Cleveland 1852.

3012 ---North wind blows free. New York: Morrow, 1949. 192p.
            Michigan--Ontario community--Underground rail-
        road.

3013 ---A star to follow. New York: Morrow, 1954. 222p.
            Frontier army post--Detroit and Arizona--1875--
        Juvenile.

3014 ---A girl of the north country. New York: Morrow,
        1957. 222p.
            Pioneering--Michigan--1850's--Juvenile.

3015 Howard, H. R. [Anonymous]. The life and adventures
        of john a. murrell, the great western land pirate.
        New York: Long, 1847. 126p.

3016 ---The life and adventures of henry thomas, the western
        burglar and murder, and the thrilling narrative of
        mrs. whipple and jesse strang. Philadelphia:
        Peterson, 1848. 141p.

3017 Howe, Edgar Watson (1854-1937). The story of a country
        town. Boston: Houghton, 1884. 413p.
            Western Kansas town--Pioneer document--Anti-
        idealistic treatment of life.

3018 Howells, William Dean (1837-1920). The leatherwood
        god. New York: Century, 1916. 236p.
            Religious fervor--Ohio frontier--1830--Good
        local color.

3019 Hubbard, Elbert (1856-1915). One day; a tale of the
        prairies. Boston: Arena, 1893. 103p.

3020 ---Time and chance; a romance and a history; being the
        story of the life of a man. East Aurora, New York:
        Roycrofters, 1899. 2 vols.
            John Brown (1800-1859)--Harper's Ferry.

3021 Hubbard, Lafayette Ronald (1911-   ). Buckskin
        brigades. New York: Macaulay, 1937. 316p.
            White lad raised by Indians--Fur trade--
        Blackfeet--Lewis and Clark--1803.

3022 Hubbard, Lucien. Rivers to the sea; an american story.
        New York: Simon, 1942. 313p.
            First novel--Steamboating--Pittsburgh to New
        Orleans.

3023 Hubbard, Margaret Ann. The hickory limb. New York:
      Macmillan, 1942. 291p.
           American Revolution--Later years--Colonel John
      Sevier--Jack Nolichucky--Great Smokies--Tennessee.

3024 ---Lone boy. New York: Macmillan, 1943. 259p.
      Western--Juvenile.

3025 ---Thunderhead mountain. New York: Macmillan, 1952.
      204p.
           Indian boy--Horse--Good regional work.

3026 Hubbard, Ralph. Queer person. New York: Doubleday,
      1930. 336p.
           Outcast Indian boy--Deaf mute with Pikuni--
      Excellent--Juvenile.

3027 Hudson, Mary Worrell (Smith). Esther the gentile.
      Topeka, Kansas: Crane, 1888. 167p.
           Anti-Mormon.

3028 Hueston, Ethel Powelson (Mrs. E. J. Best) (1889-   ).
      Star of the west; a romance of the lewis and clark
      expedition. Indianapolis: Bobbs, 1935. 372p.
           Lewis and Clark Expedition--Sacagawea--Based
      on journals.

3029 ---The man of the storm; a romance of colter who
      discovered yellowstone. Indianapolis: Bobbs, 1936.
      312p.
           John Colter (c.1813)--Romance with Sally Dale.

3030 ---Calamity jane of deadwood gulch. Indianapolis: Bobbs,
      1937. 306p.
           Black Hills--1875-1903--Air of reality.

3031 Huffman, Laurie. A house behind the mint. New York:
      Doubleday, 1969. 312p.
           First novel--Western romance--California 1875-
      1883.

3032 Hughes, Langston (1902-   ). Not without laughter.
      New York: Knopf, 1930. 324p.
           Life of black in Kansas town--Author-well
      known poet.

3033 Hughes, Mrs. Reginald pseud. Lyndon. Margaret; a
      story of life in a prairie home. New York: Scribner's
      1868. 360p.

3034 Hughes, Rupert (1872-1956). Stately timber. New York:
      Scribner's, 1939. 638p.
           Puritan New England--Virginia--Barbados--1650.

3035 Hughs, Mary (Robson) [Anonymous]. Julia ormond; or,

the new settlement. New York: Dunigan, 1846. 220p.

3036 Hulme, Kathryn (1900-   ). Annie's captain. Boston:
Little, 1961. 330p.
From sail to steam--Based on grandparents--
John M. Cavarly (1832-1895).

3037 Hummel, George Frederick (1882-1952). Heritage. New
York: Stokes, 1935. 674p.
Railroad to Warwold, Long Island--Germans move--
Good regional 1846.

3038 ---Joshua moore, american. New York: Doubleday, 1943.
456p.
Chronicle--Fortunes of Moore and family--Seven-
teenth century to 1940's.

3039 Humphrey, Mary A. (Vance). The squatter sovereign;
or, kansas in the 50's. a life picture of the early
settlement of the debatable ground. a story founded
upon memorable and historical events. Chicago:
Coburn, 1883. 354p.

3040 Hunt, Barbara. Sea change. New York: Rinehart, 1946.
270p.
First novel--Black magic--New England--1820's.

3041 Hunt, Frazier (1885-   ). Custer, the last of the
cavaliers. New York: Cosmopolitan, 1928. 209p.
George A. Custer (1839-1876) biography--
Twilight zone history and fiction.

3042 Hunt, John Clinton (1925-   ). Generations of men.
Boston: Little, 1956. 307p.
Chetopa County, Oklahoma and Chetopa Indians--
Golden Spur Award 1957 for Best Western Historical
Novel.

3043 ---The grey horse legacy. New York: Knopf,
1968. 427p.
Killing of oil rich Chetopa family--Grey Horse,
Oklahoma--1920's and 1950's--Thriller.

Hunter, Hall pseud. see Marshall, Edison

Hunter, John pseud. see Ballard, Willis Tod Hunter

3044 Hunter, Martha Eaton. "By one of her daughters".
The clifford family; or, a tale of the old dominion.
New York: Harper, 1852. 430p.
Virginia

3045 Hurst, Hawthorne. Christopher comes across. New York:
King, 1932. 249p.
Colombus is "blond Don Juan"--Humor.

235

Hutchins, Cortelle J. jt. author, see Hutchins, Frank W.

3046 Hutchins, Frank W. and Cortelle J.. <u>Sword of liberty</u>;
      <u>the story of two revolutions</u>. New York: Century,
      <u>1921</u>. 347p.
         American and French Revolutions--Sword to
      Lafayette (1757-1834).

3047 Hutchens, Mrs. Jane. <u>John brown's cousin.</u> New York:
      Doubleday, 1940. 97p.
         Pioneer Missouri family.

3048 ---<u>Timothy larkin</u>. New York: Doubleday, 1942. 279p.
         Picaresque story--Missouri family (1850-1861).

3049 Huzarski, Richard. <u>Brushland bill</u>. New York: Crowell,
      1943. 264p.
         Hunting and trapping--Northern Wisconsin--
      Juvenile.

3050 Hyndman, Mrs. Jane Andrews (Lee) (1912-   ) <u>pseud</u>.
      Wyndham, Lee. <u>Camel bird ranch</u>. New York: Dodd,
      1955. 247p.
         Southern California--Ostrich ranch--Juvenile.

3051 Idell, Albert Edward (1901-   ). The great blizzard.
      New York: Holt, 1948. 282p.
         Chronicle--Rogers family--Manhattan 1884-1888.

3052 ---Rogers' folly. New York: Doubleday, 1957. 328p.
         Bordentown, New Jersey--1844.

3053 Imlay, Gilbert (1755-1796). The emigrants, etc.; or,
      the history of an expatriated family; being a
      delineation of english manners, drawn from real
      characters, written in america. Dublin: Printed for
      C. Brown, 1794. 325p.
         Sentimental romance.

3054 Ingraham, Joseph Holt (1809-1866). Burton; or, the
      sieges. a romance. New York: Harper, 1838. 2 vols.
         1750-1812--All major historical figures appear--
      Quebec.

3055 ---Captain kyd; or, the wizard of the sea. a romance.
      New York: Harper, 1839. 2 vols.
         Pirate adventure.

3056 ---The quadroone; or, st. michael's day. New York:
      Harper, 1841. 2 vols.
         Spaniards--New Orleans--1769.

3057 ---Edward austin; or, the hunting flask. Boston:
      Gleason, 1842. 66p.

3058 ---The dancing feather; and its sequel morris graeme;
      or, the criuse of the sea-slipper. New York:
      Williams, 1845-47. 92p.

3059 ---Fleming field; or, the young artisan. a tale of
      the days of the stamp act. New York: Burgess,
      1845. 96p.
         1765--Boston.

3060 ---Grace weldon; or, frederica, the bonnet-girl. a
      tale of boston and its bay. Boston: Williams, 1845.
      108p.

3061 ---Neal nelson; or, the seige [sic] of boston. a tale
      of the revolution. New York: Williams, 1845. 48p.
         1775-1776--Washington--Conventional treatment.

3062 ---Norman; or, the privateersman's bride. a sequel

to "freemantle". Boston: 'The Yankee Office,' 1845.
48p.

3063 ---Scarlet feather; or, the young chief of the
abenaquies. a romance of the wilderness of maine.
Boston: Gleason, 1845. 66p.
Kennebec--Canadian invasion (1775-1776)--
Abnaki Indians.

3064 ---Arthur denwood; or, the maiden of the inn. a tale
of the war of 1812. Boston: Williams, 1846. 95p.

3065 ---Leisler; or, the rebel and king's man. a tale of
the rebellion of 1689. Boston: Williams, 1846. 90p.

3066 ---The silver ship of mexico. a tale of the spanish
main. New York: Williams, 1846. 98p.

3067 ---Beatrice, the goldsmith's daughter; story of the
reign of the last charles. New York: Williams,
1847. 93p.

3068 ---Blanche talbot; or, the maiden's hand. a romance
of the war of 1812. New York: Williams, 1847. 122p.

3069 ---Edward manning; or, the bride and the maiden.
New York: Williams, 1847. 120p.

3070 ---Ringold griffit; or, the raftsman of the susquehannah.
a tale of pennsylvania. Boston: Gleason, 1847.
100p.

3071 ---The surf skiff; or, the heroine of the kennebec.
New York: Williams, 1847. 98p.

3072 ---Forrestal; or, the light of the reef. a romance
of the blue waters. New York: Morning Star, 1850.
93p.

3073 ---[Anonymous]. Lafitte; the pirate of the gulf.
New York: Harper, 1836. 2 vols.
Romance--Adventure.

3074 ---Montezuma, the serf; or, the revolt of the mexitili.
a tale of the last days of the aztec dynasty.
Boston: Williams, 1845. 2 vols.

3075 ---"By a Yankee". The southwest. New York: Harper,
1835. 2 vols.
First novel--Adventure.

3076 Ingraham, Prentiss (1843-1904). Wild madge, the belle
of the brazos; or, the tenor of the trail. South
Windham, Maine: Freeman, 1881. 40p.
Western

3077   ---The girl rough riders; a romantic and adventurous
trail of fair rough riders through the wonderland
of mystery and silence. Boston: Estes, 1903. 310p.
Western

3078   ---Lafitte, the pirate of the gulf. Cleveland: Westbrook, 1931. 223p.
Pirates

3079   ---Lafitte's lieutenant. Cleveland: Westbrook, 1931.
196p.
Pirates--Romance.

3080   Inman, Henry. A pioneer from kentucky; an idyl of
the raton range. Topeka, Kansas: Crane, 1898. 160p.

3081   Iron, N. C.. Hearts forever; or, the old dominion
battle-grounds. a tale of 1782. New York: Beadle,
1867. 100p.

3082   Irving, John Treat. The hawk chief; a tale of the
indian country. Philadelphia: Carey, 1837. 2 vols.

3083   Irving, Washington (1783-1859). A history of new york
by diedrich knickerbocker, from the beginning of the
world to the end of the dutch dynasty, containing
among many surprising and curious matters, the un-
utterable ponderings of walter the doubter, the dis-
astrous projects of william the testy, the chivalric
achievments of peter the headstrong. the three dutch
governors of new amsterdam; being the only authentic
history of the time that hath ever been, or ever
will be published. New York: Inskeep, 1809. 2 vols.

3084   Irwin, Inez (Haynes) (Mrs. Will Irwin) (1873-   ).
Youth must laugh. Indianapolis: Bobbs, 1932. 402p.
    One of eight Charlestown, Massachusetts sisters
to Colorado mining area--1837-1870--Husband a
minister--Juvenile.

3085   Irwin, William Henry (1873-   ). Youth rides west.
New York: Knopf, 1925. 284p.
Western

J

J. S. of Dale pseud. see Stimson, Frederic Jesup

3086 Jackson, Charles Tenney (1874-   ). The midlanders.
Indianapolis: Bobbs, 1912. 386p.
Louisiana--Chicago--Rome, Iowa.

3087 Jackson, Charlotte E. (Cobden) (Mrs. Joseph Henry
Jackson). Mercy hicks. New York: Dodd, 1949.
241p.
California--1826--Fifteen year old girl with
father--Captain of clipper ship--Juvenile.

3088 Jackson, Frederick J.. Risky rustling. New York:
Dial, 1933. 300p.
Western

3089 Jackson, Mrs. Helen Maria (Fiske) Hunt (1831-1885).
Ramona. Boston: Roberts, 1884. 490p.
Tragic romance--Expose injustice of United
State's policy toward Indians--Southern California--
Missions--Spanish hacienda life.

3090 ---pseud. H. H.. Nelly's silver mine; a story of
colorado life. Boston: Roberts, 1887. 379p.
Juvenile

3091 Jackson, Mary E.. The spy of osawatomie; or, the
mysterious companions of old john brown. St. Louis,
Missouri: Bryan, 1881. 439p.
Kansas--1850's.

3092 Jacobs, Emma Atkins. Trailer trio. Philadelphia:
Winston, 1942. 280p.
Three on way to Idaho homestead--Modern--
Juvenile.

3093 Jacobs, Helen Hull. Storm against the wind. New York:
Dodd, 1944. 403p.
Tidewater, Virginia--Pre-Revolution--Aristocrat
agrees with colonials--Good detail.

3094 Jaeger, Carl. Verana; a tale of border life. New
York: Abbey, 1900. 101p.
Western

3095 Jahoda, Gloria. Delilah's mountain. Boston: Houghton,
1963. 310p.
American Revolution--Clinch River.

James, Dan pseud. see Sayers, James Denson

3096   James, George Payne Rainsford (1801?-1860). The old
        dominion; or, the southampton massacre. a novel.
        New York: Harper, 1856. 152p.
        1831--Nat Turner.

James, Prophet pseud. see Buck, James Smith

3097   James, Will (1892-   ). Smokey, the cowhorse. New
        York: Scribner's, 1926. 310p.
        Horse book--Author did drawings.

3098   ---Sand. New York: Scribner's, 1929. 328p.
        Western

3099   ---Uncle bill; a tale of two kids and a cowboy. New
        York: Scribner's, 1932. 241p.
        Ranch life--Juvenile.

3100   ---Three mustangeers. New York: Scribner's, 1933.
        350p.
        Western

3101   ---Home ranch. New York: Scribner's, 1935. 346p.
        Ranch life--Start to 1935.

3102   ---Flint spears, cowboy rodeo contestant. New York:
        Scribner's, 1938. 269p.
        Rodeo--Start to 1930's.

3103   ---The american cowboy. New York: Scribner's, 1942.
        273p.
        History of cowboy in fictional form.

Janet, Lillian pseud. see Cicchetti, Janet

3104   Janeway, J. B. H.. "His love for helen". New York:
        Dillingham, 1893. 314p.
        Western--Romance.

3105   Janvier, Thomas Allibone (1849-1913). The aztec
        treasure-house; a romance of contemporaneous
        antiquity. New York: Harper, 1890. 446p.
        Style of Haggard's She--Discovery of Aztec
        city.

3106   ---Santa fé's partner; being some memorials of events
        in a new-mexican track-end town. New York: Harper,
        1907. 236p.
        Mining town.

3107   Jarvis, James Jackson. Kiana; a tradition of hawaii.
        Boston: Munroe, 1857. 277p.

241

Jasper, Bob pseud. see Hogan, Robert J.

3108   Jayne, Mitchell. Old fish hawk. Philadelphia:
        Lippincott, 1970. 288p.
                Ozarks--Close of nineteenth century--Osage
        Indian.

        Jayne, Lieut. R. H. pseud. see Ellis, Edward Sylvester
        (1840-1916)

3109   Jefferson, Bradley Carter (1894-   ). Fair havens.
        New York: Macmillan, 1948. 333p.
                Eastern Texas--Discovery of oil.

3110   Jeffery, Walter. The king's yard; a story of old
        portsmouth. London: Everett, 1903. 286p.
                Based on plot of either John Hill or John
        Painter to fire Portsmouth dockyard during American
        Revolution--English version.

3111   Jenkins, Sara Lucile (1905-   ). Saddlebag parson.
        New York: Crowell, 1956. 249p.
                Florida frontier--1827--Methodist circuit rider.

3112   Jenkins, William Fitzgerald (1896-   ). The gambling
        kid. New York: King, 1933. 288p.
                Western

3113   ---Mexican trail. New York: King, 1933. 289p.
                Western

3114   ---Fighting horse valley. New York: King, 1934. 253p.
                Western

3115   ---Outlaw sheriff. New York: King, 1934. 288p.
                Western

        Jennings, Dean pseud. see Frazee, Steve

3116   Jennings, John Edward (1906-   ). Next to valour;
        a novel. New York: Macmillan, 1939. 820p.
                First novel--French-Indian War--Roger's Rangers--
        Detailed--Authentic--Scot to New Hampshire.

3117   ---Call the new world; a novel. New York: Macmillan,
        1941. 459p.

3118   ---Gentleman ranker. New York: Reynal, 1942. 565p.
                Romance--Swashbuckling--Braddock's defeat--
        French-Indian War--Shenandoah Valley.

3119   ---The shadow and the glory. New York: Reynal, 1943.
        383p.
                American Revolution--Sequel to Next To Valour--
        Portsmouth--1774-1777--John Stark.

242

3120 ---Salem frigate. New York: Doubleday, 1946. 500p.
       Barbary Pirates.

3121 ---River to west; a novel of the astor adventure.
       New York: Doubleday, 1948. 368p.
       John Jacob Astor (1763-1848)--Romance--Astoria.

3122 ---The pepper tree; a story of new england and the
       spice islands. Boston: Little, 1950. 417p.
       New England sailing--Melodrama.

3123 ---The sea eagles; a story of the american navy during
       the revolution, of the men who fought and the ships
       they sailed and the women who stood behind them.
       New York: Doubleday, 1950. 299p.
       Joshua Barney (1759-1818).

3124 ---The strange brigade; a story of the red river and
       the opening of the canadian west. Boston: Little,
       1952. 367p.
       Opening Canadian west--Very good.

3125 ---Tide of empire. New York: Holt, 1952. 309p.
       South Carolina--1800.

3126 ---Rogue's yarn. Boston: Little, 1953. 311p.
       United States v. France--Undeclared war 1790's--
       Adventure.

3127 ---Chronicle of the calypso clipper; a novel of the
       golden days of the california trade, of the great
       ocean race around cape horn, of the clipper ships
       and of the men-and women-who sailed in them.
       Boston: Little, 1955. 295p.
       1856

3128 ---Shadows in the dusk. Boston: Little, 1955. 272p.
       New Mexico--1837--Taos Indians--Mexicans.

3129 ---The golden eagle; a novel based on the fabulous
       life and times of the great conquistador hernando
       de soto, 1500-1542. New York: Putnam, 1958. 253p.

3130 ---The tall ships. New York: McGraw, 1958. 299p.
       American Navy--War of 1812 and before.

       Jepson, Ring pseud. see Latham, Henry Jepson

3131 Jerome, Ferris. High water mark; a novel. Philadelphia:
       Lippincott, 1879. 385p.
       Western prairie town.

3132 Jesse james; the life and daring adventures of this
       bold highwayman and bank robber and his no less
       celebrated brother, frank james, together with

243

the thrilling exploits of the younger boys. written
by......(one who dare not now disclose his identity).
the only book containing the romantic life of jesse
james and his pretty wife, who clung to him to the
last. [Anonymous]. Philadelphia: Barclay, 1882. 96p.

3133 Jessop, George Henry. Judge lynch; a romance of the
california vineyards. Chicago: Belford, 1889. 232p.

3134 Jewett, Sarah Orne (1849-1909). The tory lover.
Boston: Houghton, 1901. 405p.
Romance--American Revolution--John Paul
Jones.

Johansen, Margaret Alison jt. author, see Lide, Mrs.
Alice (Alison)

3135 Johnes, Winifred Wallace (Tinker). Memoirs of a
little girl. New York: Trans Atlantic, 1896. 255p.
Michigan logging.

3136 Johnson, Alvin Saunders (1874-   ). Spring storm.
New York: Knopf, 1936. 351p.
Nebraska farm--Autobiographical novel--cf.
"Story of a Country Town".

3137 Johnson, Enid and Peck, Anne Merriman. Ho for
californy! New York: Harper, 1939. 243p.
Gold Rush.

3138 Johnson, Gerald White (1890-   ). By reason of
strength. New York: Minton, 1930. 221p.
First novel--Scottish couple to North Carolina--
Very good--Romance.

3139 Johnson, James William (1885-   ). The bitteroot
trail. Caldwell, Idaho: Caxton, 1935. 342p.
Western

3140 Johnson, Josephine (1910-   ). Now in november.
New York: Simon, 1934. 231p.
Middle west farm--1920-1930--Pulitizer Prize
1935.

3141 Johnson, P. Demarest. Clauduis, the cowboy of ramapo
valley; a story of revolutionary times in southern
new york. Middletown, New York: Slauson, 1894.
206p.

3142 Johnston, Annie (Fellows) (1863-   ). The little colonel
in arizona. Boston: Page, 1905. 313p.
Juvenile

3143 Johnston, Mary (1870-1936). Prisoners of hope. Boston:
Houghton, 1898. 378p.

First novel--Colorful romance--Bacon's Rebel-
lion--Virginia.

3144 ---To have and to hold. Boston: Houghton, 1900. 403p.
Colonial Virginia--1621--One of best romances
and one of most popular--Classic form of "historical
romance".

3145 ---Audrey. Boston: Houghton, 1902. 418p.
Colonial Virginia--1727--Romantic adventure--
Blue Ridge exploration--Governor Spotswood.

3146 ---Sir mortimer; a novel. Boston: Houghton, 1904.
349p.
English sailors on Spanish Main--Romance.

3147 ---Lewis rand. Boston: Houghton, 1908. 510p.
From Constitution through Jefferson's admin-
istration--(1789-1809)--Burr's Conspiracy--Rand joins.

3148 ---The witch. Boston: Houghton, 1914. 441p.
Witchcraft from Old to New World--West Indies.

3149 ---1492. Boston: Little, 1922. 315p.
Jewish philosopher with Columbus on first
voyage--Romance.

3150 ---Croatan. Boston: Little, 1923. 298p.
Lost colony of Virginia--1587--Roanoke Island--
Romance--Virginia Dare.

3151 ---The slave ship. Boston: Little, 1924. 330p.
Slave trade--1661-1680--Good.

3152 ---The great valley. Boston: Little, 1926. 317p.
1735--Scots to Shenandoah--Very good Indian
warfare and captivity.

3153 ---The hunting shirt. Boston: Little, 1931. 256p.
Virginia frontier--1775-1880--Romance.

3154 ---Miss delicia allen. Boston: Little, 1933. 306p.
Allen (b.1834)--Virginia plantation pre-Civil
War.

3155 Jones, Alice Ilgenfritz. The chevalier de st. denis.
Chicago: McClurg, 1900. 387p.
Louisiana, early 1700's.

3156 Jones, Grover and McNutt, William. There were gaints;
a story of blood and steel. New York: Mill, 1939.
255p.
Western

Jones, H. Bedford jt. author, see Friede, Donald

245

3157   Jones, Idwal (1890-   ). <u>Vermilion</u>. New York:
        Prentice, 1947. 495p.
            Cinnabar mine--California--1846-1900--Cope
        dynasty.

3158   Jones, James Athearn. <u>Haverhill; or, memoirs of an
        officer in the army of wolfe.</u> New York: Harper,
        1831. 2 vols.
            Quebec--1759--French-Indian War.

3159   ---pseud. Murgatroyd, Captain Matthew. <u>The refugee;
        a romance.</u> New York: Wilder, 1825. 2 vols.
            American Revolution--Fantastic romance.

3160   Jones, John Beauchamp (1810-1866). <u>Wild western scenes;
        a narrative of adventures in the western wilderness;
        forty years ago, wherein the conduct of daniel boone,
        the great american pioneer is particularly described.
        also, minute accounts are given of bear hunts-deer and
        buffalo hunts desparate conflicts with the savages-wolf
        hunts-fishing and fowling adventures-encounters with
        serpents, etc.,etc.</u> New York: Coleman, 1841. 247p.
            Appeared in 1858 under <u>The Warpath</u>.

3161   ---<u>The monarchist; an historical novel embracing real
        characters and romantic adventures.</u> Philadelphia:
        Hart, 1853. 336p.
            Intrigues against George Washington.

3162   ---<u>Freaks of fortune; or, the history and adventures
        of ned lorn.</u> Philadelphia: Peterson, 1854. 401p.

3163   ---<u>Wild western scenes,--second series. the warpath;
        a narrative of adventures in the wilderness, with
        minute details of the captivity of sundry persons;
        amusing and perilous incidents during their abode
        in the wild woods; fearful battles with the indians;
        ceremony of adoption into an indian family; encount-
        ers with wild beasts and rattle snakes, etc.....</u>
        Philadelphia: Lippincott, 1856. 335p.
            Kentucky--Ohio Valley.

3164   ---<u>Wild western scenes; or, the white spirit of the
        wilderness. being a narrative of adventures, embrac-
        ing the same characters portrayed in the original
        "wild western scenes."</u> Richmond: Molsby, 1863.
        2 vols.
            Vol. 2 never appeared.

3165   ---pseud. Hazel, Harry. <u>The light dragoon; or, the
        rancheros of the poisoned lance. a tale of the
        battlefields of mexico.</u> Boston: Star Spangled,
        1848. 100p.
            Romance

3166   ---pseud. Shortfield, Luke. The western merchant;
        a narrative containing useful instructions for
        the western man of business. Philadelphia: Grigg,
        1849. 268p.

3167   Jones, John Richter. The quaker soldier; or, the
        british in philadelphia. an historical novel.
        Philadelphia: Peterson, 1858. 569p.
                American Revolution--Romance--G. Washington
        referred to as "a rebel"--Conway Cabal.

        Jones, Juanita Nuttall jt. author, see Jones, Lloid

3168   Jones, Justin. Old put; or, the days of seventy-six.
        a tale of the revolution. New York: Long, 1852.
        104p.

3169   ---The flying yankee; or, the cruise of the clippers.
        a tale of privateering in the war 1812-'15.
        New York: Long, 1853. 100p.

3170   Jones, Lloid (1908-   ) and Jones, Juanita Nuttall
        (1912-   ). Horseman of long gone river.
        Philadelphia: Westminister, 1956. 191p.
                Western--Juvenile.

3171   Jones, Madison (1925-   ). Forest of the night.
        New York: Harcourt, 1960. 305p.
                School teacher v. Frontier community--
        Tennessee--1800's.

3172   Jones, Maynard Benedict (1904-   ). The petlands.
        New York: Brewer, 1931. 341p.
                Chronicle--Three generations--Growth of Seattle,
        Washington--cf. Ferber's Cimarron.

3173   ---Swift flows the river. New York: Dodd, 1940.   449p.
                Idaho-1850's--Pioneering orphan boy with Irish
        trooper--Good on Columbia River and Valley.

3174   ---Scarlet petticoat. New York: Dodd, 1941.   306p.
                Fur trading--Pacific northwest--Early 1800's--
        Adventure.

3175   ---pseud. Jones, Nard. Oregon detour. New York:
        Payson, 1930. 283p.
                First novel--Western farm community.

3176   ---Wheat women. New York: Duffield, 1933.   334p.
                Chronicle--Three generations--Wheat in Walla
        Walla.

3177   ---Still to the west. New York: Dodd, 1946.   268p.
                Pacific northwest--Grand Coulee Dam.

Jones, Nard see Jones, Maynard Benedict (1904-   )

3178   Jones, Susan Carleton pseud. S. Carleton (1869-   ).
        Out of drowning valley. New York: Holt, 1910.
        315p.
            Romance--Prospectors--1910.

3179   Jones, Uriah James. Simon girty, the outlaw; an
        historical romance. Philadelphia: Zeiber, 1846.
        104p.
            Southwest--1709-1755.

3180   Jones, Weyman B.. Edge of two worlds. New York:
        Dial, 1968. 143p.
            Texas--1842--Juvenile.

3181   Jordan, Mildred A. (Mrs. J. Lee Bausher) (1901-   ).
        One red rose forever. New York: Knopf, 1941.
        550p.
            Baron Stiegel--1750's--Pennsylvania--Stiegel
        glass.

3182   ---Apple in the attic; a pennsylvania legend. New
        York: Knopf, 1942. 200p.
            Pennsylvania Dutch country.

3183   ---Asylum for the queen. New York: Knopf, 1948. 446p.
            Marie Antoinette--Refuge in Pennsylvania--
        cf. Gabriel, I, Thee Wed.

3184   ---Echo of the flute. New York: Doubleday, 1958.
        479p.
            Yellow fever--1793-Pennsylvania.

3185   Joscelyn, Archie (1899-   ). The golden bowl.
        Cleveland: International, 1931. 246p.
            Western

3186   ---Black horse rider. New York: Phoenix, 1935. 256p.
            Western

3187   ---The law of lonesome river. New York: Phoenix, 1935.
        255p.
            Western

3188   ---Prisoner's valley. Cleveland: World Syndicate, 1935.
        247p.
            Western

3189   ---Six gun sovereignty. New York: Phoenix, 1935. 250p.
            Western

3190   ---The king of thunder valley. New York: Phoenix, 1936.
        256p.
            Western

3191 ---Ranch of the two thumbs. New York: Phoenix, 1937.
253p.
Western

3192 ---The riding devils. New York: Phoenix, 1937. 256p.
Western

3193 ---Cottonwood canyon. New York: Phoenix, 1938. 256p.
Western

3194 ---Hoot owl canyon. New York: Phoenix, 1938. 256p.
Western

3195 ---The heart e horseman. New York: Phoenix, 1939.
249p.
Western

3196 ---Tenderfoot bill. New York: Phoenix, 1939. 256p.
Western

3197 ---Double diamond brand. New York: Phoenix, 1940.
251p.
Western

3198 ---Guns of lost valley. New York: Phoenix, 1940. 252p.
Western

3199 ---Dead man's range. New York: Phoenix, 1941. 254p.
Western

3200 ---The sawbones of desolate range. New York: Phoenix,
1941. 256p.
Western

3201 ---Satan's range. New York: Phoenix, 1942. 256p.
Western

3202 ---Yates of red dog. New York: Phoenix, 1942. 256p.
Western

3203 ---Trail to bang-up. New York: Phoenix, 1943. 250p.
Western

3204 ---Valley ranch. New York: Phoenix, 1943. 256p.
Western

3205 ---Boss of the northern star. New York: Phoenix, 1944.
256p.
Western

3206 ---Troublesome cowhand. New York: Phoenix, 1944. 256p.
Western

3207 ---Rusty mallory. New York: Phoenix, 1945. 256p.
Western

3208 ---Sign of the gun. New York: Phoenix, 1945. 256p.
Western

3209 ---Death in the saddle. New York: Arcadia, 1946. 255p.
Western

3210 ---Judge colt. New York: Arcadia, 1946. 256p.
Western

3211 ---Doomrock. New York: Avalon, 1950. 256p.
Western

3212 ---Shannahan's feud; a new western novel. Kingston,
New York: Quinn, 1950. 123p.
Western

3213 ---Hell for leather. New York: Novel Selections, 1951.
128p.
Western

3214 ---Wagons west. New York: Bourgey, 1951. 253p.
Western

3215 ---Hostage. New York: Bourgey, 1952. 256p.
Western

3216 ---Gunman. New York: Avalon, 1953. 253p.
Western

3217 ---Ride to blizzard. New York: Bourgey, 1953. 256p.
Western

3218 ---Renegade scout. New York: Avalon, 1954. 253p.
Western

3219 ---Trapper's rendezvous. New York: Avalon, 1954.
254p.
Western

3220 ---Cheyenne justice. New York: Avalon, 1955. 254p.
Western

3221 ---The sundowners. New York: Avalon, 1956. 222p.
Western

3222 ---The man from salt creek. New York: Avalon, 1957.
222p.
Western

3223 ---High prairie. New York: Avalon, 1958. 220p.
Western

3224 ---Sheriff of red wolf. New York: Arcadia, 1963. 223p.
Western

3225 ---King of silver hill. New York: Arcadia, 1964.
192p.
Western

3226 ---Storm along the rattlesnake. New York: Arcadia,
1964. 189p.
Western

3227 ---Rimrock vengeance. New York: Arcadia, 1965. 191p.
Western

3228 ---The sheriff of singing river. New York: Arcadia,
1965. 192p.
Western

3229 ---The golden river. New York: Arcadia, 1966. 188p.
Western

3230 ---Fort fear. New York: Arcadia, 1967. 188p.
Western

3231 ---pseud. Cody, Al. Empty saddles. New York: Dodd,
1946. 215p.
Western

3232 ---West of the law. New York: Dodd, 1947. 205p.
Western

3233 ---Disaster trail. New York: Dodd, 1948. 216p.
Western

3234 ---Outpost trail. New York: Dodd, 1948. 212p.
Western

3235 ---The big corral. New York: Dodd, 1949. 222p.
Western

3236 ---The marshal of deer creek. New York: Dodd, 1949.
215p.
Western

3237 ---Sundown. New York: Dodd, 1950. 220p.
Western

3238 ---Hangman's coulee. New York: Dodd, 1951. 210p.
Western

3239 ---Forbidden river. New York: Bourgey, 1952. 252p.
Western

3240 ---The thundering hill. New York: Bourgey, 1952.
253p.
Western

3241 ---Powder horn. New York: Bourgey, 1953. 253p.
Western

3242 ---Guns on the bitterroot. New York: Avalon, 1955.
256p.
Western

3243 ---The golden saddle. New York: Arcadia, 1963. 221p.
Western

3244 ---Trail of the innocents. New York: Arcadia, 1964.
191p.
Western

3245 ---pseud. Westland, Alan. The lone pine ranch. New
York: Phoenix, 1947. 254p.
Western

3246 ---pseud. Westland, Lynn. Son of the saddle. New York:
Phoenix, 1936. 254p.
Western

3247 ---Dakota marshal. New York: Phoenix, 1937. 256p.
Western

3248 ---Powdersmoke pass. New York: Phoenix, 1937. 254p.
Western

3249 ---Maverick molloy. New York: Phoenix, 1938. 255p.
Western

3250 ---King cayuse. New York: Phoenix, 1939. 254p.
Western

3251 ---The range of no return. New York: Phoenix, 1939.
256p.
Western

3252 ---Born to saddle. New York: Phoenix, 1940. 254p.
Western

3253 ---The nightmare riders. New York: Phoenix, 1940.
251p.
Western

3254 ---King of the rodeo. New York: Phoenix, 1941. 256p.
Western

3255 ---Shooting valley. New York: Phoenix, 1941. 251p.
Western

3256 ---Saddle river spread. New York: Phoenix, 1942. 251p.
Western

3257 ---Shootin' iron. New York: Phoenix, 1942. 256p.
Western

3258 ---Gunsight ranch. New York: Phoenix, 1943. 256p.
Western

3259 ---Prentiss of the box 8. New York: Phoenix, 1943.
      256p.
         Western

3260 ---Trail to montana. New York: Phoenix, 1943. 253p.
         Western

3261 ---Wagon train westward. New York: Phoenix, 1944.
      255p.
         Western

3262 ---Over the frontier trail. New York: Phoenix, 1945.
      255p.
         Western

3263 ---Prairie pinto. New York: Phoenix, 1945. 255p.
         Western

3264 ---Prairie pioneers. New York: Phoenix, 1945. 255p.
         Western

3265 ---Return to the range. New York: Phoenix, 1945. 253p.
         Western

3266 ---Long loop raiders. New York: Phoenix, 1946. 256p.
         Western

3267 ---The silver cayuse. New York: Phoenix, 1947. 256p.
         Western

3268 ---Black river ranch. New York: Phoenix, 1948. 254p.
         Western

3269 ---Home range. New York: Phoenix, 1948. 255p.
         Western

3270 ---North from montana. New York: Phoenix, 1948. 256p.
         Western

3271 ---Silvertip ranch. New York: Phoenix, 1949. 253p.
         Western

3272 ---Texas red. New York: Phoenix, 1950. 237p.
         Western

3273 ---Gun ranch. New York: Arcadia, 1962. 222p.
         Western

3274 ---The heart of texas. New York: Arcadia, 1963. 223p.
         Western

3275 ---Powdersmoke payoff. New York: Arcadia, 1963. 224p.
         Western

3276 ---Thunder to west. New York: Arcadia, 1964. 191p.
         Western

3277 ---The red gun. New York: Arcadia, 1965. 190p.
Western

3278 ---Smoke against the sky. New York: Arcadia, 1965.
191p.
Western

3279 ---Heritage in powdersmoke. New York: Arcadia, 1967.
191p.
Western

3280 Joseph, Horace G.. Bright horizons. Caldwell, Idaho:
Caxton, 1937. 253p.
Eastern Colorado--Mystery--Tries to do for
Colorado what W. Cather did for Nebraska.

Joseph, Robert jt. author, see Castle, William

3281 Judah, Charles Burnet (1902-   ). Tom bone. New
York: Morrow, 1944. 499p.
Slave trade--Late 1600's--Romance--Hero on
wrong side Bacon's Rebellion.

3282 ---Christopher humble. New York: Morrow, 1956. 320p.
Titus Oates Plot--1678--Romance--Virginia and
England.

3283 Judah, Samuel B. F. pseud. Phlogobombos, Yclept Terentius.
The buccaneers; a romance of our own country, in
its ancient day; illustrated with divers marvellous
histories, and antique and facetious episodes; gath-
ered from the most authentic chronicles and affirmed
records extant from the settlement of nieuw nederland-
ts until the time of the famous richard kid [sic]
carefully collated from the labouris researches and
minute investigations of that excellent antiquary
and sublime philosopher..... Boston: Munroe, 1827.
2 vols.

3284 Judd, Sylvester. Margaret; a tale of the real and
ideal, blight and bloom; including sketches of a
place not before described called mons cristi.
Boston: Wiley, 1845. 460p.
Transcendentalism--Massachusetts.

3285 Judson, Edward Zane Carroll pseud. Buntline, Ned.
The volunteer; or, the maid of monterey. a tale
of the mexican war. Boston: Gleason, 1847. 100p.
Romance

3286 ---Luona prescott; or, the curse fulfilled. a tale
of the american revolution. New York: Brady, 186?.
64p.
Romance

3287 ---The man-o'-war's-man's grudge; a romance of the revolution. New York: Brady, 186?. 95p.

3288 ---Sea waif; or, the terror of the coast. a tale of privateering in 1776. New York: Brady, 186?. 128p. American Revolution.

3289 ---Thayendanegea, the scourge; or, the war-eagle of the mohawks. a tale of mystery, ruth, and wrong. New York: Brady, 186?. 77p.

3290 ---The white wizard; or, the great prophet of the seminoles. a tale of strange mystery in the south and north. New York: Brady, 186?. 104p.

3291 ---Stella delorme; or, the comanche's dream. a wild and fanciful story of savage chivalry. New York: Brady, 1860. 71p.

3292 ---Life in the saddle; or, the cavalry scout. New York: Brady, 1864. 81p. Western

3293 ---Rosa, the indian captive; a story of the last war with england. New York: Hilton, 1867?. 94p.

3294 Judson, Katharine Berry. When the forests are ablaze. Chicago: McClurg, 1912. 380p. Washington--Big woods--Romance.

K

3295 Kafka, John. The apple orchard. New York: Coward,
1947. 264p.
Idaho--1860's--Communal settlement--Christian-
Socialist experiment.

3296 Kaler, James (1845-1912) pseud. Otis, James. Boys of
1745. Boston: Estes, 1895. 93p.
Juvenile

3297 ---With lafayette at yorktown; a story of how two boys
joined the continental army. New York: Burt, 1895.
303p.
Juvenile

3298 ---At the siege of quebec. Philadelphia: Penn, 1897.
362p.
Juvenile

3299 Kamban, Gudmundur I. (1888-). I see a wonderous
land; a novel. New York: Putnam, 1938. 310p.
Title is cry of Leif the Luckys viking ship--
Saga by Icelander.

3300 Kane, Harnett Thomas (1910-). Pathway to the
stars; a novel based on the life of john mcdonough
of new orleans and baltimore. New York: Doubleday,
1950. 312p.
Fictional biography of McDonough (1779-1850)--
Made fortune--Left money so slaves earn freedom--
Schools.

3301 ---The gallant mrs. stonewall; a novel based on the
lives of general and mrs. stonewall jackson.
New York: Doubleday, 1957. 320p.
Ann Morrison (1831-1915).

Kane, Jim pseud. see Germano, Peter

3302 Kantor, MacKinlay (1904-). Gentle annie; a western
novel. New York: Coward, 1942. 249p.
Western--Excellent--Dectective--Early 1900's.

3303 ---Wicked water; an american primitive. New York:
Random, 1949. 216p.
Character study of western badman--Cattlemen
v. Homesteaders.

3304 ---Warwhoop; two short novels of the frontier. New

256

York: Random, 1952. 246p.
#1 Behold Brown-Faced Men--Sioux--Nebraska--
#2 Missouri Moon--White girl loves Indian.

3305 ---Spirit lake. Cleveland: World, 1961. 957p.
Spirit Lake, Iowa--Wahpekute Indians and
massacre of settlers--1857--One of best in depth
of midwest frontier--Realism.

3306 ---Beauty beast; a novel. New York: Putnam, 1968.
382p.
South--1854.

3307 Karig, Walter. Don't tread on me; a novel of the
historic exploits, military and gallant, of commodore john paul jones...with eye-witness accounts
of his many engagements related by the then mid-
shipman manesseh fisher and here retold by walter
karig, with horace bird. New York: Rinehart, 1954.
442p.
Adventure

3308 Kauffman, Reginald Wright (1877-   ). Pirate jean.
New York: Macaulay, 1930. 322p.
Jean LaFitte--Battle of New Orleans--1815.

3309 Keene, Day and Vincent, Dwight. Chautauqua; from a
story by mauri grashin. New York: Putnam, 1960.
320p.
Iowa town--1921.

Keene, James pseud. see Cook, William Everett

Keith, Marian pseud. see MacGregor, Mrs. Mary Esther
(Miller)

3310 Kelland, Clarance Budington (1881-1964). Hard money.
New York: Harper, 1930. 474p.
Son Dutch peddler down Hudson River to New
York City--Rise in banking--1815-1845--Sequel to
This Is Gold.

3311 ---Arizona. New York: Harpers, 1939. 278p.
Western

3312 ---Valley of the sun. New York: Harper, 1940. 297p.
Western

3313 ---Sugarfoot. New York: Harper, 1942. 307p.
Western

3314 Kelleam, Joseph E. (1913-   ). Blackjack. New York:
Sloane, 1948. 268p.
Oklahoma--Oil.

257

3315 Kelley, Adelaide (Skeel) and Brearley, William H..
King washington; a romance of the hudson highlands.
Philadelphia: Lippincott, 1898. 307p.

3316 Kelley, Edith Summers. Weeds. New York: Harcourt,
1923. 333p.
Life tenant farmer on small farm in Kentucky--
Tobacco country.

3317 Kelley, Welbourn. Alabama empire. New York: Rinehart,
1957. 503p.
Panorama--Little Tallassee--Creek nation
capitol--Constitutional Era--1789-1793.

3318 Kellogg, Walter Guest (1877-1956). Parish's fancy.
New York: Day, 1929. 293p.
Descendant of Amerigo Vespucci--Heroine--
Visits America--1840-1850's.

3319 Kelly, Mrs. Eleanor (Mercein) (1880-   ). Richard
walden's wife. Indianapolis: Bobbs, 1950. 391p.
Wisconsin--Pioneering--Southern woman, children
and two black servants.

3320 Kelly, Eric Philbrook (1884-1960). Three sides of
agiochook; a tale of the new england frontier in 1775.
New York: Macmillan, 1935. 211p.

3321 ---Treasure mountain. New York: Macmillan, 1937. 211p.
Western

3322 Kelly, Florence Finch (Mrs. Allen Kelly) (1858-1939).
With hoops of steel. Indianapolis: Bowen, 1900.
342p.
Ranchers

3323 ---The delafield affair. Chicago: McClurg, 1909. 422p.
New Mexico--Political and social conditions.

3324 Kelly, James Paul. Prince izon; a romance of the grand
canyon. Chicago: McClurg, 1910. 398p.
Christian v. Aztecs driven to Grand Canyon
by Cortez.

3325 Kelton, Elmer. Buffalo wagons. New York: Ballantine,
1956. 156p.
Western

3326 ---Buffalo wagons. New York: Ballantine, 1957
156p.
Western--Golden Spur Award 1958 for Best Western.

3327 ---Shadow of a star. New York: Ballantine, 1959. 142p.
Western

258

3328 ---The texas rifles. New York: Ballantine, 1960. 159p.
Western

3329 ---Donovan. New York: Ballantine, 1961. 144p.
Western

3330 ---Bitter trail. New York: Ballantine, 1962. 156p.
Western

3331 Kendrick, Baynard Hardwick (1894-   ). The flames
of time. New York: Scribner's, 1948. 374p.
Florida--Early 1800's--Rebellion against
Spaniards--Annexation by United States.

3332 Kennedy, John Pendleton (1795-1870). Rob of the bowl;
a legend of st. inigoe's. Philadelphia: Lea, 1838.
2 vols.
St. Mary's--First capitol of Maryland--1681--
Protestant try to overthrow Lord Baltimore.

3333 ---pseud. Littleton, Mary. Horseshoe robinson; a
tale of the tory ascendancy. Philadelphia: Carey,
1835. 2 vols.
South Carolina--American Revolution--Based on
personal memoirs of events--Romantic--Virginia
school--First to deal with Revolution in the south.

3334 Kennedy, Lucy. Mr. audubon's lucy. New York: Crown,
1957. 343p.
Lucy Audubon (1788-1874)--James Audubon (1785-
1851).

3335 Kennedy, Mrs. Sara Beaumont (Cannon) (-1921).
Joscelyn chesire; a story of revolutionary days
in the carolinas. New York: Doubleday, 1902. 338p.
North Carolina--Gallant duds--Romance.

3336 ---The wooing of judith. New York: Doubleday, 1902.
399p.
Virginia--1649-1651--Romance of Cavalier refugee
in Virginia after execution of Charles I.

3337 Kennelly, Ardyth (Mrs. Egon V. Ullman). The peaceable
kingdom. Boston: Houghton, 1949. 375p.
First novel--Mormon life--Utah--1890--Death
of Young.

3338 ---Up home. Boston: Houghton, 1955. 376p.
Mormon life--1895--Sequel to Peaceable Kingdom.

3339 ---Marry me, carry me. Boston: Houghton, 1956. 433p.
Young married couple--Utah to San Francisco--
1900.

3340 Kent, Alexander. To glory we steer. New York: Putnam,
1968. 328p.

259

Last years of American Revolution--British
crew to West Indies--1782.

Kent, David pseud. see Birney, Hoffman

3341 Kent, James. The johson manor; a tale of olden time
in new york. New York: Putnam, 1877. 304p.
1755-1775.

3342 Kent, Mrs. Louise (Andrews) (1886-   ). He went with
magellan. Boston: Houghton, 1943. 200p.
Fernao Magalhães (d. 1521)--Juvenile.

3343 Kent, Madeleine Fabiola. The corsair; a biographical
novel of jean lafitte, hero of the battle of new
orleans. New York: Doubleday, 1955. 299p.
Jean LaFitte (1782-1854).

3344 Kent, William H. B. (1878-   ). The tenderfoot.
New York: Macmillan, 1942. 223p.
Western

3345 ---Range rider. New York: Macmillan, 1943. 193p.
Western

3346 Kenyon, Theda. Golden feather. New York: Messner,
1943. 390p.
Romance--Era of Charles I (1625-1649)--Cava-
liers--Indian's--Wilderness--Laud--Pym.

3347 ---Black dawn. New York: Messner, 1944. 384p.
Family chronicle--Sequel to Golden Feather--
Set after Civil War.

3348 ---That skipper from stonington. New York: Messner,
1947. 538p.
Lad to sea--War of 1812--Follows his life for
fifty years.

3349 ---Something gleamed. New York: Messner, 1948. 374p.
American Revolution--Prostitutes to British
forces in America.

3350 Kerkhoff, Johnston D.. Aaron burr; a romantic biography.
New York: Greenberg, 1931. 279p.
A. Burr (1756-1836)--Poor picture.

3351 Kerr, Alvah Milton. Trean; or, the mormon's daughter.
a romantic story of life among the latter-day saints.
Chicago: Belford, 1889. 184p.

3352 Kester, Vaughan (1869-1911). The fortunes of the land-
rays. New York: McClure, 1905. 481p.
Gold fields--1848-1900--Romantic panorama.

3353　---John o' jamestown. New York: McClure, 1907. 297p.
　　　　　John Smith (1580-1631).

3354　---The prodigal judge. New York: Grosset, 1911. 448p.
　　　　　Slave insurrection--North Carolina--Western
　　　　Tennessee--1820's and 1830's--Judge Slosum Price.

3355　Key, Alexander. Liberty or death; the narrative of
　　　　william dunbar, partisan. New York: Harper, 1936.
　　　　224p.
　　　　　American Revolution--Marion (1732-1795)in
　　　　South Carolina--Juvenile.

3356　---The wrath and the wind; a novel. Indianapolis:
　　　　Bobbs, 1949. 366p.
　　　　　Florida--1840's--St. Joseph--Slave running--
　　　　Land boom.

3357　Keyes, Mrs. Frances Parkinson (Wheeler) (1885-　　　).
　　　　The safe bridge. New York: Messner, 1934. 321p.
　　　　　Rygate, Vermont--Romance--Early nineteenth
　　　　century.

3358　---Crescent carnival. New York: Messner, 1942. 807p.
　　　　　Chronicle--Three generations--Two New Orleans
　　　　families--1890-1940.

3359　---Steamboat gothic. New York: Messner, 1952. 562p.
　　　　　Chronicle--Three generations--Romance Missis-
　　　　sippi belle and reformed gambler--Panorama.

3360　---Blue camellia. New York: Messmer, 1957. 432p.
　　　　　Crowley, Louisiana--1880's--Cheap land lure
　　　　from Illinois to Cajun country--Rice plantation--
　　　　Romance.

3361　Keyes, Harvey. The forest king; or, the wild hunter
　　　　of the adaca. a tale of the seventeenth century.
　　　　New York: Wheat, 1878. 63p.
　　　　　Mohawk Valley, New York.

3362　Kilbourn, Diana Treat. The lone dove; a legend of
　　　　revolutionary times. Philadelphia: Appleton,
　　　　1850. 281p.
　　　　　Washington--Valley Forge--Sentimental treatment
　　　　of Washington reaches high point.

3363　King, Charles (1844-1933). "Laramie"; or, the queen
　　　　of bedlam. a story of the sioux war of 1876.
　　　　Philadelphia: Lippincott, 1889. 277p.

3364　---Sunset pass; or, running the gauntlet through
　　　　apache land. New York: Lovell, 1890. 202p.
　　　　　Western

3365 ---Two soldiers and dunraven ranch; two novels.
Philadelphia: Lippincott, 1891. 263p.
Western

3366 ---A soldier's secret; a story of the sioux war of
1890; and an army portia. two novels. Philadelphia:
Lippincott, 1893. 293p.
Western

3367 ---The story of fort frayne. Chicago: Neely, 1895. 310p
Western

3368 ---An army wife. New York: Neely, 1896. 278p.
Western

3369 ---Trooper ross and signal butte. Philadelphia:
Lippincott, 1896. 297p.
Western

3370 ---Trumpter fred; a story of the plains. New York:
Neely, 1896. 201p.
Western--Neely's prismatic library.

3371 ---A trooper galahad. Philadelphia: Lippincott, 1899.
257p.
Western

3372 ---A daughter of the sioux; a tale of the indian frontier
New York: Hobart, 1902. 306p.
Western

3373 ---An apache princess; a tale of the indian frontier.
New York: Hobart, 1903. 328p.
Western

3374 ---Tonio, son of the sierras; a story of the apache war.
New York: Dillingham, 1906. 338p.
Western

3375 King, Edward Smith. The gentle savage. Boston: Osgood,
1883. 444p.

3376 ---The golden spike; fantasie in prose. Boston: Ticknor, 1886. 407p.
Northern Pacific Railroad.

3377 King, Elisha Sterling. The wild rose of cherokee; or,
nancy ward, "the pocahontas of the west". a story
of the early exploration, occupancy, and settlement
of the state of tennessee. a romance, founded on
and interwoven with history. Nashville, Tennessee:
Nashville University, 1895. 119p.

3378 King, George Suthie (1878-   ). The last slaver. New
York: Putnam, 1933. 322p.
Slave trade--1850.

3379 King, Grace Elizabeth (1852-   ). La dame de sainte
      hermine. New York: Macmillan, 1924. 296p.
          New Orleans--1718--Romance.

      King, Oliver pseud. see Mount, Thomas Ernest (1895-   )

3380 King, Rufus. Whelps of the winds; a dog story. New
      York: Doran, 1926. 309p.
          Texas--Dog--Woman.

3381 Kingsbury, Elizabeth. Prisoners of the sea; a romance
      of the seventeenth century. Philadelphia: McKay,
      1897. 480p.

3382 Kingscote, Mrs. Georgiana (Wolff) pseud. Cleeve, Lucas.
      Free soil, free soul. London: Digby, 1903. 334p.
          Boston--1755--Age of George II--Romance.

3383 Kingsley, Charles (1819-1875). Westward ho! the
      voyages and adventures of sir amyas leigh, knight,
      of burrough in the county of devon in the reign of
      her most glorious majesty queen elizabeth. Boston:
      Ticknor, 1855. 588p.
          Sea Hawks--Defeat of Armada--1575-1588.

3384 Kinkaid, Mrs. Mary Holland (Mrs. John Kinkaid) (1861-1948).
      The man of yesterday; a romance of a vanishing race.
      New York: Stokes, 1908. 318p.
          Chickasaws--Choctaws--Division of tribal land.

3385 Kinzie, Mrs. Juliette Augusta (Magill). Wau-bun, the
      "early day" in the northwest. New York: Derby, 1856.
      498p.

3386 Kirby, William (1817-1906). The chien dór. the golden
      dog; a legend of quebec. New York: Worthington,
      1878. 678p.
          Romance--Fur trade--ca.1697--Work of poet and
      folklorist.

3387 Kirk, Charles D.. Wooing and warring in the wilderness.
      New York: Derby, 1860. 288p.

3388 Kirkbride, Ronald De Levington (1912-   ). Winds,
      blow gently. New York: Fell, 1945. 313p.
          Quakers from Pennsylvania to South Carolina--
      Wage fair treatment of slaves.

3389 Kirkland, Mrs. Caroline Matilda (Stansbury) (1801-1864).
      Forest life. New York: Francis, 1842. 2 vols.
          Michigan--Pioneer life in forest.

3390 ---pseud. Clavers, Mrs. Mary. A new home-who'll follow?
      or, glimpses of western life. New York: Francis,
      1839. 317p.

Michigan--Backwoods life.

3391   Kirkland, Elithe Hamilton (1907-   ). Divine average;
        a historical novel on that period of texas history
        when "cowboy" was a phrase with a controversial
        meaning and "texians" a nationality. Boston: Little,
        1952. 378p.
              Hostility in Texas--1838--Americans, Indians,
        and Mexicans.

3392   ---Love is a wild assault. New York: Doubleday, 1959.
        502p.
              Fictional biography--Harriet (Moore) Ames--
        Pioneer woman in Texas--Based on memoirs--Frontier
        soap opera.

3393   Kirkland, Joseph (1830-1894). Zury: the meanest man
        in spring county; a novel of western life. Boston:
        Houghton, 1887. 538p.
              Illinois pioneer farm life--Important work--
        cf. Eggleston and Howe.

3394   ---The mcveys;(an episode.) Boston: Houghton, 1888.
        468p.
              Illinois prairie.

3395   Kirkman, Marshall Monroe (1842-1921). The romance of
        gilbert holmes; an historical novel. World Railway,
        1900. 425p.
              Far West-1830's--Black Hawk War-1832.

3396   Kjelgaard, James Arthur (1910-   ). Rebel siege.
        New York: Holiday, 1943. 221p.
              Carolina's--1780--Battle King's Mountain--
        Juvenile.

3397   ---The spell of the white sturgeon. New York: Dodd,
        1953. 197p.
              Wisconsin--Shores of Lake Michigan--Late
        1860's--Juvenile.

3398   ---The lost wagon. New York: Dodd, 1955. 305p.
              From Missouri to Oregon by mule team and wagon.

3399   ---Desert dog. New York: Holiday, 1956. 200p.
              Dog tale.

3400   ---Wolf brother. New York: Holiday, 1957. 189p.
              Apaches 1880's--Boy to white school and returns--
        Juvenile.

3401   ---The land is bright. New York: Dodd, 1958. 237p.
              Virginia frontier--Civil War--Romance.

3402   Klopp, Vahrah Von. Kin. New York: Dodd, 1931. 310p.

264

First novel--California 1870's--Pioneers and
outlaws--True to point of brutality--Details good.

Knibbs, Harry Herbert see Knibbs, Henry Herbert

3403 Knibbs, Henry Herbert (1874-   ). Lost farm camp.
      Boston: Houghton, 1912. 354p.
      Maine--Lumbering.

3404 ---Overland red; a romance of the moonstone cañon trail.
      Boston: Houghton, 1914. 348p.
      Western

3405 ---Sundown slim. Boston: Houghton, 1915. 356p.
      Western

3406 ---Tang of life. Boston: Houghton, 1918. 393p.
      Western

3407 ---Ridin' kid from powder river. Boston: Houghton,
      1919. 457p.
      Western

3408 ---Partners of chance. Boston: Houghton, 1921. 231p.
      Western

3409 ---Wild horses; a novel. Boston: Houghton, 1924.
      271p.
      Western

3410 ---The tonto kid. Boston: Houghton, 1936. 260p.
      Western

3411 Knight, Kim. The bulldogger. New York: Dodge, 1939.
      251p.
      Western

3412 ---Nighthawk's gold. New York: Dodge, 1939. 256p.
      Western

3413 ---Feuder's gold. New York: Dodge, 1940. 256p.
      Western

3414 ---Dangerous dust. New York: Dodge, 1941. 255p.
      Western

3415 ---Vegeance trail. New York: Dodge, 1942. 250p.
      Western

Knipe, Alden Arthur see Knipe, Emile (Benson) jt. author

3416 Knipe, Mrs. Emile (Benson) (1870-   ) and Knipe, Alden
      Arthur (1870-   ). A maid of '76. New York: Mac-
      millan, 1915. 276p.
          Girl's father a loyalist--American Revolution--
      Patriotic picture--Juvenile.

265

3417 ---A mayflower maid. New York: Century, 1920. 287p.
         Coming of Pilgrims--Orphan adopted by Myles
      and Rose Standish--Juvenile.

3418 ---The flower of fortune. New York: Century, 1922.
      354p.
         New York City after Dutch turn it over to
      English.

3419 ---The shadow captain... New York: Dodd, 1925. 347p.
         Based on notes of Launcelot Dove, Chief Lieuten-
      ant of Captain Kidd--New York 1703.

3420 Knowles, Mabel Winifred (1875-   ) pseud. Wynne, May.
         The witch finder. London: Jarrolds, 1923. 256p.
         Witches in Massachusetts--1690's.

3421 Knox, Dorthea Heness. The heart of washington. New
         York: Neale, 1909. 238p.
         Early love of George Washington.

      Knox, John Armoy, jt. author, see Sweet, Alexander Edwin

3422 Knox, Rose Bell (1879-   ). Footlights afloat. New
         York: Doubleday, 1937. 300p.
         River--Showboat--Juvenile.

3423 Kooh, Elers. The high trail. Caldwell, Idaho: Caxton,
         1952. 179p.
         People trapped in Idaho mountains.

3424 Kohl, Mrs. Edith Eudora. The land of the burnt thigh.
         New York: Funk, 1938. 296p.
         Dakota homesteading.

3425 Kramer, Harold Morton (1873-1949). The rugged way.
         Boston: Lothrop, 1911. 428p.
         Young man to northwest.

3426 Kramer, Horace. Marginal land; a novel. Philadelphia:
         Lippincott, 1939. 426p.
         City boy to Dakota ranch--Factual treatment.

3427 Krause, Herbert (1905-   ). Wind without rain.
         Indianapolis: Bobbs, 1939. 364p.
         First novel--Realistic treatment of Minnesota
      farm life--Meyer "Best treatment in farm fiction
      of...patriarchal domination of a family."

3428 ---The thresher. Indianapolis: Bobbs, 1946. 548p.
         Midwest--Wheat threshing.

3429 ---The oxcart trail; a novel. Indianapolis: Bobbs,
      1954. 507p.
         Red River settlements--1850--Serious work.

266

3430 Krey, Mrs. Laura Littie (Smith). <u>And tell of time.</u>
Boston: Houghton, 1938. 712p.
Texas--Brazos region--1865-1880's--Romantic
praise for Texas.

3431 ---<u>On the long tide.</u> Boston: Houghton, 1940. 642p.
Texas--1835-1836--From Virginia to Texas.

3432 Kringle, Kate pseud.. <u>The beautiful girl; or, burning</u>
<u>of the robber's den.</u> a tale of the revolution.
New York: New York City Publishing, 1846. 49p.

3433 Kroetsch, Robert (1927-   ). <u>The studhorse man;</u>
<u>a novel.</u> New York: Simon, 1970. 191p.
First novel.

3434 Kroll, Harry Harrison (1888-   ). <u>The keepers of</u>
<u>the house.</u> Indianapolis: Bobbs, 1940. 413p.
Mississippi--Ante bellum.

3435 ---<u>Rogues' companion; a novel of john murrell.</u> Ind-
ianapolis: Bobbs, 1943. 412p.
Fictionalized biography of famous bandit--
Natchez 1820's and 1830's.

3436 ---<u>Fury in the earth; a novel of the new madrid earth-</u>
<u>quake.</u> Indianapolis: Bobbs, 1945. 264p.
Sem-fiction--New Madrid, Missouri (1811-1812)--
Reversion to primativism on frontier.

3437 ---<u>Their ancient grudge.</u> Indianapolis: Bobbs, 1946.
326p.
Six women--Hatfield-McCoy feud.

3438 ---<u>Darker grows the valley.</u> Indianapolis: Bobbs,
1947. 400p.
Chronicle--1778-1928--From Josiah Clinch to
North Carolina to T.V.A.--Panoramic view.

Kroll, Harry H. see Sublette, Clifford jt. author

3439 Krout, Caroline Virginia pseud. Brown,Caroline.
<u>On the we-a trail; a story of the great wilderness.</u>
New York: Macmillan, 1903. 351p.

3440 ---<u>Dionis of the white veil.</u> Boston: Page, 1911. 291p.
Young novice on frontier early eighteenth
century.

3441 Kuipers, Cornelius (1898-   ). <u>Chant of the night;</u>
<u>an indian mission story.</u> Grand Rapids, Michigan:
Zondervan, 1934. 215p.
Zuñi

267

3442 Kyne, Peter Bernard (1880-1957). The valley of the
giants. New York: Doubleday, 1918. 388p.
Redwood lumbering--California.

3443 ---Tide of empire. New York: Cosmopolitan, 1928.
397p.
California Gold Rush--1846-1850.

3444   Labree, Lawrence. <u>Rebels and tories; or, the blood of</u>
<u>the mohawk!</u> a tale of the american revolution.
New York: DeWitt, 1851. 202p.
1778

A Lady of Philadelphia [Anonymous] see Carr, Mary

3445   LaFarge, Oliver (1901-1963). <u>Laughing boy</u>. Boston:
Houghton, 1929.
Navajo Indians--Pulitizer Prize 1930--Excellent.

3446   ---<u>The long pennant; a novel</u>. Boston: Houghton, 1933.
305p.
Rhode Island privateer in Caribbean--War of
1812.

3447   ---<u>The enemy gods</u>. Boston: Houghton, 1937. 325p.
Navajo Indians--1919 opens--Identification
with which culture?--Very good.

3448   <u>LaFitte; or, the baratarian chief. a tale</u>. [Anonymous]
Fall River: Hall, 1827. 70p.

3449   Laing, Alexander Kinnan (1903-   ). <u>The sea witch;</u>
<u>a narrative of the experiences of capt. roger</u>
<u>murray and others in an american clipper ship</u> during
<u>the years 1846 to 1856</u>. New York: Farrar, 1933.
487p.
Romance and adventure of real ship--Three
brothers serve on vessel.

3450   ---<u>Jonathan eagle</u>. Boston: Little, 1955. 523p.
Runaway from Stonington, Connecticut--1785-
1801--Adventure.

3451   ---<u>Matthew early</u>. New York: Duell, 1957. 372p.
Sea captain--Slave trade--Romance.

3452   Laing, Dilys (Bennett) (Mrs. Alexander Kinnan Laing)
(1906-   ). <u>The great year; a novel</u>. New York:
Duell, 1948. 285p.
First novel--Vermont farm family--1874-1950.

3453   Laird, Charlton (1901-   ). <u>Thunder on the river</u>.
Boston: Little, 1949. 310p.
Black Hawk War--Illinois--Sauk Indians--Social
history.

3454 ---West of the river. Boston: Little, 1953. 307p.
American fur trade--1830's--Upper Mississippi
River--Adventure--Picture of decline 1837.

3455 L'Amour, Louis. Crossfire trail. New York: Ace, 1954.
139p.
Western

3456 ---Kilkenny. New York: Ace, 1954. 160p.
Western

3457 ---Guns of the timberlands. New York: Jason, 1955.
182p.
Western

3458 ---The burning hills. New York: Jason, 1956. 153p.
Western

3459 ---Silver canyon. New York: Avalon, 1956. 224p.
Western

3460 ---How the west was won. New York: Bantam, 1962.
248p.
Western based on James Webb's screenplay of
same name.

3461 ---Lando. New York: Bantam, 1962. 122p.
Western

3462 ---Catlow. New York: Bantam, 1963. 122p.
Western

3463 ---Dark canyon. New York: Bantam, 1963. 120p.
Western

3464 ---Fallon. New York: Bantam, 1963. 120p.
Western

3465 ---Mohave crossing. New York: Bantam, 1964. 118p.
Western

3466 ---pseud. Burns, Tex. Hopalong cassidy and the riders
of high rock. New York: Doubleday, 1951. 191p.
Western

3467 ---Hopalong cassidy and the rustlers of west fork.
New York: Doubleday, 1951. 248p.
Western

3468 ---Hopalong cassidy and the trail to seven pines.
New York: Doubleday, 1951. 187p.
Western

3469 ---Hopalong cassidy, trouble shooter. New York:
Doubleday, 1952. 187p.
Western

3470   Lampman, Mrs. Evelyn Sibley. Treasure mountain.
       New York: Doubleday, 1949. 207p.
             Orphan Halfbreed (white-red)--Visit to Aunt
       in Oregon.

3471   Lancaster, Bruce (1896-1963). The wide sleeve of
       kwannon; a novel. New York: Stokes, 1938. 307p.
             Dutch traders to Japan--Late 1600's--Nagasaki
       Bay.

3472   ---Guns of burgoyne. New York: Stokes, 1939. 424p.
             Hessian officer in English Army tells of
       defeats at Bennington and Saratoga--Good.

3473   ---For us the living. New York: Stokes, 1940. 556p.
             A. Lincoln--Pioneer days in Indiana and Ken-
       tucky--Closes where Sherwood Anderson's play opens.

3474   ---Trumpet to arms. Boston: Little, 1944. 379p.
             Marblehead and Concord--Massachusetts--American
       Revolution--Militia--United States Army.

3475   ---Phantom fortress. Boston: Little, 1950. 310p.
             American Revolution--South--Francis Marion
       (1732-1795)--Captain from Rhode Island joins
       "Swamp Fox".

3476   ---Guns in the forest. Boston: Little, 1952. 259p.
             American Revolution--Burgoyne's invasion of
       Hudson Valley--1777.

3477   ---The secret road. Boston: Little, 1952. 259p.
             American Revolution--Washington's secret
       service--Long Island Sound-1780--Good.

3478   ---Blind journey. Boston: Little, 1953. 303p.
             American Revolution--Young patriot sent to
       Europe--Meets B. Franklin.

3479   ---The big knives. Boston: Little, 1964. 371p.
             George Rogers Clark (1752-1818)--Expedition
       to Illinois--1778-1779--Twentieth and last book--
       cf. Sinclair, Westward The Tide.

3480   ---and Brentano, Lowell (1895-   ). Bride of a
       thousand cedars; a novel of bermuda. New York:
       Stokes, 1939. 344p.
             Bermuda Island.

3481   Lancaster, F. Hewes (1871-   ). Marie of arcady.
       Boston: Small, 1909. 343p.
             Cajan people--Descendants of Acadian exiles.

       Lancaster, G. B. pseud. see Lyttleton, Edith J.

                              271

3482 Landis, Frederick (1872-1934). The glory of his
      country. New York: Scribner's, 1910. 226p.
      Woodsman--Boyhood friend of A. Lincoln.

      Landon, Louise pseud. see Hauck, Mrs. Louise Platt

3483 Lane, Carl. Fleet in forest. New York: Coward, 1943.
      369p.
      War of 1812--Battle of Lake Erie (1813)--
      Perry ship building.

3484 Lane, Mrs. Elinor (Macartney) (-1909). Mills of
      god; a novel. New York: Appleton, 1901. 337p.
      1795ca.--England,Continent and Virginia.

3485 Lane, Frederick A.. Westward the eagle. New York:
      Holt, 1955. 224p.
      Boy on whaler put ashore at Monterey--1845--
      Thomas O. Larkin (1802-1858)--Juvenile.

3486 Lane, John Haden. The birth of liberty; a story of
      bacon's rebellion. Richmond: Hermitage, 1909.
      181p.
           1676

3487 Lane, Mrs. Rose (Wilder) (1887-1968). Let the hur-
      ricane roar. New York: Longmans, 1933. 152p.
      Young married couple--Pioneering Dakota--
      1870's--Moving tale.

3488 ---Free land. New York: Longmans, 1938. 332p.
      Young married people from Minnesota to Dakota--
      1880's.

3489 Langdale, Mrs. Hazel Louise (Raybold). Mark of seneca
      basin. New York: Dutton, 1942. 215p.
      Erie Canal--Juvenile.

3490 ---Jon of the albany belle. New York: Dutton, 1943.
      212p.
      Canal--New York--1850's--Juvenile.

3491 Lange, Dietrich (1863-   ). On the trail of the
      sioux; or, the adventures of two boy scouts on the
      minnesota frontier. Boston: Lothrop, 1912. 298p.
      Juvenile

3492 ---The silver island of the chippewa. Boston: Lothrop,
      1913. 246p.
      Juvenile

3493 ---Lost in the fur country. Boston: Lothrop, 1914.
      297.
      Juvenile

3494   ---In the great wild north. Boston: Lothrop, 1915.
         278p.
              Juvenile

3495   ---The lure of the black hills. Boston: Lothrop,
         1916. 267p.
              Juvenile

3496   ---The lure of the mississippi. Boston: Lothrop,
         1917. 268p.
              Juvenile

3497   ---The silver cache of the pawnee. Boston: Lothrop,
         1918. 296p.
              Juvenile

3498   ---The shawnee's warning; a story of the oregon trail.
         Boston: Lothrop, 1919. 324p.
              Juvenile

3499   ---The threat of sitting bull; a story of the time
         of custer. Boston: Lothrop, 1920. 370p.
              Juvenile

3500   ---The raid of the ottawa. Boston: Lothrop, 1921.
         336p.
              Juvenile

3501   ---The iriquois scout. Boston: Lothrop, 1923. 308p.
              Juvenile

3502   ---The sioux runner. Boston: Lothrop, 1924. 269p.
              Juvenile

3503   ---The golden rock of the chippewa. Boston: Lothrop,
         1925. 272p.
              Juvenile

3504   ---The boast of the seminole. Boston: Lothrop, 1930.
         271p.
              Juvenile

3505   Langley, Mrs. Adria (Locke). A lion is in the streets.
         New York: McGraw, 1945. 482p.
              Rise of Huey Long--Fictional account--Political
         novel--Excellent--Louisiana.

3506   Lanham, Edwin Moultrie (1904-   ). The wind blew
         west. New York: Longmans, 1935. 481p.
              West of Ft. Worth, Texas--1875--People lured
         by railroad speculators.

3507   ---Banner at daybreak. New York: Longmans, 1937.
         497p.
              Sequel to The Wind Blew West.

3508   ---Thunder in the earth. New York: Harcourt, 1941.
      570p.
        Texas--Won Texas Institute of Letters award
     for Best Texas Book of Year-1942.

3509   Lape, Fred. Roll on, pioneers. New York: Godwin,
      1935. 310p.
      California--Gold Rush--1849.

3510   Lasswell, Mary (1905-   ). Bread for the living.
      Boston: Houghton, 1948. 262p.
      Texas border--1900-1915--Woman's life.

3511   Latham, Henry Jepson pseud. Jepson, Ring. Among the
      mormons; how an american and an englishman went to
      salt lake city and married seven wives apiece.
      their lively experience. San Francisco: San Francisco
      News, 1879. 115p.

     Lathrop, Dorothy West see Lathrop, West

3512   Lathrop, West (1892-   ). Black river captive. New
      York: Random, 1946. 307p.
      French-Indian War (1754-1763)--New Hampshire--
     Fourteen old taken by Indians--Adventure.

3513   ---Keep the wagons moving! New York: Random, 1949.
      337p.
      Two lads join wagon train on Oregon Trail--
     Juvenile.

3514   Laughlin, Ruth (Mrs. H. S. A. Alexander) (1889-   ).
      The wind leaves no shadow. New York: Whittlesey,
      1948. 321p.
      Mixed society--Santa Fé--1821-1846--Rio Grande
     Valley--Based on Doña Tules.

3515   Laurence, Margaret. The stone angel. New York: Knopf,
      1964. 308p.
      Pioneer woman in Manitoba recalls life--
     Realistic.

3516   Lauritzen, Jonreed. Arrows into the sun. New York:
      Knopf, 1943. 311p.
      Navajo country of Grand Canyon--1860's--Indians--
     Whites--Mormon--Romance.

3517   ---Song before sunrise. New York: Doubleday, 1948.
      314p.
      Spanish occupation of New Mexico--Dennis
     Julian--Half-Indian girl.

3518   ---The rose and the flame. New York: Doubleday, 1951.
      309p.
      Southwest--1680--Spaniards and Indians--Navajo
     material good.

3519   ---Suzanne. New York: Hanover, 1955. 315p.
         Oregon Trail--Daughter of half-breed sold to
         Comancheros.

3520   ---The everlasting fire. New York: Doubleday, 1962.
         474p.
         Early Mormons--Migration from Nauvoo, Illinois--
         Murder of Smith accurate--Realistic.

3521   ---Captain sutler's gold. New York: Doubleday, 1964.
         322p.
         John Augustus Sutter (1803-1880).

3522   ---The cross and the sword. New York: Doubleday,
         1965. 275p.
         Junipero Serra (1713-1784)--Juan Anza (1735-
         1788).

3523   Laut, Agnes Christina (1871-   ). Heralds of empire;
         being the story of one ramsay stanhope, lieutenant
         to pierre radisson in the northern fur trade.
         New York: Appleton, 1902. 372p.
         1650

3524   ---Freebooters of the wilderness. New York: Moffat,
         1910. 443p.
         Northwest--1910--Lawless timber--Corporate and
         political corruption.

3525   Lavender, David Sievert (1910-   ). Andy claybourne.
         New York: Doubleday, 1946. 370p.
         Farmers v. Cattlemen--1937-41.

3526   ---Red mountain. New York: Doubleday, 1963. 538p.
         Colorado--1880's.

3527   Lawson, Robert (1892-1957). Mr. revere and i; being
         an account of certain episodes in the career of
         paul revere, esq., as recently revealed by his horse,
         scheherazade, late pride of his royal majesty's
         14th regiment of foot. set down and embellished
         with numerous drawings by robert lawson. Boston:
         Little, 1953. 152p.
         Paul Revere (1735-1818).

3528   ---Captain kidd's cat; being the true and dolorous
         chronicle of wm. kidd, gent and merchant of new york,
         the late captain of the adventure galley, of the
         vicissitudes attending his unfortunate cruise in
         eastern waters, of his incarceration in newgate
         prison, of his unjust trial and execution, as nar-
         rated by his faithful cat, mcdermot, who ought to
         know. set down and illuminated by robert lawson.
         Boston: Little, 1956. 151p.
         Captain Kidd d.1701.

275

3529   ---The great wheel. New York: Viking, 1957.   188p.
       Irish lad to Wisconsin--Late 1800's.

3530   Laxness, Halldór. Paradise reclaimed. New York:
       Crowell, 1962. 253p. [Trans. by Magnusson, Magnus].
       Mormon from Iceland.

3531   Lay, Margaret Rebecca (1905-   ). Thornblossoms.
       New York: Rinehart, 1948. 248p.
       Red clay country of Georgia.

       Layton, Mark pseud. see Rush, William Marshall

3532   Lea, Tom (1907-   ). The wonderful country; a novel.
       Boston: Little, 1952. 387p.
       Western--Exceptional work--Second novel of
       artist turned writer--Own illustrations--1860-1870.

3533   ---The hands of cantú. Boston: Little, 1964. 244p.
       Sixteenth century--Ibarra mining family--
       Kingdom of Neuva Vizcaya for Philip II--Poem in
       prose--Praise of horses.

3534   Leahy, Jack Thomas (1930-   ). Shadow on the waters.
       New York: Knopf, 1960. 240p.
       First novel--Young lad in "ocean bush"--
       Olympic Peninsula.

3535   Lee, Day Kellogg. Summerfield; or, life on a farm.
       Auburn: Derby, 1852. 246p.
       Finger Lakes region, New York State.

3536   Lee, Mrs. Eliza (Buckminster) (1794-1864). Delusion;
       or, the witch of new england. [Anonymous]. Boston:
       Hillard, 1840. 160p.
       Salem, Massachusetts--1692.

3537   ---Naomi; or, boston two hundred years ago. Boston:
       Crosby, 1848. 448p.
       Quaker persecution--Fair and accurate.

       Lee, Ranger pseud. see Snow, Charles Horace

3538   Lee, Wayne C.. Prairie vengeance. New York: Arcadia,
       1954. 219p.
       Western

3539   ---Broken wheel ranch. New York: Arcadia, 1956. 220p.
       Western

3540   ---Gun in his hand. New York: Arcadia, 1964. 191p.
       Western

3541   ---The brand of a man. New York: Bourgey, 1966. 191p.
       Western

3542 ---Mystery of scorpion creek. New York: Abingdon, 1966. 191p.
      Western

3543 ---Showdown at julesburg station. New York: Bourgey, 1967. 192p.
      Western

3544 ---Trail of the skulls. New York: Bourgey, 1967. 192p.
      Western

3545 Lehman, Paul Evan. Idaho. New York: Macaulay, 1933. 285p.
      Western

3546 ---Blood of the west. New York: Macaulay, 1934. 252p.
      Western

3547 ---Son of a cow thief. New York: Macaulay, 1935. 256p.
      Western

3548 ---Texas men. New York: Green Circle, 1936. 249p.
      Western

3549 ---Valley of hunted men. New York: Green Circle, 1937. 256p.
      Western

3550 ---Wolves of the chaparral. New York: Green Circle, 1938. 250p.
      Western

3551 ---Calamity range. New York: Macaulay, 1939. 255p.
      Western

3552 ---Brand of the outlaw. New York: Hillman, 1942. 128p.
      Western

3553 ---Cow kingdom. New York: Curl, 1945. 264p.
      Western

3554 ---West of the wolverine. New York: Curl, 1946. 286p.
      Western

3555 ---Only the brave. New York: Curl, 1947. 255p.
      Western

3556 ---The devil's doorstep. New York: Dutton, 1949. 224p.
      Western

3557 ---Montana man. New York: Dutton, 1949. 219p.
      Western

3558 ---Brother of the kid. New York: Dutton, 1950. 223p.
      Western

3559 ---The siren of silver valley; a new western novel. Kingston, New York: Handi-book, 1950. 128p. Western

3560 ---Vengeance valley. Kingston, New York: Quinn, 1950. 126p. Western

3561 ---The man from the badlands. New York: Dutton, 1951. 216p. Western

3562 ---The doves of war. New York: Dutton, 1952. 224p. Western

3563 ---Fightin' sons of texas. New York: Dutton, 1953. 223p. Western

3564 ---Bullets don't bluff. New York: Ace, 1954. 155p. Western

3565 ---pseud. Evan, Paul. The twisted trail. New York: Bourgey, 1952. 256p. Western

3566 ---Outlaws of lost river. New York: Avalon, 1954. 256p. Western

3567 ---Call of the west. New York: Avalon, 1955. 253p. Western

3568 ---Gunsmoke over sabado. New York: Avalon, 1955. 256p. Western

Leighton, Lee pseud. see Overholser, Wayne D.

3569 Leighton, Mrs. Margaret (Carver). Who rides by? New York: Ariel, 1955. 218p.
American Revolution--Connecticut--Rhode Island--1780--Juvenile.

3570 Leland, John Adams. Othneil jones. Philadelphia: Lippincott, 1956. 253p.
American Revolution--War in Carolinas as seen by member of Marion's Raiders.

3571 LeMay, Alan (1899-   ). Painted ponies. New York: Doran, 1927. 304p. Western

3572 ---Old father of waters. New York: Doubleday, 1928. 329p.

278

Steamboating on Mississippi River--Romance.

3573 ---Pelican coast. New York: Doubleday, 1929. 329p.
      New Orleans--Early 1800--LaFitte.

3574 ---Bug eye. New York: Farrar, 1931. 276p.
      Western

3575 ---Gunsight trail. New York: Farrar, 1931. 335p.
      Western

3576 ---Winter range. New York: Farrar, 1932. 276p.
      Western

3577 ---Cattle kingdom. New York: Farrar, 1933. 307p.
      Western

3578 ---Thunder in the dust. New York: Farrar, 1934.
      301p.
      Western

3579 ---The smoky years. New York: Farrar, 1935. 298p.
      Western

3580 ---Empire for a lady. New York: Farrar, 1937. 303p.
      Western

3581 ---Useless cowboy. New York: Farrar, 1943. 247p.
      Western

3582 ---The searchers. New York: Harper, 1954. 272p.
      Western

3583 ---The unforgiven. New York: Harper, 1957. 245p.
      Western

3584 ---By dim and flaring lamps. New York: Harper, 1962.
      277p.
      Western

3585 Lender, Charles Franklin. Down the ohio with clark.
      New York: Crowell, 1937. 278p.
      George Rogers Clark Expedition--Juvenile.

3586 ---Pirates on the ohio; a tale of the brig st. clair
      and the indomitable commodore whipple. New York:
      Howell, 1947. 196p.
      Abraham Whipple (1733-1819)--Pioneer days
      Marietta, Ohio to New Orleans.

3587 Leonard, Elizabeth Jane. The call of the western
      prairie. New York: Library Pub., 1952. 339p.
      Western

3588 Leonard, Elmore (1925-   ). The law at randado.

279

Boston: Houghton, 1954. 240p.
Western

3589 ---<u>Bounty hunters</u>. Boston: Houghton, 1954. 180p.
Western

3590 ---<u>Escape from five shadows</u>. Boston: Houghton, 1956.
213p.
Western

3591 Leonhart, Rudolph. <u>The wild rose of the beaver</u>.
Tidioute, Pennsylvania: Needle, 1873. 111p.
Pennsylvania--1782--Indians.

3592 ---<u>The treasure of montezuma</u>. Canton, Ohio: Cassidy,
1888. 279p.

Leslie, A. <u>pseud</u>. see Scott, Leslie

Leslie, Ann George <u>pseud</u>. see Cameron, Leslie Georgiana
(1886-)

3593 Levin, Benjamin. <u>To spit against the wind</u>. New York:
Citadel, 1970. 569p.
Centers about Thomas Paine and his era--Major
figures appear.

3594 Levy, Melvin P. (1902-). <u>Last pioneers</u>. New York:
King, 1934. 368p.
Rise of town--Pacific northwest--Washington--
Alaska.

3595 Lewi, Grant. <u>Star of empire</u>. New York: Vanguard,
1935. 310p.
Middle west--Through 1920's.

3596 Lewis, Alfred Henry (1857-1914). <u>Peggy o'neal</u>.
Philadelphia: Biddle, 1903. 494p.
Fictionalized biography--Mrs. Margaret (O'Neill)
Eaton (1796-1879).

3597 ---<u>The sunset trail</u>. New York: Burt, 1905. 393p.
Western

3598 ---<u>The story of paul jones; an historical romance</u>.
New York: Dillingham, 1906. 308p.
John Paul Jones (1747-1792).

3599 ---<u>The throwback; a romance of the southwest</u>. New York:
Outing, 1906. 347p.
Western

3600 ---<u>pseud</u>. Quin, Dan. <u>An american patrican; or, the</u>
<u>story of aaron burr</u>. New York: Appleton, 1908. 335p.

280

Fictionalized biography--Burr's Conspiracy--
Western lands.

3601　Lewis, Janet. The invasion; a narrative of events
concerning the johnston family of st. mary's.
New York: Harcourt, 1932. 356p.
Eighteenth century--Michigan trader and
Ojibway wife.

3602　Lewis, John. Young kate; or, the rescue. a tale of
the great kanawha. New York: Harper, 1844. 2 vols.
West Virginia--Kanawha Valley--Frontier life.

3603　Lewis, Julius Warren pseud. Barrington, F. Clinton.
Conrado de beltran; or, the buccaneer of the gulf.
a romantic story of the sea and shore. Boston:
Gleason, 1851. 100p.

3604　---pseud. Lewis, Leon. Kit carson's last tail. New
York: Bonner's, 1891. 400p.
Dime novel tradition.

Lewis, Leon pseud. see Lewis, Julius Warren

3605　Lewis, Sinclair.[Harry] (1885-1951). The god-seeker;
a novel. New York: Random, 1949. 422p.
Presbyterian missionary to Minnesota--1840--
Sioux--Frontier society.

3606　---and Schary, Dory. Storm in the west. New York:
Stein, 1963. 192p.
Western setting--Allegory of World War II and
events leading up to it--Screenplay for MGM 1943.

3607　Liddon, Eloise (1897-   ). Some lose their way.
New York: Dutton, 1941. 352p.
Alabama-1835--Creeks threaten--Romance.

3608　Lide, Mrs. Alice (Alison). Aztec drums. New York:
Longmans, 1938. 142p.
Day of Montezuma--Juvenile.

3609　---Princess of yucatan. New York: Longmans, 1939.
187p.
Juvenile

3610　---and Margaret Alison Johansen. Dark possession.
New York: Appleton, 1934. 330p.
Charlestown, South Carolina--Early 1700's--
Pallisaded city--Juvenile.

Lieutenant Murray pseud. see Ballou, Maturin Murray

3611　Lighton, William Rheem (1866-   ). Sons of strength;
a romance of the kansas border wars. New York:

Doubleday, 1899. 242p.
Western

3612 ---Uncle mac's nebrasky. New York: Holt, 1904. 184p.

3613 ---The shadow of a great rock. New York: Putnam, 1907.
276p.

3614 ---Billy fortune. New York: Appleton, 1912. 364p.
Western

3615 ---Letters of an old farmer to his son. New York:
Doran, 1914. 212p.
Farm life.

Lin, Frank pseud. see Atherton, Gertrude Franklin
(Horn) (1857-1948)

Lincoln, Freeman jt. author, see Lincoln, Joseph
Crosby (1870)

3616 Lincoln, Jeanie Thomas (Gould). An unwilling maid;
being the history of certain episodes during the
american revolution in early life of mistress
betty yorke, born wolcott. Boston: Houghton,
1897. 263p.

3617 ---A pretty tory; being a romance of partisan warfare during the war of independence in the provinces
of georgia and south carolina, relating to mistress
geraldine moncriffe. Boston: Houghton, 1899.
268p.

3618 Lincoln, Joseph Crosby (1870-   ) and Lincoln, Freeman.
The new hope. New York: Coward, 1941. 498p.
War of 1812--Cape Codders privateering--Run
British blockade.

3619 Lincoln, Victoria. A dangerous innocence. New York:
Rinehart, 1958. 310p.
Salem, Massachusetts--Witchcraft trials--1690's.

3620 Linderman, Frank Bird (1868-1938). Lige mounts, free
trapper. New York: Scribner's, 1922. 330p.
Fur trade--Upper Mississippi River.

3621 ---Morning light. New York: Day, 1922. 330p.

3622 ---American; the life story of a great indian, plenty-
coups, chief of the crows. New York: Day, 1930.
313p.
Fictional biography--Plenty-coups (1848-1932).

3623 ---Red mother. New York: Day, 1932. 256p.

Life story of Pretty-shield, medicine woman of
Crows.

3624 ---Beyond law. New York: Day, 1933. 250p.
American Fur Company--Lige Mounts, hero.

Lindsay, Howard Arthur jt author, see Tindale, Norman
Barnett

3625 Lindsey, E. G. by E. G. L.. Marie; or, fort beauharnois.
an historic tale of early days in the northwest.
Minneapolis, Minnesota: Bausman, 1893. 176p.

3626 Linfield, Mary Barrow. Japonica grove. New York:
Doubleday, 1935. 282p.
Louisiana plantation--Post Civil War--Romance.

3627 Linford, Dee. Man without a star. New York: Morrow,
1952. 312p.
Western

3628 Linington, Elizabeth. The long watch; a novel. New
York: Viking, 1956. 377p.
American Revolution--New York--Hero is clerk
to editor of New York Courier.

3629 Lion, Hortense. The grass grows green. Boston: Houghton, 1935. 304p.
First novel--Bavarian family to America 1850-
1914.

3630 ---Mill stream. Boston: Houghton, 1937. 390p.
Home industry v. Ship builders-- 1790-1814.

3631 Lippard, George (1822-1854). Herbert tracy; or, the
legend of the black rangers. a romance of the
battlefield of germantown. Philadelphia: Berford,
1844. 168p.
Romance-- 1777--All writings much space to
George Washington--Admiration great--Dedicated to
James Fenimore Cooper.

3632 ---Blanche of brandywine; or, september the eleventh,
1777. a romance combining the poetry, legend and
history of the battle of brandywine. Philadelphia:
Zieber, 1846. 351p.
Dime novel style--Murder and seduction--Wash-
ington in Pennsylvania--Sensational and Gothic.

3633 ---Legends of mexico. Philadelphia: Peterson, 1847.
136p.
War with Mexico (1845-1848)--Romance.

3634 ---The rose of wissahikon; or, the fourth of july,
1776. a romance embracing the secret history of
the declaration of independence. Philadelphia:

Zieber, 1847. 70p.
Romance of Rose and Indian, Mayaniko.

3635 ---'Bel of prairie eden; a romance of mexico. Boston:
Hotchkiss, 1848. 88p.

3636 Lippincott, Joseph Wharton (1887-   ). The wolf king.
Philadelphia: Penn, 1933. 316p.
Rocky Mountains--Pack of wolves led by black
one--Adventure.

3637 Lipsky, Eleazar. The devil's daughter. Des Moines,
Iowa: Meredith, 1969. 633p.
California--1880's--Famous trial of era recre-
ated by lawyer author--Mark Trumbull v. "Silver
King" Lew Hagerman.

3638 Lisle, Clifton. Diamond rock; a tale of the paoli
massacre. New York: Harcourt, 1920. 301p.
1777

3639 ---Saddle bags. New York: Harcourt, 1923. 278p.
Western

3640 ---Lenape trails. New York: Harcourt, 1928. 310p.
Quaker mother and son--Pennsylvania woods.

Lisle, Seward D. pseud. see Ellis, Edward Sylvester
(1840-1916)

3641 Little, George (1791?-   ). The american cruiser;
a tale of the last war. Boston: Reynolds, 1847.
390p.
War of 1812--Dartmouth Massacre--(1812).

Littleton, Mary pseud. see Kennedy, John

3642 Llyod, John. The captain's wife. New York: Kennerley,
1908. 319p.
Arizona--Eastern girl married army officer.

3643 Locke, Charles O.. The last princess; a novel of the
incas. New York: Norton, 1954. 316p.
Spanish conquest of Peru--Inca point of view--
Tacara and lover, Tacios.

3644 ---The hell bent kid; a novel. New York: Norton, 1957.
219p.
Western

3645 ---Amelia rankin; a novel. New York: Norton, 1959.
252p.
Western

3646 Lockhart, Caroline. "Me-Smith". Philadelphia:

Lippincott, 1911. 315p.
Western

3647 ---The lady doc. Philadelphia: Lippincott, 1912. 339p.
Western

3648 ---The full of the moon. Philadelphia: Lippincott,
1914. 267p.
Western

3649 ---The man from the bitter roots. Philadelphia:
Lippincott, 1915. 327p.
Western

3650 ---The fighting shepherdess. Boston: Small, 1919.
373p.
Western

3651 ---The dude wrangler. New York: Doubleday, 1921.
319p.
Western

3652 ---The old west-and new; a novel. New York: Doubleday,
1933. 357p.
Western

3653 Lockridge, Ross Franklin (1877-1952). Raintree county...
which had no boundaries in time and space, where
lurked musical and strange names and mythical and
lost peoples, and which was itself only a name
musical and strange. Boston: Houghton, 1948. 1066p.
Indiana-- 1844-1892--Serious work.

3654 Lockwood, Mrs. Myna. Free river; a story of old new
orleans. New York: Dutton, 1942. 255p.
Louisiana Purchase--Juvenile.

3655 Lockwood, Ralph Ingersoll (1798-1855). The insurgents;
an historical novel. Philadelphia: Carey, 1835.
2 vols.
Shay's Rebellion-- 1786-1787.

3656 Lockwood, Mrs. Sarah (McNeil) (1882-   ). Fistful
of stars. New York: Appleton, 1947. 335p.
First novel--Mining and lumbering--Northern
Wisconsin-- 1880's.

3657 ---The elbow of the snake. New York: Doubleday, 1958.
261p.
Homesteading--Snake River Valley, Idaho-- 1890's.

3658 Lofts, Mrs. Norah Ethel (Robinson) (1904-   ). Here
was a man; a romantic history of sir walter raleigh,
his voyages, his discoveries and his queen. New
York: Knopf, 1936. 304p.

3659   ---Blossom like the rose. New York: Knopf, 1939.
        363p.
                New England--Religionists v. Indian's--1680--
        Romance.

3660   ---Hester roon. New York: Knopf, 1940. 457p.
                England and West Indies--1700's--Picaresque
        novel.

3661   ---Winter harvest; a novel. New York: Doubleday, 1955.
        347p.
                Donner Party--1846.

        Logan, Ford pseud. see Newton, Dwight Bennett

        Lomax, Bliss pseud. see Drago, Harry Sinclair (1888-   )

3662   Lomen, Helen and Flack, Marjorie. Taktuk, an artic boy.
        New York: Doubleday, 1928. 139p.
                Northwest Alaska--1928--Valuable for detail--
        Juvenile.

3663   London, Jack (1876-1916). Call of the wild. New York:
        Macmillan, 1903. 202p.
                Alaska adventure and comment on social Darwin-
        isim.

3664   ---White fang. New York: Macmillan, 1905. 327p.
                Adventure--Alaska.

3665   ---Burning daylight. New York: Macmillan, 1910.
        361p.
                Young man to north--"King of Klondike".

3666   ---Smoke bellew. New York: Century, 1912. 385p.
                Klondike gold craze.

3667   Long, Gabrielle Margaret Vere Campbell pseud. Bowen,
        Marjorie. Soldier from virginia. New York: Apple-
        ton, 1912. 346p.
                French-Indian War and American Revolution
        (1754-1781)--George Washington main figure.

3668   Long, Laura. Hannah courageous. New York: Longmans,
        1939. 246p.
                White River--Quaker--Underground railroad--
        Juvenile.

        Long, Leslie jt. author, see Doherty, Ethel

3669   Longstreet, Stephen (1907-   ). Eagles where i walk.
        New York: Doubleday, 1961. 477p.
                American Revolution--New York State.

3670   ---A few painted feathers. New York: Doubleday, 1963.
        397p.

3671　---War in the golden weather; a novel.　New York:
Doubleday, 1965.　470p.
French-Indian War (1754-1763)--George Washington
and General Braddock.

3672　Longstreth, Thomas Morris (1886-　　). Hide-out.
New York: Macmillan, 1947.　233p.
Concord, Massachusetts--1840's--Underground
railroad--Stagecoach.

3673　---Time flight.　New York: Macmillan, 1954.　216p.
Two teenage boys to Salem--Cotton Mather--
Witchcraft.

3674　Loomis, Noel Miller (1905-1969).　Rim of caprock.
New York: Macmillan, 1952.　202p.
Western

3675　---The buscadero.　New York: Macmillan, 1953.　200p.
Western

3676　---North to texas.　New York: Ballantine, 1955.　180p.
Western

3677　---The twilighters.　New York: Macmillan, 1955.　208p.
Kentucky and West of Mississippi River--
Early 1800's.

3678　---West to the sun.　New York: Fawcett, 1955.　176p.
Western

3679　---Johnny concho.　New York: Fawcett, 1956.　190p.
Western

3680　---Short cut to red river.　New York: Macmillan, 1958.
178p.
Western--One of his best--Golden Spur Award
1959 for Best Western.

3681　---A time for violence.　New York: Macmillan, 1960.
224p.
Western

3682　---pseud. Miller, Frank.　Tejas country.　New York:
Avalon, 1953.　256p.
Western

3683　Lorraine, A. M..　Donald adair; a novel by a young
lady.　Richmond: Cottom, 1828.　2 vols.
Valley Forge to Virginia--Romance.

3684　Lothrop, Mrs. Harriet Mulford (Stone) (1844-1924)
pseud. Sidney, Margaret.　A little maid of concord

town; a romance of the american revolution. Boston:
Lothrop, 1900. 405p.

3685 ---The judges' cave; being a romance of the new haven
colony in the days of the regicides 1661. Boston:
Lothrop, 1900. 410p.
William Goffe (1605?-1679?)--Edward Whalley
(d. 1675?).

3686 ---Little maid of boston town. Boston: Lothrop, 1910.
423p.
American Revolution--Loyalist to patriot--
Young girl--Juvenile.

3687 Lott, Milton James. The last hunt. Boston: Houghton,
1954. 399p.
First novel--Last of plains bison--1870's--
Buffalo hunters.

3688 ---Dance back the buffalo. Boston: Houghton, 1959.
406p.
Indians on Reservation--1889-1890--Wounded
Knee Creek--Based on Ghost Dance 1889.

3689 ---Backtrack. Boston: Houghton, 1965. 248p.
Cattle drive Texas to Montana 1880.

3690 Loughead, Flora (Haines) Apponyi. The abandoned claim.
Boston: Houghton, 1891. 330p.
California farming.

Lovelace, Delos Wheeler jt. author, see Lovelace, Maud

3691 Lovelace, Mrs. Maud (Hart) (1892-   ). The black
angels; a novel. New York: Day, 1926. 296p.
Travelling concert troup--Middlewest--Covered
wagon--Pre-Civil War Era.

3692 ---Early candle light; a novel. New York: Day, 1929.
322p.
Fort Snelling--Minnesota frontier--1830's--
Chippewa Indians--Domestic realism.

3693 ---The charming sally; a novel. New York: Day, 1932.
311p.
Love of Quaker for actress--1872--First legitimate theatre company to old northwest.

3694 ---and Lovelace, Delos Wheeler. One stayed at welcome.
New York: Day, 1934. 311p.
Pioneering--Romance--Post Mexican War-1850.

3695 ---Gentleman from england. New York: Macmillan, 1937.
361p.
Englishman to Crockett County, Minnesota--1865-
1875.

288

3696 Lovell, E. W.. Legacy. New York: Norton, 1934.
    339p.
        Green Bay area of Wisconsin--Decay of French
    family--Descendants of voyageurs.

3697 Lowden, Leone. Proving ground; a novel of civil war
    days in the west. New York: McBride, 1946. 455p.
    Indiana frontier.

    Loyal, C. pseud. see Burton, Maria Ampara (Ruíz)

3698 Lucas, Jay (1894-   ). The seven bar ranch. New
    York: Macaulay, 1934. 251p.
    Western

3699 ---Blaze mcgee. New York: Macaulay, 1935. 284p.
    Western

3700 ---The arizonan. New York: Green Circle, 1937. 320p.
    Western

3701 ---Boss of the rafter. New York: Green Circle, 1937.
    313p.
    Western

3702 ---The desert ranger. New York: Furman, 1939. 384p.
    Western

3703 Lull, DeLos. Father solon; or, the helper helped.
    New York: Ketcham, 1888. 367p.
        Mormon

3704 Lund, Robert (1915-   ). The odyssey of thaddeus
    baxter; a novel. New York: Day, 1957. 254p.
        Young Texan drifts to Wyoming--1870--Humor.

3705 Lundy, Mrs. Jo Evalin. Tidewater valley; a story of
    the swiss in oregon. Philadelphia: Winston, 1949.
    246p.
        Land of Free Series--Juvenile.

3706 Lutes, Mrs. Della (Thompson). Millbrook. Boston:
    Little, 1938. 330p.
        1880's--Village in southern Michigan--Main
    Street novel.

3707 ---Gabriel's search. Boston: Little, 1940. 351p.
        Michigan Early 1800's--Details of daily life.

3708 Lutz, Giles A.. Fight or run;[danger rides the kansas
    frontier.] New York: Popular Library, 1954. 192p.
    1854-1861.

3709 ---The honyocker. New York: Doubleday, 1961. 191p.
        Western--Golden Spur Award for Best Western-1962.

289

3710 ---The long cold wind. New York: Doubleday, 1962.
213p.
Western

3711 ---The golden land. New York: Doubleday, 1963. 227p.
Western

3712 ---The bleeding land. New York: Doubleday, 1965. 183p.
Western

3713 ---The hardy breed. New York: Doubleday, 1966. 192p.
Western

3714 ---Relentless gun. London: Jenkins, 1967. 159p.
Western

3715 ---Wild runs the river. New York: Doubleday, 1968.
210p.
Western

3716 Lyle, Eugene P. Jr. (1873-   ). The missourian.
New York: Doubleday, 1905. 519p.
European intervention in Mexico--1861-1867.

3717 ---The lone star. New York: Doubleday, 1907. 431p.
Texas Rebellion--To Battle of San Jacinto.

3718 ---Blaze derringer. New York: Doubleday, 1910. 314p.
Western

3719 Lyle-Smith, Alan (1914-   ) pseud. Caillou, Alan.
The walls of jolo. New York: Appleton, 1960. 311p.
United States v. Philippines--1899-1900.

Lynch, Lawrence L. pseud. see VanDeventer, Emma Murdoch

3720 Lynde, Francis (1856-1930). The helpers. Boston:
Houghton, 1899. 420p.
Western

3721 ---The master of appleby; a novel tale concerning
itself in part with the great struggle in the two
carolinas; but chiefly with the adventures therein
of two gentlemen who loved one and the same lady.
Indianapolis: Bowen, 1902. 581p.

3722 ---The king of arcadia. New York: Scribner's, 1909.
354p.
Western

3723 ---The taming of red butte western. New York: Scribner's
1910. 410p.
Western

3724 ---Branded. New York: Scribner's, 1918. 370p.
Western

290

3725 ---Mr. arnold; a romance of the revolution. Indianapolis:
      Bobbs, 1923. 326p.
         Benedict Arnold (1741-1801).

3726 ---The fight on standing stone. New York: Scribner's,
      1925. 248p.
         Western

3727 ---The tenderfoots. New York: Scribner's, 1926. 334p.
         Western

      Lyndon pseud. see Hughes, Mrs. Reginald

      Lyndon, Ross pseud. see Eisele, Wilbert Edwin

3728 Lynn, Margaret. Free soil. New York: Macmillan,
      1920. 377p.
         New England family to Kansas--1850's--Romance--
      John Brown.

3729 ---The land of promise. Boston: Little, 1927. 280p.
         Kansas--Settling--Free v. Slave.

3730 Lytle, Andrew Nelson (1902-   ). At the moon's inn.
      Indianapolis: Bobbs, 1941. 400p.
         Florida-DeSoto-1542.

3731 Lyttleton, Edith J. pseud. Lancaster, G. B.. Grand
      parade. New York: Reynal, 1943. 377p.
         Halifax, Nova Scotia--Early days.

M

M. B. pseud. see Faust, Fredrick Schiller

M. I. T. see Todd, Mary VanLennup (Ives)

3732 Maass, Edgar (1896-   ). Don pedro and the devil;
      a novel of chivalry declining. Indianapolis: Bobbs,
      1942. 634p.
            Young man with Pizarro in Peru.

3733 Mabie, Mary Louise. The long knives walked. Indiana-
      polis: Bobbs, 1932. 304p.
            Covered wagon journey across plains--Oregon
      Trail--Adventure--Romance.

3734 ---The pale survivor. Indianapolis: Bobbs, 1934.
      373p.
            English lady taken by pirates on trip to
      America--Based on Rose Marie Brudenal--Sir Henry
      Morgan (1635?-1688).

MacArthur, Burke pseud. see Burks, Arthur J.

3735 MacArthur, David Wilson (1903-   ). Traders north.
      New York: Knopf, 1952. 246p.
            First two voyages of Governor and company
      in Hudson Bay--Based on records of voyages.

3736 Macaulay, Rose. The shadow flies. New York: Harper,
      1932. 476p.
            England--Civil War--1640-1660.

3737 Macbeth, Mrs. Madge Hamilton (Lyons) (1878-1965).
      Kleath. Boston: Small, 1917. 386p.
            Klondike Gold Rush--Romance and adventure.

3738 McCague, James. Fiddle hill. New York: Crown, 1960.
      343p.
            Old Mountain Railroad--Pacific Midland Railroad.

3739 McCall, Marie (1909-   ). The evening wolves; a novel.
      New York: Day, 1949. 279p.
            Salem, Massachusetts--Witchcraft--1690's--
      Realistic.

3740 McCants, Elliott Crayton. Ninety six. New York:
      Crowell, 1930. 325p.
            American Revolution--South Carolina--Ninety
      Six is name of frontier post.

3741 McCarter, Mrs. Margaret (Hill) (1860-1938). In old
quivera. Topeka, Kansas: Crane, 1908. 139p.

3742 ---The price of the prairie; a story of kansas.
Chicago: McClurg, 1910. 489p.
Covered wagons--1860's--Romance.

3743 ---The peace of the solomon valley. Chicago: McClurg,
1911. 91p.
Kansas

3744 ---A wall of men. Chicago: McClurg, 1912. 494p.
Free soilers in Kansas--Wakarusa War--
Quantrell's Raid--Sack of Lawrence.

3745 ---Winning the wilderness. Chicago: McClurg, 1914.
404p.
Pioneering in Kansas--Two generations.

3746 ---Vanguards of the plains; a romance of the old
santa fé trail. New York: Harper, 1917. 397p.
Kansas City to Santa Fé--1840's--Role of
commerce in development of prairie area--Romance.

3747 ---The reclaimers. New York: Harper, 1918. 362p.
Western Kansas--Romance.

3748 ---Widening waters. New York: Harper, 1924. 401p.
Western

3749 McClinchey, Florence E.. Joe pete. New York: Holt,
1929. 311p.
First novel--Ojibway Indians--Northern Michigan--
Life in twentieth century.

3750 McClung, John Alexander (1804-1859). Camden; a tale
of the south. Philadelphia: Cary, 1830. 2 vols.
American Revolution--Only novel--Tradition of
Sir Walter Scott--Tarleton attacks Gates--1780--
Certain realism.

3751 McConnel, John Ludlum (1826-1862). Talbot and vernon;
a novel. New York: Baker, 1850. 513p.
Mexican War (1845-1848).

3752 McConnell, Annie Bliss. Half married; agamé gamé.
Philadelphia: Lippincott, 1887. 311p.
Frontier army post.

3753 McConville, Bernard. The gentleman on horseback.
New York: Lane, 1935. 354p.
California--1840-1850--Romance.

3754 McCook, Henry Christopher. Quaker ben; a tale of
colonial pennsylvania in the days of thomas penn.

Philadelphia: Jacobs, 1911. 336p.
1737

3755 McCoy, Samuel. Tippecanoe; being a true chronicle of
certain passages between david larrance and antoinette
o'bannon of the battle of tippecanoe in the indiana
wilderness, and what befell thereafter in old cory-
don and now first set forth by samuel mccoy.
Indianapolis: Bobbs, 1916. 295p.
Romance--1811.

3756 McCracken, Harold. Iglaome, the lone hunter. New York:
Century, 1930. 248p.
Son of Eskimo Chief--Juvenile.

3757 ---Beyond the frozen frontier. New York: Speller,
1936. 233p.
Alaska--Romance and adventure.

3758 Maccuish, David (1924-   ). Do not go gentle. New
York: Doubleday, 1960. 472p.
Mining--Montana--To World War II.

3759 McCulloch, John Herries. The splendid renegade. New
York: Coward, 1928. 373p.
John Paul Jones (1747-1792)--Romance.

3760 McCulloch, Robert W.. Me and thee. Boston: Lothrop,
1937. 257p.
Shaker Colony--Mt. Lebanon--1835--Melodrama.

3761 ---Polly kent rides west in the days of '49. Chicago:
Winston, 1940. 304p.

3762 McCutcheon, George Barr (1866-1928). Viola gwyn.
New York: Dodd, 1922. 378p.
Indiana-Kentucky frontier--1830's.

3763 MacDonald, Alexander (1818-   ). The white trail;a
story of the early days of klondike. New York:
Caldwell, 1908. 384p.

MacDonald, Allan William Colt see MacDonald, William
Colt

3764 MacDonald, Mrs. Jessica Nelson (North) (1894-   ).
Morning in the land. New York: Greystone, 1941.
408p.
English immigrants to Milwaukee--1840.

3765 McDonald, Mrs. Lucile (Saunders) (1898-   ) and Ross,
Zola Helen (1912-   ). The courting of ann maria.
New York: Nelson, 1958. 192p.
Oregon Territory--1850--Land Donation Act--
English point of view--Teenage girls.

294

3766 McDonald, Norman C. (1884-1958). Song of the axe.
New York: Ballantine, 1957. 276p.
Lumbering--Puget Sound--Jack London style--
Local color.

3767 MacDonald, William Colt (1891-   ). Rustler's paradise.
New York: Covici, 1932. 304p.
Western

3768 ---Law of the forty-fives. New York: Covici, 1933. 316p.
Western

3769 ---Six gun melody. New York: Covici, 1933. 268p.
Western

3770 ---Powdersmoke range. New York: Covici, 1934. 298p.
Western

3771 ---Riders of the whistling skull. New York: Covici,
1934. 319p.
Western

3772 ---The singing scorpion. New York: Covici, 1934. 311p.
Western

3773 ---Ghost town gold. New York: Covici, 1935. 320p.
Western

3774 ---Roarin' lead. New York: Covici, 1935. 308p.
Western

3775 ---Bullets for buckaroos. New York: Covici, 1936. 317p.
Western

3776 ---California caballero. New York: Covici, 1936. 314p.
Western

3777 ---Trigger trail. New York: Covici, 1936. 320p.
Western

3778 ---Spanish pesos; a western story. New York: Covici,
1937. 319p.
Western

3779 ---Sleepy horse range. New York: Covici, 1938. 315p.
Western

3780 ---Six shooter showdown. New York: Doubleday, 1939.
274p.
Western

3781 ---The battle at three-cross. New York: Doubleday,
1940. 280p.
Western

3782 ---Black sombrero. New York: Doubleday, 1940. 278p.
Western

3783 ---Phantom pass. New York: Doubleday, 1940. 274p.
Western

3784 ---Renegade roundup. New York: Doubleday, 1940. 302p.
Western

3785 ---Boontown buccaneers. New York: Doubleday, 1942.
274p.
Western

3786 ---The crimson quirt. New York: Doubleday, 1942. 268p.
Western

3787 ---Riddle of ramrod ridge. New York: Doubleday, 1942.
278p.
Western

3788 ---Shadow rider. New York: Doubleday, 1942. 276p.
Western

3789 ---Rebel ranger. New York: Doubleday, 1943. 246p.
Western

3790 ---The vanishing gun slinger. New York: Doubleday,
1943. 219p.
Western

3791 ---The three mesquiteers. New York: Doubleday, 1944.
214p.
Western

3792 ---Cartridge carnival. New York: Doubleday, 1945.
215p.
Western

3793 ---Thunderbird trail. New York: Doubleday, 1946.
215p.
Western

3794 ---Wheels in dust. New York: Doubleday, 1946. 273p.
Western

3795 ---Bad man's return; a three mesquiteers story. New
York: Doubleday, 1947. 192p.
Western

3796 ---Master of the mesa. New York: Doubleday, 1947.
235p.
Western

3797 ---Dead man's gold. New York: Doubleday, 1948. 224p.
Western

3798 ---Gunsight range. New York: Doubleday, 1949. 216p.
Western

3799 ---Powdersmoke justice; a three mesquiteers story.
New York: Doubleday, 1949. 222p.
Western

3800 ---The killer brand. New York: Doubleday, 1950. 222p.
Western

3801 ---Mesquiteer mavericks; a three mesquiteers story.
New York: Doubleday, 1950. 221p.
Western

3802 ---Stir up the dust. London: Hodder, 1950. 255p.
Western

3803 ---Blind cartridges. New York: Doubleday, 1951.
224p.
Western

3804 ---Ranger man. New York: Doubleday, 1951. 187p.
Western

3805 ---The galloping ghost; a three mesquiteers story.
New York: Doubleday, 1952. 192p.
Western

3806 ---Three-notch cameron. New York: Doubleday, 1952.
188p.
Western

3807 ---Law and order unlimited; a gregory quist story.
New York: Doubleday, 1953. 187p.
Western

3808 ---Lightning swift. New York: Doubleday, 1953. 188p.
Western

3809 ---Mascarada pass; a gregory quist story. New York:
Doubleday, 1954. 188p.
Western

3810 ---The comanche scalp; a gregory quist story. Philadelphia: Lippincott, 1955. 224p.
Western

3811 ---Destination danger; a gregory quist story. Philadelphia: Lippincott, 1955. 252p.
Western

3812 ---The range kid. New York: Pyramid, 1955. 158p.
Western

3813 ---The devil's drum; a gregory quist story. Philadelphia: Lippincott, 1956. 220p.

Western

3814 ---Flaming lead. New York: Pyramid, 1956. 157p.
Western

3815 ---Action at arcanum; a gregory quist story. Philadelphia: Lippincott, 1958. 192p.
Western

3816 ---Tombstone for a troubleshooter; a gregory quist
story. Philadelphia: Lippincott, 1960. 220p.
Western

3817 ---West of yesterday. New York: Bouregy, 1964. 190p.
Western

3818 ---Fugitive from fear. London: Hodder, 1966. 160p.
Western

3819 MacDonald, Zillah Katherine. Flower of the fortress.
Philadelphia: Presbyterian Bd., 1944. 231p.
King George's War (1745-1748)--Siege of Louis-
bourg (1745)--Juvenile.

3820 McDowell, Syl pseud. Gunn, Tom. The sheriff of painted
post. New York: Messner, 1935. 259p.
Western

3821 MacFarland, Raymond. The sea panther. New York:
Stokes, 1928. 309p.
Capture of Louisbourg--Pirates--Adventures.

3822 McFarlane, Peter Clark (1871-1924). Tongues of flame.
New York: Cosmopolitan, 1924. 405p.
Indian ownership--Coastal lands.

3823 McGehee, Florence. Bride of king solomon. New York:
Macmillan, 1958. 265p.
Woman raising children in Ozarks(1871-1900).

3824 McGehee, Mrs. Thomasine (Cobb) (1888-   ). Journey
proud. New York: Macmillan, 1939. 397p.
First novel--Passing of the old south plantation
to store owner--1845-1879.

3825 McGinnis, Paul (1896-   ). Lost eden. New York:
McBride, 1947. 287p.
South Seas--Eighteenth century--Hero with
James Cook (1728-1779)--To Hawaii.

McGlasson, Eva Wilder see Brodhead, Eva Wilder
(McGlasson)

3826 MacGowan, Alice (1858-   ). Judith of the cumberlands.
New York: Putnam, 1908. 406p.

298

Primitive mountain settlement--cf. with Murfree.

3827 ---A girl of the plains country. New York: Stokes,
1924. 347p.
Romance--West.

3828 ---and Cooke, Grace MacGowan. Return; a story of the
sea islands in 1739. Boston: Page, 1905. 544p.

3829 MacGregor, Mrs. Mary Esther (Miller) pseud. Keith,
Marian. A gentleman adventurer; a story of the
hudson's bay company. New York: Doran, 1924. 301p.
Hudson's Bay Company--Scots romance with half-
breed--Juvenile.

3830 McHenry, James (1785-1845). The spectre of the forest;
or, annals of the housatonic, a new-england romance.
[Anonymous]. New York: Bliss, 1823. 2 vols.
Follower of J. Cooper--Connecticut.

3831 ---The betrothed of wyoming; an historical tale.
[Anonymous]. Philadelphia: Author, (3rd Edition),
1830. 231p.
Pennsylvania--Wyoming Massacre--1778.

3832 ---Meredith; or, the mystery of the meschianza. a
tale of the american revolution. Philadelphia:
Author, 1831. 260p.
Philadelphia--British in control.

3833 ---pseud. Secondsight, Solomon. The wilderness; the youth-
ful days of washington. a tale of the west. London:
Newman, 1823. 3 vols.
Prolonged and ambitious portrayal--Early effort--
Published in Pittsburgh and Alleghany in 1848 under
title The Wilderness; or, Braddock's Time.

Machetanz, Fred jt. author, see Machetanz, Sara

3834 Machetanz, Frederick. Panuck, the eskimo sled dog.
New York: Scribner's, 1939. 95p.
Artic--Juvenile.

3835 Machetanz, Sara (Mrs. Frederick Machetanz). Rick of
high ridge. New York: Scribner's, 1952. 177p.
Alaska homesteading--Good regional piece--
Based on personal experience of author.

3836 ---and Machetanz, Fred. Barney hits the trail.
New York: Scribner's, 1950. 195p.
Juvenile

3837 McHugh, Arona. The luck of the van meers; a tradition.
New York: Doubleday, 1969. 312p.
Chronicle--Two hundred years of family--Physic-
ian studies psychic history.

McIlwraith, Jean N. jt. author, see McLennan, William

3838 McIntire, Mrs. Marguerite (Pearman). Heaven's dooryard. New York: Farrar, 1940. 308p.
Quaker from Concord to Maine--Farm--1840.

3839 McIntyre, John Thomas (1871-1951). Fighting king george. Philadelphia: Penn, 1905. 372p.
Adventure--Juvenile.

3840 ---Stained sails; a novel. New York: Stokes, 1928. 299p.
John Paul Jones--Romance.

3841 ---Drums in the dawn. New York: Doubleday, 1932. 322p.
American Revolution--Economic intrigue in France.

3842 McIntyre, Marjorie. The river witch. New York: Crown, 1955. 282p.
First novel--Mississippi and Missouri Rivers--1850.

3843 Mack, Orin. Indian gold. New York: Knopf, 1933. 244p.
Story based on Joe and Ed Hampton--1833.

3844 McKay, Allis. They came to a river. New York: Macmillan, 1941. 651p.
Columbia River--Apple industry--1900-1920.

3845 McKay, Mrs. Annie E. (Mrs. Alfred Almond McKay). A latter day saint. New York: Revell, 1893. 279p.
Mormon

3846 Mackay, Mrs. Margaret (Mack Prang) (1907-   ). Sharon; a novel. New York: Day, 1948. 269p.
Hawaii--1880's--Romance.

3847 McKee, Ruth Eleanor (1903-   ). The lord's annointed; a novel of hawaii. New York: Doubleday, 1934. 411p.
First novel--Hawaii--1820--Chronicle of three generations.

3848 ---After a hundred years. New York: Doubleday, 1935. 329p.
Hawaii (1920-1934)--Sequel to The Lord's Annointed.

3849 ---Christopher strange; a novel. New York: Doubleday, 1941. 706p.
California 1846-1900--Life on old Spanish ranch.

3850 MacKenzie, Jean Kenyon (1874-1936). The trader's wife.

New York: Coward, 1930. 158p.
New England abolition era--Wife of slave
trader--Travels with him.

3851 McKeown, Martha (Ferguson) (1903-   ). <u>Mountains</u>
<u>ahead; a novel</u>. New York: Putnam, 1961. 448p.
Wagon train--To Oregon--1847--Juvenile.

Mackie, Pauline Bradford see Hopkins, Pauline Bradford
(Mackie)

3852 MacKinnon, Mary Linehan. <u>One small candle</u>. New York:
Crown, 1956. 250p.
Farm life--New York--1850's.

3853 Mackintosh, Elizabeth (1896-1952) <u>pseud</u>. Tey, Josephine.
<u>The privateer</u>. New York: Macmillan, 1960. 279p.
Based on life of Sir Henry Morgan--Action--
Adventure.

3854 McKnight, Charles. <u>Old fort duquesne; or, captain</u>
<u>jack, the scout. an historical novel with copious</u>
<u>notes</u>. Pittsburgh: Peoples Monthly, 1873. 501p.
Romance

3855 ---<u>Simon girty; "the white savage"...a romance of the</u>
<u>border</u>. Philadelphia: McCurdy, 1880. 393p.

3856 Mackubin, Ellen. <u>The king of the town</u>. Boston:
Houghton, 1898. 152p.
Fort Ludlow, Montana.

3857 McLane, Hiram H.. <u>Irene viesca; a tale of the magee</u>
<u>expedition in the gauchipin war in texas a.d. 1812-13</u>.
San Antonio, Texas: San Antonio Printing, 1886.
548p.

3858 McLaws, Emily Lafayette <u>pseud</u>. McLaws, Lafayette.
<u>When the land was young; being the true romance of</u>
<u>mistress antoinette huguenin and captain jack middle-</u>
<u>ton in the days of the buccaneers</u>. Boston: Lothrop,
1902. 383p.
Florida border-1685.

McLaws, Lafayette see McLaws, Emily Lafayette

3859 McLean, Sydney Robertson. <u>A moment of time</u>. New York:
Putnam, 1945. 210p.
Episodic novel--Scotswoman on Massachusetts
farm--1770-1838.

3860 McLennan, William (1856-   ) and McIlwraith, Jean N.
<u>The span o' life; a tale of louisbourg and quebec</u>.
New York: Harper, 1899. 307p.
Rebellion of 1745--Maxwell, the hero is real
person.

3861 MacLeod, Alison. City of light. Boston: Houghton,
1969. 287p.
Continuation of The Hireling--A tudor tale.

3862 MacLeod, LeRoy Oliver. The years of peace. New York:
Century, 1932. 324p.
Southern Indiana rural community-- 1865- 1875--
Daily life Wabash Valley, Indiana--Anticipates
Feikma and P. Corey.

3863 ---The crowded hill. New York: Reynal, 1934. 328p.
Wabash Valley-- 1876- 1878--Sequel to Years of
Peace--Newsreel device--cf. Dos Passos.

McMeekin, Clark pseud. see Clark, Dorothy (Park)

McMeekin, Isabel (McLennan) see Clark, Dorothy (Park)
jt. author

3864 McMeekin, Mrs. Isabel (McLennan) (1895-   ). Juba's
new moon. New York: Messner, 1944. 224p.
Shadrow family--New home in Kentucky--Sequel,
Journey Cake.

3865 McNally, William James (1891-   ). House of vanished
splendor. New York: Putnam, 1932. 313p.
First novel--Chronicle--Three generations--
Rise and fall--Minneapolis- 1851.

3866 ---The roofs of elm street; a tale of the middle west.
New York: Putnam, 1936. 378p.
North Star,Minnesota--Three families--Scots--
Irish--Scandanavian's--Germans--Yankees-- 1865- 1910.

3867 McNeil, (Henry) Everett (1862-1929). The totem of
black hawk; a tale of pioneer days in northwestern
illinois and the black hawk war. Chicago: McClurg,
1914. 369p.
Northwest Illinois-- 1830's--Pioneer life--Rock
River Valley--Black Hawk War--Juvenile.

3868 ---Daniel du luth... New York: Dutton, 1926. 389p.
French exploration on Great Lakes--Journey with
Daniel G. Duluth-- 1678--Montreal to Lake Superior.

3869 McNeilly, Mildred Masterson. Heaven is too high.
New York: Hampton, 1844. 432p.
Alaska-- 1790- 1810--Russian dominance--
Aleksander Andreevich Baranov (1745- 1819).

3870 ---Great is the glory. London: Jarrolds, 1946. 352p.
Alaska

3871 ---Each bright river; a novel of the oregon country.
New York: Morrow, 1950. 308p.

302

South Carolina to Oregon--1859--Frontier life--
Homesteading.

3872 McNichols, Charles Longstreth (1895-   ). Crazy
weather. New York: Macmillan, 1944. 195p.
Arizona--114° F--American boy with Mohave friend--
Very good.

3873 McNickle, D'Arcy. The surrounded. New York: Dodd,
1936. 297p.
Indians on reservation--Western Montana--
Author brought up on Flathead Reservation--Snielemen--
Mountains of the Surrounded.

3874 ---Runner in the sun; a story of indian maize. Philadelphia: Winston, 1954. 234p.
Land of Free Series--Juvenile.

McNutt, William jt. author, see Jones, Grover

3875 Macphail, Sir Andrew (1864-   ). The vine of sibmah;
a relation of the puritans. New York: Macmillan,
1906. 432p.
English captain takes daughter to American
colonies.

3876 McSherry, James (1819-1869). Pere jean; or, the jesuit
missionary. a tale of north american indians.
Baltimore: Murphy, 1847. 256p.
Canada--1642.

3877 Madariaga, Salvador de (1886-   ). The heart of jade.
New York: Creative Age, 1944. 642p.
Mexico--Time of Monteczuma--Arrival of the
Spanish--Aztec custom and dress--Author poet and
biographer of Cortes.

3878 Madison, Marie. The witch; a novel. New Haven,
Connecticut: New Haven Publishing, 1891. 131p.
Colonial Era.

3879 Magaret, Helene (1906-   ). Who walk in pride.
Milwaukee: Bruce, 1945. 280p.
Santa Domingo--French Revolution--French planter
flees to America.

3880 Malkus, Mrs. Alida Sims (1895-   ). Raquel of the
ranch country. New York: Harcourt, 1927. 314p.
Young girl runs Texas ranch--Juvenile.

3881 ---Cavarans to santa fé. New York: Harper, 1928. 289p.
Romance--American boy and Spanish girl.

3882 ---Dragon fly of zuni. New York: Harcourt, 1928.
213p.

Romance--Squash Blossom and Blue Feather--
Juvenile.

3883 ---Pirates' port; a tale of old new york. New York:
Harper, 1929. 251p.
Romance--Juvenile.

3884 ---The dark star of itza; the story of a pagan princess.
New York: Harcourt, 1930. 217p.
Mayas--Itza--Juvenile.

3885 ---A fifth for the king; a story of the conquest of
yucatan and of the discovery of the amazon. New
York: Harper, 1931. 250p.
Spanish--Fourteen years after Cortes in Mexico--
Adventure--Juvenile.

3886 ---Stone knife boy. New York: Harcourt, 1933. 270p.
Taos Indian Boy--Juvenile.

3887 ---Eastward sweeps the current; a saga of the polynesian
sea farers. Chicago: Winston, 1938. 394p.
Polynesians to coast of America--Juvenile.

3888 ---Along the inca highway. Boston: Heath, 1941. 56p.
Peru--Juvenile.

3889 Mally, Emma Louise (1908-   ). The mockingbird is
singing. New York: Holt, 1944. 394p.
Blockade runner--New Orleans--Cattle breeding
in Texas--Railroad building.

3890 ---Abigail. New York: Appleton, 1956. 307p.
Hudson Valley girl to South--Underground railroad.

3891 Malm, Dorthea. Journal of the lady pamela foxe; being
her account of her adventures in england, in the
colony of massachusetts and at sea, together with
the story of her true love and her reflections upon
the vicissitudes of fortune, all the events narrated
having occurred in the year of our lord 17...
New York: Prentice, 1947. 278p.
Novel in diary form--Sentimental--Costume.

3892 Malvern, Gladys. If love comes. New York: Kendall,
1932. 309p.
Southern California--Early 1800's--Mission--
Indians.

3893 ---Ann lawrence of old new york. New York: Messner,
1947. 203p.
New York City--1811--Farm taken in by city--
Seventeen year old girl--Juvenile.

3894 ---Eric's girls. New York: Messner, 1949. 244p.
        New Amsterdam before change to New York City--
        Romance--Juvenile.

3895 Mancur, John Henry. Alda grey; a tale of new jersey.
        New York: Colyer, 1843. 191p.
        American Revolution.

3896 ---Christine; a tale of the revolution. New York:
        Colyer, 1843. 60p.
        Romance--Adventure--Flatbush, New York.

3897 ---The deserter; a legend of mount washington. New
        York: Colyer, 1843. 132p.
        American Revolution--Full length romance.

3898 ---Jasper crowe. New York: Colyer, 1843. 256p.
        American Revolution.

Manfred, Fredrick F. see Feikma, Fredrick

3899 Mann, Edward Beverly (1902-   ). The man from texas.
        New York: Morrow, 1931. 289p.
        Western

3900 ---The blue-eyed kid. New York: Morrow, 1932. 306p.
        Western

3901 ---The valley of wanted men. New York: Morrow, 1932.
        293p.
        Western

3902 ---Killers' range. New York: Morrow, 1933. 294p.
        Western

3903 ---Gamblin' man. New York: Morrow, 1934. 314p.
        Western

3904 ---Stampede. New York: Morrow, 1934. 299p.
        Western

3905 ---Rustlers' round-up; a "whistler" story. New York:
        Morrow, 1935. 302p.
        Western

3906 ---Thirsty range. New York: Morrow, 1935. 281p.
        Western

3907 ---El sombra. New York: Morrow, 1936. 283p.
        Western

3908 ---Comanche kid. New York: Morrow, 1937. 278p.
        Western

3909 ---With spurs. New York: Morrow, 1937. 281p.
        Western

3910 ---Shootin' melody. New York: Morrow, 1938. 310p.
Western

3911 ---Gun feud. New York: Morrow, 1939. 275p.
Western

3912 ---Troubled range. New York: Morrow, 1940. 251p.
Western

3913 ---Gunsmoke trail. New York: Morrow, 1942. 279p.
Western

3914 ---Killers' range. New York: Jefferson, 1949. 294p.
Western

3915 ---The whistler; three western noveletts. New York:
Greenberg, 1953. 188p.
Western

3916 ---pseud. Strong, Zachary. The mesa gang. New York:
Morrow, 1940. 277p.
Western

3917 Mann, Florian Alexander. Story of the huguenots; a
sixteenth century narrative. St. Augustine, Florida:
Mann, 1898. 197p.
Romance

3918 Mann, Helen. Gallant warrior; a biographical novel.
Grand Rapids: Eerdmans, 1954. 309p.
Hannah (Emerson) Duston (b.1687)--Pioneer
woman taken by Indians.

3919 Mann, Herman (1772-1833). The female review; or,
memoirs of an american young lady; whose life and
character are peculiarly distinguished; being a
continental soldier, for nearly three years, in the
late american war. During which time, she perform-
ed the duties of every department, into which she
was called, with punctual exactness, fidelity and
honor, and preserved her chastity inviolate, by the
most artful concealment of her sex. With an appen-
dix, containing characteristic traits, by different
hands; her economy, principles of domestic education
by a citizen of massachusetts. Dedham, Massachusetts:
Heaton, 1797. 258p.
Based on Mrs. Deborah (Sampson) Gannett (1760-
1827)--Sentimental treatment of G. Washington.

3920 Mann, Martha. Nathan hale, patriot. New York: Dodd,
1944. 343p.
Fictionalized biography--Juvenile.

Manning, Roy pseud. see East, Fred

Manor, Jason pseud. see Hall, Oakley Maxwell

3921 Mansfield, Mrs. Norma Bicknell. Keeper of the wolves.
      New York: Farrar, 1934. 308p.
          Alaska--Adventure and mystery.

3922 ---Boss of the ragged o. New York: Farrar, 1935.
      276p.
          Western--Juvenile.

3923 ---The girl from frozen bend. New York: Farrar, 1938.
      279p.
          Alaska--Mystery--Juvenile.

3924 The marauder; an original tale of the seventeenth
      century. [Anonymous]. New Bedford: Melcher, 1823.
      124p.
          Romance

3925 Magulies, Leo and Merwin, Samuel Jr. (1910-   ).
      The flags were three; a novel of old new orleans.
      New York: Curl, 1945. 283p.
          Chronicle--Three generations--Early 1800's.

      Margulies, Merwin jt. author, see Margulies, Leo

3926 Marion, Frances (1890-   ). Westward the dream.
      New York: Doubleday, 1948. 312p.
          From Iowa to California--1875-1914--Life in
      southern California.

3927 Marius, Richard. The coming of rain. New York:
      New York: Knopf, 1969. 448p.
          First novel--Post Civil War--Eastern
      Tennessee.

3928 Markey, Gene (1895-   ). That far paradise. New
      York: McKay, 1960. 311p.
          American Revolution--Kentucky wilderness--
      1794--Of use of General Wayne's private letters--
      Romance.

3929 Markoe, Peter (1753-1792). The algerine spy in penn-
      sylvania; or, letters written by a native of algiers
      on the affairs of the united states in america from
      the close of the year 1783 to the meeting of the
      convention. [Anonymous]. Philadelphia: Prichard,
      1787. 129p.
          Epistolary novel.

3930 Marks, Mary A. M. (Hoppus). A great treason; a story
      of the war of independence. London: Macmillan,
      1883. 2 vols.
          American Revolution--Major André and B. Arnold--
      1780.

307

3931 Marquand, John Phillips (1893-1960). Black cargoe.
New York: Scribner's, 1925. 270p.
New England clipper ship is slaver.

3932 Marquis, Thomas Guthrie (1864-1936). Marguerite de
roberval; romance of the days of jacques cartier.
London: Unwin, 1899. 250p.

3933 Marriott, Crittenden. The ward of tecumseh. Philadelphia: Lippincott, 1914. 336p.
War of 1812--Friend of Tecumseh--Girl raised
by Shawnee.

3934 Marryat, Fredrick (1792-1848). Narrative of the travels
and adventures of monsieur violet in california,
sonora, and westeran texas. London: Routledge,
1843. 3 vols.
Early California--Melodramatic--Indians travels--
Missionaries--1832-1842.

3935 Marsh, George Tracy (1876-1945). The river of skulls.
Philadelphia: Penn, 1936. 311p.
Hudson Bay--Romance--Adventure.

3936 ---Vanished men. Philadelphia: Penn, 1939. 298p.
Hudson Bay.

3937 ---Ask no quarter. New York: Morrow, 1945. 572p.
Rhode Island--Close of seventeenth century--
Indians--Privateering--Newport--Romance.

3938 Marshall, Bernard Gay (1875-   ). Redcoat and minute-
man. New York: Appleton, 1924. 277p.
American Revolution--Nineteen year old captain
under George Washington.

3939 ---Old hickory's prisoner; a tale of the second war for
independence. New York: Appleton, 1925. 254p.
War of 1812--Juvenile.

3940 Marshall, Edison (1894-1967). Seward's folly. Boston:
Little, 1924. 312p.
Purchase of Alaska--Russia--Great Britain--
United States--Romance.

3941 ---The sleeper of the moonlit ranges; a new novel.
New York: Cosmopolitan, 1925. 311p.
Alaska--Mt. Paulof erupts.

3942 ---Child of the wild; a story of alaska. New York:
Cosmopolitan, 1926. 297p.
Eskimo--Chinook.

3943 ---The dead fall. New York: Cosmopolitan, 1927. 290p.
Alaska--Melodrama.

3944   ---The deputy at snow mountain.   New York: Kinsey,
       1932.   284p.
            Alaska--Frontier.

3945   ---Benjamin blake; a novel.   New York: Farrar, 1941.
       443p.
            American Revolution--Romance.

3946   ---Great smith.   New York: Farrar, 1943.   438p.
            Picaresque story Virginia--Language of Eliza-
       bethan Era--John Smith (1580-1631).

3947   ---Yankee pasha; the adventures of jason starbuck.
       New York: Farrar, 1947.   439p.
            Romantic--Adventure.

3948   ---Castle in the swamp; a tale of old carolina.   New
       York: Farrar, 1948.   378p.
            South Carolina--1840's--Horror tale.

3949   ---Cortez and marina.   New York: Doubleday, 1963.   461p.
            Hernando Cortés (1485-1547)--Marina (ca1505-1530).

3950   ---The lost colony.   New York: Doubleday, 1964.   438p.
            Raleigh's Roanoke Colony (1584-1590).

3951   ---pseud. Hunter, Hall.   Caravan to xanadu;   a novel of
       marco polo.   New York: Farrar, 1953.   371p.
            Marco Polo (1254-1323?).

3952   ---The gentleman.   New York: Farrar, 1956.   406p.
            1840--Slaves.

3953   ---and Dazey, Charles.   In old kentucky; a story of
       the bluegrass and the mountains founded on c. t.
       dazey's play.   New York: Dillingham, 1910.   352p.
            Play written 1895.

       Marshall, Gary pseud. see Snow, Charles Horace

3954   Martin, Charles M..   Left handed law.   New York: Green-
       berg, 1936.   256p.
            Western

3955   ---Tie fast hombre.   New York: Greenberg, 1936.   255p.
            Western

3956   ---The duece of diamonds.   New York: Greenberg, 1937.
       249p.
            Western

3957   ---Gun-boss reynolds.   New York: Greenberg, 1937.
       256p.
            Western

3958   ---Law for tombstone. New York: Greenberg, 1937.
       287p.
           Western

3959   ---Lost river buckaroos. New York: Greenberg, 1937.
       255p.
           Western

3960   Martin, Mrs. Frances Gardiner (McEntee) (1906-   ).
       Pirate island. New York: Harper, 1955. 215p.
           Coastal area Virginia and Carolina--Juvenile.

3961   Martin, George Victor. For our vines have tender
       grapes. New York: Funk, 1940. 239p.
           Farm life in Wisconsin Norwegian community--
       Plain tale--Thirty-two acres--1920's.

3962   Masefield, John. Captain margaret; a romance. London:
       Richards, 1908. 405p.
           English colony at Darien--Romance of Spanish
       Main.

3963   Mason, Alfred Bishop (1851-   ). Tom strong, wash-
       ington's scout; a story of patriotism. New York:
       Holt, 1911. 313p.
           Juvenile

3964   Mason, Arthur (1876-   ). Come easy, go easy. New
       York: Day, 1933. 272p.
           Nevada gold--San Francisco earthquake--Juvenile.

3965   Mason F. VanWyck (1897-   ). Captain nemesis. New
       York: Putnam, 1931. 295p.
           Sailing story--Man cashiered from British
       Navy 1772--Turns pirate.

3966   ---Three harbours. Philadelphia: Lippincott, 1938.
       694p.
           #1 in series on American Navy in Revolution--
       Norfolk--Boston--Bermuda.

3967   ---Stars on the sea. Philadelphia: Lippincott, 1940.
       720p.
           #2 of series on American Navy in Revolution--
       Privateering--Newport--Bahamas--South Carolina--
       Companion to Three Harbours not a sequel.

3968   ---Rivers of glory. Philadelphia: Lippincott, 1942.
       572p.
           #3 in American Navy in Revolution--Boston--
       New York--Siege of Savannah.

3969   ---Valley forge; 24 december 1777. New York: Double-
       day, 1946. 30p.
           George Washington

3970 ---Eagle in the sky. Philadelphia: Lippincott, 1948.
      500p.
            #4 American Revolution series-- 1780- 1781--
      Three doctors--Last of Tetralogy.

3971 ---Cutlass empire. New York: Doubleday, 1949. 396p.
            Sir Henry Morgan--(1635?- 1688)--Eighteen years
      of his life.

3972 ---Golden admiral. New York: Doubleday, 1953. 435p.
            Sir Francis Drake (1540?- 1596)--Defeat of
      Spanish Armada (1588)--Martin Frobrisher--John
      Hawkins--Sir Philip Sidney.

3973 ---The winter at valley forge. New York: Random, 1953.
      180p.
            American Revolution--Juvenile.

3974 ---The young titan. New York: Doubleday, 1959. 621p.
            King George's War-- 1739- 1745--Siege of Louis-
      bourg--Cape Breton Island--Mayhew's settlement on
      Penobscot River--Panorama--Adventure.

3975 ---Manila galleon. Boston: Little, 1960. 495p.
            George Anson (1697- 1762)--Four year cruise
      into Pacific--Father of British Navy.

3976 ---The sea venture. New York: Doubleday, 1961. 349p.
            Jamestown--Early years--cf. Mayrant's The Land
      Beyond the Tempest--Wreck of Somers' squadron.

3977 ---Rascals' heaven. New York: Doubleday, 1964. 516p.
            Georgia colony-- 1732- 1740--James Edward Oglethorp
      (1696- 1785).

3978 ---Wild horizon. Boston: Little, 1966. 390p.
            American Revolution--Continental agent on
      Revolution frontier.

3979 ---Harpoon in eden. New York: Doubleday, 1969. 430p.
            Nantucket--Whaling--Captain and sister start
      new life in New Zealand.

3980 ---pseud. Weaver, Ward. End of track. New York:
      Reynal, 1943. 303p.
            Western--Union Pacific Railroad.

3981 Mason, Grace Sartwell (1877-   ) and Hilliard, John
      Norltern (1872-   ). The golden hope. New York:
      Appleton, 1916. 362p.
            Lure of west--Gold--Irrigation.

3982 Masters, Edgar Lee (1868- 1950). Children of the market
      place. New York: Macmillan, 1922. 469p.
            English immigrants in Illinois 1833- 1861--
      Stephen Douglas Era.

3983 ---The tide of time. New York: Farrar, 1937. 682p.
      Chronicle--First family under land grants of
      War of 1812--Ferrisburg, Illinois--Start 1822--Epic
      novel.

3984 Masters, Kelly Ray (1897-   ) pseud. Ball, Zachary.
      Dawn to new orleans. New York: Crown, 1946. 292p.
      1802--Mississippi and Ohio Rivers--Romance.

3985 ---North to abilene. New York: Holiday, 1960. 190p.
      Texas cattle drive to Kansas--Juvenile.

3986 Mathews, Cornelius (1817-1889). Behemoth; a legend
      of the mound builders.[Anonymous]. New York:
      Langley, 1839. 192p.
      Early mound builders.

3987 Mathews, John Joseph. Sundown. New York: Longmans,
      1934. 312p.
      Osage Reservation--Indian life 1930's.

3988 Matschat, Cecile (Hulse). Preacher on horseback.
      New York: Farrar, 1940. 429p.
      Mohawk Valley, New York and Michigan--1870's--
      Circuit rider--Hungarian immigrant.

3989 ---Tavern in the town. New York: Farrar, 1942. 338p.
      Family in Virginia Tidewater--Pre-Revolutionary
      days--Romance--Adventure.

3990 Matthews, Harold. River-bottom boy; a novel. New York:
      Crowell, 1942. 354p.
      Louisiana negro cotton picker to city.

3991 Maturin, Edward. Montezuma; or, the last of the aztecs.
      New York: Paine, 1845. 2 vols.
      Romance

3992 Maule, Mary Katherine (Finigan) (1861-   ). A prairie-
      schooner princess. Boston: Lothrop, 1920. 383p.
      Quakers from Ohio to Nebraska--Crossing plains--
      Juvenile.

      Maxon, Anne pseud. see Best, Mrs. Allena (Champlain)

3993 May, Earl Chapin (1873-   ). Prairie pirates. New
      York: Duffield, 1932. 360p.
      Miller's apprentice from Maryland to Illinois
      frontier--Black Hawk War--Juvenile.

3994 Mayer, Albert I.. Follow the river. New York: Double-
      day, 1969. 384p.
      Trip west 1790--Ohio River to Losantiville
      (Cincinnati) and adventures over fifty year period.

3995 Mayer, Frank. The song of the wolf. New York: Moffat, 1910. 317p.
Colorado--1880's--Eastern heroine.

3996 Mayo, Joseph. Woodbourne; a novel of the revolutionary period in virginia and maryland. in two parts. Baltimore: Baltimore Pub., 1884. 224p. 138p.
Romance

3997 Mayol, Mrs. Lurline (Bowles). The big canoe. New York: Appleton, 1933. 257p.
Haida Indians--Queen Charlotte Islands--Northwest Canada--"Vikings of Pacific"--Juvenile.

Mayrant, Drayton pseud. see Simons, Katherine

3998 Mays, Victor (1927-). Fast iron. Boston: Houghton, 1952. 190p.
Whaling--South Atlantic.

3999 Mayse, Arthur. Perilous passage. New York: Morrow, 1949. 247p.
British Columbia and Oregon--Romance--Adventure--Mystery.

4000 Meade, Richard. Big bend. New York: Doubleday, 1968. 166p.
Western

4001 Meader, Stephen Warren (1898-). Longshanks. New York: Harcourt, 1928. 243p.
A. Lincoln as boy--Juvenile.

4002 ---Away to sea. New York: Harcourt, 1931. 233p.
Boy from Rhode Island farm to sail on slave ship--Adventures--Juvenile.

4003 ---Who rides in the dark? New York: Harcourt, 1937. 281p.
New Hampshire--1815ca.--Mystery and adventure--Juvenile.

4004 ---Boy with a pack. New York: Harcourt, 1939. 297p.
Young itinerant peddler--New Hampshire to Ohio--1837.

4005 ---Clear for action! New York: Harcourt, 1940. 323p.
Maine lad to sea--1812--Impressed by British.

4006 ---Jonathan goes west. New York: Harcourt, 1946. 241p.
Sixteen year old boy leaves Maine to join father in Illinois--1845--Juvenile.

4007 ---River of the wolves. New York: Harcourt, 1948. 248p.

Maine lad taken by Indians--Canada--French-
Indian War.

4008 ---The fish hawk's nest. New York: Harcourt, 1952.
236p.
Southern New Jersey--1820's--Spanish "cut
throats" smugglers--Adventure.

4009 ---Guns for saratoga. New York: Harcourt, 1955. 207p.
American Revolution--Sea life--Juvenile.

4010 ---Buffalo and beaver. New York: Harcourt, 1960.
189p.
Rocky Mountain--Early nineteenth century--
Fur trade--Juvenile.

4011 Meadowcroft, Mrs. Enid Lamonte. By wagon and flatboat.
New York: Crowell, 1938. 170p.
Two families from Philadelphia to Losantville
(Cincinnati)--1789--Conestoga wagon--Flatboat--
Juvenile.

4012 ---Along the erie towpath. New York: Crowell, 1940.
227p.
Erie Canal--Albany to Buffalo--1823-1825--
Juvenile.

4013 Means, Florence (Crannell) (1891-   ). A candle in
the mist; a story for girls. Boston: Houghton,
1931. 252p.
Minnesota--1870's--Juvenile.

4014 ---At the end of nowhere. Boston: Houghton, 1940.
232p.
Small Colorado town--1904--Minister--Family
life.

4015 ---The rains will come. Boston: Houghton, 1954.
241p.
Hopi Indians--1885--Mores.

4016 Medary, Marjorie. Prairie anchorage. New York:
Longmans, 1933. 278p.
Family from Nova Scotia to western prairies
of United States--1855--Juvenile.

4017 Meeker, Arthur (1902-   ). The far away music.
Boston: Houghton, 1945. 308p.
Family life in Chicago--1850's.

4018 Meigs, Cornelia Lynde (1884-   ). As the crow flies.
New York: Macmillan, 1927. 299p.
Lt. Pike on Mississippi after Louisiana Purchase.

4019 ---The trade wind. Boston: Little, 1927. 309p.
Sea adventure--1760's--Juvenile

4020 ---Clearing weather. Boston: Little, 1928. 312p.
Pre-American Revolution--Sea romance and
adventure--Juvenile.

4021 ---Swift rivers. Boston: Little, 1932. 234p.
Swedes in Goose Wing River, Minnesota--1835--
Logging--Juvenile.

4022 ---The covered bridge. New York: Macmillan, 1936.
145p.
Girls winter on Vermont farm--Ethan Allen--
Pioneer story.

4023 ---Railroad west; a novel. Boston: Little, 1937.
326p.
First novel for adults--Northern Pacific Railroad from Minnesota to Yellowstone--Romance.

4024 ---The scarlet oak. New York: Macmillan, 1938. 198p.
Bordentown, New Jersey--1817--Joseph Bonaparte
(1768-1844)--Stephen Girard (1750-1831).

4025 ---Call of the mountain. Boston: Little, 1940. 258p.
Vermont youth--1830's--Clear and work farm--
cf. Fisher's Seasoned Timber.

4026 ---Mounted messenger. New York: Macmillan, 1943. 187p.
Mail routes in Pennsylvania--Philadelphia to
Carlisle--1755--Juvenile.

4027 ---The two arrows; a story. New York: Macmillan, 1949.
249p.
Maryland--1745--Juvenile.

4028 ---Fair wind to virginia. New York: Macmillan, 1955.
198p.
Williamsburg--Juvenile.

4029 Meinzer, H. A. (1918-   ) pseud. Abbott, A. C..
Branded. Cleveland: World, 1953. 223p.
Western

4030 Meller, Sidney. Roots in the sky. New York: Macmillan,
1938. 579p.
Russian Jews to California.

4031 Meloney, William Brown (1905-   ). Rush to the sun.
New York: Farrar, 1937. 275p.
First novel--Farm life New York State.

4032 Melville, Herman (1819-1891). Moby dick. New York:
Harper, 1851. 634p.
Whaling--One of greatest American novels.

4033 ---Israel potter; his fifty years of exile. New York:
Putnam, 1855. 276p.

315

Israel Potter (1744-1826?)--Revolutionary
soldier.

Melville, J. pseud. see Fraetas, Josiah A.

4034 The memoirs of lafitte; or, the baratarian pirate. a
narrative founded on fact. [Anonymous]. Providence,
Rhode Island: Spear, 1826. 125p.
Romance

4035 Mercer, Charles E.. Enough good men. New York: Putnam,
1960. 514p.
American Revolution--Classes clash--Bound boy
and girl and Philadelphia lawyer.

4036 Merrell, Elizabeth (Leigh) pseud. Merrell, Leigh.
Tenoch. New York: Nelson, 1954. 191p.
Spanish-Indian boy's journey up California--
After Cortes.

Merrell, Leigh pseud. see Merrell, Elizabeth (Leigh)

Merriman, Chad pseud. see Cheshire, Gifford Paul

4037 Merwin, Samuel (1874-1936). The road to frontenac.
New York: Doubleday, 1901. 404p.
French in Canada--1687.

4038 The meteor; or, the cutter of the ocean. a sea story
of the days of '76. (By An Old Salt) [Anonymous].
New York: Smith, 1847. 99p.
Romance

4039 Meyer, George Homer pseud. "A Native". Almiranté;
a romance of old-time caiifornia. San Francisco:
Hinton, 1890. 115p.

Michaels, Dale pseud. see Rifkin, Shepard

4040 Michener, James Albert (1907-   ). Hawaii. New York:
Random, 1959. 937p.
Chronicle--Four pointed novel--Settlement--
Arrival of whites--Social history--Fiftieth state.

4041 Miers, Earl Schenck (1910-   ). Valley in arms; a
novel of the settlement of connecticut. Philadelphia:
Westminister, 1943. 331p.
Two youngsters build home in Connecticut--
Conflict with Pequots.

4042 Milhous, Katherine (1894-   ). Snow over bethlehem.
New York: Scribner's, 1945. 98p.
Based on historical records of Moravians--
Christmas 1755--Juvenile.

4043 Millar, George Reid. <u>Crossbowman's story of the first</u>
      <u>exploration of the amazon</u>. New York: Knopf, 1955.
      354p.
           Francisco de Orellana (d. ca.1546)--From Peru
      down to Amazon--Good.

4044 Miller, Arthur (1915-   ). <u>The misfits</u>. New York:
      Viking, 1961. 132p.
           Cinema-novel--A woman and two men--Sell horses
      for dog food--Modern.

4045 Miller, Mrs. Caroline (Pafford) (1903-   ). <u>Lamb in</u>
      <u>his bosom</u>. New York: Harper, 1933. 345p.
           First novel--Georgia pioneer life--1810-1865--
      Excellent--Won Pulitizer Prize 1934.

4046 ---<u>Lebanon</u>. New York: Doubleday, 1944. 234p.
           Georgia frontier life--1800's--Young girl
      central figure.

4047 Miller, Elizabeth Jane (Mrs. Oren S. Hack) (1878-   ).
      <u>Daybreak; a story of the age of discovery</u>. New
      York: Scribner's, 1915. 430p.
           Romance of Ferdinand-Isabella Era--Moors--
      Columbus--Ponce de Leon.

      Miller, Frank <u>pseud</u>. see Loomis, Noel

4048 Miller, Helen (Topping) (1884-1960). <u>Hawk in the wind</u>.
      New York: Appleton, 1938. 256p.
           Widow operates paper mill--Carolinas.

4049 ---<u>Dark lightning</u>. New York: Appleton, 1940. 258p.
           Texas oil strike.

4050 ---<u>Dark sails; a tale of old st. simons</u>. Indianapolis:
      Bobbs, 1945. 256p.
           James Oglethorpe's attempt to settle area of
      Georgia--1730's and 1740's--Romance.

4051 ---<u>The sound of chariots; a novel of john sevier and</u>
      <u>the state of franklin</u>. Indianapolis: Bobbs, 1947.
      288p.
           American Revolution--Georgia loyalists flee
      to state of Franklin (Tennessee)--1780--John Sevier.

4052 ---<u>Trumpet in the city</u>. Indianapolis: Bobbs, 1948.
      269p.
           American Revolution--Savannah, Georgia--
      Romance--Adventure.

4053 ---<u>Born strangers; a chronicle of two families</u>.
      Indianapolis: Bobbs, 1949. 288p.
           Michigan pioneer life--To Civil War.

                              317

4054 ---Mirage. New York: Appleton, 1949. 306p.
Texas frontier--1885--Romance.

4055 ---The proud young thing. New York: Appleton, 1952.
310p.
Charlestown, South Carolina--Eighteenth century-
Romance for girls--Juvenile.

4056 ---Slow dies the thunder. Indianapolis: Bobbs, 1955.
310p.
American Revolution--South Carolina--1780--
Battle of King's Mountain--Francis Marion--Bombard-
ment of Charleston.

4057 Miller, Helen Markley. Dust in the gold sack. New
York: Doubleday, 1957. 239p.
Western--Juvenile.

4058 ---and Topping, John Dewey (1884-   ). Rebellion
road. Indianapolis: Bobbs, 1954. 287p.
Reconstruction--Alabama plantation.

4059 Miller, Joaquin. Unwritten history; life amongst the
modocs. Hartford, Connecticut: American, 1894.
445p.

4060 ---First fam'lies of the sierras. Chicago: Jansen,
1876. 258p.

4061 Miller, Mrs. May Merrill (Mrs. Justin Miller). First
the blade. New York: Knopf, 1938. 631p.
First novel--Civil War in Missouri--California
frontier--San Joaquin Valley.

4062 Miller, Tevis. Slumgullion trail. New York: Phoenix,
1935. 253p.
Western

4063 ---Blacky finn of the diamond d. New York: Phoenix,
1936. 253p.
Western

4064 ---The posse of crystal creek. New York: Phoenix,
1936. 250p.
Western

4065 ---Bullion on the range. New York: Phoenix, 1937.
256p.
Western

4066 ---The badman of vx ranch. New York: Phoenix, 1938.
255p.
Western

4067 ---Riders of the broken circle. New York: Phoenix,
1938. 255p.

Western

4068   ---Partners of the saddle. New York: Phoenix, 1939.
        255p.
        Western

4069   ---The cowhands of crystal creek. New York: Phoenix,
        1940. 254p.
        Western

4070   ---pseud. Reardon, Joseph. Blue mesa trail. New York:
        Phoenix, 1939. 253p.
        Western

4071   ---The cerro lobo. New York: Phoenix, 1941. 256p.
        Western

4072   ---Powderhorn trail. New York: Phoenix, 1941. 256p.
        Western

4073   Mills, Charles. Alexandrians. New York: Putnam,
        1952. 675p.
            Chronicle--Small Georgia town--1839-1939.

4074   Mills, Weymer Jay (1880-   ). The van rensselaers of
        old manhattan. New York: Stokes, 1907. 215p.
            Romance of colonial era.

4075   Miner, Lewis S.. Wild waters. New York: Messner,
        1946. 185p.
            Mississippi River--1840's--Boy's adventure.

4076   Minnigerode, Meade (1887-1967). Oh, Susanna!. New
        York: Putnam, 1922. 401p.
            Clipper Era--Romance.

4077   ---Cockades; a romance. New York: Putnam, 1927.
        374p.
            Last Dauphin to New Orleans--Intrigue.

4078   ---Black forest. New York: Farrar, 1937. 360p.
            Old northwest--Secured from Indians and British--
        1754-1788--Land speculation--Romance.

4079   ---The terror of peru. New York: Farrar, 1940. 305p.
            Merchant family--Eighteenth century.

4080   Mitchell, Faye L.. Pitch in his hair. New York:
        Doubleday, 1954. 224p.
            Washington territory--Thirteen year old.

4081   Mitchell, Margaret. Gone with the wind. New York:
        Macmillan, 1936. 1037p.
            First novel--Georgia--Civil War and after--
        Romance--Pulitzer Prize--1937.

319

4082 Mitchell, Ruth Comfort (Mrs. W. S. Young) (1882-1954).
      Old san francisco. New York: Appleton, 1933. 4 vols.
      Four San Francisco noveletts--1840's-1870's--
      True Love-1840's-Yankee invasion--Fire-1850's-
      Vigilante movement--Curtain-1860's-Civil War period--
      Tell Your Fortune-1870's-Days fortunes won-lost.

4083 Mitchell, Silas Weir (1829-1914). Hugh wynne, free
      quaker; sometime brevet lieutenant-colonel on the
      staff of his excellency general washington. New
      York: Century, 1897. 2 vols.
      American Revolution--Quaker attitude revealed--
      Philadelphia--Very good.

4084 ---The red city; a novel of the second administration
      of president washington. New York: Century, 1908.
      421p.
      Philadelphia--1789-1809.

4085 ---A venture in 1777. Philadelphia: Jacobs, 1908.
      120p.
      American Revolution--Pennsylvania.

4086 ---Westways; a village chronicle. New York: Century,
      1913. 510p.
      American life--1855-1865.

4087 Moberg, Vilhelm (1898-   ). [Trans. from Swedish by
      Lannestock, Gustaf]. The emigrants; a novel. New
      York: Simon, 1951. 366p.
      #1 of Trilogy Swedes to America-1850.

4088 ---Unto a good land; a novel. New York: Simon, 1954.
      371p.
      #2 of Trilogy--From Smaland, Sweden to Minnesota.

4089 ---The last letter home; a novel. New York: Simon,
      1961. 383p.
      #3 of Trilogy--Swedes to America--Does for
      Swedes what Rolvaag did for Norwegians--1840-1890.

4090 Momaday, Natachee Scott. House made of dawn. New
      York: Harper, 1968. 212p.
      First novel--Author Kiowa--Plight of American
      Indian--1945-1952.

4091 Monroe, Anne Shannon (1877-1942). Eugene norton; a
      tale of the sagebrush land. Chicago: Rand McNally,
      1900. 291p.
      Western

4092 ---Happy valley; a story of oregon. Chicago: McClurg,
      1916. 347p.
      Pioneer life in Oregon--Claim taken by eastern.

4093 ---Behind the ranges. New York: Doubleday, 1925.
343p.
Western

Monroe, Forest pseud. see Wiechmann, Ferdinand Gerhard
(1858-1919)

4094 Montague, Margaret Prescott (1878-1955). Up eel river.
New York: Macmillan, 1928. 225p.
Tony Beaver--Paul Bunyan of West Virginia
lumberman.

Montgomery, Cora pseud. see Canzeau, Mrs. William Leslie

4095 Montgomery, Rutherford George (1893-). The trail
of the buffalo. Boston: Houghton, 1939. 218p.
Juvenile

4096 ---Husky, co-pilot of the pilgrim. New York: Holt,
1942. 271p.
Alaska--Bush pilot--Juvenile.

4097 ---Trappers' trail. New York: Holt, 1943. 226p.
Arkansas River Country--Santa Fé to Alta,
California.

4098 Montross, Lynn. East of eden. New York: Harper,
1925. 299p.
Farmers' revolt--Illinois corn belt--cf. Beer's
Prairie Fire.

4099 Moody, Alan B. (1900-1944). Sleep in the sun. Boston:
Houghton, 1945. 137p.
Episodes in lives of group of poverty-stricken
Mexican families in California.

4100 Moody, Edwin F.. Bob rutherford and his wife; an
historical romance. Louisville, Kentucky: Morton,
1888. 212p.
Texas Revolution.

4101 Moody, Mrs. Minnie Hite. Long meadows. New York:
Macmillan, 1941. 657p.
Chronicle--Hite family--1705-1860's.

4102 Moon, Grace (Purdie) (Mrs. Carl Moon). Daughter of
thunder. New York: Macmillan, 1942. 184p.
Navajo--Juvenile.

4103 Moore, Amos. Lead law. New York: Macaulay, 1934.
251p.
Western

4104 ---Daredevil douglas. New York: Macaulay, 1935. 256p.
Western

4105 ---Sandy of skyline. New York: Washburn, 1935. 308p.
      Western

4106 ---A ranger rides alone. New York: Washburn, 1936.
      302p.
      Western

4107 ---Wind over the range. New York: Washburn, 1936.
      307p.
      Western

4108 ---Gunsmoke at clarion. New York: Washburn, 1937.
      303p.
      Western

4109 ---Six gun cyclone. New York: Washburn, 1937. 305p.
      Western

4110 ---Border justice. New York: Washburn, 1938. 309p.
      Western

4111 ---The two gun quaker. New York: Washburn, 1938. 303p.
      Western

4112 ---Death rides the desert. New York: Washburn, 1939.
      309p.
      Western

4113 ---Outlaw country. New York: Washburn, 1939. 305p.
      Western

4114 ---A ranger's round-up. New York: Washburn, 1940.
      305p.
      Western

4115 ---Ruckus at roaring gap. New York: Washburn, 1941.
      292p.
      Western

4116 ---Devlin's day off. New York: Doubleday, 1942. 275p.
      Western

4117 Moore, David Albert. How she won him; or, the bride
      of charming valley. Philadelphia: Peterson, 1879.
      330p.
            Pennsylvania to California gold fields.

4118 Moore, Ida L.. Like a river flowing. New York: Double-
      day, 1941. 388p.
            Chronicle--North Carolina--Early settlement to
      industrialization.

4119 Moore, Mary Olga (Mrs. C. F. Arnold). Wind-swept.
      Philadelphia: Lippincott, 1937. 320p.
            Story of Sara Kent from sixth to twenty-sixth
      year--Wyoming ranch and return.

322

4120   Moore, John Trotwood (1858-1929). Hearts of hickory;
       a story of andrew jackson and the war of 1812.
       Nashville: Cokesbury, 1926. 450p.
          Frontier romance.

4121   Moore, Lucia (Wilkins) (1887-   ). The wheel and
       the hearth. New York: Ballantine, 1953. 241p.
          Oregon Trail--Based on experience of grand-
       mother--Golden Spur Award 1954 for Best Western
       Historical Novel.

4122   Moore, Ruth. A fair wind home. New York: Morrow,
       1953. 312p.
          Pre-Revolutionary, pioneer days in Maine--
       Nathan Ellis--Francis Carnavon--Maynard Cantril.

4123   Moore, Ward (1903-   ). Bring the jubilee. New
       York: Farrar, 1953. 194p.
          What if South won Civil War?

4124   Moorehead, Warren King. Wanneta, the sioux. New York:
       Dodd, 1890. 285p.

       Morck, Paal pseud. see Rölvaag, Ole Edvart

4125   Morehouse, Mrs. Kathleen Salisbury (Moore). Rain on
       the just. New York: Furman, 1936. 319p.
          Foothills of Blue Ridge, North Carolina--
       Mt. White novel.

4126   Morey, Walt. Home is the north. New York: Dutton,
       1967. 223p.
          Alaska--Twentieth century.

4127   Morford, Henry (1823-1881). The spur of monmouth; a
       washington in arms. a historical and centennial
       romance of the revolution, from personal relations
       and documents never before made public. (by an
       expension agent). Philadelphia: Claxton, 1876.
       480p.
          George Washington--Indian John--Romance--
       Juvenile.

4128   Morgan, Emily Malbone. A lady of the olden time.
       Hartford, Connecticut: Belknap, 1896. 87p.
          Fictitious biography of Lady Alice Fenwick,
       wife of colonial governor of Fort Saybrook.

4129   Morgan, George. John littlejohn of j.; being in
       particular an account of his remarkable entanglement
       with the king's intrigues against general washington.
       Philadelphia: Lippincott, 1897. 281p.
          Valley Forge.

4130   Morris, Hilda. The main stream. New York: Putnam,
       1939. 327p.

New York State farm family--1890's-1930's--
Follows three who leave farm.

4131   Morrison, John B.. An original tale; isabella of brooke,
       contrasting the manners and customs of the early
       settlers of pennsylvania and virginia with the polish-
       ed refinements of the present age. Pittsburgh:
       Pub. by Author, 1830. 118p.
       Romance

4132   Morrow, Mrs. Honoré Willsie (McCue) (1880?-1940).
       The heart of the desert (kut-le of the desert).
       New York: Burt, 1913. 313p.
       First novel--Western--Romance.

4133   ---Still jim. New York: Stokes, 1915. 369p.
       Western

4134   ---Lydia of the pines. New York: Stokes, 1917. 357p.
       Wisconsin--Minnesota setting.

4135   ---The forbidden trail. New York: Stokes, 1919. 379p.
       Western

4136   ---Enchanted canyon; a novel of the grand canyon and
       the arizona desert. New York: Stokes, 1921. 346p.
       Western

4137   ---Judith of the godless valley. New York: Stokes,
       1922. 354p.
       Western

4138   ---The exile of the lariet. New York: Stokes, 1923.
       357p.
       Western

4139   ---We must march; a novel of the winning of oregon.
       New York: Stokes, 1925. 427p.
       Narcissa Whitman--Sir George Simpson--Governor
       of Ruperts Land.

4140   ---Beyond the blue sierra. New York: Morrow, 1932.
       341p.
       Opening overland trail--Mexico to northern
       California--1775-1776--Captain Don Juan de Anza and
       Don Antonio Bucareli.

4141   ---Argonaut. New York: Morrow, 1933. 316p.
       Woman to Alaska during Gold Rush.

4142   ---Yonder sails the mayflower. New York: Morrow, 1934.
       368p.
       Account of five weeks delay of Pilgrims--Robert
       Cushman.

4143   ---Let the king beware. New York: Morrow, 1936. 376p.
       Massachusetts tory returns to England--Adviser
       to George III--Romance--Political intrigue.

4144   Morton; a tale of the revolution. [Anonymous]. Cin-
       cinnati: Hatch, 1828. 331p.
       Romance

4145   Morton, Mary A.. Abbie saunders; a story of pioneer
       days in minnesota. Fresno, California: Pub. for
       Author, 1892. 294p.

       Morton, Stanley pseud. see Freedgood, Stanley

4146   Mosby, Mary Webster pseud. Webster, Mrs. M. M..
       Pocahontas; a legend, with historical and tradition-
       al notes. Philadelphia: n.p., 1840.[?].

       Mose, Buckskin pseud. see Perrie, George W.

4147   Motley, John Lothrop (1814-1877). Morton's hope; or,
       the memoirs of a provincial. New York: Harper,
       1839. 2 vols.
       German student's life--Romance--French-Indian
       War and American Revolution.

4148   ---Merry mount; a romance of the massachusetts colony.
       Boston: Munroe, 1849. 2 vols.
       Thomas Morton (1575-1666).

4149   Mount, Thomas Ernest (1895-   ) pseud. Cody, Stone.
       The gun with the waiting notch. New York: Morrow,
       1933. 278p.
       Western

4150   ---Dangerous gold. New York: Morrow, 1934. 279p.
       Western

4151   ---Desert silver. New York: Morrow, 1935. 284p.
       Western

4152   ---Gun-smoke cure. New York: Morrow, 1935. 284p.
       Western

4153   ---Five against the law. New York: Morrow, 1936. 283p.
       Western

4154   ---Outlaw posse. New York: Morrow, 1936. 276p.
       Western

4155   ---pseud. King, Oliver. Mustang trail. New York:
       Morrow, 1933. 271p.
       Western

4156   Moxley, Verna (Mrs. Paul Melvin Smith). Wind 'til
       sundown. Caldwell, Idaho: Caxton, 1954. 223p.

South Dakota ranch--Pioneering on former Indian
Reservation.

4157 Mudgett, Helen (Parker) (1900-   ). The seas stand watch
New York: Knopf, 1944. 391p.
Salem and New Bedford--1780-1812--Author
professional historian.

4158 Muilenburg, Walter J. Prairie. New York: Viking,
1925. 277p.
Pioneering--Great Plains--Farm--Rebellion
against parental domination.

4159 Muir, Robert. The sprig of hemlock; a novel about
shay's rebellion. New York: Longmans, 1957. 314p.

4160 Mulder, Arnold. Dominie of harlem. Chicago: McClurg,
1913. 385p.
Dutch settlement in Michigan--Twentieth century

4161 ---Bram of five corners. Chicago: McClurg, 1915. 366p.
Dutch in Michigan.

4162 Mulford, Clarence Edward (1883-1956). Bar 20; being a
record of certain happenings that occurred in the other
wise peaceful lives of one hopalong cassidy and his
companions on the range. New York: Burt, 1907. 382p.
Western

4163 ---The orphan. New York: Outing, 1908. 399p.
Western

4164 ---Hopalong cassidy. Chicago: McClurg, 1910. 392p.
Western

4165 ---Bar-20 days. Chicago: McClurg, 1911. 412p.
Western

4166 ---The coming of cassidy and others. Chicago: McClurg,
1913. 438p.
Western

4167 ---The man from bar-20; a story of the cow-country.
Chicago: McClurg, 1918. 319p.
Western

4168 ---Johnny nelson; how a one time pupil of hopalong cassidy
of the famous bar-20 ranch in the pecos valley performe
an act of knight-errantry and what came of it. Chicago
McClurg, 1920. 354p.
Western

4169 ---Bar 20-three; relating a series of startling and stren-
uous adventures in the cow-town of mesquite; of the fam
bar 20 trio, hopalong cassidy, red connors, and johnny
nelson. Chicago: McClurg, 1921. 353p.

4170 ---"Bring me his ears". Chicago: McClurg, 1922. 350p.

4171 ---"Tex"; how tex ewalt, two-gun man, philosopher, poet, and one-time companion of hopalong cassidy turned a whole community upside down, and delt retributive justice to several of windsor's leading citizens for the sake of the girl he loved. Chicago: McClurg, 1922. 323p.
Western

4172 ---Black buttes. New York: Doubleday, 1923. 318p.
Western

4173 ---Hopalong cassidy returns. New York: Doubleday, 1924. 310p.
Western

4174 ---Rustlers' valley. New York: Doubleday, 1924. 333p.
Western

4175 ---Cottonwood gulch. New York: Doubleday, 1925. 340p.
Western

4176 ---Bar 20 rides again. New York: Doubleday, 1926. 337p.
Western

4177 ---Hopalong cassidy's protége. New York: Doubleday, 1926. 349p.
Western

4178 ---Corson of the j. c.. New York: Doubleday, 1927. 340p.
Western

4179 ---Mesquite jenkins. New York: Doubleday, 1928. 306p.
Western

4180 ---Me an' shorty. New York: Doubleday, 1929. 285p.
Western

4181 ---The deputy sheriff. New York: Doubleday, 1930. 296p.
Western

4182 ---Hopalong cassidy and the eagle's brood. New York: Doubleday, 1931. 320p.
Western

4183 ---Mesquite jenkins, tumbleweed. New York: Doubleday, 1932. 321p.
Western

4184 ---The round-up. New York: Doubleday, 1933. 312p.
Western

4185 ---Trail dust; hopalong cassidy and the bar 20 with the trail herd. New York: Doubleday, 1934. 311p.
Western

4186   ---On the trail of the tumbling t.   New York: Doubleday,
         1935.   310p.
             Western

4187   ---Hopalong takes cards.   New York: Sun Dial, 1938.
         269p.
             Western

4188   ---Hopalong cassidy serves a writ.   New York: Double-
         day, 1941.   277p.
             Western

4189   ---and Clay, John Wood.   Buck peters, ranchman; being
         the story of what happened when buck peters, hopalong
         cassidy, and their bar 20 associates went to montana.
             Western

4190   Munford, Kenneth.   John ledyard; an american marco polo.
         Portland, Oregon: Binfords, 1939.   308p.
             Fictionalized biography.

4191   Munger, Dell H. (1862-   ).   The wind before the dawn.
         New York: Doubleday, 1912.   564p.
             English author writes of Kansas farm life.

4192   Munroe, Kirk (1850-1930).   The flamingo feather.   New
         York: Harper, 1887.   255p.
             Huguenots in Florida--ca.1564-1567--Juvenile.

4193   ---With crockett and bowie; or, fighting for the lone
         star flag. a tale of texas.   N. Y.: Scriber's, 1897. 34
             Juvenile

4194   Murdoch, David.   The dutch dominie of the catskills;
         or, the times of the "bloody brandt".   New York:
         Derby, 1861.   471p.
             Dutch Kaatskills scene--Romance.

4195   Murfree, Mary Noailles (1850-1922) pseud. Craddock,
         Charles Egbert.   The prophet of the great smokey
         mountains.   Boston: Houghton, 1885.   308p.
             Classic portrayal.

4196   ---The story of old ft. loudon.   New York: Macmillan,
         1899.   409p.
             French-Indian War (1754-1763)--Cherokee mas-
         sacre-1760.

4197   ---A spectre of power.   Boston: Houghton, 1903.   415p.
             French-Indian War (1754-1763)--Near Muscle
         Shoals, Tennessee.

4198   ---The amulet; a novel.   New York: Macmillan, 1906.
         356p.
             Sequel to Old Fort Loudon--Ft. Prince George-
         1763.

4199   ---The story of duciehurst; a tale of the mississippi.
New York: Macmillan, 1914. 439p.
Mississippi mansion--Post-Civil War.

Murgatroyd, Captain Matthew pseud. see Jones, James
Athearn

4200   Murphy, Edward Francis (1892-   ). Pére antoine.
New York: Doubleday, 1947. 304p.
Life Spanish priest--Attempt to move Inquisition
to New Orleans--Eighteenth century.

4201   ---Bride for new orleans. New York: Hanover, 1955. 313p.
New Orleans--Casket girls from France--1727--
Roman Catholic values and atmosphere.

4202   Murphy, Mrs. Mabel (Ansley) (1870-   ). When jefferson
was young. Chicago: Whitman, 1942. 262p.
To 1772--Romance with Martha Skelton--Juvenile.

4203   Murray, Chalmers Swinton. Here come joe mungin; a novel.
New York: Putnam, 1942. 316p.
Gullah negroes--Sea islands off coast of South
Carolina--Excellent.

4204   Murray, W. W.. Isadore; or, the captives of the
norridgewocks. n.p., 1846. 37p.
Lake Winepessauke, New Hampshire--Indian
fighting.

4205   Musick, John Roy. Columbia; a story of the discovery
of america. New York: Funk, 1892. 354p.

4206   ---Estevan; a story of spanish conquests. New York:
Funk, 1892. 399p.

4207   ---Saint augustine; a story of the huguenots in america.
New York: Funk, 1892. 319p.

4208   ---Braddock; a story of the french and indian wars.
New York: Funk, 1893. 470p.

4209   ---A century too soon; a story of bacon's rebellion.
New York: Funk, 1893. 402p.

4210   ---Humbled pride; a story of the mexican war. New
York: Funk, 1893. 462p.

4211   ---Independence; a story of the revolution. New York:
Funk, 1893. 456p.

4212   ---The pilgrims; a story of massachusetts. New York:
Funk, 1893. 368p.

4213   ---Pocahontas; a story of virginia. New York: Funk,
1893. 366p.

329

4214 ---Sustained honor; a story of the war of 1812. New York: Funk, 1893. 451p.

4215 ---The witch of salem; or, credulity run mad. New York: Funk, 1893. 389p.

4216 Myers, Henry. The utmost island. New York: Crown, 1951. 216p.
Lief Ericson to Vineland--975A.D.--Vikings v. Christianity.

4217 Myers, John Meyers (1906-   ). The wild yazoo. New York: Dutton, 1947. 378p.
Mississippi frontier--Yazoo River.

4218 ---Dead warrior. Boston: Little, 1956. 355p.
Western

4219 ---Jack swilling, founder of phoenix, arizona. New York: Hastings, 1961. 308p.
1830-1878.

4220 Myers, Peter Hamilton. The first of the knickerbockers; a tale of 1673. New York: Putnam, 1848. 221p.
Domestic narrative--Dutch and English in New York.

4221 ---The king of the hurons. [Anonymous]. New York: Putnam, 1850. 319p.
Early 1700's.

4222 ---The young patroon; or christmas in 1690. a tale of new york. New York: Putnam, 1849. 142p.
1690--Dutch manners--Manhattan.

4223 ---The prisoner of the border; a tale of 1838. New York: Derby, 1857. 378p.

4224 Myers, Virginia. Angelo's wife; a novel. Indianapolis: Bobbs, 1948. 372p.
Spanish grandees-- 1830's and 1840's--Romance.

4225 ---This land i hold. Indianapolis: Bobbs, 1951. 382p.
Americans into California--Romance.

4226 Myrick, Herbert (1860-1927). Cache la poudre; the romance of a tenderfoot in the days of custer. New York: Orange Judd, 1905. 202p.
Inspiring view of Custer.

Myrthe, A. T. see Ganilh, Anthony

N

4227 Nathan, Leonard, A wind like a bugle. New York:
Macmillan, 1954. 282p.
Kansas--Abolitionists v. Slave.

4228 Naughton, Edmond (1926-   ). McCabe; a novel. New
York: Macmillan, 1959. 146p.
Western

4229 Naylor, James Ball (1860-1945). The sign of the prophet;
a tale of tecumseh and tippecanoe. Akron, Ohio:
Saalfield, 1901. 416p.
Tecumseh (1768-1813)--Battle of Tippecanoe (1811).

4230 ---In the days of st. clair; a romance of the muskingum
valley. Akron, Ohio: Saalfield, 1902. 402p.
Campaign-1791.

4231 ---Under mad anthony's banner. Akron, Ohio: Saalfield,
1903. 394p.
Campaign-1794.

4232 ---The cabin in the big woods. Akron: Ohio: Saalfield,
1904. 239p.

4233 ---The kentuckian; a thrilling tale of ohio life in the
early sixties. Boston: Clark, 1905. 385p.

4234 Neal, Bigelow. Last of the thundering herd. New York:
Sears, 1933. 287p.
Ta-na-ha (The Buffalo) tells story--Little
Big Horn (1876)--Arikara--Bison--Juvenile.

4235 Neal, John (1793-1876). Logan a. family history.
[Anonymous]. Philadelphia: Carey, 1822. 2 vols.
Lord Dunmore's War--Yellow Creek Massacre-1774--
Author rival of J. Cooper.

4236 ---Seventy-six. Baltimore: Robinson, 1823. 2 vols.
American Revolution--Romance of passion.

4237 ---Rachel dyer; a north american story. Portland,
Maine: Shirley, 1828. 276p.
Witchcraft--Salem, Massachusetts.

4238 Neff, John C.. Maria. New York: Washburn, 1951. 201p.
One day in drought--Stricken town--New Mexico.

4239 Neider, Charles (1915-   ). The authentic death of

331

hendry jones; a novel. New York: Harper, 1956.
205p.
      Use of "Billy the Kid" myth--Relies on Burns
Saga.

4240 Neihardt, John Gneisenau (1881-   ). Life's lure.
New York: Kinnerley, 1914. 277p.
      Black Hills--Mining.

4241 ---When the tree flowered; an authentic tale of the
old sioux world. New York: Macmillan, 1951. 248p.
      Fictionalized biography of Sioux Eagle Voice--
Good.

4242 Neill, Robert. Hangman's cliff. New York: Doubleday,
1956. 352p.
      Mystery--Adventure--1780's.

Neilson, Mrs. Frances Fullerton (Jones) see Neilson,
Winthrop jt. author

4243 Neilson, Winthrop and Neilson, Frances Fullerton (Jones).
Edge of greatness. New York: Putnam, 1951. 248p.
      One day in life of Benjamin Franklin (1706-1790)
18 July 1775--Day of Braddock's defeat.

4244 Nelson, Ira Stephens (1912-   ). On sarpy creek.
Boston: Little, 1938. 298p.
      First novel--Farmers and ranchers--Montana.

4245 Nelson, John Louw. Rhythm for rain. Boston: Houghton,
1937. 272p.
      Hopi--Arizona desert--1857.

4246 Nelson, Mrs. Rhoda Louise (Smith) (1891-   ). This
is freedom. New York: Dodd, 1940. 302p.
      Mormon trek from Nauvoo to Salt Lake--Juvenile.

4247 Nelson, Truman John (1912-   ). The sin of the prophet.
Boston: Little, 1952. 450p.
      First novel--Return of slave Anthony Burns to
Virginia--Theodore Parker--1854.

4248 ---The passion by the brook. New York: Doubleday, 1953.
380p.
      Brook Farm--Utopian community.

4249 ---The surveyor. New York: Doubleday, 1960. 667p.
      John Brown (1800-1859)--Kansas 1855-1856--
Powerful novel.

Neville, Lee pseud. see Richards, Mrs. Lela (Horn)

4250 Newell, Charles Martin. Kalani of oahu; an historical
romance of hawaii. Boston: Pub. by Author, 1881.
415p.

4251 ---Kaméhaméha, the conquering king; the mystery of his birth, loves and conquests. a romance of hawaii. New York: Putnam, 1885. 399p.

4252 ---The voyage of the fleetwing; a narrative of love, wreck and whaling adventures. Boston: DeWolfe, 1886. 443p.

4253 ---pseud. Barnacle, Captain. Leaves from an old log; pehé nú-e the tiger whale of the pacific. Boston: Lothrop, 1877. 112p.

Newsom, Ed pseud. see Evans, Muriel Naomi

4254 Newton, Dwight Bennett (1916-   ). Guns of the rimrock. New York: Phoenix, 1946. 256p.
        Western

4255 ---The gunmaster at saddleback. New York: Phoenix, 1948. 256p.
        Western

4256 ---Range boss. New York: Pocket, 1949. 163p.
        Western

4257 ---Shotgun guard. Philadelphia: Lippincott, 1950. 210p.
        Western

4258 ---Six-gun gamble. Philadelphia: Lippincott, 1951. 210p.
        Western

4259 ---pseud. Bennett, Dwight. Stormy range. New York: Doubleday, 1951. 221p.
        Western

4260 ---Border graze. New York: Doubleday, 1952. 187p.
        Western

4261 ---Lost wolf river. New York: Doubleday, 1952. 190p.
        Western

4262 ---Top hand. New York: Permabooks, 1955. 186p.
        Western

4263 ---The avenger. New York: Permabooks, 1956. 149p.
        Western

4264 ---Cherokee outlet. New York: Doubleday, 1961. 190p.
        Western

4265 ---The oregon rifles. New York: Doubleday, 1962. 184p.
        Western

4266 ---Rebel trail. New York: Doubleday, 1963. 180p.
Western

4267 ---Crooked river canyon. New York: Doubleday, 1966.
212p.
Western

4268 ---pseud. Hardin, Clement. Hell bent for a hang rope.
New York: Ace, 1954. 154p.
Western

4269 ---pseud. Logan, Ford. Fire in the desert. New York:
Ballantine, 1954. 154p.
Western

4270 ---pseud. Temple, Dan. Outlaw river; a novel of the
frontier. New York: Popular, 1955. 159p.
Western

4271 Newton, John. The rogue and the witch. New York:
Abelard, 1955. 276p.
Minister--Exiles--Witchcraft.

Niall, Michael pseud. see Breslin, Howard

4272 Nichols, Walter Hammond (1866-   ). Cowboy hugh;
the odyssey of a boy. New York: Macmillan, 1927.
284p.
Boy to west--1880's--Adventure--Juvenile.

4273 ---A morgan rifleman; a story of the american revolution.
New York: Century, 1928. 308p.
Benedict Arnold (1741-1801).

4274 Nicholson, Meredith (1866-   ). The cavalier of
tennessee. Indianapolis: Bobbs, 1928. 402p.
Andrew Jackson (1767-1845)--Romance of frontier.

4275 Niles, Blair (Rice) (Mrs. Robert Niles Jr.). Day of
immense sun. Indianapolis: Bobbs, 1936. 348p.
Peru--Spanish Conquest--Pizarro--Atahualpa--
Inca lore.

4276 Niles, Blair. East by day. New York: Farrar, 1941.
330p.
Slave mutiny on "Armistad" in Cuba--1840's--
New England reaction.

4277 Niven, Frederick John (1878-   ). The lost cabin
mine. New York: Lane, 1909. 312p.
English outlaw--"Robin Hood of Far West".

4278 ---The lady of the crossing; a novel of the new west.
London: Hodder, 1919. 305p.
Romance

334

4279   ---The wolfer. New York: Dodd, 1923. 314p.
        Western

        Noel, Joseph jt. author, see Drago, Harry Sinclair

4280   Nolan, Jeannette (Covert) (Mrs. Val Nolan) (1896-   ).
        Hobnailed boots. Philadelphia: Winston, 1939. 187p.
        Clark in northwest--1778-1779--Fur trade--
        Ft. Kaskaskia.

4281   ---Treason at the point. New York: Messner, 1944. 224p.
        Benedict Arnold--Juvenile.

4282   ---Patriot in the saddle. New York: Messner, 1945.
        239p.
        Andrew Jackson (1767-1845)--Juvenile.

4283   Norris, Frank (1870-1902). The octopus; a story of
        california. New York: Doubleday, 1901. 652p.
        Wheat and railroad--San Joaquin Valley.

4284   ---The pit; a story of chicago. New York: Doubleday,
        1903. 421p.
        Speculation

4285   Norris, Hoke. All the kingdoms of earth; a novel.
        New York: Simon, 1956. 249p.
        First novel--Blacks--North Carolina.

4286   Norris, Kathleen (Thompson) (1880-1966). Certain
        people of importance. New York: Doubleday, 1922.
        486p.
        San Francisco--Gold Rush Era.

        North, Jessica see MacDonald, Mrs. Jessica Nelson

4287   North, Sterling (1906-   ). Plowing on sunday. New
        York: Macmillan, 1934. 265p.
        One year in life of farmer in southern Wisconsin--
        1913--Dairy.

4288   ---The wolfling; a documentary novel of the eighteen-
        seventies. New York: Dutton, 1969. 224p.
        Wisconsin--Wolf companion--Dutton Animal Award-
        1969.

4289   Norton, Alice Mary pseud. Norton, Andre. Yankee privateer.
        Cleveland: World, 1955. 300p.
        American Revolution--Adventure.

4290   ---Stand to horse. New York: Harcourt, 1956. 242p.
        Western--Juvenile.

        Norton, Andre pseud. see Norton, Alice Mary

4291 Norton, Frank Henry. The days of daniel boone; a romance of "the dark and bloody ground". New York: American News, 1883. 406p.

4292 Norton, Roy (1869-1917). The boomers. New York: Watt, 1914. 384p.
        Tennessee colonel--To northwest to regain lost fortune--Age sixty-five--Novelty and humor.

4293 ---The frozen trail. New York: Clode, 1932. 256p.
        Northern adventure.

4294 ---The canyon of gold. New York: Macaulay, 1935. 255p.
        Western

4295 Norvel hastings; or, the frigate in the offing. a nautical tale of the war of 1812. (By a Distinguished Novelist). [Anonymous]. Philadelphia: Hart, 1850. 143p.

4296 Norway, Nevil Shute (1899-1960) pseud. Shute, Nevil. An old captivity. New York: Morrow, 1940. 333p.
        Modern archaeologist and daughter to Greenland--Return to old days of Leif Ericson.

4297 Nott, Henry Junius (1797-1837). Novelles of a traveller, or, odds and ends from the knapsack of thomas singularity journeyman printer. New York: Harper, 1834. 2 vols.
        Realistic--cf. Longstreet, Hooper, and Baldwin.

4298 Nourse, James Duncan. The forest knight; or, early times in kentucky. New York: Ferrett, 1846. 86p.
        Romance

4299 ---Levenworth; a story of the mississippi and the prairies. Louisville, Georgia: Noble, 1848. 143p.
        Texas--Mexico-- 1815-1846.

4300 Nutt, Frances Tysen. Three fields to cross. New York: Stephen-Paul, 1948. 368p.
        First novel--Staten Island family--American Revolution--Tories and rebels--Melodrama.

4301 Nye, Nelson Coral (1907-   ). The killer of cibacue. New York: Greenburg, 1936. 255p.
        Western

4302 ---Two-fisted cowpoke. New York: Greenberg, 1936. 256p.
        Western

4303 ---The leather slapper. New York: Greenberg, 1937. 250p.
        Western

4304 ---Quick fire hombre. New York: Greenberg, 1937. 251p.
Western

4305 ---The star packers. New York: Greenberg, 1937. 252p.
Western

4306 ---G stands for gun. New York: Greenberg, 1938. 255p.
Western

4307 ---The bandit of bloody run. New York: Phoenix, 1939.
259p.
Western

4308 ---Pistols for hire; a tale of the lincoln county war
and the wests most desperate outlaw william (billy
the kid) bonney. New York: Macmillan, 1941. 196p.
Critical of Billy (1859-1881).

4309 ---Gunfighter breed. New York: Macmillan, 1942. 197p.
Western

4310 ---Salt river ranny. New York: Macmillan, 1942. 254p.
Western

4311 ---Gunslick mountain; being the final account of the
zwing hunt legend of $3,000,000 in buried plunder.
London: Foulsham, 1943. 164p.
Western

4312 ---Cartridge-case law. New York: Macmillan, 1944. 128p.

4313 ---Wild horse shorty. New York: Macmillan, 1944. 203p.
Western

4314 ---Blood of kings. New York: Macmillan, 1946. 203p.
Western

4315 ---The barber of tubac. New York: Macmillan, 1947.
203p.
Western

4316 ---Desert of the damned. New York: Dodd, 1952. 242p.
Western

4317 ---Plunder valley. New York: Ace, 1952. 147p.
Western

4318 ---Wide loop. New York: Dodd, 1952. 212p.
Western

4319 ---Come a-smokin'. New York: Dodd, 1953. 244p.
Western

4320 ---Hired hand. New York: Dodd, 1954. 217p.
Western

4321   ---The red sombrero. New York: Dodd, 1954. 218p.
        Western

4322   ---The lonely grass; a novel of the american west.
        New York: Dodd, 1955. 217p.
        Western

4323   ---The parson of gunbarrel basin. New York: Dodd, 1955.
        181p.
        Western

4324   ---Maverick marshal. New York: New American Library,
        1958. 128p.
        Western

4325   ---Long run. New York: Macmillan, 1959. 129p.
        Western--Golden Spur Award 1960 for Best Western.

4326   ---The wolf that rode. New York: Macmillan, 1960. 158p.
        Western

4327   ---Not grass alone; a novel. New York: Macmillan, 1961.
        150p.
        Western

4328   ---pseud. Colt, Clem. Gun-smoke. New York: Greenberg,
        1938. 252p.
        Western

4329   ---The shootin' sheriff. New York: Phoenix, 1938. 256p.
        Western

4330   ---The bar nothing brand. New York: Phoenix, 1939.
        255p.
        Western

4331   ---Center fire smith. New York: Phoenix, 1939. 256p.
        Western

4332   ---Hair trigger realm. New York: Phoenix, 1940. 255p.
        Western

4333   ---Trigger finger law. New York: Phoenix, 1940. 254p.
        Western

4334   ---The five diamond brand. New York: Phoenix, 1941.
        256p.
        Western

4335   ---Triggers for six. New York: Phoenix, 1941. 251p.
        Western

4336   ---The sure-fire kid. New York: Phoenix, 1942. 256p.
        Western

4337 ---Trigger talk. New York: Phoenix, 1942. 255p.
       Western

4338 ---Guns of horse prairie. New York: Phoenix, 1943.
       252p.
       Western

4339 ---Rustlers' roost. New York: Phoenix, 1943. 251p.
       Western

4340 ---Smoke-wagon kid. New York: Phoenix, 1943. 255p.
       Western

4341 ---Fiddle-back ranch. New York: Phoenix, 1944. 256p.
       Western

4342 ---Maverick canyon. New York: Phoenix, 1944. 256p.
       Western

4343 ---The renegade cowboy. New York: Phoenix, 1944. 256p.
       Western

4344 ---Gunslick mountain. New York: Arcadia, 1945. 255p.
       Western

4345 ---Once in the saddle. New York: Arcadia, 1946. 256p.
       Western

4346 ---Coyote song. New York: Curl, 1947. 224p.
       Western

4347 ---Tough company. New York: Dodd, 1952. 243p.
       Western

4348 ---Strawberry roan. New York: Dodd, 1953. 214p.
       Western

4349 ---Smoke talk. New York: Dodd, 1954. 213p.
       Western

4350 ---Quick-trigger country. New York: Dodd, 1955. 210p.
       Western

4351 ---pseud. Denver, Drake C.. The feud at sleepy cat.
       New York: Phoenix, 1940. 253p.

4352 ---Tin badge. New York: Phoenix, 1941. 256p.
       Western

4353 ---Wildcats of tonto basin. New York: Phoenix, 1941.
       254p.
       Western

4354 ---The desert desperadoes. New York: Phoenix, 1942.
       253p.
       Western

4355 ---Gun quick. New York: Phoenix, 1942. 256p.
          Western

4356 ---Breed of the chaparral. New York: McBride, 1946.
          219p.
              Western

O

4357   Oberholtzer, Sara Louisa (Vickers) (1841-1930). <u>Hope's</u>
        <u>heart bells; a romance</u>. Philadelphia: Lippincott,
        1884.   282p.
                Rural Quaker family.

4358   O'Brien, Dillon. <u>Dead broke; a western tale</u>.   St. Paul:
        Pioneer, 1866. 518p.
                Irish school teacher in Wisconsin.

4359   ---<u>Widow melville's boarding house</u>.   St. Paul: Pioneer,
        1881. 64p.
                Western

4360   O'Brien, John Sherman (1898-1938). <u>Silver chief, dog</u>
        <u>of the north</u>. Philadelphia: Winston, 1933. 218p.
                cf. <u>White Fang</u>--Juvenile.

4361   ---<u>Valiant, dog of the timberline</u>. Philadelphia:
        Winston, 1935. 218p.
                Western

4362   ---<u>Silver chief to the rescue</u>. Philadelphia: Winston,
        1937. 235p.

4363   O'Conner, Jack (1902-   ). <u>Conquest; a novel of old</u>
        <u>southwest</u>. New York: Harper, 1930. 293p.
                First novel--Arizona.

4364   ---<u>Boom town; a novel of the southwestern silver boom</u>.
        New York: Knopf, 1938. 331p.
                Western

4365   O'Daniel, Janet (1921-   ). <u>O genesee</u>. Philadelphia:
        Lippincott, 1958 [c.1957]. 350p.
                Pioneer settlement near Rochester, New York--
        War of 1812.

4366   O'Dell, Scott (1903-   ). <u>Woman of spain; a story</u>
        <u>of old california</u>. Boston: Houghton, 1934. 299p.
                Romance

4367   ---<u>Hill of the hawk</u>. Indianapolis: Bobbs, 1947. 413p.
                California (1846-1900)--March on Los Angeles
        with Kit Carson (1846-1847).

4368   ---<u>Island of the blue dolphins</u>. Boston: Houghton, 1960.
        184p.
                California island (1835-1853).

341

4369 O'Donnell, Terence (1888-1967). The lenore; a maritime
chronicle. Boston: Houghton, 1926. 325p.
Clipper ship to Canton--1857.

4370 Odum, Howard Washington (1884-   ). Cold blue moon;
black ulsysses a far off. Indianapolis: Bobbs, 1931.
277p.
Black recalls plantation days.

4371 Oemler, Marie (Conway) (1879-   ). The holy lover.
New York: Boni, 1927. 315p.
John Wesley's three years in Georgia--1735-
1738--Based on letters and journals.

4372 Ogden, George Washington (1871-1944). Tennessee tod;
a novel of the great river. New York: Barnes, 1903.
344p.

4373 ---Home place; a story of the people. New York: Harper,
1912. 364p.
Western

4374 ---The long fight. New York: Hearst's International
Library, 1915. 297p.
Western

4375 ---The rustler of wind river. Chicago: McClurg, 1917.
330p.
Western

4376 ---The land of last chance. Chicago: McClurg, 1919.
338p.
Western

4377 ---The duke of chimney butte. Chicago: McClurg, 1920.
381p.
Western

4378 ---The flockmaster of poison creek. Chicago: McClurg,
1921. 315p.
Western

4379 ---Trail's end. Chicago: McClurg, 1921. 329p.
Western

4380 ---The bondboy. Chicago: McClurg, 1922. 370p.
Western

4381 ---Claim number one. Chicago: McClurg, 1922. 352p.
Western

4382 ---The baron of diamond tail. Chicago: McClurg, 1923.
311p.
Western

4383 ---The trail rider; a romance of the kansas range. New York: Dodd, 1924. 365p.
Western

4384 ---The cow jerry. New York: Dodd, 1925. 328p.
Western

4385 ---The road to monterey. Chicago: McClurg, 1925. 371p.
Western

4386 ---The valley of adventure; a romance of california mission days. Chicago: McClurg, 1926. 356p.
Western

4387 ---West of dodge. New York: Dodd, 1926. 305p.
Western

4388 ---Short grass. New York: Dodd, 1927. 305p.
Western

4389 ---Cherokee trials. New York: Dodd, 1928. 309p.
Western

4390 ---Sheep limit. New York: Dodd, 1928. 309p.
Western

4391 ---Sooner land. New York: Dodd, 1929. 329p.
Oklahoma--Boomer Days--Sooners v. settlers.

4392 ---Wasted salt. New York: Dodd, 1930. 299p.
Newspaper man in Medicine Grove, Kansas.

4393 ---Fenced water. New York: Dodd, 1931. 302p.
Western

4394 ---Steamboat gold. New York: Dodd, 1931. 309p.
Western

4395 ---Men of the mesquite. New York: Dodd, 1932. 296p.
Western

4396 ---White roads. New York: Dodd, 1932. 304p.
Western

4397 ---A man from the bad lands. New York: Dodd, 1933. 280p.
Western

4398 ---The guard of timberline. New York: Dodd, 1934. 268p.
Western

4399 ---Deputy sheriff. New York: Dodd, 1935. 302p.
Western

4400 ---The ghost road. New York: Dodd, 1936. 264p.
      Western

4401 ---Whiskey trail. New York: Dodd, 1936. 297p.
      Western

4402 ---Stockyards cowboy. New York: Dodd, 1937. 298p.
      Western

4403 ---Windy range. New York: Dodd, 1938. 275p.
      Western

4404 ---West of the rainbow. New York: Dodd, 1942. 276p.
      Western

4405 Ogley, Mrs. Dorothy (Cleland) and Cleland, Mrs. Mabel
      (Goodwin) (1876-   ). Iron land. New York:
      Doubleday, 1946. 326p.
         Minnesota--1860's--Development of iron regions.

4406 O'Hagan, Howard. Tay john. New York: Potter, 1960.
      263p.
         Tête jaune--Yellowhead--Three section tale--
      1880--Jaspar opened up.

4407 Old fort duquesne; a tale of the early toils, struggles
      and adventures of the first settlers at the forks
      of the ohio, 1754. [Anonymous]. Pittsburgh: Cook's
      Literary Depot, 1844. 79p.
         Braddock's defeat--Stilted romance.

4408 Older, Cora Miranda (Baggerly) (Mrs. Fremont Older).
      Savages and saints. New York: Dutton, 1936. 373p.
         Rebuilding of Catholic mission--Mid 1800's--
      Romance.

4409 Oldham, Henry. The man from texas; a western romance.
      Philadelphia: Peterson, 1884. 442p.
         Kansas--Missouri--Guerrillas--Civil War.

      Olmstead, Edwin jt. author, see Graham, Lewis

4410 Olmsted, Stanley. At the top of tobin. New York:
      Dial, 1926. 497p.
         North Carolina Mountains--Death of village
      preacher and doctor.

4411 Olsen, James P.. Powdersmoke paddy. New York: Dutton,
      1940. 283p.
         First novel--Western.

4412 ---The curse of the killer. New York: Dodge, 1941.
      256p.
         Western

344

4413   ---<u>Riordan rides the range.</u> New York: Dodge, 1942.
       256p.
              Western

       O'Malley, Frank <u>pseud.</u> see O'Rourke, Frank

       O'Mara, Jim <u>pseud.</u> see Fluharty, Vernon L. (1907-   )

4414   O'Meara, Walter Andrew. <u>The trees went forth; a novel.</u>
       New York: Crown, 1947. 253p.
              First novel--Minnesota lumber-1906.

4415   ---<u>The grand portage; a novel.</u> Indianapolis: Bobbs,
       1951. 352p.
              Vermonter--Northwest fur trade (1810-1819)--
       Romance with Indian girl.

4416   ---<u>Tales of the two borders.</u> Indianapolis: Bobbs,
       1952. 197p.

4417   ---<u>The spanish bride.</u> New York: Putnam, 1954. 370p.
              Southwest--Spanish actress to New World 1700's--
       Mistress of governor.

4418   ---<u>Minnesota gothic; a novel.</u> New York: Holt, 1956.
       314p.
              Lumbering--1880-1890.

4419   Oncken, Clara. <u>Hickory sam.</u> New York: Holt, 1939.
       276p.
              Pioneer life--Illinois--1830's--Juvenile.

4420   O'Neill, Charles (1882-   ). <u>Morning time; a novel.</u>
       New York: Simon, 1949. 392p.
              Confederation period--Based on plan of General
       Wilkinson to sell out to Spain in New Orleans--
       1783-1789.

4421   Orcutt, William Dana (1870-   ). <u>Robert cavalier;</u>
       <u>the romance of sieur de la salle and his discovery</u>
       <u>of the mississippi river.</u> Chicago: McClurg, 1904.
       313p.
              Robert LaSalle (1643-1687)--Ex-Jesuit in New
       France--1670-1680.

4422   Ormar, James Allen. <u>William wakefield; a tale of the</u>
       <u>west.</u> Minneapolis, Minnesota: Tribune, 1899. 256p.
              Minnesota

4423   O'Rourke, Frank (1916-   ). <u>Action at three peaks.</u>
       New York: Random, 1948. 282p.
              Western

4424   ---<u>Thunder on the buckhorn.</u> New York: Random, 1949.
       275p.
              Western

4425 ---Black water. New York: Random, 1950. 241p.
Western

4426 ---Beyond the black hills. Philadelphia: Dorrance,
1951. 222p.
Western

4427 ---The gun. New York: Random, 1951. 275p.
Western

4428 ---Gold under skull peak. New York: Random, 1952.
214p.
Western

4429 ---Gunsmoke over big muddy. New York: Random, 1952.
238p.
Western

4430 ---Gunhand. New York: Ballantine, 1953. 149p.
Western

4431 ---Latigo. New York: Random, 1953. 177p.
Western

4432 ---Ride west. New York: Ballantine, 1953. 182p.
Western

4433 ---Violence at sundown. New York: Random, 1953. 240p.
Western

4434 ---High vengeance. New York: Ballantine, 1954. 142p.
Western

4435 ---Thunder in the sun. New York: Ballantine, 1954.
167p.
Western

4436 ---Dakota rifle. New York: Dell, 1955. 192p.
Western

4437 ---The last chance. New York: Dell, 1956. 190p.
Western

4438 ---Sequndo. New York: Dell, 1956. 192p.
Western

4439 ---Legend in the dust. New York: Ballantine, 1957.
150p.
Western

4440 ---The last ride. New York: Morrow, 1958. 250p.
Western

4441 ---The spring time fancy. New York: Morrow, 1961.
159p.
Western

346

4442 ---The swift runner. Philadelphia: Lippincott, 1969.
352p.
Western

4443 ---pseud. O'Malley, Frank. The man who found his way.
New York: Morrow, 1957. 124p.
Western

4444 ---The far mountains. New York: Morrow, 1959. 474p.
Southwest--Deterioration of Spanish control--
Juan Obregon (1801-1848)--Texas--New Mexico.

4445 Orpen, Adela Elizabeth Richards (Mrs. G. H. Orpen).
The jay-hawkers; a story of free soil and border
ruffian days. New York: Appleton, 1900. 300p.
Quantrill's Raid--Kansas.

4446 Orr, Myron David. The citadel of the lakes. New York:
Dodd, 1952. 287p.
Mackinac Island--War 1812--Astor's American
Fur Company--Romance.

4447 ---Mission to mackinac. New York: Dodd, 1956. 301p.
Pre-War of 1812--English-French Conflict.

4448 Orton, Jason Rockwood. Campfires of the red men; or,
a hundred years ago. New York: Derby, 1855. 401p.
New York City.

4449 Oskison, John Milton (1874-   ). Wild harvest; a
novel of transition days in oklahoma. New York:
Appleton, 1925. 299p.

4450 ---Black jack davy. New York: Appleton, 1926. 311p.
Oklahoma land rush--Arkansas Territory--South-
west.

4451 ---A texas titan; the story of sam houston. New York:
Doubleday, 1929. 311p.
Fictionalized biography.

4452 ---Brothers three. New York: Macmillan, 1935. 448p.
Indian territory--Oklahoma--1873-1935--Story of
three brothers--Author part cherokee.

4453 Ostenso, Martha (1900-1963). Wild geese. New York:
Dodd, 1925. 356p.
First novel--Bleak account--Scandanavian farmers
in Minnesota--Won $13,500 prize with novel--Land
greed.

4454 ---Dark dawn. New York: Dodd, 1926. 294p.
Farming--Northwest.

4455 ---The mad carews. New York: Dodd, 1927. 346p.
Wealthy family in Minnesota.

347

4456 ---Prologue to love. New York: Dodd, 1932. 265p.
Western--Melodrama.

4457 ---There's always another year. New York: Dodd, 1933.
268p.
Dakota farm life--Prairies 1930's--Romance.

4458 ---The stone field. New York: Dodd, 1937. 310p.
Chronicle--Northwest--Second and third genera-
tions--Timber and land.

4459 ---The mandrake root. New York: Dodd, 1938. 304p.
Norwegian pioneer--Midwest farm.

4460 ---O river, remember! New York: Dodd, 1943. 393p.
Norwegian settlement--Minnesota--1870-1941--
Norwegians--Irish--Red River Valley.

4461 ---Man had tall sons. New York: Dodd, 1958. 368p.
Minnesota farm.

Otis, James pseud. see Kaler, J. O.

4462 Overbaugh, DeWitt Clinton. The hermit of the catskills;
a tale of the american revolution. New York: Dillingham, 1900. 223p.

4463 Overholser, Wayne D. (1906-   ). Buckaroo's code.
New York: Macmillan, 1947. 223p.
Western

4464 ---West of the rimrock. New York: Macmillan, 1949.
213p.
Western

4465 ---Draw or drag. New York: Macmillan, 1950. 172p.
Western

4466 ---Steel to the south. New York: Macmillan, 1951.
186p.
Western

4467 ---Fabulous gunman. New York: Macmillan, 1952. 185p.
Western

4468 ---Valley of guns. New York: Macmillan, 1953. 184p.
Western

4469 ---Tough hand. New York: Macmillan, 1954. 192p.
Western

4470 ---The violent land. New York: Macmillan, 1954. 244p.
Golden Spur Award 1955 for best Western.

4471 ---Cast a long shadow. New York: Macmillan, 1955. 189p.
Western

348

4472   ---Gunlock. New York: Macmillan, 1956. 178p.
        Western

4473   ---Desperate man. New York: Macmillan, 1957. 152p.
        Western

4474   ---The lone deputy. New York: Macmillan, 1957. 144p.
        Western

4475   ---Hearn's valley. New York: Macmillan, 1958. 151p.
        Western

4476   ---The judas gun. New York: Macmillan, 1960. 148p.
        Western

4477   ---War in sandoval county. New York: Bantam, 1960.
        122p.
        Western

4478   ---The bitter night. New York: Macmillan, 1961. 155p.
        Western

4479   ---The killer marshall. New York: Macmillan, 1961.
        153p.
        Western

4480   ---The trail of billy peale. New York: Macmillan, 1962.
        180p.
        Western

4481   ---A gun for johnny deere. New York: Macmillan, 1963.
        180p.
        Western

4482   ---To the far mountains. New York: Macmillan, 1963.
        216p.
        Western

4483   ---Day of judgment. New York: Macmillan, 1965. 182p.
        Western

4484   ---Ride into danger. New York: Bantam, 1967. 121p.
        Western

4485   ---Summer of the sioux. New York: Dell, 1967. 158p.
        Western

4486   ---North to deadwood. New York: Dell, 1968. 156p.
        Western

4487   ---pseud. Daniel, John S.. Gunflame. Philadelphia:
        Lippincott, 1952. 205p.
        Western

4488   ---The nester. Philadelphia: Lippincott, 1953. 220p.
        Western

4489 ---The land grabbers. Philadelphia: Lippincott, 1955.
222p.
Western

4490 ---The man from yesterday. New York: New American
Library, 1957. 127p.
Western

4491 ---Ute country. New York: New American Library, 1959.
128p.
Western

4492 ---The gunfighters. London: Wright, 1961. 160p.
Western

4493 ---pseud. Leighton, Lee. Lawman. New York: Ballantine,
1953. 180p.
Golden Spur Award 1954 for best Western.

4494 ---Beyond the pass. New York: Ballantine, 1956. 155p.
Western

4495 ---Tomahawk. New York: Ballantine, 1958. 156p.
Western

4496 ---pseud. Stevens, Dan J.. Oregon trunk. New York:
Bourgey, 1950. 256p.
Western

4497 ---Wild horse range. New York: Bourgey, 1951. 255p.
Western

4498 ---Blood money. New York: Permabooks, 1956. 153p.
Western

4499 ---pseud. Wayne, Joseph. The sweet and bitter land.
New York: Dutton, 1950. 218p.
Western

4500 ---The snake stomper. New York: Dutton, 1951. 221p.
Western

4501 ---By gun and spur. New York: Dutton, 1952. 221p.
Western

4502 ---The long wind. New York: Dutton, 1953. 224p.
Western

4503 ---Bunch grass. New York: Dutton, 1954. 191p.
Western

4504 ---The return of the kid. New York: Dutton, 1955.
191p.
Western

4505 ---Showdown at stony crest. New York: Dell, 1957.
192p.
Western

4506 ---Pistol johnny. New York: Doubleday, 1960. 192p.
Western

4507 ---Land of promise. New York: Doubleday, 1962. 190p.
Western

4508 ---Proud journey. New York: Doubleday, 1963. 202p.
Western

4509 ---Red is the valley. New York: Doubleday, 1967. 202p.
Western

4510 ---and Patten, Lewis B.. The meeker massacre. New
York: Cowles, 1969. 136p.
Juvenile

Overholser, Wayne D. jt. author, see Cheshire, Gifford
Paul

4511 Overton, Gwendolen (1876-). The heritage of unrest;
a novel. New York: Macmillan, 1901. 329p.
Apaches--New Mexico and Arizona--Late 1800's--
Comment on United States policy--General Crook.

Owen, Caroline Dale pseud. see Snedeker, Mrs. Caroline
Dale (Parke)

4512 Owen, Robert Dale. Beyond the breakers; a story of the
present day. Philadelphia: Lippincott, 1870. 274p.

P

4513 Paddock, Cornelia (Mrs. A. G. Paddock). In the toils;
      or, martyrs of the latter days. Chicago: Dixon,
      1879. 301p.
           Mormons

4514 ---The fate of madame latour; a tale of great salt lake.
      New York: Fords, 1881. 352p.
           Anti-Mormon-- 1847- 1871.

4515 ---Saved at last from among the mormons. Springfield,
      Ohio: Farm and Fireside Co., 1881. 92p.

4516 Page, Elizabeth Merwin (1889-   ). Wagon's west;
      a story of the oregon trail. New York: Farrar,
      1930. 361p.
           Based on records of Henry Page trip to Calif-
      ornia--Epistolary form.

4517 ---Wild horses and gold; from wyoming to the yukon.
      New York: Farrar, 1932. 362p.
           1897--Based in part on memoirs of Kansas
      Gilbert.

4518 ---The tree of liberty. New York: Farrar, 1939.
      985p.
           Virginia-- 1754- 1806--cf. Mary Johnston and
      Winston Churchill.

4519 ---Wilderness adventure. New York: Rinehart, 1946.
      309p.
           Five men search for girl taken by Indians--
      1742--New Orleans--England.

4520 Palmer, Bruce and Giles, John Clifford. Horseshoe
      bend. New York: Simon, 1962. 572p.
           William Weatherford (c.1780-1824)--Half-breed
      Creek leader--Defeat by A. Jackson--Creek War 1813-
      1814--Battle of Horseshoe Bend (1814).

4521 Palmer, Mrs. Elizabeth. Up the river to danger. New
      York: Scribner's, 1940. 184p.
           Sioux trouble Minnesota during Civil War--
      Juvenile.

4522 Palmer, Mrs. Florence (Glass). Spring will come again.
      Indianapolis: Bobbs, 1940. 421p.
           Alabama-- 1880's--Cotton growers.

352

4523   Pangborn, Edgar. Wilderness of spring. New York:
       Rinehart, 1958. 374p.
              New England--1704--Two brothers orphaned by
       Indian attack.

4524   Paradise, Jean. The savage city. New York: Crown,
       1955. 319p.
              New York City--1740--Based on hysteria caused
       by girl's tale of Negro-Spanish plot to massacre
       whites.

4525   Paradise, Viola Isabel (1887-   ). Tomorrow the
       harvest. New York: Morrow, 1952. 316p.
              Small Maine community--1780's--Cape Elizabeth.

4526   Park, Charles Caldwell (1860-   ) pseud. Gray, Carl.
       A plaything of the gods. Boston: Sherman, 1912.
       260p.
              Joaquin Murrieta (ca. 1832-1853)--California
       border.

4527   Parker, Clara. An eventful night; a comedy of a
       western mining town. New York: Doubleday, 1900.
       152p.

4528   Parker, Mrs. Cornelia (Stratton) (1885-   ).
       Fabulous valley; a novel. New York: Putnam, 1956.
       379p.
              Oil Creek, Pennsylvania--1859--Discovery of oil.

       Parker, Gay pseud. see Greene, Miss M. P.

4529   Parker, Sir Gilbert H. (1862-1932). The trail of the
       sword. New York: Appleton, 1894. 277p.
              Admiral Phips to capture Quebec--Romance--
       1690-1700.

4530   ---The seats of the mighty; being the memoirs of
       captain robert moray, sometime an officer in the
       virginia regiment, and afterwards of amherst's
       regiment. New York: Appleton, 1897. 376p.
              1755-1760--French-Indian War.

4531   ---When valmond came to pontiac; the story of a lost
       napoleon. New York: Harper, 1898. 222p.
              Picturesque romance--Manners of France in
       Canadian town.

4532   ---Power and the glory; a romance of the great la salle.
       New York: Harper, 1925. 339p.
              La Salle (1643-1687).

4533   Parker, Mrs. Helen Eliza (Fitch) by H. F. P.. Constance
       aylmar; a story of the seventeenth century. New
       York: Scribner's, 1869. 347p.

                              353

New Amsterdam--Gravesend, Breuklyn--Eastward.

4534 Parker, Jane (Marsh) (1836-1913). The midnight cry;
      a novel. New York: Dodd, 1886. 298p.
      Millerites

4535 Parker, Mary Moncure. A fair maid of florida; a story
      of the spanish possession of the floridas in the
      eighteenth century. Chicago: Century, 1898. 104p.
      Romance

4536 Parkhill, Forbes. Troopers west. New York: Farrar,
      1945. 249p.
      Western

4537 Parks, Edd Winfield. Long hunter. New York: Farrar,
      1942. 270p.
            Based on story of Big-Foot Spencer, Tennessee
      hunter--Juvenile.

4538 ---Pioneer pilot; a boy's story of the first steamboat
      voyage from pittsburgh to new orleans. Indianapolis:
      Bobbs, 1947. 298p.
      Juvenile

4539 Parks, L. K.. With british and braves; story of the
      war of 1812. Cincinnati: Curts, 1898. 301p.

4540 Parrish, Anne (Mrs. Josiah Titzell) (1888-1957).
      A clouded star. New York: Harper, 1948. 242p.
            Journey on underground railroad with Mrs.
      Harriet (Ross) Tubman (1815?-1913)--To Canada.

4541 Parrish, Randall (1858-1923). When wilderness was
      king; a tale of the illinois country. Chicago:
      McClurg, 1904. 387p.
            Ft. Dearborn Massacre (1812)--Potawatomi--
      Garrison life--Romance.

4542 ---A sword of the old frontier; a tale of fort chartres
      and detroit; being a plain account of sundry adven-
      ture befalling chevalier raoul de coubert, one time
      captain in the hussars of languedoc, during the
      year 1763. Chicago: McClurg, 1905. 407p.
            Pontiac's Rebellion (1763-1764).

4543 ---Bob hampton of placer. Chicago: McClurg, 1906.
      384p.
            Little Big Horn-1876--"Abandonment theory of
      Whittaker presented".

4544 ---Beth norvell; a romance of the west. Chicago:
      McClurg, 1907. 341p.
      Western

4545 ---Prisoners of chance; the story of what befell geoffrey benteen, borderman, through his love for a lady of france. Chicago: McClurg, 1908. 423p.
Louisiana-1760's--Based on manuscript--Romance.

4546 ---Keith of the border; a tale of the plains. Chicago: McClurg, 1910. 362p.
Western

4547 ---My lady of doubt. Chicago: McClurg, 1911. 381p.
American Revolution--Romance--Adventure.

4548 ---Molly mcdonald; a tale of the old frontier. Chicago: McClurg, 1912. 403p.
1860's--Experiences of girl traveling to join father at Ft. Devere, southwest of Ft. Dodge.

4549 ---Maid of the forest. Chicago: McClurg, 1913. 427p.
Ohio--1791--Romantic adventure.

4550 ---Beyond the frontier; a romance of the early days in the middle west. Chicago: McClurg, 1915. 406p.
Journey to Ft. St. Louis from Quebec--Illinois River--Romance.

4551 ---The devil's own; a romance of the black hawk war. Chicago: McClurg, 1917. 356p.
Missouri--1832--Romance.

4552 ---Wolves of the sea; being a tale of the colonies from the manuscript of one geoffry carlyle, seaman narrating certain strange adventures which befell him aboard the pirate craft "namur". Chicago: McClurg, 1918. 355p.

4553 Paterson, Arthur Henry (1862-1928). The daughter of the nez percés. New York: Peck, 1894. 381p.

4554 ---A son of the plains. New York: Macmillan, 1895. 261p.
Western

Patrick, Joseph pseud. see Walsh, Joseph Patrick

4555 Patten, Lewis B.. Massacre at san pablo; a gold medal original. Greenwich, Connecticut: Fawcett, 1957. 142p.
Western

4556 ---Pursuit. New York: Permabooks, 1957. 152p.
Western

4557 ---Sun blade. New York: Abelard, 1958. 175p.
Western

4558 ---Top man with a gun; an original gold medal novel.
Greenwich, Connecticut: Fawcett, 1959. 144p.
Western

4559 ---Hangman's country. New York: Abelard, 1960. 180p.
Western

4560 ---Law of the gun. New York: New American Library, 1961.
128p.
Western

4561 ---Guns at gray butte. New York: Doubleday, 1963. 159p.
Western

4562 ---Giant on horseback. New York: Doubleday, 1964. 183p.
Western

4563 ---Proudly they die. New York: Doubleday, 1964. 150p.
Western

4564 ---Death waited at rialto creek. New York: Doubleday,
1966. 167p.
Western

4565 ---No god in saguaro. New York: Doubleday, 1966. 180p.
Western

4566 ---The arrogant guns. New York: Doubleday, 1967. 208p.
Western

4567 ---Bones of the buffalo. New York: Doubleday, 1967.
208p.
Western

4568 ---Death of a gunfighter. New York: Doubleday, 1968.
162p.
Western

4569 ---The red sabbath. New York: Doubleday, 1968. 188p.
Western

4570 ---Posse from poison creek. New York: Doubleday, 1969.
176p.
Western

4571 ---The youngerman guns. New York: Doubleday, 1969.
186p.
Western

4572 ---Red runs the river. New York: Doubleday, 1970. 181p.
Western

Patten, Lewis B. jt. author, see Overholser, Wayne

4573 Patterson, Burd Shippen. "The head of iron"; a romance

356

of colonial pennsylvania. Pittsburg, Pennsylvania: Walker, 1908. 360p.
John Forbes (1710-1759)--Braddock--Ft. Duquesne.

4574 Patterson, Emma Lillie. Midnight patriot. New York: Longmans, 1949. 304p.
American Revolution--Juvenile.

4575 Patterson, Frances Taylor. White wampum; the story of kateri tekakwitha. New York: Longmans, 1934. 304p.
Fictionalized biography--Mohawk girl converted to Roman Catholicism--Romance.

4576 Patterson, Norma. The man i love. New York: Farrar, 1940. 311p.
Western

4577 Patton Willoughby. Sea venture. New York: Longmans, 1959. 146p.
English to Jamestown--1609.

4578 Pattullo, George (1879-1967). The sheriff of badger; a tale of the southwest borderland. New York: Appleton, 1912. 312p.
Western

4579 Paul, Charlotte. Gold mountain. New York: Random, 1953. 307p.
Seattle--Late 1800's--Hop ranching--Smallpox.

4580 ---The cup of strength. New York: Random, 1958. 279p.
Northwest--1890--Logging.

4581 Paul, Elliot Harold (1891-   ). Lava rock. New York: Liveright, 1929. 311p.
Western mining camp--Dam in west.

4582 ---A ghost town on yellowstone. New York: Random, 1948. 341p.
Trembles, Montana-1907-1922.

4583 Paulding, James Kirke (1798-1860). Koningsmarke, the long finne; a story of the new world. New York: Wiley, 1823. 2 vols.
New Sweden

4584 ---The dutchman's fireside; a tale. New York: Harper, 1831. 2 vols.
Patroon romance--Collaboration of Washington Irving--Eulogy of yankee character.

4585 ---Westward ho! New York: Harper, 1832. 2 vols.
Daniel Boone--Solitary adventurer fleeing civilization.

4586   ---The old continental; or, the price of liberty.
       New York: Paine, 1846. 2 vols.
            New York City--American Revolution--Lower class.

4587   ---The puritan and his daughter. New York: Baker,
       1849. 2 vols.
            Virginia--New England--Seventeenth century.

4588   ---pseud. Bull-us, Hector. The diverting history of
       john bull and brother jonathan. London: Sherwood,
       1813. 135p.
            Comic account--Revolt of colonies.

4589   Pawle, Kathleen (Mrs. Dermot Darby). Mural for a
       later day. New York: Dodd, 1938. 302p.
            Founding of New Sweden on Delaware River--
       Swedes and Finns.

4590   Paxton, S. H. pseud.. The dragon in new albion.
       Boston: Little, 1953. 213p.
            Admiral Drake's visit to California coast
       1570's--Miwok Indians--Juvenile.

4591   Payne, Pierre Stephen Robert (1911-   ). The chieftain.
       New York: Prentice Hall, 1953. 312p.
            Joseph of Nez Percé (1840-1904)--Pro-Indian
       resistance--Flight to Canada 1877.

4592   ---O western wind. London: Hale, 1957. 320p.
            Massachusetts, New Plymouth.

4593   ---pseud. Cargoe, Richard. Brave harvest. New York:
       Ballantine, 1954. 168p.
            Colonial New England.

4594   ---pseud. Horne, Howard. Concord bridge. Indianapolis:
       Bobbs, 1952. 320p.
            American Revolution--Boston--Lexington—Concord--
       Romance.

       Payne, Robert see Payne, Pierre Stephen Robert (1911-   )

4595   Payne, Stephen. Raiders of the rimrock. New York:
       Avalon, 1956. 224p.
            Western

4596   PayTiamo, James. Flaming arrow's people. New York:
       Duffield, 1932. 157p.
            Acoma Indians.

       Peace, Frank pseud. see Cook, William Everett

4597   Pearce, Richard Elmo. The impudent rifle. Phila-
       delphia: Lippincott, 1951. 286p.
            Arkansas frontier--1830's--West Point graduate
       v. corrupt Indian agent--Choctaws--Comanches--Good.

                              358

4598   ---Valley of the tyrant. New York: Quinn, 1951. 123p.
        Western

4599   ---The restless border. Philadelphia: Lippincott,
        1952. 319p.
        Western

4600   Pearson, Mrs. Lorene. The harvest waits; a novel.
        Indianapolis: Bobbs, 1940. 441p.
        Mormon life--Utah.

4601   Pearson, Molly (Winston) (1876-1959) and Bullis,
        Franklin Howard (1860-   ). Injuns comin'!
        New York: Scribner's, 1935. 300p.
        Vermont family pioneering in Minnesota--1855--
        Sioux--Based on fact.

4602   Pease, Howard (1894-   ). Long wharf; a story of
        young san francisco. New York: Dodd, 1939. 219p.
        Cabin boy on father's barkentine to San Fran-
        cisco--1849--Juvenile.

4603   Peattie, Donald Culross (1898-1964). A prairie grove.
        New York: Simon, 1938. 289p.
        Saga--Missionaries--Founding of Chicago.

4604   ---Forward the nation. New York: Putnam, 1942. 281p.
        Lewis and Clark Expedition--Sacagwea (1786-1884)--
        Romance.

4605   ---and Peattie, Mrs. Louise (Redfield). Up country;
        a story of the vanguard. New York: Appleton, 1928.
        299p.
        American Revolution--To CharlesTown with bride
        to establish plantation--To west and frontier--
        Romance.

        Peattie, Mrs. Louise (Redfield) jt. author, see Peattie,
        Donald Culross

        Peck, Anne Merriman jt. author, see Johnson, Enid

4606   Peck, George Washington pseud. Bigly, Cantella.
        Aurifodina; or, adventures in the gold region.
        New York: Baker, 1849. 103p.

4607   Peck, Theodora Agnes (1882-   ). Hester of the grants;
        a romance of old bennington. New York: Fox, 1905.
        419p.
        American Revolution--Vermont.

4608   ---White dawn; a legend of ticonderoga. New York:
        Revell, 1914. 306p.
        French-Indian War--Battle of Ticonderoga (1758)--
        Scots girl--Romance.

4609 Pedersen, Mrs. Elsa. <u>Dangerous flight</u>. New York:
      Abingdon, 1960. 224p.
              Alaska--Shelter Bay Colony--Russia--Juvenile.

4610 Peeples, Samuel Anthony (1917-   ). <u>The dream ends</u>
      <u>in fury; a novel based on life of joaquin murrieta</u>.
      New York: Harper, 1949. 240p.
              (1828-1853)--Young Mexican to California--1849--
      Vengeance.

4611 ---<u>Gun feud at stampede valley</u>. New York: Avon, 1954.
      128p.
              Western

4612 ---<u>The call of the gun</u>. New York: Ace, 1955. 148p.
              Western

4613 ---pseud. Bass, Frank. <u>The angry land</u>. New York:
      Dodd, 1958. 214p.
              Western

4614 ---pseud. Ward, Brad. <u>Broken rainbow ranch</u>. New York:
      Dutton, 1950. 223p.
              Western

4615 ---<u>Canyon country</u>. New York: Dutton, 1951. 256p.
              Western

4616 ---<u>The spell of the desert</u>. New York: Dutton, 1951.
      219p.
              Western

4617 ---<u>The hanging hills</u>. New York: Dutton, 1952. 224p.
              Western

4618 ---<u>Johnny sundance</u>. New York: Dutton, 1952. 217p.
              Western

4619 ---<u>Marshal of medicine bend</u>. New York: Dutton, 1953.
      190p.
              Western

4620 ---<u>The baron of boot hill</u>. New York: Dutton, 1954.
      224p.
              Western

4621 ---<u>Trouble at tall pine</u>. New York: Dutton, 1954. 186p.
              Western

4622 ---<u>Six gun heritage</u>. New York: Dutton, 1955. 192p.
              Western

4623 ---<u>Thirty notches</u>. New York: Macmillan, 1956. 151p.
              Western

4624 ---The missourian. New York: Macmillan, 1957. 147p.
Western

4625 ---Frontier street. New York: Macmillan, 1958. 146p.
Western

4626 Peirce, Isaac. The narragansett chief; or, the adventures of a wanderer. [Anonymous]. New York: Porter,
1832. 195p.

4627 Pendexter, Hugh (1875-1940). Tiberius smith; as
chronicled by his right hand man, billy campbell.
New York: Harper, 1907. 330p.
Western

4628 ---Gentleman of the north. New York: Doubleday, 1920.
243p.
Western

4629 ---Red belts. New York: Doubleday, 1920. 346p.
Tennessee frontier.

4630 ---Kings of the missouri. Indianapolis: Bobbs, 1921.
360p.
Fur trade--1830's.

4631 ---A virginia scout. Indianapolis: Bobbs, 1922. 353p.
Messenger for Governor Dunmore--Adventure.

4632 ---Pay gravel. Indianapolis: Bobbs, 1923. 353p.
Western

4633 ---Old misery. Indianapolis: Bobbs, 1924. 389p.
Western

4634 ---The wife-ship woman. Indianapolis: Bobbs, 1925.
338p.
Girl from France to colonial Louisiana--Governor
Bienville--Adventure.

4635 ---Harry Idaho. Indianapolis: Bobbs, 1926. 315p.
Western

4636 ---The red road; a romance of braddock's defeat.
Indianapolis: Bobbs, 1927. 314p.
1755--French-Indian War--Romance.

4637 ---Bird of freedom. Indianapolis: Bobbs, 1928. 349p.
Nebraska--Homesteading--1850's-1860's--Western
thriller.

4638 ---The gate through the mountain. Indianapolis: Bobbs,
1929. 320p.
Western

4639   ---The border breed. London: Collins, 1933. 254p.
       Western

4640   ---The fighting years. London: Collins, 1933. 254p.
       Western

4641   ---The scarlet years. London: Collins, 1933. 254p.
       Western

4642   ---The blazing west. London: Collins, 1934. 252p.
       Western

       Pendleton, Ford pseud. see Cheshire, Gifford Paul

4643   Perkins, Kenneth. Ride him, cowboy. New York: Macaulay,
       1923. 314p.
       Western

4644   ---The gun fanner. New York: Macaulay, 1924. 318p.
       Western

4645   ---Gold; a novel. New York: Stokes, 1929. 315p.
       California--Whaling ships--Mystery.

4646   ---The moccasin murders. New York: King, 1931. 285p.
       Mystery

4647   ---Three were thoroughbreds. New York: Doubleday,
       1939. 280p.
       Western

4648   Perrie, Georg W. pseud. Mose, Buckskin. Buckskin mose
       [pseud]; or, life from the lakes to the pacific,
       as actor, circus-rider, dectective, ranger, gold-
       digger, indian scout, and guide. written by himself.
       New York: Hinton, 1873. 285p.

4649   Perry, Clair Willard (1887-1961) pseud. Perry, Clay, and
       Everitt, Pell John Leggett. Hell's acre; a
       historical novel of the wild east in the 50's.
       New York: Furman, 1938. 400p.
          Massachusetts ceded 1200 acres around Boston
       Corner to New York--Horse thieves.

       Perry, Clay pseud. see Perry, Clair Willard

4650   Perry, George Session. Hold autumn in your hand.
       New York: Viking, 1941. 249p.
          Southwest--Poor farmers--National Book Award
       1941--Texas Institute of Letters--Romantic and
       realistic.

4651   Perry, Stella George (Stern) (Mrs. George Hough Perry)
       (1877-   ). Defenders; a novel. New York: Stokes,
       1927. 411p.

Spain to New Orleans--To betray town to British--
Creole wife of Barataria pirate--Battle of New Orleans
1815.

4652 Peterkin, Mrs. Julia Mood (1880-   ). Black april.
Indianapolis: Bobbs, 1927. 315p.
Black life--South Carolina plantation.

4653 ---Scarlet sister mary. Indianapolis: Bobbs, 1928.
345p.
Gullah negroes--South Carolina--Chronicle of
life--Pulitizer Prize 1929.

4654 ---Bright skin. Indianapolis: Bobbs, 1932. 348p.
Black life--Sea Island--Carolinas.

4655 Petersen, Herman (1893-   ). Covered bridge. New
York: Crowell, 1950. 376p.
New York--Farming community--1865-1885.

4656 ---The road. New York: Crowell, 1952. 277p.
Boy and girl--Buried chest--Upstate New York--
1860's--Melodrama.

4657 Peterson, Charles Jacobs.(1819-1887). Agnes courtenay;
a tale of the old dominion. Amherst, Massachusetts:
Nims, 1847. 35p.

4658 ---The oath of marion; a story of the revolution.
Boston: Gleason, 1847. 50p.

4659 ---Grace dudley; or, arnold at saratoga. an historical
novel. Philadelphia: Peterson, 1849. 111p.
1777

4660 ---Kate aylesford; a story of refugees. Philadelphia:
Peterson, 1855. 356p.
Romance

4661 Peterson, Elmer Theodore (1884-   ). Trumpets west.
New York: Sears, 1934. 355p.
Chronicle--Three generations--Swedes to America--
Kansas--1853-1930's.

4662 Peterson, Henry (1818-1891). Pemberton; or, one hundred
years ago. Philadelphia: Lippincott, 1873. 393p.
André and Arnold--American Revolution.

4663 ---Dulcibel; a tale of old salem. New York: Winston,
1907. 402p.
Witchcraft

4664 Petry, Ann (Lane) (1911-   ). Tituba of salem village.
New York: Crowell, 1964. 254p.
Salem witchcraft--Juvenile.

363

4665 Pettibone, Anita. The bitter country. New York:
Doubleday, 1925. 318p.
Northwest--Salmon fishers--Lumber--School
marm.

4666 ---Light down, stranger. New York: Farrar, 1942.
310p.
Washington territory--Late 1860's.

4667 ---Johnny painter. New York: Farrar, 1944. 314p.
Washington and Oregon--1860's--Folk narrative--
Pioneer novel.

4668 Phelps, Margaret. Toby on the sheep drive. Philadelphia: Macrae, 1949. 197p.
Arizona sheep drive--Juvenile.

4669 Phil johnson's life on the plains. [Anonymous].
Chicago: Rhodes, 1888. 358p.
Adventure

4670 Philbrook, Elizabeth. Far from marlborough street.
New York: Viking, 1944. 302p.
Boston to Springfield--1793--Two hundred mile
journey--Juvenile.

4671 Phillips, Alexandra. Forever possess. New York:
Dutton, 1946. 352p.
Leisler's Revolt--1689 and 1690--New York
State--Patroons.

Phlogobombos, Yclept Terentius pseud. see Judah,
Samuel B. F.

4672 Pidgin, Charles Felton (1844-1923). Blennerhassett;
or, the decrees of fate. a romance founded upon
events in american history. Boston: Clark, 1901.
442p.
Aaron Burr (1756-1836)--Defense.

4673 ---The climax; or, what might have been. a romance of
the great republic. Boston: Clark, 1902. 335p.
A. Burr as national hero.

4674 ---Little burr, the warwick of america; a tale of the
old revolutionary days. Boston: Robinson, 1904.
396p.

4675 ---A nation's idol; a romance of franklin's nine years
of happiness at the court of france. Philadelphia:
Altemus, 1904. 348p.

4676 ---The house of shame; a novel. New York: Cosmopolitan,
1912. 244p.
Mormons

4677   Pier, Arthur Stanwood (1874-1966). The young man
       from mount vernon; a novel. New York: Stokes,
       1940. 364p.
              George Washington.

4678   Pierce, Lucy France. The white devil of verde; a
       story of the west. Dillingham, 1898. 236p.
              Mining

4679   Pierce, Ovid Williams. On a lonesome porch. New
       York: Doubleday, 1960. 237p.
              North Carolina--Reconstruction--"Top rung on
       bottom".

4680   ---The devil's half. New York: Doubleday, 1968. 287p.
              South of Civil War.

4681   Pike, Mrs. Mary Hayden (Green) (1825-1908). Agnes;
       a novel. Boston: Phillips, 1858. 509p.
              American Revolution.

4682   Pinckney, Josephine Lyons Scott (1895-   ). Hilton
       head. New York: Farrar, 1941. 524p.
              Henry Woodward (1646?-1688)--English surgeon--
       South Carolina and Barbados--1665-1686.

       Piomingo, a headman and warrior of the Muscogulie
       nation pseud. see Robinson, John

4683   Pise, Charles Constantine. Father rowland; a north
       american tale. [Anonymous]. Baltimore: Fielding,
       1829. 190p.

4684   Pittman, Mrs. Hannah (Daviess) (1840-   ). The heart
       of kentucky. New York: Neale, 1908. 267p.
              Based on Sharpe murder--1825.

4685   Place, Marian Templeton pseud. White, Dale. The johnny
       cake mine. New York: Viking, 1954. 222p.
              1873--Juvenile.

4686   ---The wild horse trap. New York: Viking, 1955. 192p.
              Western

4687   ---Vigilantes, ride! New York: Viking, 1956. 285p.
              Western

4688   ---Steamboat up the missouri. New York: Viking, 1958.
       185p.
              1860's--Juvenile.

4689   ---pseud. Whitinger, R. D.. Bitterroot basin. New
       York: Arcadia, 1955. 219p.
              Western

4690   ---High trail. New York: Avalon, 1957. 222p.
       Western

4691   Pleasants, Henry Jr. (1884-   ). Thomas mason,
       adventurer. Philadelphia: Winston, 1934. 366p.
       1736-1796.

4692   ---Mars' butterfly; a tale of the career of major
       john andré spy-extraordinary of the british army in
       the american revolution. Boston: Christopher, 1941.
       476p.
       Caricature

4693   Plowhead, Ruth Gipson. Lucretia ann on the oregon
       trail. Caldwell, Idaho: Caxton, 1931. 244p.
       Romance

4694   ---Lucretia ann in the golden west. Caldwell, Idaho:
       Caxton, 1935. 294p.
       Sequel to Lucretia Ann on the Oregon Trail.

4695   ---Lucretia ann on the sagebrush plains. Caldwell,
       Idaho: Caxton, 1936. 357p.
       Sequel to ...Oregon Trail...Golden West.

4696   Pocock, Roger S. (1865-1941). Curly; a tale of the
       arizona desert. Boston: Little, 1905. 320p.
       Anti-hero.

4697   Pollard, Eliza Frances. The green mountain boys; a
       story of the american war of independence. New
       York: Dodd, 1895. 320p.
       Adventure

4698   ---Liberty or death; a story of the green mountain boys.
       New York: Dodd, 1909. 320p.
       Romance

4699   ---New england maid. Atlanta, Georgia: Caldwell,
       1910. [?].
       American Revolution--B. Arnold and sister
       Hannah--André affair.

4700   Poole, Ernest (1880-   ). The nancy-flyer; a stage-
       coach epic. New York: Crowell, 1949. 232p.
       New England 1835--Civil War--New Hampshire.

       Poole, Richard pseud. see Wells, Lee E.

4701   Poore, Benjamin Perley. Aurora; or, the sharpshooters'
       scout. a romance of the revolution. New York:
       French, 185?. 100p.

4702   Pope, Mrs. Edith Everett (Taylor). River in the wind.
       New York: Scribner's, 1954. 392p.
       Seminole--Florida--1835-1842--Good.

4703   Porter, James A.. A prince of anahuac; a histori-
        traditional story antedating the aztec empire.
        Galion, Ohio: Crawford, 1894. 378p.
                Romance

4704   Porteus, Stanley David (1883-   ). The restless
        voyage. New York: Prentice, 1948. 257p.
                Archibald Campbell (b.1787)--Life at sea--
        Hawaiian Islands--1806-1812.

4705   Portis, Charles. True grit; a novel. New York:
        Simon, 1968. 215p.
                Ft. Smith, Arkansas--Young girl searches for
        murderer of her father.

4706   Post, Mrs. Mary (Brinker) (1906-   ). Annie jordan;
        a novel of seattle. New York: Doubleday, 1948.
        280p.
                Saga of red headed girl--1889-1917--Romance--
        Melodrama.

4707   Postl, Karl or(Postel) (1793-1864). Hope leslie; or,
        early times in massachusetts. [Anonymous]. New
        York: White, 1827. 2 vols.
                Romance

4708   ---Tokeah; or, the white rose. [Anonymous]. Philadelphia:
        Carey, 1829. 2 vols.
                Georgia frontier--Early 1800's.

4709   ---The linwoods; or, "sixty years since" in america.
        [Anonymous]. New York: Harper, 1835. 2 vols.

4710   ---pseud. Seatsfield [sic], Charles. Life in the new
        world; or, sketches of american society. [Trans. by
        Hebbe, Gustavas C.]. New York: Winchester, 1842.
        349p.

4711   ---The cabin book; or, sketches of life in texas.
        [Trans. from German by Prof. Ch. Fr. Mersch].
        New York: Winchester, 1844. 155p.

4712   ---The cabin book; or, national characteristics.
        [Trans. by Powell, Sarah]. London: Cooke, 1852.
        296p.

4713   ---Frontier life; or, scenes and adventures in the
        southwest. New York: Miller, 1857. 376p.

4714   Potter, Miss Margaret Horton (Mrs. J. D. Black) (1881-
        1911). The house of demailly; a romance. New York:
        Harper, 1901. 468p.
                1741-1748--Maryland--Versailles--French hero
        weds New England girl--Contrast New World and French
        Court.

4715 Pound, Arthur (1884-1966). Once a wilderness. New
York: Reynal, 1934. 399p.
Michigan farm life--1890's--Regional--640 acres
to industry.

4716 ---Second growth. New York: Reynal, 1935. 347p.
Sequel to Once A Wilderness.

4717 ---Hawk of detroit; a novel. New York: Reynal, 1939.
361p.
Antoine Cadillac (1656ca.-1720)--Conflicting
interest--Government monopolies--Founding of Detroit.

4718 Powell, Dawn. The bride's house. New York: Bretano's,
1929. 296p.
Ohio farm--1890's--Romance.

Power, Effie Louise jt. author, see Everson, Florence
McClurg

4719 Powers, Alfred. Chains for columbus. Philadelphia:
Westminister, 1948. 219p.
Cristoforo Colombo--Juvenile.

4720 ---Prisoners of the redwoods; an adventure story of
san francisco and the northern california coast in
the fifties. New York: Coward, 1948. 246p.
Teen-age boys to gold fields.

4721 ---Long way to frisco; a folk adventure novel of california and oregon in 1852. Boston: Little, 1951.
186p.
Juvenile

4722 Powers, Paul S. (1905-   ). Doc dillahay. New York:
Macmillan, 1949. 250p.
Arizona territory--1880's--Young doctor.

4723 Pratt, Mrs. Eleanor Blake pseud. Atkinson, Eleanor
Blake. Seedtime and harvest. New York: Putnam,
1935. 275p.
Michigan farm life--1890-1915--Daughter of
Norwegian immigrants--cf. Hamsun's Growth of the
Soil.

4724 Pratt, Theodore (1901-   ). Seminole. New York:
Duell, 1954. 170p.
Osceola-Seminole Chief (1804-1832)--From
drama Seminole.

4725 ---The white god. New York: Pyramid, 1963. 190p.
Southwest--Hohokam Indians--Coronado--1540--
Search for gold and one of cities of Cibola.

4726 ---pseud. Brace, Timothy. The barefoot mailman.
New York: Duell, 1943. 215p.

368

Florida--Miami and Palm Beach--1880's--
Frontier melodrama.

4727 Prebble, John Edward Curtis (1915-   ). <u>Spanish</u>
<u>stirrup</u>. New York: Harcourt, 1958. 158p.
Western

4728 ---<u>The buffalo soldiers</u>. New York: Harcourt, 1959.
256p.
Texas border--Close Civil War--Last hunt--
Golden Spur Award 1960 for Best Western Historical
Novel.

4729 Prentiss, Elizabeth (Payson). <u>Pemaquid; a story of old</u>
<u>times in new england</u>. New York: Anson, 1877. 370p.

4730 Prescott, John Brewster (1919-   ). <u>Journey by the</u>
<u>river</u>. New York: Random, 1954. 237p.
Wagon train through Missouri and Kansas to
Ft. Laramie, Wyoming--1848--Golden Spur Award 1955
for Best Western Historical Novel.

4731 Price, Christine. <u>Song of the wheels</u>. New York:
Longmans, 1956. 214p.
Farmers' Rebellion--New York early 1700's--
Levelers--Juvenile.

4732 Price, Eugenia. <u>The beloved invader; a novel</u>. Philadelphia: Lippincott, 1965. 284p.
#1 of Trilogy of St. Simons Island, Georgia.

4733 ---<u>New moon rising</u>. Philadelphia: Lippincott, 1969.
281p.
#2 of Trilogy of St. Simons Island--Nat Turner
Rebellion--1830's.

4734 Price, T. Buchanan. <u>Snap; the ox-train era. early</u>
<u>troubles of border trade.</u> New York: Smith, 1881.
320p.

4735 Price, Willard De Mille (1887-   ). <u>Whale adventure</u>.
New York: Day, 1960. 191p.
Juvenile

4736 Pridgen, Tim. <u>Tory oath</u>. New York: Doubleday, 1941.
371p.
American Revolution--Highland Scots of Carolinas--
Side of King--American Loyalists.

4737 ---<u>West goes the road</u>. New York: Doubleday, 1944. 226p.
Post-Revolution Era--Secession and Burr--Serious
book.

4738 Priest, Josiah. <u>A history of the early adventures</u>
<u>of washington among the indians of the west; and</u>

the story of his love of maria frazier, the exile's
daughter; with an account of the mingo prophet.
Albany, New York: Munsell, 1841. 64p.
Frontier

4739 Pritchard, Mrs. Ettie Stephens. Old farm. New York:
      Appleton, 1934. 302p.
      Farm life--1870's--Romance.

4740 Pritchett, Lulita Crawford. The cabin at medicine
      springs. New York: Watts, 1958. 195p.
      Colorado--1879--Based on author's ancestor--
      Establish Steamboat Springs--Meeker Rebellion--
      Won Franklin Watts Fiction Award--Juvenile.

4741 Proctor, Gertrude Amelia. Gleams of scarlet; a tale
      of the canadian rockies. Boston: Sherman, 1915.
      292p.
      Romance

      Prophet James pseud. see Buck, James Smith

4742 Pryor, Elinor. And never yield. New York: Macmillan,
      1942. 520p.
      First novel--Mormons--Missouri and Illinois--
      1830's.

4743 ---The double man. New York: Norton, 1957. 452p.
      Tsani war title Mankiller--White child raised
      by Cherokee--Up country from Charleston--Romance.

4744 Pryor, Sara Agnes (Rice) (Mrs. Roger Atkinson Pryor)
      (1830-1912). The colonel's story. New York:
      Macmillan, 1911. 387p.
      Southern hospitality--Simple story--Anti-
      bellum days in Virginia.

4745 Pulse, Charles K.. John bonwell; a novel of the ohio
      river valley, 1818-1862. New York: Farrar, 1952.
      436p.
      Ohio Valley--1850's--Romance.

4746 Putnam, Mrs. Ellen Tryphosa Harrington pseud. Talmon,
      Thrace. Captain molly; the story of a brave woman.
      New York: Derby, 1857. 349p.
      Romance

4747 Putnam, George Palmer (1887-1950). Hickory shirt;
      a novel of death valley in 1850. New York: Duell,
      1949. 252p.

4748 ---pseud. Bend, Palmer. The smiting of the rock; a
      tale of oregon. New York: Putnam, 1918. 328p.

4749 ---and Shipman, Mrs. Helen (Barham) (Nell Shipman)
      (1892-   ). Hot oil. New York: Greenberg, 1935.
      274p.

370

Texas and discovery of oil--Bootlegging of
petroleum.

Putnam, George Palmer jt. author, see Gragg, Frances,

4750 Putnam, Mrs. Nina Wilcox (1888-1962). The inner voice.
New York: Sheridan, 1940. 309p.
Border ruffians--Kansas--1850's--Society of
Friends--1854-1861.

4751 Pyle, Howard (1853-1911). Ruby of kishmoor. New
York: Harper, 1908. 73p.
Jamica--Pirate--Daughter and Quaker.

4752   Quick, Herbert (1861-1925). Yellowstone nights.
        Indianapolis: Bobbs, 1911. 345p.

4753   ---Vandermark's folly. Indianapolis: Bobbs, 1922.
        420p.
                #1 of Iowa Trilogy--Autobiographical in method--
        1830-1860--Erie Canal boy searches for mother--Iowa
        farm--Rich record pioneer farming--Meyer "J. Vander-
        mark one of few memorable figures in farm fiction".

4754   ---The hawkeye. Indianapolis: Bobbs, 1923. 477p.
                #2 of Iowa Trilogy--Sequel to Vandermark's
        Folly--1857-1878--Monterey Center, Iowa.

4755   ---The invisible woman. Indianapolis: Bobbs, 1924.
        488p.
                #3 of Iowa Trilogy--1880-1900.

4756   Quiller-Couch, Arthur Thomas (1863-1944). Fort amity.
        New York: Scribner's, 1904. 337p.
                French-Indian War up to American Revolution--
        Ticonderoga to Quebec--English officer in French
        station--Romance with Ojibway girl.

        Quin, Dan pseud. see Lewis, Alfred

4757   Quinn, Joseph J.. Wolf moon; a romance of the great
        southwest. Oklahoma City: Little Flower Press, 1924.
        265p.
                Oklahoma

        Quint, Wilder Dwight jt. author, see Richardson,
            George Tilton

4758   Rabl, Samuel Supplee (1895-   ). Mobtown clipper.
        Cambridge, Maryland: Cornell, 1949. 277p.
             War of 1812 to clipper ships--Privateering.

4759   Raddall, Thomas Head (1903-   ). His majesty's
        yankees. New York: Doubleday, 1942. 409p.
             Nova Scotia--Ft. Cumberland--Privateers.

4760   ---Roger sudden. New York: Doubleday, 1945. 358p.
             Nova Scotia--1700's--Halifax and Louisbourg--
        Indians--Jacobite hero.

4761   ---Son of the hawk. Philadelphia: Winston, 1950.
        247p.
             American Revolution--Nova Scotia--New England-
        ers--1775-1783--Juvenile.

4762   ---The governor's lady. New York: Doubleday, 1959.
        474p.
             Sir John Wentworth (1737-1820)--Frances Went-
        worth (1745ca.-1813)--Last Royal Governor of New
        Hampshire.

4763   Raine, William MacLeod (1871-1954). A daughter of
        raasay; a tale of the '45. New York: Stokes, 1902.
        311p.
             Western

4764   ---Wyoming; a story of the outdoor west. New York:
        Dillingham, 1908. 353p.
             Western

4765   ---Ridgway of montana; a story of today in which the
        hero is also the villain. New York: Dillingham,
        1909. 318p.
             Western

4766   ---Bucky o'connor; a tale of the unfenced border.
        New York: Dillingham, 1910. 345p.
             Western

4767   ---Texas ranger. New York: Dillingham, 1911. 337p.
             Western

4768   ---Brand blotters. New York: Dillingham, 1912. 348p.
             Western

4769   ---Mavericks. New York: Dillingham, 1912. 347p.
             Western

4770 ---Crooked trails and straight. New York: Dillingham, 1913. 339p.
Western

4771 ---The highgrader. New York: Dillingham, 1915. 321p.
Western

4772 ---Steve yeager. Boston: Houghton, 1915. 289p.
Western

4773 ---The yukon trail; a tale of the north. Boston:
Houghton, 1917. 323p.
Western

4774 ---The sheriff's son. Boston: Houghton, 1918. 345p.
Western

4775 ---A man four-square. Boston: Houghton, 1919. 286p.
Western

4776 ---The big-town round-up. Boston: Houghton, 1920. 303p.
Western

4777 ---Oh, you tex! Boston: Houghton, 1920. 340p.
Western

4778 ---Gunsight pass; how oil came to the cattle country
and brought the new west. Boston: Houghton, 1921. 331p
Western

4779 ---Tangled trails; a western dectective story. Boston:
Houghton, 1921. 323p.
Western

4780 ---The fighting edge. Boston: Houghton, 1922. 306p.
Western

4781 ---Man-size. Boston: Houghton, 1922. 310p.
Western

4782 ---Iron heart. Boston: Houghton, 1923. 288p.
Western

4783 ---The desert's price. New York: Doubleday, 1924. 354p.
Western

4784 ---Roads of doubt. New York: Doubleday, 1925. 327p.
Western

4785 ---Troubled waters. New York: Doubleday, 1925. 309p.
Western

4786 ---Bonanza; a story of the gold trail. New York:
Doubleday, 1926. 370p.
Western

4787 ---The last shot. New York: Doubleday, 1926. 186p.
     Western

4788 ---Judge colt. New York: Doubleday, 1927. 268p.
     Western

4789 ---Colorado. New York: Doubleday, 1928. 316p.
     Western

4790 ---Texas man. New York: Doubleday, 1928. 317p.
     Western

4791 ---The fighting tenderfoot. New York: Doubleday,
     1929. 354p.
     Western

4792 ---Rutledge trails the ace of spades. New York:
     Doubleday, 1930. 306p.
     Western

4793 ---The valiant. New York: Doubleday, 1930. 321p.
     Western

4794 ---Beyond the rio grande. Boston: Houghton, 1931. 282p.
     Western

4795 ---The black tolts. Boston: Houghton, 1932. 293p.
     Western

4796 ---Under northern stars. Boston: Houghton, 1932. 296p.
     Western

4797 ---For honor and life. Boston: Houghton, 1933. 277p.
     Western

4798 ---The broad arrow. Boston: Houghton, 1933. 292p.
     Western

4799 ---Roaring river. Boston: Houghton, 1934. 297p.
     Western

4800 ---The trail of danger. Boston: Houghton, 1934. 284p.
     Western

4801 ---Border breed. Boston: Houghton, 1935. 300p.
     Western

4802 ---Square-shooter. Boston: Houghton, 1935. 294p.
     Western

4803 ---Run of the brush. Boston: Houghton, 1936. 288p.
     Western

4804 ---To ride the river with. Boston: Houghton, 1936.
     283p.
     Western

4805 ---Bucky follows cold trail. Boston: Houghton, 1937.
306p.
Western

4806 ---King of the bush. Boston: Houghton, 1937. 299p.
Western

4807 ---On the dodge. Boston: Houghton, 1938. 252p.
Western

4808 ---Sons of the saddle. Boston: Houghton, 1938. 276p.
Western

4809 ---Moran beats back. Boston: Houghton, 1939. 268p.
Western

4810 ---The river bend feud. Boston: Houghton, 1939. 259p.
Western

4811 ---Riders of buck river. Boston: Houghton, 1940. 269p.
Western

4812 ---Trail's end. Boston: Houghton, 1940. 263p.
Western

4813 ---They call him blue blazes. Boston: Houghton, 1941.
250p.
Western

4814 ---The damyank. Boston: Houghton, 1942. 249p.
Western

4815 ---Justice deferred. Boston: Houghton, 1942. 257p.
Western

4816 ---Gone to texas. London: Hodder, 1943. 223p.
Western

4817 ---Courage stout. Boston: Houghton, 1944. 237p.
Western

4818 ---Arkansas guns. Boston: Houghton, 1945. 248p.
Western

4819 ---Clattering hoofs. Boston: Houghton, 1946. 274p.
Western

4820 ---Challenge to danger. Boston: Houghton, 1947. 245p.
Western

4821 ---This nettle danger. Boston: Houghton, 1947. 259p.
Western

4822 ---Saddlebum. Boston: Houghton, 1948. 248p.
Western

4823   ---The bandit trail. Boston: Houghton, 1949. 245p.
       Western

4824   ---Ranger's luck. Boston: Houghton, 1949. 281p.
       Western

4825   ---Jingling spurs. Boston: Houghton, 1950. 284p.
       Western

4826   ---Gloryhole; a rousing tale of leadville in the
       frontier days. Boston: Houghton, 1951. 245p.
       Western

4827   ---Justice comes to tomahawk. Boston: Houghton, 1952.
       249p.
       Western

4828   ---Dry bones in the valley. Boston: Houghton, 1953.
       243p.
       Western

4829   ---Reluctant gunman. Boston: Houghton, 1954. 246p.
       Western

4830   ---High grass valley. Boston: Houghton, 1955. 186p.
       Western

       Randall, Clay pseud. see Adams, Clifton

4831   Ransom, James Birchett. Osceola; or, fact and fiction.
       a tale of the seminole war. New York: Harper, 1838.
       150p.
           Seminole War--1835-1842.

4832   Rapaport, Stella F.. Reindeer rescue. New York: Putnam,
       1955. 119p.
           Rescue of whaling ship locked in ice--Eskimo
       drive reindeer to men for food--1898--Juvenile.

4833   Ratigan, William. The adventures of captain mc cargo.
       New York: Random, 1956. 245p.
           Based on Great Lakes skipper--1855--Picaresque.

4834   Rawlings, Mrs. Marjorie Kinnan (1896-1953). South
       moon under. New York: Scribner's, 1933. 343p.
           Florida backwood's life--1930.

4835   ---Golden apples. New York: Scribner's, 1935. 352p.
           Florida Cracker Company.

4836   ---The yearling. New York: Scribner's, 1938. 428p.
           Florida--Pulitzer Prize-1939--One year in
       life of boy in hammock area--Author lived in area
       for over decade--Distinguished book.

4837   ---The sojourner. New York: Scribner's, 1953. 313p.
            New York State--Farm life--1880--World War II.

4838   Raymond, James F. (1826-   ). The lost colony.
            Philadelphia: Peterson, 1891. 413p.
            Raleigh's ill-fated affair--1580's.

4839   Raymond, Rossiter Worthington pseud. Gray, Robertson.
            Brave hearts; an american novel. New York: Ford,
            1873. 284p.
            Mining--Sierra Nevada.

4840   Rayner, Miss Emma (-1926). Free to serve; a tale
            of colonial new york. Boston: Copeland, 1897. 434p.
            Manners and family life early 1700's--God-fear-
            ing folks.

4841   ---In castle and colony. Chicago: Stone, 1899. 467p.
            Swedish--Dutch--Delaware--1650's.

4842   ---Doris kingsley, child and colonist. New York:
            Dillingham, 1901. 390p.
            American Revolution--South Carolina--1776-1779.

4843   ---The dilemma of engeltie; the romance of a dutch
            colonial maid. Boston: Page, 1911. 402p.

4844   Raynolds, Robert Frederick (1902-   ). Brothers
            in the west. New York: Harper, 1931. 299p.
            First novel--West and southwest--Plains--
            Fine work.

4845   ---The quality of quiros. Indianapolis: Bobbs, 1955.
            309p.
            Exploration to Manila--1595--Isabel Barreto,
            governess of expedition--Alvara de Mendaña--Pedro
            Fernandes de Queiros.

4846   Reach, Angus Bethune (1821-1856). Leonard lindsay;
            or, the story of a buccaneer. London: Bogue, 1850.
            2 vols.
            Scots sailor--West Indies.

4847   Read, Opie Percival (1852-1939). An arkansas planter.
            Chicago: Rand, 1896. 315p.

4848   ---A yankee from the west. Chicago: Rand, 1898. 277p.
            Farm--Middle west.

4849   ---In the alamo. Chicago: Rand, 1900. 367p.

4850   ---"By the eternal"; a novel. Chicago: Laird, 1906.
            303p.
            Andrew Jackson (1767-1845).

4851 Read, Thomas Buchanan. Paul redding; a tale of the
brandywine. Boston: Tompkins, 1845. 136p.
American Revolution.

Reardon, Joseph pseud. see Miller, Tevis

4852 Reed, Ishmael. Yellow back radio broke-down. New York:
Doubleday, 1969. 192p.
Loop Garoo Kid, Negro cowboy--Pop novel--Modern
setting and past.

4853 Reed, Myrtle (1874-1911). The shadow of victory; a
romance of fort dearborn. New York: Putnam, 1903.
413p.
Frontier fort--Chicago area 1812--Anti-English.

4854 Reed, Warren. She rode a yellow stallion. Indianapolis:
Bobbs, 1950. 323p.
First novel--Chronicle--Three generations--
Wisconsin family 1846-1919.

4855 Reeder, Russell Potter. Attack on fort lookout;
a story of the old northwestern frontier. New York:
Duell, 1959. 184p.
Diary of West Point graduate to Michigan
frontier--1811--Juvenile.

4856 Rees, Gilbert. I seek a city. New York: Dutton, 1950.
316p.
Roger Williams (1604?-1683) pivot of book--
Good.

4857 Rees, James. The tinker spy; a romance of the revolution.
Buffalo, New York: Burke, 1855. 103p.

4858 Reese, John Henry. Three wild ones. Philadelphia:
Westminister, 1963. 188p.
Western--Juvenile.

4859 ---Dinky. New York: McKay, 1964. 134p.
Western--Juvenile.

4860 ---The looters. New York: Random, 1968. 177p.
Western

4861 ---Sunblind range. New York: Doubleday, 1968. 192p.
Western

4862 ---Sure shot shapiro. New York: Doubleday, 1968. 191p.
Western

4863 Reeve, Franklin D. (1928-   ). The red machines.
New York: Morrow, 1968. 191p.
One day in lives of itinerant combine crew
and families--1960.

379

4864 Regan, Rex. Camel trek. Speller, 1935. 312p.
Captain Edward Beale (1822-1893)--Twenty-five
camels--San Antonio to San Francisco-1857.

4865 Reid-Girardot, Mrs. Marion. Steve of the "bar-g"
ranch; a thrilling story of life on the plains of
colorado. New York: Broadway Pub., 1914. 287p.
Western

4866 ---Red eagle of the medicine way. Boston: Cornhill,
1922. 308p.
Western

Reiner, Max pseud. see Caldwell, Taylor (Mrs. Marcus
Reback)

4867 Remick, Martha. Richard ireton; a legend of the
early settlement of new england. Boston: Loring,
1875?. 466p.

4868 Remington, Frederic (1861-1909). Sundown leflare.
New York: Harper, 1899. 114p.
Illustrations by author--One of best of artists
of American west.

4869 ---John ermine of the yellowstone. New York: Macmillan,
1902. 271p.
Sioux v. Army--Author did illustrations.

4870 ---The way of an indian. New York: Fox, 1906. 251p.

Renard, Frances pseud. see Fox, Frances Barton

4871 Rennie, Mrs. Ysabel (Fisk) (1918-   ). Blue chip.
New York: Harper, 1953. 307p.
Arizona mining--Late nineteenth century.

4872 Repp, Edward Earl (1900-   ). Cyclone jim. New
York: Godwin, 1935. 299p.
Western

4873 ---Hell on the pecos. New York: Godwin, 1935. 323p.
Western

4874 ---Gun hawk. New York: Godwin, 1936. 294p.
Western

4875 ---Hell in the saddle. New York: Godwin, 1936. 271p.
Western

4876 ---pseud. Cody, John. Empty holsters. New York:
Godwin, 1936. 200p.
Western

4877 ---pseud. Field, Peter. Mustang mesa. New York:

380

Morrow, 1937.   284p.
Western

4878   Requa, Mark Lawrence (1865-1937).   Grubstake; a story
of early mining days in nevada, time 1874.   New York:
Scribner's, 1933.   360p.
Romance of west.

Ressler, Lillian jt. author, see Cicchetti, Janet pseud.
Janet, Lillian

4879   Reyward, Elizabeth.   The mutinous wind.   Boston:
Houghton, 1951.   210p.
Cape Cod--Early 1700's--Witchcraft and pirates.

Reynolds, Dickson pseud. see Dickson, Helen (Mrs. Helen
Campbell Dickson Reynolds)

4880   Reynolds, Helen Mary Greenwood (Campbell) pseud. Reynolds,
Dickson.   Gold in mosquito creek.   New York: Nelson,
1946.   192p.
Teenagers discover gold--Pacific northwest--
Juvenile.

4881   Rhodes, Eugene Manlove (1869-1934).   Good men and true.
New York: Holt, 1910.   177p.
Western--One of best writers in genré.

4882   ---Beyond the desert.   Boston: Houghton, 1914.   237p.
Western

4883   ---Bransford in arcadia; or the little oehippus.
New York: Holt, 1914.   236p.
Juvenile

4884   ---The desire of the moth.   New York: Holt, 1916.
149p.
Western

4885   ---West is west.   New York: Grosset, 1917.   386p.
Western

4886   ---Stepsons of light.   Boston: Houghton, 1921.   317p.
Western romance--New Mexico.

4887   ---Copper streak trail.   Boston: Houghton, 1922.   318p.
Western--Mining.

4888   ---Once in the saddle and pasó por aqui.   New York:
Houghton, 1927.   258p.
Excellent--Western.

4889   ---Trusty knaves.   Boston: Houghton, 1933.   238p.
Western

4890   ---Beyond the desert. Boston: Houghton, 1934.   237p.
       Western--El Paso and Northeastern Railroad.

4891   ---Penalosa. Santa Fe, New Mexico: Rydal, 1934.   34p.
       Diego Dionisio de Peñalosa (1624-1687).

4892   ---The proud sheriff. Boston: Houghton, 1935.   177p.
       Western--Last of his tales.

4893   Rich, Helen. The willow-bender. New York: Simon,
       1950.   277p.
            Small frontier town--Destroyed by gold mining
       project--Romance.

4894   Richard white; or, one eyed dick of massachusetts.
       a tale for the young. [Anonymous]. Boston: Light,
       1841.   106p.
            Juvenile

4895   Richards, Mrs. Clarice (Estabrook) (1875-   ).
       A tenderfoot bride; tales from an old ranch.
       New York: Revell, 1920.   226p.
            Eastern woman bride of Wyoming rancher .

4896   Richards, Mrs. Lela (Horn) pseud. Neville, Lee.
       Poplars across the moon; the story of tula kruso.
       Boston: Page, 1936.   346p.
            Mormons--Utah--Adopt two girls.

4897   Richardson, George Tilton and Quint, Wilder Dwight pseud.
       Tilton, Dwight. My lady laughter; a romance of boston
       town in the days of the great siege. Boston: Clark,
       1904.   442p.
            1775-1776.

4898   Richardson, Norval (1877-1940). Lead of honour.
       Boston: Page, 1910.   341p.
            Natchez, Mississippi--1830--Based on life of
       S. Prentiss.

4899   Richter, Conrad Michael (1890-   ). The sea of grass.
       New York: Knopf, 1937.   149p.
            Cattle kings v. nestors--cf. W. Cather, A Lost
       Lady--Excellent.

4900   ---The trees. New York: Knopf, 1940.   302p.
            #1 of Ohio Trilogy--Pioneer family from Penn-
       sylvania to virgin wilderness in southeastern Ohio--
       1790's--Authentic portrait.

4901   ---Tracey cromwell. New York: Knopf, 1942.   208p.
            "Bad woman"--Arizona mining town--1890's.

4902   ---The free man. New York: Knopf, 1943.   147p.
            Pennsylvania Dutch indentured servant becomes
       free man--Philadelphia 1770's.

4903   ---The fields. New York: Knopf, 1946. 288p.
        #2 of Ohio Trilogy--Sequel to The Trees.

4904   ---The town. New York: Knopf, 1950. 433p.
        #3 of Ohio Trilogy--Westward expansion.

4905   ---The light in the forest. New York: Knopf, 1953.
        179p.
                Rescue of fifteen year old after eleven years
        captivity with Delawares--"...authentic sensation
        of life in early America".

4906   ---The lady. New York: Knopf, 1957. 191p.
                Northern New Mexico--1880's--Violence and
        revenge--Good regional legends of New Mexico.

4907   ---A country of strangers. New York: Knopf, 1966.
        169p.
                Chronicle--White girl captive of Indians return-
        ed to white society against her will--Companion to
        Light In The Forest--Pro-Indian.

4908   Riddle, Albert Gallatin (1816-1902). Bart ridgeley;
        a story of northern ohio. Boston: Nichols, 1873.
        374p.
                Frontier

4909   ---The portrait; a romance of the cuyahoga valley.
        Boston: Nichols, 1874. 378p.
                Juvenile

4910   ---Castle gregory; a story of the western reserve
        woods in the olden times. Cleveland, Ohio: Leader,
        1884. 99p.
                Juvenile

4911   ---The tory's daughter; a romance of the northwest,
        1812-1813. New York: Putnam, 1888. 385p.
                Juvenile

4912   ---Ansel's cave; a story of early life in the western
        reserve. Cleveland, Ohio: Burrow, 1893. 249p.
                Juvenile--1813.

        Rider, Brett pseud. see Gooden, Arthur

4913   Rifkin, Shepard. Texas blood red. New York: Dell,
        1956. 192p.
                Western

4914   ---pseud. Michaels, Dale. King fisher's road. New
        York: Fawcett, 1963. 160p.
                Western

4915   Rigoni, Orlando. Brand of the bow. New York: Arcadia,
        1965. 188p.

                            383

Western

4916 ---Twisted trails. New York: Arcadia, 1965. 189p.
        Western

4917 ---Massacre ranch. New York: Arcadia, 1966. 192p.
        Western

4918 ---Showdown at skeleton flat. New York: Arcadia, 1967.
        190p.
        Western

4919 ---Six-gun song. New York: Arcadia, 1967. 188p.
        Western

4920 ---A nickel's worth of lead. New York: Arcadia, 1968.
        190p.
        Western

4921 ---The pikabo stage. New York: Arcadia, 1969. 190p.
        Western

4922 Ringwood, Mrs. Gwen (Pharis). Younger brother. New
        York: Longmans, 1959. 213p.
        First novel--Indians--Cattle.

4923 Ripley, Clements (1892-   ). Gold is where you find it.
        New York: Appleton, 1936. 331p.
        California--1870's--Farmer v. fruit grower.

4924 ---Clear for action; a novel about john paul jones.
        New York: Appleton, 1940. 310p.
        Told in first person by clerk of Jones--1773-
        1783--Climax Serapis v. Le Bonhomme Richard--Romance.

4925 ---Mississippi belle. New York: Appleton, 1942. 307p.
        New Orleans--Memphis-1830's--Widow raises
        child--Works New Orleans gambling house.

4926 Ritchie, Cicero Theodore (1914-   ). Willing maid.
        New York: Abelard, 1958. 310p.
        1740's--Louisbourg--Signourney (half-French and
        half-English) to Harvard--Romance--Adventure.

4927 Ritchie, Robert Welles. Trails to two moons. Boston:
        Little, 1920. 308p.
        Western

4928 ---Dust of the desert. New York: Dodd, 1922. 300p.
        Western

4929 Rivers, George Robert Russell. The governor's garden;
        a relation of some passages in the life of his ex-
        cellency, thomas hutchinson, sometime captain-general
        and governor-in-chief of his majesty's province of
        massachusetts bay. Boston: Knight, 1896. 259p.

18th century.

4930 ---Captain shays; a populist of 1786. Boston: Little,
1897. 358p.
Rebellion

4931 ---The count's snuff box; a romance of washington and
buzzard's bay during the war of 1812. Boston: Little,
1898. 283p.

4932 Roan, Tom. Montana outlaw. New York: King, 1934. 314p.
Western

4933 ---Whispering range. New York: King, 1934. 310p.
Western

4934 ---The rio kid. New York: Godwin, 1935. 314p.
Western

4935 ---Smoky river. New York: Godwin, 1935. 286p.
Western

4936 ---The dragon strikes back. New York: Messner, 1936.
278p.
Western

4937 Roark, Garland. Rainbow in the royals. New York:
Doubleday, 1950. 307p.
California--1850's--Sailing ships to west--
Romance.

4938 ---The lady and the deep blue sea. New York: Doubleday, 1958. 256p.
Clipper ship race--Melbourne to Boston.

4939 ---pseud. Garland, George. Doubtful valley; a novel
of traitor whites and apaches in 1880. Boston:
Houghton, 1951. 278p.
Western

4940 ---Star in the rigging; a novel of the texas navy.
New York: Doubleday, 1954. 345p.
Texas Revolution (1834-1836)--Romance.

4941 ---Bugles and brass. New York: Doubleday, 1964. 208p.
Western

4942 ---and Thomas, Charles (1903-   ). Hell fire jackson.
New York: Doubleday, 1966. 349p.
Western

Robe, Captain pseud. see Ross, Clinton

4943 Roberts, Sir Charles George Douglas (1860-1943). The
forge in the forest; being the narrative of the

385

acadian ranger, jean de mer, seigneur de briart, and
how he crossed the black abbé; and of his adventures
in a strange fellowship. Boston: Lamson, 1896. 311p.
Romance--Use of natural surroundings--Primitive
life of colonists.

4944 ---The heart of the ancient wood. New York: Silver,
1900. 276p.
Life in forests--Affectionate description.

4945 ---A sister to evangeline; a story of yvonne de lamourie,
and how she went into exile with the villagers of
grand pré. Boston: Silver, 1900. 289p.
Sequel to Forge In The Forest--1755--
Expulsion of Acadians.

4946 ---Barbara ladd. Boston: Page, 1902. 377p.
Maryland and Connecticut--1769-1778--Romance.

4947 ---The prisoner of mademoiselle; a love story. Boston:
Page, 1904. 265p.
Acadian romance--Boston captain and French
woman.

4948 ---The young acadian; or, the raid from beauséjour.
Boston: Page, 1907. 139p.
Nova Scotia--1713-1763.

4949 ---The back woodsmen. New York: Macmillan, 1909. 269p.

4950 Roberts, Charles Humphrey (1847-   ). Down the ohio .
Chicago: McClurg, 1891. 313p.
Rural life Quakers in Ohio.

4951 Roberts, Dan. The wells fargo brand. New York: Arcadia,
1964. 189p.
Western

4952 ---The cheyenne kid. New York: Arcadia, 1965. 192p.
Western

4953 ---Durez city bonanza. New York: Arcadia, 1965. 191p.
Western

4954 ---Outlaw's gold. New York: Arcadia, 1965. 190p.
Western

4955 ---Stage to link city. New York: Arcadia, 1966. 190p.
Western

4956 ---Vengeance rider. New York: Arcadia, 1966. 189p.
Western

4957 ---Wyoming range war. New York: Arcadia, 1966. 191p.
Western

4958 ---Lawman of blue rock. New York: Arcadia, 1967.
190p.
Western

4959 ---Yuma brand. New York: Arcadia, 1967. 192p.
Western

4960 ---The dawn riders. New York: Arcadia, 1968. 192p.
Western

4961 Roberts, Mrs. Edith (Kneipple) (1902-   ). Tamarack;
a novel. Indianapolis: Bobbs, 1940. 368p.
Lumbering--1890's--Decayed town--Tourists.

4962 Roberts, Elizabeth Madox (1886-1941). The time of man.
New York: Viking, 1926. 382p.
First novel--Migrant family of tenant farmer--
Good on southern life.

4963 ---The great meadow. New York: Viking, 1930. 338p.
Kentucky--Revolution era--Pioneer life--History
becomes poetry in this novel--Excellent.

4964 Roberts, Kenneth Lewis (1885-1957). Arundel; being the
recollections of steven nason of arundel, in the
province of maine, attached to the secret expedition
led by colonel benedict arnold against quebec and
later captain in the continental army serving at
valcour island, bemis heights, and yorktown. New
York: Doubleday, 1930. 618p.
#1 Chronicles of Arundel--American Revolution--
Southern Maine--Nason with Arnold-1775-1776.

4965 ---The lively lady; a chronicle of certain men of
arundel in maine, of privateering during the war of
impressments, and of the circular prison on dartmoor.
New York: Doubleday, 1931. 374p.
#3 of Chronicle of Arundel--War of 1812--Son
of hero of Arundel is hero.

4966 ---Rabble in arms; a chronicle of arundel and the
burgoyne invasion. New York: Doubleday, 1933. 870p.
#2 in Chronicles of Arundel--American Revolution--
Continental Congress is villain--Benedict Arnold is
hero.

4967 ---Captain caution; a chronicle of arundel. New York:
Doubleday, 1934. 310p.
#4 and last of Arundel Chronicle--War of 1812--
cf. Cooper and Chambers.

4968 ---Northwest passage. New York: Doubleday, 1937. 709p.
Robert Rogers (1731-1795) and St. Francis Exped-
ition--Indians--1759--Great novel.

4969 ---Oliver wiswell. New York: Doubleday, 1940. 836p.
American Revolution--View point of Loyalist.

4970 ---Lydia bailey. New York: Doubleday, 1947. 499p.
Tripoli War--Barbary pirates--Haiti Revolution--
1789-1809.

4971 ---Boon island. New York: Doubleday, 1956. 275p.
John Dean (1679-1761)--New Hampshire--1710.

Roberts, MacLennan jt. author, see Beater, Jack

4972 Roberts, Richard Emery (1903-   ). The gilded rooster.
New York: Putnam, 1947. 249p.
First novel--1863--Conflicts of four shut-in
mountain men.

Roberts, Theodore Goodridge see Goodridge Roberts,
Theodore (1877-   )

Roberts, Theodore jt. author, see Stephens, Robert
Neilson

4973 Roberts, Trev. Dead in the saddle. New York: Arcadia,
1959. 222p.
Western

4974 ---Canyon river. New York: Arcadia, 1966. 192p.
Western

4975 ---Comanche interlude. New York: Arcadia, 1966. 190p.
Western

4976 ---The hide rustlers. New York: Arcadia, 1967. 192p.
Western

4977 ---Desert campfires. New York: Arcadia, 1968. 192p.
Western

4978 Roberts, Walter Adolphe (1886-1962). Royal street; a
novel of old new orleans. Indianapolis: Bobbs,
1944. 324p.
Creole v. northern businessman--1840's--Romance.

4979 Robertson, Ben (1905-   ). Traveler's rest. Clemson,
South Carolina: Cottonfield, 1938. 268p.
Chronicle--Caldwells of South Carolina and
Tennessee--Based on real family--Texas to Oregon.

4980 Robertson, Mrs. Constance (Noyes). Seek-no-further.
New York: Farrar, 1938. 351p.
Imaginary community upstate New York--1860's--
Author grand daughter of John Humphrey Noyes,
founder of Oneida community.

388

4981   ---Fire bell in the night. New York: Holt, 1944.   342p.
           Syracuse--Underground railroad--1858-1860.

4982   Robertson, Frank Chester (1890-   ). The foreman
           of the forty-bar. New York: Barse, 1925.   319p.
           Western

4983   ---The cleanup on deadman. New York: Garden City Pub.,
           1926.   183p.
           Western

4984   ---The outlaws of flower-pot canyon. New York: Garden
           City Pub., 1926.   181p.
           Western

4985   ---The boss of the tumbling h. New York: Barse, 1927.
           308p.
           Western

4986   ---On the trail of chief joseph. New York: Appleton,
           1927.   229p.
           Western

4987   ---The fall of buffalo horn. New York: Appleton, 1928.
           232p.
           Western

4988   ---The man branders. New York: Barse, 1928.   319p.
           Western

4989   ---The silver cow. New York: Barse, 1929.   302p.
           Western

4990   ---Clawhammer ranch. New York: Barse, 1930.   294p.
           Western

4991   ---We want that range. Newark, New Jersey: Barse,
           1931.   316p.
           Western

4992   ---The trouble grabber. New York: Washburn, 1932.
           300p.
           Western

4993   ---Freewater range. New York: Washburn, 1933.   313p.
           Western

4994   ---Larruping leather. New York: Washburn, 1933.   302p.
           Western

4995   ---Outlaw ranch. New York: Washburn, 1934.   313p.
           Western

4996   ---Wild riding runt. New York: Washburn, 1934.   310p.
           Western

389

4997 ---Forbidden trails. New York: Washburn, 1935. 299p.
        Western

4998 ---The powder burner. New York: Washburn, 1935. 302p.
        Western

4999 ---Branded men. New York: Dodge, 1936. 276p.
        Western

5000 ---Fighting jack warbonnet. New York: Dutton, 1939.
        248p.
        Western

5001 ---Rip roarin' rincon. New York: Dutton, 1939. 254p.
        Western

5002 ---The firebrand from burnt creek. New York: Dutton,
        1940. 248p.
        Western

5003 ---Poison valley. New York: Dutton, 1941. 256p.
        Western

5004 ---Snake river to hell. New York: Dutton, 1941. 254p.
        Western

5005 ---Cowman's jack pot. New York: Dutton, 1942. 253p.
        Western

5006 ---The roaring sixties. London: Collins, 1942. 192p.
        Western

5007 ---Vigilante war in buena vista. New York: Dutton,
        1942. 254p.
        Western

5008 ---The noose hangs high. New York: Dutton, 1945. 219p.
        Western

5009 ---Round-up in the river. New York: Dutton, 1945.
        192p.
        Western

5010 ---The lost range. New York: Dutton, 1946. 224p.
        Western

5011 ---Rope crazy. New York: Dutton, 1948. 215p.
        Western

5012 ---The longhorns of hate. New York: Dutton, 1949.
        219p.
        Western

5013 ---Wrangler on the prod. New York: Dutton, 1950. 223p.
        Western

5014　---Hangman of the humbug.　New York: Dutton, 1951.　219p.
　　　　　Western

5015　---Saddle on a cloud.　New York: Dutton, 1952.　224p.
　　　　　Western

5016　---Where desert blizzards blow.　New York: Nelson, 1952.
　　　　　186p.
　　　　　Western

5017　---Sagebrush sorrel.　New York: Nelson, 1953.　186p.
　　　　　Western

5018　---Disaster valley.　New York: Ballantine, 1957.　160p.
　　　　　Western

5019　---Lawman's pay.　New York: Ballantine, 1957.　155p.
　　　　　Western

5020　---A man called paladin.　New York: Macmillan, 1963.
　　　　　218p.
　　　　　Western

5021　---pseud. Crane, Robert.　Thunder in the west.　New
　　　　　York: Appleton, 1934.　295p.
　　　　　Western

5022　---Wild blood.　New York: Godwin, 1935.　272p.
　　　　　Western

5023　---Stormy range.　New York: Godwin, 1936.　275p.
　　　　　Western

5024　---pseud. Field, Frank Chester.　The rocky road to
　　　　　jericho.　New York: Hillman, 1935.　288p.
　　　　　Mormon Empire.

5025　---The outlaw of antler.　New York: Dutton, 1937.　253p.
　　　　　Western

5026　---The pride of pine creek.　New York: Dutton, 1938.
　　　　　252p.
　　　　　Western

5027　---Thunder on the range.　New York: Dutton, 1938.
　　　　　247p.
　　　　　Western

5028　---Cowboy comes a-fightin'.　New York: Dutton, 1940.
　　　　　246p.
　　　　　Western

5029　---Grizzly meadows.　New York: Dutton, 1943.　256p.
　　　　　Western

5030 Robins, Edward. A boy in early virginia; or, adventures
      with captain john smith. Philadelphia: Jacobs,
      1901. 285p.
          Juvenile

5031 Robinson, Gertrude (1876-   ). White heron feather.
      New York: Harper, 1930. 299p.
          Indians--Juvenile.

5032 ---Sachim bird. New York: Dutton, 1936. 216p.
          1605--Boy rescued by Abnaki Indians--Juvenile.

5033 ---Robeen. New York: Dutton, 1938. 258p.
          Indians--North America--Juvenile.

5034 ---Winged feet; scouting for george washington. New
      York: Dutton, 1939. 311p.
          American Revolution--Juvenile.

5035 ---Sons of liberty. New York: Dutton, 1941. 248p.
          American Revolution--Juvenile.

5036 ---Catch a falling star. New York: Dutton, 1942.
      251p.
          Heroine--Daughter of captain of King's guards
      stationed at Kennebec--1693--Juvenile.

5037 ---Fox fire. New York: Dutton, 1944. 245p.
          New England--1660's--Brother and sister--Juvenile

5038 Robinson, Henry Morton (1898-   ). Water of life;
      a novel. New York: Simon, 1960. 621p.
          Chronicle of whiskey making dynasty--Three
      generations--1860-1920.

5039 Robinson, John (1782c.-1833) pseud. Piomingo, a head-
      man and warrior of the Muscogulee nation. The
      savage. Philadelphia: Manning, 1810. 312p.

5040 Robinson, John Bunyan. The serpent of sugar creek
      colony; a temperance narrative of pioneer life
      in ohio. Philadelphia: Johnson, 1885. 128p.

5041 Robinson, John Hovey (1825-   ). The boston con-
      spiracy; or, the royal police. a tale of 1773-75.
      Boston: Dow, 1847. 110p.
          Boston Tea Party and later.

5042 ---Redpath; or, the western trail. a story of frontier
      life and adventure. New York: French, 185?. 84p.
          Romance

5043 ---The royal greens; or, the scout of the susquehanna.
      a tale of the valley of wyoming. New York: French,
      185?. 100p.
          Romance

392

5044 ---Black ralph, the forest fiend! or, wonders of the west. a tale of wood and wild. Boston: National, 1851. 97p.

5045 ---The white rover; or, the lovely maid of louisiana. a romance of the wild forest. New York: French, 1851. 100p.

5046 ---The lone star; or, the texas bravo. a tale of the southwest. Boston: Gleason, 1852. 100p.

5047 ---Marion's brigade; or, the light dragoons. a tale of the revolution. Boston: Gleason, 1852. 100p.
        South Carolina.

5048 ---The rebel spy; or, the king's volunteers. a romance of the siege of boston. Boston: Gleason, 1852. 100p.
        1775-1776.

5049 ---Rosalthe; or, the pioneers of kentucky. a tale of western life. Boston: Gleason, 1853. 100p.

5050 ---Silver-knife; or, the hunters of the rocky mountains. an autobiography. Boston: Spencer, 1854. 168p.

5051 ---The buckeye ranger; a tale of the kansas hunting grounds! New York: Brady, 186?. 79p.

5052 ---The maid of the ranche; or, the regulators and moderators. a story of life on the texan border. New York: Brady, 186?. 100p.

5053 ---Pathaway; or, the mountain outlaws. a tale of the northern hunting grounds. New York: Brady, 186?. 127p.

5054 ---The round pack; a tale of the forked deer. New York: Brady, 186?. 72p.

5055 ---Whitelaw; or, nattie of the lake shore. a tale of the ten mile trace. New York: Brady, 1861. 83p.

5056 ---Mountain max; or, nick whiffles on the border. a tale of the bushwackers in missouri. New York: Brady, 1862. 77p.

5057 ---Nick whiffles, the trapper guide. a tale of the northwest. New York: Carleton, 1877. 412p.

5058 Robinson, Mrs. John Hovey. Evelyn, the child of the revolution. a romance of real life. Boston: Hotchkiss, 1850. 104p.

5059 Robinson, Rowland Evans (1833-1900). Danvis folks. Boston: Houghton, 1894. 349p.
        Vermont

5060 ---A hero of ticonderoga. Burlington, Vermont:
Shanley, 1898. 187p.
Vermont

5061 ---In the green wood. Burlington, Vermont: Shanley,
1899. 163p.
American Revolution--Vermont.

5062 ---A danvis pioneer; a story of one of ethan allen's
green mountain boys. Boston: Houghton, 1900. 214p.

5063 Robinson, Solon. Me-Won-I-Toc; a tale of frontier life
and indian character. New York: New York News,
1867. 133p.
Michigan and Illinois.

5064 Robinson, William Henry (1867-   ). Thirsty earth.
New York: Messner, 1937. 288p.
Arizona--Choya River Valley--1890's--Irrigation
project.

5065 Rodney, George Brydges (1872-   ). In buff and blue;
being certain portions from the diary of richard
hilton, gentleman of haslet's regiment of delaware
foot, in our ever glorious war of independence.
Boston: Little, 1897. 206p.
American Revolution.

5066 ---Jim lafton, american. New York: McCann, 1920. 276p.
Juvenile

5067 ---The coronado trail. New York: Clode, 1932. 256p.
Western

5068 ---The creed of the range. New York: Clode, 1932. 256p.
Western

5069 ---The crimson brand. New York: Watt, 1932. 256p.
Western

5070 ---The open trail. New York: Clode, 1932. 256p.
Western

5071 ---The canyon trail. New York: Clode, 1933. 256p.
Western

5072 ---The mormon trail. New York: Clode, 1933. 247p.
Western

5073 ---The tenderfoot. New York: Clode, 1933. 252p.
Western

5074 ---The apache trail. New York: Clode, 1934. 255p.
Western

5075 ---Beyond the range. New York: Clode, 1934. 256p.
Western

5076 ---The glory hole. New York: Clode, 1934. 254p.
Western

5077 ---Coyote currency. New York: Clode, 1935. 256p.
Western

5078 ---Riders of the chaparral. New York: Greenberg, 1935.
250p.
Western

5079 ---The vanishing frontier. New York: Greenberg, 1935.
247p.
Western

5080 ---Frontier justice. New York: Greenberg, 1936. 256p.
Western

5081 ---Badland trail. New York: Phoenix, 1937. 233p.
Western

5082 ---The sidewinder trail. New York: Greenberg, 1937.
248p.
Western

5083 ---Coyote valley. New York: Phoenix, 1938. 248p.
Western

5084 ---Guns of smoky fork. New York: Phoenix, 1938. 256p.
Western

5085 ---Gunpowder heritage. New York: Arcadia, 1939. 256p.
Western

5086 ---Raiders of the cherokee strip. New York: Phoenix,
1940. 253p.
Western

5087 ---Maverick medico. New York: Phoenix, 1941. 250p.
Western

5088 ---Tumbleweed trail. New York: Phoenix, 1941. 256p.
Western

5089 ---Frayne of the lying y. New York: Phoenix, 1942.
256p.
Western

5090 ---The seco bonanza. New York: Phoenix, 1942. 254p.
Western

5091 ---Cheyne of the rocking k. New York: Phoenix, 1943.
256p.
Western

5092 Roe, Azel Stevens. The star and the cloud; or, a
      daughter's love. New York: Derby, 1857. 410p.
      New Jersey--Pre-Revolution.

5093 Roe, Edward Payson. Near to nature's heart. New
      York: Dodd, 1876. 556p.
      American Revolution--Hudson Highlands.

5094 Roe, Vingie Eve (Mrs. R. C. Lawton) (1879-   ).
      The maid of the whispering hills. New York: Dodd,
      1912. 405p.
      Romance

5095 ---The heart of the night wind; a story of the great
      northwest. New York: Dodd, 1913. 395p.
      Oregon--Girl befriended by Indians--Lumber--
      Romance.

5096 ---The primal lure; a romance of fort lu cerne. New
      York: Dodd, 1914. 350p.

5097 ---Tharon of lost valley. New York: Dodd, 1919. 299p.
      Romance

5098 ---Val of paradise. New York: Dodd, 1921. 253p.
      Western

5099 ---Nameless river. New York: Duffield, 1923. 278p.
      Western

5100 ---The splendid road. New York: Duffield, 1925. 303p.
      Oregon Trail--1849.

5101 ---Flame of the border. New York: Doubleday, 1933.
      296p.
      Western

5102 ---Sons to fortune. New York: Doubleday, 1934. 307p.
      Romance--Sacramento, California--Gambling.

5103 ---Black belle rides the uplands. New York: Doubleday,
      1935. 276p.
      Western

5104 ---Guns of the round stone valley. New York: Mill,
      1938. 254p.
      Western

5105 ---Dust above the sage. New York: Mill, 1942. 251p.
      Western

5106 ---The great trace; a novel. Philadelphia: Macrae,
      1948. 256p.
      Western

5107   ---West of abilene. Philadelphia: Macrae, 1951. 255p.
        Western

5108   Roe, Wellington. The tree falls south. New York:
        Putnam, 1937. 241p.
        Kansas--Farmers and droughts.

5109   Rölvaag, Ole Evart (1876-1931). Peder victorious;
        a novel. [Trans. by Solum, Nora O.]. New York:
        Harper, 1929. 350p.
        Sequel Giants In The Earth.

5110   ---pseud. Morck, Paal. Giants in the earth; a saga
        of the prairie. New York: Harper, 1927. 465p.
                Norwegian settler--South Dakota--1873-1891--
        Great account pioneer on plains.

5111   Rogers, Cameron (1900-   ). Manila galleon. New
        York: Appleton, 1936. 232p.
                Manila--1621--Romance--Spain in Philippines.

5112   Rogers, John Rankin pseud. Rogers, S. L.. The graftons;
        or, looking forward. a story of pioneer life.
        Chicago: George, 1893. 115p.

5113   Rogers, Robert Cameron (1862-1912). Will o' the wasp;
        a sea yarn of the war of '12. New York: Putnam,
        1896. 269p.

        Rogers, S. L. pseud. see Rogers, John Rankin

5114   Rollins, Alice Marland (Wellington). The story of a
        ranch. New York: Cassell, 1885. 190p.
                Kansas

5115   Rollins, Philip Ashton (1869-1950). Jinglebob; a true
        story of a real cowboy. New York: Scribner's, 1927.
        262p.
                Standard reference on legendary America--cf.
        Adams' Log of Cowboy.

5116   ---Gone haywire; two tenderfoots on the montana cattle
        range in 1886. New York: Scribner's, 1940. 269p.
                Based on personal experience.

5117   Root, Corwin. An american, sir; a novel. New York:
        Dutton, 1940. 383p.
                War of 1812--Romance.

5118   Roripaugh, Robert A.. Honor thy father. New York:
        Morrow, 1963. 287p.
                Western Heritage Wrangler Award for Outstanding
        Western Novel-1964.

5119   Rosenholtz, Jennie. Upon thy doorpost. New York:

397

Bloch, 1936. 167p.
Wisconsin--Pioneering settlement--Jewish family.

5120 Ross, Clinton. The scarlet coat. New York: Stone, 1896. 309p.
Yorktown

5121 ---pseud. Robe, Captain. Chalmette; the history of the adventures and love affairs of captain robe before and during the battle of new orleans. written by himself. Philadelphia: Lippincott, 1898. 264p.

5122 Ross, Lillian Bos (1898-). The stranger; a novel of the big spur. New York: Morrow, 1942. 282p.
First novel--First year of married life--Kansas girl and rancher--1870 to Monterey area of California.

5123 ---Blaze allan. New York: Morrow, 1944. 281p.
Sequel to The Stranger--Big Sur, California--1890's--Romance--Frontier.

5124 Ross, Margaret Isabel (1897-). Kaga's brother; a story of the chippewas. New York: Harper, 1936. 221p.
Boy with expedition to Sioux and Chippewa--Trading--Sault Ste. Marie--1826--Juvenile.

5125 ---Wilderness river; adventure in the fur trapping country. New York: Harper, 1952. 214p.
Northwest Fur Company--Juvenile.

5126 Ross, Zola Helen (1912-). Bonanza queen; a novel of the comstock lode. Indianapolis: Bobbs, 1949. 358p.
Virginia City, Nevada--Silver boom.

5127 ---Reno crescent. Indianapolis: Bobbs, 1951. 299p.
Nevada--1860's covered wagon--Newspaper--Sheep ranch--Saloon--cf. Bess Aldrich.

5128 ---The green land. Indianapolis: Bobbs, 1952. 287p.
Pacific northwest--Northern Pacific Railroad to Portland.

5129 ---Cassy scandal; a novel. Indianapolis: Bobbs, 1954. 278p.
Seattle--1800's--Fire--Race riots.

Ross, Zola Helen see McDonald, Mrs. Lucile (Saunders) jt. author

5130 Rounds, Glen. Pay dirt. New York: Holiday, 1938. 149p.
Black Hills--Mining--Tall tale.

5131　Rowland, Henry Cottrell (1874-1933).　Hirondelle.
　　　　New York: Harper, 1922.　321p.
　　　　　　War of 1812--Privateering.

5132　Rowson, Susanna (Haswell).　Charlotte; a tale of truth.
　　　　Philadelphia: Humphreys, 1794.　2 vols.

5133　---Reuben and rachel; or, tales of old times.　Boston:
　　　　Manning, 1798.　2 vols.

5134　---Charlotte's daughter; or, the three orphans.　a
　　　　sequel to charlotte temple.　Boston: Richardson,
　　　　1828.　184p.

5135　Royall, Anne (Newport).　The tennessean; a novel found-
　　　　ed on facts.　New Haven: Printed for Author, 1827.
　　　　372p.

5136　Royle, Edwin Milton.　The silent call.　New York:
　　　　Scribner's, 1910.　392p.
　　　　　　Sequel to Squaw Man.(Drama)

5137　Rucker, Mrs. Helen.　Cargo of brides.　Boston: Little,
　　　　1956.　459p.
　　　　　　First novel--Brides to Washington Territory--
　　　　1865 on.

5138　---The wolf tree.　Boston: Little, 1960.　307p.
　　　　　　Lumber--San Francisco family.

5139　Rud, Anthony Melville.　The second generation.　New
　　　　York: Doubleday, 1923.　318p.
　　　　　　First novel--Scandanavians in America--Farm
　　　　in Wisconsin.

5140　---The sentence of the six-gun.　New York: Doubleday,
　　　　1926.　184p.
　　　　　　Western

5141　Runbeck, Margaret Lee.　Hope of earth.　Boston: Houghton,
　　　　1947.　559p.
　　　　　　Man and wife to Illinois--Panic of 1837--
　　　　Prairie--Religion and patriotism.

5142　Runkle, Bertha Brooks (Mrs. Louis H. Bash).　The
　　　　scarlet rider.　New York: Century, 1913.　386p.
　　　　　　Romance--American Naval officer escapes from
　　　　England--Dashing--George III.

5143　Rush, William Marshall (1887-　　).　Wheat rancher.
　　　　New York: Longmans, 1946.　247p.
　　　　　　Western

5144　---pseud. Layton, Mark.　Silver spurs; the story of a
　　　　montana cattle ranch.　New York: Mill, 1947.　216p.
　　　　　　Western

399

5145 ---Red fox of the knapoo; a tale of the nez perće
      indians. New York: Longmans, 1949. 279p.
      1872-1877--Juvenile.

5146 Russ, Wilma. Quivering earth; a novel of the ever-
      glades. New York: McKay, 1952. 248p.
      1900--Girl left after Seminole raid--Raised
      by swamp derelict--Romance.

5147 Russell, John. Claudine lavalle; or, the first convict.
      The mormoness; or, the trials of mary maverick.
      Alton, Illinois: Courier, 1853. 89p.

5148 Ryals, J. V.. Yankee doodle dixie; or, love the light
      of life. an historical romance illustrative of
      life and love in old virginia country home, and
      also an explanatory account of the passions, pre-
      judices and opinions which culminated in civil war.
      Richmond, Virginia: Waddey, 1890. 532p.

5149 Ryan, Don. The warrior's path. London: Duckworth,
      1937. 303p.
      Virginia boy taken by Lenape--Pontiac.

5150 ---The devil's brigadier. New York: Coward, 1954.
      312p.
      Fictional version of two Harpe brothers--
      Loyalist father murdered by nationalists--Trail of
      vengeance--1787.

5151 Ryan, Marah Ellis (Martin) (1860-   ). A pagan of
      the alleghanies. Chicago: Rand, 1891. 297p.

5152 ---Told in the hills; a novel. Chicago: Rand, 1891.
      362p.
      Montana and Idaho.

5153 ---Squaw élouise. Chicago: Rand, 1892. 240p.
      Columbia River.

5154 ---The flute of the gods. New York: Stokes, 1909.
      338p.
      Pueblo Indians--Sixteenth century.

5155 ---The dancer of tuluum. Chicago: McClurg, 1924.
      210p.
      Yucatan Indians.

S

S.E.H. see Heald, Mrs. Darah E.

5156   Sabatini, Rafael (1875-1950). The carolinian. Boston:
       Houghton, 1925. 414p.
          American Revolution--South Carolina--Young
       rebel member of Sons of Liberty.

5157   ---Black swan. Boston: Houghton, 1932. 311p.
          Pirates--Caribbean--Spanish Main.

5158   ---Columbus; a romance. Boston: Houghton, 1942. 430p.
          Based on love of Columbus and Beatrice Enriquez.

5159   ---The gamester. Boston: Houghton, 1949. 310p.
          John Law (1671-1729)--Stock manipulation--
       1715-1720.

5160   Sabin, Edwin Legrand (1870-   ). Bar b boys; or, the
       young cow punchers. New York: Crowell, 1909. 386p.
          Western--Juvenile.

5161   ---Range and trail; or, the bar b's great drive.   New
       York: Crowell, 1910. 445p.
          Western--Juvenile.

5162   ---The circle k; or, fighting for the flock.   New York:
       Crowell, 1911. 305p.
          Western--Juvenile.

5163   ---Old four-toes; or, hunters of the peaks.   New York:
       Crowell, 1912. 350p.
          Juvenile

5164   ---With carson and frémont; being the adventures, in
       the years 1842-'43-'44, on trail over mountains and
       through deserts from the east of the rockies to the
       west of the sierras, of scout christopher carson and
       lieutenant john charles frémont, leading their brave
       company including the boy oliver. Philadelphia:
       Lippincott, 1912. 301p.
          Juvenile

5165   ---On the plains with custer; the western life and
       deeds of the chief with the yellow hair, under whom
       served boy bugler ned fletcher, when in the troublous
       years 1866-1876 the fighting seventh cavalry helped
       to win pioneer kansas, nebraska, and dakota for white
       civilization and today's peace. Philadelphia:

401

Lippincott, 1913. 308p.
Juvenile

5166 ---Treasure mountain; or, the young prospectors. New
       York: Crowell, 1913. 294p.
       Juvenile

5167 ---Buffalo bill and the overland trail; being the story
       of how boy and man worked hard and played hard to
       blaze the white trail, by wagon train, stage coach
       and pony express, across the great plains and the
       mountains beyond, that the american republic might
       expand and flourish. Philadelphia: Lippincott,
       1914. 384p.
       Juvenile

5168 ---Kit carson days, 1809-1868. Chicago: McClurg, 1914.
       669p.
       Juvenile

5169 ---Scarface ranch; or, the young homesteaders. New
       York: Crowell, 1914. 297p.
       Juvenile

5170 ---Gold seekers of '49. Philadelphia: Lippincott, 1915.
       335p.
       Juvenile

5171 ---The boy settler; or, terry in the west. New York:
       Crowell, 1916. 301p.
       Juvenile

5172 ---With sam houston in texas; a boy volunteer in the
       texas struggles for independence, when in the years
       1835-1836 the texas colonists threw off the unjust
       rule of mexico, and by heroic deeds established
       under the guidance of the bluff sam houston, their
       own free republic which today is the great lone star
       state. Philadelphia: Lippincott, 1916. 319p.
       Juvenile

5173 ---The great pike's peak rush; or, terry in the new
       gold fields. New York: Crowell, 1917. 253p.
       Juvenile

5174 ---General crook and the fighting apaches, treating
       also of the part borne by jimmie dunn in the days
       1871-1886. Philadelphia: Lippincott, 1918. 301p.
       Juvenile

5175 ---On the overland stage; or, terry as a king cub.
       New York: Crowell, 1918. 293p.
       Juvenile

5176 ---Lost with lieutenant pike. Philadelphia: Lippincott,
       1919. 314p.

Juvenile

5177 ---Opening the iron trail; or, terry as a "vipay" man. New York: Crowell, 1919. 273p.
Juvenile

5178 ---Into mexico with general scott. Philadelphia: Lippincott, 1920. 316p.
Juvenile

5179 ---Desert dust. Philadelphia: Jacobs, 1922. 313p.
Juvenile

5180 ---The rose of santa fé. Philadelphia: Jacobs, 1923. 309p.
Juvenile

5181 ---The city of the sun. Philadelphia: Jacobs, 1924. 316p.
Juvenile

5182 ---With george washington into the wilderness. Philadelphia: Lippincott, 1924. 297p.
Juvenile

5183 ---White indian. Philadelphia: Jacobs, 1925. 320p.
Juvenile

5184 ---Rio bravo; a romance of the texas frontier. Philadelphia: Macrae, 1926. 334p.
Juvenile

5185 ---In the ranks of old hickory, when with the western riflemen in defence against attack from within and without, young and old of all degrees united under andrew jackson to make the republic's borders safe. Philadelphia: Lippincott, 1927. 351p.
Juvenile

5186 ---"Old" jim bridger on the moccasin trail; a tale of the beaver west and of the men who opened the mountains. New York: Crowell, 1928. 316p.
Juvenile

5187 ---Klondike pardners; where in are told the haps and mishaps of two fortune-seekers who in the klondike stampede hit the trail of rain and mud, snow and ice, mountains, lakes and rivers, for six hundred miles so that rainbow's end in a frozen land of "gold is where you find it" if you don't quit first. Philadelphia: Lippincott, 1929. 286p.
Juvenile

5188 ---Mississippi river boy. Philadelphia: Lippincott, 1932. 317p.
Juvenile

5189 Sabran, Jean (1908-   ) pseud. Deleuze, Bernard.
      The vengeance of don manuel. New York: Putnam,
      1952. 314p.
          Chile--1811--Spanish colonial era--French
      prize Prix de Lecteurs.

5190 St. Clair, A. S.. Senora ines; or, the american vol-
      unteers. a tale of the mexican wars. Boston:
      Gleason, 1848. 100p.
          Romance

5191 Safford, Henry Barnard (1883-1956). That bennington
      mob. New York: Messner, 1935. 303p.
          1777--Action leading to Battle of Bennington--
      Green Mountain Boys.

5192 ---Mr. madison's war. New York: Messner, 1936. 316p.
          War of 1812--From view of Vermont boy--Romance.

5193 ---Tristam bent. New York: Coward, 1940. 311p.
          Englishman raised in Holland--Spy on Dutch in
      New World--1632 and after.

5194 ---Tory tavern. New York: Penn, 1942. 389p.
          American Revolution--Espionage--Son of Tory
      family for patriots.

5195 Sage, William (1864-   ). Maid of old virginia; a
      romance of bacon's rebellion. New York: Revell,
      1915. 367p.
          1676--Romance--Melodrama.

5196 The salem belle; a tale of 1692. [Anonymous]. Boston:
      Tappan, 1842. 238p.
          Witchcraft

5197 Salem witchcraft; or, the adventures of parson handy,
      from punkapog pond. [Anonymous]. New York: Bliss,
      1875. 71p.

5198 Saltzman, Eleanor. Ever tomorrow. New York: Coward,
      1936. 309p.
          Chronicle--Three generations--German-American
      farmer--Southern Iowa.

5199 Sandburg, Carl (1878-1967). Remembrance rock. New
      York: Harcourt, 1948. 1067p.
          Chronicle--From Pilgrims into nineteenth century.

5200 Sanders, Charles Wesley. Ten thousand dollars reward.
      New York: Garden City Pub., 1924. 116p.
          Western

5201 ---Trouble range. New York: Watt, 1925. 304p.
          Western

404

5202 ---The avenger. New York: Watt, 1926. 302p.
      Western

5203 ---The crimson trail. New York: Watt, 1927. 314p.
      Western

5204 ---Riders of the oregon. New York: King, 1932. 256p.
      Western

5205 ---Blotted brands. New York: King, 1933. 282p.
      Western

5206 ---The lone fighter; mournful martin makes his bow.
      New York: King, 1933. 287p.
      Western

5207 ---Killer's code. New York: King, 1934. 290p.
      Western

5208 ---Mournful martin. London: Collins, 1937. 252p.
      Western

5209 Sanders, Jacquin. The fortune finders. New York:
      Appleton, 1956. 246p.
      Vermont farmer to Nevada--Gold rush.

      "Sandette" pseud. see Walsh, Marie A.

5210 Sandoz, Mari (1907-1966). Slogum house. Boston: Little,
      1937. 400p.
      Pioneering days in Nebraska--One of best writers
      in this area--Brutal book.

5211 ---The tom walker; a new novel. New York: Dial, 1947.
      372p.
      Chronicle--Three generations--Midwestern life--
      1860's-1940's.

5212 ---Winter thunder. Philadelphia: Westminister, 1954.
      61p.
      Juvenile

5213 ---Miss morissa, doctor of the gold trail; a novel.
      New York: McGraw, 1955. 249p.
      Woman doctor--North Platte Region--cf. Cather's,
      Archbishop--1870's.

5214 ---The horse catcher. Philadelphia: Westminister,
      1957. 192p.
      Young Cheyenne's struggle to be non-warrior
      in warrior tribe--Superb.

5215 ---Son of the gamblin' man; the youth of an artist.
      a novel. New York: Potter, 1960. 333p.
      John Jackson Cozad--Robert Henri (1865-1929)--
      Founder of Cozad, Nebraska.

5216 Sanford, Ezekiel. The humours of eutopia; a tale of
      colonial times. [Anonymous]. Philadelphia: Carey,
      1828. 2 vols.

5217 Sanford, John B.. Seventy times seven; a novel. New
      York: Knopf, 1939. 195p.
          Upstate New York farmer--Murder.

5218 Santee, Ross (1889-1965). Sleepy black; the story of
      a horse. New York: Farrar, 1933. 250p.
          Western

5219 ---The bubbling spring. New York: Scribner's, 1949.
      300p.
          West and western life--Post-Civil War Era.

5220 ---Rusty, a cowboy of the old west. New York: Scribner's,
      1950. 240p.
          Western

5221 ---Hard rock and silver sage. New York: Scribner's,
      1951. 224p.
          Arizona--1910--Very good.

5222 ---Lost pony tracks. New York: Scribner's, 1953. 303p.
          Boy wrangler--Cowboy frontier life--Semi-fiction.

5223 Saratoga; a tale of the revolution. [Anonymous].
      Boston: Cummings, 1825. 2 vols.
          Romance

5224 Sass, Herbert Ravenel. War drums. New York: Double-
      day, 1928. 293p.
          English girl to colonies to search for her
      lover.

5225 ---Look back to glory. Indianapolis: Bobbs, 1933.
      360p.
          Charleston, South Carolina--Pre-Civil War.

5226 ---Emperor brims. New York: Doubleday, 1941. 312p.
          South Carolina--1715--Creeks and uprising.

5227 Saunders, Anna M., by A Daughter of Nebraska. Golden-
      Rod; a story of the west. Lincoln, Nebraska:
      Golden-Rod Pub., 1896. 134p.
          Romance

5228 Savage, Elizabeth. Summer of pride; a novel. Boston:
      Little, 1961. 308p.
          Modern day ranch life--Family story.

5229 Savage, Les. Treasure of the brasada. New York:
      Simon, 1947. 238p.
          Western

406

5230   ---The doctor at coffin gap.   New York: Doubleday,
        1949. 219p.
          Western

5231   ---The hide rustlers.   New York: Doubleday, 1950. 219p.
          Western

5232   ---The wild horse.   New York: Fawcett, 1950. 153p.
          Western

5233   ---Land of the lawless.   New York: Doubleday, 1951.
        192p.
          Western

5234   ---Shadow riders of the yellowstone.   New York: Double-
        day, 1951. 220p.
          Western

5235   ---Outlaw thickets.   New York: Doubleday, 1952. 192p.
          Western

5236   ---Last of the breed.   New York: Dell, 1954. 192p.
          Western

5237   ---Silver street woman.   New York: Hanover, 1954. 351p.
          Western

5238   ---Teresa.   New York: Dell, 1954. 256p.
          Western

5239   ---The phantom stallion.   New York: Dodd, 1955. 178p.
          Western

5240   ---Return to warbow; an original western.   New York:
        Dell, 1955. 159p.
          Western

5241   ---Hangtown.   New York: Ballantine, 1956. 155p.
          Western

5242   ---Once a fighter.   New York: Pocket, 1956. 150p.
          Western

5243   ---The royal city.   New York: Hanover, 1956. 381p.
          Santa Fe--Pueblo Revolt--1680--Death march.

5244   ---Beyond wind river.   New York: Doubleday, 1958. 192p.
          Western

5245   ---Doniphan's ride.   New York: Doubleday, 1959. 236p.
          First Missouri Volunteers--Mexican War.

5246   ---pseud. Stewart, Logan.   War bonnet pass.   New York:
        Fawcett, 1950. 164p.
          Western

5247 Savage, Thomas. The pass. New York: Doubleday, 1944.
269p.
Western

5248 ---Lona hanson. New York: Simon, 1948. 306p.
Western

5249 Sayers, James Denson. Eagle trail. New York: Bouregy,
1951. 255p.
Western

5250 ---pseud. Bardwell, Denver. Gun-smoke in sunset valley.
New York: Godwin, 1935. 288p.
Western

5251 ---Killers on the diamond a. New York: Godwin, 1935.
278p.
Western

5252 ---Beyond midnight chasm. New York: Godwin, 1936.
277p.
Western

5253 ---Rancho bonita. New York: Godwin, 1936. 282p.
Western

5254 ---Rivers westward. New York: Hillman, 1939. 272p.
Western

5255 ---Coyote hunter. New York: Doubleday, 1940. 277p.
Western

5256 ---Prairie fire. New York: Doubleday, 1940. 274p.
Western

5257 ---Calamity at devil's crossing. New York: Bouregy,
1952. 255p.
Western

5258 ---pseud. James, Dan. Gun thunder on the rio. New
York: Godwin, 1935. 295p.
Western

5259 ---Rustlers on the smoky trail. New York: Godwin,
1936. 287p.
Western

5260 ---Stranger at storm ranch. New York: Godwin, 1936.
281p.
Western

5261 ---West of the sunset. New York: Hillman, 1939. 287p.
Western

5262 ---Trouble at choctaw bend. New York: Bouregy, 1952.
255p.
Western

5263 ---Shadow guns. New York: Avalon, 1953. 254p.
           Western

5264 ---Gunsmoke mesa. New York: Avalon, 1955. 253p.
           Western

5265 Scarborough, Dorothy (1878-1935). In the land of
           cotton. New York: Macmillan, 1923. 370p.
              First novel--Tyranny of King Cotton--Plan-
           tation contrasted with tenant farmer.

5266 ---The wind. New York: Harper, 1926. 337p.
              Virginia girl to Texas plains--Portest against
           hardship.

5267 ---Can't get a red bird. New York: Harper, 1929.
           408p.
              Texas--Cotton farmer--Homestead law--Farm
           organizations.

5268 ---The stretchberry-smile. Indianapolis: Bobbs, 1932.
           326p.
              Early attack on tenant farming.

5269 Schachner, Nathan. The king's passenger. Philadelphia:
           Lippincott, 1942. 413p.
              Bacon's Rebellion--Virginia--1676--cf. Scrugg's
           Man Cannot Tell.

5270 ---The sun shines west. New York: Appleton, 1943.
           508p.
              "Bleeding Kansas"--1854-1861.

5271 Schaefer, Jack Warner (1907-   ). Shane. Boston:
           Houghton, 1949. 214p.
              Western--Homestead--Wyoming--cf. Wister's
           Virginian.

5272 ---Company of cowards. Boston: Houghton, 1951. 203p.
              New Mexico frontier--Post-Civil War.

5273 ---The canyon. Boston: Houghton, 1953. 132p.
              Cheyenne--Little Bear--Legendary story.

5274 ---Old ramon. Boston: Houghton, 1960. 102p.
              Boy to learn sheepherding.

5275 ---Monte walsh. Boston: Houghton, 1963. 501p.
           Western

5276 ---Mavericks. Boston: Houghton, 1967. 184p.
              Old cowboy tells of mustangs.

5277 ---The short novels of jack schaefer. Boston: Houghton,
           1967. 525p.

Shane--First Blood--The Canyon--The Kean Land--
Company of Cowards.

Schary, Dory jt. author, see Lewis, [Harry] Sinclair

5278   Schindall, Henry. Let spring come. New York: Appleton,
        1953. 311p.
        American Revolution--Young Virginian during
        first year.

5279   Schisgall, Oscar (1901-   ) pseud. Cole, Jackson.
        Gun justice. New York: Watt, 1933. 288p.
        Western

5280   ---The ramblin' kid. New York: Watt, 1933. 286p.
        Western

5281   ---The outlaws of caja basin. New York: Watt, 1934.
        256p.
        Western

5282   ---The cholla kid. New York: Watt, 1935. 256p.
        Western

5283   ---The outlaw trail. New York: Watt, 1935. 255p.
        Western

5284   ---Black gold; a story of the texas rangers. New York:
        Caslon, 1936. 254p.
        Western

5285   ---Six gun stampede. New York: Dodge, 1937. 252p.
        Western

5286   ---Lone star law. New York: Mill, 1939. 256p.
        Western

5287   ---Lone star silver. New York: Mill, 1939. 256p.
        Western

5288   ---Lone star legion. New York: Mill, 1940. 243p.
        Western

5289   ---Lone star terror. New York: Mill, 1940. 256p.
        Western

5290   ---Lone star treasure. New York: Arcadia, 1944. 255p.
        Western

5291   ---The valley of revenge. New York: Arcadia, 1944.
        256p.
        Western

5292   ---The frontier legion. New York: Arcadia, 1945.
        256p.
        Western

5293 ---Haunted valley. New York: Arcadia, 1945. 256p.
        Western

5294 ---The devil's legion. New York: Arcadia, 1946. 255p.
        Western

5295 ---pseud. Hardy, Stuart. The man from nowhere. New
        York: Macaulay, 1935. 253p.
        Western

5296 ---Arizona justice. New York: Green Circle, 1936.
        254p.
        Western

5297 ---Montana bound. New York: Green Circle, 1936. 251p.
        Western

5298 ---The mountains are my kingdom. New York: Green Circle,
        1937. 253p.
        Western

5299 ---The miracle at gopher creek. New York: Green Circle,
        1938. 243p.
        Western

5300 ---Trouble from texas. New York: Macaulay, 1938. 253p.
        Western

5301 Schlytter, Leslie. The tall brothers. New York:
        Appleton, 1941. 449p.
        Wisconsin--Lumbering.

5302 Schmidt, Mrs. Sarah Lindsay. New land; a novel for
        boys and girls. New York: McBride, 1933. 317p.
        Wyoming--1930's--Morgan twins--Juvenile.

5303 ---Ranching on eagle eve. New York: McBride, 1936.
        374p.
        Ranch in Rockies--Future farmers of America--
        Juvenile.

5304 ---The secret of silver peak. New York: Random, 1938.
        334p.
        Girl and goat ranch--Juvenile.

5305 ---Shadow over winding ranch. New York: Random, 1940.
        298p.
        Colorado ranch--Juvenile.

5306 Schofield, William Greenough (1909-   ). Ashes in
        the wilderness; a novel. Philadelphia: Macrae,
        1942. 317p.
        Roger Williams--King Philip's War (1675-1676)--
        Based on diary of Captain Benjamin Church--Romance.

411

5307   Schoonover, Lawrence L.. The revolutionary. Boston:
       Little, 1958. 495p.
          John Paul Jones (1747-1792)--Good.

5308   ---Key of gold; a novel. Boston: Little, 1968.   279p.
          Jewish family--House of Baruch--Granada (1492)
       to New World--Doctors--1400-1600--Episodic.

5309   Schoonover, Shirley. Mountain of winter; a novel.
       New York: Coward, 1964.   256p.
          First novel--Set in Finnish enclave in timber-
       land of upper middlewest.

5310   Schorer, Mark (1908-   ). A house too old. New York:
       Reynal, 1935.   305p.
          Saga--Wisconsin town--1835-1935--Established
       by two Hungarian noblemen.

5311   Schrag, Otto. The locusts. [Trans. from German by
       Winston, Richard]. New York: Farrar, 1943.   565p.
          Pioneer life--Utah and Kansas--1870's--Mormons--
       Mennonites--Mining--Locusts.

       Schreiner, Tin pseud. see Broderick, Therese

5312   Schultz, James Willard (1859-   ). With the indians
       in the rockies. Boston: Houghton, 1912.   227p.
          Boy's adventures--Uncle fur trader--Head of
       Missouri River with Blackfeet.

5313   ---The quest of the fish-dog skin. Boston: Houghton,
       1913.   218p.
          Juvenile

5314   ---On the warpath. Boston: Houghton, 1914.   244p.
          Juvenile

5315   ---The gold cache. Boston: Houghton, 1917.   189p.
          Juvenile

5316   ---Lone bull's mistake; a lodge pole chief story.
       Boston: Houghton, 1918.   207p.
          Indian "man without country".

5317   ---Running eagle the warrior girl. Boston: Houghton,
       1919.   311p.
          Juvenile

5318   ---The dreadful river cave; chief black elk's story.
       Boston: Houghton, 1920.   243p.
          Juvenile

5319   ---In the great apache forest; the story of a lone
       boy scout. Boston: Houghton, 1920.   224p.
          Juvenile

412

5320 ---The war trail fort; further adventures of thomas fox and pitamakan. Boston: Houghton, 1921. 192p.
Juvenile

5321 ---Seizer of eagles. Boston: Houghton, 1922. 229p.
Juvenile

5322 ---The trail of the spanish horse. Boston: Houghton, 1922. 212p.
Juvenile

5323 ---The-danger trail. Boston: Houghton, 1923. 295p.
Juvenile

5324 ---Plumed snake medicine. Boston: Houghton, 1924. 244p.
Juvenile

5325 ---Sahtaki and i. Boston: Houghton, 1924. 305p.
Juvenile

5326 ---Questers of the desert. Boston: Houghton, 1925. 224p.
Juvenile

5327 ---Sun woman; a novel. Boston: Houghton, 1926. 244p.
Romance--Blackfoot.

5328 ---William jackson indian scout; his true story told by his friends. Boston: Houghton, 1926. 200p.
Juvenile

5329 ---Red crow's brother; hugh monroe's story of his second year on the plains. Boston: Houghton, 1927. 208p.
Juvenile

5330 ---A son of the navahos. Boston: Houghton, 1927. 200p.
Juvenile

5331 ---In enemy country. Boston: Houghton, 1928. 234p.
Juvenile

5332 ---Skull head the terrible. Boston: Houghton, 1929. 207p.
Juvenile

5333 ---The white beaver. Boston: Houghton, 1930. 272p.
Juvenile

5334 ---Alder gulch gold. Boston: Houghton, 1931. 147p.
Juvenile

5335 ---Friends and foes in the rockies. Boston: Houghton, 1933. 174p.
Juvenile

413

5336   ---Gold dust. Boston: Houghton, 1934. 244p.
        Juvenile

5337   ---The white-buffalo robe. Boston: Houghton, 1936.
        221p.
        Juvenile

5338   ---Stained gold. Boston: Houghton, 1937. 217p.
        Juvenile

5339   ---Short bow's big medicine. Boston: Houghton, 1940.
        201p.
        Juvenile

5340   Schumann, Mrs. Mary. Strife before dawn. New York:
        Dial, 1939. 440p.
                Fort Pitt menaced by Pontiac--Quakers--Simon
        Girty--Logan--Clark--Dunmore's War.

5341   ---My blood and my treasure. New York: Dial, 1941.
        439p.
                Oliver Perry (1785-1819)--War of 1812.

5342   Schuyler, Montgomery. The pioneer church; or, the
        story of a new parish in the west. New York: Hurd,
        1867. 211p.

5343   Scoggins, Charles Elbert. White fox. Indianapolis:
        Bobbs, 1928. 170p.
                Last of Aztecs plays part of Montezuma.

        Scott, Alexander Leslie see Scott, Leslie

        Scott, Bradford pseud. see Scott, Leslie

5344   Scott, Mrs. Evelyn (1893-   ). Migrations; an ara
        besque in history. New York: Boni, 1927. 337p.
                Tennessean to California gold fields--Moral
        novel.

5345   Scott, John Reed (1869-   ). The imposter; a tale of
        old annapolis. Philadelphia: Lippincott, 1910. 330p.
                Romance of colonial days.

5346   Scott, Mrs. Lena Becker. Dawn boy of the pueblos.
        Philadelphia: Winston, 1935. 198p.
                Young silversmith--Zuni--Pueblo--cf. Armer's
        Waterless Mountain.

5347   Scott, Leslie (1893-1950). Longhorn empire. New York:
        Arcadia, 1954. 221p.
        Western

5348   ---The desert rider. New York: Arcadia, 1955. 223p.
        Western

5349 ---The trail builders. New York: Arcadia, 1956. 223p.
Western

5350 ---Boothill town. New York: Arcadia, 1957
224p.
Western

5351 ---Panhandle pioneer. New York: Arcadia, 1957. 223p.
Western

5352 ---Tombstone showdown. New York: Arcadia, 1957. 223p.
Western

5353 ---Lone star cowboy. New York: Arcadia, 1959. 220p.
Western

5354 ---Brant of texas. New York: Arcadia, 1960. 224p.
Western

5355 ---Deadline for sheriffs. New York: Arcadia, 1960.
223p.
Western

5356 ---Showdown trail. New York: Arcadia, 1960. 224p.
Western

5357 ---pseud. Cole, Jackson. Lone star law. New York:
Mill, 1939. 256p.
Western

5358 ---Lone star silver. New York: Mill, 1939. 256p.
Western

5359 ---Haunted valley. New York: Arcadia, 1945. 256p.
Western

5360 ---Gun-blaze; a jim hatfield western. New York: Pyramid,
1955. 127p.
Western

5361 ---pseud. Leslie, A.. Arizona ranger courage. New
York: Gateway, 1942. 256p.
Western

5362 ---Phantom riders. New York: Arcadia, 1945. 256p.
Western

5363 ---The border raiders. New York: Arcadia, 1946. 256p.
Western

5364 ---Iron men and gold. New York: Arcadia, 1946. 224p.
Western

5365 ---pseud. Scott, Bradford. Guns of silver valley.
New York: Dodge, 1937. 253p.
Western

5366 ---The cow puncher. New York: Gateway, 1942. 256p.
　　　 Western

5367 ---Walters of the flying w. New York: Arcadia, 1943.
　　　 256p.
　　　 Western

5368 ---The trail herd. New York: Arcadia, 1944. 256p.
　　　 Western

5369 ---The range rider. New York: Arcadia, 1945. 256p.
　　　 Western

5370 ---Desert gold. New York: Arcadia, 1946. 256p.
　　　 Western

5371 ---Frontier doctor. New York: Arcadia, 1946. 256p.
　　　 Western

5372 ---Gold for the dead. New York: Arcadia, 1947. 224p.
　　　 Western

5373 ---Silver city. New York: Arcadia, 1953. 221p.
　　　 Western

5374 ---Dead in texas. New York: Arcadia, 1958. 222p.
　　　 Western

5375 Scott, Natalie Anderson (1900-1957). The husband.
　　　 New York: Dutton, 1949. 270p.
　　　　　 Massachusetts--1740's--Marriage and sex--Good
　　　 picture pre-Revolution America.

5376 Scott, Reva (Holdaway) (1900-   ). Samuel brannan
　　　 and the golden fleece; a biography. New York:
　　　 Macmillan, 1944. 462p.
　　　　　 Fictional biography of Mormon leader--Samuel
　　　 Brannan (1819-1889)--Reported California gold
　　　 discovery.

5377 Scowcroft, Richard. Children of the covenant. Boston:
　　　 Houghton, 1945. 292p.
　　　　　 Chronicle--Conflict of Mormon families through
　　　 generations.

5378 Scruggs, Philip Lightfoot. Man cannot tell. Indianap-
　　　 olis: Bobbs, 1942. 396p.
　　　　　 Bacon's Rebellion (1676)--Indentured servant.

Sealsfield, Charles (1793-1864) pseud. see Postl, Karl

5379 Seaman, Mrs. Augusta (Huiell) (1879-   ). Mamselle
　　　 of the wilderness; a story of la salle and his pion-
　　　 eers. New York: Sturgis, 1913. 405p.
　　　　　 La Salle--Mississippi River--Pioneering colony--
　　　 Juvenile.

Sears, Baldwin pseud. see Young, Elizabeth Guion

5380 Sears, Clara Endicott (1863-   ). The great pow-wow;
the story of the nashaway valley in king philip's war.
Boston: Houghton, 1934. 288p.
1675-1676.

5381 Sears, Edmund Hamilton. Pictures of the olden time,
as shown in the fortunes of a family of pilgrims.
Boston: Crosby, 1857. 342p.
Three tales--Domestic life.

Seatsfield, Charles pseud. see Postl, Karl

5382 Seawell, Molly Elliot. The berkeleys and their neighbors.
New York: American News, 1888. 232p.

Secondsight, Solomon pseud. see McHenry, James

Sedges, John pseud. see Buck, Pearl

5383 Sedgwick, Catharine Maria (1789-1867). The travellers;
a tale designed for young people. New York: Bliss,
1825. 171p.
Family travels--Montreal--Quebec--Niagara--New
York--Juvenile.

5384 ---Hope leslie; or, early times in massachusetts.
New York: White, 1827. 2 vols.
Domestic novel--Primitive life New England
homestead--Prolific writer.

5385 ---The linwoods; or, "sixty years since" in america.
New York: Harpers, 1835. 2 vols.
New York--New England--Sentimental romance--
Portrayal of Washington as good as Cooper's The Spy--
Her father knew Washington.

5386 Seely, Howard. A nymph of the west; a novel. New
York: Appleton, 1888. 232p.

5387 ---A border leander. New York: Appleton, 1893. 168p.

5388 Seifert, Shirley Louise (1889-   ). Land of tomorrow;
a legend of kentucky. New York: Mill, 1937. 320p.
Chronicle--Three generations--Early nineteenth
to 1930's--Virginia and Kentucky--Aristocrats.

5389 ---The wayfarer; a novel. New York: Mill, 1938. 396p.
Based on life of John Cotter of New York--To
west--1850-1870--Stock farming.

5390 ---River out of eden; a novel. New York: Mill, 1940.
432p.
French up the Mississippi River to St. Anne de
Chartres--1763--Romance.

5391 ---Waters of the wilderness; a novel. Philadelphia:
Lippincott, 1941. 523p.
George Rogers Clark (1752-1818)--Romance--
Sister of Spanish governor of St. Louis--1778-1780.

5392 ---Those who go against the current; a novel. Phil-
adelphia: Lippincott, 1943. 612p.
Manuel Lisa (1772-1820)--Opening of Missouri
River--Louisiana Purchase.

5393 ---Captain grant. Philadelphia: Lippincott, 1946.
606p.
Fiction based on early life of U. S. Grant
(1822-1885)--Ends with start of Civil War--Sympathetic

5394 ---Proud way. Philadelphia: Lippincott, 1948. 316p.
Courtship of Varina Howell and Jefferson Davis--
Natchez plantation--1843-1844.

5395 ---The turquois trail. Philadelphia: Lippincott, 1950.
409p.
Based on diary of Susan Magofin (1827-1855)--
Overland journey from Missouri to Mexico--1845.

5396 ---The three lives of elizabeth. Philadelphia: Lippincott, 1952. 287p.
Missouri frontier--1820--Washington, D. C.

5397 ---Let my name stand fair. Philadelphia: Lippincott,
1956. 414p.
American Revolution--Nathaniel Greene (1742-
1786)--Catherine Greene.

5398 ---Destiny in dallas. Philadelphia: Lippincott, 1958.
288p.
Role of Alexander and Sarah Cockrell in Dallas--
1858.

5399 Selby, John (1897-   ). Island in the corn. New York:
Rinehart, 1941. 404p.
#2 of Trilogy--Wisconsin--Fox River--1880's
and 1890's--Sequel to Elegant Journey.

5400 ---Elegant journey. New York: Rinehart, 1944. 371p.
#1 of Trilogy--Southern frees slaves--Starts
over in Wisconsin--1840's.

5401 Sellingham, Ella J. H.. The hero of carillon; or,
fort ticonderoga in 1777. Ticonderoga, New York:
Bryan, 1888. 195p.

5402 Seltzer, Charles Alden (1875-1942). The two-gun man.
New York: Outing, 1911. 349p.
Western

418

5403 ---The coming of the law. New York: Outing, 1912.
378p.
Western

5404 ---The boss of the lazy y. Chicago: McClurg, 1915.
346p.
Western

5405 ---The trail to yesterday. New York: Burt, 1915. 363p.
Western

5406 ---The range boss. Chicago: McClurg, 1916. 333p.
Western

5407 ---The vengeance of jefferson gawne. Chicago: McClurg,
1917. 344p.
Western

5408 ---"Firebrand" trevison. Chicago McClurg, 1918. 325p.
Western

5409 ---The ranchman. Chicago: McClurg, 1919. 319p.
Western

5410 ---The trail horde. Chicago: McClurg, 1920. 345p.
Western

5411 ---"Beau" rand. Chicago: McClurg, 1921. 311p.
Western

5412 ---"Drag" harlan. Chicago: McClurg, 1921. 280p.
Western

5413 ---Square deal sanderson. Chicago: McClurg, 1922.
323p.
Western

5414 ---West! New York: Century, 1922. 312p.
Western

5415 ---Brass commandments. New York: Century, 1923. 301p.
Western

5416 ---The way of the buffalo. New York: Century, 1924.
318p.
Western

5417 ---Channing comes through. New York: Century, 1925.
429p.
Western

5418 ---Last hope ranch. New York: Century, 1925. 335p.
Western

5419 ---The gentleman from virginia. New York: Doubleday,
1926. 300p.

419

Western

5420 ---<u>The valley of the stars</u>. New York: Century, 1926.
350p.
Western

5421 ---<u>Land of the free</u>. New York: Doubleday, 1927. 318p.
Western

5422 ---<u>The mesa</u>. New York: Doubleday, 1928. 293p.
Western

5423 ---<u>Mystery range</u>. New York: Doubleday, 1928. 303p.
Western

5424 ---<u>The raider</u>. New York: Doubleday, 1929. 294p.
Western

5425 ---<u>The red brand</u>. New York: Doubleday, 1929. 294p.
Western

5426 ---<u>Gone north</u>. New York: Doubleday, 1930. 298p.
Western

5427 ---<u>A son of arizona.</u> New York: Doubleday, 1931.
315p.
Western

5428 ---<u>Double cross ranch</u>. New York: Doubleday, 1932.
310p.
Western

5429 ---<u>Clear the trail</u>. New York: Doubleday, 1933. 309p.
Western

5430 ---<u>West of apache pass</u>. New York: Doubleday, 1934.
309p.
Western

5431 ---<u>Silverspurs</u>. New York: Doubleday, 1935. 277p.
Western

5432 ---<u>Kingdom in the cactus</u>. New York: Doubleday, 1936.
272p.
Western

5433 ---<u>Parade of the empty boots</u>. New York: Doubleday,
1937. 296p.
Western

5434 ---<u>Arizona jim</u>. New York: Doubleday, 1939. 279p.
Western

5435 ---<u>War on wishbone range</u>. New York: Doubleday, 1939.
303p.
Western

5436 ---Treasure ranch. New York: Doubleday, 1940. 273p.
       Western

5437 ---So long, sucker. New York: Doubleday, 1941. 276p.
       Western

5438 Serdy, Kate. Listening. New York: Viking, 1936. 157p.
       Ramapo Valley--Dutch coloniah house--1656.

5439 Service, Robert William (1874-1958). The trail of '98;
       a northland romance. New York: Dodd, 1911. 514p.

5440 Sessler, Jacob (1899-   ). Saints and tomahawks.
       New York: Pyramid, 1940. 246p.
       Pennsylvania--1736-1760--Moravian settlements.

5441 Seton, Anya (Mrs. Hamilton Chase). My theodosia.
       Boston: Houghton, 1941. 422p.
       Mrs. Theodosia (Burr) Alston (1783-1813)
       daughter of A. Burr--Love for Meriwether Lewis.

5442 ---Dragonwyck. Boston: Houghton, 1944. 336p.
       Van Ryan estate on Hudson River--New York
       City 1830-1850--Victorian melodrama.

5443 ---The turquoise. Boston: Houghton, 1946. 377p.
       Santa Fé Cameron--Daughter of Scot-Spanish
       marriage--1850's--Scenario approach.

5444 ---The hearth and the eagle. Boston: Houghton, 1948.
       464p.
       Chronicle--Marblehead, Massachusetts--Earliest
       to present.

5445 ---Foxfire. Boston: Houghton, 1950. 346p.
       Western

5446 ---The winthrop woman. Boston: Houghton, 1958. 586p.
       Elizabeth Winthrop, niece of governor--Puritan
       "Bible Commonwealth".

5447 ---Devil water. Boston: Houghton, 1962. 526p.
       Radcliffe and Byrd families--Jacobite Rebellion.

5448 Seton, William (1835-1905). Romance of the charter oak;
       a picture of colonial times. New York: O'Shea, 1871.
       2 vols in one.
       Hartford, Connecticut--Charter hidden from
       colonial governor.

5449 ---The pride of lexington; a tale of the american
       revolution. New York: O'Shea, 1874. 365p.
       Romance

421

5450   Settle, Mary Lee (Mrs. Douglas Newton). O beulah
        land; a novel. New York: Viking, 1956. 368p.
                #1 of Virginia Series--Virginia frontier--
        1754-1775--Land on Proclamation Line.

5451   ---Know nothing; a novel. New York: Viking, 1960.
        334p.
                #2 of Virginia Series--West Virginia--Pre-
        Civil War--Romance.

5452   The seven brothers of wyoming; or, the brigands of
        the revolution. [Anonymous]. New York: Long,
        1850. 114p.
                Romance

5453   Seymour, Alta Halverson. Galewood crossing. Phil-
        adelphia: Westminister, 1945. 212p.
                Pioneer story--Ohio to Wisconsin--Juvenile.

5454   Shackelford, Miss E. A. B. by E.A.B.S.. Virginia
        dare; a romance of the sixteenth century. New
        York: Whittaker, 1892. 207p.

5455   Shafer, Donald (1881-   ). Smoke fires in schoharie.
        New York: Longmans, 1938. 357p.
                Chronicle--Three generations--Palatine Germans--
        New York State--Indians--1713-1782.

5456   Shaftel, George Armin. Golden shore; a novel of the
        conquest of california. New York: Coward, 1943.
        370p.
                1840--Romance--Adventure.

        Shapiro, Herbert Arthur see Arthur, Herbert

5457   Sharon, Thomas. By a Western Man. Viola; or, life
        in the northwest...this book illustrates the peculair
        habits and customs of the people...with incidents of
        the minnesota massacre. Chicago: McCabe, 1874. 422p.

5458   Shaw, Adèle Marie and Shaw, Albert Judson. The coast
        of freedom; a romance of the adventurous times of
        the first self-made american. New York: Doubleday,
        1902. 466p.
                Sir William Phips (1651-1694)--Governor of
        Massachusetts--Witchcraft--Cotton Mather.

        Shaw, Albert Judson jt. author, see Shaw, Adèle Marie

5459   Shaw, Margaret. Inherit the earth. Indianapolis:
        Bobbs, 1940. 437p.
                Indentured girl--Whig--Revolution Era--Married
        Loyalist--To Nova Scotia--Romance.

5460   Shay, Edith (Foley) (Mrs. Frank Shay) and Smith, Katharin

                                422

The private adventure of captain shaw. Boston:
Houghton, 1945. 255p.
Cape Cod sea captain--1793.

5461 Shay, Frank (1888-   ). Pirate wench (mary read; the
      pirate wench). New York: Washburn, 1934. 329p.
      Romance

5462 Shecut, John Lewis Edward Whitridge. Ish-Noo-Ju-Lut-
      Sche; or, the eagle of the mohawks. a tale of the
      seventeenth century. New York: Stickney, 1844.
      312p.
      New York

5463 ---The scout; or, the fast of st. nicholas. a tale
      of the seventeenth century. New York: Stickney,
      1844. 312p.

5464 Shedd, George Clifford (1877-1937). The princess of
      the forge. New York: Macaulay, 1910. 356p.
      Mining camp.

5465 ---In the shadow of the hills. New York: Macaulay,
      1919. 319p.
      San Mateo, New Mexico--Irrigation.

5466 ---Rustlers of the basin. Philadelphia: Penn, 1940.
      276p.
      Western

5467 Shellabarger, Samuel (1888-   ). Captain from castile.
      Boston: Little, 1945. 632p.
      Spain and Mexico--1519-1540--Conquistadores--
      Romance.

5468 ---Lord vanity. Boston: Little, 1953. 467p.
      Europe and New World--1750-1763--Adventure and
      romance.

5469 Shelton, Jess. Hangman's song; a novel. Philadelphia:
      Chilton, 1960. 314p.
      Western frontier--Missouri--Arkansas--Pawnee
      Strip.

5470 Shepard, Odell (1884-1967) and Shepard Willard Odell
      Hold fast gaines. New York: Macmillan, 1946. 647p.
      Panorama--Hero American raised by Indian family--
      1783-1865.

5471 ---Jenkin's ear; a narrative attributed to horace
      walpole, esq.. New York: Macmillan, 1951. 474p.
      Anglo-Spanish War (1739-1748)--Epistle form--
      1739-1741.

Shepard, Willard Odell jt. author, see Shepard, Odell

5472 Shepherd, Daniel. _Saratoga; a story of 1787._ New
York: Fetridge, 1856. 400p.
Indian warfare--Hudson Valley.

5473 Sherman, Herbert LeRoy. _The king of cuba._ New York:
Neely, 1899. 326p.
Spanish-American War.

5474 Shetzline, David (1936-   ). _De Ford._ New York:
Random, 1968. 217p.
Western

5475 Shiflet, Kenneth E.. _The convenient coward._ Harris-
burg, Pennsylvania: Stackpole, 1961. 308p.
Marcus A. Reno (1835-1889)= Hero--George Custer=
Villain--Little Big Horn-1876.

5476 Shindler, Mary Stanley Bunce (Palmer) Dana _pseud._ Dana,
Mary S. B.. _Charles morton; or, the young patriot._
a tale of the american revolution. New York:
Dayton, 1843. 236p.
Romance

Shipman, Mrs. Helen (Barham) Nell Shipman jt. author,
see Putnam, George Palmer

5477 Shipman, Louis Evan. _D'Arcy of the guards; or, the_
fortunes of war. Chicago: Stone, 1899. 237p.
American Revolution.

5478 Shore, William. _The witch of spring._ New York:
Pellegrini, 1950. 348p.
New Orleans--1835--Sex--Murder--Revolution--
Magnolias.

Short, Luke _pseud._ see Glidden, Fred

Shortfield, Luke _pseud._ see Jones, John Beauchamp
(1810-1866)

5479 Shrake, Edwin. _Blessed mcgill._ New York: Doubelday,
1968. 234p.
Western

5480 Shrewder, Col. H. Clay _pseud.._ _The carpet-bagger;_
an autobiography. Washington: Polkinhorn, 1884.
236p.
Salt Lake City.

5481 Shrimpton, Charles. _The black phantom; or, woman's_
endurance. _a narrative connected with the early_
history of canada and the american revolution.
New York: Miller, 1867. 358p.

5482 Shuey, Lillian (Hinman). _David of juniper gulch;_

424

a story of the placer regions of california.
Chicago: Laird, 1894. 413p.

Shute, Nevil pseud. see Norway, Nevil Shute

Sidney, Margaret pseud. see Lothrop, Mrs. Harriet
   Mulford (Stone) (1844-   )

5483   Simms, Jeptha Root (1807-1883). The american spy;
       or, freedom's early sacrifice. a tale of the
       revolution, founded upon fact. Albany, New York:
       Munsell, 1846. 63p.
              Defense of Nathan Hale (1755-1776).

5484   Simms, William Gilmore (1806-1870). Guy rivers; a
       tale of georgia. New York: Harper, 1834. 2 vols.
              First of Border Romance--Georgia frontier--
       1820's--Hubbell, "...central figure in literature
       of the Old South".

5485   ---Yemassee; a romanace of carolina. New York: Harper,
       1835. 2 vols.
              First of Colonial Romances--Expansion seen from
       Indian perspective--South Carolina.

5486   ---The partisan. New York: Harper, 1835. 2 vols.
              First of Revolutionary Romance--Carolina scenes.

5487   ---Mellichampe; a legend of the santee. New York:
       Harper, 1836. 2 vols.
              Second of Revolution Series--Sequel to Partisan--
       South Carolina--Marion and Tarleton.

5488   ---Richard hurdes; or, the avenger of blood. Philadel-
       phia: Carey, 1838. 2 vols.
              Second of Border Series--Revised version in
       1855 as, Richard Hurdis; a tale of Alabama.

5489   ---The damsel of darien. Philadelphia: Lea, 1839.
       2 vols.
              Spanish conquest of Peru--Romance.

5490   ---Border beagles; a tale of mississippi. Philadelphia:
       Carey, 1840. 2 vols.
              Third of Border Series--Sequel to Richard Hurdis...

5491   ---The kinsmen; or, the black riders of congaree.
       a tale. Philadelphia: Lea, 1841. 2 vols.
              Third of Revolution Series--Also published
       as The Scout.

5492   ---Beauchampe; or, the kentucky tragedy. a tale of
       passion. Philadelphia: Lea, 1842. 2 vols.
              Border Series--Sequel to Charlemont....

425

5493 ---Helen halsey; or, the swamp state of conelachita.
      a tale of the borders. New York: Burgess, 1845.
      216p.
          Border Series--Appeared later as The Island
      Bride.

5494 ---The lily and the totem; or, the hugenots in florida.
      a series of sketches, picturesque and historical of
      coligni, in north america, 1562-1570. New York:
      Baker, 1850. 470p.
          Colonization--Florida, Georgia and South Carolina.

5495 ---Katherine walton; or, the rebel of dorchester. an
      historical romance of the revolution in carolina.
      Philadelphia: Hart, 1851. 186p.
          Fourth of Revolution Series--Charleston, South
      Carolina.

5496 ---As good as a comedy; or, the tennesseean's story.
      Philadelphia: Hart, 1852. 251p.
          Border Series.

5497 ---The sword and distaff; or, "fair, fat and forty".
      a story of the south at the close of the revolution.
      Charleston: Walker, 1852. 591p.
          Fifth of Revolution Series--Appeared later as
      Woodcraft.

5498 ---The forayers; or, the raid of the dog days. New
      York: Redfield, 1855. 560p.
          Sixth of Revolution Series.

5499 ---Charlemont; or, the pride of the village. a tale
      of kentucky. New York: Redfield, 1856. 447p.
          Border Series.

5500 ---Eutaw, a sequel to the forayers; or, the raid of
      the dog days; a tale of the revolution. New York:
      Redfield, 1856. 582p.
          Seventh and last of Revolution Series.

5501 ---The cassique of kiawah; a colonial romance. New
      York: Redfield, 1859. 600p.
          Colonial Series--Indian warfare in Carolinas.

5502 ---pseud. Cooper, Frank. Vasconselos; a romance of
      the new world. New York: Redfield?, 1853. 531p.?
          Colonial Series--De Soto--Florida.

5503 Simon, Mrs. Charlie May (Hogue) (Mrs. John Gould
      Fletcher) (1897-   ). Robin on the mountain.
      New York: Dutton, 1934. 178p.
          Ozark folk--Homesteading--Juvenile.

5504 ---Lost corner. New York: Dutton, 1935. 202p.
          Ozark chronicle--Juvenile.

426

5505 ---The faraway trail. New York: Dutton, 1940. 213p.
Covered wagon--Tennessee to Arkansas--1850's.

5506 ---Younger brother; a cherokee indian tale. New York:
Dutton, 1942. 182p.
Juvenile

5507 ---Joe mason, apprentice to audubon. New York: Dutton,
1946. 215p.
Mississippi River--Cincinnati to New Orleans--
1820--Juvenile.

5508 Simons, Katherine Drayton Mayrant (1892-   ) pseud.
Mayrant, Drayton. The red doe. New York: Appleton,
1953. 278p.
American Revolution--Juvenile.

5509 ---Always a river. New York: Appleton, 1956. 282p.
Puritan school teacher to Carolina--Romance--
1695.

5510 ---The land beyond the tempest. New York: Coward,
1960. 282p.
Bermuda and Jamestown--Early years--Somer's
squadron heading for Virginia--Wrecked on Bermuda.

5511 Simonsen, Sigurd Jay (1891-   ). Among the sourdoughs.
New York: Fortuny's, 1940. 153p.
Mining

5512 ---The clodhopper. New York: Fortuny's, 1940. 146p.
Danes to Minnesota.

5513 ---The mongrels. New York: Diana, 1946. 238p.
Sandville, Minnesota--1885--Development of
community to 1929.

5514 Simpson, Charles H.. Life in the far west; or, a
dectective's adventures among the indians and the
outlaws of montana. Chicago: Rhodes, 1896. 264p.
Romance

5515 ---Life in the mines; or, crime avenged; including
thrilling adventures among the miners and outlaws.
Chicago: Rhodes, 1898. 343p.

Sims, John pseud. see Hopson, William L.

5516 Sims, Mrs. Marian (McCamy) (1899-   ). Beyond
surrender; a novel. Philadelphia: Lippincott,
1942. 492p.
South Carolina--Reconstruction.

5517 Sinclair, Mrs. Bertha (Muzzy) (1874-1940) pseud.
Bower, B. M.. Chip of the flying u. New York:

427

Dillingham, 1906. 264p.
Western

5518 ---Her prairie knight, and rowdy of the "cross 1".
New York: Dillingham, 1907. 314p.
Western--Reissued as Range Dwellers.

5519 ---The lure of the dim trails. New York: Dillingham,
1907. 210p.
Western

5520 ---The range dwellers. New York: Dillingham, 1907.
265p.
Western

5521 ---The lonesome trail. New York: Dillingham, 1909.
297p.
Western

5522 ---The long shadow. New York: Dillingham, 1909. 320p.
Western

5523 ---The happy family. New York: Dillingham, 1910.
310p.
Western

5524 ---Good indian. Boston: Little, 1912. 372p.
Western

5525 ---Lonesome land. Boston: Little, 1912. 322p.
Western

5526 ---The gringos; a story of old california days in 1849.
Boston: Little, 1913. 350p.
Western

5527 ---The uphill climb. Boston: Little, 1913. 283p.
Western

5528 ---Flying u ranch. New York: Dillingham, 1914. 260p.
Western

5529 ---The ranch at the wolverine. Boston: Little, 1914.
356p.
Western

5530 ---The flying u's last stand. Boston: Little, 1915.
353p.
Western

5531 ---Jean of the lazy a. Boston: Little, 1915. 322p.
Western

5532 ---The heritage of the sioux. Boston: Little, 1916.
312p.
Western

428

5533 ---The phantom herd. Boston: Little, 1916. 325p.
Western

5534 ---The lookout man. Boston: Little, 1917. 321p.
Western

5535 ---Starr, of the desert. Boston: Little, 1917. 312p.
Western

5536 ---Cabin fever; a novel. Boston: Little, 1918. 290p.
Western

5537 ---Skyrider. Boston: Little, 1918. 317p.
Western

5538 ---Rim o' the world. Boston: Little, 1919. 349p.
Western

5539 ---The thunder bird. Boston: Little, 1919. 317p.
Western

5540 ---The quirt. Boston: Little, 1920. 298p.
Western

5541 ---Casey ryan. Boston: Little, 1921. 242p.
Western

5542 ---Cow country. Boston: Little, 1921. 249p.
Western

5543 ---The trail of the white mule. Boston: Little, 1922.
278p.
Western

5544 ---The parowan bonanza. Boston: Little, 1923. 305p.
Western

5545 ---The voice at johnnywater. Boston: Little, 1923.
300p.
Western

5546 ---The bellehelen mine. Boston: Little, 1924. 308p.
Western

5547 ---The eagle's wing; a story of the colorado. Boston:
Little, 1924. 296p.
Western

5548 ---Desert brew. Boston: Little, 1925. 311p.
Western

5549 ---Meadowlark basin. Boston: Little, 1925. 302p.
Western

5550 ---Black thunder. Boston: Little, 1926. 312p.
Western

5551 ---Van Patten. Boston: Little, 1926. 289p.
Western

5552 ---The adam chaser. Boston: Little, 1927. 274p.
Western

5553 ---White wolves. Boston: Little, 1927. 297p.
Western

5554 ---Hay-wire. Boston: Little, 1928. 306p.
Western

5555 ---Points west. Boston: Little, 1928. 325p.
Western

5556 ---Rodeo. Boston: Little, 1929. 309p.
Western

5557 ---The swallow fork bulls. Boston: Little, 1929.
317p.
Western

5558 ---Fool's goal. Boston: Little, 1930. 308p.
Western

5559 ---Tiger eye. Boston: Little, 1930. 293p.
Western

5560 ---Dark horse; a story of the flying u. Boston: Little,
1931. 286p.
Western

5561 ---The long loop. Boston: Little, 1931. 274p.
Western

5562 ---Laughing water. Boston: Little, 1932. 290p.
Western

5563 ---Rocking arrow. Boston: Little, 1932. 310p.
Western

5564 ---Open land. Boston: Little, 1933. 304p.
Western

5565 ---Trails meet. Boston: Little, 1933. 292p.
Western

5566 ---The whoop-up trail. Boston: Little, 1933. 308p.
Western

5567 ---The flying u strikes. Boston: Little, 1934. 304p.
Western

5568 ---The haunted hills. Boston: Little, 1934. 290p.
Western

5569   ---The dry ridge gang. Boston: Little, 1935. 294p.
        Western

5570   ---Trouble rides the wind. Boston: Little, 1935.
        299p.
        Western

5571   ---Five furies of leaning ladder. Boston: Little,
        1936. 301p.
        Western

5572   ---Shadow mountain. Boston: Little, 1936. 295p.
        Western

5573   ---The north wind do blow. Boston: Little, 1937.
        295p.
        Western

5574   ---Pirates of the range. Boston: Little, 1937. 275p.
        Western

5575   ---The wind blows west. Boston: Little, 1938. 288p.
        Western

5576   ---The singing hill. Boston: Little, 1939. 299p.
        Western

5577   ---A starry night. Boston: Little, 1939. 313p.
        Western

5578   ---Man on horseback. Boston: Little, 1940. 295p.
        Western

5579   ---The spirit of the range. Boston: Little, 1940.
        302p.
        Western

5580   ---Sweet grass. Boston: Little, 1940. 295p.
        Western

5581   ---The family failing. Boston: Little, 1941. 305p.
        Western

5582   ---Border vengeance. New York: Bouregy, 1951. 255p.
        Western

5583   ---Outlaw moon. New York: Bouregy, 1952. 255p.
        Western

5584   Sinclair, Bertrand William (1878-   ). Raw gold;
        a novel. New York: Dillingham, 1908. 311p.
        Western

5585   ---The land of the frozen suns; a novel. New York:
        Dillingham, 1910. 309p.
        Western

5586 ---Big timber; a story of the northwest. Boston:
Little, 1916. 321p.
Western

5587 ---North of fifty-three. Boston: Little, 1916. 345p.
Western

5588 ---Burned bridges. Boston: Little, 1919. 308p.
Cree Indians.

5589 ---Wild west. Boston: Little, 1926. 288p.
Western

5590 ---Gunpowder lightning. Boston: Little, 1930. 298p.
Western

5591 Sinclair, Harold (1907-   ). American years; a novel.
New York: Doubleday, 1938. 411p.
Chronicle--Thirty years--Illinois town--First
settler to A. Lincoln era.

5592 ---The years of growth 1861-1893. New York: Doubleday,
1940. 415p.
Illinois town--1861-1893.

5593 ---Westward the tide. New York: Doubleday, 1940. 359p.
George Rogers Clark--Vincennes and Ft. Pitt--
cf. Lancaster's, Big Knives.

5594 ---The horse soldiers. New York: Harper, 1956. 336p.
Civil War--West.

5595 ---The cavalryman. New York: Harper, 1958. 342p.
Western--Sequel to Horse Soldiers.

5596 Sinclair, John L. (1902-   ). In time of harvest.
New York: Macmillan, 1943. 226p.
Family from Oklahoma to New Mexico--Homestead-
ing--Dirt farming southwest.

5597 ---Death in the claimshack. Denver: Sage, 1947. 133p.
Western

5598 Singmaster, Elsie (Mrs. Harold Lewars) (1879-1958).
The long journey. Boston: Houghton, 1917. 190p.
Germans to Mohawk Valley--Juvenile.

5599 ---Rifles for washington. Boston: Houghton, 1938.
321p.
With Washington to Yorktown--Juvenile.

5600 ---A high wind rising. Boston: Houghton, 1942. 206p.
Conrad Weiser in Pennsylvania--1728-1755.

432

5601 ---I heard of a river; the story of the germans in pennsylvania. Philadelphia: Winston, 1949. 209p.
Land of Free Series--Swiss Mennonites to Pennsylvania--Juvenile.

5602 Skelton, Charles L.. Riding west on the pony express. New York: Macmillan, 1937. 196p.
Western--Juvenile.

5603 Skinner, Constance Lindsay (-1939). Silent scot, frontier scout. New York: Macmillan, 1925. 234p.
Juvenile

5604 ---Becky landers; frontier warrior. New York: Macmillan, 1926. 234p.
Kentucky frontier.

5605 ---The white leader. New York: Macmillan, 1926. 219p.
General Wilkinson--Early 1800's.

5606 ---Andy breaks trail. New York: Macmillan, 1928. 199p.
Western

5607 ---Derby barnes, trader. New York: Macmillan, 1932. 244p.
Western Pennsylvania--1750--Adventure--Juvenile.

5608 ---Red man's luck. New York: Coward, 1930. 251p.
Juvenile

5609 ---Rob roy; the frontier twins. New York: Macmillan, 1934. 218p.
Juvenile

5610 Slaughter, Frank Gill (1908-). The golden isle. New York: Doubleday, 1947. 373p.
African slave trade--Spanish Florida--Fernandino on Amelia Island--1817.

5611 ---Sangaree. New York: Doubleday, 1948. 306p.
Post-American Revolution--Land tenanting--Georgia--Romance.

5612 ---Fort everglades. New York: Doubleday, 1951. 340p.
Second Seminole War (1835-1840)--Doctor in Everglades--Romantic triangle.

5613 ---Storm haven. New York: Doubleday, 1953. 282p.
Florida cattle drive--Civil War.

5614 ---Apalachee gold; the fabulous adventures of cabeza de vaca. New York: Doubleday, 1954. 254p.
Based on Cabeza de Vaca--1528-1536--Fabulous journey--Based on his record--Juvenile.

433

5615   ---Flight from natchez. New York: Doubleday, 1955.
        284p.
              American Revolution--Loyalists' flight from
        Natchez--1781--Romance.

5616   ---The warrior. New York: Doubleday, 1956. 255p.
              Osceola, Seminole Chief (1804-1838)--Seminole
        War (1835-1842)--Florida.

5617   ---The mapmaker; a novel of the days of prince henry,
        the navigator. New York: Doubleday, 1957. 320p.
              Andrea Bianco (El Hakim)--Venetian mapmaker.

5618   ---pseud. Terry, C. V.. Buccaneer surgeon. New York:
        Garden City, 1954. 309p.
              Spanish Main--Days of Sir Francis Drake 1580's.

5619   Sleight, Mary Breck. An island heroine; the story of
        a daughter of the revolution. Boston: Lothrop,
        1898. 432p.
              Romance

        Slocombe, Edwin M. see Fernald, Helen Clark jt. author

5620   Small, Austin J.. The frozen trail. Boston: Houghton,
        1924. 305p.
              Klondike--Gold seeking.

5621   Small, Sidney Herschel (1893-   ). The splendid
        califorians. Indianapolis: Bobbs, 1928. 323p.
              Spanish rancheros--Early nineteenth century.

5622   Smith, Mrs. Alice (Prescott). Kindred. Boston:
        Houghton, 1925. 344p.
              French-Indian War--English spy.

5623   Smith, Arthur Douglas Howden (1887-   ). The eagle's
        shadow. Philadelphia: Lippincott, 1931. 311p.
              Intrigue in America to effect escape of Napoleon
        from St. Helena.

5624   ---Conqueror; the story of cortés and montezuma and
        the slave girl, malinal. Philadelphia: Lippincott,
        1933. 360p.
              Hernando Cortés (1485-1547)--Montezuma II--
        Emperor of Mexico (ca.1480-1520).

5625   ---Alan breck again; being the account of the adventures
        of ian macdonnell, of new york, and his foster-
        brother, ho-no-we-na-to, son of the onodaga royaneh,
        in the course of a journey to scotland in the year
        1755, and of their experiences with the famous
        jacobite agent, alan breck stewart, and the notorious
        spy, pickle, as likewise, of their attempt to recover

the loch arkaig treasure on behalf of prince charles stuart, miscalled the young pretender, the which narrative has been edited and englished by arthur d. howden smith. New York: Coward, 1934. 303p.

5626 ---The dead go overside. New York: Greystone, 1938. 388p.
       Provincetown seaman sails with slave ship-- 1820's.

5627 ---pseud. Grant, Allen. The doom trail. New York: Bretano's, 1922. 312p.
       Great Britain v. France--Fur trade--Early 1600's--Albany--French posts--Good.

5628 ---Beyond the sunset. New York: Bretano's, 1923. 291p.
       Sequel to The Doom Trail--Adventure--Long journey.

5629 ---Porto bello gold. New York: Bretano's, 1924. 330p.
       Pirates--Romance.

5630 Smith, Chard Powers. Artillery of time. New York: Scribner's, 1939. 853p.
       Upper New York State--1850-1865--Lathrop family.

5631 Smith, Gilbert (Mrs. Mary Gilbert Smith). The green mountain boys ride. New York: Appleton, 1932. 257p.
       Ethan Allen--Struggle against New York land speculators--Juvenile.

5632 Smith, Harry Allen (1907-   ). Mister zip. New York: Doubleday, 1952. 252p.
       Satire on western movies and stories.

5633 Smith, Helen Butler pseud. Stuart, Hester. A modern jacob. Boston: Lothrop, 1888. 209p.
       From eastern farm to west.

5634 Smith, Henry Justin (1875-   ). Señor zero. New York: Harcourt, 1931. 337p.
       Based on legend of boy stowaway with Columbus on first voyage.

Smith, Katharine jt. author, see Shay, Edith(Foley)

5635 Smith, Laban C. (1911-   ). No better land. New York: Macmillan, 1946. 311p.
       First novel--Wisconsin farm--1906.

5636 Smith, Leonard K.. Forty days to santa fé. Boston: Little, 1938. 325p.
       Western--Juvenile--Better than most adult ones.

5637 Smith, Mary Stuart (Harrison). Lang syne; or, the wards of mount vernon. a tale of the revolutionary era. New York: Alden, 1889. 133p.

5638 Smith, Michael pseud. Casender, Don Pedro. The lost virgin of the south. a tale of truth, connected with the history of the indian war in the south, in the years 1812-13-14 and 15. Tallahassee, Smith, 1831. 327p.

5639 Smith, Minna Caroline (1860-   ). Mary paget; a romance of old bermuda. New York: Macmillan, 1900. 326p.
    Wreck of "Sea Venture"--used by Shakespeare in "The Tempest"--Established church v. Puritanism.

5640 ---Red top ranch; a story of ranch life in wyoming. New York: Dutton, 1907. 213p.
    Western

5641 Smith, Richard Penn (1799-1854). The forsaken; a tale. Philadelphia: Grigg, 1831. 2 vols.
    Howe's evacuation of Philadelphia.

5642 Smith, Ruel Perley (1869-1937). Prisoners of fortune; a tale of massachusetts bay colony. Boston: Page, 1907. 392p.
    Pirates--Treasure--Romance.

5643 Smith, Samuel Robert. Daniel north of wyoming valley. Wilkes-Barre, Pennsylvania: 1897. 144p.
    1775-1800.

5644 Smith Titus Keiper. Altruria. New York: Altruria Pub., 1895. 120p.
    Utopian community in west.

5645 Smith, William A.. Who is responsible? a story of american western life. Boston: Lothrop, 1883. 270p.

5646 Smith, William Fielding. Diamond six. New York: Doubleday, 1958. 383p.
    Fictional biography--Wesley Smith (1829-1902)--Texas Ranger--Owned Diamond Six Ranch.

5647 Snedeker, Mrs. Caroline Dale (Parke) (1871-   ). The town of the fearless. New York: Doubleday, 1931. 351p.
    European background and establishing New Harmony--Related to Sethway...and The Beckoning Road.

5648 ---Uncharted ways. New York: Doubleday, 1935. 340p.
    Mary Dyer, Quaker in Massachusetts (d.1660)-- Romance--Nantucket Island.

5649 ---pseud. Owen, Caroline Dale. Sethway; a romance of the new harmony community. Boston: Houghton, 1917. 413p.
Indiana--Owenites--Pioneer days.

5650 ---Downright dencey. New York: Doubleday, 1927. 314p.
Young Quaker--Nantucket--1810-1820--Juvenile--Good.

5651 ---The beckoning road. New York: Doubleday, 1929. 326p.
New Harmony, Indiana--1850's--Related to Sethway...

5652 Snell, George Dixon. Root, hog, and die. Caldwell, Iadho: Caxton, 1936. 418p.
Mormonism--Rise and fall--1830-1930.

5653 Snelling, Mrs. Anna L.. Kabosa; or, the warriors of the west. a tale of the last war. New York: Adee, 1842. 320p.
Great Lakes--War of 1812.

5654 Snider, Charles Henry Jeremiah (1879-   ). In the wake of the eighteen twelvers; fights and flights of frigates and fore-'n'-afters in the war of 1812 on the great lakes. London: Lane, 1913. 291p.
Based on logs and letters of War of 1812.

5655 ---Under the red jacket; privateers of the maritime provinces of canada in the war of 1812. London: Hopkinson, 1928. 268p.
Romance

5656 Snow, Charles Horace (1877-   ). The rider of san felipe. Boston: Hale, 1930. 285p.
Western

5657 ---The sheriff of chispa loma. Philadelphia: Macrae, 1931. 290p.
Western

5658 ---Don jim. Philadelphia: Macrae, 1932. 287p.
Western

5659 ---The silent shot. London: Wright, 1932. 282p.
Western

5660 ---Stocky of lone tree ranch. Philadelphia: Macrae, 1932. 274p.
Western

5661 ---Tamer of bad men. London: Long, 1932. 287p.
Western

5662 ---Beyond arizona. London: Wright, 1933. 284p.
         Western

5663 ---The invisible brand. Philadelphia: Macrae, 1933.
         283p.
         Western

5664 ---The scorpion's sting. London: Wright, 1933. 284p.
         Western

5665 ---The gold of alamito. London: Wright, 1934. 286p.
         Western

5666 ---The high graders. London: Long, 1934. 288p.
         Western

5667 ---Hollow stump mystery. London: Wright, 1934. 251p.
         Western

5668 ---Cardigan cowboy. Philadelphia: Macrae, 1935. 268p.
         Western

5669 ---The sign of the death circle. London: Wright, 1935.
         254p.
         Western

5670 ---Six-guns of sandoval. Philadelphia: Macrae, 1935.
         286p.
         Western

5671 ---Argonaut gold. Philadelphia: Macrae, 1936. 288p.
         Western

5672 ---The trail to abilene. Philadelphia: Macrae, 1937.
         282p.
         Western

5673 ---The vilgilantes of gold gulch. Philadelphia: Macrae,
         1937. 269p.
         Western

5674 ---Border feud. Philadelphia: Macrae, 1938. 287p.
         Western

5675 ---Guns along the border. Philadelphia: Macrae, 1939.
         270p.
         Western

5676 ---Riders of the range. Philadelphia: Macrae, 1939.
         286p.
         Western

5677 ---Outlaws of red canyon. Philadelphia: Macrae, 1940.
         263p.
         Western

5678   ---<u>Sheriff of yavisa</u>. Philadelphia: Macrae, 1941.
      252p.
      Western

5679   ---<u>Wolf of the mesas</u>. Philadelphia: Macrae, 1941.
      264p.
      Western

5680   ---<u>The brand stealer</u>. Philadelphia: Macrae, 1942.
      249p.
      Western

5681   ---<u>Outlaws of sugar loaf</u>. Philadelphia: Macrae,
      1942. 256p.
      Western

5682   ---<u>Rebel of ronde valley</u>. Philadelphia: Macrae, 1943.
      256p.
      Western

5683   ---<u>Renegade ranger</u>. Philadelphia: Macrae, 1943. 256p.
      Western

5684   ---<u>Horsethief pass</u>. Philadelphia: Macrae, 1944. 248p.
      Western

5685   ---pseud. Ballew, Charles. <u>Red gold</u>. London: Long,
      1932. 288p.
      Western

5686   ---<u>The cowboy from alamos</u>. Philadelphia: Macrae, 1933.
      288p.
      Western

5687   ---<u>The gambler of red gulch</u>. London: Long, 1933.
      287p.
      Western

5688   ---<u>One crazy cowboy</u>. New York: Morrow, 1933. 302p.
      Western

5689   ---<u>The bandit of paloduro</u>. New York: Morrow, 1934.
      291p.
      Western

5690   ---<u>Cowpuncher</u>. New York: Morrow, 1934. 293p.
      Western

5691   ---<u>Smugglers' ranch</u>. Philadelphia: Macrae, 1934.
      315p.
      Western

5692   ---<u>Texas spurs</u>. New York: Loring, 1935. 241p.
      Western

5693   ---The treasure of aspen canyon. New York: Loring,
        1935. 264p.
           Western

5694   ---Frontier regiment. London: Wright, 1939. 284p.
           Western

5695   ---Rim-fire in mexico. London: Wright, 1939. 251p.
           Western

5696   ---pseud. Marshall, Gary. Flaming six guns. London:
        Wright, 1934. 288p.
           Western

5697   ---The watchers of gold gulch. London: Wright, 1934.
        288p.
           Western

5698   ---One fightin' cowboy. London: Wright, 1935. 282p.
           Western

5699   ---Raiders of the tonto rim. New York: Hartney, 1935.
        283p.
           Western

5700   ---pseud. Lee, Ranger. Thundering hoofs. New York:
        Greystone, 1937. 332p.
           Western

5701   ---Rebel on the range. New York: Greystone, 1938.
        292p.
           Western

5702   ---The red gash outlaws. New York: Greystone, 1939.
        279p.
           Western

5703   ---Badland bill. New York: Phoenix, 1941. 256p.
           Western

5704   ---The bar d boss. New York: Phoenix, 1943. 255p.
           Western

5705   Snow, Donald Clifford (1917-   ). The justicer.
        New York: Rinehart, 1960. 255p.
           Western

5706   Sorensen, Mrs. Virginia (Eggersten) (1912-   ).
        Little lower than angels. New York: Knopf, 1942.
        427p.
               First novel--Mormons--Nauvoo--Just before
        death of Smith and Utah Trek--Good--#1 of Mormon
        Series.

5707   ---On this star. New York: Reynal, 1946. 275p.

#2 of Mormon Series--Temple City, Utah-1920.

5708 ---The neighbors; a novel. New York: Reynal, 1947.
311p.
      Colorado sheep country.

5709 ---The evening and the morning. New York: Harcourt,
1949. 341p.
      #3 of Mormon Series--Scots-Irish to Utah--
Twentieth century.

5710 ---The proper gods. New York: Harcourt, 1951. 309p.
      Yaqui Indians--Mexicans--American.

5711 ---The house next door; utah 1896. New York: Scribner's,
1954. 223p.
      #4 of Mormon Series.

5712 ---Many heavens; a new mormon novel. New York: Harcourt,
1954. 352p.
      #5 of Mormon Series--1890's.

5713 ---Kingdom come. New York: Harcourt, 1960. 497p.
      #6 of Mormon Series--1850.

5714 Southworth, Ella. Sarah de vaughn; a story of the
times of aaron burr. New York: Dean, 1858. n.p.
      Romance

5715 Southworth, Mrs. Emma Dorothy Eliza (Nevitite).
The curse of clifton; a tale of expiation and
redemption. Philadelphia: Hart, 1853. 2 vols.
      Romance

5716 ---The fatal marriage. Philadelphia: Peterson, 1863.
487p.
      1755-1775.

5717 Sparhawk, Frances Campbell. A chronicle of conquest.
Boston: Lothrop, 1890. 239p.
      Carlisle School for Indians, Pennsylvania.

5718 ---Onoqua. Boston: Lee, 1892. 263p.
      Montana--Indians--Whites.

5719 ---Senator intrigue and inspector noseby. a tale of
spoils. Boston: Red-Letter, 1895. 162p.

5720 Speare, Mrs. Elizabeth George. Calico captive.
Boston: Houghton, 1957. 274p.
      French-Indian War--1750's--Based on diary of
Susan Johnson--Very good.

5721 ---The prospering. Boston: Houghton, 1967. 372p.
      Missionary in Stockbridge, Massachusetts--1750's-
1760's.

5722   Spearman, Frank Hamilton (1859-1937). Whispering smith. New York: Scribner's, 1906. 421p.
        Western

5723   ---The mountain divide. New York: Scribner's, 1912. 319p.
        Western

5724   ---Nan of music mountain. New York: Scribner's, 1916. 430p.
        Western

5725   ---Laramie holds the range. New York: Scribner's, 1921. 374p.
        Western

5726   ---Hell's desert. New York: Doubleday, 1933. 322p.
        Western

5727   ---Gunlock ranch. New York: Doubleday, 1935. 310p.
        Western

5728   ---Carmen of the rancho. New York: Doubleday, 1937. 328p.
        Western

5729   Spears, John Randolph. The fugitive; a tale of adventure in the days of clipper ships and slaves. New York: Scribner's, 1899. 325p.
        Romance

5730   Spence, Hartzell (1908-   ). Bride of the conqueror; a novel. New York: Random, 1954. 336p.
        1500's--Peru--Panama--Romance.

5731   Spencer, Cornelia. China trader. New York: Day, 1940. 362p.
        Early days--Macao and Canton factories.

        Spencer, Mrs. George E. pseud. see Spencer, William Loring (Nuñez)

5732   Spencer, William Loring (Nuñez). A plucky one. New York: Cassell, 1886. 353p.
        Nevada mining camp.

5733   ---Calamity jane; a story of the black hills. "By Mrs. George E. Spencer". New York: Cassell, 1887. 172p.
        Western

5734   Sperry, Armstrong. All sail set; a romance of the "flying cloud". Chicago: Winston, 1935. 175p.
        Boston lad works for Donald McKay--1851--Maiden voyage to San Francisco--Juvenile.

5735 ---Wagons westward; the old trail to santa fé. Chicago: Winston, 1936. 276p.
Wagon train--1846--Juvenile.

5736 ---Little eagle, a navajo boy. Philadelphia: Winston, 1938. 102p.
Juvenile

5737 ---No brighter glory. New York: Macmillan, 1942. 429p.
Astor's fur outposts on Columbia River--1810--Juvenile.

5738 ---Storm canvas. Philadelphia: Winston, 1944. 301p.
War of 1812--Juvenile.

5739 ---Danger to the windward. Philadelphia: Winston, 1947. 241p.
South Seas--Early 1800's--Juvenile.

5740 ---The black falcon; a story of piracy and old new orleans. Philadelphia: Winston, 1949. 218p.
Jean La Fitte--Juvenile.

5741 ---River of the west; the story of the boston men. Philadelphia: Winston, 1952. 182p.
Robert Gray's trip around Horn to Columbia River--Juvenile.

5742 Sperry, Portia Howe and Donaldson, Lois. Abigail. Chicago: Whitman, 1938. 196p.
From Kentucky to Brown County, Indiana--Juvenile.

5743 Spicer, Bart. The wild ohio. New York: Dodd, 1953. 328p.
French émigrés flee French Revolution to Scioto Company land--Gallipolis--1790.

5744 ---Brother to the enemy. New York: Dodd, 1958. 308p.
John Champe (1752-1798) sent to New York City to get B. Arnold--Based on memoir of Light Horse Harry Lee.

5745 Spielhagen, Friedrich (1829-1911). The german pioneers; a tale of the mohawk. Chicago: Henneberry, 1891. 250p.
Romance

5746 Springer, Mary Elizabeth. "Lady hancock"; a story of the american revolution. New York: Blanchard, 1900. 267p.
Romance

5747 ---Dolly madison; a story of war of 1812. New York: Bonnell, 1906. 244p.
1772-1849.

5748   Spur, George Graham. The land of gold; a tale of
        '49. illustrative of early pioneer life in califor-
        nia and founded upon fact. Boston: Williams, 1881.
        271p.
                Romance

5749   ---A fight with a grizzly bear; a story of thrilling
        interest. Boston: Pub. by Author, 1886. 26p.
                Adventure

5750   Stackpole, Edouard A. (1905-   ). Smuggler's luck;
        being the adventures of timothy pinkham of nantucket
        island during the war of the revolution. New York:
        Doubleday, 1931. 310p.

5751   ---Madagascar jack; the story of the nantucket whaler,
        being the account of obed c. folger, thirteen years
        of age, who went to the south seas with whalemen
        and found there many adventures as well as sperm
        whales. New York: Morrow, 1935. 308p.

5752   ---Privateer ahoy! a story of the war of 1812. New
        York: Morrow, 1937. 310p.
                Juvenile

5753   ---Mutiny at midnight; the adventures of cyrus hussey
        of nantucket aboard the whaleship glove in the
        south pacific from 1822-1826. New York: Morrow,
        1939. 245p.
                Juvenile

5754   Stafford, John Richard (1874-   ). When cattle king-
        dom fell. New York: Dodge, 1910. 374p.
                Western--Juvenile.

5755   Stanford, Alfred Boller (1900-   ). Navigator; the
        story of nathaniel bowditch. New York: Morrow,
        1927. 308p.
                1773-1838--Juvenile.

5756   Stanley, Edward (1903-   ). Thomas forty; a novel.
        New York: Duell, 1947. 307p.
                Former bond servant--Westchester County--
        With Armand's Partizan legion.

5757   ---The rock cried out. New York: Duell, 1949. 311p.
                Herman Blennerhasset (1764?-1831) and A. Burr.

5758   Stanley, Harvey. Pilate and herod; a tale illustrative
        of the early history of the church of england in
        the province of maryland. Philadelphia: Hooker,
        1853. 2 vols.
                1632-1661.

5759   Stapleton, Patience (Tucker). Kady. Chicago: Belford,
        1888. 403p.

444

Colorado Rockies.

5760 ---Babe murphy. Chicago: Belford, 1890. 280p.
Colorado to Texas.

5761 Stead, Robert James Campbell (1880-   ). Cowpuncher.
New York: Harper, 1918. 331p.
First novel--World War I.

5762 Steele, Wilbur Daniel (1886-   ). That girl from
memphis. New York: Doubleday, 1945. 470p.
Western--Arizona silver camp 1890's-1930--
Beula City.

5763 ---Diamond wedding. New York: Doubleday, 1950. 309p.
1835-1919--Long story of man of the west--Good.

5764 Steele, William Owen (1917-   ). Wilderness journey.
New York: Harcourt, 1953. 209p.

5765 ---Tomahawks and trouble. New York: Harcourt, 1955.
213p.

5766 ---We were there on the oregon trail. New York:
Grosset, 1956. 177p.
1843.

5767 Steelman, Robert. Apache wells. New York: Ballantine,
1959. 159p.
Western

5768 ---Call of the artic. New York: Coward, 1960. 316p.
Charles F. Hall (1821-1871)--Explorer of far
north--Greely Artic Expedition--1881-1884--Juvenile.

5769 Stegner, Wallace Earle (1909-   ). Remembering
laughter. Boston: Little, 1937. 154p.
First novel--Farm life in Iowa--cf. Ethan Frome.

5770 ---The big rock candy mountain. New York: Duell, 1943.
515p.
1906-1942--Family on the move--Far west and
Alaska.

5771 Steinbeck, John Ernest (1902-   ). Cup of gold; a
life of henry morgan, buccaneer with occasional
reference to history. New York: McBride, 1929.
269p.
Adventure

5772 ---The grapes of wrath. New York: Viking, 1939. 619p.
Southwest farmers and share croppers off to
California--1930's--Excellent.

5773 ---East of eden. New York: Viking, 1952. 602p.

Family from Connecticut to California--Civil
War to World War I.

5774 Stephens, Mrs. Ann Sophia (Winterbotham) (1813-1886).
Mary derwent; a novel. Philadelphia: Peterson,
1858. 408p.
Wyoming Valley, Pennsylvania.

5775 ---Malaeska; the indian wife of the white hunter.
New York: Day, 1860. 254p.
First dime novel.

5776 ---The rejected wife. Philadelphia: Peterson, 1863.
436p.
New England--B. Arnold villain--Secret marriage.

5777 Stephens, Charles Asbury (1845-1931). The ark of 1803;
a story of louisiana purchase times. New York:
Barnes, 1904. 340p.

5778 Stephens, Robert Neilson (1867-1906). The continental
dragoon; a love story of philipse manor-house.
Boston: Page, 1898. 299p.
New York State.

5779 ---Philip winwood; a sketch of the domestic history
of an american captain in the war of independence...
written by his enemy in war, herbert russell....
presented a new by robert neilson stephens. Boston:
Page, 1900. 412p.
1763-1786.

5780 ---The road to paris; a story of adventure. Boston:
Page, 1901. 552p.
1760-1780--Adventures in Revolution.

5781 ---and Roberts, Theodore. A soldier of valley forge;
a romance of the american revolution. Boston: Page,
1911. 328p.

5782 Stephenson, Henry Thew. Patroon van volkenberg; a
tale of old manhattan in the year sixteen hundred
and ninety-nine. Indianapolis: Bowen, 1900. 360p.

5783 Stephenson, Howard. Glass. New York: Kendall, 1933.
284p.
Ohio ca.1900--Agriculture v. Industry--Gas
and glass.

5784 Sterling, Charles F.. Buff and blue; or, the privateers
of the revolution. New York: Graham, 1847. 128p.
Long Island.

5785 ---The red coats; or, the sack of unquowa. a tale of
the revolution. New York: Williams, 1848. 111p.

446

5786   Stern, Philip VanDoren (1900-   ) pseud. Storme, Peter.
        The drums of morning. New York: Doubleday, 1942.
        625p.
                Abolitionist--1837-1865--Good.

5787   Sterne, Mrs. Emma (Gelders) (1894-   ). White swallow.
        New York: Duffield, 1927. 158p.
                Indians, North America.

5788   ---Drums of monmouth. New York: Dodd, 1935. 287p.
                American Revolution--Philip Freneau (1752-1832)--
        Battle of Monmouth--1778--New York--New Jersey.

5789   ---Some plant olive trees. New York: Dodd, 1927.
        312p.
                Alabama--Napoleonic exiles form the Vine and
        Olive Colony--Demopolis--Early 1800's.

5790   Steuber, William F.. The landlooker. Indianapolis:
        Bobbs, 1957. 367p.
                Wisconsin frontier--1871.

        Steven, Margaret Dean (1911-1918) pseud. see Aldrich,
        Bess

        Stevens, Dan J. pseud. see Overholser, Wayne D. (1906-   )

5791   Stevens, Elizabeth Welty. Ann of bar ton ranch.
        New York: Knopf, 1938. 196p.
                Wyoming--Juvenile.

5792   Stevens, James Floyd (1892-   ). Brawny-man. New
        York: Knopf, 1926. 323p.
                Lumber--Northwest.

5793   ---Big jim turner; a novel. New York: Doubleday, 1948.
        275p.
                West--Early 1900's.

5794   Stevens, Mrs. Sheppard (Pierce) (1862-   ). The
        sword of justice. Boston: Little, 1899. 275p.
                Huguenot colony in Florida--1562-1565--France
        v. Spain.

5795   Stevens, Sheppard. In the eagle's talon; a romance
        of the louisiana purchase. Boston: Little, 1902.
        475p.
                American and Paris--1803.

5796   Stevenson, Burton Egbert (1872-1962). A soldier of
        virginia; a tale of colonel washington and braddock's
        defeat. Boston: Houghton, 1901. 325p.
                1754-1773.

5797   ---The heritage; a story of defeat and victory. Boston:
        Houghton, 1902. 324p.

American Revolution--1776-1781--General St.
Clair--Fallen Timbers.

5798   Stevenson, Janet. The ardent years; a novel. New York:
       Viking, 1960. 374p.
       Fictional biography of Fanny Kemble (1809-1893)--
       South.

5799   Steward, Davenport. Rainbow road. Atlanta: Tupper,
       1953. 283p.
       Georgia Gold Rush--1820's--Authentic.

5800   ---Caribbean cavalier. New York: Dutton, 1957. 253p.
       Romance--1739-1744--Spanish and English conflict
       in New World.

5801   Stewart, Anne. Song of the stars. New York: Phoenix,
       1937. 251p.
       Penniless girl reclaims Colorado gold mine.

5802   Stewart, Mrs. Catherine (Pomeroy). Three roads to
       valhalla. New York: Scribner's, 1948. 307p.
       Jacksonville, Florida--Reconstruction.

5803   Stewart, Charles David (1868-   ). The wrong woman.
       Boston: Houghton, 1912. 285p.
       Texas sheep ranch--Romance.

5804   Stewart, George (1892-   ). Reluctant soil. Caldwell,
       Idaho: Caxton, 1936. 363p.
       Widow with two small children--Farm south-
       western Idaho--1900-1920.

5805   Stewart, George Rippey (1895-   ). Ordeal by hunger;
       the story of the donner party. New York: Holt,
       1936. 328p.
       1846.

5806   ---East of the giants; a novel. New York: Holt, 1938.
       478p.
       1837--Daughter of New England sea captain to
       California--Elopes with Spanish ranch owner--Died 1861.

5807   Stewart, Sir William George Drummond (1796-1871).
       Edward warren. London: Walker, 1854. 724p.
       Fictious autobiography--Carson v. Sherman duel.

       Stewart, Logan pseud. see Savage, Les

5808   Stickney, Mary Etta (Smith). Brown of lost river;
       a story of the west. New York: Appleton, 1900. 309p.
       Wyoming

5809   Stiles, Pauline. Doctor will. Indianapolis: Bobbs,
       1949. 343p.

448

California frontier town--1880-1900.

5810 Stillson, Florence Georgeanna Merchant. Doris; a story
      of 1778. Danbury, Connecticut: Published for private
      circulation, 1891. 96p.
           Connecticut

5811 Stilwell, Hart. Border city. New York: Doubleday,
      1945. 276p.
           Western

5812 ---Uncovered wagon. New York: Doubleday, 1947. 309p.
           Texas early 1900.

5813 Stimpson, Herbert Baird. The tory maid; being an
      account of the adventures of james frisby of fairlee,
      in the county of kent, on the eastern shore of the
      state of maryland, and sometime officer in the mary-
      land line of the continental army during the war of
      the revolution. New York: Dodd, 1899. 245p.

5814 Stimson, Frederic Jesup (1855-1943) pseud. J. S. of Dale.
      King noanett; a story of old virginia and massachusetts
      bay. New York: Scribner's, 1896. 327p.
           Devon settlers--Bacon's Rebellion--1676--
      Ingram's Rebellion--King Philip's War--1675-1676.

5815 ---My story; being the memoirs of benedict arnold,
      late major general in the continental army and
      brigadier-general in that of his britannic majesty.
      New York: Scribner's, 1917. 622p.

5816 Stockton, Frank Richard (1834-1902). Kate bonnet;
      the romance of a pirate's daughter. New York:
      Appleton, 1902. 420p.
           Eighteenth century.

5817 Stoddard, William Osborn (1835-1925). The talking
      leaves; an indian story. New York: Harper, 1882.
      336p.

5818 ---Red beauty; a story of the pawnee trail. Phil-
      adelphia: Lippincott, 1887. 368p.

5819 ---The red mustang; a story of the mexican border.
      New York: Harper, 1890. 284p.

5820 ---Little smoke; a tale of the sioux. New York:
      Appleton, 1891. 295p.

5821 ---Mart satterlee among the indians. New York: Bonner's,
      1891. 238p.

5822 ---Guert ten eyck; a hero story. Boston: Lothrop, 1893.
      258p.

449

5823 ---On the old frontier; or, the last raid of the iriquois. New York: Appleton, 1893. 340p.

5824 ---The red patriot; a story of the american revolution. New York: Appleton, 1897. 275p.

5825 ---The lost gold of the montezumas; a story of the alamo. Philadelphia: Lippincott, 1898. 309p.
       1836

5826 ---The noank's log; a privateer of the revolution. Boston: Lothrop, 1900. 337p.

5827 ---Jack morgan; a boy of 1812. Boston: Lothrop, 1901. 353p.

5828 ---The errand boy of andrew jackson; a war story of 1814. Boston: Lothrop, 1902. 327p.

5829 ---Ahead of the army. Boston: Lothrop, 1903. 302p. Mexican War (1845-1848).

5830 ---The spy of yorktown; a story of arnold and washington in the last year of the war of independence. New York: Appleton, 1903. 229p.
       1781

5831 ---The fight for the valley; a story of the siege of fort schuyler and the battle of oriskany in the burgoyne campaign of 1777. New York: Appleton, 1904. 250p.

5832 --Two cadets with washington. Boston: Lothrop, 1906. 341p.
       American Revolution.

Stone, Cody pseud. see Mount, Thomas Ernest

5833 Stone, Eugenia. Free men shall stand. New York: Nelson, 1944. 264p.
       1730's--Peter Zenger--Juvenile.

5834 Stone, Mrs. Grace (Zaring) (1896-   ). The cold journey. New York: Morrow, 1934. 336p.
       Deerfield Raid--Massachusetts 1704.

5835 Stone, Irving (1903-   ). Immortal wife; the biographical novel of jessie benton fremont. New York: Doubleday, 1944. 456p.
       1824-1902--Romance.

5836 ---The president's lady; a novel about rachel and andrew jackson. New York: Doubleday, 1951. 338p.

5837 ---Those who love; a biographical novel of abigail and
john adams. New York: Doubleday, 1965. 662p.
Closes in 1801--End of presidency.

5838 Stone, William Leete. Mercy disborough; a tale of
new england witchcraft. [Anonymous]. Bath, New York:
Underhill, 1844. 98p.

5839 Stong, Philip Duffield (1899-1957). State fair.
New York: Century, 1932. 266p.
First novel--Iowa farm life.

5840 ---Buckskin breeches. New York: Farrar, 1937. 366p.
Mississippi-Iowa trek--1837--Grandfather's
memoirs.

5841 ---Cowhand goes to town. New York: Dodd, 1939. 85p.
Ranch life--Juvenile.

5842 ---Ivanhoe keeler. New York: Farrar, 1939. 309p.
Midwest--1840--Picaresque tale.

5843 ---The iron mountain. New York: Farrar, 1942. 310p.
Minnesota mining.

5844 ---Missouri canary. New York: Dodd, 1943. 78p.
Juvenile

5845 ---Jessamy john. New York: Doubleday, 1947. 271p.
John Law (1671-1729).

5846 ---Forty pounds of gold. New York: Doubleday, 1951.
218p.
Panorama--Frontier life--Iowa to California--
1850's.

5847 ---Return in august. New York: Doubleday, 1953. 256p.
Sequel to State Fair.

5848 ---The adventure of "horse" barnsby. New York: Doubleday, 1956. 192p.
California gold fields--Satire on "pseudo-
historical novel of old west".

5849 Stork, Charles Wharton. On board old ironsides, 1812-
1815, a rope yarn epic. Mill Valley, California:
Wing's, 1948. 92p.
Juvenile

5850 Storke, Francis Eugene. Mr. de lacy's double. New
York: Continental, 1898. 306p.
Part of story on Mississippi riverboat.

Storme, Peter pseud. see Stern, Philip VanDoren

5851 Storrs, Lewis Austin. Koheleth; a novel. New York:
        Dillingham, 1897. 265p.
            Whaling--New London, Connecticut.

5852 Stouman, Knud (1889-   ). With cradle and clock.
        New York: Harper, 1946. 292p.
            New York--1702--"Male midwife".

5853 Stover, Herbert Elisha. Song of the susquehanna.
        New York: Dodd, 1949. 275p.
            French-Indian War--Pennsylvania.

5854 ---Men in buckskin. New York: Dodd, 1950. 311p.

5855 ---Powder mission. New York: Dodd, 1951. 278p.
            American Revolution--Expedition from Ft. Pitt
        to New Orleans--Romance--Adventure.

5856 ---The eagle and the wind. New York: Dodd, 1953. 308p.
            American Revolution--Central Pennsylvania.

5857 Stowe, Mrs. Harriet Elizabeth (Beecher) (1811-1896).
        Uncle tom's cabin; or, life among the lowly.
        Boston: Jewett, 1852. 2 vols.
            Attack on institution of slavery.

5858 ---Dred; a tale of the great dismal swamp. Boston:
        Phillips, 1856. 2 vols.
            Anti-slavery manifesto--Also known as Nina
        Gordon.

5859 ---The minister's wooing. New York: Derby, 1859.
        578p.
            Rhode Island--Romance--1750-1800.

5860 ---Old town folks. Boston: Fields, 1869. 608p.
            Portraits of bygone society and people--ca.1800.

5861 Strabel, Thelma. Storm to the south. New York:
        Doubleday, 1944. 342p.
            California and Peru ca.1820--Swashbuckling.

5862 Strachey, Mrs. Rachel (Costelloe) (1887-   ) pseud.
        Strachey, Ray. Marching on. New York: Harcourt,
        1923. 385p.
            Feminist and abolitionist movements--Michigan
        1840's--Kansas.

      Strachey, Ray pseud. see Strachey, Mrs. Rachel
        (Costelloe)

5863 Straight, Michael Whitney. Carrington; a novel of
        the west. New York: Knopf, 1960. 374p.
            Biography fictional form--Henry Beebee Carring-
        ton (1824-1912)--Fetterman Ambush--1866--Wyoming.

5864 ---A very small remnant. New York: Knopf, 1963.
232p.
Indian conflict--Sand Creek--1864--Edward
Wynkoop (b. 1836)--Major J. Chivington (1821-1894).

5865 Strange, Oliver. The law o' the lariat. London:
Newnes, 1931. 256p.
Western

5866 ---The range robbers. New York: MacVeagh, 1931. 303p.
Western

5867 ---Lawless; an adventure of sudden, the outlaw. New
York: Dial, 1933. 309p.
Western

5868 ---Outlaw breed. New York: Doubleday, 1934. 309p.
Western

5869 ---Outlawed. Boston: Lothrop, 1936. 305p.
Western

5870 ---Sudden rides again. New York: Doubleday, 1939.
280p.
Western

5871 ---Sudden takes charge. New York: Sun Dial, 1940.
280p.
Western

5872 Strange, Robert (1796-1854). Eoneguski; or, the cherokee
chief. a tale of past wars. Washington: Taylor,
1839. 2 vols.
Cherokee from North Carolina to west of
Mississippi River.

5873 Stratemeyer, Edward (1862-1930). With washington in
the west; or, a soldier boy's battles in the wilderness. Boston: Lee, 1901. 302p.
1755--Juvenile.

5874 Strawn, Arthur (1900-   ). The road to granada; a
story of adventure. in the days of the moorish wars
in spain. New York: Warren, 1931. 278p.
Moorish Wars in Spain--Help Columbus get
precious map--Romance.

5875 Street, James Howell (1903-   ). Oh, promised land.
New York: Dial, 1940. 816p.
Georgia to Mississippi--1794-1817--Founding
of Natchez--War of 1812--Romance.

5876 ---Tap roots. New York: Dial, 1942. 593p.
Sequel to Oh, Promised Land--Anti-slavery
section of Mississippi.

5877　Stribling, Thomas Sigismund (1881-1965).　Teef tallow.
　　　　New York: Doubleday, 1926.　405p.
　　　　Lance County, Tennessee--"hill folks".

5878　---The forge.　New York: Doubleday, 1931.　525p.
　　　　#1 of Series Old South-Alabama.

5879　---The store.　New York: Doubleday, 1932.　571p.
　　　　#2 of Old South-Alabama--Sequel to The Forge--
　　　　1880's.

5880　---The unfinished cathedral.　New York: Doubleday,
　　　　1934.　383p.
　　　　#3 of Alabama Trilogy--1930's.

5881　Stringer, Arthur John Arbuthnott (1874-　　). Power.
　　　　Indianapolis: Bobbs, 1925.　308p.
　　　　Pioneer railroad man.

5882　---The wolf woman.　Indianapolis: Bobbs, 1928.　331p.
　　　　Adventure

5883　---The wife traders; a tale of the north.　Indianapolis:
　　　　Bobbs, 1936.　319p.
　　　　Romance

5884　---The lamp in the valley; a novel of alaska.　Ind-
　　　　ianapolis: Bobbs, 1938.　314p.
　　　　Romance

5885　Strong, Clara Lathrop.　Forfeit; a novel.　Boston:
　　　　Houghton, 1912.　313p.
　　　　Romance Puritan New England--Late seventeenth
　　　　century--Witchcraft.

Strong, Zachary pseud. see Mann, Edward Beverly

5886　Stuart, Colin pseud..　Shoot an arrow to stop the wind.
　　　　New York: Dial, 1970.　272p.
　　　　First novel--Montana town--1926--Sixteen year
　　　　old "breed".

5887　Stuart, Henry Longan.　Weeping cross; an unwordly
　　　　story.　New York: Doubleday, 1908.　497p.
　　　　New England--1650--Irish bond servant work
　　　　for Cromwell--Long Meadow Massacre.

Stuart, Hester pseud. see Smith, Helen Butler

5888　Stuart, Jesse (1907-　　).　Trees of heaven.　New York:
　　　　Dutton, 1940.　340p.
　　　　Land rented to squatter--Kentucky mountain--
　　　　Good.

Stuart, Matt pseud. see Holmes, Llewellyn Perry

5889   Stuart, Ruth McEnery (1856-1937). <u>Sonny</u>. New York:
        Century, 1896. 135p.

5890   ---Napoleon jackson; the gentleman of the plush rocker.
        New York: Century, 1902. 132p.

5891   Styron, William (1925-   ). <u>The confessions of nat</u>
        <u>turner</u>. New York: Random, 1967. 428p.
                Slave uprising--Virginia--1831--Nat Turner
        (1800?-1831)--Psychological for 1967--Social for
        1831--Pulitzer Prize 1968.

5892   Sublette, Clifford MacClellan (1887-   ). <u>The scarlet</u>
        <u>cockerel; a tale wherein is set down a record of the</u>
        <u>strange and exceptional adventures of blaise de</u>
        <u>breault and martin belcastle in the new world, as</u>
        <u>members of an expedition sent out by the great coligny</u>.
        Boston: Little, 1925. 293p.
                French in Carolina--Won $2,000 <u>Atlantic Monthly</u>
        Prize for best tale in manner of late Charles Board-
        man Hawes.

5893   ---<u>The bright face of danger; a tale, wherein are re-</u>
        <u>lated the adventures of francis havenell, of hookset</u>
        <u>hundred in henrico county, virginia during the days</u>
        <u>of bacon's rebellion</u>. Boston: Little, 1926. 321p.
                1676--Romance.

5894   ---<u>Golden chimney</u>. Boston: Little, 1931. 304p.
                Richest of Colorado silver lodes--Tale of
        Marcellus Bassett.

5895   ---<u>Greenhorn's hunt</u>. Indianapolis: Bobbs, 1934. 241p.
                Missouri Fur Company--Juvenile.

5896   ---and Kroll, Harry Harrison (1888-   ). <u>Perilous</u>
        <u>journey; a tale of the mississippi river and the</u>
        <u>natchez trace</u>. Indianapolis: Bobbs, 1943. 418p.
                Boy searches for "Pa"--Life of river towns--
        1820's.

5897   Suckow, Ruth (1892-   ). <u>Country people</u>. New York:
        Knopf, 1924. 213p.
                Chronicle--Three generations--German-American
        family--1850--Pennsylvania to Iowa.

5898   ---<u>The odyssey of a nice girl</u>. New York: Knopf, 1925.
        364p.
                Girl of soil to city.

5899   ---<u>The folks</u>. New York: Farrar, 1934. 727p.
                Details farm life--Small Iowa town--1914-1934.

5900   Sullivan, Alan (1868-   ). <u>Three came to ville marie</u>.
        New York: Coward, 1943. 329p.

French in Canada--Late seventeenth century--
Romance.

5901 ---The fur masters. New York: Coward, 1947. 244p.
Canadian fur trade--Early nineteenth century--
Hudson's Bay Company.

Summerfield, Charles pseud. see Arrington, Alfred

5902 Summers, Richard Aldrich (1906-   ). The devil's
highway. New York: Nelson, 1937. 299p.
Eusebio Francisco Kiño (1644-1711)--Southwest
to lower California--Missions--Romance--Juvenile.

5903 ---Conquerors of the river. London: Oxford, 1939.
195p.
John Wesley Powell (1834-1902)--Down Colorado
River--Juvenile.

5904 ---Cavalcade to california. London: Oxford, 1941. 256p.
Juan Bautista de Anza (1735-1788)--Juvenile.

5905 ---The battle of the sierras. New York: Oxford, 1943.
235p.
Railroad construction--Juvenile.

5906 ---Vigilante; a novel. New York: Duell, 1949. 211p.
San Francisco--1856--Crooked politics--Career
of president of California Senate.

5907 Sumner, Mrs. Cid Ricketts (1890-   ). Sudden glory;
a novel. Indianapolis: Bobbs, 1951. 326p.
Mississippi family life (1879-1880)--Passing
of plantation.

5908 Sutcliff, Rosemary. Lady in waiting. New York: Coward,
1957. 253p.
Sir Walter Raleigh (1552?-1618)--Elizabeth
(Throckmorton) Raleigh.

5909 ---Rider on a white horse. New York: Coward, 1959.
320p.
Anne (Vere) Fairfax (d. 1665)--Thomas Fairfax
(1612-1671).

Sutherland, John jt. author, see Byrd, Sigman

5910 Sutton, Mrs. Margaret. Palace wagon family; a true
story of the donner party. New York: Knopf, 1957.
210p.
Told from point of view of one of the survivors--
Letters of Reed family base--1846--Juvenile.

5911 Swain, Virginia (Mrs. Philip Stong) (1899-1968).
The dollar gold piece. New York: Farrar, 1942. 438p.

Kansas City--Early growth--1887.

5912   Swanson, Neil Harmon (1896-   ). The flag is still
        there. New York: Putnam, 1933. 140p.
            Battle of Baltimore--1814.

5913   ---The judas tree. New York: Putnam, 1933. 360p.
            Siege of Ft. Pitt--1763--Romance--cf. Unconquered.

5914   ---The phantom emperor. New York: Putnam, 1934. 391p.
            James Dickinson's effort at empire--1836.

5915   ---The first rebel; being a lost chapter of our history
        and a true narrative of america's first uprising
        against english military authority and an account
        of the first fighting between armed colonists and
        british regulars, together with a biography of colonel
        james smith who...led the pennsylvania rebellion....
        recounted from contemporary documents by neil h.
        swanson. New York: Farrar, 1937. 393p.
            Scots-Irish uprising in Pennsylvania 1763-1767.

5916   ---The forbidden ground. New York: Farrar, 1938. 445p.
            American Revolution--Sequel to Judas Tree--
        Detroit and regions north and west--Romance--Fur trade.

5917   ---The silent drum. New York: Farrar, 1940. 507p.
            Sequel to Forbidden Ground--Ft. Pitt--1760's.

5918   ---The perilous fight; being a little known and much
        abused chapter of our national history in our second
        war of independence and a true narrative of the
        battle of godly wood and the attack on fort mchenry,
        more suitably described as the battle of baltimore...
        to which is added some notice of the circumstances
        attending the writing of the star spangled banner...
        recounted mainly from contemporary records by neil
        h. swanson. New York: Farrar, 1945. 555p.
            Effect is that of fiction--1814.

5919   ---Unconquered; a novel of the pontiac conspiracy.
        New York: Doubleday, 1947. 440p.
            Sequel to Silent Drum--Pontiac's Conspiracy--
        1763-1765--Romance.

5920   Swarthout, Glendon Fred. They came to cordura. New
        York: Random, 1958. 213p.
            Last mounted charge of United States Cavalry
        against an enemy--Pershing's "Punitive Expedition"--
        1916--Ojos Azules, Mexico--Strong novel.

5921   Sweeny, Mrs. Sarah Louisa (Banning). Harvest of the
        wind. Caldwell, Idaho: Caxton, 1935. 291p.
            Kentucky--Kansas migration--1850's--Kansas-
        Nebraska Bill--Romance.

5922 Sweet, Alexander Edwin (1841-1901) and Knox, John Armoy
      (1851-1906). On a mexican mustang through texas
      from the gulf to the rio grande. Hartford, Connecticut
      Scranton, 1883. 672p.

5923 Swift, Hildegarde. The railroad to freedom; a story of
      the civil war. New York: Harcourt, 1932. 364p.
          Harriet Tubman(1815?-1913).

      Switzer, A. Jennie see Switzer, Jennie (Bartlett)

5924 Switzer, Jennie (Bartlett) by A. Jennie Bartlett.
      Elder northfield's home; or, sacrificed on the
      mormon altar. a story of the blighting curse of
      polygamy. New York: Brown, 1882. 319p.
          Appeared later under different titles.

5925 Sykes, Hope Williams. Second hoeing. New York: Putnam,
      1935. 309p.
          German-Russian workers--Sugar beet--Colorado-
      1930's.

5926 Sylvester, Harry (1908-   ). Dayspring. New York:
      Appleton, 1945. 294p.
          Penitents--New Mexico--Flagellation ceremony.

5927 [Tabb, T. T.]? pseud. Virginian. Rose-hill; a tale
      of the old dominion. Philadelphia: Key, 1835.
      208p.
              West Virginia.

5928 Tales of an american landlord; containing sketches of
      life south of the patomac. [Anonymous]. New York:
      Gilley, 1824. 2 vols.
              "One of first novels to attempt picture of
      Virginia life"--Religious.

5929 Tallant, Robert (1909-   ). The voodoo queen; a novel.
      New York: Putnam, 1956. 314p.
              Marie Laveau (1794-1881)--Quadroon--Voodoo
      leader--New Orleans.

      Talmon, Thrace pseud. see Putnam, Mrs. Ellen Tryphosa
      Harrington

5930 Tarkington, Booth (1869-1946). The two vanrevels.
      New York: McClure, 1902. 351p.
              Comedy--Indiana abolitionists--Mexican War
      (1845-1848).

5931 ---Cherry. New York: Harpers, 1903. 178p.
              College days before American Revolution--
      Nassau Hall.

5932 Taylor, Benjamin Franklin. Theophilustrent; old
      times in the oak openings. Chicago: Griggs,
      1887. 250p.
              Michigan--1815-1820.

5933 Taylor, David. Lights across the delaware. Phil-
      adelphia: Lippincott, 1954. 336p.
              #1 of Revolution Series--Events leading to
      Battle of Trenton-1776.

5934 ---Farewell to valley forge. Philadelphia: Lippincott,
      1955. 378p.
              #2 of Revolution Series--Two young people
      spies for G. Washington--Lee's plot--Battle of
      Monmouth.

5935 ---Sycamore men. Philadelphia: Lippincott, 1958.
      386p.
              #3 of Revolution Series--Francis Marion (1732-
      1795)--Battle of Camden, King's Mountain and Eutaw
      Springs.

5936 ---Storm the last rampart. Philadelphia: Lippincott,
1960. 384p.
#4 of Revolution Series--Andŕe and Arnold--
End of war--1780-1781.

5937 ---Mistress of the forge. Philadelphia: Lippincott,
1964. 350p.
Foundry--Pennsylvania--1775-1865.

5938 Taylor, Grant. Caravan into canaan. Philadelphia:
Lippincott, 1934. 320p.
Western

5939 ---Guns of salvation valley. Philadelphia: Lippincott,
1934. 302p.
Western

5940 ---Whip ryder's way. Philadelphia: Lippincott, 1935.
304p.
Western

5941 ---Gunsmoke hacienda; a novel. Philadelphia: Lippincott,
1936. 301p.
Western

5942 Taylor, James Wickes. The victim of intrigue; a tale
of burr's conspiracy. Cincinnati: Robinson, 1847.
120p.
Romance

5943 Taylor, Mary Imlay. Anne scarlett. Chicago: McClurg,
1901. 350p.
Salem witchcraft.

5944 Taylor, Robert Lewis. The travels of jaimie mcpheeters.
New York: Doubleday, 1958. 544p.
Picaresque tale--To California gold fields--
1849-1852--Based on journals of Joseph Middleton,
Louisville physican--Excellent--Pulitizer Prize-1958.

5945 ---Journey to matecumbee. New York: McGraw, 1961.
424p.
Escape from Kentucky to Florida Keys--1870--
In a way companion to Travels of Jaimie McPheeters.

5946 ---Two roads to guadalupé. New York: Doubleday, 1964.
428p.
Picaresque novel--Mexican War--Fourteen year
old runs away to enlist in U. S. Army.

5947 Taylor, Ross McLaury (1909-   ). Brazos; an historical
novel of the southwest 1876-1885. Indianapolis:
Bobbs, 1938. 329p.
Cattle drive--Balanced account.

460

5948   ---The saddle and the plow; an historical novel of texas.
        Indianapolis: Bobbs, 1942. 308p.
        Sequel to Brazos--Novel of land.

5949   Taylor, Winchcombe. Ram; being the tale of one ramillies
        anstruther 1704-55. New York: St. Martin's, 1960.
        463p.
            To Georgia with Oglethorpe--1704-1755--Ends
        with Braddock's defeat.

5950   Teal, Angeline (Gruey). John thorn's folks; a study
        of western life. Boston: Lee, 1884. 187p.

5951   Tebbel, John William (1912-   ). The conqueror; a
        novel. New York: Dutton, 1951. 352p.
            Sir William Johnson (1715-1774)--British
        superintendent--General of Indian Affairs in North
        America--Based on his life--Romance.

5952   ---Touched with fire. New York: Dutton, 1952. 447p.
            Robert LaSalle (1647-1687).

5953   Teilhet, Darwin Le Ora (1904-   ). Steamboat on the
        river; a novel. New York: Sloane, 1952. 256p.
            1822-1833--Narrator serves on steamboat--
        Sangamon River.

5954   ---Road to glory. New York: Funk, 1956. 279p.
            Franciscan missions--Last year of Junipero
        Serra (1713-1784)--1783.

        Temple, Dan pseud. see Newton, Dwight Bennett

5955   Templeton, Frank. Margaret ballentine; or, the fall
        of the alamo. a romance of the texas revolution.
            1836

5956   Templeton, John. Charlie eagletooth's war. New York:
        Morrow, 1969. 224p.
            Indian uprising--Sociological implications--
        cf. Huffakers', Nobody Loves a Drunken Indian--
        Contemporary.

5957   Tempski, Armine Von (Mrs. A. L. Ball). Hula; a romance
        of hawaii. New York: Stokes, 1927. 368p.

5958   ---Dust; a novel of hawaii. New York: Stokes, 1928.
        323p.

5959   ---Fire; a novel of hawaii. New York: Stokes, 1929.
        344p.

5960   ---Lava; a saga of hawaii. New York: Stokes, 1930.
        301p.

461

5961   ---Hawaiian harvest. New York: Stokes, 1933. 337p.

5962   ---Ripe breadfruit. New York: Dodd, 1935. 376p.
       Hawaii

5963   ---Pam's paradise ranch; a story of hawaii. New York:
       Dodd, 1940. 333p.
       Juvenile

5964   Tenney, Edward Payson. Constance of acadia; a novel.
       Boston: Roberts, 1886. 368p.
       New France--Constance (Bernon) La Tour basis
       for account.

5965   ---Agatha and the shadow; a novel. Boston: Roberts,
       1887. 321p.
       Puritans--Colonial Era.

5966   Terhune, Albert Payson (1872-1942). Black gold. New
       York: Doran, 1922. 297p.
       Northern California--Dogs--Romance--Mystery.

5967   ---Grudge mountain. New York: Harper, 1939. 289p.
       Dog--Adventure--Mystery.

5968   Terhune, Mary Virginia (Hawes) (1830-1922) pseud.
       Harland, Marion. Judith; a chronicle of old virginia.
       Philadelphia: Our Continent Pub., 1883. 391p.

5969   ---His great self. Philadelphia: Lippincott, 1892.
       355p.
       Colonial Virginia--Colonel Byrd.

5970   ---A long lane. New York: Hearst's, 1915. 363p.
       Northern New Jersey--Dutch--1650's.

5971   Terrell, John Upton (1900-   ). Plume rogue; a novel
       of the pathfinders. New York: Viking, 1942. 498p.
       Trek of men and women from St. Louis to Colum-
       bia River.

5972   Terrell, Upton. The little dark man. Chicago: Reilly,
       1934. 309p.
       Western

5973   ---Adam cargo. Chicago: Reilly, 1935. 245p.
       Western

5974   Terrett, Courtenay (1901-   ). The white cheyenne.
       New York: Dodd, 1949. 311p.
       Montana ranch life--1900--Juvenile.

       Terry, C. V. pseud. see Slaughter, Frank Gill

5975   Terry, J. William (1895-1966). A restless breed.

Cleveland: World, 1956. 254p.
First novel--Western Reserve--1856--New Hartford, Ohio--Episodic.

Tey, Josephine pseud. see Mackintosh, Elizabeth

5976 Thackeray, William Makepeace (1811-1863). The
virginians; a tale of the last century. London:
Bradbury, 1858-59. 2 vols.
1756-1783--Early career of George Washington--
Virginia--Sequel to Henry Esmond--Appeared serially
in Harper's Monthly Magazine --Treatment of Washington
unconventional for era.

Thane, Elswyth pseud. see Beebe, Elswyth

Thanet, Octave pseud. see French, Alice

5977 Thayer, Tiffany Ellsworth (1902-   ) pseud. Ellsworth,
Elmer. Call her savage. New York: Kendall, 1931.
316p.
Daughter of Texas pioneer family--Call her
Nasa--Color her sex.

Thickstun, Frederick pseud. see Clark, Frederick
Thickstun

5978 Thomas, Mrs. Anna Lloyd (Braithwaite) (1854-   ).
Nancy lloyd; the journal of a quaker pioneer. New
York: Frank-Maurice, 1927. 192p.
Pennsylvania--1680-1700--Diary of caring for
ten members of family--Founding of colony--Mrs.
Hannah Hill (1666-1726?).

Thomas, Charles jt. author, see Roark, Garland

5979 Thomas, Frederick William. East and west. Philadelphia:
Carey, 1836. 2 vols.
Kentucky--Mississippi River and Ohio River.

Thomas, Kate pseud. see Bull, Katherine Thomas (Jarboe)

5980 Thomas, William Henry. The whaleman's adventures in
the sandwich islands and california. Boston: Lee,
1872. 444p.

5981 Thomason, John William (1893-   ). Gone to texas.
New York: Scribner's, 1937. 274p.
Late 1860's--Romance--Adventure--Humor--South
Texas.

5982 Thomes, William Henry. On land and sea; or, california
in the years 1843, '44, and '45. Boston: DeWolfe,
1884. 351p.

5983　Thompson, Daniel Pierce (1795-1868). The green mountain
　　　　boys; a historical tale of the early settlement of
　　　　vermont. Montpelier, Vermont: Walton, 1839. 2 vols.
　　　　1757-1775--Romance--Juvenile.

5984　---Locke amsden; or, the schoolmaster. Boston: Mossey,
　　　　1847. 231p.
　　　　Vermont frontier life.

5985　---The rangers; or, the tory's daughter. a tale,
　　　　illustrative of the revolutionary history of vermont,
　　　　and the northern campaign of 1777. Boston: Mussey,
　　　　1851. 2 vols.
　　　　George Rogers Clark--1779.

5986　---Gaut gurley; or, the trappers of umbagog. Boston:
　　　　Jewett, 1857. 360p.
　　　　Maine frontier life.

5987　---The doomed chief; or, two hundred years ago. Phil-
　　　　adelphia: Bradley, 1860. 473p.

5988　Thompson, James Myers (1906-　　　). Heed the thunder;
　　　　a novel. New York: Greenberg, 1946. 297p.
　　　　Nebraska--1940's.

5989　Thompson, Maurice (1844-1901). Alice of old vincennes.
　　　　Indianapolis: Bowen, 1900. 419p.
　　　　Old northwest--1778--Adventure.

5990　Thompson, Thomas. Broken valley. New York: Doubleday,
　　　　1949. 224p.
　　　　Western

5991　---Sundown riders. New York: Doubleday, 1950. 224p.
　　　　Western

5992　---Gunman brand. New York: Doubleday, 1951. 191p.
　　　　Western

5993　---Shadow of the butte. New York: Doubleday, 1952.
　　　　189p.
　　　　Western

5994　---King of abilene. New York: Ballantine, 1953. 181p.
　　　　Western

5995　---The steel web. New York: Doubleday, 1953. 189p.
　　　　Western

5996　---Trouble rider. New York: Ballantine, 1954. 164p.
　　　　Western

5997　---Brand of a man. New York: Doubleday, 1958. 188p.
　　　　Western

5998   ---Bitter water.   New York: Doubleday, 1960.   188p.
        Western

5999   ---Bonanza; one man with courage.   New York: Media,
        1966.   253p.
        Western

        Thorne, Hart pseud. see Carhart, Arthur Hawthorne

6000   Thorpe, Francis Newton (1857-1926).   The spoils of
        empire; a romance of the old world and the new.
        Boston: Little, 1903.   421p.

6001   Thruston, Lucy Meacham (Kidd) (1862-   ).   Mistress
        brent; a story of lord baltimore's colony in 1638.
        Boston: Little, 1901.   352p.

6002   Thurston, Mary Worthy and Breneman, Muriel pseud.
        Breneman, Mary Worthy.   Land they possessed.   New
        York: Macmillan, 1956.   335p.
                Dakota territory--1880's--Ukranian and American
        settlers--Farm and small town life.

6003   Tibbetts, Pearl Ashby (Mrs. R. R. Tibbetts).   Land
        under heaven.   Portland, Maine: Falmouth, 1937.
        296p.
                Aroostook County, Maine--Pioneer life--Conquest
        of wilderness.

6004   Tibbles, Thomas Henry.   Hidden power; a secret history
        of the indian ring, its operations, intrigues, and
        machinations.   revealing the manner in which it
        controls three important departments of the united
        states government.   a defense of the u. s. army
        and a solution of the indian problem.   New York:
        Carleton, 1881.   356p.

6005   Tiernan, Mary Spear (Nicholas) (1836-1891).   Homoselle.
        Boston: Osgood, 1881.   367p.
                Life on James River--1830-1860.

6006   ---Suzette; a novel.   New York: Holt, 1885.   306p.
                Richmond life.

        Tilton, Dwight pseud. of Richardson, George Tilton
        and Quint, Wilder Dwight see Richardson, George
        Tilton

6007   Tindale, Norman Barnett (1900-   ) and Lindsay, Harold
        Arthur (1900-   ).   Rangatira, the high-born; a
        polynesian saga.   New York: Watts, 1959.   208p.
                Reconstruction of migration of Polynesians
        from Hawaii to New Zealand--Juvenile.

6008   Tippett, Thomas (1894-   ).   Horse shoe bottoms.

New York: Harper, 1935. 298p.
Illinois mining--1870--Labor novel.

6009 Titus, Harold (1888-   ). Bruce of the circle a.
Boston: Small, 1918. 294p.
Western

6010 ---Last straw. Boston: Small, 1920. 288p.
Western

6011 ---Spindrift; a novel of the great lakes. New York:
Doubleday, 1925. 326p.
Adventure

6012 ---The man from yonder. Philadelphia: Macrae, 1934.
272p.
Adventure--Lumber.

6013 ---Black feather. Philadelphia: Macrae, 1936. 285p.
Fur trading.

6014 Tobenkin, Elias (1882-   ). The house of conrad.
New York: Stokes, 1918. 375p.
Chronicle--Three generations--German immigrant
family--1868.

6015 Todd, Helen (1912-   ). So free we seem; a novel.
New York: Reynal, 1936. 369p.
Missouri frontier--Young couple--Husband left--
Returns after fourteen years.

6016 Todd, Mary Van Lennup (Ives) by M. I. T.. Deborah,
the advanced woman. Boston: Arena, 1896. 233p.
Mormons--Salt Lake City--Early days.

6017 Tolbert, Frank Xavier. The staked plain. New York:
Harper, 1956. 272p.
Texas 1870--Fictional account of real people--
South Plains Indians--Lonnie (Llano Etacado) Nabos
son of scout Gehugh Nabors--Antelope Commanche.

6018 Tomkinson, Grace. Welcome wilderness; a novel. New
York: Washburn, 1946. 289p.
American Revolution--New England loyalists
to maritime province close of war.

6019 Tomlinson, Everett Titsworth. Exiled from two lands.
Boston: Lee, 1898. 119p.
French to Canada late 1700's.

6020 ---The young minute-man of 1812. Boston: Houghton,
1912. 343p.
Juvenile

6021 Tompkins, Walter A.. Thundergust trail. New York:

Phoenix, 1942. 256p.
Western

6022 ---Border bonanza. New York: Phoenix, 1943. 256p.
Western

6023 ---Texas tumbleweed. New York: Phoenix, 1943. 256p.
Western

6024 ---The scout of terror trail. New York: Phoenix, 1944.
256p.
Western

6025 ---Trouble on funeral range. New York: Phoenix, 1944.
256p.
Western

6026 ---Flaming canyon; a western novel. Philadelphia:
Macrae, 1948. 239p.
Western

6027 ---West of texas law. Philadelphia: Macrae, 1948.
285p.
Western

6028 ---Manhunt west. Philadelphia: Macrae, 1949. 254p.
Western

6029 ---Rimrock rider. Philadelphia: Macrae, 1950. 256p.
Western

6030 ---Roy rogers and the ghost of mystery rancho; an
original story featuring roy rogers, famous motion
picture star as hero. Racine, Wisconsin: Whitman,
1950. 250p.
Western

6031 ---Border ambush. Philadelphia: Macrae, 1951. 254p.
Western

6032 ---Prairie marshall. Philadelphia: Macrae, 1952.
249p.
Western

6033 ---Gold on the hoof. Philadelphia: Macrae, 1953.
221p.
Western

6034 ---Texas renegade. Philadelphia: Macrae, 1954. 219p.
Western

6035 ---SOS at midnight. Philadelphia: Macrae, 1957. 223p.
Western

6036 Toner, Raymond John. Midshipman davy jones; being the log of his adventures aboard diverse frigates; sloops of war, and other fighting craft of the united states navy; together with an account of his captivity in, and escape from, the islands of bermuda, during the late war with great britain, 1812-1815. wherein may be discovered to those of nautical mind, sundry time-honored naval customs, and the routine observed aboard united states men of war. to the adventurous, a recounting of gallant deeds of iron men in wooden ships. written and illustrated by lieutenant (j.g.) raymond j. toner. Chicago: Whitman, 1938. 328p.

6037 ---Meeheevee; being an account of the commerce-raiding cruise of the united states frigate essex into the south pacific seas under the command of captain david porter, u. s. navy anno 1812-1814; written and illustrated by lieutenant (j.g.) raymond j. toner. Chicago: Whitman, 1940. 319p.

Topping, John Dewey jt. author, see Miller, Mrs. Helen (Topping)

6038 Tourgée, Albion Winegar (1838-1905). Figs and thistles; a western story. New York: Fords, 1879. 538p.

6039 ---Button's inn. Boston: Roberts, 1887. 418p. Joseph Smith--Mormons--New York State.

6040 Towner, Ausburn. Chedayne of kotono; a story of the early days of the republic. New York: Dodd, 1877. 606p.
Wyoming Valley, Pennsylvania.

6041 Townsend, George Alfred. Katy of catoctin; or, the chain-breakers. a national romance. New York: Appleton, 1886. 567p.
From John Brown's raid to death of A. Lincoln.

6042 Townshend, Richard Baxter. Lone pine; the story of the lost mine. New York: Putnam, 1899. 400p.
Pueblo Indians--1870's.

6043 Trace, John. Rough messa. New York: Doubleday, 1940. 277p.
Western

6044 ---Trigger vengeance. New York: Doubleday, 1940. 272p.
Western

6045 ---Range of golden hoofs. New York: Doubleday, 1941. 270p.
Western

6046 Tracy, Don (1905-   ). Chesapeake cavalier.

New York: Dial, 1949. 376p.
   Virginia--Seventeenth century--Young indentured
boy--Jamestown--Good.

6047   ---Crimson is the eastern shore. New York: Dial, 1953.
440p.
   Maryland--War of 1812.

6048   ---Roanoke renegade. New York: Dial, 1954. 367p.
   Raleigh's lost colony--1580's.

6049   ---Carolina corsair. New York: Dial, 1955. 375p.
   Edward Teach (d. 1718).

6050   ---Cherokee. New York: Dial, 1957. 376p.
   War in the Smokies--Suti-young Cherokee Chief--
Two Fallen Panthers Chief (1807-1808)--Romance.

6051   Tracy, Edward B.. Great horse of the plains. New York:
Dodd, 1954. 215p.
   Western

   Traver, Robert pseud. see Voelker, John

6052   Trowbridge, John Townsend (1827-1916). Cudjo's cave.
Boston: Lothrop, 1891. 504p.
   Tennessee--Underground railroad.

6053   Troyer, Howard William (1901-   ). The salt and the
savor. New York: Wyn, 1950. 284p.
   Indiana--Pioneer days to Civil War--Daily life.

6054   Truax, Rhoda (Mrs. R. H. Aldrich). Green is the
golden tree; a novel. Indianapolis: Bobbs, 1943.
306p.
   Founding of Utopian community upstate New York--
"Elysian Field"--Post-Civil War.

6055   The true narrative of the five years' suffering and
perilous adventures by miss barber, wife of "squatting
bear," a celebrated sioux chief. [Anonymous].
Philadelphia: Barclay, 1872. 108p.

6056   Trumball, Annie Eliot. Mistress content craddock. New
York: Barnes, 1899. 306p.
   Colonial New England.

6057   Tucker, George. The valley of shenandoah; or, memoirs
of the graysons. New York: Wiley, 1824. 2 vols.
   Early 1800's--Hubbell "...The Virginia Clarissa
Harlowe."

6058   Tucker, Nathaniel Beverley (1784-1851). George balcombe;
a novel. [Anonymous]. New York: Harper, 1836. 2 vols.

6059 Tucker, St. George. Hansford; a tale of bacon's rebellion
       Richmond, Virginia: West, 1857. 356p.
       1676--Thomas Hansford (d.1677).

6060 Tufts, Anne. Rails along the chesapeake. New York:
       Holt, 1957. 223p.
       Baltimore--1830's--Juvenile.

6061 Tupper, Tristram. Jorgensen. Philadelphia: Lippincott,
       1926. 267p.
       Railroad building--Mountains--Romance.

6062 Turnbull, Mrs. Agnes (Sligh) (1888-   ). The rolling
       years. New York: Macmillan, 1936. 436p.
       Chronicle--Three generations--American family
       in Scottish community--Western Pennsylvania--1870-
       1910--Farm life.

6063 ---The day must dawn. New York: Macmillan, 1942.
       483p.
       Revolution Era--Western Pennsylvania--Family
       life--Simon Girty--Indians.

6064 Turpin, Waters Edward (1910-   ). These low grounds.
       New York: Harper, 1937. 344p.
       Chronicle--Four generations of negroes--
       Eastern shore Maryland--1850-1930's.

6065 Tuttle, Hudson (1836-1910). Clair; a tale of mormon
       perfidy. Chicago: n.p., 1881. (?).
       Wright, "Listed in Coyle".

6066 Tuttle, Wilbur C. (1883-   ). Reddy brant, his
       adventures. New York: Century, 1920. 285p.
       Western

6067 ---Straight shooting. New York: Garden City, 1926.
       181p.
       Western

6068 ---Thicker than water; a story of hashknife hartley.
       Boston: Houghton, 1927. 306p.
       Western

6069 ---The morgan trail; a story of hashknife hartley.
       Boston: Houghton, 1928. 308p.
       Western

6070 ---Sad sontag plays his hunch. New York: Doubleday,
       1928. 179p.
       Western

6071 ---The red head from sun dog. Boston: Houghton, 1930.
       290p.
       Western

6072 ---The valley of twisted trails. Boston: Houghton, 1931. 269p.
Western

6073 ---Mystery at the jhc ranch. Boston: Houghton, 1932. 238p.
Western

6074 ---Silver bar mystery. Boston: Houghton, 1933. 243p.
Western

6075 ---Rifled gold. Boston: Houghton, 1934. 272p.
Western

6076 ---Santa dolores stage; a story of hashknife hartley. Boston: Houghton, 1934. 273p.
Western

6077 ---Hashknife of stormy river. Boston: Houghton, 1935. 252p.
Western

6078 ---Tumbling river range. Boston: Houghton, 1935. 252p.
Western

6079 ---Hashknife of the double bar 8. Boston: Houghton, 1936. 244p.
Western

6080 ---Henry the sheriff. Boston: Houghton, 1936. 283p.
Western

6081 ---Bluffer's luck. Boston: Houghton, 1937. 251p.
Western

6082 ---The keeper of red horse pass. Boston: Houghton, 1937. 252p.
Western

6083 ---Wandering dogies. Boston: Houghton, 1938. 244p.
Western

6084 ---Wild horse valley. Boston: Houghton, 1938. 248p.
Western

6085 ---The medicine-man; a hashknife story. Boston: Houghton, 1939. 284p.
Western

6086 ---Singing river. Boston: Houghton, 1939. 252p.
Western

6087 ---Ghost trails. Boston: Houghton, 1940. 275p.
Western

6088 ---Shotgun gold. Boston: Houghton, 1940. 226p.
Western

6089 ---The tin god of twisted river. Boston: Houghton,
1941. 242p.
Western

6090 ---Mystery of the red triangle. Boston: Houghton,
1942. 248p.
Western

6091 ---The valley of vanishing herds; a hashknife hartley
story. Boston: Houghton, 1942. 248p.
Western

6092 ---Hidden blood. Boston: Houghton, 1943. 244p.
Western

6093 ---The wolf pack of lobo butte. Boston: Houghton,
1945. 197p.
Western

6094 ---The trouble trailer. Boston: Houghton, 1946. 199p.
Western

6095 ---Renegade sheriff. New York: Bouregy, 1953. 256p.
Western

6096 ---Thunderbird range. New York: Avalon, 1953. 255p.
Western

6097 ---Mission river justice. New York: Avalon, 1955.
256p.
Western

Twain, Mark pseud. see Clemens, Samuel

6098 Twombly, Alexander Stevenson. Kela, the surf-rider;
a romance of pagan hawaii. New York: Fords, 1900.
402p.

6099 Tyler, Royall. The algerine captive; or, the life and
adventures of dr. updike underhill. [pseud.] six
years a prisoner among the algerines. Walpole,
New Hampshire: n.p., 1797. 2 vols.

6100 Tynan, James J.. The great divide. New York: Grosset,
1925. 293p.
Western based on MGM movie.

6101 Tyson, John Audrey (1870-   ). The stirrup cup.
New York: Appleton, 1903. 208p.
American Revolution--Pennsylvania and New
York--1777--Aaron Burr--Theodosia Prevost.

472

U

6102 Ullman, Allan and Bloom, Rolfe. The naked spur. New
      York: Random, 1952. 175p.
          Western--Based on movie scenaria.

6103 Ulyatt, Kenneth (1920-   ). North against the sioux.
      New York: Prentice, 1967. 224p.
          1860's--Ft. Philip Kearney--Ft. Laramie--
      Powder River.

6104 Underhill, Ruth Murray (1884-   ). Hawk over whirl-
      pools. New York: Augustin, 1940. 255p.
          Papago--Desert Indians of Arizona--Good.

6105 Upchurch, Boyd. The slave stealer; a novel. New
      York: Weybright, 1968. 382p.
          Slave story--Pre-Civil War--Underground rail-
      road.
6106 Updegraff, Mrs. Florence Maule. Blue dowry. New
      York: Harcourt, 1948. 271p.
          Pre-Revolution--Connecticut farm.

6107   Vachell, Horace Annesley (1861-1955). Spragge's
          canyon; a character study. New York: Doran,
          1915. 320p.
             Pioneer family--Ranch life.

6108   Vaczek, Louis C.. River and empty sea. Boston:
          Houghton, 1950. 372p.
             Quebec--1671.

6109   Vance, Wilson J.. Big john baldwin; extracts from the
          journal of an officer of cromwell's army recording
          some of his experiences at the court of charles I
          and susequently at that of the lord protector and
          on the fields of love and war, and finally in the
          colony of virginia edited with sparing hand by
          wilson vance. New York: Holt, 1909. 375p.
             1642-1660--Journal seventeenth century English-
          man.

6110   Van Deventer, Emma Murdoch pseud. Lynch, Lawrence L..
          A mountain mystery; or, the outlaws of the rockies.
          Chicago: Loyd, 1887. 600p.
             Western

6111   Van De Water, Frederic Franklyn (1890-1968). Reluctant
          rebel. New York: Duell, 1948. 442p.
             #1 of Vermont Series--Ethan Allen--Green
          Mountain Boys v. Yorkers and British--New Hampshire
          Grants--1711--To Battle of Ticonderoga.

6112   ---Catch a falling star. New York: Duell, 1949. 362p.
             #2 of Vermont Series--American Revolution--
          Sequel to Reluctant Rebel--Ends-1780-1781--Vermont.

6113   ---Wings of the morning. New York: Washburn, 1955.
          335p.
             #3 of Vermont Series--1777-1791--New Yorkers
          v. Vermonters.

6114   ---Day of battle. New York: Washburn, 1958. 365p.
             #4 of Vermont Series--Ticonderoga to Battle
          of Bennington--1777.

6115   Van Every, Dale (1896-   ). Westward the river.
          New York: Putnam, 1945. 275p.
             First novel--1790's--Louisiana from Spain to
          France--Hero-Kentucky settler.

6116   ---The shining mountains. New York: Messner, 1948.
       407p.
                Lewis and Clark Expedition--1803-1804--Good.

6117   ---Bridal journey. New York: Messner, 1950. 311p.
                1778--Trip from Tidewater to Ohio frontier
       outpost--Romance and adventure.

6118   ---The captive witch. New York: Messner, 1951. 362p.
                Opening American west--1779--Vincennes--
       Romance.

6119   ---The trembling earth. New York: Messner, 1953.
       310p.
                Missouri--1811--Lead mining--Earthquake.

6120   ---The voyagers. New York: Holt, 1957. 347p.
                American frontier--1780's--Ohio and Mississippi
       Rivers--White woman taken by Sioux--Good work.

6121   ---Scarlet feather. New York: Holt, 1959. 315p.
                Frontier life--1785--Kentucky.

6122   Van Schaick, George Gray (1861-   ). Son of the
       otter. Boston: Small, 1915. 345p.
                Hudson's Bay Company trader--Ahteck wife of
       Peter McLeod--Agent at Grand Lac--Romance.

6123   Van Zile, Edward Sims (1863-1931). With sword and
       crucifix; being an account of the strange adventures
       of count louis de sancerre, companion of sieur de
       la salle on the lower mississippi....1682. New
       York: Harper, 1900. 298p.

6124   Varble, Mrs. Rachel Margaret (McBrayer). Romance
       for rosa. New York: Doubleday, 1946. 276p.
                London Company--Virginia--Juvenile.

       Vaughn, Carter A. pseud. see Gerson, Noel Bertram
       (1914-   )

6125   Venable, Clarke (1892-   ). All the brave rifles.
       Chicago: Reilly, 1929. 369p.
                1836--Events leading to Texas Revolution.

6126   Venable, William Henry (1836-1920). A dream of empire;
       or, the house of blennerhassett. New York: Dodd,
       1901. 344p.
                Burr's scheme.

       Vernon, Charles pseud. see Craven, Braxton

       Vestal, Stanley pseud. see Campbell, Walter

       Vic St. L. (Jeune Hopkins) pseud. see Hopkins, Squire D.

6127 Victor, Mrs. Metta Victoria (Fuller). Mormon wives; a narrative of facts stranger than fiction. New York: Derby, 1856. 326p.

Vincent, Dwight jt. author, see Keene, Day

6128 Vining, Mrs. Elizabeth (Gray) (1902-   ). Meggy macintosh. New York: Doubleday, 1930. 274p.
Scotch girl to America--1775--Carolina--Juvenile.

6129 ---Jane hope. New York: Viking, 1933. 276p.
Chapel Hill, North Carolina--Juvenile.

6130 ---The virginia exiles. Philadelphia: Lippincott, 1955. 317p.
American Revolution--Quakers in Philadelphia--Loyalty oath.

Virginian see Tabb, T. T.

6131 Voelker, John pseud. Travers, Robert. Laughing white fish. New York: McGraw, 1965. 312p.
Lawyer author has lawyer plead case of Laughing White Fish--Indian girl claiming share of iron mine--Michigan--1870's.

6132 Vogdes, Walter. A great man. New York: Longmans, 1929. 310p.
From southern New Jersey to California--1850's--Life of '49 ers.

6133 Von Hagen, Victor Wolfgang (1908-   ). The sun kingdom of the aztecs. Cleveland, World Pub., 1958. 126p.
Juvenile

6134 Von Hesse, Maxeda Ferguson (1913-   ). Inherit the wind. New York: Morrow, 1943. 282p.
Based on sordid life of Seminole Indians--Everglades, Florida.

6135 Von Ziekursch, Theodore. White trail's end. Philadelphia: Macrae, 1925. 285p.
North country--Lumber.

W

6136 Wagner, Elby. <u>Partners three</u>. New York: Crowell,
1928. 295p.
Alaska--Prospecting--Adventure.

6137 Waite, Carlton. <u>A silver baron; a novel</u>. Boston:
Arena, 1896. 325p.
Colorado

6138 Waldman, Emerson. <u>The land is large</u>. New York:
Farrar, 1938. 379p.
Jewish immigrant from Russia to Mississippi
plantation.

6139 Walker, Ambrose. [Anonymous]. <u>The highlands; a tale
of the hudson</u>. Philadelphia: Printed for Author,
1826. 156p.
Late--1700's.

6140 Walker, Jesse. [Anonymous]. <u>Fort niagra; a tale of
the niagra frontier</u>. Buffalo: Steele, 1845. 156p.
Part II.

6141 ---<u>Queenston; a tale of niagra frontier</u>. Buffalo,
Steele, 1845. 151p.
Part I.

6142 Walker, Mrs. Mildred (Mrs. F. R. Schemm) (1905-   ).
<u>Fireweed</u>. New York: Harcourt, 1934. 314p.
First novel--Michigan--Lumber--Scandanavians.

6143 ---<u>Winter wheat</u>. New York: Harcourt, 1944. 306p.
Montana ranch--cf. <u>Growth of the Soil</u>.

6144 ---<u>The quarry</u>. New York: Harcourt, 1947. 407p.
Vermont--Civil War to 1914.

6145 ---<u>The curlew's cry</u>. New York: Harcourt, 1955. 382p.
Montana--1905-1940's--Pioneer days.

6146 Walker, Turnley. <u>The day after the fourth</u>. New York:
Appleton, 1958. 345p.
Western

6147 Wall, Mary Virginia. <u>The daughter of virginia dare</u>.
New York: Neale, 1908. 194p.
Pocahontas (d.1617)--Virginia Dare (b.1587).

6148 Wallace, Lewis (1827-1905). <u>The fair god; or, the last
of the 'tzins. a tale of the conquest of mexico</u>.

477

Boston: Houghton, 1873. 586p.
Archaelogical reconstruction of Mexican life--
Spanish Conquest--1519-1520.

6149 Wallace, Willard Mosher (1911-   ). Jonathan dearborn;
a novel of the war of 1812. Boston: Little, 1967.
376p.
Hartford Convention.

6150 Walsh, John Henry (1879-   ). Cam clarke. New York:
Macmillan, 1916. 309p.
Washtucna, Washington--One year in life of
frontier town.

6151 Walsh, Joseph Patrick pseud. Patrick, Joseph. King's
arrow. Philadelphia: Lippincott, 1951. 380p.
Smuggling--1758-1770--Romance--Adventure.

6152 Walsh, Marie A. pseud. "Sandette". A romance of the
great salt lake. New York: Carleton, 1878. 384p.

6153 Walters, Raube. The hex woman. New York: Macaulay,
1931. 320p.
Witchcraft--Pennsylvania Dutch--1850's--Good.

6154 Walworth, Alice. Lost river. New York: Dodd, 1938.
303p.
First novel--Reconstruction Mississippi River
plantation.

6155 ---Indigo bend. New York: Doubleday, 1954. 314p.
Natchez--Reconstruction.

6156 Walworth, Mansfield Tracy. Hotspur; a tale of the
old dutch manor. New York: Carleton, 1864. 324p.
New York

Walz, Mrs. Audrey jt. author, see Walz, Jay

6157 Walz, Jay and (Mrs.) Audrey pseud. Bonnamy, Francis.
The bizarre sisters. New York: Duell, 1950. 371p.
Based on scandal involving some members of
Randolph family of Virginia--Strong.

Ward, A. B. pseud. see Bailey, Mrs. Alice Ward

6158 Ward, Austin N. [pseud.?]. The husband in utah; or,
sights and scenes among the mormons, with remarks
on their moral and social economy. by austin n.
ward [pseud.?]. edited by maria ward [pseud.?].
New York: Derby, 1857. 310p.

Ward, Brad pseud. see Peeples, Samuel Anthony

478

6159   Ward, Christopher Longstreth (1868-1943). Strange
        adventures of jonathan drew, a rolling stone during
        his travels through massachusetts, connecticut,
        rhode island, new york, pennsylvania, virginia, ohio,
        indiana, illinois, missouri, and kentucky in the
        years 1821-1824. together with some account of the
        people he met, the things they did and said, the
        songs they sang and the roads they travelled as taken
        down by christopher ward esq.. New York: Simon,
        1932. 399p.
              Picaresque--Drawn from Ash's Travels.

6160   ---Yankee rover; being the story of the adventures of
        jonathan drew during his travels in the south and
        far west by road, river and trail in the years 1824-
        1829, together with some account of the people he
        met white, black and red, good,bad and indifferent,
        his friends and enemies and what they did or tried
        to do. as taken down by christopher ward esq..
        New York: Simon, 1932. 323p.
              Sequel to Strange Adventures...--To Santa Fé.

6161   Ward, Mrs. Florence Jeannette (Baier) (1886-   ).
        Dales acre. New York: Dutton, 1939. 308p.
              Early nineteenth century--Fifty miles out of
        Chicago--Family life.

6162   Ward, Mrs. Maria [pseud.?]. Female life among the
        mormons. a narrative of many years' personal
        experience. by the wife of a mormon elder recently
        from utah. New York: Derby, 1855. 449p.
              Sabin attributes this to Mrs. Benj. G. Ferris.

6163   Ware, Clyde. The innocents. New York: Norton, 1969.
        240p.
              Old prospector and half-wild girl--Old west.

6164   Ware, Edmund. Rider in the sun. Boston: Lothrop,
        1935. 197p.
              Boy from eastern home to western ranch.

       Ware, John Fleming jt. author, see Hogeboom, Amy

6165   Warinner, Emily V.. Voyager to destiny; the amazing
        adventures of manjiro, the man who changed worlds
        twice. Indianapolis: Bobbs, 1956. 267p.
              Manjiro Nakahama to America.

6166   Warren, Charles Marquis (1912-   ). Only the valiant.
        New York: Macmillan, 1943. 327p.
              Cavalry--Indians--Army post--Old west.

6167   ---Valley of the shadow. New York: Doubleday, 1948.
        255p.
              Western

6168 Warren, Israel Perkins. Chauncey judd; or, the stolen
      boy. a story of the revolution. New York: Warren,
      1874. 314p.
          Juvenile

6169 Warren, Lella (1899-   ). Foundation stone. New York:
      Knopf, 1940. 754p.
          Chronicle--Pioneering in Alabama--1820;s through
      reconstruction--cf. Gone With The Wind.

6170 Warren, Robert Penn (1905-   ). World enough and
      time; a romantic novel. New York: Random, 1950.
      512p.
          Reconstruction of nineteenth century murder
      case--Kentucky--1820's--Philosophical.

6171 ---Band of angels. New York: Random, 1955. 375p.
          Chronicle--Amantha Star--Sold as slave--
      Kentucky plantation.

6172 Warren, William Stephen (1882-   ). Tony gay on the
      longhorn trail. Philadelphia: McKay, 1949. 205p.
          Western--Juvenile.

6173 Warriner, Edward Augustus by a broad churchman.
      Victor la tourette; a novel. Boston: Roberts, 1875.
      406p.
          Religion--Michigan frontier.

6174 Washburn, Charles Ames. Philip thaxter; a novel.
      New York: Rudd, 1861. 350p.
          California--mining.

6175 Wason, Robert Alexander (1874-   ). Happy hawkins.
      Boston: Small, 1909. 352p.
          Western

6176 ---Happy hawkins in the panhandle. Boston: Small, 1914.
      492p.
          Western

6177 Waterhouse, Benjamin. A journal of a young man of
      massachusetts, late a surgeon on board an american
      privateer who was captured at sea by the british in
      may eighteen hundred and thirteen. Boston: Rowe,
      1816. 228p.

6178 Waterhouse, E. B.. Serra, california conquistador; a
      narrative history. Los Angeles: Parker, 1968. 290p.
          Junipero Serra (1713-1784).

6179 Waters, Frank (1902-   ). The wild earth's nobilty.
      New York: Liveright, 1935. 454p.
          #1 of Colorado Mining Trilogy--1875-1900.

480

6180 ---Below grass roots. New York: Liveright, 1937.
523p.
#2 of Colorado Mining Trilogy.

6181 ---The dust within the rock. New York: Liveright,
1940. 534p.
#3 of Colorado Mining Trilogy.

6182 ---People of the valley. New York: Farrar, 1941.
309p.
Spanish-Americans forced from ancestral homes
by government dam.

6183 ---The man who killed the deer. New York: Farrar,
1942. 311p.
Pueblo Indians--1940--Cultural conflict--
Excellent.

Waters, Frank jt. author, see Branch, Houston, River
Lady, 1942. Diamond Head, 1948.

6184 Waters, Gladys Poe (Mrs. Chester E. Smedley) (1886-   ).
Fairacres; a novel of the shepherd family and the
founding of independence, missouri. Denver, Colorado:
Univ. of Denver Press, 1952. 463p.
1826--Good--Based on family experience.

6185 Watson, Augusta (Campbell) (1862-   ). The old
harbor town; a novel. New York: Dillingham, 1892.
275p.
1781--New London.

6186 ---Dorothy the puritan; the story of a strange delusion.
New York: Dutton, 1893. 341p.
Salem, Massachusetts--1691.

6187 Watson, Sally. The hornet's nest. New York: Holt,
1967. 246p.
From Island of Skye to Williamsburg--Juvenile--
Distinguished book.

6188 Watson, Virginia Cruse (1872-   ). The princess
pocahontas. Philadelphia: Penn, 1916. 306p.
Juvenile

6189 ---With cortes the conqueror. Philadelphia: Penn,
1917. 332p.
Juvenile

6190 ---With la salle the explorer. New York: Holt, 1922.
366p.
Juvenile

6191 ---Manhattan acres; the story of a new york family.
New York: Dutton, 1934. 287p.

481

Chronicle--Ten generations--Van Kampen family--
1577-1933--Growth of Manhattan.

6192 ---Flags over quebec; a story of the conquest of canada.
New York: Coward, 1941. 217p.
French-Indian War (1755-1763)--Juvenile.

6193 Watters, Augustus. The vale of rampo; a new jersey idyl.
Newark, New Jersey: Hardham, 1886. 127p.

6194 ---A newark knight; a romance. Newark, New Jersey:
Hardham, 1888. 151p.

6195 ---The puritans; or, newark in the olden time. an
historical romance. Newark, New Jersey: n.p.,
1894. 107p.

6196 Watts, Mrs. Mary Stanberry (1868-   ). Nathan burke.
New York: Macmillan, 1910. 628p.
Ohio--1840-1860--Soldier--Mexican War.

6197 Way, Mrs. Isabel Stewart. Seed of the land. New York:
Appleton, 1935. 293p.
Life on midwest farm.

Wayne, Joseph pseud. see Overholser, Wayne D.

Weaver, Ward pseud. see Mason, F. Van Wyck

6198 Webb, Barbara (1898-   ). Aletta laird. New York:
Doubleday, 1935. 304p.
American Revolution--Bermuda--Romance.

6199 Webb, Jack pseud. Grady, Tex. High mesa. New York:
Dutton, 1952. 223p.
Western

6200 Webb, James Plimell (1903-   ). Riley dawson. New
York: Dodd, 1950. 245p.
Recreation Kentucky mountain life--Juvenile.

6201 Webber, Charles Wilkins (1819-1856). Old hicks, the
guide; or, the adventures in the camanche country
in search of a gold mine. New York: Harper, 1848.
356p.
Western--Melodrama.

6202 ---The gold mines of the gila. New York: Dewitt, 1849.
2 vols.
Sequel to Old Hicks.

6203 ---The prairie scout; or, agatone the renegade. New
York: Dewitt, 1852. 288p.
Wright, "In part Gold Mines of The Gila."

482

6204 ---The wild girl of the nebraska. Philadelphia:
     Lippincott, 1852. 87p.
          Romance

6205 Webber, Everett (1907-   ) and Webber, Olga (1910-   ).
     Rampart street. New York: Dutton, 1948. 318p.
     New Orleans--1800's--Romance.

6206 ---Bound girl. New York: Dutton, 1949. 314p.
     Kansas--Missouri border--1865ca.--Romance.

     Webber, Olga jt. author, see Webber, Everett

6207 Weber, Mrs. Lenora (Mattingly) (1895-   ). Wind on
     the prairie. Boston: Little, 1929. 276p.
          Juvenile

6208 ---Rocking chair ranch. Boston: Houghton, 1936. 210p.
          Western--Juvenile.

6209 Weber, William Louis. Josh. New York: McGraw, 1969.
     256p.
          First novel--Southern boy--Adventures--Civil
     War Era.

6210 Webster, J. Provand. Children of wrath. London:
     Routledge, 1889. [?].
          Virginia--1687-1697.

     Webster, M. M. pseud. see Mosby, Mary Webster

6211 Weiner, Willard. Morning in america. New York: Farrar,
     1942. 303p.
          American Revolution--Charles Lee--Debunked as
     fascist--cf. Oliver Wiswell.

6212 Weir, James (1821-   ). Lonz powers; or, the regulators.
     a romance of kentucky. Philadelphia: Lippincott,
     1850. 2 vols.
          Pioneer justice.

6213 ---Simon kenton; or, the scout's revenge. an historical
     novel. Philadelphia: Lippincott, 1852. 195p.
          Boone's companion--1790's--Carolina frontier.

6214 ---The winter lodge; or, vow fulfilled. an historical
     novel. Philadelphia: Lippincott, 1854. 231p.
          Sequel to Simon Kenton.

     Welch, Ronald pseud. see Felton, Ronald Oliver

6215 Weld, John (1905-   ). Don't you cry for me; a novel.
     New York: Scribner's, 1940. 494p.
          To California--1846--Based on Donner Party.

6216 ---The pardners; a novel of the california gold rush. New York: Scribner's, 1941. 349p.

6217 ---Sabbath has no end; a novel of negro slavery. New York: Scribner's, 1942. 329p.
South Carolina--1815.

6218 Wellman, Manly Wade (1905-   ). Candle of the wicked. New York: Putnam, 1960. 317p.
Fort Scott--Independence Road--Kansas--1873.

6219 Wellman, Paul Iselin (1898-1966). Broncho apache; a novel. New York: Macmillan, 1936. 303p.
1886--Massai escaped from Geronimo train--Illinois to Arizona--Return to home.

6220 ---Jubal troop. New York: Doubleday, 1939. 583p.
1886-1916--Career of Jubal Troop--West--Panorama.

6221 ---Angel with spurs. New York: Lippincott, 1942. 508p.
Joseph Shelby (1830-1897)--One thousand men to Mexico--Juarez--Maxmillan--1860's.

6222 ---The bowl of brass. Philadelphia: Lippincott, 1944. 319p.
#1 of Titrology--South western, Kansas--Conflict for county seat--1880's.

6223 ---The walls of jericho. Philadelphia: Lippincott, 1947. 423p.
#2 of Tetrology--Kansas--Plains country.
#3 is The Chain (1949)--Religious novel.

6224 ---The iron mistress. New York: Doubleday, 1951. 404p.
James Bowie (1805-1836).

6225 ---The comancheros. New York: Doubleday, 1952. 286p.
New Orleans gambler and Texas ranger--Catch Comancheros.

6226 ---Jericho's daughters; a novel. New York: Doubleday, 1956. 380p.
#4 of Tetrology--Story of woman.

6227 ---Ride the red earth; a novel. New York: Doubleday, 1958. 448p.
Louis St. Denis (1676-1744)--France and Spain in southwest--Melodramatic.

6228 ---Magnificent destiny; a novel about the great secret adventure of andrew jackson and sam houston. New York: Doubleday, 1962. 479p.
Biographical novel--Heroic Jackson.

484

6229 ---The buckstones; a novel. New York: Trident, 1967.
436p.
1820's-1830's--Bonded servant--"Perils of
Pauline" style.

6230 Wells, Evelyn. A city for st. francis. New York:
Doubleday, 1967. 374p.
Second Anza Expedition--1770's--Establish
San Francisco--Good--Based on true experience.

6231 Wells, Helena. The step mother; a domestic tale from
real life. by a lady. London: n.p., 1789. 2 vols.
Loyalist from South Carolina to London--Didactic--
Sentimental.

6232 Wells, Lee E. pseud. Poole, Richard. Danger valley.
New York: Doubleday, 1968. 207p.
Western

6233 ---Gun vote at valdoro. New York: Doubleday, 1969.
Western

6234 Welton, Miss A. E.. Cora; a tale of right and wrong.
a novel of today. New York: Ogilvie, 1891. 187p.
Early Omaha.

6235 Welty, Eudora (1909-   ). The robber bridegroom.
New York: Doubleday, 1942. 185p.
Natchez country early 1800's--Romance bandit
chief and daughter of Mississippi plantation owner.

6236 Wendt, Lloyd. Bright tomorrow. Indianapolis: Bobbs,
1945. 304p.
Gann, Dakota--Farm town.

6237 Wertenbaker, Charles Christian (1901-   ). The barons.
New York: Random, 1950. 579p.
Chronicle--One hundred and twenty-five years--
Industrial family.

6238 Wescott, Glenway (1901-   ). The grandmothers; a
family portrait. New York: Harper, 1927. 338p.
Chronicle--Wisonsin family--1840-1900.

6239 West, Jessamyn. Friendly persuasion. New York: Harcourt,
1945. 214p.
First novel--Quakers--Indiana--1860's.

6240 ---The witch diggers. New York: Harcourt, 1951. 441p.
Southern Indiana--1899--Farm.

6241 ---South of the angels. New York: Harcourt, 1960.
564p.
San Francisco--New farming and new housing--
Pioneering.

6242 ---Leafy rivers. New York: Harcourt, 1967. 310p.
Ohio frontier--Early 1800's--Feminine view.

6243 ---Except for me and thee. New York: Harcourt, 1969.
320p.
Quaker Indiana family--Sequel to Friendly
Persuasion.

West, Tom pseud. see East, Fred

6244 West, Ward. Halfway to timberline. New York: Greenberg,
1935. 246p.
Western

6245 Westcott, Jan (Vlachos) (1912-   ). Captain for
elizabeth. New York: Crown, 1948. 358p.
Thomas Cavendish (1555?-1592)--Third round
world trip--Sea adventure.

6246 ---Captain barney; a novel. New York: Crown, 1951.
286p.
American Revolution--Joshua Barney (1759-1818)--
Romance.

6247 Western border life; or, what fanny hunter saw and
heard in kanzas and missouri. [Anonymous]. New York:
Derby, 1856. 408p.

Westland, Alan pseud. see Joscelyn, Archie

Westland, Lynn pseud. see Joscelyn, Archie

6248 Westley, George Hembert (1865-   ). The maid and
the miscreant. Boston: Mayhew, 1906. 217p.
Puritan colony and English rogue.

6249 Wetherell, June (Mrs. Daniel Platt Frame). The glorious
three. New York: Dutton, 1951. 320p.
From Connecticut to Puget Sound area--1840's--
Romance and tragedy--Boundary dispute.

6250 Whalen, William Wilfrid. Golden squaw; being the story
of mary jemison, the irish girl stolen by the indians
from buchanan valley, adams county, pennsylvania in
1758. a story too strange and grim not to be true.
Philadelphia: Dorrance, 1926. 228p.

6251 Wharton, Thomas Issac. A latter day saint; being the
story of the conversion of ethel jones. related
by herself. New York: Holt, 1884. 200p.
Mormon

6252 Wheelwright, Jere Hungerford. Kentucky stand. New
York: Scribner's, 1951. 279p.
Baltimore boy to Kentucky--1777-1792.

486

6253 Whipple, Maurine (1904-   ). The giant joshua.
        Boston: Houghton, 1941. 637p.
            Settle Dixie Mission--Mormons--Desert Utah--
        1860's.

    White, Dale pseud. see Place, Marian (Templeton)

6254 White, Ethel. Bear his mild yoke; the story of mary
        dyer, a quaker martyr in early new england. Nash-
        ville: Abingdon, 1966. 255p.
            d.1660.

6255 White, Mrs. Georgia (Atwood) pseud. Atwood, Dascomb.
        Free as the wind. New York: Liveright, 1942. 331p.
            Family chronicle--Hollanders to Michigan--
        1850-1940.

6256 White, Helen Constance (1896-   ). Dust on king's
        highway. New York: Macmillan, 1947. 468p.
            Inland route from Sonora to California--1771-
        1781--Francisco Garcés (1738-1781).

6257 White, Leslie Turner (1903-   ). Look away, look away.
        New York: Random, 1944. 326p.
            Southerners from south to Brazil--Based on
        letters and records--Post-Civil War Era.

6258 ---Lord johnnie. New York: Crown, 1949. 298p.
            London and New York City--Eighteenth century.

6259 ---Log jam. New York: Doubleday, 1959. 284p.
            Lower Peninsula-1870's--Logging--Romance.

6260 White, Samuel Alexander (1885-   ). Empery; a story
        of love and battle in rupert's land. New York:
        Outing, 1913. 332p.
            Hudson's Bay Company--Adventure and mystery.

6261 ---Ambush. New York: Doubleday, 1920. 244p.
            Hudson's Bay Company--Romance and adventure.

6262 White, Stewart Edward (1873-1946). The claim jumpers;
        a romance. New York: Appleton, 1901. 284p.
            Western

6263 ---The westerners. New York: McClure, 1901. 344p.
            Sioux--Frontiersmen--Plains.

6264 ---The blazed trail. New York: McClure, 1902. 413p.
            #1 of Logging Series--Michigan.

6265 ---Conjurer's house; a romance of the free forest.
        New York: McClure, 1903. 260p.
            Hudson's Bay Company v. free traders.

                            487

6266   ---The riverman. New York: McClure, 1908. 368p.
       #2 of Logging Series--Romance.

6267   ---The rules of the game. New York: Doubleday, 1910.
       644p.
       #3 of Logging Series--California Sierras.

6268   ---The cabin. New York: Doubleday, 1911. 282p.
       Sierras--Cabin home at 6,500 feet.

6269   ---Gold. New York: Doubleday, 1913. 437p.
       #1 of California Trilogy--'49ers via Panama.

6270   ---The gray dawn. New York: Doubleday, 1915. 395p.
       #2 of California Trilogy--Vigilantes-1851-1856.

6271   ---The rose dawn. New York: Doubleday, 1920. 369p.
       #3 of California Trilogy--1880's.

6272   ---Story of california gold; the gray dawn, the rose
       dawn. New York: Doubleday, 1927. 1204p.
       California Trilogy in single volume--cf. Quick's
       Trilogy on Iowa.

6273   ---The long rifle. New York: Doubleday, 1932. 537p.
       #1 of Andy Burnett Trilogy--Rocky Mountain
       men 1820's--Second series on California.

6274   ---Ranchero. New York: Doubleday, 1933. 302p.
       #2 of Andy Burnett--Spanish in California--
       1832.

6275   ---Folded hills. New York: Doubleday, 1934. 479p.
       #3 of Andy Burnett Series--Spanish girl and
       American--Settle on hidalgo--Mexican War.

6276   ---Wild geese calling. New York: Doubleday, 1940.
       577p.
       Lumberjack--1890's--Seattle to Southern Alaska.

6277   ---Stampede. New York: Doubleday, 1942. 275p.
       #4 of Andy Burnett Series--Squatters threat
       to ranch.

6278   ---and Devighne, Harry. Pole star. New York: Doubleday,
       1925. 452p.
       Russian Fur Company--Alaska Aleskandr Baranov
       (1745-1819)--Espionage--Romance.

6279   White, William Allen (1868-1944). In the heart of a
       fool. New York: Macmillan, 1918. 615p.
       1865-1914--Establish town of Harvey.

6280   White, William Patterson (1884-   ). The owner of
       the lazy d. Boston: Little, 1919. 324p.
       First novel--Western.

488

6281 ---Hidden trails. New York: Doubleday, 1920. 335p.
     Western

6282 ---Lynch lawyers. Boston: Little, 1920. 387p.
     Western

6283 ---Paradise bend. New York: Doubleday, 1920. 287p.
     Western

6284 ---The heart of the range. New York: Doubleday, 1921.
     313p.
     Western

6285 ---The rider of the golden bar. Boston: Little, 1922.
     391p.
     Western

6286 ---The wagon wheel. Boston: Little, 1923. 320p.
     Western

6287 ---Twisted foot. Boston: Little, 1924. 329p.
     Western

6288 ---The buster. Boston: Little, 1926. 384p.
     Western

6289 ---Sweetwater range. Boston: Little, 1927. 334p.
     Western

6290 ---Cloudy in the west. Boston: Little, 1928. 369p.
     Western

6291 ---Adobe walls. Boston: Little, 1933. 300p.
     Western

Whitinger, R. D. pseud. see Place, Marian (Templeton)

6292 Whitlock, Brand (1869-1934). The stranger on the
     island. New York: Appleton, 1933. 268p.
        Exiled Mormons--Beaver Island--King Gorel
     religious sect--1850's.

6293 Whitmore, Walter. Wilburn; or, the heir of the manor.
     a romance of the old dominion. Cincinnati: n.p.,
     1852. 104p.

6294 Whitney, Janet (Payne) (Mrs. G. G. Whitnen) (1894-   ).
     Judith. New York: Morrow, 1943. 340p.
        Philadelphia--1792--Romance.

6295 ---The quaker bride. Boston: Little, 1954. 309p.
     Juvenile

6296 Whitson, Denton. The governor's daughter. Indianapolis:
     Bobbs, 1952. 322p.

French-Indian War--Clytie Delancey, acting governor of New York is hero--Romance.

6297 Whitson, Rolland Lewis. Rolinda; a tale of the mississinewa. Columbus, Ohio: Champlain, 1898. 356p.

6298 Whittier, John Greenleaf (1807-1892). Leaves from margaret smith's journal in the province of massachusetts. Boston: Ticknor, 1849. 224p.
        In form of pretended diary--English girl visits colony--1678-1679.

6299 Wibberley, Leonard Patrick O'Connor (1915-   ). John treegate's musket. New York: Farrar, 1959. 188p.
        Juvenile

6300 Wickersham, James Alexander. Enoch willoughby; a novel. New York: Scribner's, 1900. 356p.
        Pioneering Quakers in Ohio.

6301 Widdemer, Margaret. Lani. New York: Doubleday, 1948. 276p.
        Hawaii, Australia, South Pacific-1889--Romance.

6302 ---Red cloak flying. New York: Doubleday, 1950. 306p.
        Sir William Johnson (1715-1774)--Irish girl--Romance.

6303 ---Lady of the mohawks. New York: Doubleday, 1951. 304p.
        Molly Brant--Sir William Johnson--French-Indian War--Romance.

6304 ---Prince in buckskin; a story of joseph brant at lake george. Philadelphia: Winston, 1952. 184p.
        Brant (1742-1807)--Battle of Lake George-1755.

6305 ---The golden wildcat. New York: Doubleday, 1954. 314p.
        Indian diplomacy 1750's--French, British, Iriquois, Mohawk.

6306 ---The great pine's son; a story of the pontiac war. Philadelphia: Winston, 1954. 182p.
        Juvenile

6307 ---Buckskin baronet. New York: Doubleday, 1960. 350p.
        Albany, New York--Eve of Revolution.

6308 Wiechmann, Ferdinand Gerhard (1858-1919) pseud. Monroe, Forest. Maid of montauk. New York: Jenkins, 1902. 164p.

New Amsterdam and Long Island--Dutch v. English--
1650's.

6309 Wight, Frederick (1902-   ). The chronicle of aaron
      kane. New York: Farrar, 1936. 559p.
           Chronicle of sea--Aaron Kane (1838-1935)--
      Romance.

6310 Wilcox, Marrion. Sénora villena; and gray: an old
      haven romance. Two volumes in one. New York:
      White, 1887. 179p. and 262p.

6311 Wilder, Mrs. Laura (Ingalls). Little house on the
      prairie. New York: Harper, 1935. 200p.
           Juvenile

6312 Wilder, Robert (1901-   ). Bright feather; a novel.
      New York: Putnam, 1948. 408p.
           Seminole War--1835-1842--Osceola--Romance.

6313 ---Wind from the Carolinas. New York: Putnam, 1964.
      635p.
           Chronicle--Six generations--1790-1920--South
      Carolina to Bahamas.

6314 Wiley, Calvin Henderson. [Anonymous]. Alamance; or,
      the great and final experiment. New York: Harper,
      1847. 151p.

6315 Wiley, Richard Taylor (1856-   ). Sim greene, a
      narrative of the whiskey insurrection; being a
      setting forth of the memoirs of the late david
      froman, esq. by richard t. wiley. Philadelphia:
      Winston, 1906. 380p.
           1794

      Wilkins, Mary Eleanor see Freeman, Mrs. Mary Eleanor
      (Wilkins)

6316 Willard, Caroline McCoy (White). Kin-da-shon's wife;
      an alaskan story. New York: Revell, 1892. 281p.

      Willard, Mrs. Eugene S. see Willard, Caroline McCoy
      (White)

6317 Willette, Dorothy Davis. The spear penny; a novel.
      New York: Coward, 1949. 283p.
           Welsh family to America-1800's.

6318 Williams, Ben Ames (1889-1953). The strumpet sea.
      Boston: Houghton, 1938. 338p.
           South Seas--Missionaries, pearlers, whalers--
      1868.

6319 ---Thread of scarlet. Boston: Houghton, 1939. 374p.

#2 of Series--War of 1812--Privateer fights
British frigate--Romance.

6320 ---Come spring. Boston: Houghton, 1940. 866p.
#1 of Series--Maine-American Revolution--Good.

6321 ---The strange woman. Boston: Houghton, 1941. 684p.
#3 of Series--Maine--War of 1812--Civil War.

6322 ---Time of peace, september 26, 1930-december 7, 1941.
Boston: Houghton, 1942. 750p.
#4 of Maine Series.

6323 Williams, Catherine Read (Arnold) (1790-1872). The
neutral french; or, the exiles of nova scotia.
Providence, Rhode Island: The Author, 1841. 2 vols.
Acadian exiled by British--1755.

6324 Williams, Cecil Brown (1901-   ). Paradise prairie.
New York: Day, 1953. 372p.
Oklahoma--Farm life--Central area--Dunkards.

6325 Williams, Henry Llewellyn. Joaquin (the claude duval
of california); or, the marauder of the mines. a
romance founded on truth. New York: Dewitt, [187-?].
160p.

6326 Williams, John Edward (1922-   ). Butcher's crossing.
New York: Macmillan, 1960. 239p.
Western Kansas--End of Buffalo Era--Colorado
Mountains.

6327 Williams, Mary Floyd. Fortune, smile once more!
Indianapolis: Bobbs, 1946. 312p.
Australian gambler to San Francisco-1850's.

6328 Williamson, Edward Hand. The quaker partisans; a
story of the revolution. Philadelphia: Lippincott,
1869. 294p.

6329 Williamson, Thames Ross (1894-   ). The earth told
me. New York: Simon, 1930. 350p.
Alaska tundra--Stark work.

6330 ---On the reindeer trail. Boston: Houghton, 1932.
242p.
Juvenile

6331 ---The woods colt; a novel of the ozark hills. New
York: Harcourt, 1933. 288p.
Arkansas--Good.

6332 ---D is for dutch; a last regional novel. New York:
Harcourt, 1934. 266p.
Pennsylvania Dutch-1930's.

492

6333 Willis, John R.. Carleton; a tale of seventeen hundred and seventy-six. Philadelphia: Lee, 1841. 2 vols.
Battle of White Plains--Son of Tory--Joins Patriots.

Willoughby, Barrett see Willoughby, Mrs. Florance (Barrett)

6334 Willoughby, Mrs. Florance (Barrett). Rocking moon; a romance of alaska. New York: Putnam, 1925. 360p.
Aleuts and descendants of Russians--Fox farm.

6335 ---The trail eater; a romance of the all-alaska sweepstakes. New York: Putnam, 1929. 400p.

6336 ---Spawn of the north. Boston: Houghton, 1932. 349p.
Alaska

6337 ---River house. Boston: Little, 1936. 389p.
Alaska

6338 ---Sondra o'moore. Boston: Little, 1939. 320p.
Alaska--Fishing industry.

6339 ---The golden totem; a novel of modern alaska. Boston: Little, 1945. 314p.

6340 Wills, Grace E. (1887-   ). Murphy's bend. Philadelphia: Westminister, 1947. 287p.
Susquehanna River--Early 1800;s--Romance--Underground railroad.

Willsie, Honoré McCue see Morrow, Mrs. Honoré (McCue) Willsie

6341 Wilson, Mrs. Augusta Jane (Evans) (1835-1909). Inez; a tale of the alamo. New York: Harper, 1855. 298p.
1836--One of few early novels--Anglo-American v. Mexicans in southwest.

6342 Wilson, Charles Morrow (1905-   ). Acres of sky. New York: Putnam, 1930. 340p.
Ozark youth.

6343 ---A man's reach. New York: Holt, 1944. 288p.
Archibald Yell (1797-1847)--From North Carolina to Arkansas--Governor--Maria Yell (niece of Andrew Jackson).

Wilson, Charlotte pseud. see Baker, Mrs. Karl (Wilson)

6344 Wilson, Clyde. Our bed is green. New York: Ballou, 1934. 288p.
First novel--Southern mountains--cf. Maristan Chapman.

6345 Wilson, Harry Leon. The lions of the lord; a tale of the old west. Boston: Lothrop, 1903. 520p.
      Popular novel rè Mormons.

6346 Wilson, John Fleming (1877-1922). The land claimers. Boston: Little, 1911. 291p.
      Oregon timberlands.

6347 Wilson, Margaret (1882-   ). The able mclaughlins. New York: Harper, 1923. 262p.
      Scottish colony in Iowa-1860-70's--Pulitizer Prize-1924.

6348 ---The valiant wife. New York: Doubleday, 1934. 309p.
      War of 1812--Impressment.

6349 ---The law and the mclaughlins. New York: Doubleday, 1936. 308p.
      Sequel to Able McLaughlins.

6350 Wilson, Marian Calvert. Manuelita; the story of san xavier del bac. New York: United States Book Co., 1891. 305p.
      Father Kino era.

6351 Wilson, Neil Compton (1889-   ). Galleon bay; a novel. New York: Morrow, 1968. 274p.

6352 Wilson, William Edward (1906-   ). Abe lincoln of pigeon creek; a novel. New York: Whittlesy, 1949. 288p.
      Frontier boyhood--Riverboat.

6353 Wilson, William Robert Anthony (1870-   ). A rose of normandy. Boston: Little, 1903. 378p.
      La Salle--Henri de Tonty.

6354 Winther, Sophus Keith. Take all to Nebraska. New York: Macmillan, 1936. 305p.
      #1 of Nebraska Trilogy--Danish farmers to Massachusetts then Nebraska-1898-1908.

6355 ---Mortage your heart. New York: Macmillan, 1937. 333p.
      #2 of Nebraska Trilogy--Sequel Take All To Nebraska--Rent farmers 1906-1917.

6356 ---This passion never dies. New York: Macmillan, 1938. 289p.
      #3 of Nebraska Trilogy--Sequel to Mortgage Your Heart.

6357 Winthrop, Theodore (1828-1861). Edwin brotheroft. Boston: Ticknor, 1862. 3rd Edition. 369p.
      Battle of New York--Romance.

494

6358   ---John brent. Boston: Ticknor, 1862. 359p.
Mormons in Utah--Adventure and romance.

Winwar, Frances pseud. see Grebanier, Mrs. Frances
(Vinciguerra) (1900-   )

6359   Wire, Harold Channing. Mountain man. New York:
Crowell, 1929. 305p.
Western

6360   ---Marked man. New York: Appleton, 1934. 266p.
Western

6361   ---Indian beef. New York: Doubleday, 1940. 279p.
Western

6362   ---North to the promised land. Philadelphia: Westminister, 1948. 187p.
Last cattle drive--Boy tells tale--Juvenile.

6363   Wise, Evelyn Voss. As the pines grow. New York:
Appleton, 1939. 256p.
Minnesota farm town--1910-1920.

6364   ---Mary darlin'. New York: Appleton, 1943. 257p.
Minnesota woman.

6365   Wister, Owen (1860-1938). Lin mclean. New York:
Harper, 1898. 277p.
First of his western novels.

6366   ---The virginian; a horseman of the plains. New York:
Macmillan, 1902. 504p.
One of best westerns written by anyone at
anytime.

6367   The witch of new england; a romance. [Anonymous].
Philadelphia: Carey, 1824. 217p.
Wright, written by "John Cadwalder McCall".

6368   Wolford, Nelson and Shirley. Green grow the rushes.
New York: Dodd, 1954. 243p.
Mexican War (1845-1848)--Romance.

6369   Wonsetler, Mrs. Adelaide (Hill) and Wonsetler, John.
Me and the general. New York: Knopf, 1941. 299p.
War of 1812--Juvenile.

6370   ---Liberty for johanny. New York: Longmans, 1943.
278p.
American Revolution--Mennonite lad--Juvenile.

Wonsetler, John jt. author, see Wonsetler, Mrs. Adelaide
(Hill)

6371 Wood, Charles Seely (1845-1912). On the frontier with st. clair; a story of the early settlement of the ohio country. Boston: Wilde, 1902. 343p.

6372 ---The sword of wayne; a story of the way he smote the indians and brought them to sue for peace. Boston: Wilde, 1903. 370p.

6373 ---"Don't give up the ship!" New York: Macmillan, 1912. 314p.
    War of 1812--Juvenile.

6374 Woodman, Mrs. Jean. Glory spent. New York: Carrick, 1940. 347p.
    Mormonism-1930's.

6375 Woodville, Fanny. Edward wilton; or, early days in michigan. n.p., n.d. 124p.

6376 Woodworth, Samuel (1785-1842). The champions of freedom; or, the mysterious chief, a romance of the nineteenth century, founded on the events of the war, between the united states and great britain which terminated in march, 1815. New York: Baldwin, 1816. 2 vols.
    Moral romance--Amorphous--War of 1812.

6377 Woolson, Constance Fenimore (1840-1894). East angels. New York: Harper, 1886. 591p.
    Georgia homelife before Civil War.

6378 Wormser, Richard Edward (1908-   ). The lonesome quarter. New York: Mill, 1951. 250p.
    Western--Better than most--Warm people--Small ranch.

6379 ---Battalion of saints. New York: McKay, 1960. 312p.
    Mormons from Council Bluffs, Iowa to New Mexico for service Mexican War.

6380 Wright, C. W.. Joe cummings; or, the story of the son of a squaw in search of his mother. written by himself. Boston: Cupples, 1890. 329p.

6381 Wright, Caleb Earl. [Anonymous]. Wyoming; a tale. New York: Harper, 1845. 123p.
    Pennsylvania

6382 ---Rachael craig; a novel connected with the valley of wyoming. Wilkes-Barre, Pennsylvania: Baur, 1888. 308p.
    Pennsylvania

6383 Wright, Edmund pseud. Narrative of edmund wright [pseud.]; his adventures with and escape from the knights of the golden circle. Cincinnati: Hawley, 1864. 150p.

Colonial frontier.

6384 Wright, Harold Bell (1872-   ). <u>The shepherd of the</u>
        <u>hills; a novel</u>. New York: Burt, 1907. 351p.

6385 ---<u>Winning of barbara worth</u>. Chicago: Book Supply Co.,
        1911. 511p.
              Desert of Colorado River.

6386 Wright, James North. <u>Where copper was king; a tale</u>
        <u>of the early mining days on lake superior</u>. Boston:
        Small, 1905. 352p.
              1860's.

6387 Wyatt, Mrs. Geraldine (Tolman) (1907-   ). <u>Wronghand</u>.
        New York: Longmans, 1949. 206p.
              Western--Juvenile.

6388 Wyckoff, Nicholas Elston (1906-   ). <u>Braintree mission;</u>
        <u>a fictional narrative of london and boston 1770-1771</u>.
        New York: Macmillan, 1957. 184p.
              American Revolution--Offer John Adams an
        Earldom--Very good.

6389 ---<u>The corinthians; a novel</u>. New York: Macmillan,
        1960. 293p.
              Mormons--1850's--Illinois and Missouri.

6390 Wylie, Ida Alexa Ross (1885-1959). <u>Ho, the fair wind;</u>
        <u>a novel</u>. New York: Random, 1945. 373p.
              Martha's Vineyard--Close of Civil War.

Wyndham, Lee <u>pseud</u>. see Hyndman, Mrs. Jane Andrews (Lee)

Wynne, May <u>pseud</u>. see Knowles, Mabel

6391   Yates, Elizabeth (Mrs. William McGreal) (1905-   ).
       Hue and cry. New York: Coward, 1953. 248p.
       New Hampshire--1836-1837--Rural--Horse thieves.

6392   Yerby, Frank (1916-   ). The foxes of harrow. New
       York: Dial, 1946. 534p.
       New Orleans gambler--Plush romance--1825.

6393   ---The golden hawk. New York: Dial, 1948. 346p.
       Picaresque--Day of buccaneers--Late seven-
       teenth century.

6394   ---Benton's row. New York: Dial, 1954. 346p.
       Renegade from Texas-1842.

6395   ---Bride of liberty. New York: Doubleday, 1954. 219p.
       American Revolution--Romance.

6396   ---Jarrett's jade; a novel. New York: Dial, 1959.
       342p.
       American Revolution and earlier--Savannah--
       Romance.

6397   Yordan, Philip. Man of the west. New York: Simon,
       1955. 240p.
       Western

6398   Yore, Clement (1875-   ). Raw gold. New York:
       Garden City Pub., 1926. 181p.
       Western

6399   ---Trigger justice. New York: Macaulay, 1928. 306p.
       Western

6400   ---Hard riding slim magee. New York: Macaulay, 1929.
       300p.
       Western

6401   ---Dusty dan delaney. New York: Macaulay, 1930. 311p.
       Western

6402   ---Ranger bill. New York: Macaulay, 1931. 319p.
       Western

6403   ---The two gun kid. New York: Macaulay, 1932. 254p.
       Western

6404   ---The six-gun code. New York: Macaulay, 1932. 320p.
       Western

6405 ---Mississippi Jimmy. New York: Macaulay, 1933. 320p.
      Western

6406 ---Rider of the red ranges. New York: Macaulay, 1933.
      310p.
      Western

6407 ---The valley of grim men. New York: Macaulay, 1934. 315p.
      Western

6408 ---Trigger slim. New York: Macaulay, 1934. 252p.
      Western

6409 ---Hard country and gold. New York: Macaulay, 1935.
      313p.
      Western

6410 Yorktown; an historical romance. [Anonymous]. Boston:
      Wells, 1826. 2 vols.

6411 Young, Elizabeth Guion pseud. Sears, Baldwin. Homestead
      ranch. New York: Applton, 1922. 296p.
      Western prairie--Romance--Humor.

6412 Young, Gordon Ray (1886-   ). Hurricane williams.
      Indianapolis: Bobbs, 1922. 342p.
      Western

6413 ---Days of '49. New York: Doran, 1925. 425p.
      Western

6414 ---Fighting blood. New York: Doubleday, 1932. 308p.
      Western

6415 ---The devil's passport. New York: Century, 1933.
      300p.
      Western

6416 ---Red clark o' tulluco. New York: Doubleday, 1933.
      309p.
      Western

6417 ---Red clark rides alone. New York: Doubleday, 1933.
      301p.
      Western

6418 ---Red clark of the arrowhead. New York: Doubleday,
      1935. 303p.
      Western

6419 ---Red clark on the border. New York: Doubleday,
      1937. 287p.
      Western

6420 ---Red clark, range boss. New York: Doubleday, 1938.
      271p.
      Western

6421   ---Red clark, two-gun man.   New York: Doubleday, 1939.
       271p.
                Western

6422   ---Red clark for luck.   New York: Doubleday, 1940.
       270p.
                Western

6423   ---Red clark takes a hand.   New York: Doubleday, 1941.
       277p.
                Western

6424   --- Iron rainbow.   New York: Doubleday, 1942.   271p.
                Western

6425   ---Tall in the saddle.   New York: Doubleday, 1943.
       277p.
                Western

6426   ---Red clark at the showdown.   New York: Doubleday,
       1947.   219p.
                Western

6427   ---Red clark in paradise.   New York: Doubleday, 1947.
       222p.
                Western

6428   ---Quarter horse.   New York: Doubleday, 1948.   224p.
                Western

6429   ---Red clark to the rescue.   New York: Doubleday,
       1948.   222p.
                Western

6430   ---Wanted—dead or alive!   New York: Doubleday, 1949.
       220p.
                Western

6431   Young, Mary Stuart (Mrs. Louis G. Young).   The griffins;
       a colonial tale.   New York: Neale, 1904.   182p.

6432   Young, Samuel.   Tom hanson, the avenger; a tale of
       the backwoods embracing the history legends and
       romance of the "country around the head of the
       ohio".   Pittsburgh: Cook, 1847.   199p.

6433   Young, Stanley.   Young hickory; a story of the frontier
       boyhood and youth of andrew jackson.   New York:
       Farrar, 1940.   271p.
                Juvenile

6434   Young, Stark (1881-1963).   Heaven trees.   New York:
       Scribner's, 1926.   286p.
                Gracious plantation life contrasted with Vermont--
       Pre-Civil War.

6435 ---So red the rose. New York: Scribner's, 1934. 431p.
Southern aristocracy--Mississippi--Pre-Civil
War.

6436 Zara, Louis (1910-   ). This land is ours. Boston:
Houghton, 1940. 778p.
Panorama--1755-1835--Pioneer with Clark, Wayne,
Dearborn.

6437 ---Blessed is the land. New York: Crown, 1954. 393p.
Jews from Brazil to New Amsterdam--1654-1681.

6438 Ziegler, Isabelle Gibson. The nine days of father
serra. New York: Longmans, 1951. 242p.
Nine days that founder of mission in California
waited for ship.

6439 Zietlow, E. R.. These same hills. New York: Knopf,
1960. 251p.
South Dakota--Farm country.